GABRIEL'S EXTINGUISHING THE ATOMIC HELL SERIES

THE MIRACLE OF THE HOLY QURAN

THE QURAN PREDICTS, PHENOMENALLY CHARACTERIZES, AND AVERTS THE ATOMIC HELL

YOUSUF GABRIEL

EDITED BY KHALID MEHMOOD MALIK

No part of this book may be used or reproduced by any means, graphic, electronic, or mechanical, including photocopying, recording, taping or by any information storage retrieval system without the written permission of the publisher except in the case of brief quotations embodied in critical articles and reviews.

Author Credits:
Also, by Yousuf Gabriel: "Gabriel's Islamic Bomb" 1st Edition May 1991. Published by: Progressive Publishers Zaildar Park, Ichra, Lahore, Pakistan. Phone: 411142.

Because of the dynamic nature of the internet, any web addresses or links contained in this book may have changed since publication and may no longer be valid. The views expressed in this work are solely those of the author and do not necessarily reflect the views of the publisher, and the publisher hereby disclaims any responsibility for them.

The author of this book does not dispense medical advice or prescribe the use of any technique as a form of treatment for physical, emotional, or medical problems without the advice of a physician, either directly or indirectly. The intent of the author is only to offer information of a general nature to help you in your quest for emotional and spiritual well-being. In the event, you use any information in this book for yourself, which is your constitutional right, the author and the publisher assume no responsibility for your actions.

Any people depicted in imagery are models, and such images are being used for illustrative purposes only.

Publisher: Khalid Mehmood Malik, Canada.
khalidmalikpk@gmail.com
Save Future Generations From Nuclear Hell | Facebook
SaveFutureGeneration@khalidmalikpk1 | Twitter

Copyright © 2022 Khalid Mehmood Malik
All rights reserved.
ISBN: 9798780971283
Imprint: Independently published

DEDICATION

By the infinite grace and boundless mercy of Allah, this series of volumes is my original work. The discoveries from the Quran and the application of scientific facts are my own and are entirely unknown to anyone, whether Muslim or non-Muslim. For that, I praise the most Benign and Merciful Allah forever, eternally. Thus, it is all my responsibility. Again, Allah is praised. I am convinced that the light therein will ultimately extinguish the fire of atomic hell and save this humankind and the other innocent creatures on earth from atomic doom. I speak this not without reason. It is remarkable work, and I have the blessings of the Merciful Creator of this world. I present the fruit of my forty years' labor to humankind, and my reward is with my Beneficent Allah for this gift to humanity.

'Gabriel's Extinguishing the Atomic Hell Series' is dedicated by the servant of humanity to all humankind on the face of this globe regardless of caste, color, creed, country, race, or religion. Hypnotized by the witch of 'nuclear energy', beguiled and bewitched humankind, under the spell of the goddess of wealth, is standing right on the brink of the flaming nuclear pyre, awaiting nuclear holocaust to be roasted alive in the nuclear hell.

YOUSUF GABRIEL
September 13, 1980.

~~*~*~*

'GABRIEL'S EXTINGUISHING THE ATOMIC HELL SERIES' AT A GLANCE
BOOK-1
VOLUME-1
THE FIRST ERUPTION OF GABRIEL'S ARGUMENT AGAINST THE ATOMIC HELL
The Quran predicts, phenomenally characterizes, and averts the atomic hell
VOLUME-2
The Quran predicts and characterizes the technical knowledge of nuclear science
VOLUME-3
QURAN VERSUS ANCIENT AND MODERN ATOMISM
PART-1 Quran versus the ancient atomism of Democritus
PART-2 Quran versus Bacon's modern atomism
BOOK-2
VOLUME-4
An essay on Bacon's life referred to his philosophy
VOLUME-5
Democritus enkindles, Abraham extinguishes the atomic hell (the logical consequence of Baconian Anti-Christic spirit and philosophy)
VOLUME-6
QURAN VERSUS THE PHILOSOPHY OF THE 'UNSCIENTIFIC SCIENTIST PHILOSOPHER'
PART-1
Quran, the ancient atomism of Democritus, and the twelve pages of 'The Mysterious Universe'
PART-2
Quran versus the philosophy of the 'Unscientific Scientist Philosopher'
VOLUME-7
ATOMIC ENERGY FOR PEACE
PART-1 Atomic energy for peace: a curse
PART-2 The case of the atomic energy for peace in the Court of 'Lord Justice Science'
VOLUME-8
The relation between the Quran and the Bible
VOUME-9
A Quranic design of the neutralizer of the atomic hell and my mission therein

NOTE: The survival of humankind in particular and other species in general on the face of this globe depends on the burning issue of nuclear energy. This series consists of two books (nine volumes) on the same subject in chronological order. All the volumes form an unbreakable entity and are tight-knit. The following volumes are interlinked with the preceding volumes and could be well understood by knowing the previous volumes. To get a comprehensive perspective and understanding of this subject, the reader should study the nine volumes in a sequence as a whole.

~~*~*~*

ABOUT THE AUTHOR AND HIS MISSION

On February 17, 1917, the author was born in the Awan tribe, in a small remote village Khabbeki, Soan Sakeser Valley, Khushab. It is a tract that now forms part of Pakistan. There are three strange coincidences. First of all, February 17, according to the Bible, is the date of the eruption of Noah's deluge though of water, against this present one of nuclear fire. Hence, it is a strange coincidence with the day and the month of Noah's deluge. Secondly, Lenin's Revolution started in 1917. Thirdly, it was the era of the years of World War I.

Who knew other than the Providence that it was in the author's destiny to fight someday with the present-day fiery deluge of nuclear fire and prepare another Noah's ark in human history to save humanity from the deluge of atomic fire? He was a research scholar, philosopher, philanthropist, linguist, theologian, mystic, Orator, and Urdu poet.

He left the school in grade-8 but engaged in constant study and meditation after that. However, he privately secured an MA degree in Islamic Studies from the 'University of the Punjab', Lahore, Pakistan. He spent years 1955 to 1959 in his native village experimenting with the possibilities of manufacturing Portland cement on small scales after receiving a license from the 'West Pakistan Department of Industry', Lahore, and succeeded in the experiment.

In 1964, he served as an interpreter in the United Arab Republic (UAR) [1] Cultural Center Lahore, Pakistan. He also functioned as the translator of their cultural bulletin. From 1968 to 1972, he worked as a 'Research Officer' in the 'Ulema Academy, Auqaf-Department, Lahore, Pakistan' and was retired at 55. From 1972 to the last day of life, he struggled in Wah Cantt, Pakistan, day in, day out, arranged the materials, and then wrote the Books of 'Gabriel's Extinguishing the Atomic Hell Series'.

Throughout his life, the author saw specific visions of great authenticity in line with his mission of saving humankind from grievous nuclear doomsday. In the year 1942 in which Enrico Fermi succeeded in opening the gate of atomic fire on this humankind by his successful realization of Uranium fission chain reaction in Chicago, America; the author, in Mussayyib near Baghdad (Iraq), in a vision was recommended by the Green-turbaned saint 'Al-Khidr' [2] to Abraham for the Abrahamic Mission that of warning this world about the atomic hell, and exposing the actual reality of the nuclear problem and teaching this world the methods of escaping the grievous atomic doom. He was in that vision shown extraordinary great signs of Allah. In the same era and at the same place, he saw the Crucifix in another vision.

From 1942 to 1982, like a man pre-possessed, the author took to study and engaged himself in intellectual pursuit day in, day out. He learned the history and literature in English, Arabic, Persian, and Urdu languages. In ancient and modern philosophy, he was well-educated. He studied Mathematics with every branch, Arithmetic, Geometry, and Algebra. About science, particularly nuclear science, he was thoroughly knowledgeable. He was well-versed in the Scriptures, like the Quran and the Bible, the Old and the New Testament.

He exerted to gain knowledge year after year. And indeed, it was all without a school and a teacher in circumstances that no Bunyan could have the heart to describe and achieve that which no Freud could have a method to analyze. In 1961, he stumbled upon discovering the prophetic warning of the Quran about the atomic hell. Thereby he realized his theme and set to the research in the subjects involved therein. In 1963, in a debate with renowned German scholar Ms. Annemarie Schimmel, his theme got approval and had the stamp of genuineness and authenticity. In 1972, he set himself to writing till in 1982 he brought his work to its finish. He has produced Literature in English and Urdu about six thousand pages. Besides Urdu prose and poetry and one book, 'Gabriel's Islamic Bomb' (English), hundreds of the author's articles have been published in Pakistan in Urdu and English newspapers.

'Gabriel's Extinguishing the Atomic Hell Series' comprises the interpretation of the prophecy of the Quran about the atomic hell, a work regarding which author's conceit was that not even Bacon, Darwin, and Einstein combined could have produced. However, remember, the foundation of this work is not on any claim or pretension of the author himself. Nor is it even on the divine authority of the Quran. Instead, he based his work on science and logic, which must be the criterion. On

January 05, 2006, the author departed without seeing in his lifetime the publication of his life-long ordeal to save humanity from nuclear hell.

May his soul rest in peace. Aameen.

~~*~*~*

---

[1] **The United Arab Republic** [(U.A.R.) Arabic: الجمهورية العربية المتحدة] was a sovereign state in the Middle East from 1958 to 1971. Initially, it was a political union between Egypt (including the occupied Gaza Strip) and Syria from 1958 until Syria seceded from the union after the 1961 Syrian coup — leaving a rump state. Egypt continued to be known officially as the 'United Arab Republic' until 1971. Egyptian President Jamal Abdel Nasser led the republic. The U.A.R. was a member of the 'United Arab States', a loose confederation with the 'Mutawakkilite Kingdom of Yemen', dissolved in 1961.

[2] **'Al-Khidr'** (Arabic: also transcribed as 'Khidr', 'Khizr', 'Khizar') is a mystical figure that some believe described in the Quran as a righteous servant of God possessing great wisdom or mystic knowledge. Because of the linguistic similarities between the name 'Al-Khidr' and the Arabic word for green 'al-akhdar', the meaning of the name is often taken colloquially and sometimes academically to be 'the Green One' or 'the Verdant One'. For a detailed reference/description of 'Al-Khidr', please read Book-2/volume-9/chapter-12: ['Al-Khidr' recommended me to 'Abraham' for Abrahamic Mission].

~~*~*~*

"THE QURAN PREDICTS ATOM BOMB"

BY: ALLAMA MUHAMMAD YOUSUF GABRIEL

(A BOOK REVIEW)

The theme of the book revolves around the word 'Al-Hotama' of Surah 'Al-Homaza'. The author, who calls himself Gabriel, appears to be fulfilling a Gabrielic mission of forewarning the fellow humans of impending hazards of a nuclear age and has convincingly portrayed the Quranic philosophy to avert the potential catastrophe. He has painstakingly tried to establish that not only Quran predicts an atom bomb but also spells out the course to be followed if the danger of the nuclear explosion is to be averted. He believes to have found this warning in the Quran and feels duty-bound to make this known to the whole vast mankind. The author seems to be saying in chorus with Bertrand Russell that "Since Adam and Eve ate the apple, man has never refrained from any folly of which he was capable.", and the end is the atomic explosion.

In his enthusiasm to link up atom bomb with Quran, the author goes to the extent of saying that nuclear energy in itself is destructive no matter for whatever purpose it is harnessed. Here then, he seems to have loosened his otherwise sound grip on the seriousness befitting a serious subject. Writing with feverish energy, deep anguish, and extreme abhorrence for nuclear weapons, he does not hesitate to condemn the development of nuclear energy even though it is for the benefit of mankind. He maintains that even the peaceful uses of nuclear energy are quite hazardous due to irradiations emanating from its use. Here then, the author seems to forget that this is an objection against the basic methodology of entire science. It is the inherent characteristic of science to willingly lend itself to any use. Nuclear energy, like any other department of science, is no exception and can equally be applied both for the prosperity and destruction of mankind. One would have wished that in dealing with such a serious subject, Gabriel should not have been unmindful of the vast potential which nuclear energy holds to solve the menacing problems of hunger, disease, and dwindling power resources.

Sentences like the one, "Whether for a powerhouse or an atomic bomb, every nucleon shot in the heart of an atom to generate nuclear energy is like a deadly shaft driven through the heart of people's peace and existence", appear to give the impression of a zealous writer taking the subject a bit too far.

Gabriel's style in dealing with the subject is literary but not hackneyed or cliché-ridden. His description of the 'Unscientific Scientist Philosopher' has a remarkable original expressiveness about itself and provides a deep insight into the chemistry of the mind of such people. Though not formally educated in the field of nuclear science, his grasp of the subject and understanding of its delicacies is indeed marvelous.

While going through this book, one gets the impression that the writer's financial limitations clash with his commitment to the subject he holds so dear. He admits to having written the book in "frightening circumstances". It is indeed remarkable that this could not deter him, and despite utter dejection, he looks forward with confidence to the emergence of a new dawn when the Quranic warning about the atomic bomb will be heeded to.

The book, it is hoped, will be welcomed by the intellectual circles as a valuable contribution to the understanding of that fine blend of Quran and science which Gabriel so ardently maintains is inevitable for the progress, nay for the very survival of mankind.

(FARHATULLAH)
Pakistan Atomic Energy Commission
June 26, 1974.

~~*~*~*~*

AUTHOR'S NOTE REGARDING
THE REVIEW OF MR. FARHATULLAH

In his valuable review, the worthy reviewer has maintained that because humankind could advantageously put nuclear energy to peaceful purposes, therefore, the objections of the author to such a use seem to have taken "the subject a bit too far". The reviewer had indeed a right to hold any opinion. But I think the answer to the problem better is sought in the resultant amount of advantage or loss in the long run. Whether we generate this energy for peace or war, nuclear energy's noxious and debatable feature is its radiological hazard. Until, therefore, we check this hazard thoroughly, the fear thereof exists. It is difficult to assess this hazard today when a few new atomic plants are in operation. But the problem shall appear in its earnestness only when in time hundreds or thousands of atomic plants shall be operating in the world. Therefore, let the scientists put up a challenging endeavor to ensure hundred percent checks on the leakage of radiations and bring absolute joy to my heart if I lived by then.

The reviewer, alluding to my antipathy toward nuclear energy, even humankind generated it for its benefit, has considered it equivalent to negating the methodology of fundamental science.
He said:

"Nuclear energy, like any other department of science, is no exception and can equally be applied both for the prosperity and destruction of mankind."

I, on my part, have clearly stated in the book and have made an exception in favor of nuclear science only, due only to the unbearably noxious and intolerably destructive hazards of nuclear energy. Unfortunately, this just objection stands as long as the radiological hazards exist. Therefore, the scientific community should only focus on one point: the guarantee of checks on atomic radiations. It will be far better than sentimentally defending an un-defendable issue.

YOUSUF GABRIEL

~~*~*~*~*

MINISTRY OF INFORMATION, PAKISTAN
(A BOOK REVIEW)
'Gabriel's Extinguishing the Atomic Hell Series'
The Miracle of the Holy Quran: The Quran predicts, phenomenally characterizes, and averts the Atomic Hell.

(1) Allama Mohammad Yousaf Gabriel's manuscripts viz. "Quran Predicts Atom Bomb" and "Unscientific Philosophy of Scientist" have been thoroughly studied in BNR & R (Bureau of National Research and Reference). The views of Atomic Energy Commission have also been taken into consideration.

(2) Our view is that the subject matter of the manuscripts is really thought-provoking. The author has built his entire thesis on the Sura "Al-Homaza (Quran: 104)". The word on which the vital interpretation of his thesis has been made is the word "Al-Hotama". He has found certain similarities between the description of Al-Hotama in the aforementioned Sura and the stages accompanying the scientific process of atomic blast. It is felt by the Bureau that this thesis needs propagation throughout the world including the non-Muslim countries. This will attract the Muslims as well as the non-Muslims to pay heed to the modern appeal of the Holy Quran. This will, no doubt, be a service to Islam.

(3) But the Bureau has certain reservations as well on the manuscripts. The author's view that the Atomic Energy should not be used even for peaceful purposes, should be deleted from the main thesis. Similarly the invectives hurled at the modern scientists are too serious to be included in any manuscript on a scientific subject. This will unnecessarily antagonise them.

(4) It is, therefore, proposed that a pamphlet describing his main thesis in precise and un-emotive language may be published by a Government agency and then distributed to our foreign missions abroad for circulation in respective countries. Needless to mention that a book on scientific phenomena should be written in the modern scientific prose style. For this purpose his three articles published in the daily Nawa-i-Waqt are more convincing than the manuscript written in his idiosyncratic style. Our feeling is that the translation of these articles published in the form of a pamphlet will serve the purpose.

(M. E. H. Khilji)
Deputy Director
August 29, 1974.

~~*~*~*

LETTER OF THE AUTHOR ADDRESSED TO

MR. ZULFIQAR ALI BHUTTO

THE THEN PRIME MINISTER OF PAKISTAN

Dear Mr. Bhutto, Zulfiqar Ali,

Whether it is folly to write this to you or it is an act of opportune wisdom, I know not, but I am impelled only to unburden my overwhelmed mind by telling you, and I think it my duty to tell you, that despite all the circumstantial pressures --- neighborly and international --- and despite all the necessities, emergencies and essentialities entailed by this present epoch, the ATOMIC ENERGY --- apart from its appendages like atomic bombs, etc. --- is not an ENERGY but a curse; the atomic weapons not weapons but abomination, means of wholesale annihilation of the entire mankind.

If, then it is not for any sort of pressure from any quarters locally, like Senator Brien McMahonian pressure on President Truman, which I think there is not; be advised, I pray, and wait and see; slacken thy pace in your initiative --- a very sincere initiative though --- but based on innocence. Why I write this and why I should write it, or why yet this writing I but cannot help. I say no country is going to benefit from atomic energy. See the signs, and know that this mysterious disease is now prevalent here and there, if not exactly the atomic radiation sickness, it certainly is the harbinger, the gorgon sister of radiation sickness, and has precisely the same symptoms, not only similar but the same. I do not want to write, but my pen is being forcibly dragged on this paper. I want to be as short, curt, pert, and brief. Look upon the map of Pakistan and see that profusion of the hydroelectric possibilities, and judge if there be any necessity for atomic energy. But no, go ahead with whatever you people want to go and do. It was my great misfortune. The age blinded by the wrath of Providence; will they hear? Have I told you, or do you want to understand? Is it wise on my part? Is it of use to say these things on this level: A storm and a beetle? Would you condescend to call me in, and it is not a request, not so much as desire, but only to make clear what I have said. And (it depends upon) your discretion, your convenience, your will, and pleasure.

It is not Pakistan that is the object of my attention with its three reactors and an Atomic Energy Commission in Islamabad. My targets are those huge stockpiles that can destroy this world 30 times. But what pains me is that a country like, say, Pakistan, with only dubious hopes to derive some substantial benefit from atomic energy, becomes the subject of the hazards which atomic energy is sure to bring with its appearance. However, don't try to be carried away by my sentiments and consider my wailing just a side note in that big organ that is at present sending its peals all over the world. I will feel most content if I receive no reply. I will be most happy if all this is treated as simply absurd, either by your secretary or yourself, but pray hesitate to make it the butt of ridicule or a casual joke amidst your friends.

Yours most sincerely,
Allamah Muhammad Yousuf Gabriel
C/O Khalid General Stores,
Main Bazaar, Wah Cantt.
February 23, 1976.

~~*~*~*

LETTER OF THE AUTHOR ADDRESSED TO MR. RONALD REAGAN THE THEN PRESIDENT OF THE U.S.A.

To,
Mr. Reagan,
The President of the U.S.A.

This is a letter to you from Allama Muhammad Yousuf Gabriel. Read it with care and attention for the truths that are based on solid scientific and logical grounds. Therein is nothing fanatic, nor is there anything fantastic. The time that is the best of judges will prove the validity of the facts, seemingly so illusive and impracticable to a generation hypnotized by the influence of the fast-approaching grievous nuclear doom; the logical and scientific consequence of the process of atomism. Let the President of America know:

(1) That this mankind now is inevitably doomed to the flames of atomic hell. There is no alternative left but either to vanish suddenly under the hails of atomic bombs, deservedly, or to perish under the stings of deadly radiations of the reactors of the atomic energy for peace in a lingeringly miserable manner, also deservedly. There is no power on earth to save mankind from the flames of nuclear Jehannah (hell). No Reagan-Brezhnev conferences about no-nuclear war or armament cuts will succeed despite the most genuine efforts on both sides. The nuclear war may be delayed but not annulled forever. These movements, which you see stirring among the public against the atomic weapons, will prove to be a part of the punishment in the form of confusion, anarchy, disturbance, and rifts between the public and their governments. The threat of atomic weapons could not be hissed away by the reaction of collective fear. "The Fate of the Earth" by Jonathan Schell [1] is a good book, but it is no more than a hue and cry to frighten the people into 'Anti-Atomic Bomb' cries. The need rather is of discovering the basic causes of the nuclear trouble, a line which has not been described by any of the great Anti-Nuclear writers and philosophers of this age.

(2) That this mankind is doomed to nuclear flames on scientific and logical justice, and neither the heavens will cry nor will the angels take to mourning if this mankind is destroyed in the atomic

conflagration. The mistake of the old American who stamped the earth saying, "America is indestructible", is a typical mistake of the denizens of this present age. Who could convince the poor old American that America could be destroyed by the nuclear cannonade without giving him time to stamp the earth by his foot twice? I feel no joy in saying this. If, I being a mere human, am saddened by the affair, how Allah, the Merciful Creator of man, could not be expected to have a soft corner about mankind in His heart, despite the justification of the nuclear punishment.

(3) That, it was due to the sheer kindness of the Allah of Mercy, that in the year 1942 (my 25th year), and the year in which Enrico Fermi had by his successful realization of the Uranium fission chain reaction opened the gate of atomic fire on mankind, I was assigned the 'Abrahamic Mission' of warning and saving this mankind from the annihilation in the flames of atomic hell. I had then but negligibly insignificant knowledge. But thereafter, like a man pre-possessed, I learned languages, works of literature, philosophies, sciences, and Scriptures, indeed without a school or a teacher and in circumstances which no Bunyan could have a heart to narrate, while no Freud was there to analyze the method of my intellectual achievement or to believe the possibility of such accomplishment. The result of my struggle appeared ultimately in 1982 in the form of 'Gabriel's Extinguishing the Atomic Hell Series', unpublished and awaiting publication.

My conceit of this work is that it is the only guidance for this mankind to escape the all-consuming flames of the nuclear Jehannah (hell). Also that all the celebrities of this modern age combined would find it hard to produce the like of it, which I did single-handed without a school or a teacher. The treatment of atomic science therein would cause an Einstein to stand aghast with wonder, while a Russell would be lost in a revere at the treatment of the philosophy of modern atomism.

(4) That the nuclear confusion and nucleo-political anarchy will increase till the explosion eventually occurs. But there is a lot of difference between the war with conventional weapons and the war with nuclear weapons. They who say that the survival of mankind is possible after a partial or even total atomic war are only blinded by the

hypnotizing effect of nuclear doom. When the defense analysts of America call the view of complete extinction of human species resulting from the atomic war expressed by poor Jonathan Schell as plain wrong, do they mean that until the complete extinction of human species as a result of the atomic war were a verity, they would care a little about the possibility of atomic war? The whole thing appears as tragic. What course could then be adopted in these circumstances is the question, judging from the situation, that no one country alone could do anything to avoid nuclear trouble? My honest opinion is that my books should be published and read by the entire mankind. Thereby men will understand the true reality of the affair and will, therefore, come together to chalk out some collective program to rid this world of the nuclear threat. The efficacy of my plan may be doubted. But there is no possible alternative left but to move on the path in chains to the brink of the blazing atomic hell, then to be cast therein into the eternal atomic hell of the next world. The name of the Quran may sound objectionable to those who have no faith in the Quran. But surely this world, once it has had a glimpse of the fiery giant Atumbumb [2] and felt its nasty breath, will be willing to rush into the lap of the devil himself if there were some hope of refuge there. But science, it is, and not the Quran, that has furnished the criterion of judgment in this wok while the Bible, particularly the Gospel of Christ, has found a proper place of respect as a twin with the Quran justly.

    Mr. President! My object in sending to you this letter has been to inform you of the situation as is in my view. And I have written nothing anywhere without the testimony of facts. Remain witness, therefore, that I have informed you. I will anxiously await your reply to know your views. And please acknowledge the receipt of my letter at your earliest, for time is short and margin narrow. And in the end, let us say: May Allah save this world from the atomic conflagration. (Aameen)

WARNING

Remember that if this my work is lost, the last and the only hope of mankind to escape the atomic doom is lost too. It is not only the leaves of the manuscripts of my Anti-Nuclear work that the white-ants will eat, but it is also the destiny of a race hypnotized by a grievous doom that they will eat. I have neither wealth, no property, nor even a house. And surely, I should have none because I have been engrossed in an unprofitable pursuit throughout, having neither time nor mind to attend to my worldly business. If this mankind fails to rescue my Anti-Nuclear manuscripts at once, the painful decree of atomic ruin will be executed ultimately. I remind the dignitaries of this world of Einstein's now historic letter, which he sent on August 22, 1939, to the President Roosevelt of America, inviting the President's attention to the possibility of building a nuclear bomb a million times more powerful than the conventional one. The suggestion was accepted, and the world now stands in terror, trembling before the bomb. I have to invite their attention now, on April 22, 1982, to the possibility of an escape from the nuclear doom through my Anti-Nuclear works. All the heaps of wealth all over the world could be saved from the atomic bombs by spending a negligible part on the publication of these manuscripts. It is hardly a wise policy to accumulate riches and discard at the same time the side of preventive efforts in a nuclear world.

Yours Sincerely,
Allama Muhammad Yousuf Gabriel,
Khalid Chappal Stores, Nawab-Abad,
Wah Cantt, Distt. Rawalpindi, Pakistan.
May 05, 1982.

~~*~*~*~*

---

[1] **'The Fate of the Earth'** is a 1982 book by Jonathan Schell. This "seminal" description of the consequences of nuclear war "forces even the most reluctant person to confront the unthinkable: the destruction of humanity and possibly most life on Earth". The book revitalized the Anti-Nuclear movement and instigated the nuclear freeze movement.

[2] This appellation **'Atumbumb'** of the word 'atom bomb' was devised by the author. In fact, during conversation/discussion with close friends, he usually enjoyed using this nickname instead of 'atom bomb' to stress the word regarding its expression and meaning. He said that the word 'Atumbumb' bears and conveys the genuine expressions of the wrath and severity of terribleness associated with the atom bomb's explosion. The reader will come across this word at some places throughout this series.

~~*~*~*~*

FOREWORD

The scenario on the globe map shows that the flames of nuclear war may burst at any moment. [1] Have you ever thought about what happens if (Allah forbid) nuclear war starts today? Will we repeat the history of Hiroshima and Nagasaki on a global scale with the resultant nuclear holocaust? Or even luckily, if nuclear war does not start, what will this so-called nuclear energy for peace do with our future generations? Will the incidents of Chernobyl and Fukushima continually be repeated on the face of this globe with an inevitable result of genes' mutation by radiations and our future generations be born as monsters and chimeras? [2] How much more this flawed humanity on the face of this globe has to witness in the future? Will our earth become T. S. Eliot's 'The Waste Land'? How long can we (the common masses of the world) wink at the mad pursuit of the governments worldwide for nuclear nukes and nuclear energy? Dr. Rosalie Bertell has said:

"We know we face extinction if nuclear war ever begins. We face the same extinction even if the bombs never fall. The production alone of nuclear energy and nuclear weapons is initiating the death crisis of our species."

(Dr. Rosalie Bertell; 'No Immediate Danger: Prognosis for a Radioactive Earth')

Similarly, Director-General World Health Organization (WHO) issued the bold statement, Margaret Chan, saying, "There is no safe, low level of radiation", echoes the same situation.

Mr. Yousuf Gabriel completed the subject 'Gabriel's Extinguishing the Atomic Hell Series' of two books comprising nine volumes in 1982 regarding the same burning issue of nuclear threat to the globe. He trumpeted the doomsday of this 'Science-guided Baconian culture progress' in this book and emerged with a unique resolution of the nuclear dilemma from the Holy Quran. He boasted that the Quran has the solution to the problem of all nuclear ills. In his own words from the book:

"The Quran has claimed to contain every example for humankind. If, then, the example of the destruction of just the froward tribes of Sodom and Gomorrah have found a mention in the Quran, how someone could expect that the Quran should omit the wholesale destruction of whole humankind by the atomic hell? What could be the destruction of those little tribes against this universal destruction produced by the atomic hell? What was the torture of those condemned tribes against the torment and agony caused by the nuclear hell?"

Providence made him look into the far future with the same ideas and opinions before Dr. Rosalie Bertell and Margaret Chan. The purpose was to save this humankind from nuclear doomsday. This series covers philosophy, religion, Scriptures, nuclear science, ancient atomism, modern atomism, history, literature, and much more, all fused. This work is a fusion of ancient and modern knowledge. Also, it is a contrast and comparison of Oriental and Western knowledge and philosophy. This philanthropist philosopher based his work on a prophecy (instead, a warning) of Scripture regarding nuclear hell: the atomic bombs and atomic radiations. The author believed this work's publication would bring about a revolution of thought in people of this age worldwide regarding their attitude toward nuclear energy, its hazards, and its adoption, whether for war or peaceful purposes. The primary source of the prophecy and its resultant philosophy is the Holy Quran.

However, the Holy Bible has also been quoted and found its relevant honorable place in founding the philosophy presented in this work. The crux of the matter is that faith has disappeared from the society of present-day materialistic slandering wealth-accumulators. The author's primary focus is on reviving faith to regain the lost bliss and avoid nuclear hell. This work sets the future safe course to be adopted by humanity.

Moreover, hopefully, this will ultimately save this globe and, along with it the humanity from the impending nuclear doom that is fast approaching in the form of a nuclear World War III. These are not merely the words of a fanatic, but every volume, chapter, paragraph, sentence, or even word of this work is open for debate for the intelligentsia to get critical appreciation with positive criticism purely on the criterion of merit only. It is based totally on the touchstone of logic, reason, and present-day nuclear science scientific facts.

In the words of the author himself:

"I base my work on knowledge in this age of knowledge. Therefore, I established my argument throughout based on science and logic. And remember that in my works in which I have treated the Quran, I have not based the work on the divine authority of the Quran; science and logic constitute the criterion of judgment."

Along with its resultant hazardous nuclear bombs and radiations, this nuclear energy is the outcome of Baconian [3] philosophy given by Francis Bacon (1561–1626), an English philosopher, statesman, scientist, jurist, and author. He preferred natural philosophy (science) over moral philosophy (based on religion). His philosophy was that of the right of man's dominion over Mother Nature for material benefit and utility, which has eventually brought humanity to the brink of nuclear devastation. However, according to all revealed religions, Allah reserved dominion over Mother Nature only for Himself. For humankind is only utility and glorification of Allah. This contrast between the right of either man's or Allah's dominion over Mother Nature is the primary point on which the author's philosophy concentrates in this work in the light of the Holy Quran and the Holy Bible.

This work is the outcome of a spiritual vision (dream) through which the author was assigned by Providence, in 1942, the 'Abrahamic Mission' to save this humanity and all species on earth from nuclear fire and doomsday. Abraham (Prophet Hazrat Ibraheem) faced the 'biological fire' of Namrud, [4] whereas present-day humankind is facing this 'nuclear fire' lit by the 'slandering wealth accumulators' of this nuclear age. In the same year, 1942, atomic physicist Enrico Fermi opened the gates of nuclear hellfire on earth with the successful fission chain reaction conducted in Chicago. We have seen the most horrible results (ever in human history) of this successful fission chain reaction in Hiroshima, Nagasaki, Chernobyl, and most recently in Fukushima. And nobody knows what it will bring the next?

The people of Italy deserve salutations who have consistently voted against the adoption of nuclear energy, whether for war or so-called peaceful purposes. Also, praised be the spirit of the government of Germany for closing some of their nuclear reactors after the most recent tragedy of Fukushima. They have announced that by 2022, they will shut down all of the nuclear reactors in Germany. People of India have already started a protest and debate in this regard. Most recently, on July-13/2013, organized by online social media, a rally billed as an "innocent stroll" of just 1000 protesters on the streets of Jiangmen (100km from Hong Kong) prompted the government of China to cancel the "Jiangmen Uranium Plant" project. In a country like China, where public protests are usually severely curtailed, just within 24 hours of the street protest, the people's government of Heshan decided to respect the public opinion that opposed the plan and canceled the project altogether. The project would have provided enough fuel for around half of China's atomic energy needs. In this 'Anti-Nuclear Energy' rally, the protesters chanted slogans and waved banners saying, "We want children, not atoms", with a realistic, rational approach.

But what about other nations around the globe? This nuclear energy has intoxicated most of them like wine as they lay there in a drunken stupor and have lost all their wisdom. Even the tragic incidents of Hiroshima, Nagasaki, Chernobyl, and Fukushima have not opened their eyes. Are these four catastrophic incidents not enough to open their eyes regarding the adoption of nuclear energy? Shockingly, they are still insanely obsessed with the enthusiastic pursuit of nuclear energy. This nonsense stubbornness will devour their children ultimately. The nuclear hell is in front of them, and they are happily ready to jump into it as if some unseen mysterious power has put a blinder on their eyes. Nations need the knowledge, wisdom, and awareness in this regard, and which this work provides in the best possible manner.

Moreover, this unbiased work is in universal interest addressed to humanity, all religions, beliefs, or dogmas: without discrimination between Jews, Christians, Muslims, Hindus, Buddhists, believers, non-believers, pagans, and even atheists. Throughout this work, the author looks like a philanthropist, 'a servant of humanity', concerned with the safety of humanity from nuclear bombs and nuclear radiation. In this regard, he based his perspective on the conviction that when the nuclear bomb explodes, it kills humanity and not the followers of a specific faith or religion, without any discrimination between black, brown, and white. It will kill Jews, Christians, Muslims, Hindus, Buddhists, believers, non-believers, pagans, and atheists alike with the same fire and intensity, at the same time, level, and place. And it will destroy synagogues, churches, monasteries, mosques, pagodas, and temples with equal severity and intensity. It did the same in Hiroshima, Nagasaki, Chernobyl, and Fukushima and will do the same in the future.

The same is the case with nuclear radiation: They will devour all humanity. No nuclear bomb is a Jews bomb, a Christian bomb, an Islamic bomb, Communist bomb, or Hindu bomb: Rather, it is neither a bomb nor a weapon of war; it is, as the author describes it, "the wrath of Allah enkindled for sinful humanity". And this work of the author describes how humanity can avert it.

Another exciting feature of this work is that an illiterate person miraculously produced it who never went to a college or university or visited any teacher. Instead, it is purely the outcome of his self-study, research, and effort, an exciting research case for future historians and scholars. However, later on, he got his Post Graduate degree in Islamic Studies from the 'University of the Punjab', Lahore, Pakistan as a private candidate. This scholarly work written with a missionary purpose is the outcome of 30 years (1942-1972) of learning and research and ten years (1972-1982) of writing manuscripts, with a sum of 40 years of a long ordeal. The author became sick due to prolonged and never-ending severe exertion. He led a life of poverty throughout his life career. Being away from the modern centers of learning of the West, he lived in a remote region of the world. It was an atmosphere not conducive to his lofty philosophy and theme and for the publication of his work. Due to a lack of resources and means, he could not approach West and get it published. He departed in 2006 without seeing the fruit of his life-long struggle. But he has left his work in the form of a legacy for this generation to benefit from it. Or they can keep it in a museum for future generations to benefit from when deemed fit for their needs. But then it will be too late.

A prophecy (warning) of the Holy Quran about nuclear hell is the basis of this work. It is yet unknown to the world. This prophecy of the Holy Quran is a miracle undeniable in the whole of human history. It will be fantastic to listen that more than fourteen centuries ago, the Holy Quran had opposed the ancient atomism of Democritus and the modern materialistic atomism of Francis Bacon, which appeared after fourteen centuries.

The Holy Quran has described the characteristics of the age in which it was supposed to appear. It has also given the characteristics of the people who would become the victims of nuclear fire, the outcome of either nuclear explosions or nuclear radiation. It has predicted complete nuclear phenomena with the minutest of details and has given the causes of its appearance, the remedial measures, and solutions to avoid this nuclear doomsday. It has described the complete scientific behavior of nuclear radiation and even portrayed a picture of the nuclear explosion with its characteristic scientific features. In short, it has described the whole nuclear phenomena in its entirety.

This series is a case of dwindled religion and diminished faith versus science. Since the birth of science, religion and science have always been at loggerheads with each other. People must resolve at last a conflict passing through a span of centuries. Neither of the two can triumph and prevail. So why should we not assume a balanced approach in this strife? It looks that a new World War of arguments will start between religion and science with the philosophy of adopting a midway presented in this series.

In volume-6, you will find Darwin's philosophy of evolution of man's base ape-like origin and Sir James Jeans' philosophy of the 'Unscientific Scientist Philosopher' (as expressed in 'The Mysterious Universe'); both together on one side. The Holy Quran alone will be on the other side, entering into a debate with Darwin and the 'Unscientific

Scientist Philosopher'. It will be in the shape of an exciting and eye-opening dialogue astonishing enough to render the reader speechless.

This work is a fusion of atomism (ancient and modern), Scriptures (The Bible and the Quran), philosophy, theology, literature, history, and modern nuclear science. In the author's words, this "key to the future destiny of this now doomed humankind" needs to be published and distributed throughout the world to get the critical appreciation of the intelligentsia worldwide and bring a universal revolution of thought in this matter. Present worldwide violence, strife, chaos, unrest, hatred, torment, and fights among the world's nations have ultimately brought humanity to the brink of nuclear World War, resulting in a nuclear holocaust. This work can bring light, hope, and unity amongst all nations on the focal point of their attitude toward adopting nuclear energy in the present circumstances.

In the end, the author has provided "A Quranic design of the neutralizer of the atomic hell". It is a 'formula' for the nullification of nuclear fire, which has its foundation in the soil of ethics. In the light of this formula, the world's nations can chalk out a program to reach a certain point of agreement not to follow nuclear energy either for war or peaceful purposes and ban it altogether.

If humankind adopts nuclear energy for war purposes, it will eradicate whole humanity and other species on the face of the earth. If nations adopt it for peaceful purposes, people should mentally prepare themselves for their near and dear ones or future generations to be born chimeras and monsters. Instead, it has already started even in the present age. Watch the videos of Chernobyl babies born after the Chernobyl accident or monster babies born after using Depleted Uranium bombs: a long sad story to tell. Just visualize the future scenario of the globe when all the energy resources are exhausted because of the rapid progress that is in progress. Nuclear energy will only be the resource left. Powerhouse to airplanes, trains, buses, cars, and even motorbikes will have independent nuclear reactors as energy sources.

Will humanity not be surrounded by nuclear radiation as it is surrounded by electromagnetic waves these days? Will these tiny nuclear reactors not be exploding everywhere after completing their physical age? The ultimate result will be radiation sickness for human beings with their genes mutated, multiplying through marriages, and their future generations giving birth to their offspring as monsters and chimeras; a horrible scene to describe. The author wants to display such a scenario to humankind in the nick of time, employing the Holy Quran's warning.

The majority of the believers on the face of this globe, particularly all the Muslim community, believe in the second coming of Jesus Christ. According to this belief, he will appear at the end of the world as a Saviour of humanity. He will relieve humankind from the shackles of all the miseries. What could be miserable more than the nuclear holocaust of all humanity and all other species on the face of this earth to be roasted alive in nuclear hell? If Christ appears today, what will he do to save humanity? Being Saviour, he will undoubtedly save humankind from this nuclear doom and nuclear hell. He will struggle to stop the nuclear World War III. In the words of the author:

"Christ, in his first coming, had struggled against the ancient atomism of Democritus. So, if he appears today in his second coming, he will have to struggle against this modern atomism of Bacon."

Hopefully, this work will pave the way for Christ's mission as a Saviour produced under the supervising eye of Providence within forty years. According to the author's expectations, a time will come that the compelling needs of humanity will force all nations to translate this work into their respective languages around the globe.

The author of this work had been in contact with Bertrand Russell regarding the uncertain nuclear world. Bertrand Russell was also a great advocate against nuclear energy, and he had a keen insight into the threat of nuclear conflict. He believed that abolishing war only would end the nuclear threat. Along with other scientists like Albert Einstein, he appealed to end disputes and quarrels and abolish war, but all these appeals failed. In contrast, Yousuf Gabriel believes that the appeals of philosophers and scientists, Anti-Nuclear movements, movements for peace, and campaigns for nuclear disarmament only cannot avoid the impending nuclear threat. He believes that nations cannot abolish war in any way. History has proved it. He asserts that something solid and practical needs to be done based on the touchstone of logic, reason, philosophy, and scientific argument, which should appeal to and convince humankind.

In light of the prophecy/warning of the Holy Quran regarding nuclear hell given fourteen centuries ago, he provides the solution that you cannot avoid the nuclear threat unless you eradicate the root causes of the emergence of nuclear hell. The Holy Quran has pointed out these root causes responsible for the emergence of nuclear phenomena and tells us how to avert nuclear hell. Russell based his work regarding nuclear disarmament on philosophy and appeals only. In contrast, Yousuf Gabriel based his approach on philosophy, appeal, and Holy Scriptures (the Holy Bible and the Holy Quran). It will appeal to the followers of these two great revealed religions, Christianity, and Islam. Moreover, it can help in bringing them closer together.

Russell focused his efforts mainly on the use of nuclear energy for war and opposed it. In contrast, Yousuf Gabriel is absolutely against this two-edged sword of nuclear energy, i.e., nuclear energy for war and peace. Two eye-opening incidents in recent history have proved it; 'Chernobyl' and, most recently, 'Fukushima'. In his works in 1982, he had already predicted such incidents caused by nuclear energy for so-called peace, whereas these incidents happened afterward in 1986 and 2011, respectively.

Russell died disappointed regarding the future destiny and end of humankind in nuclear hell. On the contrary, Yousuf Gabriel is optimistic about the future of humankind that this prophecy of the Holy Quran will ultimately save this humankind from nuclear doomsday.

Proceeding through this series, in the course of reading, you will know that on March 1, 1954, the Castle Bravo test explosion at Bikini Atoll in the Pacific Ocean revealed a harsh truth on nuclear powers to their terror. They discovered that neither the aggressor nor the defender was safe from the radiological hazard of this 'treacherous slave' atom bomb or Hydrogen bomb.

"It could also rebound towards its own master who unleashed it on his foe and thus bring about the ruin of both, nay, even of other neutral people all over the globe."

Most recently, with the tragedy of Fukushima, Mother Nature disclosed to humanity on the face of the globe another disastrous outcome of atomic energy for peace. Whereas in the catastrophe of Chernobyl, only the populations of neighboring districts were involved in paying the price of the misfortune, here in the case of Fukushima, the whole of humanity is at stake. In 2021, ten years after the three reactors melted in the Fukushima nuclear disaster in 2011, the crisis has not ended yet. The worst water discharge contaminated with radioactive substance with a too high level of radiation leaking into the sea from Fukushima nuclear plant is a predicament that will haunt humanity for decades because this radioactivity will contaminate the ocean life that humans eat.

This radioactive plume of water from Fukushima is a dilemma concerned with whole humanity worldwide. Because if these traces of radioactive pollution, started from Japan, in the sea have been recorded in Canadian continental waters in Vancouver, British Columbia on one side; on the other hand, they are hitting Alaska and the West coast of North America. [5] Onwards, contaminants may disperse eastwards on Pacific currents. In this way, these radiations may 'encompass' the world's oceans, a perpetual headache for humanity. This 'encompassing feature of radiation' on the local and global level is the spirit of this work. The author discussed it minutely in the light of the prophecy of the Quran in this series.

Another key feature of this work is the severe criticism of 'slandering/backbiting', 'wealth-accumulation', and a 'belief in the eternity of the life of this world' as prohibited by the Holy Quran in this subject prophecy. These traits, which have become part and parcel of this present-day nuclear age, are the fundamental root cause of the problem and ultimately have brought this humanity to the brink of nuclear hell. In this slandering wealth accumulators' world, in the words of Dr. Rosalie Bertell, "Scientists are economic prisoners" with "money-based goals" who are not concerned with the safety of humanity from nuclear threats and radiation and don't disclose the complete truth.

In this context, it will not be inappropriate to refer to the following worth mentioning three reports that emerged on the scene. The first and second reports are concerned with the 'wealth accumulation' and the poverty and plight of humanity regarding inequality of wealth distribution worldwide. At the same time, the third one concerns the hazardous nature of nuclear (ionizing) radiation and closely relates to the safety of humanity and its children.

(A) The first report is from Jeremy Hobbs, Executive Director "Oxfam International" published: January 19, 2013.

Here are some excerpts from this report:
— Annual income of the richest 100 people is enough to end global poverty four times over.
— The $240 billion net income in 2012 of the richest 100 billionaires would be enough to make extreme poverty history four times over.
— The richest one percent has increased its income by 60 percent in the last 20 years, with the financial crisis accelerating rather than slowing the process.
— Oxfam warned that 'extreme wealth and income is not only unethical; it is also economically inefficient, politically corrosive, socially divisive, and environmentally destructive'.
— We can no longer pretend that the creation of wealth for a few will inevitably benefit the many – too often, the reverse is true.
— Concentration of resources in the hands of the top one percent depresses economic activity and makes life harder for everyone else – particularly those at the bottom of the economic ladder.

— In a world where even basic resources such as land and water are increasingly scarce, we cannot afford to concentrate assets in the hands of a few and leave the many to struggle over what's left.

— Members of the richest one percent are estimated to use as much as 10,000 times more carbon than the average U.S.A. citizen.

(www.oxfam.org)

(B) The second report is from "Oxfam International" too, published on January 20, 2014. Here are some excerpts from this report.

WORLD'S RICHEST ONE PERCENT
CONTROL HALF OF GLOBAL WEALTH

Given the scale of 'rising wealth concentrations', opportunity capture and unequal political representation are serious and worrying trends.

For instance:

— Almost half of the world's wealth is now owned by just one percent of the population.

— The wealth of the one percent richest people in the world amounts to $110 trillion.

— That's 65 times the total wealth of the bottom half of the world's population.

— The bottom half of the world's population owns the same as the richest 85 people in the world.

— Seven out of ten people live in countries where economic inequality has increased in the last 30 years.

— The richest one percent increased their share of income in 24 out of 26 countries for which we have data between 1980 and 2012.

— In the U.S.A., the wealthiest one percent captured 95 percent of post-financial crisis growth since 2009, while the bottom 90 percent became poorer.

This massive concentration of economic resources in the hands of fewer people presents a significant threat to inclusive political and economic systems. Instead of moving forward together, people are increasingly separated by economic and political power, inevitably heightening social tensions and increasing the risk of societal breakdown.

(www.oxfam.org)

— Oxfam says that if trends continue, the rich will get richer, and the poor will get poorer.

— In September, a University of California, Berkeley study found that the wealthiest 1 percent of Americans saw their incomes grow by 31.4 percent over the period 2009 to 2012, while the other 99 percent experienced just 0.4 percent growth. Last month, the Pew Research Center published a study that found income inequality in the U.S.A. was at its highest since 1928, the year before the start of the Great Depression."

(www.npr.org)

(C) The third report is from Marion Odell. Here are some excerpts from this report:

— Until May 12, 2011, the World Health Organization (WHO) always followed the lead of the International Atomic Energy Agency (IAEA) on nuclear health effects issues as there is a 1959 agreement that WHO would accept the findings of that organization. This agreement is still in effect and hopefully will be rescinded soon. However, this most likely will need some considerable political pressure from the public. ... On that day in May, history was made when courageous WHO Director-General Margaret Chan said, "There is no safe, low level of radiation." This was very exciting news for those of us who have been working so diligently over many years to get people and governments to understand this simple fact that has been very well-researched and scientifically proven over and over, that there is no safe level of nuclear (ionizing) radiation. There has been no significant media attention paid to this announcement. We learned about it through emails from other NGOs. This gives us some concern as there is sure to be opposition from the nuclear industries and governments that want nuclear power and/or nuclear weapons. It is imperative that we support this tremendously important pronouncement and spread the message far and wide. This is a breakthrough that will impress the public because of the prestige of the World Health Organization and the integrity of the Director-General, Dr. Margaret Chan.

(www.iicph.org)

— Dear Dr. Chan: For those of us in the Non-Governmental Organization (NGO) community that have been working for so many years to awaken the public and politicians to the dangers to the health of ionizing radiation, your pronouncement that radiation is always dangerous and there are no safe, low levels of radiation is very welcome! .... 'Millions of lives have already been adversely affected by ionizing radiation. Our descendants are unlikely to escape the effects even if all proliferation of ionizing radiation should cease today'. Therefore it is vital to warn, teach, and prevent even very low exposures.

[Marion Odell's letter to Director-General WHO Dr. Margaret Chan (www.iicph.org)]

An essential aspect of this work is that neither the root causes nor the resolution of the nuclear dilemma is in politics; instead, they are in theology. The foundation of this work is based on Holy Scriptures, religion, theology, philosophy, literature, history, atomism, and modern nuclear science. Hence readers should keep them aloof and not amalgamate and link this work with any global political scenario regarding the widespread intoxicated zest of adoption of nuclear energy (whether for war or so-called peaceful purpose) shown by some nations around the globe. Instead, this remarkable work is here to implore all humanity on the face of this earth to a one-point plan of raising the voice and saying a big "No" to 'Nuclear Energy', whether for war or so-called peaceful purpose.

Read the words of the author:

"Humankind has the solace of 'No-Atomic-War' pacts, and these are not reliable. They have the satisfaction of safeguards against nuclear radiation, and no safeguards could be a guarantee against nuclear radiation. What hope of peace is there in a world of many nations and diverse considerations, mainly when the devil is at large to hatch his plots to bring about the ruin of the human race. The atomic war in such circumstances may at any time start and seal the doom of miserable humanity."

At first, 'Gabriel's Extinguishing the Atomic Hell Series' comprised fourteen volumes written between 1972 and 1982. The plan was to publish them step by step, one by one, and separately in a sequence. Unfortunately, the author could not make it happen in his lifetime. During the process of revision and composition, the numbers and names of the volumes have changed, and now, at last, this series emerges comprising the final nine volumes packed in two books. The idea is to give the reader the comprehension of the subject as a whole in one place. Because of this reason, while studying these books, the reader will find some repetitions (particularly quotations in successive volumes). Taking some of these echoes out while giving these volumes the shape of two books would have damaged the context, link, and subject. But the purpose of these recurrences is to emphasize the critical nature of this burning issue of nuclear energy. The author was pretty aware of readers' concerns in this regard.

He justified these repetitions for the sake of stress on his subject of critical nature in the following words.

"The name of the atomic bomb is indeed terrible. The very mention of this name strikes terror in the heart of flawed helpless humanity. But worse is another face of nuclear energy, a facet that I might have repeated a hundred times in this work. And which I would never feel tired of repeating as long as I live and breathe, quite unmindful of the charge of unnecessary repetition, namely, the lethal effect of the inherent and inescapable ionizing radiations of nuclear energy generated for war or peaceful purposes. I observe a general tendency in humanity's responsible guides with much heartfelt grief, which can move any sincere-hearted person to genuine resentment. This tendency is to underestimate the radiological hazard of atomic radiation on the plea of obtaining much-needed power from nuclear energy. Of course, it will be with a guilty conscience if I skip this fundamental reality without declaring it at the top of my voice to the whole of the human species."

Last but not least, a critical factor that needs to be noted by the reader is that this work is not a sermon of a traditional preacher who is preaching or trying to preach some specific dogma to the followers of other creeds to convert them. On the contrary, it is an unbiased and neutral analysis of the dilemma and addresses humanity purely on a universal basis without any discrimination between the beliefs. Therefore, to feel delighted, the reader should read it with the same impartial and dispassionate spirit without any blinders of prejudice on the eyes against any religion.

All the readers of this series will not be believers in the Holy Quran. The author was prudent enough in this regard, and he has given a detailed answer to this question in this work. But here, just to give the reader a bird's-eye view, I feel compelled to quote three brief paragraphs from this work as follows.

(1) "Now, please listen. The devil may effectively whisper in your ears: 'Do not hearken to it; it is the Quran, a book in which you do not believe.' Unfortunately, the word of this arch-seducer of people, 'the Satan', may please you, but it is against the dictates of wisdom and may eventually prove fatal. It may bring about grievous consequences but alas then. O, ailing soul! Suppose you could approve the physical treatment of the body by a doctor apparently of a faith different from yours. Why then deny life if vouchsafed by a piece of advice appearing in a book in which you do not formally

believe. But, maybe, this bit of advice is in no way contrary to the Scripture in which you might have believed. There is an overflowing cup of life-giving elixir, pure and celestial; whosoever shall accept it shall do so to his good, and whoever shall reject the same shall reject it to his hurt. Blessed are they who take up the word, the truth, wherever found, and rejoice therein." [6]

(2) "The views expressed therein are hot, not, however, as hot as the nuclear explosion; are indeed stingy but not so as the stings of deadly radiations; and are unpleasant yet not, as unpleasant as the spectacle of cancer-ridden human beings turned chimeras. However, who is to blame for all this embarrassment? Not I. I have said only which the Quran has said, attested indeed and confirmed by science. And that which the Bible and the Gospel of Jesus have said.

Again, the name of the Quran may not sound very pleasant to some. However, what I can assure you is one thing. Once this humankind has had a mere glimpse of that gruesome, called the fiery giant Atumbumb, it would not be capable of finding itself hesitant to fly even into the lap of the devil himself for refuge, if some hope of refuge appeared there. Quran, after all, is a book of guidance and claims a Divine Origin and has a right to guide humankind toward peace.

However, though the Quran has initiated the case, science has furnished the proof thereof. The Bible has had a due share in the work and has found a place of honor. Nay, even the Hindu philosophy of Maya and the Buddhist philosophy of Nirvana have received treatment therein. If Christ, the Mehdi, the Kulkai Autar, or Buddha were today, they would be most zealous in publishing and propagating this work in every language worldwide."

(3) "My heartfelt conviction is that the people worldwide, irrespective of their caste, color, creed, country or religion, inclination, aptitude, or considerations, will view this prophecy with the regard it deserves. They will lend their sympathies to it in the name of humanity and for the sake of their own home, health, children, and all. Because the nuclear explosion respects no such thing: It is a conjoint foe; let us make it a common cause. Or else this common foe will leave nothing. Nay, but you will not even have a chance to mourn your dear and near ones. May Allah bless you with understanding and endow you with wisdom that you may discern the facts and avoid the approaching calamity. Aameen."

No prior knowledge of science is necessary for the reader to understand this work perfectly. May the author's soul rest in peace, and Allah bestows upon humankind wisdom to shun this nuclear 'Leviathan' [7] and save this earth from nuclear doomsday. Furthermore, as presented in this work, may Allah make the state of affairs around the globe conducive to fulfilling the author's life-long dream and cherished wish for global peace. Aameen.

Khalid Mehmood Malik
Hamilton/Stoney Creek,
Ontario, CANADA.
October 25, 2021.

~~*~*~*

---

[1] In this regard, please read (out of many) the following five latest news updates.

(A) NORTH KOREA THREATENS NUCLEAR STRIKE ON WHITE HOUSE: If the U.S.A. threatens North Korea's survival, the country will fire nuclear-armed rockets, says director of the military's General Political Bureau: (July 29, 2014) … A top-ranking North Korean military official has threatened a nuclear strike on the White House and Pentagon after accusing Washington of raising military tensions on the Korean peninsula. Hwang, who holds the rank of vice marshal in the Korean People's Army, said a recent series of South Korea-U.S.A. military drills, one of which included the deployment of a nuclear-powered U.S.A. aircraft carrier, had ramped up tensions.

"If the U.S.A. imperialists threaten our sovereignty and survival --- our troops will fire our nuclear-armed rockets at the White House and the Pentagon - the sources of all evil," Hwang said in his speech broadcast on Monday on state television. (www.telegraph.co.uk)

(B) NORTH KOREA THREATENS 'GANGSTER' U.S.A. WITH NUCLEAR STRIKES, CYBER WARFARE; RULES OUT TALKS: (February 04, 2015): North Korea on Wednesday ruled out further negotiations with the United States, and threatened to react with nuclear strikes and cyber warfare to any U.S.A. attempt to ignite "a war of aggression." (www.ibtimes.com)

(C) UKRAINE CONFLICT: PUTIN 'WAS READY FOR NUCLEAR ALERT'

President Vladimir Putin has said he was ready to put Russia's nuclear weapons on standby during tensions over the crisis in Ukraine and Crimea. --- On putting Russia's nuclear weapons into a state of combat

readiness, Mr. Putin said: "We were ready to do this." "[Crimea] is our historical territory. Russian people live there. They were in danger. We cannot abandon them," he added. [(www.bbc.com) / (March 15, 2015)]
(D) DOOMSDAY CLOCK SET AT 3 MINUTES TO MIDNIGHT By MONEY MORNING STAFF REPORTS – (3/6/2015) & (3/15/2015): The Earth's "Doomsday Clock' just jumped up to 23:57 in January 2015 - just three minutes from midnight, or complete global disaster. ... That's the first time we have moved this close to collapse in 21 years.

The Bulletin of Atomic Scientists Executive, which has been setting the iconic clock since 1947, cited <u>extraordinary and undeniable threats to the continued existence of humanity</u> behind the move, adding that "<u>the probability of global catastrophe is very high</u>." ... One of the things the Doomsday Clock measures is what's pushing the globe to a crisis point. In the past that's been global conflicts, unstable financial markets, nuclear threats, and environmental catastrophes. ... Should the rise of attacks on the U.S.A. dollar and conflicts across the Middle East and Russia serve as a warning sign that Doomsday is approaching? ... According to Jim Rickards, the CIA's Asymmetric Warfare Advisor, the answer is yes. In a startling interview he reveals that all 16 U.S.A. Intelligence Agencies have begun to prepare for actual <u>World War III</u>. Making matters worse, his colleagues believe it could begin within the next 6 months. However, the ground zero location for this global conflict is what makes his interview a must-see for every American.

(http://moneymorning.com/ext/articles/rickards/doomsday.php?iris=329207)
(E) RUSSIA TO TARGET DENMARK'S WARSHIPS IF IT JOINS MISSILE SHIELD – AMBASSADOR (Sun March 22, 2015)
(Reuters) - Danish warships will be a target for Russian nuclear weapons if the Scandinavian country joins NATO's missile defence programme, Russia's ambassador to Denmark told the newspaper Jyllands-Posten.

"If that happens, Danish warships will be targets for Russian nuclear missiles," Vanin said in an interview published on Saturday.

(http://in.reuters.com)
The ambassador wrote: "I do not think that the Danes fully understand the consequences if Denmark joins the U.S.A.-led missile defence shield. If that happens, Danish warships become targets for Russian nuclear missiles. Denmark will be part of the threat to Russia."

(www.cityam.com)

[2] Greek Mythology: **Chimera** is a fire-breathing she-monster usually represented as a lion, goat, and serpent composite.

[3] **Baconian:** It is a term coined by the author meaning 'of Bacon'. The reader will frequently come across this term throughout this work.

[4] **Namrud** (**Arabic:** النمرود an-Namrood) was the king of Shinar, the son of Kush, and the great-grandson of Prophet Nuh. He intended to burn the Prophet Ibraheem on the pyre but failed because Allah made the fire cold. His daughter Sara later married Ibraheem.

[5] LOW-LEVEL RADIATION FROM JAPAN ON B.C. SHORES
By Canadian Press: APRIL-06/2015
VICTORIA — Radiation from the leaking Fukushima nuclear reactor in Japan has been detected on the shores of Vancouver Island. --- Scientists say it's the first time since a tsunami in Japan four years ago that radiation has been found on the shorelines of North America.

(http://www.msn.com)

[6] In this regard, please refer to Book-2/volume-9/chapter-6: "Address to the Jews, Christians, Hindus, Buddhists, and the Communists" for an exciting incident described by the author. Read the meaningful dialogue cautiously that took place between the British Ambassador and the author.

[7] **Leviathan:** It is a sea monster mentioned in the 'Book of Job' in the Bible, where it is associated with the forces of chaos and evil. The author has associated this 'Leviathan' with the nuclear phenomena. Its description will be of genuine interest to the reader and the scientists due to such features of the 'Leviathan' as seen in the atomic bomb and other igneous devices of modern science concerning the natural phenomena and man's control over the forces of Mother Nature. In this regard, please refer to Book-2/volume-8/chapter-5: 'The Bible's and Quran's relative frame of reference'.

~~*~*~*~*

PROLOGUE

GABRIEL TRUMPETS THE DOOMSDAY OF THIS SCIENCE-GUIDED BACONIAN CULTURE PROGRESS

Fellow humans! It is my destiny to greet you with a terrific warning. It is time now to trumpet the doomsday of this science-guided, Baconian culture of progress. Adopt atomic energy for peace, and nuclear annihilation of this world is a certainty. Ban the atomic energy, and the result is the cessation of this Economico-Industrial setup. Hopes, expectations, and optimism of the scientists and the non-scientists to the contrary are but a dream whose interpretation is a blazing hell of nuclear Jehannah (hell). Progress, atomic energy, and atomic bombs are trinity interlinked. The disappearance of one implies the disappearance of the other two. The annulment of the atomic war entails the abolition of atomic energy as well as of this progress. Be not surprised. The flames of atomic hell are more surprising.

This modern progress has its own peculiar and particular features and characteristics. It is a process functioning per particular laws, and it has its specific stages and results. It is organized, systematic, continuous, ever-increasing, and infinite. It is exclusively a matter of the world. Moreover, because it is a matter of the world and ever-increasing, it must gradually occupy man's mind and time, expelling the otherworld's thought. Besides, because it is infinite, it must ultimately dismiss the idea of the otherworld entirely from man's mind and time, and because the otherworld is the basis of faith and revealed religion, the faith, and revealed religion thus would be expelled from man's mind and time. It is not difficult to observe this transition. That religion only could allow this sort of progress which was willing to sign the warrant of its exile; therefore, either religion or this progress. Men may accept willingly or be helpless to accept a life of progress without religion, but this modern culture is of ultimate ruin. Again, it is continuous, ever-increasing, and infinite greed and necessity. Ever-increasing anarchy, endless conflict, burning discontent in an atmosphere of mistrust, distrust, and immorality will ultimately result in a universal war of a race of hungry, enraged cannibals, to mean universal destruction. Are you happy?

Again, the energy is the spirit of this progress. In a natural sequence, chemical, electrical and nuclear energy have appeared in this progress. The fuels of chemical nature having been exhausted in time, and the humankind helplessly entangled in the net of Economico-Industrial setup, nevertheless will be forced to choose between the alternatives, namely, either to adopt atomic energy to atomic ruin or, let the Economico-Industrial setup freeze with the resulting disastrous famine, transient though. It appears that humankind will adopt the course of atomic energy to nuclear ruin. Nuclear ruin or no nuclear ruin; thus, the result of this modern progress in every way is the ruin, the universal ruin.

Refer to the prophecy about the 'Messiah-id-Dajjaal' (Anti-Christ), [1] a marvel of a prophecy made by the Holy Prophet of Islam (peace be upon him). You will have no difficulty finding to your horror that this Baconian culture of modern progress shows every feature that the Prophet of Islam (peace be upon him) ascribed to the left-eyed, donkey-ridden monster that is the Anti-Christ. It is possible to regard this modern science as a result thereof having the same features. Yet I say not to you that it is the same 'Messiah-id-Dajjaal', though it will destroy this world if humankind does not eliminate it beforehand.

This modern progress has grown upon Bacon's philosophy of modern atomism, and poor Blake was not amiss when he said:

"If what Bacon says is right, what Christ says is false?"

Francis Bacon, the greatest benefactor of humankind, did to the posterity of Adam on earth what the devil had previously done to their progenitor in Paradise. The proof now is no longer a secret. Christ, in his first coming, had struggled against the ancient atomism of Democritus. So, if he appears today in his second coming, he will have to struggle against this modern atomism of Bacon.

In the age of full-fledged atomic energy for peace, everything from a power-house to a private car will have its private reactor. The exploding reactors will be making a worldwide bonfire of radiation and changing this earth into a vast hospital of radiation sickness. The governments, tottering under economic pressure, will indicate the failure of Baconian progress in fulfilling its promises of plenty and self-sufficiency. Given the circumstances as they now prevail, no alternative appears for this humankind but either to vanish under the hail of atomic bombs suddenly and deservedly or perish under the deadly stings of atomic radiations; slowly, lingeringly, miserably in the form of cancer-ridden chimeras.

This world will see the ultimate futility of 'America-Russia-Peace-Treaties', nuclear deterrence, and freeze on nuclear weapons' movements, just as it has seen the futility of the strong Einstein-Russell appeals in the past. This race of Baconian locusts will not rest till it has reached the zones of nuclear spray. These monuments of science (appearing so formidable and enduring) and worldwide Economico-Industrial setup will disappear as if by the touch of a magic wand at the appearance of the atomic bombs. There is another possibility that life on earth may become extinct by the long-term effects of atomic energy radiation for peace. As a result, humans will leave behind them, these monuments abandoned, and habitations of the human race as the memorials of a misguided species.

Remember! This atomic hell is the wrath of Allah enkindled as retribution, though it is not Allah that will rain the atomic bombs from the heavens; it is the man himself that will. You will be surprised if I tell you that severe punishment is the consequence of evils like 'slander', 'engrossment in the pursuit of wealth', and 'undue confidence in this worldly life'. Yet the fact is even so. It is a punishment for this modern progress. Because there is no protection possible against the wrath of Allah, no protection is possible from this atomic hell which is the atomic bombs and the atomic radiations. Castaway, every hope of ever discovering any means of protection from the atomic bombs or atomic radiations. I speak this not at haphazard. Nor is this in any way the alarmist view. It is the verdict of matter-of-fact science, inaudible to those only that are doomed. Terrible are the effects of radiation, even if unaccompanied by a fearful blast of the atomic bomb. Will you understand? Ask the scientist for an answer if he can show you any cause for hope. Nor does he hope that there would be no atomic war on any basis. Again, to think that this earth will be a place worth living in after a total or a partial war is a thought which reflects little sagacity. And further, to expect that humankind will survive the age of the full-fledged atomic energy for peace or that humankind of that age will find it worth living is an expectation that only is a delusion.

The present age is the age of origin-seeking Darwin, and the mind-analyst Freud noted distinctly for her scientific research, rational criticism, and hair-splitting attitude. It is hard to believe that the full attention of such an age should be exclusively entangled in the fruits of the nuclear problem, utterly unmindful of the roots. The destruction of atomic weapons is like the act of picking up the fruits of a tree in a season. These fruits will again grow in the next season. Hence, if the desire is to demolish fruit, you have to strike at the root of the tree.

Humanity may find the roots of the nuclear problem in the soil of ethics. Science is only an instrument. Unfortunately, there has not been an author in the modern age whose attention has been drawn towards this fact on which depends the solution of the entire problem. Focus on the fundamental causes, therefore, if you intend to solve the nuclear problem. [2] Greed is the root, this progress is the body, and the nuclear bomb is the tree's fruit. Radiation may be regarded as a nuclear fragrance. Chant the Christ's 'Sermon on the Mount' to scare the grisly, this fiery giant Atumbumb away.

On the other hand, every sage and every ignoramus of this age prescribes more production and self-sufficiency as the sole remedy of all the present ills, as if adding fuel to the kiln could extinguish the fire. It is a strange logic and far worse than the witch doctor of the past ages of superstition. Now is the time to discover the root causes of the nuclear problem and expose the actual reality. Present humankind is deplorably ignorant of nuclear science and needs teaching and education in this regard. The plight and existence of the human species and entire life on earth are staked now on the subject of nuclear science. The fruit of my life-long endeavor, 'Gabriel's Extinguishing the Atomic Hell Series', can serve the purpose well.

This series comprises the interpretation and explanation of the prophecy of the Quran about the atomic hell that is the atomic bombs and atomic radiations and the hellish atmosphere of the atomic culture. The theory of relativity was the discovery of Einstein himself and was unknown to the scientist or the non-scientist. Similarly, discovering this prophecy in the Quran is indeed by the Grace of Almighty Allah my own, and known to none in the world, Muslim, or non-Muslim.

The prophecy has about 36 words, covering the entire philosophy of modern atomism and modern atomic science. The text of the prophecy is as follows.

"Woe to every backbiter, defamer, who amasseth wealth (of this world) and arrangeth it (against the future). He thinketh that his wealth will render him immortal. Nay, for verily, he will be cast into Al-Hotama. And what could teach thee what Al-Hotama is? It is the fire of Allah enkindled which leapeth up unto the hearts. It is (a fire) closed in on them in outstretched columns."

(Quran: 104 'Al-Homaza')

Now, let a philosopher read this prophecy and see for himself if the description of this modern Baconian, materialistic culture of science-guided progress as is given by the Quran in a manner so succinct and yet so comprehensive is not remarkable. Let the atomist read the characterization of the atomic phenomena as appears in this prophecy, and he can discern and discover for himself in these 36 words of the prophecy the basic, distinctive, and distinguishing characteristics of atomic phenomena that distinguish it from the rest of the phenomena, e.g., chemical, electrical, and physical. I have discovered every distinguishing characteristic of the nuclear phenomena that science has discovered and recorded in my work. Will this world, now approaching the brink of its nuclear doom, consider this claim my challenge? Moreover, will it condescend to examine its validity by reading my work? Or, I don't know, whether this world is doomed to perish in a nuclear holocaust? And will, therefore, persist in the pride of its knowledge and regard my work as not worth considering, for this earth's ultimate fate is known only to Allah. But what is known to me is that every claim I make is based on factual proof strictly. It is not possible for me in this brief address to explain things in detail.

Remember! You will hear in this address things that might appear to you as hyperbolic, embellishment, fulminatory, boisterous, boastful, overpowering, and even like a rant. Yet, in reality, there is no such thing. The facts described therein are too great to avoid the suspicion of hyperbolism. Calling a hill, a mountain is not hyperbolic, though naming a little fish a whale or a tiny ant a giant elephant is exaggerated. Again, if it were possible to render hyperbolic the description of the atomic bomb explosion itself, the attempt would have sounded pleasant in the ears of a citizen of an atomic that is a superpower. Yet, the same thing might not appear so pleasant to the would-be victims of that bomb. It is my destiny to deal with a world drunk with the inebriating wine of progress in such a way that even the description of its ill effects and its destructive phenomena is prone to sound hyperbolic in their ears.

Firstly, know that the Baconian culture of progress described by this prophecy of the Quran would leave Bertrand Russell stunned with wonder. For, no better and more accurate description of this wealth-accumulating and pre-planning process of this modern progressive and world-loving humankind could be expected in an age fourteen centuries in the past when no trace of the philosophy of atomism existed. Similarly, the scientific characterization of the atomic phenomena, which is the most modern and the most complex of the phenomena, in just about 36 words, is a feat not probable for even an Einstein to achieve undoubtedly in the presence of atomic science. This scientific characterization of the atomic phenomena given by a Scripture fourteen hundred years in the past in an age of no science is a fact not likely to fail in casting Einstein himself in a trance.

Thus, through this prophecy of the Quran, a Russell and an Einstein, the greatest intellects of their time, would be able to understand the difference and distance between the greatest human intellects and divine intelligence. If my claim to the characterization of the nuclear phenomena by the Quran fourteen centuries ago be valid, then what reason remains with the scientist or skeptic to deny the miraculous aspect of this prophecy of the Quran even though science itself rejected the possibility of the miraculous? The prophecy has given out the 'slander', the 'engrossment in the pursuit of wealth accumulation', and the 'love of this worldly life' as evils. People don't esteem these as evil in this age. But, on the other hand, they regard them as desirable, innocent, guiltless, and essential, no doubt the sole object of man's life.

Secondly, it was not for Plato or Aristotle to see or establish a sequential link between the materialistic philosophy of atomism and the appearance of the atomic hell, that is, the atomic bombs and atomic radiations. However, people recognized both these celebrities as the most chronic antagonists of the ancient atomism of Democritus. Indeed, the discovery of this link that the prophecy has seen fourteen hundred years before the appearance of the fact will throw Plato, and Aristotle stunned with wonder. To them, also the difference and the distance between the greatest of human intellects and the divine intelligence might appear clearly.

However, the most beneficial aspect of the prophecy is to mention the causes of the appearance of the atomic hell. Thereby we see that only by removing the causes mentioned could their effects be removed. To wit, by removing this modern progress, the danger of nuclear annihilation could be removed. Thus, we understand that the destruction of humankind in the nuclear hell is not a decree pre-ordained, but instead is an affair of the condition and could be avoided. You might be surprised to know that the Quran has in this prophecy pointed out the causes of the appearance of the atomic hell for the first time in this world. This modern age is the era of scientific research, philosophical inquiry, critical appreciation, origin-seeking Darwins and Darwinians, hair-splitting Freuds, and Freudians. But you will be surprised even more to learn that no philosopher has ever tried to peep into the causes of the nuclear trouble in this modern age. No philosophical inquiry whatsoever has ever been conducted to investigate the root causes of the nuclear fruit. Instead, the full attention of the thoughtful people is engaged in avoiding the atomic war and putting the atomic energy to peaceful purposes. No one has hitherto pointed out that the inquiry of the nuclear problem takes us right into the heart of ethics.

No man in this age has ever doubted the correctness of this modern progress and the validity of this Baconian culture. The tree of progress to them is beneficial, valid, and correct. The nuclear problems are only like thorns that humankind can remove. That is why when everyone hears the cry of more production and further progress to self-sufficiency as the remedy for all ills, the cry never strikes anyone that is meant only to add fuel to the kiln to extinguish the fire. The necessity was to cut the root of the tree. Even Russell saw a Paradise of bliss for this humankind in the course of progress through atomic energy in case this humankind forgot its quarrels.

I have yet another surprise for you, namely, that humankind's existence and future well-being are now staked on two points. While on both these scores, the humanity of this age of knowledge and science is generally ignorant. One of these is the root causes of the nuclear problem. The other, of course, is atomic science. The first that is the causes of the nuclear crisis is known to none except me in today's entire world. The second, atomic science, is known only to the atomists, while the non-scientist intelligentsia, including the most learned ones, is ignorant about it. Another point is that only the Quran should point out the primary causes of nuclear trouble to this age to show the difference and the distance between the human intellect and the divine intelligence.

Severe no doubt might appear the measure prescribed by the Quran, namely, the complete eradication of this modern system of progress to eliminate the danger of nuclear ruin. Yet, appearing drastic only to a generation steeped and knocked deep into the Baconian marsh of this modern progress; a generation inebriated by the wine of wealth and physical comforts and being helplessly dragged in the net of a universal Economico-Industrial setup like fish toward the nuclear harbor to be roasted there, along with their children, in the nuclear ovens. Drastic indeed, but only until the horrifying squadrons of fiery giant Atumbumb and the pestering swarms of deadly radiations have appeared to consume this world.

The great English philosopher, late Bertrand Russell, died in disappointment about the end of this modern humankind. But, unfortunately, the little gold pamphlet which he so very kindly sent me in 1964 contained only one sentence which read:

"Since Adam and Eve ate the apple, man has never refrained from any folly of which he was capable."

The pamphlet contained a few caricatures that indicated that war and suppression were the most manifests of human follies in the sight of Russell. I judge that, even if war is completely abolished from this world in the presence of atomic energy for peace for this progress, humankind will perish under the stings of radiations in an age of full-fledged atomic energy for peace. Everything will have its reactor in that age, from a power-house to a private car, and the exploding reactors will make a universal bonfire of radiations.

Russell died in disappointment, and so would have I. Still, thanks to my discovery of the prophecy of the Quran, which fostered hope and expectation in my heart. I produced a work based on the prophecy that might save this world from the tragic atomic doom. Nobody knows better than me how dearly I miss Russell and Einstein. How helpful they would have proved to me by making a due appreciation of my work to benefit this world.

Some people say, well, we must die one day. What difference it would make if by atomic bombs or atomic radiations. They appear to be mistaken. They not only forget the untold and unheard-of miseries that are associated with the nuclear affair but also, they are ignorant of yet another extremely horrible fact. They do not know that this nuclear affair is not restricted to this transient world only, but it moves onward, onto the next eternal world, where an eternal atomic hell lies in wait. The temporal atomic hell of this world is only the replica and the representation of that eternal atomic hell waiting in the next eternal world. That eternal atomic hell is called by the Quran by the name of 'Hotama' in the prophecy under issue, just as ordinary fire represents the ordinary hell of the next world. We understand that the evils responsible for the appearance of this transient atomic hell, as we can see them, are the same as are mentioned by the prophecy for the punishment in the 'Hotama' of the next world. They, therefore, who deserved the transient atomic hell of this present world, even if they chanced to escape this atomic hell unscathed to the next world, there they will find the 'Hotama', the eternal atomic hell awaiting them without any possibility of escape.

Also, this humankind now appears apprehensive of the danger of atomic war only. Still, it is ignorant and unmindful that even now, in the absence of the atomic war, it is in a sort of a hell unfelt due to the hypnotizing and inebriating influence of the increasing wealth, physical comforts, and indeed the hope of self-sufficiency and security. Only if they could observe their discontent, apprehension, fear, frustration, heart-burning, worry, panting, sweating, running, rushing, hustling, and bustling, sufferings, sorrows, and misery. Till, in the wilderness of this progress and quest of self-sufficiency, they have fallen prey to atomic vultures to perish. Moreover, that might not mean even an end to their misery because the eternal atomic vultures will welcome them in the next world.

Now, I will tell you something about my work: the interpretation of the prophecy of the Quran about the atomic hell in nine volumes, as mentioned before. You will hear in this respect things appearing as hyperbolic and boastful, but time will prove that they are statements; just, exact, and sober. This work, brethren, is, as you too will know in time, the only light, and the sole guidance in this world to lead this distressed humankind out of the nuclear hell. My work is Noah's ark for this deluge of atomic fire. No Anti-Nuclear movement in this world and no endeavor to revive religion can ever succeed in this age without adopting the guidelines and basic principles given in this work.

The views expressed therein are hot, not, however, as hot as the nuclear explosion; are indeed stingy but not so as the stings of deadly radiations; and are unpleasant yet not, as unpleasant as the spectacle of cancer-ridden human beings turned chimeras. However, who is to blame for all this embarrassment? Not I. I have said only which the Quran has said, attested indeed and confirmed by science. And that which the Bible and the Gospel of Jesus have said.

Again, the name of the Quran may not sound very pleasant to some. However, what I can assure you is one thing. Once this humankind has had a mere glimpse of that gruesome, called the fiery giant Atumbumb, it would not be capable of finding itself hesitant to fly even into the lap of the devil himself for refuge, if some hope of refuge appeared there. Quran, after all, is a book of guidance and claims a Divine Origin and has a right to guide humankind toward peace.

However, though the Quran has initiated the case, science has furnished the proof thereof. The Bible has had a due share in the work and has found a place of honor. Nay, even the Hindu philosophy of Maya and the Buddhist philosophy of Nirvana have received treatment therein. If Christ, the Mehdi, the Kulkai Autar, or Buddha were today, they would be most zealous in publishing and propagating this work in every language worldwide. This work has no forerunner and may have no followers. I conceit that all the intellectual celebrities of the age combined would find it hard to produce the like of it which I have indeed by the Grace of Merciful Allah produced single-handed and alone.

Fellow humans! This Baconian culture is proved to be false, and its end now is apparent. You may hereafter wander in the wilderness of this Baconian culture for centuries in quest of self-sufficiency and in the hope of peace and control over this nuclear problem, to be the prey of nuclear vultures only. An ever-increasing feeling of hunger and poverty will be your lot despite the mountainous heaps of commodities. Ever-increasing and endless anarchy, strife, discontent, fear, mistrust, arson sabotage, and homicide will prevail worldwide. You see now everywhere the battling and rattling of nations, sects, and individuals. These strifes will not abate but will forever increase, till the fire has spread worldwide and has assumed international character and has involved the entire world in bringing about the destruction of the entire life on earth.

Fellow humans! Times are coming when you sigh and wish for the atomic war to rid you of a life unbearably miserable. It has fallen to my miserable lot to remind you of the terrific denunciations of Prophet Moses. He warned with these admonitions the children of Israel on Mount Gerizim and Mount Ebal in his last address to his people, in case they failed to listen to the voice of God, their Lord. These denunciations cause anyone to shudder, and human history has failed to produce another address like that. Just read the Bible, 'Deuteronomy' chapter-28. [3] In this respect, I have to inform you, today it is not the Jewish race only. It is the entire humankind that may be seen as the victims of the terrible denunciations made against the children of Israel in the address of Moses. For instance:

"Is not the rain of this earth now the powdery nuclear fall-out, and will it not continue to fall on earth till this entire humankind is destroyed?"

However, read the entire content of chapter-28.

Fellow Humans! I make a universal and earnest appeal to you in the name of humanity to publish my work and implore you to show sense and cast away all prejudice to consult safety. I may not make any divine pretensions or claim titles like the Christ, the Mehdi, the Kulkai Autar, or Buddha. Nevertheless, I am bound to inform you that these volumes I have produced after a life-long struggle under the supervising eye of the Providence just as Noah had built his ark under the supervising eye of the Providence. Therefore, there is no alternative for you now but to publish these volumes or be prepared for nuclear ruin. If you assume indifference, you will see the mysterious Providence at work against you to bring calamities upon you from sources that might be secret and unknown to you. Fear Allah, therefore, and show sense.

Jews! You are the guides, the leaders, and the masters of this age of Baconian culture. Indeed, you have found your Messiah in this Anti-Christic, Baconian culture, and you are the hierarchs of this worldwide, Anti-Christic, Baconian culture. All the rest of the nations are your proselytes. Beware, therefore, and repent. Read chapter-28 of 'Deuteronomy' and try to assess the portion and proportion of your destruction when the final moment arrives.

Christians! You are the victims of the Baconian culture of modern materialistic atomism, the un-Christian, Anti-Christian, and Anti-Christic culture. Remember! You stand accused of spreading it worldwide and, consequently, dragging behind you the entire world into the flames of the atomic hell, the logical and scientific consequence of the Baconian culture. Beware, therefore, repent and read Christ's 'Sermon on the Mount'. Know that the Christian banners planted on the Moon or Mars refer to the glory, neither Christianity nor Christ, but of atomism, Francis Bacon and Anti-Christ. The banner on the moon is Ozymandias's reminiscence.

Muslims! You slavish followers of this philosophy of modern progress have come to consider this modern progress as an article of your faith and compatible with the views of the Quran. You are the victims of a misunderstanding that will cast you into the flames of the atomic hell in this world and the next world. Can you think that the teachings of the Quran could lead its followers into the nuclear Jehannah? Misunderstanding emanates from the fact that you fail to differentiate between the purpose of the Quran given to 'Ghaur-Fil-Aayaat' (the contemplation of the works of Allah) and the purpose which Baconian progress has adopted. The same may be said of 'Taskhir-il-Kaayinaat' (the conquest of Mother Nature). The Quran points upward in this respect while this Baconian progress, as may be seen, not only points downward toward the earth but even changes its adopters into earthworms. Read the Quran in comparison with the Baconian philosophy, and you will see the difference.

The Quran never was a book of materialism despite its license for the human necessities of life. Suppose you fail to realize even in the presence of the most manifest of the proofs that is this atomic hell. In that case, you will only see the fact in the flames of the nuclear Jehannah, 'Al-Hotama', as the Quran has with miraculous appropriateness called it. Read the chapter 'Al-Homaza' and dread. You are being guided aright in these lines and indeed for your benefit lest you say tomorrow, nobody told you. My views can be attested by every authentic commentator of the Quran, from Abdullah Ibn-Abbas to Shabbir Ahmad Usmani. Your helplessness in this universal Economico-Industrial setup is an excuse not acceptable to the inexorable laws of Mother Nature.

Muslims! Regarding the nuclear problem, you are entangled in the same net with the entire humankind that is fast approaching nuclear Jehannah. My work is based on the direct interpretation of the Quran itself, corroborated by science in these volumes. Hence, it appears natural that I should appeal to you, particularly those who claim to be the followers of the Quran.

Muslims! I have to say a lot to you in this challenging situation of the world. Yet so grievous is the peril and such utterly hopeless and deplorable is the situation in which I find myself fallen, that words begin to fail me. My more courageous than twenty lions' heart begins to sink in dismay. Seldom was a servant of humanity fallen in a difficult situation and so peculiarly queer as I have amidst this inebriated by the Anti-Christic deceit. I have produced a miracle of the Quran greater than which nobody ever produced on earth. It is a miracle greater than raising the dead.

Yet, I see a veil cast on the eyes of even followers of the Quran by blinding intoxication of love for wealth and physical comforts. They turn a deaf ear to my appeals for help. With a burning zeal in their hearts to publish it as a light to the world to save humankind from nuclear doom and as an honor to the word of Allah, Muslims ought to throng me. But, on the other hand, I see the Muslim nation uninterested and in a mood of indifference.

Muslims! I need not recite to you the terrible denunciations of Moses that he made against Israel's children. The prophecy of the Quran about 'Al-Hotama' is in itself terrible enough. My work is the interpretation of the prophecy of the Quran about the atomic hell. It is the only guidance and hope of escaping the most painful and most disgraceful end in the burning flames of the nuclear Jehannah, both in this transient world and the next eternal world. I will only say that failing to publish it, you will thus deprive humankind of the light and guidance therein. Then here in this world, you will feel yourself sitting on a muffled mouth of a live volcano. The worst kind of calamities and vicissitudes from unknown and unseen sources will be your lot till the final moment of the universal wholesale destruction of this world has arrived.

You will see yourself being dragged with the tail of the Baconian West into the dazzling flames of the nuclear Jehannah, the enkindled wrath of Allah. You will fall in this nuclear Jehannah, as helplessly and as slavishly as you have followed the Baconian West in adopting the Baconian progress, in apparent contradiction to the word of the Quran. Moreover, on the Day of Judgment, you will stand before the throne of Allah, answerable for neglecting the publication of the guidance of the Quran and failing humankind in the moment of greatest peril and distress. If the nuclear Jehannah consumes this world of Allah without having published this prophecy of the Quran about the atomic hell, then it is you and not the non-Muslim nations that will bear the brunt of the blame.

Beware, therefore. Fear Allah and repent. There still is some little margin left for repentance for those who may feel inclined to repentance. Remember, if the Muslims make the Islamic world a prison to my interpretation of the prophecy of the Quran about the atomic hell, the Providence will demolish the wall of the prison that the Quran may burst through.

Muslims! I have no power over you, just as I have no power over anyone else but let the word of the Quran count if you believe in the Quran. I admit to your right to ascertain the authenticity and validity of my work. I am aware of my obscurity. I invite you to judge my work. I will give you every quarter in that respect. But I inform you that to judge my work; you have to call in a number of the leading physicists and Radiobiologists worldwide to attest the authenticity of the Quranic characterization of the atomic phenomena found in the prophecy about the nuclear hell. Also, you have to call in some noted philosophers, particularly that of atomism worldwide, to attest the truth of the Quranic description of the philosophy of modern atomism as is to be found in the prophecy about the nuclear hell. A number of the Quran's commentators who have a Quranic commentary to their credit should also be included. Why should the Muslims grudge such a conference when many conferences are held annually in the Islamic world for purposes and topics that may well be regarded as comparatively superfluous? Why do my nine volumes not be published by the Islamic world when hundreds of books are annually published, which, if published or not, would make not the slightest difference to this world?

Muslims! Have no apprehensions and no misapprehensions. I am not going to plunge you in any instantaneous practical revolution by the publication of these volumes. Nay, but it is only publishing a few volumes, first original and then in translations in every language. The seed therein will gradually grow, and the publishers will have the credit. Then, knowing the reality, nations will gradually chalk out some collaborative program to rid this world of nuclear danger.

Muslims! I had an intention to side-track you and save you the trouble of publishing my work. Still, I expect difficulties due to the general Baconian helplessness of this humankind, mainly due to the name of the Quran. Neither I have the mind nor find myself in a position in present circumstances to say to you to do this, or do not do that. But I cannot desist from saying that being Muslims, it is not your role to follow the world into the atomic hell blindly. Instead, your role is to oppose nuclear weapons, dissolve the nuclear problem, and stand against these evils manfully like true Muslims to save this humankind from nuclear doom. The world will be grateful to you for your kindness. It is far better than being cast into the nuclear pit like a filth basket and consumed. No better gift of the Islamic world to this distressed humankind in the 15th century Hijra program could be than the set of this work of mine published. No one country alone could do much against this nuclear problem. Therefore, let us teach humankind the reality of the nuclear problem so that the nations coming together would chalk out a joint, gradual program to rid this world of nuclear danger.

Hindus and Buddhists! I remind you that both the Hindu philosophy of Maya and the Buddhist philosophy of Nirvana are opposed to this Baconian philosophy of modern atomism and this modern progress. Also, the palanquin of this modern progress crashes right into the flames of the 'Promanu-Narkh' that is the 'Hotama' or 'atomic hell'.

Atomists! I implore you to come to your senses and realize your responsibility in this nuclear affair. You must declare to the world the uncontrollability of nuclear power and doubtfulness of any discovery that might bring the nuclear affair within the control of man. Preach to the world the horrible aspects of nuclear hazards. Instead of designing still more destructive atomic bombs and more powerful reactors, leave this noxious profession, take up some other employment somewhere, and make it your mission to teach your fellow humans the nefarious reality of the nuclear affair. Instead of dying of cancer in a hospital, die as a missionary of a humanitarian cause. Tell the world that the atomic bomb is not a weapon, but it is the wrath of Allah, and that the atomic war is not a war but is the wholesale destruction of life on earth.

Despite all this inducement, the present generation of humankind may not be willing to publish this work. Then, I pray that at least preserve this work in some museum. Hence, perhaps some future generation, being in acute distress and grievous danger, might seek the guidance contained therein and emerge from the atomic pit which their preceding generations bequeathed to them as a legacy. If, however, a meter is invented to measure the continuous deterioration of the world's nuclear situation, humankind could continually measure the increasing need for my work in direct proportion. [4]

Why should a man in my position and circumstances ever undertake a work of this nature and undergo such a lengthy and afflictive ordeal? Why not a Russell or a William James if not a Darwin or a Spinoza? No one in the world can give a satisfactory answer to this question except him, who has been whipped through this ordeal. That is, I, my miserable self. Why should I sacrifice every ambition? Why should I sacrifice every desire? Why should I submit myself to so excruciating an experience while hundreds of thousands of highly learned persons with dozens of degrees from reputable universities existed in this age of knowledge and science? Now, when I look back at my forty years' long intellectual pilgrimage, I see no John Bunyan that could find a heart to narrate my pilgrimage. I fail to discern a Sigmund Freud that could own a method to subject the manner of my intellectual attainment to psychoanalysis. Mine has been an experience that fails to find a precedent in the history of thought provided that someone examined my particular case minutely.

My answer to this question, though simple, is that I was born on February 17, 1917, with a destiny to fight this deluge of atomic fire and save this world. February 17, according to the Bible, is the date of the eruption of Noah's deluge though of water against this present one of fire. In my childhood, I saw specific visions that I now understand to be of great authenticity and presaging significant universal events in line with my mission of saving humankind from grievous doom in the flames of atomic hell. In 1942, the great Italian Physicist Enrico Fermi opened the gate of atomic fire on humankind by discovering the formula of 'Open Sesame' by his successful realization of the Uranium fission chain reaction in Chicago, America. It was my 25th and the fateful year. I was in Mussayyib, a place near Baghdad, in Iraq. In a vision, I was recommended by the Green-turbaned saint 'Al-Khidr' to Abraham for the Abrahamic Mission to warn this world about the atomic hell, expose the nuclear problem's actual reality, and teach this world the methods of escaping the grievous atomic doom. I was in that vision shown extraordinary great signs of Allah. In the same era and at the same place, I was shown the crucifix in another vision. I, at that time, had but little knowledge and extremely meager education.

But, after that, as a man prepossessed, I took to study. I learned languages and works of literature, English, Arabic, Persian, and Urdu; Philosophies, ancient and modern; Mathematics with its every branch, Arithmetic, Geometry, and Algebra; Sciences to the nuclear science; Scriptures, the Quran, and the Bible, the Old and the New Testament; year after year, indeed without a school and a teacher, and always obliged to work for my subsistence and the subsistence of a respectable family.

Till in 1961, I stumbled upon discovering the Prophetic warning of the Quran about the atomic hell. Thereby I realized my theme and set to the research in the subjects involved therein. You will wonder from where I received the books for study from the beginning of my course to its end forty years later. I leave this point to you to wonder about it. Books, however, in hundreds on various topics I received, and I read to absorb them, meditate on the points contained therein, and make them a piece with my mind. Then, in 1972, I set myself to writing till in 1982 I brought my work to its finish. I have another three thousand pages of writings on various topics in Urdu and Persian besides these English writings, all hitherto unpublished and all in the form of manuscripts. You can judge my labor and industry, but you cannot know of my sufferings and afflictions.

Now, I have the key to humankind's future destiny and all these invaluable treasures of knowledge in my hand, which never added a groat or a penny to my pocket. But I stand groping in darkness in an indifferent world, fearing that these manuscripts will be eaten away by white-ants because I have no home, property, health, or wealth to secure these voluminous writings. Let this, however, be known to humanity that if these manuscripts are eaten away by the white-ants, it is not merely the leaves of paper but the future destiny of humankind that the white-ants will eat away.

Remember that I place no claim on my dreams or visions. Regard all that as my personal affair. What I insist upon is the perusal of my works on their merit. If my works are published, I would prefer to be forgotten myself by humanity. However, know that this work has its power and thrust. A work claiming the power to destroy all these stockpiles of atomic bombs and all these arsenals of conventional weapons ought as a rule to have its power, in fact, weightier than the stockpiles it has to destroy. Therefore, if this world found wanting in cooperation for the publication of this work, nations will be subjected by the mysterious hand of Providence to miseries, sufferings, and calamities emanating from unknown secret sources, open, and manifest.

"One event occurred in 1945," wrote Truman, the President of America in his Memories (1956), "of such magnitude that it was to revolutionize our relations with the world and usher in a new era for humanity, the 'fruits' and 'goals' and 'problems' of which we cannot even now fully grasp. It was the atomic bomb."

Nothing is hidden any longer about the 'fruits' and 'goals' and 'problems' of the atomic bomb. The atomic destiny of this humankind is apparent. In this utter darkness flashed the declaration of Benjamin Creme about the appearance of the new Christ. On April 24, 1982, Benjamin Creme declared in leading newspapers of the Western countries that the new Christ lived among the Pakistani community of

Brick Lane, East London, and was to declare himself soon. According to Benjamin Creme, the new Christ was the name of the 'Christ Lord Maitreya', the 'Mehdi', the 'Messiah', the 'Kulkai Autar', and the 'Buddha' in his fifth appearance, and that the mission of his appearance was to stop the World War III. The significance of this declaration of 1982 was equal to, if not more significant than the appearance of the atomic bomb, the nuclear giant Atumbumb.

Let me declare outright that whatever might have been the guiding media of Benjamin Creme, I and only I was the object of Benjamin Creme's declaration. It is neither the name nor the title with which Benjamin Creme addressed his Saviour; instead, his mission counts. To stop World War III, which means to annul the possibility of the nuclear ruin of the world, is my mission and mine alone in the world at these present times. The name or title Benjamin Creme has assigned to the expected Saviour of this present world; namely, the 'Christ Lord Maitreya', the 'Mehdi', the 'Messiah', the 'Kulkai Autar', or the 'Buddha' does not matter. It may even prove detrimental to the actual mission, which in itself is incredibly tremendous.

Refer to the Gospel about the second coming of Christ. He said:

"Then if any man shall say unto you, Lo here is Christ, or there; believe it not. For there shall arise false Christs, and false prophets, and shall shew great signs and wonders; insomuch that, if it were possible, they shall deceive the very elect. Behold, I have told you before. Wherefore if they shall say unto you, Behold, he is in the desert; go not forth: behold, he is in the secret chambers; believe it not. For, as the lightning cometh out of the east, and shineth even unto the west, so shall also the coming of the Son of man be. For wheresoever the carcass is, there will the eagles be gathered together."

(The Bible: New Testament: Matthew 24:23-28)

Also, read the entire chapter-24 and with care. There is a whole world of interpretation and explanation therein. However, here I have no time to go into detail. Exert yourself to understand.

The failure of Benjamin Creme in finding his new Christ among the Pakistani community of Brick Lane, East London, disproved the possibility of any pre-planned scheme or planting a person there beforehand or a conspiracy against any nation. The success of Benjamin Creme in spotting out his new Christ there in Brick Lane would have meant to the world a mere hoax and a plot. Also, even Christ would have failed in gaining acceptance of the Christian and the non-Christian world. Long before Benjamin Creme's declaration, I had yearned for London for the presentation of my case there, but the lack of means had prevented me. In all probability, I would have stayed in the Pakistani ghetto of Brick Lane, East London, and Benjamin Creme would have had no difficulty in recognizing me there.

Nevertheless, if I presented myself like that to the world, it would have ruined my mission in the ensuing controversy about the title of Christ. However, the declaration of Benjamin Creme has proved beyond any doubt that none in the world today existed to claim the title of Christ. None in the world today exists to claim the mission of annulling the possibility of the nuclear ruin of the world except me. Hence, I declare to the world my mission without considering the nomenclature specificity in these present circumstances and this present attitude of humankind about divinity or spiritual ordainment.

Why did Benjamin Creme's guiding media fail to point out the exact whereabouts of the object of his prophecy? For, when his colleague Chris Kellan searched for the new Christ among the Pakistani community of Brick Lane in East London, England, I was among the Pakistani community of Nawab Abad, Wah Cantt District Rawalpindi, Pakistan; fuming, fretting, and chafing about my mission. The answer to this question is as follows.

Had Benjamin Creme's satellite led him to where I then was, just as the star of the wise men of the East had led them where the child Christ then lay in Bethlehem and had Benjamin Creme pointed me there out by declaring me as the 'Mehdi', that would have meant to be a Judas Kiss. I, just like every other pretender to the title of 'Mehdi' among the Muslims these days, would have come to a grievous instantaneous end. The media would have published the affair as a conspiracy of some Western Anti-Islamic lobby against the Islamic world.

However, the most baffling question is why Benjamin Creme had not ensured his prophecy's object beforehand in London before venturing at so costly and fierce a declaration to the world? Indeed, he could not be regarded as so devoid of sense. After throwing the expecting world into convulsions, why should he confess his failure to find his new Christ in Brick Lane? The only possible answer to this question could be that the scheming hand of Providence deluded him into such a baffling mistake. But why? Was it only to see Benjamin Creme's declaration made to the world? Again, how come? Because if Benjamin Creme had done a search beforehand and had failed to spot his object in Brick Lane, he indeed would have abandoned his intention while Providence intended to bring my mission into the presence of the world through Benjamin Creme's declaration.

Benjamin Creme did neither lie nor was he a victim of a false hallucination. Upon me now, it is to vindicate his honor before the world and to assuage his pangs of agony. Let him communicate with me at my address. Let him know that I sent him letters on June 23, 1982, C/O Information Centre Amsterdam; Tara Press London; Tara Centre New York; and Tara Centre N. Hollywood, U.S.A. [5] I do not know whether these reached him or not. Nor do I know in what state of mind he is now. I call upon him to cheer up. His name will go in history like a sparkling star in the new age, Allah willing indeed.

Poor Benjamin Creme's declaration of the appearance of Christ was, as could have been expected, lost in the jeers of a skeptical crowd. [6] The world still entertains hopes in science and political sagacity to avoid atomic war. The atomic weapons are still locked up in stockpiles and, but a few reactors are at present functioning throughout the world. They could accept Christ only when the degree of their panic has reached a mark where they will cry in panic for a Saviour. Maybe only under the hail of atomic bombs will humankind realize the reality of this Baconian culture and the necessity of a Saviour, but then it will be too late. No Saviour could neutralize the irreparable ill-effects of nuclear war.

If Christ descended from Heaven in these days, he would find himself in the custody of border post as a derelict with no passport and without nationality and, therefore, a person ingratiate. Mehdi would have a short shift among the Muslims. Messiah of Jews would be required to sit on the throne of David and restore the kingdom to the Jews. Kulkai Autar will find it hard to fix his role in India, while Buddha will see his entire previous realm occupied by Socialists. Also, remember that all of them are Anti-Materialistic. They can't allow particularly this Baconian modern progress judging it to be the root cause of all the trouble and a basis for the nuclear ruin. It is unrealistic to expect any of them to come to a compromise with this Baconian culture. Moreover, no joy is there for Christ in the Christian banners planted on the Moon or Mars. They reflect the glory not of Christ but Francis Bacon.

The world should realize that neither these stockpiles can be evaporated, nor the spiritual breath and mere prayers could dissolve this nuclear problem. Nay, but a practical revolutionary substantial basis is necessary to neutralize this process that has reached this nuclear annihilation stage. Humankind has to conduct a worldwide seismic revolution on the principle of antithesis, and it will be as great and universal as it has been that has brought this world to the brink of nuclear ruin. This revolution will need a book of guidance that I have produced after life-long labor. Christ, too, will need a book like this to guide the revolution. It is high time, however, for a spiritual Saviour to arrive because this world now stands on the brink of utter ruin, and the atomic war may at any moment begin to declare the end of this world. What will that Deliverer come for after the ruin? Whom will that Redeemer then address? Will he then address the cities in ruins? Whom will that Rescuer then guide? Will he then guide the lurking radiations?

People of this age! You are people callous-hearted and merciless without precedent in human history. The proof is your atomic bombs, incendiary bombs, and plague bombs. If these bombs destroy you, it is only justice since you have made them yourself to destroy fellow humans. However, the Merciful Allah still has shown His special mercy in producing a work of guidance that I have produced in this Dark Age. Show gratitude, therefore, and accept this work of mine and publish it that perhaps you might be saved from a most disgraceful end in the flames of the nuclear Jehannah (hell).

On May 5, 1980, I sent an article to fifteen of the leading physicists worldwide. The article contained the scientific characterization of the atomic phenomena found in an antique book, the Quran. I sent the characterization on condition that if the Physicists attested it, I would declare to the world the formula of neutralizing the fire of atomic hell as is contained in the same book. The reader may find the article and names of these celebrities in Book-2/Volume-9, Chapter-1 & 2, respectively, of this 'Gabriel's Extinguishing the Atomic Hell Series'. Cast a glance at the list, and you'll see the essence of the world of Physicists represented therein. None of them sent me either the attestation or rejection. Three only, namely, Shirley Petty, Secretary to Dr. Edward Teller; Statens Stockholm; and R. S. Pease of England, acknowledged the receipt of my article for which I bless them and give them thanks.

Let all these Physicist addressees know that my article was a historical and epoch-making one. It envisaged the end of an age and the beginning of a new different one, and it was a wonder of scientific characterization. If it had reached them and is still with them, let them read it. If they peruse it with that care, they possess the knowledge required to appreciate it. It will gain significance day by day. My offer to them still holds for not only these fifteen but for the entire community of scientists. Times are coming that the community of the scientists will be of the most enthusiastic votaries of my views about science.

On May 5, 1982, I sent letters to fifteen dignitaries worldwide described in the following list.
(1) Presidents of America, Russia, and Libya.
(2) Prime Ministers of India, Canada, and Japan.

(3) King of Saudi Arabia, His Majesty King Khalid; may he be blessed by Allah, he is no more with us.
(4) Religious heads, Ayatullah Khomeini of Iran, and His Holiness the Pope of Rome.
(5) Excellencies of Kuwait, Abu-Dhabi, Bahrain, Dubai, and Sharjah.
(6) The Secretary-General of UNO Mr. Javier Perez De Cuellar.

Of these, one only hitherto has replied, namely, the Prime Minister of Canada. I heartily thank him and bless him.

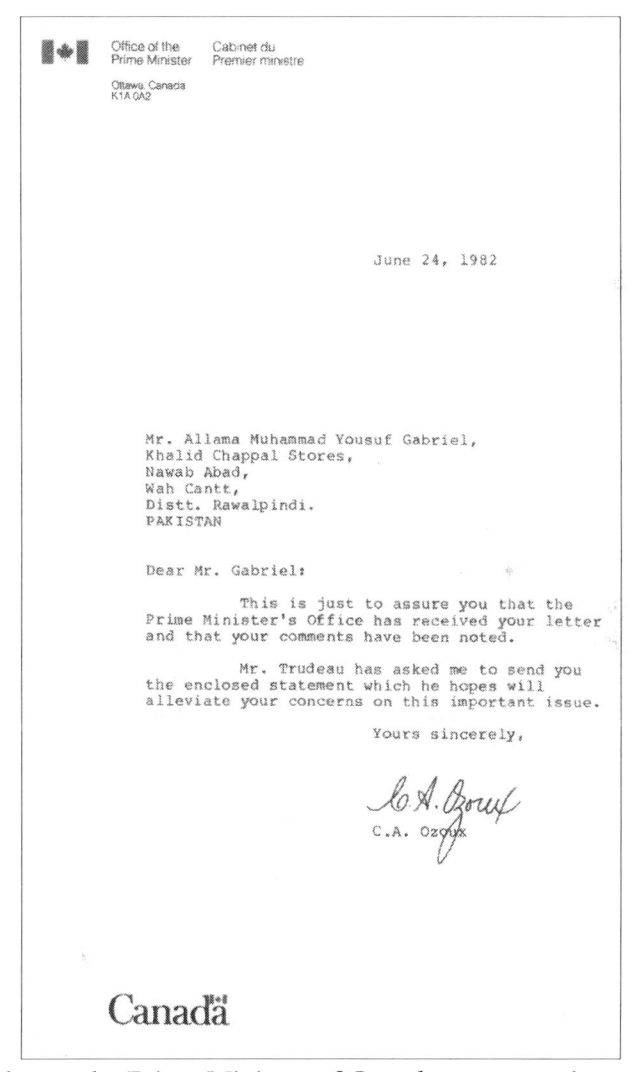

>
> **Office of the Prime Minister / Cabinet du Premier ministre**
> Ottawa, Canada
> K1A 0A2
>
> June 24, 1982
>
> Mr. Allama Muhammad Yousuf Gabriel,
> Khalid Chappal Stores,
> Nawab Abad,
> Wah Cantt,
> Distt. Rawalpindi.
> PAKISTAN
>
> Dear Mr. Gabriel:
>
> This is just to assure you that the Prime Minister's Office has received your letter and that your comments have been noted.
>
> Mr. Trudeau has asked me to send you the enclosed statement which he hopes will alleviate your concerns on this important issue.
>
> Yours sincerely,
>
> C.A. Ozoux
>
> Canada

The letter, the Prime Minister of Canada, wrote to the author.

Although it is quite natural that a letter from an obscure citizen could hardly gain the attention of so high ranking and pre-occupied personages as these. Yet, the eye of a connoisseur could hardly fail to judge the exceptional character of the epistle. Unfortunately, however, letters considered of little significance are not presented to such high dignitaries. If they received my letters and are still with them in the record, I pray, let them be as kind as to read these, for they hold the destinies of this humankind and their respective countries. My request still holds, and I expect them to perform their role in this affair according to their high office and influence.

In my letter to the Secretary-General of UNO, I had requested him to invite me to attend the second session of UNO about the Armament Race. But I received no reply. I ask Mr. De Cuellor one question. How much success has that session achieved? Nay, let Mr. De Cuellor note that the result of the 22nd session will be no better. It was for me alone to speak there if they aimed at any light or result.

To some of these my dignified addressees, I had appealed for funds to publish my work. With all the respect, I request them to realize that having wealth and ignoring the preventive measures against the atomic war is no wise policy. One atomic war will destroy all the existing wealth on earth, while a bit of wealth spent on publishing my work may save all the rest. My request for funds still holds. I apologize to the rest of the nations' Heads that I could not send my letter to them. It was only because my means did not allow me. How I managed to pay for the postage for the letters I sent is a tale too sad to tell.

During the last few months, I sent the list of the names of my books to several publishers in England and America. Some sent their apologies and good wishes, and others did not reply. Perhaps the names of the books are too formidable for a publisher of these times to consider. While my obscurity perhaps added to their doubts, and maybe there are other factors too. Nevertheless, it is hard for me to ignore their business or sentimental considerations. In their case, I can neither behave like a despot nor can feign myself inconsiderate. However, what they cannot see at this stage, and I see, is that these my works are immortal and of genuine universal interest. The entire world will long read them. At least the first edition will go, as they say, like hotcakes all over the earth. After that, the merit of the work will be the factor.

Though I have no complaint against the publishers, I have a very genuine complaint against the newspapers of the West, particularly of Britain and America. Although these esteemed papers of the West have a reputation for granting a right of the view to everyone without any prejudice, they have not considered it fit for publication even a single word of all that I have hitherto sent to them. Therefore, I request them to correct their attitude toward me despite all the apparent pungency and causticity of views.

In the end, I invite the attention of the elites of this world to the historic letter which Einstein wrote to Mr. Roosevelt, the then President of America, on August 2, 1939. He invited the President's attention to the possibility of making a bomb, million times more potent than the conventional bomb, as then was indicated by some work of Fermi and Szilard on Uranium fission. The U.S.A. government seriously explored the possibility, and of course, they made the bomb successfully, before which the entire humankind now stands trembling in terror for life. On July 21, 1982, today I invite the attention of horrified humankind to the possibility of destroying that terrific bomb as is indicated by the prophecy of the Quran about the atomic hell.

Farewell now, fellow humans! I appeared in this world as a stranger. I lived all this life in this world like a stranger. My sojourn on this earth may end at any moment. I have no exceptional quality to show except sincerity and sympathy. How dearly I wish that you recognized it before my departure. I bless you and pray to Allah that He saves you from the dreadful atomic doom and may you and your children live in peace and prosperity and the memory of Allah and the otherworld forever. Aameen. If my work is not published during my lifetime, it will undoubtedly be published one day to save the world from nuclear doom. So, try to preserve it for the sake of your children, children's children, children's children. Farewell to you all and Goodbye.

YOUSUF GABRIEL
July 21, 1982.

~~*~*~*~*

---

[1] **'Messiah-Id-Dajjaal'**, also known as 'Al-Masih ad-Dajjal'. Dajjal (Arabic: المسيح الدجّال, romanized: al-Masih ad-Dajjal) is an evil figure in Islamic eschatology described as 'the false messiah', 'liar', 'the deceiver', 'the deceiving messiah'. He is said to have come from several different locations but generally from the East, usually between Syria and Iraq, comparable to the Christian understanding of the appearance of the 'Anti-Christ' in Christian eschatology. He is Christ's enemy expected by medieval Christianity to appear before the end of the world. In this

regard, please study Book-2/volume-5/chapter-5: [Anti-Christic features of Baconian culture and 'Messiah-Id-Dajjaal'].

[2] "The best way to solve any problem is to remove its cause."
(Martin Luther King: 'Stride Towards Freedom', 1964)

[3] In this regard, for a detailed description of chapter-28 of Deuteronomy from the Bible with particular reference to, and relevance with this age of atomic energy for peace, please study Book-2/volume-7/part-1/chapter-3: 'The terrific warning of Moses to the people of Israel involves the entire human race in this modern age'.

[4] It looks that the author was unaware of the Doomsday Clock. [The **Doomsday Clock** is a symbolic clock face, representing a countdown to possible global catastrophe (e.g., nuclear war or climate change). It has been maintained since 1947 by the members of the Science and Security Board of the Bulletin of the Atomic Scientists, who are in turn advised by the Governing Board and the Board of Sponsors, including 18 Nobel Laureates. The closer they set the clock to midnight, the closer the scientists believe the world is to global disaster. Originally, the clock, which hangs on a wall in the Bulletin's office in the University of Chicago, represented an analogy for the threat of global nuclear war; however, since 2007 it has also reflected climate change and new developments in the life sciences and technology that could inflict irrevocable harm to humanity. The most recent officially announced setting—three minutes to midnight (11:57 pm)—was made on January 22, 2015, due to climate change, the modernization of nuclear weapons in the United States and Russia, and the problem of nuclear waste.]
(http://en.wikipedia.org)

[5] Please refer to the next page for the "Letter of the author addressed to Mr. Benjamin Creme".

[6] For the latest updates of Benjamin Creme's declaration of the appearance of Christ, please visit his website: (www.share-international.org).

~~*~*~*

LETTER OF THE AUTHOR
ADDRESSED TO MR. BENJAMIN CREME

Mr. Benjamin Creme,

Allah's Blessings and His Boundless Mercy.

Accept my heartfelt sympathy for your remorse due to your failure in discovering the New Christ, Lord Maitreya, though you were not amiss in your prediction. The object of your prediction, however, was not among the Pakistani community in Brick Lane of East London, England, but it was among the Pakistani community in Nawab-Abad, Wah Cantt/District Rawalpindi, Pakistan. You failed to make sure beforehand of the presence of the New Christ in Brick Lane because, in that case, you would have been obliged to abandon your prediction, yet Providence desired the declaration of your prediction to be made. I was the object of your prediction. Every clause of your prediction applied to me in truth. Since long before your advertisement, I had desired to be in London, but the lack of means had prevented my journey, indeed for good. In case you had spotted me in Brick Lane, the whole affair would have been regarded by the world as a pre-planned scheme. Also, my appearance as the Christ would have started a worldwide controversy --- not to speak of the non-Christians, even the Christians would not have agreed on the claim of Christ. The resultant disturbance would have marred my mission which you have very accurately pointed out to the jeering crowd in Kings Cross in London, to be the annulment of the possibility of the Third-World-War that is the nuclear ruin of the world.

Again, if your satellite had led you to the place where I then was in Pakistan, just as the star of the wise men of the East had led them to where the Child Christ lay in Bethlehem, and you had declared me as Mehdi, your act would have proved to be as Judas Kiss for me, for I would have forthwith been killed, and the affair would have been published as a deep conspiracy of the Anti-Islamic lobby of the West to cause factious disturbances among the countries of the Islamic World. The mysterious hand of Providence deluded you in your search for the object of your prediction to save the situation. Your advertisement, however, proved beyond any doubt that none at present was in this world to claim the title of Christ.

If you refer to your advertisement, you will find that there is a condition that does not apply to me and for which I do not qualify myself. Space would not allow me to explain all that. But there is one point therein which I will not apply to myself, namely, the title of the Christ. I will say 'NO' to that. Instead of involving myself in nomenclative controversy which might ruin the prospect of my mission that is the annulment of the possibility of the nuclear ruin of the world, I will insist on that light and guidance which is in my six volumes of "Extinguishing the Atomic Hell Series", and eight miscellaneous volumes on the same topic that lead to a world, free from nuclear danger. No alternative now is left for this humanity but either to perish under the atomic bombs and atomic radiations or to follow the guidance in these volumes and be saved from the atomic doom. Allah has special mercy on a world that deserved the painful atomic ruin and humankind whose nuclear wholesale destruction no heavens would cry.

It was in 1942, my 25th year, and the year in which the great Italian Physicist Enrico Fermi had succeeded in opening the gate of atomic fire on this world by his successful realization of Uranium fission chain reaction in Chicago, that I was in Mussayyib, a place in Iraq recommended in a vision by the Green Turbaned Saint 'Al-Khidr' to Abraham for the 'Abrahamic Mission' of warning this world against the atomic hell. I was shown in that vision unusually great signs of Allah. In the same period and at the same place, I was shown the crucifix in a vision. I, at that time, had little knowledge and meager education. But thereafter, like a prepossessed man, I commenced studies and learned languages, works of literature, philosophies, sciences, and Scriptures, indeed without a school or a teacher and always obliged to work for my subsistence, till in 1961 I discovered the theme of my mission and in 1972, I set to writing till in 1982 I completed my work in the form of a series of six volumes and eight miscellaneous volumes, all in English and all unpublished.

No Anti-Nuclear movement or revival of religion in the world could succeed without adopting the guidelines given in these volumes. This work may be regarded as 'Noah's Ark' for this deluge of atomic fire. No John Bunyan can find a heart to narrate the afflictions of my forty years' long intellectual pilgrimage. Nor is there a Freud to find a method to subject my intellectual attainment to a psycho-analysis. My life-long engrossment in a materially unprofitable pursuit did neither leave mind nor time to attend to my worldly side, and hence I find myself now without a home, wealth, property, or anything. If these manuscripts are eaten away by white-ants, it is not merely the leaves of paper that they eat away, but it is the destiny of a race that they destroy. London now is my place, and I cannot go there to explain my case before the scientists and philosophers. I sent an article to fifteen of the leading atomists of the world, including Edward Teller, the maker of the Hydrogen Bomb, in 1982, and none replied. I sent letters to fourteen of the Heads of States, including His Holiness Pope John Paul-II, in May 1982, and none hitherto has sent a reply. Let these manuscripts at least be preserved in some museum that perhaps some future generation in distress may avail their light to emerge from the atomic pit.

If you find it interesting, and this could vindicate your honor of an actual benefactor of humankind, then communicate with me. And if you will so desire, I will send to you my declaration, as well as my opening speech in type and, if you will wish, also taped in my voice. Time is short, and I am on my last legs. Sorrow, suffering, and affliction have been and still are my lot.

With best regards,

Yours Sincerely,

Allama Muhammad Yousuf Gabriel,
Khalid Chappal Stores, Nawab-Abad,
Wah Cantt, Distt. Rawalpindi,
Pakistan.
June 21, 1982.

~~*~*~*

REMINISCENT GLIMPSES

"Some recent work by E. Fermi and L. Szilard, which has been communicated to me in manuscript, leads me to expect that the element uranium may be turned into a new and important source of energy in the immediate future ... I believe therefore that it is my duty to bring to your attention the following facts and recommendations: In the course of the last four months it has been made probable -- through the work of Joliot in France as well as Fermi and Szilard in America -- that it may become possible to set up a nuclear chain reaction in a large mass of uranium, by which vast amounts of power and large quantities of new Radium like elements would be generated. Now it appears almost certain that this could be achieved in the immediate future. This new phenomenon would also lead to the construction of bombs, and it is conceivable -- though much less certain -- that extremely powerful bombs of a new type may thus be constructed. A single bomb of this type, carried by boat and exploded in a port, might very well destroy the whole port together with some of the surrounding territory."

(Letter from Albert Einstein to President Franklin Delano Roosevelt about the possible construction of nuclear bombs: August 2, 1939)

"Now, mark the hope and the intention of this great scientist and see his expectation of the possibility of a weapon, a million times more destructive than the conventional bombs. A bomb a million times more potent than the conventional bomb is the ideal of a member of a community (the scientific community) that is acclaimed as the benefactor community of humankind. Mark also the uncertainty of the expression of this greatest of the scientists and mark in comparison the unfaltering and decisive mode of expression of the prophecy of the Quran.

Again, observe that when writing his letter to the President of America, Einstein himself was unaware of the catastrophic hazards of radioactivity to be incident on atomic energy. Nevertheless, his eye had caught the destructive capacity of the atomic bomb itself. As you will gradually understand better, you will yourself be able to find the difference not only between the doubtful expression of Einstein in his letter against the clear-cut and decisive mode of the expression of the prophecy but also between the limitations of the human mind and the infallible omniscience of the Quran that has given in its prophecy; a final, decisive and complete word on the entire subject of atomic energy in only fourteen words. The profundity of the word of Allah in this respect is unique and indeed beyond human power."

(Yousuf Gabriel)

~~*~*~*

"On August 2, 1942, Man achieved here the first self-sustained chain reaction and thereby initiated a controlled release of Nuclear Energy."

(The inscription at Stagg Field, University of Chicago)

"Our mind wanders towards the Stagg Field, the University of Chicago in America, where the inscription mentioned above catches our eye on the wall of the first atomic reactor of Fermi, the great Italian physicist. Our mind wondered at this so high-toned acclamation of man's triumph and with it emerged before the eye of our mind a picture of the ruin of humankind involved in unimaginable miseries of atomic war and atomic radiations of the atomic energy for peace, all wrapped up in an atmosphere of a most grievous doom of man. We heard that the inscription in question had been torn down lately. But alas! Before they have torn down man's heart, who will tear down all the nuclear reactors along with the nuclear stockpiles of the world? Humankind cannot attain this goal until man's heart shuns greed of wealth and gold and cleanse itself of the slander."

(Yousuf Gabriel)

~~*~*~*

"The explosive force of nuclear fission has changed everything except our modes of thinking, and thus we drift towards unparalleled catastrophe. We shall require an entirely new pattern of thinking if humankind is to survive."

(Albert Einstein, 1946)

~~*~*~*

"Had I known that the Germans would not succeed in producing an atomic bomb, I would not have lifted a finger…I do not know how the Third World War will be fought, but I can tell you what they will use in the Fourth—rocks!"

(Albert Einstein)

~~*~*~*

"The idea of achieving security through national armament is, at the present state of military technique, a disastrous illusion… The armament race between the U.S.A. and the U.S.S.R., originally supposed to be a preventive measure, assumes hysterical character. On both sides, the means to mass destruction are perfected with feverish haste---behind the respective walls of secrecy. The H-Bomb appears on the public horizon as a probably attainable goal…If successful, radioactive poisoning of the atmosphere, and hence annihilation of any life on earth, has been brought within the range of technical possibilities… At the end, there beckons more and more clearly general annihilation."

('Arms can bring no security'; by Albert Einstein)

~~*~*~*~*

"I am absolutely convinced that no 'wealth' in the world can help humanity forward, even in the hands of the most devoted worker in this cause. The example of great and pure characters is the only thing that can produce fine ideas and noble deeds. Money only appeals to selfishness and always tempts its owners irresistibly to abuse it. Can anyone imagine Moses, Jesus, or Gandhi armed with the money-bags of Carnegie?"

(Albert Einstein: 'The World As I See It', Page-21)

~~*~*~*~*

"One event occurred in 1945 of such magnitude that it was to revolutionize our relations with the world and usher in a new era for humanity, the 'fruits' and 'goals' and 'problems' of which we cannot even now fully grasp. It was the atomic bomb. With it came the secret of how to harness nuclear energy."

('The Memoirs of Harry S. Truman, President of America: Atom Problems Arise', 1956)

"The results of the event of 1945 might have been a little ambiguous in the year 1945. Nevertheless, in 1956 the 'fruits' and 'goals' and 'problems' of the event of 1945 could in no way be considered ambiguous.

The 'fruits' of the event in 1945 were atomic bombs, Hydrogen bombs, hell bombs, super bombs, atomic missiles, ionizing radiations, warts, cysts, cancers, hemorrhages, genetic disorders, and chimerical babies. The 'goal' simply is a mutual destruction of life after a continued spell of untold miseries and afflictions. Its 'problems' are constant fear, infinite apprehension, eternal dread, and universal anarchy."

(Yousuf Gabriel)

~~*~*~*~*

"We will not prematurely or unnecessarily risk the costs of worldwide nuclear war in which even the fruits of victory would be ashes in our mouth."

(President John F. Kennedy)

~~*~*~*

"I call upon the scientific community in our country, those who gave us nuclear weapons, to turn their great talents now to the cause of mankind and world peace, to give us the means of rendering those nuclear weapons impotent and obsolete."

(Ronald Reagan: 'National address', March 23, 1983)

~~*~*~*

"A nuclear war cannot be won and must never be fought."

(Reagan-Gorbachev principle)

~~*~*~*

[The verdict of Bertrand Russell is:

"Since Adam and Eve ate the apple, man has never refrained from any folly of which he was capable."

The pamphlet in which this verdict of Russell has appeared bears cartoons that show that Russell did understand the cause of the destruction of men, namely, greed and tyranny. Russell, as is well-known, was a grand champion of humanity against the atomic war. But, though his verdict on the end of humankind is a clear-cut one, his endeavor against the fundamental causes of greed lacked the necessary sharpness of a view. His topic was simply hooked under the weight of the overwhelming circumstances prevailing in the world. And his heart might have wept at his helplessness as well as of the world in such circumstances.]

(Yousuf Gabriel)

~~*~*~*

"You may reasonably expect a man to walk a tightrope safely for ten minutes. It would be unreasonable to do so without accident for two hundred years."

(Bertrand Russell on nuclear weapons)

~~*~*~*

"If atomic bombs are to be added as new weapons to the arsenals of a warring world, or the arsenals of nations preparing for war, then the time will come when mankind will curse the names of Los Alamos and Hiroshima. The people must unite, or they will perish."

(J. Robert Oppenheimer)

~~*~*~*

"If you are asking, 'Can we make them more terrible?' the answer is yes. If you are asking, 'Can we make lots more of them?' the answer is yes. If you are asking, 'Can we make them terribly more terrible?' the answer is, probably."

(Robert Oppenheimer's response to a question regarding significant limitations in the future of nuclear weapons)

~~*~*~*

[J. Robert Oppenheimer {remembered as "The Father of the Atomic Bomb" (1904-1967)} ... later recalled that, while witnessing the explosion, he thought of a verse from the Hindu holy book, the Bhagavad Gita: "If the radiance of a thousand suns were to burst at once into the sky that would be like the splendor of the mighty one..." ... Years later he would explain that another verse had also entered his head at that time; namely, the famous verse; "Kalo Asmi Loka-ksaya-krit Pravardho, Lokan Samartum iha Pravattah" and was quoted by Oppenheimer after the successful detonation of the first nuclear weapon.

He translated it as **"Now I am become Death, the destroyer of worlds, come to annihilate everyone."**

Oppenheimer later would be persuaded to quote again in 1965 for a television broadcast: "We knew the world would not be the same. A few people laughed, a few people cried. Most people were silent. I remembered the line from the Hindu Scripture, the Bhagavad-Gita; Vishnu is trying to persuade the Prince that he should do his duty, and to impress him, takes on his multi-armed form and says, 'Now I am become Death, the destroyer of worlds, come to annihilate everyone.' I suppose we all thought that, one way or another."]

(Wikipedia, the free Encyclopedia)

~~*~*~*

"We believe that no nation has the right to use such a bomb, no matter how righteous its cause. This bomb is no longer a weapon of war but a means of extermination of whole populations. Its use would be a betrayal of all standards of morality and of Christian civilization itself. ... to create such an ever-present peril for all the nations of the world is against the interests of Russia and the United States. ... In the meantime, we urge that the United States, through its elected government, make a solemn declaration that we shall never use the bomb first."

(A statement by F. Seitz, George Braxton Pegram, F. W. Loomis, Hans Albrecht Bethe, C. C. Lauristen and others of the American Physical Society issued on February 4, 1950, in New York)

~~*~*~*

"After the initial blast shock wave passed (picking up gravel and sand from the beach), we were allowed to turn around and view the atomic cloud. ... It was an awesome sight! The cloud was 'mushroom-shaped', with the top of the cloud white. The 'shaft' was crimson and black. The cloud was growing upward at a very high rate, upwards through 30,000 feet or more. ... When the Bomb went off, I could see flashes of light - like lightning in the sky, and several minutes later could hear rumbling like thunder - all from 180 miles away. Wow! ... The power released is almost impossible to describe. I wish the leaders of all countries could experience this revelation of power, so they could better decide on NOT USING ATOMIC WEAPONS. If an atomic war is ever started, that will be the end of civilization, as we know it to be. Controlled atomic warfare is not a viable choice. Seeing a test blast is a humbling experience. ... I had the opportunity to fly over the remains of island 'Mike', where the first Hydrogen bomb was detonated in 1954. There is no island Mike there anymore - just a hole in the coral reef, where island Mike was. ... It is over two miles in diameter! ... It is difficult to comprehend that so much material was vaporized from the explosion. ... ... But I have had a concern about radiation exposure. As of now, there seems to be no problem for me or my children. Only time will tell. I can only hope these tests were effective in determining that Atomic Warfare is an impossible method of confrontation. Since many nations have atomic weapons, none of us can afford to use them. The use would only destroy the world."

('A Helicopter Mechanic's Memory of Eniwetok Marshall Islands'; by Harry L. Francis)

~~*~*~*~*

"We know we face 'extinction' if nuclear war ever begins. We face the same extinction even if the bombs never fall. The production alone of nuclear energy and nuclear weapons is initiating the death crisis of our species."

('No Immediate Danger: Prognosis for a Radioactive Earth'; by Dr. Rosalie Bertell)

~~*~*~*~*

"The probable fate of our species is 'extermination by poisoning'."

(Dr. Rosalie Bertell)

~~*~*~*~*

"There is no safe, low level of radiation."
[Margaret Chan, Director-General World Health Organization (WHO): www.iicph.org]

~~*~*~*

"Millions of lives have already been adversely affected by ionizing radiation. Our descendants are unlikely to escape the effects even if all proliferation of ionizing radiation should cease today. Therefore it is vital to warn, to teach, and to prevent even very low exposures."

(Letter to Director-General WHO Dr. Margaret Chan from Marion Odell: www.iicph.org)

~~*~*~*

"Both Religion and science require a belief in God. For believers, God is in the beginning, and for physicists, He is at the end of all considerations. … To the former, He is the foundation, to the latter, the crown of the edifice of every generalized world view."

(Max Planck)

~~*~*~*

"...I may say that in my opinion true Science and true Religion neither are nor could be opposed."

(Sir John William Strutt, Lord Rayleigh; Quoted in James Joseph Walsh, Religion and Health, 1920)

~~*~*~*

"In a nuclear war, there would be no victors, only victims."

(Pope Benedict-XVI)

~~*~*~*

"Nuclear weapons must be banned. A general agreement must be reached on a suitable disarmament program, with an effective system of mutual control."

(Pope John XXIII-1963)

~~*~*~*

"Abolishing nuclear weapons is not a narrowly partisan or nationalistic issue; it is an issue of fundamental moral values that should unite people across national and ideological boundaries."

(Most Reverend Edwin O'Brien, U.S.A. Catholic Bishops, July 2009)

~~*~*~*

"The best way to solve any problem is to remove its cause."

(Martin Luther King: 'Stride Towards Freedom', 1964)

~~*~*~*

AN APPEAL OF
NOTE-WORTHIES TO HUMANKIND

However, in his lifetime, Albert Einstein was destined to see the results of his erroneous suggestion in his letter to President Roosevelt about the possible construction of nuclear bombs: August 2, 1939. So, then this conscience-smitten physicist was obliged in the face of the impending dangers of atomic bombs to sound a warning to humankind crying:

"Here, then, is the problem which we present to you, stark and dreadful and inescapable: Shall we put an end to the human race, or shall mankind renounce war? People will not face this alternative because it is so difficult to abolish war. ... There lies before us if we choose continual progress in happiness, knowledge, and wisdom. Shall we, instead, choose death because we cannot forget our quarrels? We appeal as human beings to human beings: Remember your humanity, and forget the rest. If you can do so, the way lies open to a new Paradise; if you cannot, there lies before you the risk of 'universal death'."

(An extract from 'The Russell-Einstein Manifesto', issued in London, July 9, 1955, under the signature of Max Born, Percy W. Bridgman, Albert Einstein, Leopold Infeld, Frederic Joliot-Curie, Herman J. Muller, Linus Pauling, Cecil F. Powell, Joseph Rotblat, Bertrand Russell, Hideki Yukawa)

Were it not for the charge of ingratitude on our part, despite all the great names involved, this heartfelt appeal of the essence of the scientists and philosophers of the world was no more than an absurd piece of touching rhetoric that lacked both the scientific and philosophical worth. For, how little these great celebrities could be seen to understand the topic they so touchingly warned against in their most pathetic appeal to humankind. There is not so much as an illusion of genuine root causes of trouble as pointed out by the Quran distinctly and briefly in its prophecy.

These gentlemen seem to beat about the bush all the while in their warning. They spoke of banning the war, which is an impossibility in the present greedy, materialistic, and competitive setup in a world that suffered from world mania. They hoped that humankind in these circumstances might be able to relinquish war and forget their quarrels, yet they said not a word about the actual root of these quarrels. Instead, they confined their whole thought to the danger of atomic bombs. At the same time, they completely closed their eyes from the greater danger of atomic radiation. Otherwise, they would never have uttered things like "continual progress in happiness, knowledge, and wisdom" in the presence of atomic energy. For that reason, not one person could grant either their wish to ban atomic war or "continual progress in happiness, knowledge, and wisdom" as long as the primary causes of slander and greed existed in the world.

The only truth in their appeal, namely, the 'universal death', could be found to countenance the fact. But, despite all their sincerity and sympathy, it hardly needs to state that the appeal of these luminaries was doomed to fall on deaf ears worldwide. The stockpiles went on increasing without a scruple on the part of their builders. The test explosions continued as they continue to this day despite the most alarming warnings of the scientists.

~~*~*~*~*

AN APPEAL OF THE SCIENTISTS MOST WANTED BUT NOT FORTHCOMING AS YET

"The last and final appeal which we now make to you is that the atomic energy, whether used for war or peace, is equally destructive. Renounce, therefore, every thought of utilizing this energy source, or be prepared to meet the wholesale destruction of a kind as painful as has no precedent in whole human history. Try to make yourself content with less plenty, nay even with scarcity, nay even if you are in the danger of dying of hunger, and immediately destroy every source of atomic energy before it has a turn to annihilate you. It will be our last appeal to you and our last warning, which will also be your last chance to escape from the atomic net. Take heed, therefore, and consult your safety before it is too late. You have been warned and adieu."

~~*~*~*~*

We do not know whether such a warning of the scientists will ever come or not, but if ever there was the most critical time for such a warning, it is now, for hereafter the warning itself be too late. However, the scientist is as reticent as a bird under the hypnotizing gaze of a serpent. The influence of a very miserable doom is fascinating. Anyone can see it most distinctly at present in the attitude of the scientists' community, who still seem to entertain false hopes of one day bringing the atomic radiations under control.

~~*~*~*~*

TWO PROBABLE POST-ATOMIC WAR CONFLAGRATION EPITAPHS OF HUMANITY DEVISED BY THE AUTHOR OF 'GABRIEL'S EXTINGUISHING THE ATOMIC HELL SERIES'

(1)

An epitaph on the grave of humankind destroyed by the atomic bombs or decayed by atomic radiations after a continued spell of atomic energy for peace:

"Here lies a race of **backbiters** and **defamers** that did amass the **wealth** of this world and arranged it against future and thought that they were to live forever in this world, forever increasing in riches. Nay, but they were cast into the fire of atomic hell; the fire that leaped up over their **hearts** and it encompassed them in **outstretched columns** till both, they and their wealth were consumed."

(2)

Another epitaph could well be read with feasibility:

"Beneath these ruins lie rotten and fossilized bones and heaped up smoldering ashes of a leprous, cancer-ridden race of chimerical monsters. They once flourished as human beings on this earth as the honorable vicegerents of Allah. As the chosen creation and a species capable of surpassing angels of Heaven, they enjoyed their Creator's greatest favors and were created in **His (own) Image** [1] who breathed into them of **His Spirit**. [2] However, eventually forgetting their high-ranking place and the predetermined purpose of their creation on earth, they engrossed themselves in the pursuit of wealth as the sole object of their life. Considering this world as their perpetual abode, they developed an attitude of **backbiting** and **slander** with the ever-increasing greed of **wealth**. Unable to check their excessive greed and slandering disposition, forgetting their mission on earth, and forsaking their home in Heaven, shaking their atomic tridents, they fell on one another, in a fit of wrathful fury like wild animals and furious beasts. They were thus in a mad frenzy destroyed mutually and were one and all consumed and turned their earth into the universal grave. Wronged by no one, they brought all this on themselves by their own hands. The ruins of once flourishing habitations exist all over the earth still, to tell a sad story indeed to shining stars at midnight."

(THE SAD AUTHOR)

~~*~*~*

---

[1] The Bible repeatedly says that God created man on His (own) **Image**:
(a) "And God said, Let us make man in our image, after our likeness:"
(Genesis 1:26)
(b) "So God created man in His own image, in the image of God created he him; male and female created he them."
(Genesis 1:27)
(c) "Whoso sheddeth man's blood, by man, shall his blood be shed: for in the image of God made he man."
(Genesis 9:6)

[2] The Quran repeatedly says that Allah breathed into man His (own) **Spirit**:
(a) "And (remember) when thy Lord said unto the angels: Lo! I am creating a mortal out of potter's clay of black mud altered. So, when I have made him and have breathed into him of My Spirit."
(Quran 15:28-29)
(b) "Then He fashioned him and breathed into him of His Spirit."
(Quran 32:9)
(c) "And when I have fashioned him and breathed into him of My Spirit."
(Quran 38:72)

~~*~*~*

~~*~*~*~*

"How many were the gardens and the water springs that they left behind, and the corn lands and the goodly sites and pleasant things wherein they took delight! Even so (it was), and We made it an inheritance for other folks, and the heaven and the earth wept not for them, nor were they reprieved."

(Quran 44:25-29)

~~*~*~*~*

GABRIEL'S EXTINGUISHING THE ATOMIC HELL SERIES

THE MIRACLE OF THE HOLY QURAN

THE QURAN PREDICTS, PHENOMENALLY CHARACTERIZES, AND AVERTS THE ATOMIC HELL

BOOK-1

YOUSUF GABRIEL

TABLE OF CONTENTS

BOOK-1

VOLUME-1
THE FIRST ERUPTION OF GABRIEL'S ARGUMENT AGAINST THE ATOMIC HELL
The Quran predicts, phenomenally characterizes, and averts the atomic hell 83

VOLUME-2
The Quran predicts and characterizes the technical knowledge of nuclear science 259

VOLUME-3
QURAN VERSUS ANCIENT AND MODERN ATOMISM ... 585
PART-1 Quran versus the ancient atomism of Democritus 591
PART-2 Quran versus Bacon's modern atomism 635

A WORD WITH THE INTELLECTUALS REGARDING THE PROPHECY OF THE QURAN

~~*~*~*~*

THE TEXT OF THE PROPHECY OF THE QURAN ABOUT 'AL-HOTAMA' (THE HELL OF THE 'HOTAMA') THAT IS THE 'ATOMIC HELL'

بِسْمِ اللَّهِ الرَّحْمَٰنِ الرَّحِيمِ

وَيْلٌ لِّكُلِّ هُمَزَةٍ لُّمَزَةٍ ۝ الَّذِي جَمَعَ مَالًا وَعَدَّدَهُ ۝ يَحْسَبُ أَنَّ مَالَهُ أَخْلَدَهُ ۝ كَلَّا ۖ لَيُنبَذَنَّ فِي الْحُطَمَةِ ۝ وَمَا أَدْرَاكَ مَا الْحُطَمَةُ ۝ نَارُ اللَّهِ الْمُوقَدَةُ ۝ الَّتِي تَطَّلِعُ عَلَى الْأَفْئِدَةِ ۝ إِنَّهَا عَلَيْهِم مُّؤْصَدَةٌ ۝ فِي عَمَدٍ مُّمَدَّدَةٍ ۝

"Wail-Ul-Likul-Le-Homazat-Il-Lomazate, Nillazi Jammah Malan-Wa-Addadah. Yahsabo Anna Ma-Lahu Akhladah. Kalla La-Yunbazanna Fil Hotamah. Wa Maa Adraaka Maa Al-Hotama? Naarullah-Il-Muqadah. Allati Tattalio Alal Afedha. Innaha Alaihim Musadah. Fi Amadim Mumaddadah."

(Quran: 104 'Al-Homaza'/Roman Arabic text)

"Woe unto every slandering traducer who gathereth (wealth of the world) and arrangeth it. He thinketh that his wealth will render him immortal. Nay, but verily he will be cast into Al-Hotama. Ah, what will convey unto thee what Al-Hotama is? (It is) the fire of Allah kindled, which leapeth up over the hearts. Lo! It is closed in on them in outstretched columns."

(Quran: 104 'Al-Homaza')

Here is another translation of the same verses as follows.
"Woe unto every backbiter, defamer who heapeth up riches and prepareth the same (for the time to come). He thinketh that his riches will render him immortal (that is, his riches will remain with him forever). By no means. He shall surely be cast into Al-Hotama (the crushing fire). And what shall cause thee to understand what Al-Hotama is? (That is how crushingly terrible this fire is? And how incomprehensibly complex is its phenomena?). (It is) the kindled fire of Allah, which leapeth up onto the hearts. Verily it is a fire closed in on them in outstretched columns."

(Quran: 104 'Al-Homaza')

Read this little chapter. 'Philosophically', it covers the entire field of modern Baconian atomism. Furthermore, 'Scientifically', it covers the entire nuclear phenomena. It happens to be the only guidance in the world today that leads this world out of the nuclear hell and this modern materialism that is the mother of nuclear hell.

Now, fellow humans, read the above-quoted Prophetic warning of the Quran and see and judge for yourself what you have found in it. Then reserve your judgment in your mind.

If you happen to be a <u>scientist</u>, read it from the perspective of science and reserve your judgment in your mind. If you are a <u>philosopher</u>, read it from the viewpoint of philosophy and reserve your judgment in your mind. If you are <u>literate</u> or <u>poet</u>, read it from your perspective and reserve your judgment in your mind. The following chapters of 'Gabriel's Extinguishing the Atomic Hell Series' will perhaps startle you out of your previous judgment of the warning of a Scripture and turn you into an embodiment of wonderment. The <u>general reader</u>, strangely enough, needs no previous knowledge of atomic science.

My dear scientist! You have read the text of the previous Prophetic warning with due care. You might have made a judgment of the situation in the light of scientific knowledge. We assure you that 'fourteen' original words describing the fire of 'Al-Hotama' in the prophecy contain all the knowledge that science could now or ever in the future show about the subject of nuclear energy. Indeed, even much besides, as will forever remain beyond human ken in this particular sphere. Therein these fourteen words, you will view the extent of an Omniscient mind if you possess already all or most of the knowledge of nuclear science that has been furnished hitherto by science.

My dear philosopher! If you have with due care read the 'eighteen' words that have appeared about the characteristics of the 'backbiter' and 'defamer' in the prophecy, then rest assured that these few words have contained in them all the characteristics of the modern atomistic materialism. There, in these eighteen words, you shall view the encompassing powers of an Omniscient mind.

Moreover, in the prophecy, in its completeness, you shall find a miracle of brevity, simplicity, and clarity unknown in any product of the human mind, whether you be a scientist or a philosopher.

My dear literate, my dear historian, poet, mathematician, or any other non-scientist scholar! We are sorry for you, for the whole thing may appear to you like a straightforward narrative and no more than a mere denunciation of the fire of 'Al-Hotama' against the 'slandering wealth-accumulator'. Perhaps, nearly the same might be said of the scientist and the philosopher at their first glance of the prophecy. Throughout 'Gabriel's Extinguishing the Atomic Hell Series', we endeavored to make things as clear and comprehensive as possible. Even the last layman among the entire humankind will not be left unacquainted with the subject. We should not deprive him of extraordinary and important intelligence like this, on which the question of life and death and joy and misery of this humankind depended.

The difficulty of the theme has been extreme, and the course of inquiry has been arduous. It has been a passage through a fantastic world. To judge this point, we request every scientist and philosopher to read the text of the prophecy by himself and record whatever scientific or philosophical knowledge he could find from the words of the prophecy before reading this work. Then let him read this work and compare the initial record and the knowledge shown in this work. Then it is for Darwin to sit with brows knit with wonder as to how so much knowledge could have been packed in so few words, a treat indeed that the Omniscience of Allah alone could achieve. Atomists' astonishment at so much knowledge packed in so few words of the prophecy will surpass their wonder at releasing such a tremendous amount of energy packed in so small a particle as the atom.

Non-Muslims are not well acquainted with the Quran, and Muslims are the followers of the Quran. Nevertheless, as far as the affair of this particular prophecy is concerned, there happens to be a slight distinction between the non-Muslims and the Muslims. The discovery and the treatment of this prophecy will appear equally novel to the Muslims.

~~*~*~*

VOLUME-1

THE FIRST ERUPTION OF GABRIEL'S ARGUMENT AGAINST THE ATOMIC HELL

THE QURAN PREDICTS, PHENOMENALLY CHARACTERIZES, AND AVERTS THE ATOMIC HELL

TABLE OF CONTENTS

VOLUME-1

PREFACE:
THE QURAN SOUNDS ITS NUCLEAR WARNING ABOUT THE ATOMIC HELL AND PREDICTS, PHENOMENALLY CHARACTERIZES, AND AVERTS IT 87

Chapter-1
Nuclear (atomic) theory 109

Chapter-2
The history of atomism 113

Chapter-3
'Hotama': The Quran predicts,
phenomenally characterizes, and averts the atomic hell 132

Chapter-4
The early commentators of the Quran and 'Al-Hotama' 197

Chapter-5
The prominent points of the Prophetic warning of the Quran 206

Chapter-6
The efficacy of the warning of the Quran about the atomic hell 210

Chapter-7
The characteristics of those doomed to atomic hell 221

Chapter-8
The atomic bomb is the wrath of Allah and not a weapon 227

Chapter-9
Accumulation of wealth and wealth worship 229

Chapter-10
How to avert the atomic danger in the light of the Quran 233

Chapter-11
The concluding word 253

PREFACE

THE QURAN SOUNDS ITS NUCLEAR WARNING ABOUT THE ATOMIC HELL AND PREDICTS, PHENOMENALLY CHARACTERIZES, AND AVERTS IT

I found this warning about the atom bomb in the Quran, and now it has become a duty incumbent on me, as my faith implies, to make it known to the whole vast humankind. My duty, however, is to warn only, and then it remains for them to do as they would deem fit. Whether humankind chooses to plunge into atomic hell ablaze, themselves along with their children to be roasted alive, one and all, in a world of cancer-ridden monsters, or by avoiding the atomic hell, move on the path of peace and safety to their ultimate destination. How little did the atomists know when engaged in the study of nuclear energy that what they were doing? They did no more than apply the keys to the gate of atomic hell, a gate which they eventually did succeed in throwing wide open. The powers then appeared to round up the lowing humankind from every side like mad cowboys towards this mighty gate of atomic hell and whipping them mercilessly with a show of chivalry, of course, endeavored to push them through the gate with promises of bliss inside: gardens, palaces, rivers, peace, prosperity and indeed everything that could be the desire of one's heart. What else it could be, if not sheer madness, that they disbelieve in the promises of Allah about the gardens in the next world as mere fantasy, whereas they believe in the promises of bliss in the nuclear energy in this world.

The prophecy of the Quran about the atom bomb that is the atomic hell, fortunately enough for humankind, is in the form of a warning and is based on cause and effect, deed and consequence, and not at all a decree pre-ordained. The Quran has manifestly given the causes responsible for the emergence of nuclear power and its consequent fruit, the hell bomb. The danger, therefore, could undoubtedly be averted through repentance and removal of the fundamental causes which Quran has enumerated in the most explicit of terms. The Merciful Allah could pardon the sins of a sinner on repentance even a little while before death. Similarly, the danger even could be averted a little before the atomic holocaust has taken place. Once the atomic holocaust has commenced, nothing but ruin, both of this and the otherworld is sure.

The prophecy or warning about atomic hell in the Quran is primarily interpreted as and assumed to be an event of the next eternal world. Still, just as fire and garden are there in this world to represent Hell and Heaven, respectively, this atom bomb on earth represents the atomic hell of the next world with the difference indeed. The victims of the atom bomb on earth might taste death. In contrast, the victims of the atomic hell of the next world are doomed to burn therein forever without ever dying. If, on the one hand, they will suffer the punishment of burning in the atomic fire in this world, on the other hand, they will be hurled into the atomic hell in the next world to burn therein eternally.

Also, among the victims of the atom bomb in this world, there might be innocent people. However, the inmates of the atomic hell in the next world will be persons judged individually and found deserving of the particular punishment. Innocent believers may fall victims along with other wicked people whose evil deeds have incurred the wrath of Allah and the subsequent chastisement. According to His promise, Allah will compensate them on the Day of Judgment for undeserved sufferings. Likewise, those innocent people who unluckily fell victims to the atom bomb in this world would find ample compensation in the next world for their loss and suffering in this world, through Allah's abounding mercy.

Also, not to oppose the atomic bomb and its causes is punishable guilt. None, therefore, appears to be saved. Allah, however, is ever Merciful and may take mercy on those guilty of reticence against the atomic bombs due to their powerlessness.

I may be a man more than or at least as enlightened as you might be. Pray now, do not call me superstitious, fanatic, or a bigot in any way if I venture to place before you a fact, curious though and strange indeed, yet neither is anyway impossible nor fantastic. To wit that during my ordeal of writing this book that you will now read, an ordeal very gruesome, blood-curdling, and extremely horrible, you may wonder what I say. A book which you may think is not significantly different in any way from many other books, yet, there might be persons in this very world possessed of sight clear enough to discern the truth of my ordeal in the pages of this book. They might hear the shrieks, cries, laments, and thunders of a different kind not to be found in many other books. I wrote this book in frightening circumstances, even adverse, more than Great Milton's when he wrote his 'Paradise Lost'.

However, I want to tell you that I have remained throughout the subject of two strange powers while writing this curious book. One of these powers, I found to be helpful in a mysterious way and working like an undercurrent; a very encouraging power indeed. The other power was aggressive, hostile, cunning, and mischievous. It has always been in a state of extreme exasperation and furious to the point of dreadful frenzy. It was a perfect fright, a picture of horror, fury insatiate, and a terrifying witch with fearful teeth and fiery eyes. It was covered all over with hair, always in excitement and a bullying mood, as if in readiness to snatch away my papers right from my hands, but would not dare due to the awful majesty of Allah in whose service I moved. Think me not at all unaware of the age in which I live: a purely materialistic age in which a thing like this would be deemed a mere hallucination and fantasy, something sheerly unbelievable. But what if the spiritual lights have been dimmed to a faint glimmer? What if the celestial edge of the human mind has been dulled to extreme bluntness? Yet, the human intellect is not as blurred as not realizing the truth of my statement if I explain the thing a little further.

Brethren and fellow human beings! The power which I say was helpful to me was the personification of the merit of present-day humanity. This power endeavored to lead them away from their impending doom that is the atomic hell. In contrast, the other power which was hostile towards me was the personification of the guilty part of the conduct of present-day humankind. It endeavored to the utmost of its ability to drag them towards the pit of punishment ablaze with atomic hell. Both these powers incessantly struggled in a tug of war. They will decide the fate of humanity accordingly, whichever of these two powers would finally succeed. Do you understand it now? I think not the understanding of some sage extraordinary is required to comprehend such a simple thing.

However, the question arises: why did these powers think me to be a fit object of their attention? The answer is equally simple: both these powers realized the worth of warning of the Quran, which I held in hand and was engaged in its presentation to humankind. So great has been worth this warning in the eyes of the devil that the fiend has been in mourning ever since I undertook this work. He has done all that was in his power to deter me from my enterprise. Humankind may shake dizzy heads at the sound of this warning. They may ponder over the problem, realize the folly, repent, and thus save themselves. However, this is not at all to the liking of this constant enemy (devil) of the sons of Adam. So overzealous had the devil been in endeavors against me that, but for abounding grace of Almighty Allah, shredded pages of my book might have been scattered all over the plain that was the scene of a battle fought centuries ago between Alexander the Great and the brave Porus.

Now that I have done my part, it remains for me only to wonder what pranks this resourceful fiend will play with humankind in the matter of their acceptance of this book and their subsequent conduct in hearing the warning of Allah, their Creator, about the atom bomb. Therefore, our hearty prayer today ought to be: My Allah give us wisdom such that we may be saved from the atomic hell and so also our children and all humankind. That which I have suffered was necessarily the part of my training and will always be.

That the Quran has prophesied about the atom bomb must naturally come as a surprise to the world. A miracle has happened in an age of no miracles. It indeed is a miracle of no ordinary kind, in no way less extraordinary than raising the dead from the graves. Indeed, something has been raised to life that laid dead and buried in its grave for no less than fourteen centuries. The sound of call has appeared at the most auspicious moment when humanity is standing, ready to leap into the nuclear hell they have created. Only if humanity would condescend to listen and pay heed to this resounding trumpet of the Most Beneficent Allah, the Most Merciful Creator of humankind, they may still with certainty avert a most painful end.

Judging from the present state of distressed humankind and the nature of horrors that stand in readiness to fall upon it, nations could justly consider that no topic is of a more momentous import or in any way of a graver aspect than the nuclear energy and atom bomb. Unfortunately, it is most neglected and entirely ignored by humankind. Far more grievous is the aspect of the perfidious nuclear radiation in comparison with the atomic blast and raging fires. These radiations constitute a hazard of quite a different nature, that of far more severe nature to humanity. Humankind has the solace of 'No-Atomic-War' pacts, and these are not reliable. They have the satisfaction of safeguards against nuclear radiation, and no safeguards could be a guarantee against nuclear radiation. What hope of peace is there in a world of many nations and diverse considerations, mainly when the devil is at large to hatch his plots to bring about the ruin of the human race. The atomic war in such circumstances may at any time start and seal the doom of miserable humanity.

The only sure way of eradicating the danger of atomic warfare lay in removing fundamental causes responsible for the appearance of the atomic bomb. The worth of the warning of the Quran about the atom bomb manifested itself most conspicuously in the enumeration of causes of the emergence of the atom bomb. This warning of the Quran ought to be deemed a God-sent opportunity at a most critical juncture. If humankind failed to recognize its true worth, there could not be a precedent as unhappy as that in the whole history of the human race.

The devil is as free in this age of confusion as it never was in the past. Its chances of success are as significant in this age of constant tumult and unrest as were never before. We will tell a story about the devil even at the risk of incurring old-fashioned and outmoded titles. The story, however, may be interesting, instructive, and to the point, and one which reveals the extent of the ingenuity of the methods adopted by the devil in bringing about the ruin of persons. I fear that in the presence of such a resourceful villain, the most genuine and well-meant efforts of Nixons and Kosigans to banish the atomic warfare might well be doomed to final frustration.

The story starts as follows.

Once a man remonstrated with the devil to create all the broil and clamor amongst people to break the world's peace. To which the fiend replied, "Brother! I do no more than dab the wall with a syrupy finger, and the rest of it all humans do by themselves."

He beckoned the man to follow him and straightway went to the shop of a confectioner. The confectioner sat busily preparing sweetmeats. The devil stood silently, watching for a while. Then stealthily dipped his little finger in the syrup, silently entered the shop, just made a little dab on a wall by his syrupy finger and retired to an obscure corner within and there sat himself down, secretly musing.

Presently a few flies gathered on the dab. A lizard popped up from somewhere and sat lurking silently behind the flies. The cat of the confectioner mysteriously emerged and crouched behind the lizard. Then, outside came a customer to buy sweetmeats for his children, and along with him, his bulky dog came smelling and sniffing all the way. The dog sensed the cat's presence inside and at once fixed its anxious eyes upon it and stood wagging its tail in excitement.

The scene was by now set, and then deep suspense for a while ensued. The moment at last arrived. The lizard suddenly made a jump on the flies. The cat, like a flash, pounced upon the lizard. The dog at once swooped down on the cat. The exasperated owner of the cat threw his syrupy ladle at the dog and maimed it forthwith. The angry master of the maimed dog struck the exasperated owner of the cat with the club on the head and killed him on the spot.

The plot was by now well on its way to final success. The police naturally arrived in the wake. And then the awful creak of the hinges of the jail door, and the hanging noose, and the widowed women with orphaned children, and life-long mourning, etc., etc., you could imagine after that.

The devil leaving his seat and approaching its complainant, who stood with his eyes wide open in wonder at the mysterious play, slightly patted his shoulder and, peeping deep into his startled eyes, said:

"Look, friend, I just dabbed the wall with a syrupy finger, and the rest is all done by humans themselves. So why then is the whole blame on me for what others do?"

Humankind today is in a state of great distress everywhere, both in the East and the West. Heart-burning, anxiety, and frustration are everywhere as common and cheap, both in the castle and the cottage, as the wind now blows. The spell of science is over, and the panic is increasing amongst humanity in exact proportion to the relative increase in material progress. The higher the piles of commodities, the deeper the sense of poverty; the greater the number of factories, the greater the fear of hunger. The much-repeated terms of modern times, namely, peace, progress, plenty, and prosperity, have come to assume the forms perverted in reality. The scientific progress indeed gave a delighting swing in the beginning when Lord Macaulay and, along with him, an innumerable host of masterminds had nothing but praises for the fruitful philosophy of the modern age of science.

Francis Bacon, the supposed initiator of the modern philosophy of fruit and the recognized trumpeter of the modern age, was unanimously hailed as the greatest philosopher of his times and the true benefactor of all humanity. But alas! The short-sighted followers of Bacon had taken too short-sighted a view of Baconian philosophy, discarded the Grand Trunk Road of a balanced outlook, and had fallen instead on the delusive paths of exclusive, ungodly terrestrial materialism (lacking spiritual) towards immediate gain. Then, naturally, the honey gradually assumed a bitter taste, and the illusion of a fast-approaching Paradise began to show signs of a deceptive mirage. The reaction of Mother Nature, against those who had proceeded to achieve Mother Nature's conquest for material gains only within this world and in the absence of spiritual considerations, began to appear in a vengeful mode. This reaction inwardly stirred up heart-burning discontent and frustration in the minds. Outwardly it led them on the paths that ended in front of the horrible horror, the atom bomb.

Slander, backbiting, mutual mistrust and distrust, excessive greed, and complete engrossment in a systematic accumulation of wealth of this world, and an exaggerated and undue confidence in wealth amounting to worship, in short, all the qualities fused altogether which the Quran has given out as requisites of the appearance of the atom bomb, finally have appeared in the form of nuclear energy and its corollary the atomic bomb, together with their issuing fragrance, the atomic radiations. Once hailed as a great boon, nuclear energy turned out to be a bane and not at all a boon, a feature which darkened even the brighter aspects of science, and which eventually is just to be feared as the killer of science itself along with the human race.

If not abolished in time and not supplanted by some harmless means of power, this nuclear energy will destroy the world. There is no doubt about it. But, on the other hand, do I exaggerate my fears? I say, go! Ask a scientist. I am not a fanatic. I have a balanced mind, just as balanced as anyone would wish, for I see humanity playing like an ostrich. I am engaged only in shooing them out and away from this sand in which they now stand with their heads buried deep and eyes closed, imagining themselves safe in their blindness and thinking that just as they cannot see the approaching wolf, the wolf also is not seeing them.

Suppose every single soul today living on this earth turns Shakespeare by some miracle, and they chafe themselves at the bit in their combined effort to describe the horrors of the atomic war. In that case, they will never be able to succeed in their enterprise. If every one of these turns Dante to make a combined effort to portray the atomic hell in their 'Secular Tragedy' against Dante's 'Divine Comedy', they will also fail. Yet this present-day world is full of misunderstandings, misconceptions, and illusions regarding the atomic hell. Just as no one can see one's face, this present-day humankind cannot see the truth of their own making, which is the atomic hell.

The tragedy of this present humankind, however, is a little different. People, despite their knowledge of the facts, do as if they knew it not. The atomic bomb, known to them, is not a weapon of defense, nor even a means of war; instead, it is the means of wholesale destruction of life on earth. Though as yet, they know not that the atomic bomb is the wrath of Allah enkindled against them, and they are busy building their stockpiles afresh or are engaged in improving their existing stockpiles. They take their stockpiles as a deterrent to atomic war. Here, the doubt appears in the quality of their understanding because they could hardly find another more evident delusion than this. Their behavior, however, in this respect becomes like that of a species of ostriches hypnotized by the influence of the impending doom they are by themselves busily bringing upon themselves.

Humanity, only if it had a little faculty of imagining the horrors of nuclear power, whether used for war or peace, would have preferred poverty and indigence without nuclear power to plenty and opulence with nuclear energy. Humanity has tolerated the conventional bombs and air-raids against the facilities provided by science, but nuclear energy has become a killer of all hope. Unfortunately, general humanity knows little about the nefarious features of nuclear energy. They will forever be absorbed in their problems of the necessities of life, food, and clothing. They will eventually be driven like herds of cattle into the atomic pit after a painful existence in an atom-ridden age.

Let the 'rational scientist' and 'wise politician' dare stand up to humankind and declare at the top of their voice that:
(1) "Atomic-ridden science will soon throw all despicable forms of witchcraft of the dark ages, and obnoxious magical arts, along with their disgusting features, into shades."
(2) "All the toil, labor, patience, perseverance, sacrifices of hundreds of past generations of humanity, and a history-long endeavor to build up a civilization worthy of man will soon be ultimately destroyed by a tiny little invisible atom, merely due to the folly of the most knowledgeable and most enlightened age of the whole history of humankind on earth."

It is a painful reflection, and it reminds me of a tiny distich of Wordsworth:

"To let a creed, built in the 'heart' of things,
Dissolve before a twinkling 'atomy'."

Indeed the 'creed built in the heart of things' has been let to 'dissolve before a twinkling atomy', and we just say, wonderful Wordsworth. The bliss of science has turned into a curse because humanity has discarded the element of faith, and science has become prey to certain untoward philosophies if we could rightly apply the word philosophy to them.

Now, if Humanity:
(1) Persist in playing simply like an ostrich and do nothing to restore faith to its proper place.
(2) Do not re-establish faith in Allah and Resurrection in the human mind.
(3) Do not depose wealth from the usurped godhead to its proper place, that of a sheer necessity.
(4) Do not divert science towards correct channels.
(5) Do not banish nuclear energy.

Then, let all the tape recorders be kept in readiness to record the outcry of harassed humankind, like the outcry of the enraged Northumberland in Shakespeare's King Henry-IV, which is as follows.

"Now bind my brows with iron; and approach

> The rugged'st hour that time and spite dare bring
> To frown upon the enraged Northumberland!
> Let heaven kiss earth! Now let not Nature's hand
> Keep the wild flood confined! Let order die!
> And let this world no longer be a stage
> To feed contention in a lingering act;
> But let one spirit of the first-born Cain
> Reign in all bosoms, that, each heart being set
> On bloody courses, the rude scene may end,
> And darkness be the burier of the dead!"
>
> ('King Henry-IV'; Part-2; Act-I/Scene-I)

But Northumberland lived at different times. The maddening circumstances, heart-rending afflictions, inexpressible sufferings, and unpredictable calamities of our modern age have dwarfed the troubles of any previous age to a mere speck and just a storm in a tea-cup. Eventually, the outcry of the modern Northumberland will be more painful and pathetic, and indeed far louder due to hundreds of thousands of resounding loudspeakers producing a din and uproar of an unprecedented kind unknown to Northumberland.

Just imagine all the radios of the world magnifying the outcry of the modern desperate Northumberland, crying before the declaration of atomic warfare, as follows.

> "Now lock this world in atomic hell,
> And spark up the flint-hearted retribution
> To ablaze the destiny of a miserable race;
> Now, let design expire, purpose fail, and order die,
> And now let the winked out an edifice
> Of this tottering universe kiss the earth,
> Now, let at last the long-sought notion of
> A fortuitous concourse of contending atoms prevail,
> O, relentless Nemesis!
> Unsheathe thy uncompromising sword,
> And thou much wronged Mother Nature!
> Unleash thine innumerable hosts
> Of dazzling adders with mortal tongues,
> Blazing vipers with hissing venoms,
> Fiery demons with gurgling thunders,
> Screaming witches with a thousand spouting flames,
> Snake-headed gorgons with a million petrifying visages,
> Wriggling billions of meteoric stinging elephant scorpions;
> To be set on a rancorous, ravenous, and ungrateful species,

These slanderous slaves of wealth and the world,
Unpitying murderers of body and the soul,
Ill-advised, misguided, and proud destroyers
Of science, civilization, art, religion, culture, humanity, and all,
Now, stir thy vengeance,
And let loose thine all-devouring hell,
On their once flourishing abode,
And turn this globe into a pandemonium of reeking deserts,
Smoldering debris, whirling storms of scorching sands,
Amidst the resounding peals of devil's jeering laughter,
A foe, over-joyed at so dire a spectacle of ruin,
So ignominious an end of his old adversary,
Adam's unwise posterity,
And call this hell the atomic hell
Creation of their own hands."

(Yousuf Gabriel)

Moreover, let this be clear to innocent humankind that nuclear energy is essentially poisonous. The lethal radiations, alpha, beta, gamma rays, and neutrons are inherent in the very nature of atomic energy. These lethal radiations, insidiously and without the knowledge of their victims, cause incurable damage and unspeakable harm to human health. Their presence in the body is only known when the die has already been cast. These radiations cannot be ejected from the body once they have entered therein. They are no doubt far more dangerous than any other poison known to man, including arsenic, strychnia, and cyanides, and if you allow me to talk a little Greek and less Latin to you, it would be said, that:

"The atomic radiations are 'thanatoid perfidia'. If all the 'venenum' of the 'thanatoid' nature within the 'regalimen' of poison is distilled, it will never approach the mark of atomic radiations, and above all else, these radiations are 'thanatoid perfidia' sans; 'theriaca Andromachi'." [1]

Now, in plain language, it all means that the atomic radiations are death-like and treacherous, and poisonous snakes such as there happen to be no antidote for their poison. Indeed, medical men worldwide have hitherto failed to find any effective treatment of radiation sickness. However, they have succeeded in transplanting hearts. These atomic radiations kill. It is a fact that may not perhaps have mattered too much. However, unfortunately enough, they are the sure harbingers of a race of monsters begetting monsters multiplying in a cancer-ridden world with a thousand sexual diseases and disorders and chimerical developments. Just ask the scientist. He will attest to the truth of my statement. It also may come as a piece of strange news to the innocent and ignorant part of humanity that these radiations distort and destroy human genetic constitution both in males and females and create genetic troubles of the worst imaginable kind.

These radiations are extraordinarily perfidious and may keep lurking in the human body generation after generation without any sign whatsoever in a most surreptitious manner. Then suddenly may reveal their presence in the birth of a 'poor monster baby', born abnormal and piteously staring at the face of its panic-stricken parents. [2]

Any atomic plant or reactor situated anywhere in any part of the world is a dangerous sign because it unfailingly emits radiation no matter for what purpose the particular plant works. There is no question whatsoever of the purpose, whether peaceful or bellicose. Thus, the atomic plant is entirely innocent of the phrase, "The atomic energy for peaceful purposes." Such a phrase is mere self-deception and could only satisfy human beings who have a natural capacity for feigning themselves deaf, blind, or mad.

I say that: "The atomic energy knows only to emit toxic radiations whenever or wherever generated: whether for giving light to a city with peaceful and civilized intentions or taking the life out of it with aims that are savage and belligerent."

A man these days may dive into a river and come out dry, but no man can generate atomic energy and hope to remain healthy or immutable. Therefore, safeguards and precautions against the ill-effects of atomic radiations cannot be relied upon even if of the most efficient order. Dumping the refuse of fissile materials has been a headache and plague and will, in all probability, forever remain so. [3]

I am not inventing these facts about the radiations and then telling you. The scientists themselves are loudest in proclaiming all these facts, and even so, to deaf humanity. These scientists are extremely honest fellows in matters concerned with science. However, if humankind pretends deafness against their cries, they cannot be held responsible for that. Yet, scientists are putting up their utmost endeavor for the advancement of atomism and nuclear energy. If all their enthusiasm emanates from pecuniary necessities, that is quite a different matter. But suppose they honestly believe that they are doing service to science or humanity by propagating nuclear energy. In that case, I can tell with utmost certainty that they neither do any service to science nor humanity. Instead, they are procuring death for both science and humanity and themselves. Let them, therefore, reflect alone on the matter and see if there is some truth in what I say.

The primary reason given in favor of nuclear energy is that it constitutes an inexhaustible source of power. Be it even so. But is the deal acceptable to any human being worth the same if we tell him both the pros and cons of the matter?

I ask that: "Would you choose to die a leper yourself and bequeath to your posterity monstrosity in heritage in return for nuclear power? Or would you not prefer a healthy life for yourself and a healthy legacy for your children to the power that companies derive from nuclear energy?"

However, suppose you persist in having plenty of food and clothing. Then do we need to tell you that no doubt nuclear energy brings plenty, but side by side with penalty as well, indeed? Yes! The plenty, not of eatables only, but also the plenty of pain, panic, disease, and distress in the form of penalty. Is it not appropriate to say instead that it is not only the plenty but also the penalty of pain, panic, disease, and distress? As a foul play on your part, Providence will impose a penalty. But, it will not be you; instead, your future generations will pay back the price for this plenty of food and clothing with plenty of pain, panic, disease, and distress.

And if even then you vote for nuclear energy, is there no mental doctor in your neighborhood that may test the soundness of your brain? Moreover, is there no insurance company in your vicinity that may insure your head for a thousand measures of nuclear energy in hard currency?

I request that: "Let the scientists and governments tell the masses worldwide all about nuclear energy, and then let there be a census to see how many of them vote in favor of nuclear energy? How many mothers want their children to turn monsters for a few additional morsels of food? How many fathers there are who like to be hurled into the atomic hell along with their children that they may get a few additional calories of food?"

Again, I ask, have all the energy sources been exhausted that they are clamoring for nuclear energy? We request the enthusiasts that if they are bent on bringing martyrdom to humanity, let them choose another field and renounce such ideas as nuclear suicide. Better still, keep this unique honor to them and leave innocent humankind alone. The entire responsibility of the ill-application of science and misuse of wealth and the consequent misery, sufferings and afflictions, hazards, and dangers, lay solely on the head of those unfortunate people who left faith out as a source of unending troubles and impedance to progress and went headlong into exclusively worldly pursuits. Instead of implementing reforms in their religion if it existed in a state of corruption, they just decided to cut at its root. They then proceeded on the way to progress unhampered and free, little knowing that in this way, they had thrown the load on one side only of the pack-horse and had thus upset the balance.

How little did they realize in their blind zeal for progress that people were not a clay model only and made of two elements: the body (matter) and soul (mind)? This makeup of two elements was human beings' basic constitution. How could then, one half of it and perhaps the better half, that is, the soul (mind), be entirely discarded and left to starve without food, a prey to a hundred and one disorders. But they certainly did discard the soul (mind). Instead, they lavished all their attention on the body (matter). The result was that humanity which had sustained its existence through untold calamities, catastrophes, and disasters for thousands of years during its long and troubled history in the past, has arrived at the brink of sure and shameful destruction within a few centuries in this modern, science-guided age.

Science-Religion conflict at the very outset of the Renaissance of the West has been an unhappy affair that has proved disastrous in the long run to the humankind at large. The atrocities of an authoritative Church might indeed have been unbearable, while the rational and benevolent character of science might have seemed a great boon. But thanks to the absence of faith that the unfortunate survivors of the atomic conflagration, unfortunate by their survival itself, sitting like haggard and a wretched group of bald vultures in a desolate desert, on top of a stinking heap of smoldering debris and choking fumes, might be heard as saying with a sad sigh:

"Alas for us, perhaps the amenities of beneficent science were a mere delusion. Perhaps it was at some accursed hour that ill-starred humankind had adopted the course of science. Alas for us! Perhaps the inhuman atrocities of the cruel Clergies were preferable to this. O, death benign, why hast thou spared us, miserable creatures? Pray, condescend once to visit us, and relieve this wretched medley of a painful existence. We envy the owners of these swollen and stinking bodies. We wish we were in their place killed and saved this unbearable existence."

We earnestly hope that neither scientists nor politicians will treat these sentiments as mere mockery. But for blinding dazzle of a pre-ordained decree of cruel fate blinded their eyes, and they are foredoomed along with the whole of humankind to an unfortunate end. It is my heart that speaks, and the voice of a heart only the foredoomed can pretend not to hear, and blind only can deny the presence of the sun in the heavens. Pray, I implore you, now awake from your slumber and see what lies ahead over the horizons of humanity.

Today, the world is thirsty for peace and contentment amidst this maddening uproar and heart-breaking drudgery of Godless materialism. Humankind today pines for long-lost faith in this immoral and unspiritual age, and they now yearn after a world in which science and religion may exist side by side in perfect reconcilement. They find themselves unable to disown science, and they feel a sense of emptiness in their mind due to the absence of faith. They cannot relinquish science without the risk of uprooting the whole economic structure of the world, and they cannot now long renounce faith, for science has been long misused due merely to the absence of the element of faith. Unfortunately, science and religion have been kept at loggerheads since the birth of modern science and modern civilization. Their reconcilement, therefore, seems now a matter of many difficulties.

The general opinion on this matter is that it might be difficult. Yet certain conditions may be fulfilled to make it possible; namely, that science and religion, wealth and Allah, body and soul, matter and mind, this world, and the next world, are allotted the places due to them in an atmosphere of faith. This atmosphere of faith is faith in Allah, the Day of Judgment, the life in Heaven, and under the complete Sovereignty of the Creator. Therefore, science ought to become a servant to faith and wealth, a mere means and necessity. Every act ought to reflect the thought of the Judgment of Allah.

Such re-organization may seem challenging, but when faith is there, nothing is complicated. You will see the world astonished to witness that nuclear energy, now so formidable a problem, will be dissolved before 'a creed built in the heart of things', and the stockpiles of the atom bombs will evaporate and disappear like mist before the rays of the rising sun. You will also see that humankind could live happily enough without the agency of nuclear energy. Nations will defend territories even without atom bombs. The sinking boat of humanity will be sailing again in calm and tranquil waters. Alack, the day. It is not at all possible to affect a compromise between these two.

But, on the other hand, suppose faith is not brought back amidst humankind and matters are allowed to deteriorate gradually till at last the stage of atomic conflagration has approached, and atomic fire has consumed unfortunate humanity. Then, of course, those responsible for this unprecedented heinous deed shall be answerable for it before Allah, the Master of all those innocent as well as to deserving creatures who have most mercilessly been cast into the atomic hell. It shall not be possible for guilty of so terrible a crime to escape the wrath of the Creator and the severity of His vengeance. It is an uncommon evil to bring the world to such a tragic end, a world that might have taken millions of years to reach its present state of perfection. A garden planted by the Creator and watered and pruned for ages, and at last, when the season of its blossoming arrived, it was blighted by those for whose sake it was prepared. How woeful a day of the tragic end shall choke the laughter and turn merriments into the gloom. When beating hearts fail, and the wailing souls caught in the blizzard of atomic bombs shall forever be silenced amidst the groaning flames of all-consuming atomic hell.

It was in 1961 that I discovered this warning about the atomic bomb in the Quran. I sat in my study engrossed in writing my book 'The Mind of the Quran'. During my perusal of the Holy Quran, the secret, just like a flash, dazzled the eye of my mind. It indeed was a discovery, more startling and more important than all the most significant discoveries of science united, including the atom bomb itself, and far more vital than Galileo's astronomy, Darwin's biology, Newton's gravity, and Einstein's special relativity. Allah, at last, had taken mercy on miserable humankind and had risen to the occasion. The mighty hand of truth had eventually appeared to give battle to the pernicious tendencies that led the helpless humanity like dumb, mute, and blind victims to atomic shambles.

I was dead sure about the truth of the prophecy. But to satisfy a skeptic world, it was necessary to provide proof in exact accord with the prevailing spirit of the age, the age of science. Scientific proof, therefore, was essential. Judging from the particular complexity, novelty, and ambiguity of the topic of the atom bomb, it was pretty natural that the prophecy within the Quran remained a secret to be only discovered after the actual object of the prophecy had made its appearance before the world. The prophecy was a wonder in itself, and the wonder was further augmented by the aptness of the commentaries of the earliest commentators of the Quran, namely, the Sahabah [disciples of the Holy Prophet (peace be upon him)]. They had the honor of hearing from the mouth of Prophet (peace be upon him) himself.

In this age, scientific proof is a criterion for judging everything. It was justly feared that without scientific proof and a perfect corroboration of the prophecy by the facts of nuclear science, the whole affair would be treated as mere fantasy. Therefore, my certainty would prove of little avail either to myself or the world at large. Nor could the affair be left away without a deep sense of gross injustice and a great wrong to humankind. It is not hard for anyone endowed with average understanding to realize both the urgency of the matter and the influential role such a prophecy could play in saving humankind from dreadful doom. It was a sure neutralizer of the atom bomb and an efficacious antidote against all the poisonous characteristics that tended towards humanity's wholesale destruction through nuclear weapons. This prophecy was a sure means of survival and hope for the revival of humanity, a guarantee against the painful extinction of human species, a miracle of miracles, and a priceless boon of the Beneficent and Merciful Allah. The prophecy possessed my soul so that I thought no toil, labor, or sacrifice would be too much for a matter so great and beneficial to fellow human beings. I believe that I did all I could in my humble way to achieve the scientific proof of the prophecy and lend it a form presentable to humanity due to many years' toil and labor, and perhaps sweat and tears if you can understand.

My difficulties are great and many. The ones that concerned me personally, I need not mention. Nevertheless, the main challenging incident on the topic itself has come to present itself in a formidable form: the proper appreciation of the subject entails a set of pre-requisites not generally found together in a single person. It is hard to find one endowed simultaneously with a thorough understanding of science and that of Quran and Arabic language and endued with a truthful mind, perspicuous intellect, and keen sense of sympathy for the worldwide humanity. Darwin's philosophy is generally and justly considered as a complicated subject and implies deep understanding. Yet, that philosophy would not impose conditions of so diversified a nature for its genuine appreciation as this prophecy under discussion would essentially impose. Men of the scientific caliber that of, say, Albert Einstein; and the philosophical caliber, say, that of Bertrand Russell; and the theological caliber, say, that of His Holiness would indeed be available. But none of these could claim a thorough knowledge of either the Quran or the Arabic language, and also that they may be specialists only in their respective fields.

On the other hand, although there would not be a shortage of men learned in the Quran and the Arabic language within the Islamic counties, a few could be justly expected to be well-versed in science or modern knowledge. Indeed, and yet, no mistaken notion of over-estimated and insurmountable difficulties of the matter be entertained. Such high qualifications which we have desired are required only for a critical appreciation of the subject. Persons so highly gifted would be enraptured by the topic and thrown into ecstasies according to their capacity. Otherwise, there is no such intricacy to baffle an average understanding as far as a general understanding of the subject is concerned. Being situated in a place far removed from all the acknowledged centers of science and learning and the scientific and philosophical societies, I am obliged to rely on the intelligentsia's good sense and charitable thoughts worldwide. Whosoever has recognized the truth of this prophecy or a warning; it is well in the broad interest of the humanity that the same be treated with sympathy and be given the publicity it rightly deserves that perchance they may reflect and be saved. The circumstances of humanity today warrant a broader and broader outlook. Let not our petty considerations in any way veil our understanding or obscure our vision when we see that the very existence of humankind is at stake.

My heartfelt conviction is that the people worldwide, irrespective of their caste, color, creed, country or religion, inclination, aptitude, or considerations, will view this prophecy with the regard it deserves. They will lend their sympathies to it in the name of humanity and for the sake of their own home, health, children, and all. Because the nuclear explosion respects no such thing: It is a conjoint foe; let us make it a common cause. Or else this universal foe will leave nothing. Nay, but you will not even have a chance to mourn your dear and near ones. May Allah bless you with understanding and endow you with wisdom that you may discern the facts and avoid the approaching calamity. Aameen.

Now, in the end, please pay attention, for I am about to say something important: lest you say tomorrow, nobody told you. Suppose atomic conflagration destroyed this garden of Allah and all His creatures. In that case, on the Day of Judgment, the Creator shall call to account everyone responsible for the catastrophe. The enraged Creator of the world then is well-justified in avenging Himself on the criminals. His Mercy also finds no bounds. He may forgive everyone, but we must consider our deeds.

Suppose atom bombs consume Allah's world without this prophecy of the Quran, having received publicity which this rightly deserves, due either to my laziness or helplessness or the neglect of those in a position to cooperate in this matter. In that case, we shall be answerable before Allah on the Day of Judgment. Allah may ask the atomic powers or others, having had a share in the atomic devastation of the world, whether they had received the warning of the Quran and had considered the methods of averting the atomic danger contained therein? To which they may reply negatively. I then may be questioned by Allah, what I had done in making the prophecy known to humankind? If I, then say that I did whatever was within my powers. I researched and sought scientific proof and then wrote the books, but no cooperation came from anywhere. The Muslims excused themselves, for they thought they had their problems of a material nature more important and showed utter indifference. And I, not being myself in a position to cope with the situation single-handed in an age of printing presses and publications, found myself quite helpless. The non-Muslim powers were remote from me and out of my reach, and I could not afford to approach them. The thing, therefore, was lost.

Then Allah may question the Muslims. They may answer they did not understand the topic of the prophecy, and they had many other problems before them to solve. Allah may then display the atomic hell before their eyes and explain to them the text of His prophecy, and they may then learn a practical lesson soon. Suppose this prophecy has reached all the four corners of the world, and it could be achieved only through the cooperation of all concerned. Then after that, the world has not heeded Allah's word and has failed to remove the causes that the Quran has given out as responsible for the emergence of nuclear energy and the atom bomb. In that case, nuclear fire has consequently consumed humankind or has turned it into monsters. Those who have done duty to give due publicity to this prophecy shall be absolved from guilt, and the responsibility shall be shifted on to the negligent part of humanity.

Do you now understand, or will the terrific blast of the atom bomb only start you thinking? However, will that then avail you aught? Will these Muslims only understand after they have received a practical bath in the nuclear hell?

Now, please listen. The devil may effectively whisper in your ears: 'Do not hearken to it; it is the Quran, a book in which you do not believe.' Unfortunately, the word of this arch-seducer of people, 'the Satan', may please you, but it is against the dictates of wisdom and may eventually prove fatal. It may bring about grievous consequences but alas then. O, ailing soul! Suppose you could approve the physical treatment of the body by a doctor apparently of a faith different from yours. Why then deny life if vouchsafed by a piece of advice appearing in a book in which you do not formally believe. But, maybe, this bit of advice is in no way contrary to the Scripture in which you might have believed. There is an overflowing cup of life-giving elixir, pure and celestial; whosoever shall accept it shall do so to his good, and whoever shall reject the same shall reject it to his hurt. Blessed are they who take up the word, the truth, wherever found, and rejoice therein.

It indeed is most proper that a work of this nature be subjected to extreme scrutiny. But a few elites and few only throughout this vast world will be able to judge, for an enterprise of this nature entailed Einsteinian scientific genius, the Socratic sight of discernment, Darwinian depth of thought, a deep insight into the inner heart of the Scripture under discussion, and a penetrating eye to observe the trends, tendencies, ideas, problems, and answers to the problems of the modern age. It is a gruesome ordeal, and a grim fact turned grimmer because, but a few could judge while the applause of the generality of humankind would be but an echo of the recognition by the few elites, in a pioneer work with no model, no precedent.

I do not know when this book will be published. Someone may, in the meantime, try to write on the topic in the light of my two articles, namely, 'The Quran and the atomic hell' published in the daily 'Pakistan Times', dated 20-2-1963; and Urdu 'Atom Bomb Ka Dhamaaka, Azzab-e-Elahi hai' (i.e., atomic bomb explosion, the wrath of Allah), published in the daily 'Mashrique'(Urdu), Lahore, Pakistan, dated 5-7-1970; and also several lectures delivered by me before various audiences. However, let me warn such people that it is the most complex and delicate of all topics. It is factual to be feared that such writers, despite best intentions, may throw the whole thing into utter confusion resulting in irreparable loss to the topic and consequently humankind itself. Therefore, this work has to be scrutinized by the most competent judges worldwide, and it is destined to become the by-word throughout as the sole hope of doomed humanity in which the Yousuf Gabriel is to figure as the martyr. Peace be with you all.

YOUSUF GABRIEL
February 07, 1974.

~~*~*~*~*

---

[1] [Meanings of these Latin words are as follows.
Thanatoid: mortal, deadly   **Perfidia:** treacherous
Venenum: poison, drug   **Regalimen:** realm   **sans:** without
Theriaca: an antidote considered a panacea to a poison
Theriaca Andromachi: Flourished in the 1st century, Andromachus was a Greek physician to the Roman emperor Nero. He is credited with the invention of the famous antidote for poison now known as 'theriaca Andromachi'.]

[2] **JELLYFISH BABIES:** In 1996, Lijon Eknilang from Rongelap Atoll told the International Court of Justice how she and other Marshallese women had given birth to 'monster babies': 'One woman on Likiep gave birth to a 'child with two heads'. There is a young girl on Ailuk today with 'no knees, three toes on each foot and a missing arm'. Her mother had not been born by 1954, but she was raised on a contaminated atoll. The most common birth defects have been 'jellyfish babies', born with no bones in their bodies and with transparent skin. We can see their brains and hearts beating. The babies usually live for a day or two before they stop breathing.' 'Nuclear Weapons: a history, reprinted with permission from New Internationalist, June 2008'.

[(www.newint.org); with special thanks to Ian McKelvie.]
NOTE: The author believed that because of the genetic effects of perfidious nuclear radiation on the human body, this transformation of the human species to monstrous chimeras would start after a couple of generations but unfortunately, it has already started in the present generation. See the photos of a large number of these poor monstrous human babies at the end of this series (Book-2).

[3] HOW DO YOU DISMANTLE A NUCLEAR SUBMARINE?
By Paul Marks: March 30, 2015
When nuclear-powered submarines reach the end of their lives, dismantling them is a complicated and laborious process. Paul Marks investigates.

At the end of their useful lives the subs essentially become floating nuclear hazards, fizzing with lethal, spent nuclear fuel that's extremely hard to get out. --- Some of the strangest industrial graveyards on the planet have been created – stretching from the U.S.A. Pacific Northwest, via the Arctic Circle to Russia's Pacific Fleet home of Vladivostok.
"An aquarium of radioactive junk" — The Kara Sea, a submarine graveyard

These submarine cemeteries take many forms. --- In the Kara Sea north of Siberia, they are essentially nuclear dumping grounds, with submarine reactors and fuel strewn across the 300m-deep seabed. Here the Russians appear to have continued, until the early 1990s, disposing of their nuclear subs in the same manner as their diesel-powered compatriots: dropping them into the ocean. --- The Soviets turned the Kara Sea into "an aquarium of radioactive junk" says Norway's Bellona Foundation, an environmental watchdog based in Oslo.

The seabed is littered with some 17,000 naval radioactive waste containers, 16 nuclear reactors and five complete nuclear submarines – one has both its reactors still fully fuelled. --- The Kara Sea area is now a target for oil and gas companies – and accidental drilling into such waste could, in principle, breach reactor containments or fuel rod cladding, and release radionuclides into the fishing grounds, warns Bellona's managing director Nils Bohmer. --- Russian reactors have been stored in the harbor at Vladivostok. --- Official submarine graveyards are much more visible: you can even see them on Google Maps or Google Earth. Zoom in on America's biggest nuclear waste repository in Hanford, Washington, Sayda Bay in the arctic Kola Peninsula, or the shipyards near Vladivostok and you'll see them. There are row after row of massive steel canisters, each around 12m long. They are lined up in ranks in Hanford's long, earthen pits awaiting a future mass burial, sitting in regimented rows on a Sayda Bay dockside, or floating on the waters of the Sea of Japan, shackled to a pier at the Pavlovks sub base near Vladivostok. --- Although the reactor machinery – steam generators, pumps, valves and piping – now contains no enriched uranium, the metals in it are rendered radioactive by decades of neutron bombardment shredding their atoms.

Floating menace: At Pavlovks, near Vladivostok, 54 of the canisters are still afloat and at the mercy of the weather. --- When nuclear submarines reach the end of their lives, some of their hulks remain dangerously radioactive. --- Russia has so far decommissioned 120 nuclear submarines of the Northern Fleet and 75 subs from its Pacific Fleet. In the U.S.A., meanwhile, 125 Cold War-era subs have been dismantled. --- Even with high security, radioactive material can occasionally escape – sometimes in bizarre ways. For instance both I.N.L. and Hanford have suffered unusual radiation leaks from tumbleweeds blowing into waste cooling ponds, picking up contaminated water, and then being blown over the facility's perimeter by the wind. ---The Russian Navy is planning to launch several new submarines. --- The U.S.A. is not alone: Russia has four new nuclear subs under construction at Severodvinsk and may build a further eight before 2020. "Despite limited budgets Russia is committed to building up its nuclear fleet again," says Bohmer. China is doing likewise.

(http://www.bbc.com)

~~*~*~*~*

CHAPTER-1

NUCLEAR (ATOMIC) THEORY

Humankind has used flowing water as a source of energy and also got energy from burning wood and charcoal for a long time. The first is gravitational energy, and the second is chemical energy (essentially electrical in origin). An entirely new energy process, roughly a million times more powerful than any chemical process, has been discovered in recent years. This energy source lies in the 'nuclear force', which operates between atomic nuclei constituents, protons, and neutrons. Observe that, unlike gravitational and chemical energy, the harnessing of nuclear energy (also called atomic energy) demands deep insight and considerable progress in fundamental science as distinct from the empirical arts and crafts. After a gruesome struggle for centuries, the discovery and manipulation of nuclear energy have been possible in acquiring systematized knowledge, continuous scientific progress, and an elaborate economic system.

All matter consists of atoms. The atoms are further coagulated into molecules. All atoms consist of a central core, called the nucleus, that is, the heart, around which the electrons revolve, like planets that revolve around the sun. All nuclei are built from two fundamental particles, protons, and neutrons. The neutron is electrically neutral. The proton has a positive charge equal to and opposite the charge of an electron. A neutron is slight, one part in 759 --- heavier than a proton which has 1836 times the mass of an electron. A neutron outside the nucleus is an unstable particle: it has a 'half-life' of about a quarter of an hour. It decays into a proton and an electron.

THE ATOM

The mass number (A) of a nucleus is the number of neutrons and protons. The number of protons defines the atomic number (Z) of the nucleus. The atomic number is characteristic of an element; for example, it is 1 for Hydrogen, 38 for Strontium, and 92 for Uranium. For the same element, nuclei can have different values of the mass number (A). They are called isotopes of the given element. A nuclear species (nuclide) is specified by assigning Z and A values; thus, Z=92, A=235, generally written as Uranium-235 (U-235). Uranium-238 contains 92 protons and 146 neutrons, making a total of 238 nucleons. A 'nucleon' stands for either a proton or a neutron. The protons and neutrons are most strongly bound in nuclei of moderate mass numbers, and the binding is relatively weak in heavy and light nuclei. It is on this account that heavy nuclei liberate energy on fission and light nuclei on fusion.

Some elements may have the same atomic number: the number of protons but may have different mass numbers, that is, the different number of neutrons contained in the nuclei. For example, the atomic number of Chlorine is 17 that means the Chlorine nucleus has 17 protons. However, one Chlorine atom may have 18 neutrons to make the mass number 35, while another Chlorine atom may have 20 neutrons to make the mass number 37. Yet, they are the atoms of Chlorine and are called isotopes. This particular kind of variation is of interest to us in this work because the isotopes represent different states of a nucleus that is the atom's heart. These hearts are, in a way, in a state of disturbance. The atomic weight is the relative weight of the atom.

FISSION PROCESS

Fission means the division of a nucleus into smaller nuclei. Of all the fissile materials, Uranium-235 has been discovered as the most suitable for fission purposes. If we break a Uranium nucleus into two nuclei of nearly the same size, it releases energy. The process in which a heavy nucleus such as Uranium is broken into two intermediate nuclei with the release of energy is called a 'fission reaction' or 'nuclear fission'.

When an isotope of Uranium-235 is bombarded with slow neutrons, fission takes place spontaneously. The neutron strikes at the heart of the Uranium atom. It splits the nucleus into two approximately equal daughter nuclei, say Krypton and Barium nuclei, knocking out 2 or 3 (the average is 2.5) neutrons from the nucleus of the U-235 atom. These two or three knocked-out neutrons strike in turn at the heart of 2 or 3 other atoms and knock out 2 or 3 neutrons each, and so on so forth; the process continues. It is then said that a fission chain reaction is built up until the whole mass of U-235 becomes incandescent and eventually explodes with wrath. For the hearts of the atoms disturbed to an ultra-natural extremity, the resultant commotion has approached a limit where the natural sustenance becomes an impossibility.

FUSION PROCESS

In the fusion process, simply lighter nuclei are fused. A fusion process can be realized in various ways, e.g., by bombarding light elements with charged particles obtained from cyclotron and other high-energy-particle accelerators. However, the fusion process becomes possible only at exceedingly high temperatures of the order of millions of degrees. The fusion bomb (Hydrogen bomb) utilizes this temperature in achieving fusion reaction. From our point of view, the simplest explanation of fusion reaction could be that nucleus (heart) of an atom is fused with the nucleus (heart) of another atom, and the energy is released when the two hearts crush together.

However, the infamous feature of the whole matter is radiation. The fission reaction essentially emits this radiation as alpha, beta, gamma rays, and neutrons. These radiations are undetectable by the five senses and are not only poisonous but perniciously, rather wickedly poisonous. They not only kill, but they also cause leprosy, cancer, and inheritable monstrosity. These radiations make no difference whether the nuclear (atomic) energy is produced for peaceful purposes or as a weapon of war for wholesale destruction. Thus, a phrase like 'nuclear energy for peaceful purposes' is only a misnomer and a self-deception, rather a blindness of deluded humanity. It is a contradiction in terms.

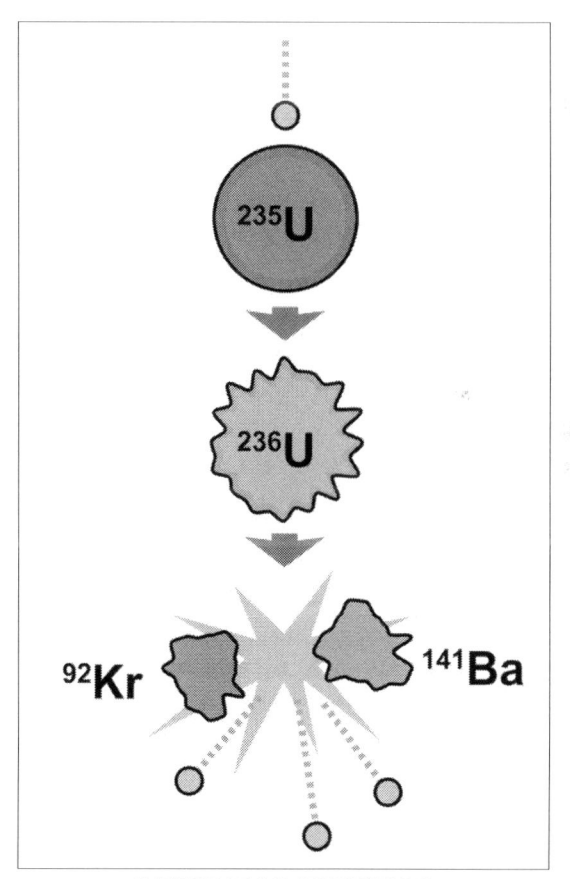

NUCLEAR FISSION
(https://commons.wikimedia.org/wiki/File:Nuclear_fission.svg)

FISSION CHAIN REACTION
(https://commons.wikimedia.org/wiki/File:Fission_chain_reaction.svg)

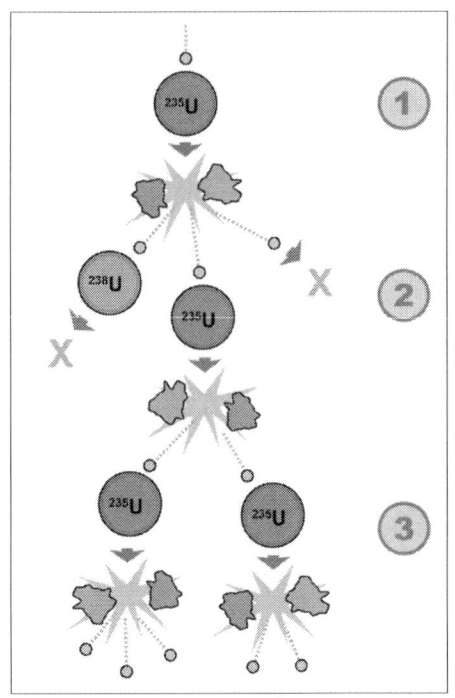

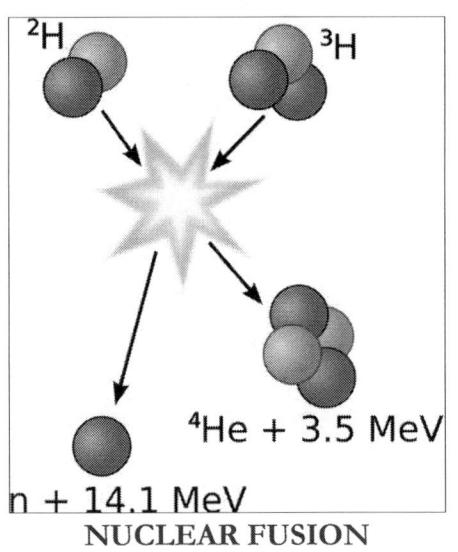

NUCLEAR FUSION
(https://commons.wikimedia.org/wiki/)

~~*~*~*

CHAPTER-2

THE HISTORY OF ATOMISM

We now produce a brief history of atomism, from atom to the atomic bomb. The reader will get some idea of the course atom has traversed during its long journey in twenty-five centuries towards its final, rather the first stage of the Hiroshima and Nagasaki destination. Moreover, when the Quran revealed this warning about the atom bomb, not a vestige of such theory as 'Atomism' remained anywhere in the world; not to speak of Arabia proper, the inhabitants of which being entirely ignorant then and innocent of any type of Greek philosophy, rather any philosophy. This fact makes the prophecy indeed more remarkable.

After a doubtful and controversial existence, the theory of atomism had breathed its last at the hands of the overwhelming pressure of Stoicism, an opposed school of thought, and Christianity, a religion even more strongly antagonistic towards atomism. In the circumstances, when the theory of atomism did not even exist, a prophecy about an atom bomb would seem like an arrow shot in space without any visible target. The arrow, however, was shot, which traveled on its way to its target out of sight. At last, in the fourteenth century of its travel, it struck its target in 1945 in Hiroshima and Nagasaki. Even then, it remained out of sight of humankind. Finally, about sixteen years after, it arrived at its destination when in 1961, I discovered it in the Holy Quran, indeed by the Grace of Almighty Allah.

The Quran had also prophesied the victory and prevalence of the defeated Greeks against the decisively victorious Persians. According to Edward Gibbon, the famous author of 'The History of the Decline and Fall of the Roman Empire', nothing could be more remote from this prophecy's fulfillment when the Quran ventured it. Because of the circumstances at that time, there seemed not the most negligible probability of Greeks fighting back to defeat Persians. Nevertheless, the Greeks repulsed Persian forces and drove them out of the Greek territories but went further to the throne of the Persian Emperor and forced him to accept the conditions of a treaty most disgraceful to him. Thus, the prophecy of the Quran about improbability was fulfilled in a short time. [1]

But on the other side of the scale is the prophecy of the Quran about the atom bomb, which took more than thirteen centuries for fulfillment. The theory of atomism lay buried for centuries, fathoms deep in obscurity when the Quran made a prophecy about its fruits, that is, the atomic bomb and radiations. Centuries more elapsed in a state of humanity, tending farther and farther away from the atmosphere, which could be favorable to the revival of atomism. The time arrived at last when humanity discovered the grave of atomism by some strange chance. The scientists revived atomism with a flurry that gradually came to pervade every branch of science.

Eventually, at a decisive stage, it took on an unexpected turn and fell on a way that ultimately and again quite unexpectedly led to the production of the atomic bomb. Nay, even the atomic bomb was not quite assuredly predictable during all its consecutive stages of development, and it was believed as a certainty only after the scientists finally tested it. However, it proved practicable and proved its actual efficacy and efficiency in the smoke-ridden ruins of Hiroshima and Nagasaki and indeed put the spirit of Christian mercy in the crucible. Was it not so? Ask Ronald Arbuthnott Knox. [2]

THE AUTHOR OF ATOMISM

The scientists generally attribute the theory of atomism to Democritus (ca. 460 BCE – ca. 370 BCE) of Abdera in Thrace, Greece. He was a younger contemporary of Socrates and nicknamed 'the laughing philosopher' because he found in human life matter only for laughter against Heraclitus (535 BCE – 475 BCE). The later tradition called Heraclitus the 'weeping philosopher' because he always found in human life matter for tears. The theory of atomism is attributed to Democritus though not he, but Leucippus was its actual originator. We know little about Leucippus except that he was a Milesian (most probably born in 'Miletus') and flourished about 440 BC.

"Leucippus or Leukippos (first half of 5th century BC) was the first Greek to develop the theory of atomism — the idea that everything is composed entirely of various imperishable, indivisible elements called atoms — which was elaborated in far greater detail by his pupil and successor, Democritus."

(Wikipedia, the free Encyclopedia)

Democritus received the credit because he was responsible for developing the system and making it known. Both Leucippus and Democritus were atheists. Due to the hatred, it caused in the people's minds, this atheism was primarily responsible for rejecting the theory of Leucippus and Democritus. It is remarkable to note that, when this theory of atomism was discovered and adopted in modern times, they did not revive associated atheism along with it. But somehow and unfortunately, of course, this atheism has found its way into the minds of the modern atom-ridden skeptics, although in a guise most astonishingly queer.

THE EARLY VIEWS OF THE ATOMISTS

Following are the views of the early atomists about atomism.
(1) The atoms are indivisible and indestructible.
(2) They move about in all directions in a fortuitous concourse in an otherwise empty space.
(3) Atoms and space are all that exist.
(4) Differences of shape distinguish different kinds of atoms, but individual atoms are too small to be noticed by the senses.
(5) The arrangement makes the things we touch and see atoms in groups. The change consists of nothing but their arrangements. There is no alteration in the atoms themselves.
(6) The motion of an atom persists until checked, presumably in collision with another atom since the theory itself denies any other cause.

The last one is the most significant of all the atomists' ideas. It foreshadows the law of inertia which states that motion needs no cause to preserve it. The cause is necessary only to produce changes in motion. If a thing moves, it will continue to move without changing speed or direction until something forces it to slow down, accelerate, or deviate from its path. This notion is the foundation of Newtonian mechanics. It is opposed to Aristotle's view that a body comes to rest unless something keeps it going.

The atomists say that once the atoms get a start, invariable mechanical laws determine their subsequent motions. The state of the universe depends only upon its previous state. Its present decides its future. Here is the philosophy of Determinism in its extreme form. The moral implications arising from the necessary denial of free will are evident and disturbing. Unfortunately, philosophies that are the product of the human mind are mostly fragmentary in form and far too limited in scope. Human knowledge is of a nature fragmentary, and human vision is minimal. The philosophers see an elephant just as the legendary ten blind men of Hindustan (India) had once seen it. Therefore, interpretations of such philosophies are susceptible, too many and diverse, having even opposite conclusions, and generally following the predisposition of the interpreters' minds.

Further, such philosophies are the reflections of the disposition of the mind of their makers themselves. In an attempt to prove the omnipresence of the Creator and His design and order, Aristotle's mind thought it essential to subject the atom to the controlling hand of the Creator in its motion. In contrast, to show the absence of the Creator, design, and control, Democritus imparted the qualities to the atom such as would prove fortuitous concourse of atoms in a world without any design or purpose. Neither Aristotle nor Democritus could see anything beyond this in the atom. In the presence of faith, everything seems to one's mind converging towards the Creator. Whereas in the absence thereof, everything seems to be running away from Him. We see many a raging storm raised in a teacup during discussions of these subtle philosophies.

So short is man's vision that Darwin saw no harm to faith in all his philosophy, as apparent from his genuine remonstrance. However, was his philosophy as innocent as he thought it to be in the haze of his zeal to discover the truth? We could discuss this fascinating topic at length, but we are, I am afraid, deviating from our actual topic, the history of atomism. What pranks imagination has not played with the human mind? What part corrupt and selfish amongst religious leaders have not played in driving the people away from the faith and creating disgust and hatred of religion in their hearts? How often have two persons said the same thing without understanding each other and disputing all the same?

THE ATOMS OF DEMOCRITUS AND THE IDEAS OF PLATO

Like Plato, Democritus held the eternal and ultimate reality as the object, not of senses but the understanding. Still, he considered the nature of this reality very differently from Plato. The nature of this reality consisted of atoms of inseparable and imperishable bodies of sizes too small that our senses could not detect. They differed from one another in shape (whence he could call them by the same name as Plato gave to his ultimate realities of ideas or forms) and moved about in a vacuum or void. However, the two worlds were different.

THE GREATEST CONTEMPORARY THINKERS CONDEMN ATOMISM

The greatest contemporary thinkers cast the significant influence of Aristotle into the scale against adopting such a theory as atomism. Moreover, the greatest philosopher of ancient time, Socrates' disciple and master of Aristotle, Plato, also vehemently opposed atomism. Mathematicians and Astronomers made significant scientific progress in mathematics and astronomy during the two hundred years that followed the death of Aristotle in 322 BC.

These two centuries were made illustrious by names like Euclid of Alexandria, Greek mathematician, often referred to as the 'Father of Geometry' (300 BC), Eratosthenes of Cyrene (276 BC–195 BC), Archimedes of Syracuse (287 BC–212 BC), and Hipparchus (190 BC–120 BC). Euclid wrote 'Elements' that was the textbook of Geometry for two thousand years. Eratosthenes first used the method to determine the size (circumference) of the earth. Archimedes discovered the principle of the lever. Hipparchus has been called the true 'Father of Astronomy'.

Though these were years of significant progress, yet none of these great thinkers so much as condescended to take the name of atomism, not to speak of any research, investigation, or inquiry. Francis Bacon was the trumpeter of this modern age. Also, he was the greatest, ablest, and most eloquent advocate of atomism. He disagreed with Aristotle on many points. However, he stood in perfect agreement with Aristotle condemning the blindness of atomism to the evidence of design in the world, as afforded by the existence of the structure too elaborate ever to be explained satisfactorily by a fortuitous concourse of atoms. Bacon seemed to be keenly sensible of the danger that lay in attempts to start our investigations considering the purpose of nature of which we are about too likely to take a very short-sighted view. The apprehensions of Bacon, unfortunately, proved only too true. His followers divorced the spiritual side of the affair entirely in due course and fixed full attention on immediate material gains. Hence, the result was a worldwide discontent, and the remedy prescribed was the raining of atomic bombs, releasing ionizing radiations, plagues, poisonous gases, and fires.

THE EPICUREANS ADOPT ATOMISM AS A SYMBOL

Amidst universal rejection by all great minds, however, a philosophical school adopted atomism as a fundamental part of their system. This attraction of atomism for this school was not its scientific utility so much as its apparent inconstancy with the doctrine of the divine government of the world, which they regarded as the source of the worst evil that affected humankind, namely, fear of death and of what may come after it. No doubt, scientific men have combined a belief in the atomic constitution with the divine government in more modern times. Still, they have held the atoms to be (as one of them, James Clerk Maxwell put it) manufactured articles, and the world to include immaterial beings that were not composed of atoms at all. It seems, however, that this idea, unfortunately, did not work satisfactorily.

Once they opened the gate of atomism, the atoms forced out the invisible thought of the immaterial beings, and sheer atomism attained complete sway. There are reasons for it being far too conspicuous. Anything which could not lend itself to an atomic explanation was discarded as unreal and, therefore, undesirable because, unluckily, they desired it so. The ancient atomists, too, as their inner wish so desired, had held the atoms to be eternal and that nothing existed that was not an assemblage of atoms except the void in which the atoms moved. We find ourselves quite at a loss to understand how the whole world of mind was left out of sight to intellect as Democritus and some of his followers possessed? Except for doubtful notions, these atomists moved into atoms to the extent of sublimity. They thought that specific atoms constructed even the 'thought' itself. These particular atoms were tremendously subtle in the assemblage of different patterns.

Still, again their avowed atheism and their notion of the absence of design negates our view. We should, therefore, search for the reasons for their views in some other field. Democritus was a younger contemporary of Socrates. Illustrious men like Socrates, Plato, and Aristotle flourished in a community in that era. It is hard to believe that such extreme dullness, and blindness to the scheme of design in creating the universe, could be found in men like Democritus hailing from the same community and possessing an intellect in no way contemptibly inferior to their illustrious contemporaries above mentioned. It proves that faith is the exceptional boon of Allah and does not depend on either knowledge or intellect.

Epicureans' school of thought adopted atomism as a remedy against the terrors of religion. To this school, the terrors of religion might have seemed quite formidable. Suppose Epicureans have been raised from graves and started living in the present age of their choice. Then, the spectacle of the atomic grizzly will expel the theory of atomism and terror of death from their heads. Life has created these herds of atomic grizzlies amongst modern humans as a reward for labors exhausted in the perfection of atomism.

Epicurus, the founder of the Epicurean school and the chief rival of Zeno (the founder of Stoicism), recommended the rational pursuit of pleasure. He believed and taught that there was no life after death. Epicurus did not preach that one should make the most of his life; eat, drink, and be merry, for tomorrow we die, and there is no Resurrection. Instead, he recommended refined pleasures and moderation. However, followers did not follow his ideal, and excess became the order of his adherents. To employ moderation seems quite harsh in the absence of dread of death and the Judgment in the hereafter. We wish that the natures of many persons were refined enough to pursue refined pleasure, but that, alas, is not the case. The sensualists found a good chance in the teachings of Epicurus to claim for their lives the sanction of Epicurean principle that pleasure is the chief good at which alone it is reasonable to aim, and the name of the Epicurean very early became a synonym for a sensualist and a reproach.

EPICUREANS HAD NO REGARD FOR THE SCIENTIFIC ASPECT OF ATOMISM

Both Zeno (the founder of Stoicism) and Epicurus (the founder of Epicureanism) are chiefly interesting as outstanding examples of men who shaped their opinions without regard for truth according to the needs of their ethical systems. 'Epicurus adopted atomism, not for its scientific merit but because its materialism supported his denial of a spiritual life after death'. The Roman poet and philosopher Lucretius was an eminent follower of Democritus. He did much by his epic philosophical poem on Epicureanism 'De Rerum Natura' (translated into English as 'On the Nature of Things', or 'On the Nature of the Universe') to make atomism known.

Yet although the founder seemed to the poet worthy of being called a god, and as man's deliverer from the superstitious terrors; to a consistent Epicurean, the intellectual and scientific activity, except so far as it served to dissipate the superstitious dread, it could hardly be more than a refined pastime. It is not surprising that the Epicureans contributed little to the advancement of science or philosophical inquiry. They adopted as their own the atomic theory of Democritus. Still, in their hands, it was neither enabled to meet the objections which may be raised against it as a theory of the ultimate nature of reality nor made to exhibit its great capacities as an instrument of scientific description and discovery.

THE APOSTLE PAUL IN ATHENS ENCOUNTERS THE REPRESENTATIVES OF STOICS AND EPICUREANS

The Epicurean school was confronted from its cradle by the Stoic, the opponent of atomism. The Stoic gradually prevailed, although, for a considerable period, these two schools divided the allegiance of a majority of thoughtful persons in the countries, which at the beginning of the Christian era formed the heart of the Roman Empire.

Remember that the philosophers whom the Apostle Paul is related to (The Bible: Acts-17) have encountered on his visit to Athens were representatives of Epicureans and Stoics.

YOUSUF GABRIEL

THE APOSTLE PAUL IN ATHENS AND HIS INTERESTING ENCOUNTER WITH EPICUREANS AND THE STOICS

"Then certain philosophers of the Epicureans, and the Stoicks, encountered him. And some said, What will this babbler say? Other some, He seemeth to be a setter forth of strange gods: because he preached unto them Jesus and the Resurrection. And they took him, and brought him unto Areopagus, saying, May we know what this new doctrine, whereof thou speakest, is? For thou bringest certain strange things to our ears: we would know therefore what these things mean. (For all the Athenians and strangers who were there spent their time in nothing else, but either to tell or to hear some new thing.) Then Paul stood in the midst of Mars' hill and said, ye men of Athens, I perceive that in all things ye are too superstitious. For as I passed by and beheld your devotions, I found an altar with this inscription, TO THE UNKNOWN GOD. Whom, therefore, ye ignorantly worship, him declare I unto you. God that made the world and all things therein, seeing that he is Lord of heaven and earth, dwelleth not in temples made with hands; Neither is worshipped with men's hands, as though he needed anything, seeing he giveth to all life, and breath, and all things; And hath made of one blood all nations of men for to dwell on all the face of the earth, and hath determined the times before appointed, and the bounds of their habitation; That they should seek the Lord, if haply they might feel after him, and find him, though he be not far from every one of us: For in him we live, and move, and have our being; as certain also of your own poets have said, For we are also his offspring. Forasmuch then as we are the offspring of God, we ought not to think that the Godhead is like unto gold, or silver, or stone, graven by art and man's device. And the times of this ignorance God winked at; but now commandeth all men everywhere to repent: Because he hath appointed a day, in which he will judge the world in righteousness by that man whom he hath ordained; whereof he hath given assurance unto all men, in that he hath raised him from the dead. And when they heard of the Resurrection of the dead, some mocked: and others said, We will hear thee again of this matter. So Paul departed from among them. Howbeit certain men clave unto him, and believed: among which was Dionysius the Areopagite, and a woman named Damaris, and others with them."

(The Bible: New Testament: Acts 17:18-34)

This preaching of Apostle Paul did not augur well for Epicureanism. For, with the introduction of Christianity in those parts began the sharp decline of Epicureanism. Epicureanism later ended in its dissolution, and hence along with it, the disappearance of atomism.

NOT THE EPICUREANS BUT STOICS POPULAR WITH ROMANS

It was not surprising that of all the Greek Schools, the Stoic was the one that made itself more at home among the Romans who, in less than two centuries after the death of Zeno, the founder of that school, had become the masters of the Greek-speaking world. Love of knowledge and delight in beauty, the indulgence of subtle doubts, and the cultivation of refined pleasures were all alike uncongenial to the Roman temper. These traits were inclined to charge their representatives among Greek professors of philosophy with a frivolity, dangerous to the sense of discipline and public duty, which had hitherto been the mainstay of the Roman state. However, such suspicions were less aroused by the Stoics than by any of their rivals. Stoicism's moral and religious temper thus won it a special welcome in Rome. Also, 'The Sense of Justice and Law' in the temper of the Roman people was particularly agreeable to the Stoic philosophy. This temper marked out the Romans for justice and law amongst all the nations of antiquity. And the stability of society has ever since been built based on the Roman legal system. The Stoics, rather than either the Epicureans or the Skeptics, exercised, in the long run, the most expansive influence in an era seeking religious faith. They explained it by their attitude of devout acquiescence in the predestined or providential order of the universe.

BOTH THE STOICISM AND CHRISTIANITY WERE AT ONE AGAINST THE EPICUREANISM AND THE ATOMISM

Both Stoicism and Christianity were against Epicureanism and atomism in their exacting standards of conduct and faith in the divine government of the world. Moreover, while the Epicureans saw an eternal play of atoms in the course of nature without any predestined plot, the Stoics and Christians alike looked forward to a conflagration in which the current frame of things would perish.

CHRISTIANITY WAS COMPLETELY TRIUMPHANT WHILE STOICISM VANQUISHED

By the 5th century AD, the period of struggle among numerous competitors ended in the complete victory of Christianity. Atomism consequently disappeared along with Epicureanism. Christianity had by that time become the state religion of the Roman Empire. Christianity had extinguished every other candle by then. The whole Empire, including the emperor, had embraced the Christian religion.

QURAN PROPHESIED ABOUT THE ATOM BOMB IN THE SO-CALLED 'DARK AGES' OF THE WEST

Generally, Ca. 500 to 1000 AD is known as the 'Dark Ages' of Europe. This period is considered the West's dark ages: neither because Christianity was on the wane nor the Christian doctrine of hatred of the material world was suspected on the decline. Instead, intellectual activity during that period regarding the acquirement of knowledge and learning had been missing. Any inclinations towards atomism were yet out of the question. Somewhat the absence of intellectual activities had hardened Christianity's attitude against atomism or any such creed, which in their eyes inclined towards the material world.

Moreover, even if the Christian community had felt the worldly desire inwardly, there was no reason to suspect them of any inclinations towards atomism in its outward appearance. Since the religious sense of Christians was then at least as strong as to expel any thought of a system associated with atheism such as atomism was. At that time, no one could even dream that anything like atomism could ever find its revival in this world. By the 4th century AD, Christianity had become the state religion of the Roman Empire. By the fifth century, every trace of the opposition from any other school of thought vanished entirely.

In the seventh century, the darkness of the dark ages of the West was on the increase. In the first decade of that century, the Holy Quran produced the prophecy about the atomic bomb. It was revealed in a country that had on its credit, as the memory of the historian could take his thought back into history, the ages of darkness. This prophecy of the Quran was to remain dormant for more than thirteen centuries awaiting its fulfillment. No human intelligence could venture at this prophecy with utmost surety even a day before the 1st of December-1942 when Italian scientist Fermi achieved the first successful fission chain reaction in Chicago. It took more than two years after this achievement to build a workable atom bomb. And only about three years before the successful chain reaction, Einstein could not assume a tone of certainty in his letter to President Roosevelt. He only had assumed the possibility of the construction of bombs far more potent than conventional bombs by utilizing the phenomenon of Uranium fission.

ATOMISM REVIVED

In the 4th Century BC, Aristotle had thrown the weight of his authority against the atomic theory. When Galen, the celebrated physician of the 2nd century AD, added his veto to that of Aristotle, atoms suffered an eclipse that was to last for some fourteen centuries. The eclipse was, however, cleared at last. The philosophies of Plato and Aristotle, which had employed the faculties of the ablest of men, held the throne for centuries together, were at last destined to fall.

These philosophies had worn many shapes. They had mingled themselves with many creeds. They had survived revolutions in which empires, religions, languages, and races had perished but were fated at last to leave before the new philosophy of 'fruit', 'utility', and 'progress'. Aristotle was deposed, and Plato was confined. The caravan of the West, led by Francis Bacon, 'Buccinator Novi Temporis', the 'Trumpeter of the Modern Age', raising the flag of science and chanting 'De Rerum Natura', moved on to the conquest of the realm of Mother Nature for the good of humankind in general, with atomism acting as their guide and interpreter all along.

After its long disappearance, the knowledge of the atomic theory was derived from a relic, the poem of Lucretius (ca. 99 BC – ca. 55 BC). In this poem, he logically organized as well as brilliantly exposed the earlier views of the atomists. In light of the information derived from a relevant piece of this poem, 'De Rerum Natura', Pierre Gassendi (1592-1655), the Provencal philosopher and a Roman Catholic priest, introduced the views of Greek atomists. The Christian Church had imposed intolerable austerity on its followers, exempting the ecclesiastical leaders who lived like princes. There had also been an equally unbearable urge to enjoy the feast that Mother Nature had spread before them.

Last but not least, besides this, perhaps a misunderstood example of Islam had prepared the Christian world to accept atomism. The tyrannical Church applied the whip while able men like Francis Bacon took the lead, and atomism came into view. Gradually and systematically, it gained the field altogether.

FRANCIS BACON'S ATTEMPT IN BALANCING ATOMISM AND SPIRITUALISM NOT SUCCESSFUL EVENTUALLY

Francis Bacon's design was, by means of inquiries, some of which should be experimental like those of Alchemists but purged from all superstitious taint and directed not towards immediate gain but towards a thorough-going knowledge, vastly to increase in the long run the dominion of man over Mother Nature. To enjoy such a dominion was, he held, the original destiny of our race. However, Bacon's believers ignored his discretion, and unfortunate men soon inclined towards immediate gains. So, they discarded entirely Bacon's higher ideal. Nor was Bacon's attempt in adding the practical side of natural philosophy to the spiritual philosophy of Christianity successful, for men left off the spiritual side entirely and adopted the material side. Lord Macaulay has highly extolled Bacon's bringing into view the practical side of the material and fruitful side of the natural philosophy against the barren philosophy of ancient Greek masters. Still, unfortunately, the desired effects have not been achieved due to men's forsaking the spiritual and moral side of the affair and inclining to the material side only. Thus, everything spiritual and moral having vanished, the field remained exclusively for atomism, dangerously unbalanced.

DALTON'S RESEARCH IN THE FIELD OF ATOMISM

Newton and Boyle believed that matter was atomic, but the atomic theory was not systematically adopted in chemistry until John Dalton (1766-1844) took it up. Dalton's modernization of the long-neglected atomic theory marked the end of the previous epoch, which had begun with Nicolaus Copernicus (1473-1543) three centuries ago.

Dalton's chief contentions are as follows.

(1) Matter consists of atoms that cannot be created or destroyed. The chemical change consists of the combination of previously apart atoms or the separation of those combined. There is no change in the atoms themselves.

(2) The atoms of a given element are all exactly alike, and they differ, practically in weight, from those of any other element.

It has been necessary to extend and modify his original hypotheses, but they still play a vital part in chemical theory in the modern dress.

THE THEORY OF ATOMISM FALLS ON ITS PATH TO ATOM BOMB UNEXPECTEDLY

The atomic theory fell on the path of the atom bomb with the almost accidental discovery of X-rays on November 8, 1895, by the German physicist Wilhelm Conrad Roentgen (1845-1923). This discovery initiated a period of unprecedented progress in physical science. In seeking a possible connection between phosphorescence and X-rays, by a mere chance, the French physicist Antoine Henri Becquerel (1852-1908) chose Uranium Nitrate as the substance for investigation. And he was led unexpectedly in 1896 to the discovery of radioactivity. This discovery of radioactivity, in its turn, soon led to the discovery of Radium by Pierre Curie (1859-1906) and Madame Marie Sklodowska Curie (1867-1934).

In 1905, Albert Einstein enunciated the theory of special relativity and, as a consequence of it, established the equivalence between mass and energy. The outstanding work of Ernest Rutherford (1871-1937) on radiations (named by him as alpha, beta, and gamma rays) emitted from radioactive bodies eventually led to the concept of the atom as made up of a central core, the nucleus (that is the heart) with electrons revolving around it; "a solar system in miniature". Niels Henrik David Bohr (1885-1962) incorporated the Quantum hypothesis of Max Planck (1858-1947) and Albert Einstein into Rutherford's atom model and thus formulated his far-reaching Quantum theory of the atom.

In 1919, Rutherford, for the first time, achieved the disintegration of an element (Nitrogen) by bombarding it with alpha particles. Patrick Blackett soon provided a cloud chamber photograph of the same process. Sir James Chadwick (1891-1974), working in Rutherford's laboratories, discovered the neutron in 1932. In the same year and laboratory, Sir John Douglas Cockcroft (1897-1967) and Ernest Thomas Sinton Walton (1903-1995) brought about the first artificial nuclear transmutation by bombarding Lithium with protons accelerated to less than a million volts. Discoveries followed in rapid succession.

In 1938, the phenomenon of Uranium fission was discovered by the German physical chemists Otto Hahn (1879-1968), [regarded as 'the father of nuclear chemistry' and the 'founder of the atomic age'] and Fritz Strassmann (1902-1980). The extraordinary significance of the discovery was soon realized and led to a period of intense activity in the study of atomic nuclei. By 1940, more than a hundred papers had appeared on this subject. Soon after, the whole subject went underground, and no further reference appeared in open scientific literature till the end of the war.

The fundamental discoveries leading to the realization of atomic energy came practically all from Western Europe. However, it was not Western Europe but the U.S.A. to first harness this fundamental knowledge to practical ends with its colossal industrial and scientific resources. U.S.S.R. soon followed the U.S.A. in the enterprise. However, all the peculiar features of this probable destroyer of humankind are no longer a secret that in the early days of its appearance were. This probable destroyer of humankind is an open challenge to humanity, and it is staring fiercely at the frightened humankind. They say much about putting it to peaceful purposes, but peace and nuclear power cannot co-exist.

HISTORIC LETTER OF EINSTEIN TO PRESIDENT ROOSEVELT OF AMERICA

On August 2, 1939, Albert Einstein wrote his now-famous letter to President Roosevelt. He drew the President's attention to the possibility, as indicated by some work of Fermi and Szilard, of utilizing the phenomenon of Uranium fission for the construction of a mighty (weight for weight) bomb of a new type, a million times more potent than conventional bombs.

"A single bomb of this type, carried by boat and exploded in a port, might very well destroy the whole port together with some of the surrounding territory," said Einstein.

The U.S.A. government decided to explore the possibility seriously. Enrico Fermi successfully realized a (slow neutron) fission chain reaction in the Graphite-pile built in a converted squash court of the University of Chicago's Stagg-field on December 2, 1942. It is a landmark in the history of nuclear science. It led to the construction of a gigantic plant at Hanford on the banks of the Columbia River to produce Plutonium. Followed by the diffusion of Uranium, they built a plant to produce Uranium-235 from natural Uranium on Oakridge. Another plant at Oakridge produced Uranium-235 employing the principle of electromagnetic separation. The designing of a workable atom bomb was entrusted to the New Los Alamos Laboratory (New Mexico), working under the leadership of J. Robert Oppenheimer (1904-1967), [remembered as 'the father of the atomic bomb']. They produced three atomic bombs by the middle of 1945. One made of Plutonium was tested on the ground at the Alamogordo sands on July 16, 1945. This test was named the 'Trinity Test'. They dropped the other two on Hiroshima and Nagasaki on August 6 and 9, 1945.

Enrico Fermi, who had successfully achieved the first fission chain reaction, failed to protect against the harmful reaction of radiation he had played with and soon succumbed to radiation sickness and left this world to exchange sorrows with the victims of Hiroshima and Nagasaki in Heaven.[3] We are not aware of the topic and trend of these close friends at their meeting. However, it seems probable that at the sheer sight of their old friend Fermi, the victims of Hiroshima and Nagasaki might have taken fright. And breaking into a stampede emitting wild shrieks, and screaming 'atomy', 'atomy', disappeared in every direction and leaving poor Fermi, the great servant of humanity in a sudden surprise and a profoundly thoughtful mood at this so unusual behavior of these strange victims of the Hiroshima and Nagasaki.

HIROSHIMA-NAGASAKI TRAGEDY

August 6, 1945, is an unforgettable date. On the early morning of this tragic day, the first atomic (U-235) bomb, 'Little Boy', fell on Hiroshima, killing 66,000 men and injuring another 69,000. The second atomic (Pu-239) bomb 'Fat Man' was dropped on Nagasaki on August 9, 1945. The number killed was 39,000 and injured 25,000. The two bombs were about the same power, equivalent to 20 kilotons of TNT, but due to somewhat uneven terrain in Nagasaki, casualties were less there than in Hiroshima.

Bombs exploded at about 2000 feet above ground to obtain, as nearly as possible, the maximum area of damage under the blast of the explosion.

The death rate was above 90 percent within half a mile of ground zero (the point on the ground immediately below the burst), above 50 percent between half a mile and one and a half miles. Structural damage was complete, including the collapse of earthquake-resistant reinforced concrete buildings, within half a mile from ground zero. It destroyed most of the houses within one and a half miles. Houses up to two miles were severely damaged and slightly damaged up to about three miles. Because of the very high temperatures produced, the explosion emitted intense heat radiation causing fatal burns (and almost instantaneous deaths due to the intense heat and shock of the 'Heat-Flash') to exposed persons within about three-quarters of a mile, from ground zero.

In Hiroshima, the Uranium-235, a 20-kiloton bomb, killed 66,000 persons and injured 69,000, and in Nagasaki, 39,000 were dead and 25,000 wounded by the Plutonium-239, 20-kiloton bomb. In general, most of the casualties were due to the combined effects of burns and mechanical injuries. However, estimates show about 60 percent of deaths (almost 75% of all casualties) were caused by burning through 'Heat-Flash' and fires. About 20% of deaths were due to physical injuries from falling structures and flying debris (resulting from blast damage). 20% of deaths were due to other causes, including nuclear radiation (gamma rays). Radiation, too, is fire originally. Out of Hiroshima's 75,000 houses, it entirely burnt about 55,000 and utterly destroyed 7000.

The damages such as these indeed sounded terrible, and the figures were imposing at first. Still, the later developments in nuclear weapons have dwarfed the Hiroshima-Nagasaki bombs into mere toy bombs. The damages expected from the giant thermonuclear bombs are of a pretty different caliber. They destroy not cities but states.

Moreover, for the large-scale nuclear attack, please refer to the U.S.A. June 15, 1955, Operation alert mock civil defense exercise mentioned in a subsequent chapter, wherein 'Hotama' as 'a fire closed in on them' is explained.

HELL-BOMB PRODUCED

The first Soviet atomic, ordinary fission (like the Hiroshima bomb) took place in August 1949. On September 23, 1949, President Truman announced that the U.S.A. government had incontrovertible proof that the Russians had detonated a fission device. The U.S.A. government immediately decided to go ahead with the thermonuclear bomb (the so-called 'H' or Super bomb). On January 31, 1950, Truman publicly announced to continue work to determine the feasibility of the Hydrogen bomb. On March 10, 1950, he directed the atomic energy commission with David E. Lilienthal as Chairman and its general advisory committee with J. Robert Oppenheimer as Chairman to produce the Hydrogen bomb. However, their opinions about the speed and scale of efforts to the Super bomb sharply divided. After seeing the catastrophes in Hiroshima and Nagasaki, the scientists put their conscience perhaps to the severe test; even the considerations of the national defense could with some difficulty induce some scientists to produce yet another even more terrific atomic bomb than the Hiroshima pattern.

Conscience, after all, smites and, its stings may be painful. Yet there was another consideration, namely, that producing more powerful atomic bombs was no remedy for the great wrong which had been done already by the production of nuclear weapons. The production of a more powerful atomic bomb no doubt meant to bring even greater destruction on their people, for a more incredible bomb would be retaliated by yet the most incredible bomb.

The plea of national defense, however, superseded every other consideration. A brilliant and enthusiastic atomist, Mr. Edward Teller (1908-2003), known colloquially as 'the father of the Hydrogen bomb', successfully experimented with the thermonuclear device at Marshal Islands on November 1, 1952. While the science of destruction advanced by many leaps and bounds, the earth sighed at so single an achievement.

On November 1, 1952, the U.S.A. first tested the thermonuclear device at Marshal Islands (MIKE) in the Pacific Ocean. Russia followed suit. The first Soviet thermonuclear explosion took place in August 1953. The U.S.A. set off a powerful thermonuclear explosion at Bikini Atoll on March 1, 1954; the energy of the explosion was equivalent to about 15 megatons of TNT. In November 1955, the Russians had a thermonuclear explosion about as powerful as the U.S.A. test of March 1954. Britain, France, China, India, and Israel came in the wake like the legendary. One after another, they displayed the unique trick of setting off a nuclear bonfire and joined the big ones of atomic powers.

Necessity expelled the mercy from the hearts of men. None would like to stay behind, forgetting how many tasks they could achieve with the money spent on a single atomic bomb to destroy people? They might have fed quite a lot of hungry bellies. Funds used to produce nuclear bombs could have been spent contributing clothes to numerous naked bodies and giving medical treatment to several sick persons. Moreover, they could use that money to turn into smiles, various tearful eyes, and save countless distressed families from ruin.

NO ONE IS SAFE FROM THE RADIOLOGICAL HAZARD

On March 1, 1954, during the 'Castle Bravo' [4] test explosion at Bikini Atoll in the Pacific Ocean, an unfortunate fact dawned on the atomic powers to their horror: the atomic bomb was a very 'treacherous slave'. It could also rebound towards its own master who unleashed it on his foe and thus bring about the ruin of both, nay, even of other neutral people all over the globe.

It so happened that a Japanese fishing boat, 'Daigo Fukuryu Maru' ('Lucky Dragon-5'), [5] having a crew of 23, was lying at a distance of 90 miles from the testing site. The misfortune of this boat appeared in the form of powdery fallout of the explosion. It began to settle on it to announce to the world that the thermonuclear bomb constituted a severe radiological hazard for everyone who lived on earth. The frightened crew of the boat rushed towards Japan and sailing a distance of 2,000 miles in about 13 days, reached the port, all sick with radiations. There, the radio operator died after a few months, but they saved the rest eventually.

It was, however, proved beyond any doubt that no one should deem himself safe from the radiological hazard of nuclear energy all over the globe. The news about the potential hazard of radioactive fallout from thermonuclear weapons burst out of deep secrecy. Twenty-three Japanese fishermen announced to the world the first fateful news about the lurking catastrophe that lay in wait for all of us. All the official secrecy proved inept, and the mysterious Providence of Allah decided otherwise. When the secret came out through the channels, the shock to the world opinion rivaled the Hydrogen bomb blast itself. Though the world opinion soon slumbered again on the bed of rosy problems these days to wait for the real shock of the actual atomic war. Nothing sort of that could have alarmed them.

We bring this chapter to an end with the following questions.

Do you want this civilization to remain, or do you want it to go? Is there no sensible man among you to inform you about the dangers of nuclear power? Or do you know but overlook the hazard intentionally as if you are tired of existence? Pray, die if you want to, but do not die a death which would prove a Darwin to be in the right in his surmise of your origin. Then a monkey needs to say to his mate:

"What a contemptible species among the monkeys, these humans that even don't have a tail and still call themselves a race of monkeys."

~~*~*~*

[1] For the detailed description of this prophecy, refer to Book-1/Volume-2/Chapter-1/'Introductory'.

[2] **Ronald Arbuthnott Knox** (February 17, 1888 - August 24, 1957) was an English theologian, priest, and crime writer. His book 'God and the Atom' is an ethical and philosophical analysis of the shock of the atomic bomb, its use against Hiroshima and Nagasaki, and the moral questions arising from there.

[3] As a result of heavy exposures to radiation, **Fermi** died at age 53 of stomach cancer in Chicago, Illinois, and was buried at Oak Woods Cemetery. Two of his graduate students who assisted him in working on or near the nuclear pile also died of cancer. Fermi and his team knew that such work carried considerable risk, but they considered the outcome so vital that they forged ahead with little regard for their safety. Eugene Wigner wrote, "Ten days before Fermi had died, he told me, 'I hope it won't take long.' He had reconciled himself perfectly to his fate."

[4] Hired later by the Nuclear Claims Tribunal to research and report on the economic damage caused by the testing, Economist and Crisis Consultant Randall Bell writes in his book, Strategy 360, "Bravo had an explosive force equal to nearly 1,000 Hiroshima-type bombs. It vaporized the test island, parts of two other islands, and left a mile-wide crater in the lagoon floor. In total, nearly 70 acres of the Bikini Atoll vaporized by the nuclear testing." Bravo was estimated as being equivalent to approximately 15 megatons of TNT, while the Hiroshima bomb was estimated at 13 kilotons. Randall Bell also notes, "Many of the landowners and local people accompanied me back to Rongelap and Rongerik, where much of the nuclear fallout came down. John, an older man, stood on his former home site in Rongelap and told me that he had gotten up early to make coffee and the sun had not yet come up. Suddenly, the sky lit up like it was the day. He could see the large mushroom cloud rising off the horizon from Bikini and, soon after, he felt the blast of the shock wave. Later, as the entire village gathered, they

watched the radioactive gray ash fall on them, their houses, and their children. John did not express any anger, only deep sorrow that his one-year-old daughter died from leukemia soon after Bravo." Among those contaminated were the 23 crewmembers of the Japanese fishing boat Lucky Dragon-5.

[5] '**Daigo Fukuryu Maru**' ('Lucky Dragon-5') was a Japanese tuna fishing boat exposed to and contaminated by nuclear fallout from the United States' Castle Bravo thermonuclear device test on Bikini. Atoll, on March 1, 1954. The boat, along with its 23 fishermen aboard, as well as their catch of fish, was contaminated. They returned to Yaizu, Japan, on March 14. The crew members, suffering from nausea, headache, burns, pains in the eyes, bleeding from the gums, etc., were diagnosed with acute radiation syndrome and admitted to two Tokyo hospitals. On September 23, chief radio operator Mr. Aikichi Kuboyama, 40, died — the first Japanese victim of a hydrogen bomb. He left these words: "I pray that I am the last victim of an atomic or hydrogen bomb." … The sky on the west lit up like a sunrise. Eight minutes later, the sound of the explosion arrived, with fallout several hours later. The fallout, fine white flaky dust of calcined coral with adsorbed highly radioactive fission products, fell on the ship for three hours. The fishermen scooped it into bags with their bare hands. The dust stuck to surfaces, bodies, and hair; after the radiation sickness symptoms appeared, the fishermen called it death ash.

[2-5 above (Wikipedia, the free Encyclopedia)]

~~*~*~*

CHAPTER-3

'HOTAMA'

THE QURAN PREDICTS, PHENOMENALLY CHARACTERIZES, AND AVERTS THE ATOMIC HELL

THE PROPHECY OF THE QURAN ABOUT THE ATOMIC HELL

It is the most interesting, astonishing, and absorbing topic of a universal nature and one of most momentous import. Still, I would no longer give a bare skeleton in so brief a chapter and hardly even all the basic features. [1] I, on my part, have no reason to doubt that the topic will be most welcomed everywhere humanity exists. In this brief chapter, I cannot show more than a mere glimpse of all that I have to deliver to this world.

According to factual and scientific analysis, this world is undoubtedly doomed to a universal ruin in the flames of the atomic hell, naturally, justly, and deservedly. Despite all the wishful thinking, optimism, and behavior like an ostrich, this world must either vanish suddenly under the hail of atomic weapons, deservedly, or perish slowly, lingeringly, and miserably under the swarms of the atomic radiations, also deservedly. No protection from either atomic bombs or atomic radiation is a possibility. No peace treaties will be of everlasting avail in an atmosphere of ever-increasing and never abating universal anarchy till the scientific process of this modern Baconian atomism working under unfailing and inexorable natural laws has reached its final stage and burst into the flames; all-consuming flames of atomic hell, atomism via atom to atomic hell. Such a surmise may appear so terrible and so pessimistically denunciative.

Then know that Late Bertrand Russell too had arrived at the same conclusion in 1964 when he communicated to me a single sentence which read:

"Since Adam and Eve ate the apple, man has never refrained from any folly of which he was capable."

Thus, to Bertrand Russell, this world was doomed to atomic ruin. I, too, like Bertrand Russell, would have died in disappointment about the end of this humankind. However, by the sheer Grace of Almighty

Allah, in 1961, my discovery of the Prophetic warning of the Quran about atomic hell that stumbled upon me rescued me from a similar fate. Thereby I realized that an escape from nuclear ruin was possible for humankind in the light of the warning of the Quran. This discovery of the Prophetic warning of the Quran about atomic hell hitherto is unknown either by any Muslim or a non-Muslim worldwide.

An antique book fourteen centuries in the past treated the subject of atomic science. It scientifically characterized the nuclear phenomena giving such characteristics as distinguishing it from the rest of the phenomena, e.g., chemical, and electrical, would come as no mild surprise to the modern atomist and Radiobiologist. Also, in the same era and context, the fact that the same book should characterize the culture of modern Baconian atomism would cast the modern philosopher in reverie. Again, the same book in the same passage should constitute a link between atomism and the atomic hell of the atomic bombs and atomic radiations and would leave Aristotle and Plato, the two celebrated antagonists of atomism, stunned with wonder. The affair is such that it serves as an outstanding example to show the difference between the human and divine intellect; the difference which the intellects of the caliber of Einstein, Russell, Aristotle, and Plato would best see, they being some of the most outstanding intellects among the human beings.

Thus, this Prophetic warning of the Quran is the only hope in all-pervading, universal, and ever-increasing darkness in the world. The harbingers of modern progress are dragging this world willy-nilly towards the brink of atomic hell to be consumed. Something unbelievable, but the truth is that the Quran has prophesied about the atomic hell. This prophecy is a miracle in atomic science and modern atomism philosophy, undeniable by the scientist or the philosopher. This 36-word prophecy has taken me 3000 pages to interpret in decades at a stretch. It is irrefutable proof of the Quran's Divine Origin and is like Noah's ark in this fiery deluge of atomism being the sole means to escape this painful atomic end of humankind. The Quran has exposed the reality of this Baconian progress and its logical end, the atomic hell, in a way that no atomic scientist and philosopher, including Russell, hitherto has done. I miss Russell, Albert Einstein, and Sir James Jeans as the judges and critics.

No activists can effectively conduct any movement in this world against the atomic threat, nor could any religion be completely revived or effectively promulgated without adopting the basic guidelines provided by this prophecy of the Quran. Moreover, know that this temporal atomic hell represents the eternal atomic hell of the next world that the Quran names as 'Hotama'. They who deserved this temporal atomic hell, Allah would also cast them into the eternal atomic hell ('Hotama') of the next world, for the causes of both are identical.

Fourteen centuries ago, when neither a trace nor any signs of the future revival of the ancient Greek atomism were present worldwide, a Scripture (the Holy Quran) characterized the Baconian philosophy of modern atomism and the modern Baconian progress. At the same time, it described the modern atomic phenomena giving out such characteristics as distinctively distinguish it from every other chemical or electrical phenomenon. It portrayed an atomic bomb explosion phenomenon and strangely and phonetically called the atomic fire by the same name as the modern scientist gave it, 'Hotama' or 'Otama'. Would it not come as a surprise or a wonder, rather a miracle manifest, and at least as great as raising the dead, if not greater?

And that the Quran infers the appearance of the atomic bomb and atomic radiations from the characteristics of Baconian culture giving out the atomic hell as the consequence of the characteristics of Baconian progress, is a priori for no human intellect, not even a Plato or an Aristotle. Both these superior intellects of all human history have been antagonistic toward ancient Greek atomism. They had themselves exerted against atomism. Yet if they ever would happen to read this inference of the Quran, they would fall on their faces before the Allah of the Quran and worship in wonder at such a unique marvel of intelligence. The most beneficial side of this miraculous prophecy of the Quran is the revelation of the causes of the appearance of atomic hell, which the Quran has enumerated. Only by removing these causes could humanity avert the threat of atomic annihilation and eliminate the danger of atomic ruin. There is no other way out. The scientist and the politician are utterly helpless in this matter.

QURAN TREATS BACONIAN ATOMISM AND THE ATOMIC HELL

The Quran characterizes the Baconian progress of modern atomism and characterizes the nuclear phenomena and gives the causes of the appearance of the atomic hell of atomic bombs and radiations to avert the atomic threat. Bacon's philosophy of modern atomism is a complete antithesis of revealed religion. The result of Baconian philosophy, this modern progress, being unbalanced and un-proportional to the basic design of creation, has naturally brought this world to the verge of inevitable atomic annihilation. The Quran now takes up the field to extinguish the atomic hell and save humankind.

Following is the translation of the full text of the prophecy of the Quran. Everyone is requested to read it carefully. Only then can one find out how much nuclear science the Quran could have in these few words. I have revealed this secret now. The explanation of these 36 words has cost me three thousand pages, about nine hundred thousand words in English, and decades of toil and labor, day in, day out. Nevertheless, this discovery is mine by the Grace of Allah, and I have no forerunner in this field and no model. The Quran says:

"Woe to every slandering traducer (backbiter, defamer) who amasseth wealth (of this world) and arrangeth it (against the future). He thinketh that his wealth will render him immortal. Nay, for verily he will be cast into Al-Hotama (the crusher), and what could teach thee what Al-Hotama (the crusher) is? It is the fire of Allah enkindled which leapeth up onto the hearts. It is (a fire) closed in on them in outstretched columns."

(Quran: 104 'Al-Homaza')

This version is the full text of the warning (prophecy) about the atom bomb. Please read it carefully and see what you understand from it. Yet, it is much regrettable that the translation of whatever quality and howsoever grand a language would never portray the original picture as a rule. [2] Moreover, caused by the unavoidability of remaining as close to the original in translating as the peculiar nature of a Scripture demands, we may compare the translation to the minced meat of a slaughtered body, worth millions when alive. However, firstly the characteristics of those doomed to atomic hell are enumerated. Then the atomic phenomenon has been characterized with all its subtle and distinctive features, and lastly, we will portray the phenomenon of the actual atomic explosion.

THE WARNING ABOUT THE ATOMIC HELL

Know that it is a warning and not a decree pre-ordained. Therefore, it is avoidable by removing the actual causes of the tragedy. These causes enumerated explicitly in the warning text are responsible for the emergence of the atomic bomb and nuclear energy. Let this also be known that this warning has primarily alluded to the next world that is the eternal atomic hell in the next eternal world. Still, just as the fire and the garden represent hell and heaven on earth, this atom bomb represents the atomic hell of the next world on earth.

As you can see, the warning text is miraculously brief and concise yet is most evident and comprehensive. The tones are oracular. How clearly and entirely all the inconsistencies responsible for the atom bomb's appearance and the particular characteristics and distinctive features of the nuclear phenomena have been described, and how precisely have the atomic explosion been portrayed — all in thirty-six words only. We repeat the text thereof.

LET THE READER SEE THE ASPECTS OF THE ROPHECY/WARNING

(1) THE CHARACTERISTICS OF THOSE, ATOMIC-HELL BOUND

"Woe to every slandering traducer (backbiter, defamer) who amasseth wealth (of this world) and arrangeth it (against the future). He thinketh that his wealth will render him immortal. Nay, for verily he will be cast into Al-Hotama (the crusher), and what could teach thee what Al-Hotama (the crusher) is?"

(2) THE CHARACTERISTICS AND THE DISTINCTIVE FEATURES OF 'AL-HOTAMA'

"It is the fire of Allah enkindled which leapeth up onto the hearts."

(3) THE PORTRAYAL OF THE ATOMIC BOMB EXPLOSION

"It is (a fire) closed in on them in outstretched columns".

However, before we proceed into the further detailed description of the prophecy, let us see first what 'Hotama' means.

'HOTAMA'

'Hotama' means a hell of fire generated by nuclear, that is, atomic energy with all its attributes, namely, the 'heat radiation', 'blast', and 'radioactive fallout' united. The word 'Hotama', etymologically speaking, is derived from its root verb 'Hatama', which means 'to break something into pieces'. Borrowing the language of the scientist, we could say, 'the process of atomizing'.

Further inquiries into the grammatical conjugations reveal that the inflective form 'Ha**tt**ama' that is 'Hatama' with 't' doubled assumes a sense of more significant impact. Thus, it means to 'shatter', 'smash', or 'dash to pieces'.

The next inflection, '**Ta**hattama', '**Ta**' having been prefixed to 'Hattama' means, 'to break-up', 'to go to pieces', or 'to wreck'. And so also would mean the inflection '**In**hatama' that is '**In**' prefixed to the basic word 'Hatama'.

Further, 'Hutaam' and 'Hitma' are nouns and mean 'smithereens', 'pieces', 'particles' etc. We can see the fascinating use of the word 'Hutaam' in the phrase 'Hutaam-ud-Duniya', the 'vanities of the world'. We call these 'Hutaam' metaphorically since they are perishable and must one day disintegrate. Again, the wreckage of a ship is called by the Arab 'Hutaam-us-Safina'.

THE RESEMBLANCE BETWEEN THE QURAN'S 'HATAMA' AND THE 'ATOM' OR THE 'ATOMOS' OF THE SCIENTIST

The word 'Hatama' (حطمة) purely is of Arabic origin. The scientists adapted the word used as 'Atom' from the Greek word 'Atomos'. 'Atomos' means: 'not-cuttable', 'indivisible', and 'indestructible'.

We will now make our utmost endeavor to show the phonetic resemblance and disparity regarding meanings and purport between the two words 'Hatama' of the Quran and 'Atom' or 'Atomos' of the scientist. This phonic resemblance amounting to astonishing identity is no secret that we have to divulge. Yet, judging from the nature of the topic and impending necessity, we are obliged to show it. We can attribute the slight phonic difference between 'Hatama' and the 'Atom' or 'Atomos' to the phonic peculiarities of the two different people with slightly variant vocal organs and accentual variations. Moreover, this difference can also be due to the difficulties of transliteration.

It may surprise the reader if he knows that the Arabic alphabet contains no letter that we could exactly call 'T'. For example, as it is pronounced by the people of England proper or certain other parts of the world, in words like **T**ap, **T**est, **T**ip, **T**op, or **T**ucker, etc.

Arabic has two alternative letters: soft 'T' (ت) and '**TUA**' (ط). The '**T**' of this '**TUA**' is not the hard one; instead, it is soft. However, this '**TUA**' is pronounced not as ordinary soft '**T**' but literally as '**TUA**'. Keeping this testy discussion in mind, we note that although the Arabic alphabet contains the same letter '**H**' as pronounced in English '**H**at', it has another character that may sound like '**H**' to a foreigner. Yet, it is a pity that we cannot precisely transliterate it into English. Also, as far as my knowledge goes, we cannot precisely transliterate it into any language spoken globally. Hence, it needs the practice to be correctly pronounced by a foreigner. This peculiar letter is between '**H**' (ح) and '**KH**' (خ) used in '**H**atama' and is not simple '**H**'.

However, without falling into such minute complexities, we should conclude that the word we have transliterated as 'Hatama' with 'H' is strictly not the exact representation of the word we mean it to stand for. That is, the Arabic 'Hatama' and the actual pronunciation of the word 'Hatama' we have spoken about by 'TUA' having preceded by that untranslatable character and that we are always obliged to write as '**H**' in a foreign language, is far near to the 'A**TUA**MA' in pronunciation and not 'HATAMA'.

If the reader happens to be so lucky to have an Arab in his neighborhood, let him ask this Arab friend to pronounce the word 'HATAMA' as the actual Arabic word that this 'Hatama' stands for. You will hear him say something like 'A**TUA**MA' with a strange accent on the first 'A', sounding something between 'H' and 'KH'.

By this minute description, we mean to show the miraculous nature of this coincidence that of the phonic resemblance of these two words, that is, the Arabic 'HATAMA' and Greek 'ATOMOS', if coincidence we may justly call it, for it is a miracle manifest that of the Omniscient Allah. The resemblance between these two elementary words is the key to the door and a clue to the inner secret of prophecy. I say this on personal experience since, but perhaps I would have never let into the real mystery of this phonic resemblance.

THE QURAN IS EXACT, BUT THE SCIENTIST IS WRONG

By saying that the scientist is wrong in a particular aspect, I do not mean to injure anyone's feelings for whom I feel sincere regard. Still, I feel obliged to point out a slight error that the scientist is aware of and has had a remarkable mystery concealed beneath it.

By the Greek word, 'Atomos' is necessarily meant something: 'not-cuttable', 'indivisible', and 'indestructible'. The same is the meaning of the word 'Atomos' in the Greek language, and the same was meant by early Greek atomists when they used the word 'Atomos'. The modern scientist adapted the term 'Atomos' as 'Atom' with the same significance. Still, scientists split the atom into sub-atomic parts such as neutrons, protons, electrons, positrons, etc. Therefore, the 'Atom' remained no more like 'Atom'. It has changed its character. It was no more, 'not-cuttable'.

Nevertheless, the point that interests us most is: Was the scientist unmindful of this fundamental change of the character of 'Atom'? Did he not realize the necessity of changing the term with the change of the quality? Was the earth allowed to retain its previous designation that is 'flat' after knowing that it was not flat but 'round'? Was it again allowed to retain its previous quality as 'stationary' after discovering it was not stationary; instead, it 'rotated' on its axis and 'revolved' around the sun?

The answer is 'No'. 'Flat' was changed to 'round' and 'stationary' to 'rotating' or 'revolving'. Why not then, the question arises, the scientists changed word 'Atom' for some other correct word whereas Greek, Latin and all the dictionaries of Europe laid open before them, even though we could not suspect shortage of talent amongst the scientist community? Why then did they not change the word 'Atom' and allow this misnomer to continue? Was the scientist unmindful of this serious flaw, or did he neglect the discrepancy? No.

We find Sir James Jeans regretting this error, on page 45 of his admirable book, 'The Mysterious Universe' as saying:

"Then, just as the nineteenth century was drawing to a close, Sir J. J. Thomson and his followers began to break up the 'atom', which now proved to be no more uncuttable, and so no more entitled to the name of 'atom' than the molecule to which the name had previously been attached."

Sir James Jeans tells us this was the case when the 19th century was drawing to a close. However, we have seen the 'atom' shattered into pieces entirely by scientists during the first half of the twentieth century. Yet, the 'atom' retained its previous name as if it were its unbreakable birthright. All this seems strange. Nevertheless, the fact that excites far greater wonder than all this is that scientists had called up a conference to discuss this very question of the error in the name of the 'atom'. Did they discuss the matter? The answer is, "Yes, they did. They did discuss it."

However, did they change the name of 'atom'? The answer is "No".

The question arises, why was it so? However, after discussing the matter, we do not know why they decided to let the 'atom' remain as is. It may seem extraordinarily strange to anyone acquainted with the hard-headed nature of science and consequently the scientist. As a rule, the scientist, the adherent of science principles, could not be expected to call 'atom' as 'atom', which was not 'atom' but actually 'tom' then, which is precisely the opposite scientist condescended to call it. Why did all this happen? Scientists subject themselves to the charge of a gross violation of the rules of science. How did they happen to slight and ignore the fundamental spirit thereof? It is an exciting situation, and there lay behind it a fact far more formidable than at first is to be suspected.

Moreover, you might ask, what is that fact so astoundingly tremendous to justify so loud a clamor as this? The answer is the Power that was so pleased to place the prophecy in the Quran about the 'atom bomb' had superimposed itself on the minds of the scientists in their conference that they so decided to let the 'atom' remain as it is. They decided this at the eleventh hour and dropped the question when they had reached the last rung of their proceedings.

We are desirous to ask this question from anyone who would be skeptical about this assumption: Why, if this was not the reason, then the scientists dropped the question to violate the very spirit of science and, of course, in vivid contradiction to common sense, nay even in violation of the general principle of a world in which no one would ever call 'ugly' the 'beautiful' or 'dark' the 'white' except in satirical sense?

Again, the question arises: Why was Providence so over particular and so very much interested in the name of 'atom' that it remains as it is? The answer to this question is that this apparent phonic resemblance between two words, namely, 'Hatama' of the Quran and 'Atom' of the scientist, was desired to remain as is. Due to this phonic resemblance only, one could discover the prophecy about the atom bomb contained in the Quran. However, for this resemblance, the mind's eye could perhaps not be directed to the inner mystery.

As I have already said, based on my personal experience, this apparent phonic resemblance between these two words enticed me into the actual bosom of the secret. By the grace of Almighty Allah, I discovered it and then corroborated the facts by the exact characteristics of the phenomena in practice. It remains only to say now in this respect that the terminology of the Quran is exact and correct. The word 'Hatama', as is used by the Quran, implies 'being cuttable' and not otherwise. At the same time, Providence has mystified the scientist that he may persist in error.

THE QURAN SAYS, "WHAT COULD TEACH THEE WHAT 'AL-HOTAMA' (THE CRUSHER) IS?"

This expression of surprise implies the undetectable complication, extreme terribleness, and unspeakable horror of nuclear phenomena. We, the unfortunate inhabitants of this age, were doomed to experience this horror. However, what we have hitherto seen of this hellish monstrosity in Hiroshima and Nagasaki is but a negligible fraction, while the actual blazing hell of the atomic bombs is still farther away but fast approaching. The atom bombs hitherto dropped on human habitations have merely been toy bombs compared to the giants that lately have developed in this civilized age. These giants are resting in their dungeons to be raised only at the right moment for all-out destruction of humanity. Those unfortunate people could only narrate the horror's actual extent, who had the chance of a practical experience, like those of Hiroshima and Nagasaki.

Yet, it is something that could not evade human imagination completely. A well-known fact is that the atomic bomb, whether fission or fusion, is a dreadful and horrifying combination of an all-consuming hell of blazing fires, deafening thunderclaps, striking lightning, raging tempests, devastating earthquakes, and invisible storms of deadly radiations. In short, it is an inexplicable 'Jehannah' (hell) ablaze on the ruins of this world. This fact, at least the educated class of humanity knows very well.

Stately buildings, gigantic forts, and giant castles are pulled down and razed to the ground amidst a world of huts of the poor, a world of living human beings a few moments ago, now turned into charred dead bodies. Millions of them mingled with the burnt remains of the beast and the brute. The atomic assaults, to a lesser degree, would bestow on the survivors, agonizing disorders like cancers, chafing ulcers, the curse of monstrosity, and a painful and embarrassing end.

Also, if you will allow me to be a little antique, I should say: the imagination shudders, heart bleeds, and the pen weeps, not only of man but also of the heavens along with man. Yet, if humanity worldwide would pretend to be blind to this global holocaust of nuclear cannonade now tending towards their home and health, then what could be said except that, "Alas! For ill-fated humankind".

THE QURAN DESCRIBES THE NUCLEAR PHENOMENA

The Quran has described the nuclear phenomena with such accuracy, analyzed its characteristics with minute precision, and discerned its distinctive features with so strange a peculiarity that might surprise the modern reader, particularly the scientist. We may well describe a truth without being suspected of resorting to an ancient and old-fashioned style of rhetoric. We say that the description of the characteristics of the nuclear phenomena by the Quran would throw the scientist and the philosopher into ecstatic moods, provided indeed if the faculty of the imagination of these celebrated geniuses have not been wholly dulled and dried up.

Even the fathers of the atomic bomb had to depend on practical experimentation to learn the characteristics of their invention. In contrast, the Quran contained all that knowledge and something more than that past fourteen centuries since men possessed knowledge of thermodynamics no more than that derived from the lime kiln or fire that glowed in the hearth.

We could expect the proper appreciation of this point only from great atomists of the caliber of Albert Einstein, Enrico Fermi, Robert Oppenheimer, Edward Teller, and others of note. The Quran contained all this most accurate scientific data about the nuclear phenomena long before the scientists even had heard the name of the 'Uranium fission', nay even the very name of Uranium itself.

Let someone approach any one of these renowned men of the realm of science and ask him: how much did he know about the various characteristics of the nuclear phenomenon, e.g., its Heat-Flash, enclosing features, its column raising idiosyncrasy, its radiations, and their heart-reaching tendencies, and the global extent of the radiological hazards of the fallout before the actual experimentation of various processes? The Quran has enumerated and explained all these characteristics of nuclear energy with such talent and clearness that could be the wonder and delight of atomists.

Following are the prominent features of the Quran's warning.

(1) It is the only guidance for humankind to escape atomic doom. But, unfortunately, scientists and politicians are helpless.
(2) This warning is a miracle that neither scientist nor skeptic can find a reason to deny or refute even though science has neither belief nor sight in the miraculous or supernatural.
(3) It is the first time in this modern age that the Quran has exposed the actual reality of Baconian philosophy and Baconian progress and the logical and scientific hazards impending on them. It appears impossible to reach the heart of the ultimate reality without reading this analysis by the Quran.
(4) Bertrand Russell himself appears to be approaching reality but only viewing the inward trouble's outward ripples and seeing the danger just in war. They who prescribe more production as the remedy of the Baconian ills appear only adding fuel to the kiln to extinguish the fire. The Quran has diagnosed the disease and has prescribed the correct remedy, namely, the complete eradication of this Baconian progress. No campaigners could successfully or effectively conduct any movement against the atomic threat except by adopting the guidelines given by the Quran in its warning.
(5) Endeavors to revive religion in this Baconian entangled culture and the presence of this ever-increasing progress will be of dubious and partial success. Religion will find difficulties presented by this Baconian system and contend with the ever-increasing attention of its votaries fixed on the progress. Moreover, we observe that religion is proving ineffective in this world's gradual drift toward atomic hell. When the atomic hell comes, it will neither leave the religion nor its votaries. Therefore, revivers of religion must understand this warning of the Quran to chalk out their program in the light of its guidelines.
(6) This warning of the Quran is Noah's ark in this fiery deluge of modern atomism and is like the Rod of Moses for these inventions of science.

(7) This Prophetic warning about the atomic hell has furnished undeniable and irrefutable proof of the Divine Origin of the Quran. None but Allah could know these facts fourteen centuries ago.

Read the prophecy from the Quran mentioned above with care. Try to find a resemblance between the description of 'Al-Hotama' given by the Quran and the characteristics of atomic fire. This prophecy about 'Al-Hotama' has existed in the Quran ever since its revelation. According to the characterization and causes of the appearance of phenomena, I found it to apply to worldly atomic hell.

Atomic energy is of recent origin compared to chemical and electrical energy. Atomic energy has specific essential distinctive characteristics in comparison to other types of energy. These characteristics distinguish atomic energy from other types of energy.

The Quran has treated nuclear phenomena and has described the essential distinguishing characteristics of atomic energy and called it 'Al-Hotama', a hell of the next eternal world and, therefore, eternal. The atomic hell of this temporal world is the temporal representation of the 'Hotama' of the next eternal world just as ordinary fire is the temporal representation of the hell of the next eternal world in general, and so also is garden the representation of the Paradise of the next eternal world.

The Quran has claimed to contain every example for humankind. If, then, the example of the destruction of just the froward tribes of Sodom and Gomorrah have found a mention in the Quran, how someone could expect that the Quran should omit the wholesale destruction of whole humankind by the atomic hell? What could be the destruction of those little tribes against this universal destruction produced by the atomic hell? What was the torture of those condemned tribes against the torment and agony caused by the nuclear hell?

Some may be cast into the atomic hell undeservedly along with those deserving ones, but then Allah has the power and the mercy to compensate for this loss in the next world. According to Quran, the causes of the punishment in 'Al-Hotama' are 'slander', 'wealth accumulation', and 'belief in the eternity of life of this world'. This belief means the solicitude in the durability of the material works of this world as if one hoped to live here forever.

We can classify the prophecy into two parts.

FIRST PART OF THE PROPHECY

We cannot leave the first part of this warning of the Quran about the atomic hell un-mentioned, for both the parts form an indissoluble entity and are interlinked inseparably.

Also, we cannot complete the topic without the treatment of the warning in toto. The text of the first part of the warning is as follows.

"Woe to every backbiter, defamer, who amasseth wealth (of this world) and arrangeth it (against the future). He thinketh that his wealth will render him immortal. Nay, for verily he will be cast into Al-Hotama."

Herein then may be found the characterization of this culture of modern science-guided Baconian atomism. These characteristics of slander, engrossment in wealth accumulation, and faith in the eternity of this process of wealth accumulation are the particular characteristics of this modern Baconian culture and form the fundamental cause of the appearance of the atomic hell, that is, the nuclear bombs and the nuclear radiations. Indeed, Aristotle and Plato, though intensely antagonistic to the theory of Atomism, could not have seen so far as to find a link between atomism and atomic bombs. Again, this point differentiates between the greatest of the human intellects and the divine intelligence. Quran could see so far.

We will now show that the characteristics mentioned above are precisely the characteristics of this modern culture of Baconian atomism.
(1) The Quran says, **"Backbiter and defamer."**
Now, the doctrines of atomism, both ancient and modern, are slander against the revealed religion. In ancient Greek atomism, the doctrine of the fortuitous concourse of atoms meant slanderous denial for the religious doctrines of the divine government of the world. Further, the doctrine of the indestructibility of atoms and the consequential eternity of this universe implied an impossibility of Resurrection. On the other hand, the doctrine of the pursuit of natural philosophy as the actual business of man on earth and the prohibition of moral philosophy in the case of modern atomism of Bacon meant a slanderous denial of the fundamental religious doctrine of man's trial on the earth. It thus implied a rejection of morality, law, divine government, Resurrection, and all. The rejection of miraculous and supernatural by the Baconian critics of the Bible on the criterion of science and rationalism and the reduction of the person of Jesus Christ himself to a mere fable is reminiscent of the essential slanderous attitude of the philosophy of atomism.

This age is of 'slander'. The universal slander, intellectualized and named 'propaganda', is a peculiar feature of this age. The transformation of the meanings of the word 'slander' to 'propaganda' in the present modern age furnishes peculiar proof of the prevalence of 'slander' in this age. This age in itself is conspicuous for the habit of intellectualized slander, carping, backbiting, and defaming. Nothing therein escapes the fangs of slander except wealth. No two persons meet but to slander the third. People discuss no subject except in terms of direct or indirect slander. The critical attitude of modern rationalism has been tampered with slander by the intrinsic slanderous attitude of atomism.

(2) The Quran says, **"He amasseth wealth of this world and arrangeth it against the future."**

And indeed, no better or accurate definition and description of this science-guided, worldwide, continuous, systematic, organized, ever-increasing, and infinite process of wealth accumulation and its systematic arrangement for the future known by the name of progress of this modern age could be expected. This fact is as transparent as could hardly need any more explanation. Just observe this modern Baconian industrial and economic setup and people's engrossment in wealth accumulation and continuous future economic link ad infinitum that is a peculiar and particular feature of this age.

(3) The Quran says, **"He thinketh that his wealth will render him immortal."**

Mark the faith of this age in the infinite continuity of this progress through five-year plans to the ultimate goal of self-sufficiency. And see their solicitude about the continuity and stability of the monuments of progress and property. They believe and behave as if they have to live forever in this world. The belief of this age in the eternity of this progress and process of wealth accumulation is universal. This belief is unshakeable even in the presence of wholesale atomic destruction. So also, was the belief of ancient atomism in the eternity of this universe.

(4) The Quran says, **"Nay, for verily he will be cast into the 'Hotama' (that is into the atomic crusher)."**

Atomic hell of the atomic bombs and atomic radiations is the unpreventable and logical end of these characteristics. No surer proof now is needed that the belief in the eternity of this progress is false in the presence of the self-destructive character of this Baconian progress and the presence of the atomic bombs and atomic radiations and the anarchical exhaustion of harmless resources of energy.

The Quran has calculated the course of the Baconian atomistic progress with utmost surety and accuracy. The Quran has falsified the notion of eternity of the 'backbiting wealth accumulator', and the end of the 'slandering wealth accumulator' in the atomic hell is a must. The only alternative is redemption through the cessation of this progress.

Belief or disbelief is not a consideration in this particular matter. However, the stay of the believer in the 'Hotama' will be as long as Allah will wish, but the disbeliever shall have to remain therein forever and eternally. Now, the characteristics of 'Hotama' are identical to those of the atomic fire. Quran pointed out causes of punishment in 'Al-Hotama' similar to those of the appearance of nuclear fire with its brood of manifestations. The Quran only has pointed towards the right direction for the remedy. Various sages of this age give out more production as the remedy as if they prescribe the addition of fuel as the extinguishing agent in case of raging fire.

This Prophetic warning of the Quran, the last and only ray of hope, needs to be taken as the conclusive argument of Providence to humankind. No power on earth can save now this world from wholesale atomic destruction except by the removal of those causes which the Quran has given out as the causes of the punishment in 'Al-Hotama' and subsequently of the appearance of the atomic hell, namely, the atomic bombs and the atomic radiations on this earth.

Even if they escaped the atomic war and atomic radiation, the people of this particular age would not escape the 'Hotama', the nuclear hell of the next eternal world, because the causes of both this transient atomic hell and the eternal atomic hell ('Al-Hotama') are the same. This world's transient atomic hell represents the eternal 'Hotama' of the next eternal world. This temporal atomic hell comprising atomic bombs and radiations is the transitory prototype of 'Al-Hotama', the eternal atomic hell of the next eternal world.

SECOND PART OF THE PROPHECY

For me, now, it is to prove that the essential characteristics of atomic fire are the basic characteristics of 'Al-Hotama' and vice versa. The causes of the punishment in 'Al-Hotama' are the causes of the appearance of atomic energy on earth. It is surprising to note that the characteristics of 'Al-Hotama' given by the Quran are those characteristics of atomic fire that distinguish it from other types of fire, either in principle or degree in some cases.

Again, and surprisingly, it is that a Scripture should predict, describe, and warn against the atomic hell fourteen centuries ago in an age of no science. We reserve professional appreciation of the prophecy for scientists and philosophers. However, there is also the surprise for the layman.

What would have been Einstein's state of mind at the nuclear description of the atomic fire by the Quran is not very difficult to guess. He simply would not believe his eyes and his ears first. He would be lost in reverie since it was for a mind of the level of Einstein to understand the exact nature of the description of the characteristics. He might also view the extent of nuclear knowledge of the Thinker that made the prediction. Indeed, suppose the human knowledge of nuclear science today or even after be regarded as a lamp. In that case, knowledge of the Quran in this respect appears as a distinct luminous star visible in any part of the universe to guide the sailor, astronaut, or the solitary traveler lost in the desert.

The text of the second part of the warning is as follows.

"And what could teach thee what Al-Hotama (the crusher) is? It is the fire of Allah enkindled which leapeth up onto the hearts. It is (a fire) closed in on them in outstretched columns."

Following are the description and characterization of nuclear phenomena given by the Quran. Mark the characteristics that distinguish the nuclear phenomena from all the rest of the phenomena.

MUTUAL CORROBORATION OF 'HOTAMA' AND 'ATOMIC HELL'

Following is the description of the fire of 'Hotama' given by the Quran.
(1) "It is 'Hotama'."
(2) "It is the fire of Allah enkindled which leapeth up unto the hearts. It is a fire closed in on them in outstretched columns."
(3) The questioning mode, "What could teach thee what 'Al-Hotama' is?" displays the thrilling intricacy and frightfulness of the phenomena.

Following, then, are the characteristics.

THE CHARACTERIZATION OF THE NUCLEAR PHENOMENA GIVEN BY THE QURAN

(1) That, it is 'Hotama'. 'Hotama' literally means a crusher.
(2) That, it is a 'fire'.
(3) That, it is a 'fire of Allah kindled'.
(4) That, it is a 'fire which leaps up unto the hearts'.
(5) That, it is a 'fire which is closed in on them'.
(6) That, it is a 'fire closed in on them in outstretched columns'. That is, it shows 'encompassing' characteristics, and it raises 'outstretched columns'.
(7) That, 'such phenomena are too complex and terrible', just as is apparent from the question, "What could teach thee what 'Al-Hotama' is?"

These are unerringly the characteristics of the nuclear phenomena that distinguish it from all the other phenomena, e.g., chemical, and electrical.

In light of atomic science, we have now to show that these are precisely the characteristics of the atomic phenomena. We will treat each point individually to show these characteristics as shown by the atomic fire, believing that those who do not know atomic science will follow the theme also. The atomist and the textbooks of atomic science could confirm the validity of the facts of atomic science included.

We will now bring these facts against the facts observed and brought to light during the practical experimentation of the nuclear phenomena.

(1) **THE QURAN SAYS, 'HOTAMA' THAT IS A 'CRUSHER'.** The atomic fire and nuclear phenomena both are crushers. The Quran has used the word 'Hotama'. 'Hotama' is purely an Arabic word and is a qualitative noun derived/formed from the root verb 'Hatama', which means 'break anything into pieces' or 'to shatter it'.

Thus, 'Hotama' is a descriptive noun and means a 'breaker' or a 'crusher'. The sound of the word 'Hotama' recalls to our mind the word 'Atoma'. Mark the phonetic resemblance between the two, though one is purely Arabic, and the other is an adaptation from the Greek word 'Atomos', which means 'not-cuttable'.

Thus, the word 'Atom' has assumed the meaning contrasting with 'Hotama', which means 'to break something to pieces'. Yet both are concerned with the same action, that of breaking. We need not remind the scientist that the word 'Atom' is a misnomer, for 'Atom' has been cut and deserves no more to be called 'Atom'. The scientists had, after breaking the 'Atom', assembled and discussed the inconsistency.

Yet after some discussion, they left the word 'Atom' as it was. This particular point of retaining the word 'Atom' may or may not be of particular scientific interest to our theme. Yet, this phonetic resemblance of the two words, 'Hotama' and 'Atoma', adds some interest in a way. It may serve as the formula of open sesame to the gate of that tremendous atomic mystery that lay concealed in the words of the prophecy.

The scientist has adopted the word 'Atom' from the Greek word 'Atomos'. That means which is 'not-cuttable'. Therefore, as the scientist uses, the word atom seems to be a misnomer since they have broken an atom into subatomic parts, e.g., electrons, protons, neutrons, positrons, etc.

On the other hand, the word used by the Quran, 'Hattama', is correctly used. As mentioned above, it is surprising that the scientists gathered in a conference to coin some applicable term in place of 'atom'. Still, after discussion, they decided to leave the thing as it was, all in contradiction to the essential spirit of science and its dictates.

In this context, we could, with plausibility, make a conjecture. The same Power that had placed the prophecy about the atom bomb in the Quran also managed the scientist's mind to let 'Atom' remain 'Atom' due to the phonic resemblance between 'Atom' and 'Hatam'. So that when the time came, the discovery of the secret in the prophecy be made possible. This phonic resemblance between these two keywords served as the clue without which even the most scrupulous corroboration of the descriptive facts contained in the prophecy would find a little strict recognition.

Now, we will show that atomic energy, from its beginning and generation to the last reactions of its radiations, is a series of crushing (breakings).

(a) THE ATOMIC ENERGY IS THE BINDING ENERGY OF THE ATOM

Mark the atomic energy that appears by breaking the binding of the atomic nucleus. Powerhouses generate only atomic energy in this manner and none other. The atom's binding, which keeps the nucleons of the atomic nucleus packed close together, is broken, and energy is released. Thus, the binding of the atomic nucleus is crushed, and the energy is released.

No matchstick, no sparkling system, and no fuel are required to produce atomic fire. This ignition without a matchstick is the distinguishing feature of atomic fire from any other type of fire. No one can ignite any other type of fire in this manner.

(b) ATOMIC FIRE IS AN ABSOLUTE 'CRUSHER'

The atomic phenomena may be regarded as the absolute crusher since its breaking and crushing is absolute. Atoms once crushed could not be reconstructed by a method of synthesis. Nucleus, once disintegrated, could not be rearranged in its original form by any means or methods. We observe that the crushing is done by the consumption of chemical fire too. However, there is a difference between the two. In the case of a chemical fire, nuclei of the atoms remain untouched and intact. By some synthetic method, there is the possibility of reproduction of the substance so consumed. In the case of the atomic disintegration, the nuclei of the atoms are so disintegrated as there is no possibility hitherto of the nuclear re-arrangement, for the basic nuclear structure of atoms is crushed.

Moreover, we see that the atomic radiation attacks the cell's nucleus and breaks the chromosomes, which the chemical fire could not perform. So complete is the crushing involved in the atomic actions and reactions that the atomic fire destroys the atom's nuclear structure, the 'basic building block of the universe'. It also destroys the cell nucleus, which is called the 'basic unit of life'. Hence, we can specify the atomic phenomena as 'absolute fire', which again is a characteristic that distinguishes the atomic phenomena from all the rest.

(c) ALL THE THREE MANIFESTATIONS OF THE ATOMIC BOMB EXPLOSION, NAMELY, 'INITIAL HEAT-RADIATION', 'BLAST', AND 'NUCLEAR RADIATIONS' ARE THE 'CRUSHERS'

The 'initial heat-radiation' crushes the hearts of its victims at the time of explosion though it has not the time enough to burn them. So, it kills them through shock. As the name implies, the 'blast' crushes the most robust buildings to dust. The 'nuclear radiations' do so as it is their norm. They crush the atomic nuclei of the inanimate matter. Thus, they produce changes in the order of the atomic nuclei to cause transmutations. In the living bodies, they crush the nucleons out of the atomic nuclei, and in the cell nuclei, they crush the chromosomes.

(d) THE ATOMIC RADIATIONS AS THE 'CRUSHER'

As mentioned above, radiations knock out electrons from the atoms and eject nucleons from the atomic nuclei. They cause transmutations of atoms by crushing and changing the order of the atomic nuclei.

(e) THE ATOMISTS MARK THE 'CRUSHING' TRAIT OF ATOMIC ENERGY

'Hotama' literally means a 'breaker', a 'crusher' just as the term 'Bremsstrahlung'. When Germans named the continuous spectrum of rays 'Bremsstrahlung', which means 'braking radiation', the atomists regarded the term as highly descriptive.

This particular crushing characteristic is a distinguishing feature of nuclear phenomena, and strangely enough, is to be found in none other chemical, electrical, or gravitational phenomena. Unlike other energy generation processes, we generate nuclear energy distinctively by crushing (the binding of) the atom's nucleus, and complete crushing occurs. Nucleus, once disintegrated, can never be re-arranged in its original form by any means of synthesis. While in no other phenomena nucleus is so much touched. The basic building block of the universe, the 'atom', and the basic unit of life, the 'cell', are involved in atomic crushing.

Furthermore, nuclear radiations crush the atomic nuclei, causing atoms' transmutations and breaking the cell nuclei chromosomes. The 'Heat-Flash' of the atomic bomb explosion crushes the 'heart' of its victims while the 'blast' crushes buildings and the 'radiations' of atomic bombs crush the atomic nuclei and the cell nuclei irreparably. That is why atomic physics books are replete with terms like 'bombarding', 'crushing', 'smashing', 'hitting', 'breaking', etc., in the description and explanation of the actions and reactions in atomic phenomena.

During his famous experiment of bombarding the gold foil with alpha particles, the crushing attitude of alpha particles astonished Rutherford so much that he recorded it as the most incredible event that ever happened to him in his life:

"It was the most incredible event that ever happened to me in my life. It was almost as incredible as if you fired a 15-inch shell at a piece of tissue paper, and it came back and hit you", wrote Rutherford in his diary.

That indicates a conspicuous realization of the particular feature of crushing observable in the nuclear phenomena on the scientist's part. But mark the phonetic and functional identity between scientist's 'Atomic' and Quran's 'Otamic' or 'Hotamic', which simply is miraculous. 'Atom' no longer means something indestructible, while 'Otama' of the Quran means a destroyer, yet both are expressive of the act of breaking. Do mark the sound of the two words. It appears to be one word. Is this a mere coincidence? No. The exact characterization of the atomic phenomena by the Quran excludes the possibility. Instead, it appears that He, who coined the term 'Otama', had before His eyes, indeed supernaturally penetrating eyes, the entire theme of atomic phenomena and all the future ages. The term 'Otama' being neither Greek nor English enhances the wonder at being so similar term as 'Atomic' even in the Arabic tongue. What other name could one give to this fact if not a miracle? The tremendousness of the crushing capacity of the atomic bomb and atomic radiations is as conspicuously significant that needs no allusion.

(f) RADIOBIOLOGICAL TERMS INDICATIVE OF THE '<u>CRUSHING</u>' TRAIT OF RADIATIONS

The classic books of Radiobiology are replete with phrases, similes, and sentences describing the actions and reactions of radiations to indicate the crushing trait of the radiations. The examples are as: 'the target concept', 'direct action', 'indirect action', 'snapping the cable with a bullet', 'breaking the chromosomes', and sentences like "radiations hit the cell like a sledgehammer and crush them," etc.

(2) THE QURAN SAYS, "HOTAMA IS <u>A FIRE</u>."

The nuclear explosion is 'fire'. It has two main constituents, namely, the 'Heat-Flash' and the 'ionizing radiations'. Both these are fire. The 'Heat-Flash' is the initial radiation, more dazzling than the sun. It appears at a minute fraction of a second on detonation and lasts for but two seconds.

The 'ionizing radiations', alpha, beta, gamma rays, and neutrons, are inherent in the atomic explosion and appear as fission products. There is indeed the blast as powerful as an earthquake, but it is only an associated effect. Moreover, colossal fires consume whole cities, but they are started through convection or due to damaged electrical appliances. Sixty percent of deaths and seventy-five percent at least of all casualties in Hiroshima were due to fire.

The atomic energy is fire too. Atomic energy from the beginning to the end is fire. In its generation stages, it is the heat. The initial heat radiation of the atomic bomb is fire. Radiations, too, are fire. The discoverer of radioactivity himself, Becquerel was the first to experience the burn on his skin next to the pocket he had carried a vial of Radium.

Edward Teller and Dr. Albert L. Latter wrote on Page-156 of their book "Our Nuclear Future: Facts, Dangers, and Opportunities":

"A vicious dragon (reactor) will spit radioactive 'fire'."

In X-ray therapy, radiotherapists use the term 'crossfire of radiation' in radiation treatment. Chemical fire, too, is a fire, but what is the chemical fire to the fire of atomic energy, which (latter) is of the order of millions of degrees, and no container on earth can be found to contain it. Tremendous fires are started due to the tremendous heat spread in the atmosphere after the atomic bomb explosion. Yet, such fires are not part of the atomic explosion, and we do not treat them as atomic but chemical.

Today, the atomists and humanity know that nuclear energy and nuclear phenomena are fire, the whole fire, and nothing but fire. However, the atomist also knows that the nuclear device's initial radiations on detonation, the radiations called 'Heat-Flash', and the ionizing radiations are the only ingredients that constitute the nuclear explosion. This 'Heat-Flash' produces intense heat, and the temperatures developed by its heat are of the order of a million to tens, even hundreds of millions of degrees. Indeed, there are other fires also: fires colossal in magnitude and devastating that consume whole cities. However, they start through the convection of heat produced by the initial radiation and damaged electrical appliances or the adjacent buildings on fire. A terrific blast of the order of an earthquake occurs and constitutes an unspeakable hazard to the dwellings and human life. However, in light of the modern energy theory, it could be taken as a part of energy itself or cited as an associated effect of the explosion fire. It is thus practically proved that the nuclear phenomena are fire.

(3) THE QURAN SAYS, "HOTAMA IS <u>A FIRE OF ALLAH</u>."

We know that the atomic phenomenon is concerned with energy, and the energy is heat, fire, etc. We may prove the atomic phenomenon as Allah's fire because certain evils produce it as retributive punishment. Atomic fire, too, is the fire of retribution. Scientific research has discovered the atomic fire whose object has been to gain dominion over Mother Nature for material benefit. The atomic fire, therefore, has appeared as retribution. It is not energy; instead, it is wholesale destruction and a curse. The atomic bomb is not a defense weapon, but the excessive desire for wealth and physical comforts has blinded humankind, and the doom is grievous.

This point involves no complexity. Atomic phenomena produce energy; energy produces heat, and heat produces fire. The association of fire with atomic bombs and radiation is a well-known fact. However, why Allah would associate this particular fire with His name is the question? The colossal magnitude of atomic fire, as well as its problem, might be the consideration. Also, if this humankind is consumed eventually by the flames of the atomic bombs or the effects of radiation, then rightly this fire may be regarded as the retribution and wrath of Allah enkindled. This rage of Allah is a fact that takes every thoughtful man's mind to the 'causes' and the 'effects' of this significant problem. Will this humankind be able to avoid the atomic war forever? Will it guard itself against the hazards that are incident on the existence of the factor of atomic radiations? Such are the questions that demand every man's attention endowed with the faculty of thought.

The fire of 'Hotama' has appeared as the wrath of Allah and as retribution. It emerged because of a set of inconsistencies that the Quran has enumerated as 'slander', 'backbiting', 'complete engrossment in wealth accumulation', and 'wealth worship'. The intensity of the flame, magnitude of the fire, and extent of the destruction, all are so great that we could reasonably attribute it to the name of Allah. The Hiroshima bomb developed a temperature of million degrees Celsius. Regular high yield bombs develop temperatures of the order of tens of millions of degrees Celsius.

In contrast, for the triggering of thermonuclear bombs, the temperatures developed are of the order of hundreds of millions of degrees Celsius. Such temperatures are not earthly but solar and stellar. The earliest commentators of the Quran correctly defined 'Al-Hotama', for instance, as:

"A kind of a hell in which whatever we cast; the sheer intensity of the flame reduces it to powder."

We can summarize this fire as follows.

(a) A SORT OF PUNISHMENT

It is a sort of punishment and is retributive. It appears as a chastisement of Allah for certain particular inconsistencies on the part of human beings. This punishment results from a continuous process of science misguided and ill-applied due to a particular misguiding philosophy that was tampered with blasphemous and worldly faithlessness, apostasy, and skepticism. The fire of atomism consequently appears as a symbol of Allah's wrath, and the Quran has enumerated such untoward tendencies of humanity responsible for the emergence of such a fire. These widespread worldly trends include a defamatory nature and character, excessive love for wealth accumulation, and great faith in wealth. The inconsistencies, unfortunately, happen to be a particular trait of this modern age of ours.

(b) ABNORMAL INTENSITY OF THE TEMPERATURES

The abnormal intensity of the temperatures developed in nuclear processes and unusually vast magnitudes of the atomic fire and the considerable extent of its devastation, when judged against the ordinary types of fire, would with much plausibility be attributed to the name of Allah, the Great.

These characteristics of the atomic fire are of such caliber as justly cause human imagination to reel so much that it would have been hard for anyone to believe if humanity had not witnessed them. Just imagine a temperature of 1500 degrees Celsius at white heat that turns clay into molten slag flowing like a liquid. Then, try to imagine a temperature of a million degrees Celsius. The thing is perhaps just beyond human imagination. It only could be remembered as a mathematical computation.

Nevertheless, the story does not come to an end with a mere million. The atomic bomb dropped on Hiroshima developed a temperature of a million degrees. However, the little high yield atomic bomb develops temperatures of tens of millions of degrees.

Further, in triggering the Hydrogen bomb (the so-called Hell bomb), the developed temperatures are of the order of hundreds of millions of degrees. Such temperatures are not earthly but are supposed to be related to such heavenly bodies as are meant for burning, e.g., the sun and the stars. In the heart of the sun or the stars, such temperatures are likely to be found.

The fires, therefore, of the solar or stellar nature to be found on humble earth would seem something unnatural. Such fires could neither be controlled for peaceful purposes nor could anybody contain them in some container on earth. We simply do not find any container on earth that could hold fires with such intense temperatures to evaporate every matter to the gaseous state. It seems pretty plausible, therefore, to attribute such a fire to the name of Allah.

(c) THE UNBELIEVABLE MAGNITUDE

Barely a couple of pounds of Uranium-235 produces energy equivalent to 20 thousand tons of ordinary chemical TNT. A thousand kilograms (one metric ton) of Uranium-235 would liberate energy equivalent to 20 million tons of TNT. This energy is of the order of large-scale natural phenomena such as hurricanes and earthquakes. To create such natural phenomena as hurricanes and earthquakes in the pre-nuclear age was considered an act of Mother Nature and not of man. Therefore, it certainly is not without some real plausibility if we attribute such a fire to the name of Allah.

(d) THE EXPLOSIVE ENERGY

The explosive energy produced by a single 15 megaton (15 million tons) thermonuclear (Hydrogen) bomb far exceeds all the explosive energy produced collectively during the whole history of humankind.

(e) THE HEAT-FLASH

The 'Heat-Flash', its subsequent fires, and the blast of a single 20 megaton thermonuclear bomb destroy the largest cities in the world. The radioactive fallout of such a bomb would lay waste areas equal to states: to wit an area a little less than five hundredth part of the whole surface of the earth. Therefore, to wit, suppose that we symmetrically detonate five hundred such bombs on the surface of the earth. In that case, it is not difficult to imagine that it would obliterate every single sign of life from the planet after a painful existence, though for a while.

Unfortunate survivors, if any, would envy the doom of those dead in a dungeon horrible on all sides round as a colossal furnace flamed. Still, from those flames, no light but rather darkness visible, to discover sights of woe, the regions of sorrow, doleful shades, where peace and rest can never dwell, hope never comes that comes to all. However, rather endless torture still urges in a fiery deluge fed with ever-burning Uranium un-consumed.

John Milton has delineated the description of hell in the following words.
>"At once as far as angel's ken he views
>The dismal situation waste and wild,
>A dungeon horrible, on all side round
>As one great furnace flamed, yet from those flames
>No light, but rather darkness visible
>Served only to discover sights of woe,

Regions of sorrow, doleful shades, where peace
And rest can never dwell, hope never comes
That comes to all; but torture without end
Still urges, and a fiery deluge, fed
With ever-burning sulphur unconsumed."

('Paradise Lost', Book-1, by John Milton)

(f) ATOMIC RADIATIONS

Nuclear energy is not only destructive as a weapon of war, but in a way, it is also lethal if restricted to peaceful purposes due to its inherent and inseparable atomic radiation. These radiations may bring about a death quick enough, or they may allow their victim a painful existence somewhere in a cancer hospital for some time and then put him to a lingering and painful death. The ionizing radiations of nuclear energy, whether generated with peaceful views or for war purposes, are always there and fatal to human health. By and by, it will turn humanity into cancer-ridden freaks. Nobody has found any remedy hitherto for the perils of radioactivity.

(4) THE QURAN SAYS, "HOTAMA IS A FIRE WHICH LEAPS UP UNTO THE HEARTS."

This point presents a fascinating study and must be read with attention, for the fires generally are supposed to burn the body, but a fire which 'leaps up unto the heart' without having first burnt the body sounds a bit strange. Here is a particular characteristic of the atomic phenomena, which may be regarded as one most distinct characteristic and distinguishes the atomic phenomena from other phenomena.

THE ATOMIC FIRE LEAPS UP UNTO THE 'NUCLEI'
(a) 'NUCLEUS' AND THE 'HEART'

This point of the Quran that the atomic fire 'leaps up unto the hearts' is proved simply calling the atomic phenomena by its characteristic name that of the 'nuclear phenomena'. We name the nuclear phenomenon 'nuclear' because its actions appear in the nucleus (heart) of the atom. It is very well-known that the actions do not occur in the atom's nucleus in other chemical and electrical phenomena. The nucleus there in all non-atomic phenomena remains untouched to the end. The atomic phenomena, actually the nuclear phenomena, has their actions within the nucleus. Also, the scientists use the words 'nucleus' and 'heart' synonymously, indeed orthodoxly, and Quran is not amiss in using the word 'hearts' for 'nuclei'.

However, how we can prove the point of 'leaping up unto the hearts' is the question? The Quran has used the word 'hearts' while scientists have coined the term 'nucleus'. Identity, therefore, has to be found between the two words. These two words, the 'nucleus' and 'heart' are synonymous. The Arab Lexicographers have translated this modern word 'nucleus' as 'heart', and both show specific characteristics and functional resemblance. Both are delicate and sensitive. If they die, the body dies with them. We have to exert no toil in proving our point. The Quran has not spoken amiss. The scientists themselves frequently call the 'nucleus' like 'heart' and indeed appropriately, and the practice continues in the standard textbooks of atomic physics. Some of the scores of examples in the following statements will suffice, which we find in the standard textbooks of atomic physics.

(i) Edward Teller, in 1939, spoke of "obtaining energy from the heart of atom" in his lecture delivered on atomic energy. ('The Hydrogen Bomb: The Men, the Menace, the Mechanism'; by James R. and Blair, Clay Jr. Shepley, Pages 18-49)

(ii) "Each fast particle comes from the breakup of the very heart of a single atom (the nucleus) of the radioactive material." (Physics, Physical Science Study Committee Second Edition, D.C. Heath and Company, Lexington, Massachusetts, July 1965, Page-130)

(iii) "How many nuclear heart-beats are in the lifetime of a radioactive nucleus which lasts only billionth of a second?"

(Ibid-Page 21, Short Problems)

(iv) Even the part of the reactor in which atomic energy generation takes place is called the 'heart of reactor'. ('Our Nuclear Future'; by Edward Teller and Dr. Albert L. Latter; quote 'heart of reactor' referred from the photograph of the Reactor)

Thus, the point of the Quran is proved by merely uttering the word 'nuclear'.

(b) 'NUCLEI' THAT ARE 'HEARTS' INVOLVED IN THE NUCLEAR ENERGY GENERATION PROCESS

Nuclear energy is generated even on the same principle that is the attack on the 'heart'. When we look into nuclear energy generation processes, we find the same formula, of the 'leaping up of the fire over the hearts' on work. How come it is so? The entire field of action of the nuclear phenomena is in the 'nuclei'. In any other phenomena, the process of energy generation never touches the nucleus. In atomic energy generation, the 'nuclei' of atoms are involved in the fission and fusion process.

(i) FISSION PROCESS

Let us first have a view of the fission process of energy generation. In the fission process, the atomic particles 'leap up unto the nuclei' that are the 'hearts' of the atoms. We see a neutron, for example, to assail the nucleus (heart) of the atom in a pile of fissile material and knock out two neutrons. As if in a retaliative mood, these knocked-out neutrons further strike at the 'hearts' of other atoms and knock out two neutrons each. The knocked-out neutrons in continued succession keep on knocking out two neutrons each in turn. This process continues multiplying the number of knocked-out neutrons, so the fission chain reaction is built until the whole mass of the fissile matter becomes red hot and explodes in wrath at the 'hearts' of the atoms having been disturbed.

Finally, the cup of the patience of enraged mass overflows, and it explodes itself with terrible violence. Now we know how the neutrons attack the 'hearts' of atoms, and we generate nuclear energy within the 'hearts' of atoms. Thus, it means that nuclear energy not only tends 'leaping up over the hearts' after we generate it, but it also is generated in a similar process that of 'leaping up over the hearts'.

(ii) FUSION PROCESS

The exact process we see at work in the fusion process of nuclear energy generation. In this case, simply two atoms of lighter nuclei are taken, and the 'heart' (nucleus) of one atom we forcibly crush into the 'heart' (nucleus) of the other atom; the 'hearts' break and give out the heat (energy). In other words, the 'nuclei' ('hearts' of atoms) are crushed together in the fusion process, which liberates energy. In the fusion process, the atomic fire obtained from the fission device targets the 'nuclei' of the fusile material.

(iii) THE TERM 'THERMONUCLEAR'

It will be learned with no mild surprise that the Quran has only, and precisely translated the term 'thermonuclear' as the scientist applied himself when it (the Quran) says that nuclear energy is a fire which 'leaps up over the hearts'. How is it? It is thus!

The word 'thermo' means 'of heat', that is, fire. The word 'nuclear' is the adjective of 'nucleus' which means 'heart'. Thus, the word 'nuclear' means something connected with 'heart'. The complete term that is 'thermonuclear' would then mean, "A fire which is related to the heart." Scientists coined this term accurately. They confirmed employing fantastic aptness what Quran said in this respect.

The scientist says: "A fire related to the heart."

The Quran says: "A fire which leaps up over the hearts."

Such an act of anticipation on the part of the Quran would seem nothing short of a marvel.

Both fission and fusion in atomic energy generation occur within the 'nuclei'. Still, the best and the clearest spectacle of 'leaping up onto the nuclei that are the hearts' by the fire of atomic energy we see in the 'thermonuclear' process wherein the inner fission device produces the necessary temperature. Then the process directs the heat unto the 'nuclei' of the outer fusile material, that is, the 'hearts' of the hydrogen atoms where it 'leaps up unto the nuclei' of Hydrogen atoms and fuses them in groups of four. Mark the term 'thermonuclear' in this context: It means "heat connected with 'nucleus' (heart)".

This distinguishing characteristic discriminates the atomic phenomena, for, in no other phenomena, the 'nucleus' of the atom is involved. The scientist's term "thermo-nuclear" is the scientific version of the Quran's expression, that is, "A fire which leaps up unto the nuclei that are the hearts."

(c) NUCLEAR RADIATIONS LEAP UP UNTO THE 'NUCLEI' THAT ARE 'HEARTS'
(i) EFFECTS OF RADIATIONS IN INANIMATE AND LIVING BODIES

The nuclear radiations do characteristically attack the nuclei of the atoms of the material through which they pass. In inanimate matter, they change the order of the nuclei of the atoms and thus cause transmutations of atoms. In living bodies, they leap up unto (attack) the nuclei of the atoms, and they eject nucleons from there. They attack the nuclei of the cells and break the chromosomes. They show a remarkable and preferential attraction for the 'heart' and all related to the 'heart' within the body.

(ii) THE EFFECT OF RADIATIONS IS BEYOND THE CONTROL OF BRAIN AT THE LEVEL OF 'HEART' OF LIFE ITSELF

Radiations affect the coordination of function at a level where it is beyond the control of the brain in a living body nearest to the 'heart'. One can assume that they attack at the very 'heart' of life itself.

(iii) RADIATIONS' EXCEPTIONAL ATTRACTION TOWARD ALL THAT IS RELATED TO THE 'HEART' IN THE BODY

Bone marrow and all blood-forming organs are more sensitive to the effect of radiations than the brain, the nerves, and the muscles. The blood relation of bone marrow and blood-forming organs with the 'heart' is well-known.

The nuclear radiations alpha, beta, gamma rays, and neutrons are inherent in the very nature of the atomic explosion. The scientists nicknamed these radiations 'bone-seekers' because they tended to seek and reach the bones through the bloodstream. There, they attack the bone marrow. Now, the function of the bone marrow is to generate blood. The nuclear radiations render the bone marrow incapable of generating blood. They attack the blood and destroy its red and white corpuscles, depriving its nourishing qualities and rendering it (instead) a source of torment to the 'heart' due to its poisoned state. Thus, the blood supply to the 'heart' stops, and the heart thus dies of starvation and torment. All the blood-forming organs are a desirable target of radiation. The relation between blood-forming organs, blood and heart, and bone marrow and blood are well-known. The attack of the radiations, therefore, is being directed towards the 'heart'.

In truth, the radiations attacking the blood-forming organs play something of a war strategy with the 'heart'. They besiege it and stop its blood supplies by destroying the existing quantities and preventing the replenishment by destroying the blood-producing capacities of organs until, at last, the 'heart' succumbs to starvation and expires in acute agony.

Recent research on the effects of radiation has revealed that the brain, nerves, and muscles are the least sensible parts of the body to the effects of radiation. Again, this fact would establish radiations' greater relative affinity for the 'heart', and all that more directly connects with it.

(iv) **EFFECTS OF RADIATIONS ON THE MULTI-CELLULAR AND UNI-CELLULAR ORGANISMS**

The multi-cellular organisms are more sensitive to the effects of radiations than the entire unicellular organisms. Multicellular organisms have more perfected hearts and lungs and more elaborated circulatory and respiratory systems. Unicellular organisms have less perfect hearts and lungs and less elaborated circulatory and respiratory systems. All multicellular organisms are more sensitive to the effects of radiations than all unicellular organisms. And it is without any exception. The relation of the circulatory and respiratory systems to the 'heart' through the blood is also known. This fact also proves the conclusive attraction of radiations for the 'heart', and everything directly connected with the 'heart'. This view is my personal opinion. No scientist has said any such thing.

(v) **RELATION BETWEEN OXYGEN AND RADIATIONS**

Oxygen is related to the 'heart' through blood. The action of radiations in the absence of Oxygen is retarded. Scientists have discovered that the presence of Oxygen perceptibly enhances the action of radiations, whereas its absence noticeably retards their action. The role of Oxygen is the aeration and purification of blood in the lungs. The connection of Oxygen with the heart is a fact of common knowledge. Muscles, nerves, and the brain are the least sensitive organs to radioactivity, whereas the heart and those connected to the heart are most sensitive to the effect. It proves a particular affinity of these radioactive rays for the 'heart'.

(vi) **THE SYMPTOMS OF RADIATION SICKNESS**

The symptoms of radiation sickness are leukemia, a disease of blood; hemorrhage that is blood leaking, a disease of the blood; fever, also connected with blood; nausea and vomiting also linked with the 'heart'.

(d) **HEAT-FLASH AND RADIATIONS OF ATOMIC BOMB**

As stated earlier, the 'Heat-Flash' is the initial radiation that appears on the atomic bomb's detonation within a fraction of a second. It appears similar to a dazzle brighter than that of the sun. It travels with the speed of light 186,000 miles per second and lasts for about two seconds. It strikes the bodies of exposed persons within its effective range and burns their skin dark or brown, while within a particular zone (nearer to the site of detonation), it kills its victims instantaneously on the spot. It leaves its victims having severe to minor painful skin burns of various degrees at greater distances outside this zone. The 'Heat-Flash' of the atomic bomb explosion that strikes the body of the exposed persons with a crushing impact like lightning on the body and has not enough time to penetrate beneath the skin kills the 'heart' of the victim though through shock to the 'heart'.

We know that persons who have got their skins burnt in an accident do not essentially die on the spot. We may save them with proper treatment. We know that 'Heat-Flash' penetrates neither beneath the skin of victims who may survive its effects nor those killed on the spot. It does not penetrate beneath the skin of its victims because of its concise duration, namely, two seconds or so. How does it then kill some of its victims on the spot if it has not penetrated their body, which remains un-impaired? The answer is that it kills by heat which has entered the lungs and has choked the 'heart' to death. Its heat through the lungs of its victim enters the breast, and with its heat and shock, which is indeed unbearably terrible, it affects the 'heart' and chokes it to instantaneous death.

The terrible shock also plays a considerable role, along with the heat, in bringing about instantaneous death. Thus, it is that the nuclear fire 'leaps up over the hearts', and without first burning the body, kills its victim by affecting the 'heart', which expires due to exceeding unbearable agony and terror. There are other fires, colossal, and devastating that are because of the atomic explosion. They burn persons' bodies to charcoal and kill. But these fires are not a part of the original body of the atomic explosion and are only caused afterward through convection due to the tremendous heat radiated by the explosion, initially in the form of 'Heat-Flash'. The 'blast' of the atomic bomb is a terrible crusher of structures, while the 'radiations' of the atomic bomb explosion carry out the process of crushing in the usual way. We observe the first two features also in the conventional bombs. However, what do the conventional bombs wreak the crushing to that wrought by the atomic bomb? The radiations of the atomic bomb explosion 'leap up unto the nuclei' of the atoms as usual.

(e) 'NUCLEAR' AND 'THERMONUCLEAR' 'CRUSHER'

We may call nuclear fire the 'nuclear crusher' because it leaps up unto the nuclei and crushes them. Because in the thermonuclear process, its fire leaps up unto the nuclei of the atoms of the fusile material and crushes them, it may be called the 'thermonuclear crusher'. This term 'thermonuclear' is the inter-translation of the words of the Quran, namely that, "It is a fire which leaps up unto the hearts." 'Thermo' means 'heat' and 'nuclear' means "that which connects with the nuclei that are hearts."

(f) A DISTINCTIVE FEATURE OF THE ATOMIC FIRE WHICH DISTINGUISHES IT FROM OTHER TYPES OF FIRE: (THAT IS) 'NUCLEUS'

It is not by coincidence that the scientist named 'nucleus' to a specific part of the atom. The name given to the central core of the atom is most appropriately a 'nucleus'. Moreover, what is the meaning of 'nucleus' if it is not the 'heart', the central core, the 'kernel'? The 'nucleus' means the central core, the 'heart'; and the 'nucleus' of the atom indeed is the 'heart' of the atom; that the nuclear fire springs from 'nucleus' and that the actions of the nuclear fire take place in the nuclear zones, is a feature exclusively characteristic of nuclear fire. The chemical fire never reaches the nuclear zones. As regards this heart-atom relation, Wordsworth was not amiss when he lamented:

"To let a creed built in the 'heart' of things,
Dissolve before a twinkling 'atomy'."

('Excursions' by Wordsworth)

The little couplet of Wordsworth represents our point in the best of manner. We could say it as follows.

"To let a universe built in the nuclear system,
Dissolve before tempting energy."

(g) THE RAGING FIRES OF DISCONTENT

Last but not least is the fire of discontent, frustration, and anxiety that is furiously raging in every heart without exception throughout the vast world today. Who could be unaware of the fire of discontent which is raging today in every human heart? The cause of this heart-burning emanates from the present materialistic age with its peculiar 'slander' and 'backbiting', 'excessive engrossment in the accumulation of wealth' and 'wealth worship'; the very same characteristics also cause the emergence of nuclear weapons.

This fire has, in every era, pestered and tormented poor human hearts. Yet, in this particular modern age of atomism, due partly to the peculiar setup of this exclusively materialistic age and partly due to the absence of faith and moral and spiritual values, it has assumed alarming proportions. To the problems of necessities of life should be added the dread of atomic bombs—and even more than the nuclear bombs that of atomic radiations. Worst is the plight of those whose lot have fallen more thorns but fewer flowers for the fruit of modern science and its progress.

Therefore, it is not without some aptness if the first cry emitted by the newborn baby at its birth, we interpret as saying: "Alas for me! What shall I do to save my body? How Shall I ever exist to solve the painful riddle of material necessities in a world poisoned by radiations?" While the first cry of a baby who was born in some pre-modern age, we could have interpreted it as saying: "Alas for me! What shall I do to save my soul in a world full of snares and pitfalls? Oh, how shall I be able to go safely back to my home in Heaven, whence I came?"

The intensity of such tormenting worries about one's material existence in the absence of spiritual relief, patience, moral fortitude, and faith has made the life of human beings extremely miserable both in the East and in the West. So crushing is the pressure and so fast increasing is the tempo that sooner or later a stage may arrive so that persons in acute frustration might prefer death to this life. Then perhaps they may hail the flashing dazzle of the atomic bomb as a surer redeemer of man from all this formidable host of miseries and unbearable agonies of a painful existence. They perhaps may prefer a sudden end through an atomic blast to a lingering death which their existence actually would be.

Perhaps no pen on earth could describe, and no imagination could honestly portray the life of humanity surrounded by atomic plants and plagued by nuclear radiation. It will be a race of horrible monsters and haggard apparitions, dreading their shadows and mistaking their cry for a smile and a smile for a cry, thinking of themselves as smiling but crying and taking themselves as crying but smiling. Darwin's perception is not needed to know that they must be most unfit for survival if that be the plight. Further, nobody requires the impulse of a Freud to realize that such a race would undoubtedly prefer an atomic holocaust to the tormenting anxiety. The faster the end, the better.

So fast is the process of changing the human mind these days, a change for the worse indeed that a man goes to bed in an attitude quite typical and serene, with perhaps a thought or two of pity and sympathy in the heart. However, to your horror, you will see him, all of a sudden, coming out of his bed, panting with a fury boiling in his breast, his eyes blood-shot with wrath, cursing himself violently and everyone. You will see him scolding himself hysterically to have done good or some kind act to anyone in the past and swearing never to do any such thing to anyone whosoever, from that very moment onward. Lull him to sleep and then wait for yet another surprise. Amid sleep, he shall come out of his bed again and swearing bitterest vows to snatch everything from everyone in the world; aye, the first thing tomorrow morning, by the early sunrise. Just lull him to sleep, and perhaps the scared sun will never again arise in this world.

We can compare the present world with T. S. Eliot's 'Waste Land', where there is no joy of wealth left, nor is patience for poverty found. But, the joy of wealth and patience for poverty both have joined with worry in mourning. Every emotion has joined every other emotion, and all have fused into one that is the worry. Tears, sighs, hearty laughter have all disappeared. [3] Mind today is a barren desert with nothing but worry blowing in every direction over seething fumes. Judging from these fast-changing attitudes of persons, it is not difficult to realize the probability of a chance occurrence. A time may not be very far when to the actual misfortune of humankind, a man blinded by an uncontrollable fit of rage, in some unavoidable situation, may cast the destiny of wretched humanity into the atomic hell. The most solemn pleaders of peace and unbreakable treaties may at such a moment prove a singed hair and crumble to dust, hurling a race headlong into a blazing hell from which there is no coming back.

THE STATE OF POST-ATOMIC WAR HUMANITY
Alas for us! Brother human-beings! Would this be the end? I wish it had been so; a complete end, the whole life on earth has gone to a perfect sleep after a short spell of terror, a storm of shrieks, and then a complete silence: no one to mourn, no one to be mourned; no one to cry, no one to be cried for; this world to be the abode of silence; terror silenced into muteness forever. However, is it so? Is it going to be the end of all misery? No, it is not so. The atomic holocaust is not going to be the final remedy. Death will not prevail ultimately, and people shall survive the atomic conflagration. They will have to taste the fruits of their scientific deeds further still and see a hell within a hell in a hellish world, the result of their greed, power, wisdom, genius, and ambition.
Let us picture a spectacle of the state of post-atomic war humanity.

The heavens will witness the folks tasting the extremes of pain and agony by festering ulcers, paining cancers, and leprous wounds.

Hordes of populaces will be stinking like skunks and covered with swarms of pestering flies, buzzing, and biting swarms of flies licking the pus all over. Just imagine the state of persons stark naked, and their minds stark mad and shattered into pieces; unable to get food and unable to search or procure something to eat; shivering with cold but having neither clothing nor even a matchstick to stir the fire and warm them. It will be a nightmare: a frightful dream when they will have the saddest thoughts of their past glory but will see instead the burnt and charred skeletons of the symbols of their past glory, outstanding achievements, the caterpillars, and the aircraft spread all over as reminders of a dreadful past, telling a silent tale of shame and folly. In short, the physical state of the people will be inexpressible, and that of their minds incredibly miserable and strange, neither raving in madness nor crying in sorrow.

The word gloom, not indeed, no word could express people's state. What happened? How, where, and why? Neither death nor even life is there. People forget the notion of death and the thought of life. What is death, and what is life? What we were, and what we are? What are we, and what is this? What are these dark images? And those sparkling ones? What is this that moves? And that does not move? Blurred; everything blurred in a post-atomic war ruin.

Now, imagine if this is the state of post-atomic war humanity. Nevertheless, the actual state we are not able to express. Nay, even if all the great pens and all the great minds of humanity that ever existed on this earth join together to express the state of post-atomic-war humanity, would not be able to describe a shred. The thing itself is just beyond expression. Of course, equally beyond expression is the pigheadedness and stubbornness of this present folly-ridden self-conceited and ill-starred generation of ours. What if I cry my throat sore, nay, if all the well-meaning individuals throughout the present humankind join in a chorus to cry their throats sore, who is going to heed their exertion? This knowledge-drunk and power-eaten generation of dark-hearted, brain-ridden commuters of wretched humanity will never stop until it has found the bottom of the affair.

However, let us now stop that we may talk here to this group of a picture of misery, these men of a post-atomic era sitting in a group, as survivors of the atomic war. No, they are not in a mood to talk. They just look at us and stare, and they turn their eyes away from us in disgust. Look, here comes a man, one of them. He seems to be a bit more loquacious.

"Hey man, here, all hail! How now, what have you to say? What are your impressions about all this?"

No, this man in his face has more of a wild surprise than any desire to talk.

"Hey man," we said, "What is your impression about all this?"
"Gentlemen, why do you ask me? This whole world, these haggard faces and all here is an impression in itself. Are you blind? Can you not see it? Or do you joke?"

"No man, we certainly are not in a mood to joke but pray tell us your impression."

"Right then, if you ask my impressions, then listen. My impression is that every unprincipled princely priest that had a share in making Christianity a dread be skinned alive before my very eyes that I may hear his shrieks. My impression is that every man who had a hand in the revival of atomism at the expense of faith should be brought right here before me and skinned alive with this very blunt knife I have in my hand. And then cast before my eyes into the fire, here in this smoldering debris that I may smell the stench of his burning flesh and fat.

My impression is that you should bring all those responsible for worldly greed, misery, negligence, and insensibility from the Muslim community, I say right here, and bring the Quran along with them. Bring in a passage in which the Quran has described the atomic hell. Then hell on that same pattern, to the minutest detail, be prepared. At that point, bring right here every one of those lovers of this world who failed in doing their duty towards humankind by withholding light of the Quran, neither abiding by it themselves nor giving it to anyone else. So that I might see the truth of that Scripture come true with my own eyes, the Scripture that meant to oppose atomic war and to save humankind from every conflagration and to lead the caravan of humanity to their destination in peace and prosperity. As were devoured the bodies of its followers, I have seen the leaves of that same book consumed by the leaping flames of the atomic fire.

Moreover, my impression is that every dared scientist who made the atomic bomb, and every devilish politician who aided and abetted the enterprise, should be brought here and directly before my eyes, speared to death, and flung into this endless sea of seething fumes.

And that helpless man, Yousuf Gabriel, in whose inanimate hands the greatest of Prophetic warnings remained unpublished, bare his back and mercilessly lash him till he breathed his last amidst a raging tempest of jeering hovels.

These are my impressions, gentlemen. And now, please, we will be grateful to you to the deep most nucleus of our heart if you could guide us to some way that we could put this painful existence of ours to an end. O benevolent death, O beneficent death, we call you, pray be so kind as to pay so much as a visit to these sooty shambles here and relieve us from this torture forever."

However, it may be erroneous to assume that the maladies of greed, discontent, and distress were of only recent origin and did not exist in any pre-modern age. Complete contentment of freedom from greed or distress never was the lot of folks since the appearance of humanity on earth. This earth has never been an abode of pure bliss. The very nature of people ingrained the love of wealth and the world. The worry of material needs and the thought of luxury and enjoyment have constantly pestered the human mind. Pain and fear have always been companions of people.

Thousands of years ago, this earth had population scantily, and large tracts of land, pastures, meadows, and jungles lay vacant and unobserved. The worry of material needs and a sense of scarcity, distinction of poverty and luxury did not exist amongst humankind. There was no problem with the population; instead, the increase in population was the aim. There was no shortage of land; instead, men to plow the land wanted, and of course, peace and security to make harvesting possible.

There is a difference between the modern and pre-modern ages. In every pre-modern era, there existed a philosophy of Anti-Materialistic nature in some form or the other. That philosophy constantly reminded men about the transitoriness and treachery of this life as against the eternal life hereafter. That philosophy also preferred spiritual to the material and celestial to the terrestrial. To soften the severity of man's natural greed and excessive desire for worldly things and power, that philosophy of denunciation and self-abnegation always preferred mind to matter, soul to the body, and otherworld to this world.

In contrast, casting away every consideration of death, the otherworld, the Day of Judgment, mind, spirit, morality, and all, this present modern age has headlong plunged itself into materialism entirely and exclusively for the pursuit of the world's material necessities. There is no thought of this world's transient, unreliable, and deceitful nature, its snares, pitfalls, or the Last Judgment of Allah on the Day of Resurrection, which is denied and not dreaded.

For modern societies, the standards of success and failure culminate in death and nothing whatsoever hereafter. People, therefore, have become daring in sin and betrayal. Nothing exists there to have some beneficial effect of bringing much-needed relief from the constant struggle of a purely materialistic type of life. Also, nothing exists to alleviate the pains and sorrows of a materialistic mind except the remedies of material nature, which, instead of affecting the desired relief, further accentuate the disorder and thus aggravate the matter and make things worse. It is just as to add fuel to put the fire out.

In contrast, due to the particular philosophy of world-hatred, belief in the transitory nature of this life, and hope in the life to come, the men of pre-modern ages bore hardships, calamities, and vicissitudes of life with patience and perseverance. A few more days and all this would come to an end, they would think, and another life after this awaits; a life worthy of more significant consideration than this temporary stay here on this earth. They ventured at great sacrifices due to their hope in the reward in a better and reliable world. They did everything with a submissive eagerness and devout acquiescence and thus achieved mitigation of pain and misery.

We shudder at the thought of atrocities perpetrated by those who appeared in long past simple times as tyrants, those clever hypocrites who played upon the simplicity and superstition of the ignorant people and sold falsity in the guise of sainthood. But they, who had suffered on their hands, perhaps had little to complain. Partly because besides the false pretenders of sainthood, there always existed, at least some genuine saints, partly because they thought everything that happened was merely transitory and, therefore, not much important.

But what about our modern world? The false saints of the past have appeared in modern apparel and repeating the same history. At least the crafty priest of the past did not create for his victims something like atomic hell. He did not at least fill the world with atomic radiations: this lurking death; unseen, untouched, untasted, unheard, and un-smelt; and this raging hell of discontent was not so. It never raged with such fury in past ages despite the horrific tyranny of both priest and the prince, besides oppressive needs, and necessities of life.

Now, reform, and not the destruction of that philosophy of the past, is the need of the hour. Let men search for a philosophy that could strike up a balance between extremes. Let the spiritual balance the material. Otherwise, the load thus unbalanced would take humanity down to the bottom of the sea of miseries. Either do this, or people should prepare to live in a world replete with fiery scorpions and stinging snakes and die a death at which the heavens even may shudder.

People today are raving mad after the material world, material progress, material comfort, material safeguards, material remedies in a braying hell of materialism that is raging with unprecedented enthusiasm. They are, under the modern system, compelled to go headlong into material pursuits. They have chained themselves with the chains prepared by themselves and are being dragged on to nuclear hell by a sort of willing helplessness. Nobody can stay out. The dragging column of humanity would crush under the feet, anyone stopping to look behind.

Indeed, everything seems to have left the human mind except a worry about food, clothes, abode, and every material necessity of life. History fails to produce any past age in which people were so hard-pressed by the necessities of life. They have shunned the spiritual in favor of the physical and made material worldly pursuit the object of their lives. They have forsaken faith to achieve this object, severed themselves from Allah, and forgotten everything about death and all that is in the hereafter. They have broken ties with the past for this object and subjected their future to imminent risks and dangers unprecedented in the whole history of human adventure and have sacrificed their very hope in life in Heaven.

Yet the question is that have they achieved their object despite all these unusual and wholesale exertions in search of worldly necessities? The answer after having summed up everything is, unfortunately, "No."

In the modern age of materialism, men of Macaulay's intellect had nothing but unending praises for Francis Bacon, the trumpeter of the modern age and an able advocate of atomism. At that point, after a few pleasant whirls and inebriating swirls on the wheel of the material progress, the speed of the wheel gradually increased to such alarming proportions that tormenting dizziness seized the whirling heads of swirling humanity. At last, their eyeballs startled out of sockets due to extreme effort to keep hold of the flying wheel.

And what is our state of affairs now? We are still hungry. We want clothes, medicines, and all other material necessities of life. We see before us the horror of the atomic monster with its flaming eyes and poisonous breath to devour us all. Devour us all? But in place of what? It is all in response to our request for food to fill our hungry bellies, garments to conceal our shame, medicines to cure our ills, and fees for our school-going children, blah-blah.

We are obliged to present an analogy between this state of humanity today and a stanza written by Percy Bysshe Shelley in 1820. He was not amiss when he drew a picture of the plight of the present-day humankind of this modern age, though without his knowledge, in the following words.

"We look before and after,
And pine for what is not;
Our sincerest laughter with some pain is fraught;

Our sweetest songs are those that tell of saddest thought."

['To a Skylark'; by Percy Bysshe Shelley (1792 – 1822)]

Alas for us! When I recall the state of character of people of Allah in these parts of the world only about a half-century ago, those persons seem to me angels, or at least human beings compared to the prying wolves and cunning foxes of today. These panting, prowling, ravaging, and ransacking wolves in packs are sans thought, regard, peace, humanity, pity, mercy, and charity.

Humankind, in its whole pre-modern history, shunned, hated, and quelled the advancement of science. Right from Socrates, Plato, and Aristotle to every sensible philosopher of the pre-modern age, there has not been one who has not detested the appearance of science. The advancement of science and the thought of material progress on science lines have never been to the liking of humankind in past human history. The things as they stand today, at least, furnish proof of the better judgment of those ignorant people of the past. It is only once in all the human history that is in this modern age that science had a chance to display its worth, that today it has the entire field solely to itself.

However, unfortunately, that which the ancient people had dreaded in science has come true. People indeed have plunged themselves into the material world. It seems as if they are lost forever, and these worldly pursuits have irrevocably taken over them. They have not shown the ability needed to keep things in balance.

The leaders of science and the scientific world have thought of faith as an enemy and, therefore, directed all their endeavors towards eradicating it, little realizing that faith was indispensable to man. Thus, things have reached a stage where we can see them today with horror. Yet, the things are not past cure. There is still only one chance provided that the blindness of humanity does not prevail to the end: a dreadful end indeed.

There is darkness all around. All that light of Adam, Noah, Abraham, Moses, Jesus, and Mohammed (peace be upon them all), has disappeared behind the illusive veil of modern knowledge. This modern-day knowledge constitutes a basket of bread, one dilated, unappeasable belly wrapped up in the dark, lusty, selfish, miserable, and squeamish brain. It is a gastric knowledge related to the stomach only comprising gastric philosophy, thought, attention, and gastric considerations in a gastric world. Its maladies are gastric, its remedies also gastric. Its joys, sorrows, worries, and delights, smiles, grim, and frowns are all gastric. Its problems, like population, are one and all of a gastric nature, and so are the keys, clues, and solutions of a character, basically, gastric.

Besides, the Hydrogen bomb is a scientific remedy for the population's problem. Is it not of a gastric smell and hue? Is not the Hydrogen gas of a gastric origin? Gastric is the light of this age of lights, and so is its darkness of a gastric nature. Is not the problem of population gastric? The problems of the current age are Gastroenteric: its leaders are gastronomes, and its science is gastronomy. Hence, its philosophy ought to bear the name of Gastronomic. In gastronomy, it has its origin, and Gastronomic shall ultimately dissolve it just as water dissolves salt.

Yet, there is still a chance of light in this blinding darkness. Yes, there is still a chance if the people of the present age once again kindle the torch of faith. Recall to your dazed and dizzied mind the part that the Christian training played in the past to bring about the success of the Renaissance of the West and subsequent scientific progress. Without that training, the West could never have achieved the modern scientific enterprise despite the tyrannical priest and the corrupted Church, the dark superstition, and fanatic bigotry.

Indeed, all the pre-requisites of their success: the spirit of contemplative research, the honesty of purpose, faculty of concentration, sense of clean business, patience, perseverance, humility, sympathy, cooperative attitude, acquiescence in mutual coordination, a charitable disposition, humane considerations, and several other traits were bestowed on the people of the West by their religion and were impinged upon their minds during their past ecclesiastical training for many centuries. Without these qualities, their success in their great enterprise would not have been only dubious but uncertain. Do they not see that their movement after reaching a certain pinnacle at dizzying height is now going to tumble them down on the ground? This tumbling will be because people had excluded faith from their affair and that reminiscent features bestowed of their past faith had gradually dwindled and disappeared?

Minute scrutiny reveals some shining features of modern civilization, so much so that its destruction despite such good qualities would be due merely to the lack of faith and incorrigible hard-headedness of some of its guides and leaders. And it seems a real tragedy. It has a thirst for knowledge and an aptitude for discerning the truth regardless of all the weight of authority to the contrary; a scientific method and rational attitude as against legend and myth; a sense of human liberty and fundamental human rights; a clean sense of business and most scrupulous honesty in trade and transaction; a sense of cleanliness, order, justice, sympathy, and punctuality; a constant endeavor to bring about physical comfort and material welfare and a perpetual campaign against poverty, disease, and ignorance; a remarkable quality of patience, perseverance and fortitude and a heartfelt desire for peace, plenty, progress, and prosperity. All these are commendable desires and worthy ambitions, and humane considerations.

However, an exceptionally great and rare virtue is their exercise of sagacity to judge a thing, weigh it, and readily accept the same if found sound and correct, even if not to their inner liking. No less remarkable are their trends against disposition and tyranny and their sense of human equality, equity, and democracy, though there be exceptions everywhere.

Alas! This beautiful civilization is now going. No power beneath this sky can rescue it from utter destruction unless modern civilization removes fundamental flaws and consequent corruption in time. These dominant errors are the habit of slander, backbiting, and the resultant mistrust and distrust, wholesale engrossment in material pursuits, and accumulation of wealth in an atmosphere completely devoid of moral and spiritual values and wealth worship. It is needless to say that people shall become sober and serene if they eliminate faults. Then, the veils of darkness shall automatically be removed from their eyes. And the thoughts of nuclear power will be cast away and forgotten, and people will have more significant consideration of their next life in Heaven and the Day of Judgment. Thus, nuclear energy and its formidable offspring, the atom bomb, will disappear, leaving humankind in eternal peace and safety. Atomic power, which humankind now considers a boon, then will appear as an abomination and monstrosity unbearable.

(5) **THE QURAN SAYS, "HOTAMA IS A FIRE <u>CLOSED IN ON THEM</u>."**

Please bring your imagination into play and enact the scene of an atomic explosion of, say, a twenty-megaton bomb. There is a column ten miles high, three miles across like the central pole of a tent. This column is topped by a mushroom-shaped lid, a hundred miles across. Around this column, imagine a hollow, transparent cylinder eighty miles in diameter, ten miles high, and covered with the hundred miles mushroom-shaped lid of the column. This imaginary enclosure is indeed the effective range of the bomb in question.

The interior of this eighty miles wide cylinder comprises 'Heat-Flash', blast waves interwoven with invisible radiation rays, interspersed with colossal fires and flying incandescent debris amidst shattering buildings, toppling spires of lofty churches, all enveloped in whirling clouds of a stridden smoke and choking fumes, and indeed unwholesome odor of burning bodies of men, women, children, birds, and beasts in an atmosphere of wails unheard, groans un-cared, and cries un-responded in an enclosure eighty miles around and ten miles high.

Nevertheless, the description of the enclosure is not yet complete. There is yet another storey above this awe-inspiring edifice. Raise your head and see the central three miles wide column that has shot upward from the mushroom-lid towards the higher regions above the troposphere into the stratosphere another ten miles. In those regions, the head of the column spreads itself into a thin layer of radioactive fallout driven by the prevailing streams of winds around the earth like satellites for about ten years. This radioactive fallout gradually settles down on the land, contaminating vegetation and water sources, turning human beings into chimeras and monsters begetting monsters. Thus, we see that the 'fire' of 'Hotama' has even enclosed the whole earth.

Also, the atomic explosion starts with 'Heat-Flash' within a fraction of a second, then comes the 'blast', and lastly, the 'ionizing radiations'. All this takes place at the most in ten seconds. The effective range of the explosion may be as far as eighty miles. Who could, therefore, get out of that effective range within a fraction of a second or even ten seconds? Judging from the number of affected persons, which may run into millions, the evacuation of such massive masses of people that might have survived the 'Heat-Flash', the 'blast', and are affected by 'radioactive fallout', seems an impossibility even for the most industrialized countries. To avoid the severe hazard, the people affected by fallout must move to safer places within a day or two. Again, whereto are they to be evacuated? Where is a safer place to be found in case of war? In short, it is a fire closed in on them.

DISTINCTIVE 'ENCOMPASSING' CHARACTERISTICS OF THE NUCLEAR FIRE

The nuclear phenomena show distinctive encompassing characteristics. Also, nuclear fire has encompassing features too as follows.

(a) The atomic bomb explosion assumes the form of an inverted cauldron. Its local fallout forms yet another enclosure around the first. The global fallout of the megaton thermonuclear bomb forms a global enclosure.

(b) The tenacity of bone-seeking radioactive materials is well-known. No procedure or technique can expel the bone-seeking radioactive substances from the bones even after the patient's death.

(c) Cancers have appeared from six to thirty years after the actual radiation exposure. All this time, the radiations have kept the victim encompassed.

(d) Despite the attack of radiations on the cell in its resting stage, the appearance of effect in anaphase is a well-known fact. The radiations attack the cell in its resting stage, but their impact appears only in the anaphase of the cell.

(e) If one organ is irradiated, the radiations encompass the whole body.

(f) Frogs, if lethally irradiated and kept in a dormant state at a low temperature just above freezing point, will, instead of dying in the usual time interval of three to six weeks, survive for many months. However, as soon as the irradiated frogs/animals are warmed up, they begin to show radiation symptoms and die in the same interval (three to six weeks) as those that are warm (not cooled) after irradiation. Radiations have laid a siege to the irradiated animals that are cooled.

(g) The Radiobiologists have sensed this encompassing feature of radiation. A fact proved it. Forty years ago, Alexander Haddow suggested that the cancer-producing action of the cancer-producing substances may result from prolonged interference with average growth. However, it only is a suggestion without scientific proof. Yet, it suggests the suspicion of the Radiobiologist regarding the encompassing trait of radiations.

(h) Radiations encompass humankind, even all species, nay even the plants to generations to their extinction through long term radio-genetic effects. Genes mutated by radiations move secretly from generation to generation till they manifest their existence in some generations in the form of abnormal birth; this abnormality being inheritable increases in kinds and numbers through marriages. This phenomenon of genes' mutations passed on to the next generations applies to every animal and plant species. It means that radiations have kept their siege over them for ages. There is the possibility that radiations might continue their siege to the extinction of all life on earth. Nay, even after radiations have driven life to its colossal grave of earth, they would keep on the encompassment of that enormous tomb, that is this earth, to millions of years indeed, according to the 'half-life' of the wide-spread radioactive substances.

(i) THE SCENE OF THE HELLISH 'ENCOMPASSMENT' OF THIS EARTH BY RADIATIONS IN THE AGE OF FULL-FLEDGED 'ATOMIC ENERGY FOR PEACE'

Just imagine the scene of a world in some future age when every power-house, factory, ship, submarine, railway engine, airplane, bus, even every private car will have its independent reactor. [4] The leakage and the frequent explosions of old reactors worldwide will fill it with radiation. This earth will appear like a colossal globe encompassed by the net of radiations that would continue even when life has been made extinct on earth by the effect of radiations.

This world then, for a period before the extinction of life, will resemble so exactly the atomic hell that no keen-sightedness of a Socrates will be needed to see it so or call it so. Nor is it impossible now, even before the state has in reality appeared, to imagine the actual state that will then be prevailing, naming that state as the atomic hell.

These are some of the facts mentioned above, which indicate the distinct encompassing features of nuclear phenomena. Now, this fire is, 'A fire closed in on them'. The Sahabah that are the companions (disciples) of the Holy Prophet (peace be upon him) said:

"It is a fire, enkindled in a huge edifice with a roof on arched vaults supported by columns of vast extent."

Now, let us see in detail in the light of the practical facts of nuclear phenomena that whether this fire is, 'A fire closed in on them'.

(j) THE HEAT-FLASH

The 'Heat-Flash', already described as initial radiation of atomic explosion, is the radiation that appears within a fraction of a second on detonation. It travels with the speed of light that is 186,000 miles per second. It lasts for only about two seconds or so. It is the only original body of atomic explosion besides nuclear radiation. It begins within a fraction of a second on detonation and, after only two seconds, disappears. However, within these two seconds, it completes its burning of the people's skin in its effective range.

The other effects of the atomic explosion, the 'blast' and the atomic 'radiations', complete their process within ten seconds at the most. The atomic explosion begins within a fraction of a second and is complete within ten seconds. The effective range of the atomic explosion might be as far as eighty miles.

Now, what are the means to carry folks out of the effective range (zone) of the atomic explosion within a fraction of a second or two seconds or ten seconds? No, but the die is cast, and Providence has spun the destiny of unfortunate people within that enclosure. There is no exit in case of the atomic explosion. They are in a pan, a fold, an enclosure, or an inverted huge cauldron; indeed, the 'fire is closed in on them'.

(k) RADIOACTIVE FALLOUT

The story does not come to an end with this eighty miles' enclosure of atomic fire. The area of radioactive fallout is even of a vaster extent. It may be 7000 square miles or 100,000 square miles; nay, even it could be as large as the whole surface of the earth. The March 1956 test explosion (a 15-megaton bomb) resulted in radioactive fallout of 7000 square miles.

Depending on meteorological conditions and particularly the wind velocities, the hazard may cover up to 100,000 square miles.

All the persons in the fallout area must have exposure to a hefty dose of deadly radiation. They must be evacuated to a safer place within a day or so, following detonation, if they are to escape serious consequences, but alas! The evacuation of so large a mass of the population in so short a time is not a probability. It cannot be considered a practical thing even for a highly industrialized country. Further, where would be found a safe area, particularly in case of war, to provide shelter to such a massive mass of evacuated people? Alas! The "fire (of atomic explosion) has been closed in on them". It is a fire so treacherous as to turn back on the house of its master who a few moments ago had unleashed it on his foe, and then after having consumed the home of his enemy, it would turn back on him and reduce his home also to a heap of hot ashes.

(l) 'HOTAMA': A HUGE EDIFICE OF FIRE

The companions of the Holy Prophet (peace be upon him) had described the 'Hotama' as "a fire, enkindled in a huge edifice with a roof on arched vaults supported by columns of vast extent". Like the companions described, the atomic explosion is undoubtedly a massive fire tower with a roof on arched vaults supported by columns of vast extent.

We shall now describe how it happens. Let us take, for example, a nominal high yield fission bomb (surface burst).

Suppose the bomb detonates. See the fireball being in close contact with the earth; it has produced a gigantic crater a mile in diameter. Now, the fireball is rushing upwards, expanding, and cooling. It now has assumed the diameter of three miles, strong upward air currents follow the rapidly rising ball, carrying dust and debris. In a few minutes, the explosion cloud has reached the tropopause at the height of 40 thousand feet. The temperature inversion in the atmosphere has met here, which has considerably slowed down its upward motion. See, the cloud has exactly expanded into a 'mushroom' 100 miles in diameter and placed on top of a stem of diameter like fire-ball (3 miles). The central portion of the cloud (head of the stem) continues to push forward, reaching 80 thousand feet in about 10 minutes. Because of the marked increase in temperature due to height in the higher stratosphere levels, the central portion cannot go beyond 100,000 feet (20 miles). Then, the head of the stem changes into a thin layer by the stream of the prevailing current of air.

This current of the air shall keep this layer of fallout in circulation around the earth for many years, say ten years. During this period, the fallout particles will gradually settle all over the earth; on crops, plants, soil, water sources, etc. This fallout being radioactive will affect everything it will come in contact with and produce terrific results. The cow will eat the crop, you will drink its milk, and the milk is radioactive. The next generation or any other future generation will be born in the form of monsters. The disease of cancer will widely spread. The plight of humanity will then be most miserable. Alas for them.

However, let us revert to our edifice of the atomic bomb.

We have portrayed the picture of the atomic explosion to you. Please bring that picture before the eye of your mind and see a column three miles in diameter, ten miles high, and a mushroom 100 miles in diameter resting on top of it. Since the effective range of such a bomb would be about 40 miles around, imagine a hollow, transparent, cylindrical column 40 miles in diameter, rising upward to meet the lower edge of the 100 miles' mushroom, covering this 40 miles' cylinder like a lid! Itself resting on the central three-mile round column, which stands like the central pole of a tent.

Now, the picture of the atomic edifice is complete, and it is all fire; how majestic, how awe-inspiring. However, just have a peep into the interior of it. O! What havoc fires are playing therein? A storm of fires is raging and consuming everything, and mad earthquakes are furiously pulling down buildings. Men, women, children, and brutes are being roasted alive for the feast of the devil and so on in 'A fire closed in on them'; a fire from which there happens to be no exit, no emergency door.

Nevertheless, our picture of the edifice is not yet complete. Yet, we have not fully described it. Further, this phenomenon has also built an earth-wide edifice. Just look up and see above the mushroom. The upper column of the upper storey of the edifice is resting on the head of the lower central column and rising further ten miles into the stratosphere. There, its head melts into a layer of fallout that keeps on circulating the earth for ten years.

Now, keeping this double-storeyed edifice into view, just see, all over the earth, the atom bombs symmetrically planted and then detonated simultaneously. Explode at once, say 10,000 atom bombs. Watch 10,000 columns rising to the height of ten miles, and there see the mushrooms-like arched vaults resting on top of these 10,000 central columns. And then see, from every column, another column shooting upwards and reaching a height of twenty miles and there spreading itself into a layer of fallout. Then see this fallout spreading and joining in, making a perfect spherical roof above the earth, the whole of it. The picture is now complete.

Just see the 'edifice with its majestic columns', its mighty 'mushroom-arched vaults', and its 'universal roof', and inform the inhabitants of Mars if there be any, of this grand achievement of denizens of the earth. Or if you be as touched at this fate as to cry, then retire to a corner and weep to your heart's content and wonder how the "fire is closed in on them", all of them including yourself, in a universal, worldwide enclosure.

(m) OPERATION ALERT: A MOCK EXERCISE OF NUCLEAR ATTACK

If there is still any doubt about this 'closing-in-on' nature of this fire, we will refer to 'Operation Alert' of the U.S.A. It was a mock exercise of a nuclear attack that proved atomic fire's 'closing-in-on' character beyond any doubt. Read the following.

"It was assumed that 61 cities were struck by 61 bombs varying in size from a Nominal bomb to a five-megaton bomb. The warning time (that is, the advance information of the attack) allowed was about three hours. Based on the data collected by the bomb damage assessment group of the federal civil defense administration, it was estimated that at the end of the first day of the attack, more than 8 million people would have been killed, and another 8 million would have died a few weeks later. About a quarter of the deaths would have been caused by radioactive fallout. It was also estimated that the attack would have damaged more than 11 million dwelling units and rendered about 25 million people homeless. In New York alone, a five-megaton bomb (surface burst) would have killed about 3 million people (38 percent of the population) and injured another 23 percent. Of every 8 New Yorkers, about three were estimated killed and two injured. Civil Defence officials said that the nation was far from being ready to withstand a nuclear attack."

('Operation Alert'; June 15, 1955; the first U.S.A. National-wide civil defense exercise based on a mock attack using nuclear weapons)

Who could withstand the nuclear attack when the 'enkindled fire of Allah' was 'closing in on them'? But, of course, this was a mere mock attack, and unluckily the things in an actual nuclear attack with real atom bombs raining on the heads of blinded people would be not relatively so easy to imagine, and there, neither would be the bomb assessment groups to assess the damages nor the civil defense officials to give their opinions about the readiness of nation.

To this is to be added the following information to understand the international 'closing-in-on-them' character of the nuclear fire. When referring to a full-scale nuclear assault, Lt. General James Gavin (Chief of the U.S.A. Army Research & Development) in his testimony to the U.S.A. Senate Sub-Committee, investigating comparative AirPower, is reported to have said:

"Current planning estimates run on the order of several hundred million deaths that would be either way depending on which way the wind blew. If the wind blew southeast, they would be mostly in the U.S.S.R., although they would extend into the Japanese and perhaps down into the Philippine area. If the wind blew the other way, they would extend well back into western Europe."

Thus, it would mean that no one, friend or foe or neutral, would deem himself safe from the deadly radiological hazard, no matter in which part of the earth one lived. The atomic fire has been 'closed in on them' from every side, and nobody could impose a check on the wind.

(6) **THE QURAN SAYS, "HOTAMA IS A FIRE CLOSED IN ON THEM IN <u>OUTSTRETCHED COLUMNS</u>."**

An 'outstretched column' and the 'mushroom top' are characteristic features of the atomic explosion. One such column, twenty miles high and three miles across, we have already mentioned. Still, the column of water raised in case of a shallow underwater explosion presents the most spectacular view.

(a) **THE 'OUTSTRETCHED COLUMN' OF THE ATOMIC BOMB EXPLOSION**

The 'outstretched column' has become the symbolical representation of the atomic bomb explosion. The 'outstretched column' optically distinguishes the atomic bomb explosion from the conventional bomb explosion. Everybody knows the fact and recognizes it.

(b) **RADIOACTIVE ATOMIC PARTICLES RAISE 'COLUMNS' TOO**

Besides the symbolically distinctive feature of the 'outstretched columns' associated with the atomic bomb explosion, the nuclear phenomena have yet another side in this respect. That is, we may regard the world of radioactivity as a world of 'columns'. It is not only the atomic bomb explosion that raises the 'columns'; the radioactive atomic particles also raise 'columns' by themselves. A single Uranium-235 fission liberates comparatively tremendous energy equal to 200 MeV.

If a copper atom has to traverse a height of one inch only, it has to move a distance equal to 100 million times its diameter. We find that an alpha particle that is much smaller than the copper atom in size and whose radius is of the order of about 1.9×10^{-13} cm can rise to a height from 3 to 7 centimeters. Thus, the particle has traversed a distance equal to millions of millions of times its diameter. The 4 cm rise of the alpha particle will appear as a formidable column if the particle size is seen compared to the height it has assumed. A football rising into the air in the same ratio to its size would move far out into outer space. Gamma rays, despite their extreme smallness, traverse a distance of 200 yards in the air. This ratio is further formidable, rather inexpressibly large. Beta Rays move several yards in the air. The neutron in the process of the fission chain reaction of U-235 has to move a distance more than ten thousand times its size while rising from one nucleus to another, yet the absorbing nucleus checks the neutron; otherwise, it can traverse a greater distance if left to move unchecked.

It means that raising 'columns' is inherent in the norm of the atomic phenomena itself and is not confined to the atomic bomb explosion only. Further, we find the cosmic rays falling in showers on earth from outer space. These cosmic rays present a spectacle of unique 'columns' in showers, having formidable heights that may cause man's imagination to reel. Remember that so fast is the speed of the atomic particles (gamma rays move with the speed of light) that a rising particle would appear like the flash of lightning, although rising like a column. The scientist has not viewed this point from this angle as yet. This point is more critical than the unification of natural forces, perhaps due to its correct direction.

We have sometimes written in this chapter 'columns of vast extent'. This translation does not seem to be the most exact of the word which the Quran uses. The nearer translation might seem to be 'outstretched columns' just as a pot maker draws the clay pot upward while molding on his wheel. The Quran always would use a primary expression and suppose tomorrow it is proved that the phenomenon has built up a column over every little, microscopic nucleon in fission. This column will not be of a vast extent, although we may judge it like that in proportion to the size of the nucleon. These, however, are sheer subtleties.

Let us proceed with our point.

A column is a characteristic feature of an atomic explosion. The terrific fireball rises upward, dragging behind it a column of fission products, vaporized dust, and debris. It is a fascinating scene to behold. Sensations of awe and wonder unite to impart to the spectator's mind who witnesses this enkindled wrath of Allah. Indeed, it is a strange inexpressible feeling. But wow! It is a column of so great a rising, so majestically to such formidable heights. If the reader remembers aright, we have described one such column previously, which could be recalled to mind if desired.

A column is an essential feature of the atomic explosion in air, surface, underground, or underwater burst. However, in the cases of deep underground or deep underwater bursts, it may be muffled up by the enormous weight of earth or water. The shallow underwater burst presents the most spectacular view of the column. Between 1946 and 1958, twenty-three nuclear devices were detonated at Bikini Atoll, beginning with the 'Operation Crossroads' series in the summer of 1946. The Bikini Atoll (1946) test (Baker) was a shallow underwater explosion.

Generally, in the shallow underwater burst, the detonation takes place at a depth of about 50 feet. The first thing seen in 'Baker' was a flash of light, much less luminous than for air burst as the fireball broke through the water surface. A column of water in the form of a hollow cylinder (plume) with a straight stem rushed upwards. In 15 seconds, it was a mile high and attained its maximum height of about a mile and half within a minute; the stem was one-third of a mile in diameter, and the 'mushroom head' about a mile and half across; the water contained in the column was of the order of a million tons.

Due to the explosion force, the water present in the plume was in a state of clear drops and carried the subdivision further as the water column began to fall after it had attained its maximum height. There rolled out a white ring of mist, named 'base surge', at a speed of about fifty miles per hour from the base of the column. This 'base surge' was an unexpected phenomenon. After about three minutes of the explosion, rain began to fall from the bottom of the expanding surge, and soon the outward spreading slowed down and altogether stopped in another two minutes. The base probably covered a total area of more than five square miles. It carried some fission products, but a significant fraction was probably in the mushroom top.

(7) A DESCRIPTION OF THE HELL OF 'HOTAMA' BY THE HOLY PROPHET OF ISLAM (PEACE BE UPON HIM)

The Holy Prophet (peace be upon him) said (Quoted from 'Tafsir al-Jalalayn'):

(a) "Allah will send over the victims, the angels equipped with 'covers of fire', and 'nails of fire', and 'columns of fire'. They will cover the doomed with 'covers of fire', and will transfix them with 'nails of fire', and will 'stretch the columns of fire upward over them'. The entire phenomenon will be made so over airtight that no trace of delight shall enter from outside, nor a trace of agony will escape from inside. Allah will forget them on His throne and will cut them off from His mercy. The inmates of Paradise will begin to enjoy the boons of Allah. The inmates of hell will cease to cry for help, and speech will come to an end. Their speech will then be (as the sound of) inhaling and exhaling".

(b) "The angel gets hold of the victim and, placing him over the knee, breaks him like a wooden stick and then casts him into the fire."

It is hardly possible to find another description of the atomic bomb explosion phenomenon as realistic and exact. The atomic bomb explosion is like a 'cover of fire'; the radiation rays are like the 'nails of fire' which transfix the unfortunate inmates of the atomic hell. The 'columns of fire stretched upward' miles high are the columns of the atomic bomb explosions. Know that these factors will be present in the age of atomic energy for peace, even in the absence of nuclear war and the explosions of atomic bombs. The form, though, of these factors will be different.

(8) THE QURAN SAYS, "WHAT COULD TEACH THEE WHAT 'AL-HOTAMA' IS?"

This question implies the strangeness of the phenomena as well as its terribleness. The Quran, however, proceeds with the description of 'Al-Hotama'. It is a miraculous description. But, just as the Quran has said, the topic is too deep, too high, and far too intricate. Science, philosophy, theology, the Quran, and the Arabic language are necessary to appreciate it fully.

The early commentators of the Quran have said that the questioning mode of the Quran in this question implies indescribable dreadfulness of the phenomena of 'Al-Hotama'.

The terribleness of the atomic bombs and the atomic radiation is no secret. To this may be added the unrevealable and unusual complexity of the subject of nuclear phenomena. Therefore, today every atomist and every Radiobiologist may be put forth the question: "What could teach thee what nuclear science is?"

Indeed, the complexity of nuclear science is so baffling and may remain forever baffling. Moreover, nuclear science knowledge is so scanty that the answer would invariably be as "Nothing". [5]

(9) THE CAUSES OF PUNISHMENT OF 'AL-HOTAMA' ARE THE SAME AS CAUSES OF THE APPEARANCE OF ATOMIC FIRE ON EARTH

The Quran says:

"Woe to every backbiter, defamer, who amasseth wealth (of this world) and arrangeth it (against the future). He thinketh that his wealth will render him immortal. Nay, for verily he will be cast into Al-Hotama."

These are the causes given out by the Quran for the punishment of 'Al-Hotama'. The atomic fire is the production of science whose object has been wealth accumulation and a struggle to remain forever rich, increasing the riches in a systematic, continuous, infinite, and eternal manner with all the interest in this world only. Backbiting and defaming are inherent in the very nature of atomism, which is the philosophy of this age.

Mark the perversion of the critical attitude of the modern rationalism, which anyone could see to border on slander, and that the struggle for the dominion over Mother Nature to obtain material benefits as the object of man's life; it is that has ultimately resulted in the appearance of the atomic fire. Moreover, dreadful enough, the identity between the causes of this transient atomic hell and the eternal 'Hotama' of the next eternal world implies inescapable and eternal punishment in 'Hotama' for those who deserved punishment in this transient atomic hell even if they escaped it for any reason.

(10) THE ATOMIC ENERGY IS THE SCIENTIFIC AND LOGICAL CONSEQUENCE OF THE THREE CAUSES MENTIONED BY THE QURAN

The Quran says:

"He will verily be cast into Al-Hotama."

Just as the three ingredients of gun powder produce the gun powder, the three causes of the atomic fire produce atomic fire. The causes given by the Quran are 'slander', 'wealth accumulation and perpetual struggle in increasing the riches', and a 'belief in the eternity of this process of wealth accumulation'.

(11) THE RECOMMENDATION OF THE ADOPTION OF ATOMIC ENERGY IS UNSCIENTIFIC, ITS ADOPTION DISASTROUS

One can sue the atomist in the court of science for his gross violation of the dictates of science in recommending the adoption of atomic energy. [6] Scientists must not subject any force of Mother Nature to man's service without first achieving control over that force and producing protection against the pernicious effects. Atomic energy has a special place in this respect. It has special insidious hazards that amount to the total extinction of life on earth and untold miseries and unheard-of afflictions. At present, nuclear scientists have very meager knowledge of nuclear science and have little control over it, while the hazards in atomic energy are unique.

Judging from the nature of the subject, it appears that there is little hope for attaining the required knowledge of the subject and obtaining the required control over it. People should judge the question of knowledge because there is no certainty even in the permissible dose of radiation, and it may prove erroneous in the future with catastrophic results. Radiation is harmful in any amount, and the only possible method of protection against it is by entirely and materially covering the source of radiation. The atomic reactors tend to explode and inundate neighboring districts with the flood of radiation, while the states leave people at the mercy of elements.

Scientists have discovered no sure cure for radiation sickness, and none is in view. The genetic effects of radiation are irreparable and irreversible, and nobody can do anything about that most crucial factor. No one can detect mutated genes. No one can do anything after mutated genes manifest their existence with disastrous effects that may end in the extinction of all life on earth.

These and many more facts are known to the scientist, but he appears to treat the adoption of atomic energy as an experiment of 'research-cum-material' benefit. That is, at the same time to conduct the nuclear experiment on 'human guinea pigs' and to avail the material advantage of the atomic energy. This attitude is suicidal in the particular case of atomic energy. No, but the scientists must complete the experiment first in the laboratory, and after that, one should think about adopting atomic energy.

Firstly, proof of safety through experimentation and then adoption is the verdict of science itself. The experiment of atomic energy means the involvement of the entire world in wholesale destruction. Alas, the scientist, like other people of this age of atomistic materialism, is blinded by the influence of three causes of the appearance of atomic hell. Otherwise, the problem is not so difficult to understand.

If, however, humanity will adopt atomic energy for peace or war without first fulfilling the requisite conditions stated above, then no prophet is required to predict the disastrous ruin of this world. This disaster may come either through atomic bombs or the long-term effects of the radiations of nuclear energy for peace in a slow decaying manner.

(12) **THIS PROPHETIC WARNING OF THE QURAN IS A MIRACLE**

Suppose this characterization of the atomic phenomena, the most complex of the natural phenomena, is correct, and it certainly is correct. What reason remains there for a scientist to deny the possibility of a miracle? How could he deny this miracle of the Quran?

Again, if none other than Allah Himself could know the phenomena of the atomic hell at the time of the revelation of the Quran, then indeed no one needed any more irrefutable proof of the Divine Origin of the Quran. This warning of the Quran is a miracle undeniable by the scientist or the philosopher. It is the only light to guide the world out of the atomic pit.

Fourteen centuries ago, a Scripture characterized modern Baconian atomism and nuclear phenomena and inferred the atomic bomb from Baconian atomism. These facts have shattered the notion of science's denial of supernatural and miraculous. Thus, it has left the scientist in a fix regarding his allegiance to the delimiting doctrines of materialistic science.

The future destiny of this world and humankind depends now on this warning of the Quran. It is the only guidance and the only hope, and it is Noah's ark for this atomic deluge of fire and is the Rod of Moses for the magic serpents of this science. It is the extinguisher of the fire of atomic hell and the neutralizer of the atomic bombs. It renders the atomic radiations innocuous by the method of eradication. The thirty-six words of this prophecy of the Quran, which appear in the original text, have taken me volumes to explain. The Quran has left nothing of this Baconian world of atomism in this prophecy. Is not this a miracle, then?

This prophecy of the Quran has furnished irrefutable proof of the Divine Origin of the Quran in history. Praised be the Merciful Allah. Neglect it, and then from this transient replica of 'Hotama' from this world, you go right into the eternal 'Hotama' of the next world; the causes of both are the same. The loss of this transient world is transient but dread the eternal punishment in the next eternal world. I wish you could judge.

(13) **'HOTAMA': THE VIEW OF ATOMIC HELL ENJOYED**

We have brought our discussion of 'Al-Hotama' to an end. We have displayed a corroboration by practical facts of the entire nuclear phenomena and the phenomenon of the nuclear explosion. The whole thing has received a scientific treatment as we promised at the outset and has borne a countenance aptly to be recognized by the scientist. Therefore, let us proceed to celebrate this most outstanding ever achievement of the human mind, this deadliest harbinger of death and wholesale destruction, namely, the 'atom bomb', and enjoy for a while its awe-inspiring flourish proudly.

Please close your eyes and imagine yourself sitting on Mount Everest, the loftiest peak of the tallest mountain on earth. The whole earth is before your eyes, but you are shivering with cold. Yes, indeed, there is much cold over there. However, see the marvel of the mind, the like of which the scientist has not discovered; yes, it is a marvel, this human mind. The lofty peak which Sir John Hunt was only able to conquer after great hardships amongst torturous hosts of blood-sucking leeches and amidst blinding blizzards, and indeed loss of human life, you can feel under your very feet. You can touch the pole of that flag that Colonel Hunt planted there as a victory sign.

Indeed, the great atomists subjected themselves to risks and hazards to conquer the loftiest pinnacle of mount atomism and revive the giant Atumbumb, which lay dormant in his cave 'nuclear energy', snorting. They caged and brought it to the earth as a magnificent piece of the exhibition.

We can sit and close our eyes and imagine a genuine display of unusual feats of our giant Atumbumb. We need not in any way take so much trouble as to travel to the much disturbed and without peace mosquito-infested Bikini Atoll or Marshal Islands in the Pacific Ocean. Please see the imaginary display of nuclear phenomena and then send your report that we may read. In the meantime, we will occupy ourselves with some writing.

Thank you, Sir, we have received your valuable report, and we reproduce the same that others may read. Following is the text of the report.

Wise leaders of all the nations that occupy any part of this earth of Allah agreed unanimously about humankind's instantaneous destruction, which they honestly believed to have outgrown and far too old and overpopulated. It was the right time. These wise leaders reiterated that some new species had a chance to appear and grow. They also agreed unanimously to a suggestion made by a very system-loving member of that grand assembly of nations of the world called UNO that this highly merciful act of destroying this miserable humanity could occur per some pre-planned and well-organized system. The points of this very innovative proposal were as follows.

"Firstly, humanity should be accorded the honor of being dispatched with atom bombs of the choicest kind. Secondly, on a pre-agreed time and point, the atomic bombs should be planted in exact symmetry all over the face of the earth without depriving any part whatsoever of this privilege. Thirdly, the bombs should be exploded simultaneously at the zero-hour as all members agreed on a most democratic basis. Finally, they should well advertise the exact time of explosion lest someone, due to ignorance, remains in some underground cell and miss the unique flavor of the first sparkle of the great 'Heat-Flash'."

There was a rumor that the scheme caused a great commotion in the low animal world, but they decided to completely ignore the objections of such low creatures as stupid beasts. Ten thousand bombs, twenty megatons each, were at once offered by more illustrious powers. Soon they announced three awards for the powers that had donated the highest number of the choicest atom bombs very kindly and were offered atomic wreaths of exquisite beauty for their graves. The bombs were then transported to the appointed places by air in a manner unusually swift and exact contradiction to the general tradition of the wriggling UNO. They planted bombs with a grand ceremony in their proper places like the trees of the legendary Garden of Eden. Engineers now were waiting anxiously for the zero-hour, which at last arrived.

The much eagerly awaited hour arrived at last. Anxious humanity rushed out of homes with shouts of joy and hurrahs. They detonated all the bombs simultaneously. The earth shook, mountains trembled, the remotest heavens echoed the gurgling thunders, and you saw to your amazement 10,000 colossal columns majestically rising in perfect symmetry and with perfect majesty over the entire face of the earth. Then, over-awed by enchanting grandeur of spectacle as in a dream, and to have a better view of the whole scene, you pressed the button and reached Mars along with your observatory, with the speed of light.

Sitting on the planet Mars, you beheld through your telescope, in quite an ecstatic mood, the fascinating scene of beautifully rising columns and their spectacular mushrooms and their delightful colors. You thought that perhaps a world of grandest palaces was in the process of creation for the souls of all the deceased emperors, kings, and lordly princes of the past. Or else, the earth was in the process of transformation into a universal amphitheater to exhibit interplanetary boxing bouts, tiger-man fights, interstellar centenary, and theatrical competitions, or cultural shows.

It seemed all wonderful. Columns develop mushroom tops, mushrooms dilating and uniting like lofty clouds and forming a complete spherical roof over the earth, supported by massive pillars of fascinating hues and colors. Every column rises and a grand palace eighty miles across, rising around it to the ultimate height of ten miles, illuminated with dazzling lights, various degrees, and diverse hues of illumination.

Then to your absolute inward joy and admiration, you saw the commencement of the upper storey. The heads of columns shot upwards and reached a height of twenty miles. At that point, the tops of the columns began to dissolve and spread in glistening sheets of mercuric shades. The sheets gradually kept spreading and joined together to form the roof of the upper storey in a spherical form but visible to you the half of it only in the form of a hemisphere.

Wow! How beautiful is the scene thou spectators on Mars? How fascinating and enchanting, but pray condescend to descend a bit lower and come down to earth. The dazzling lights that thou seest in these princely chambers are the burning pyres of human beings. These majestic edifices which thou thinketh to be the royal palaces are massive, eighty miles across and ten miles high inverted cauldrons, containing fires mingled with human bodies, millions of them; men, women, and children. But sparkling in your view is neither the grand assemblage of royal palaces nor even some great theater.

"It is only the 'Hotama', the atomic hell ablaze and ready to devour a race of backbiters and slanderers that are greedily engaged in gathering the wealth of the world and adoring it to the degree of worship." Yet it is an amphitheater in a way; an amphitheater rose at the Gaza of modernity by the modern Philistines on columns of greed and designed and constructed by modern science. On these columns, brethren! Stands leaning the great 'Atomic Samson' with his hands around these massy pillars watching for the occasion to say to these philistine lords of modern times who have put the nuclear Samson to a display of his strength to peaceful purposes:

"Hitherto Lords, what your command imposed for peaceful enjoyment, I have performed working your nuclear reactors, power-houses, and mighty ships. Now, on my own accord, the other trial I mean to show you of my strength, yet grand as with amaze shall strike all who behold."

Uttering this, straining all his nerves, he would bow as with the force of the wind. He would tug and shake those massy pillars with horrible convulsions to and fro till they would come down and draw the whole sky-high and sky-wide roof after them with a burst of deafening thunder upon the heads of all those who sat beneath: the presidents, prime ministers, scientists, philosophers, priests, and doctors along with earth's inhabitants, turning the whole world into:

"A dungeon horrible, on all sides round,
As one great furnace flamed; yet from those flames
No light; but rather darkness visible
Served only to discover sights of woe,
Regions of sorrow, doleful shades, where peace
And rest can never dwell, hope never comes
That comes to all, but torture without end
Still urges, and a fiery deluge, fed
With ever-burning sulphur unconsumed.
Such place Eternal Justice has prepared

> For those rebellious; here, their prison ordained
> In utter darkness, and their portion set,
> As far removed from God and light of Heaven
> As from the centre thrice to th' utmost pole.
> Oh, how unlike the place from whence they fell!"

(John Milton's description of Hell in the 'Paradise Lost')

And if you think it to be a royal palace, then it is like the palace which a widowed Queen of ancient Egypt had built on the bank of Nile in remote antiquity to avenge herself on the unwearied murderers of her husband. There she invited them to feast and, going out of the hall on some pretext, closed the door from outside and opened the water duct she had pre-arranged. Water rushing into the hall drowned them one and all, and the hall turned into their graves. In the same way, Mother Nature may also avenge those who had murdered her laws and principles.

Science today holds complete sway over all humankind, and the bodies, as well as the minds of humanity, are in its grip. So strong is its hold on human thought these days, and so profoundly set are its roots in the economic fabric of the world of today that it could not be uprooted without at the same time completely upsetting the whole economic structure of the world.

Yet, on the other hand, the unprecedented havoc which the science itself will play with humankind sooner or later, perhaps sooner, is a calamity of nature far worse that amounts to the wholesale destruction of all of the unfortunate race. It has already prepared its hell; that is the atomic hell. This hell is of the worst kind, and it is now in the process of accumulating fuel and awaiting some pretext for enkindling the fire. It is a hell in which people will at once perish, but the survivors may have no joy to live in a world that has witnessed the atomic hell. Poor wretched lepers, these survivors will have a reason to envy the doom of those who perished in that hell and got rid of existence.

However, ask science, and it will tell you the facts and absolve itself from all guilt and instead throw all the blame on your head and quite justly so. It is not the science, but it is you that have been guilty of systematically misapplying and ill-applying it. Science is but a slave. She is there to obey your commands.

You set out to conquer the realm of Mother Nature for the material well-being of humankind in general. Still, you completely forgot the sentimental side of the affair so that material gain only remained the whole purpose of your research and your practical application of science. The Providence, for your neglect of faith and your complete discard of moral and spiritual values and complete disregard of Resurrection and the Day of Judgment, looked askance at you. Your ill luck and misfortune favored your excessive greed. Such channels were by chance opened for you that you found your ultimate goal of the atomic hell before you within a period of the only half-century from 1895 through the discovery of X-rays by Roentgen to 1942 through Fermi's achievement of fission chain reaction.

You adopted wealth as your deity, and you forsook God, the Giver of wealth but your wealth only made the construction of a costly and destructive affair that is 'atom bomb' possible for you. If you sit down and think for a while coolly, you perhaps will realize the truth of these things.

As I have mentioned at the start of this chapter, the late Bertrand Russell, the well-known English philosopher, was utterly disappointed regarding the nuclear issue. The pamphlet of golden hue which he sent me on 21 April-1964 in response to my outcry about the impending atomic danger to slumbering humanity, contained only one sentence, namely:

"Since Adam and Eve ate the apple, man has never refrained from any folly of which he was capable."

The pamphlet in which this verdict of Russell has appeared bears cartoons that show that Russell did understand the cause of the destruction of men, namely, greed and tyranny. Russell, as is well-known, was a grand champion of humanity against the atomic war. But, though his verdict on the end of humankind is a clear-cut one, his endeavor against the fundamental causes of greed lacked the necessary sharpness of a view. His topic was simply hooked under the weight of the overwhelming circumstances prevailing in the world. And his heart might have wept at his helplessness as well as of the world in such circumstances.

This pamphlet contained some very interesting caricatures to constitute the history of humankind. Firstly, it showed Adam and Eve holding one half of the apple each, and there the serpent was seen lurking with its forked tongue above them. Then two towers were shown, on which stood men in a mood of confrontations equipped with arms and weapons of diverse kinds, and below them was shown a man, made into a horse with another man riding him.

Was the sage, then, right in his surmise? Was this world going to end with the atom bomb and the unfortunate humanity certainly destined to perish through atomic conflagration? Was the thing finally settled, and no hope left there? Was the disease past all cures or any hope of a remedy left there? Such were the questions that arose in my mind.

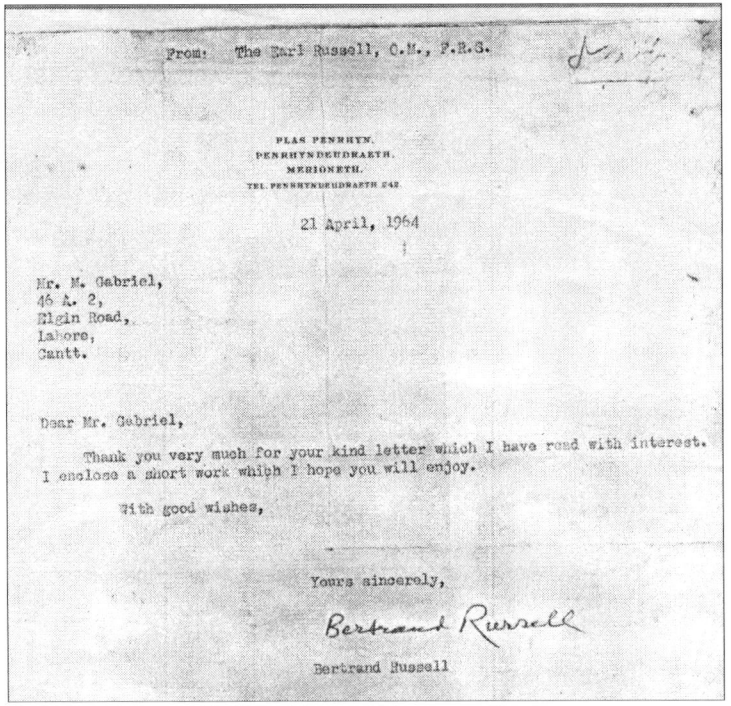

> From: The Earl Russell, O.M., F.R.S.
>
> PLAS PENRHYN,
> PENRHYNDEUDRAETH,
> MERIONETH.
> TEL. PENRHYNDEUDRAETH 242
>
> 21 April, 1964
>
> Mr. M. Gabriel,
> 46 A. 2,
> Elgin Road,
> Lahore,
> Cantt.
>
> Dear Mr. Gabriel,
>
> Thank you very much for your kind letter which I have read with interest. I enclose a short work which I hope you will enjoy.
>
> With good wishes,
>
> Yours sincerely,
>
> Bertrand Russell

Bertrand Russell's letter addressed to the author dated 21 April-1964.

After a lot of thinking, I said to myself: well, humanity might have been doomed to atomic hell. I do not know. Nor is it in my power to stop them from jumping into the pyre if they would so choose. However, the thing which indeed is in my power is to set up a hue and cry. I will cry my throat sore till no more crying is possible like the bereaved parents of Lucy Gray in Wordsworth's poem when they lost all hope in the last terrifying footprint of Lucy in the treacherous snow to show that they had lost the poor child forever.

I will keep on crying till the cruel hand of inevitable death has ultimately closed my eyes. Then no doubt, it is pretty perceptible that a species that would not abstain from the folly of swallowing arsenious pills of deadly poison like Uranium-235 would die despite specific knowledge. Alas, for me! How could they be expected to heed a warning of anyone but ours is to cry. To cry our throat sore, till we can cry no more, just a duty of a fellow human being towards fellow human beings, till death parts us forever. However, this crying might not be as easy as it may seem. They may say they would but use nuclear energy for peaceful purposes and escape its harm. But something alike was said by the infidel son of Noah. In response to the pleas of his father to embark on the boat, he said:

"I will hide myself to the top of these mountains to escape the flood."

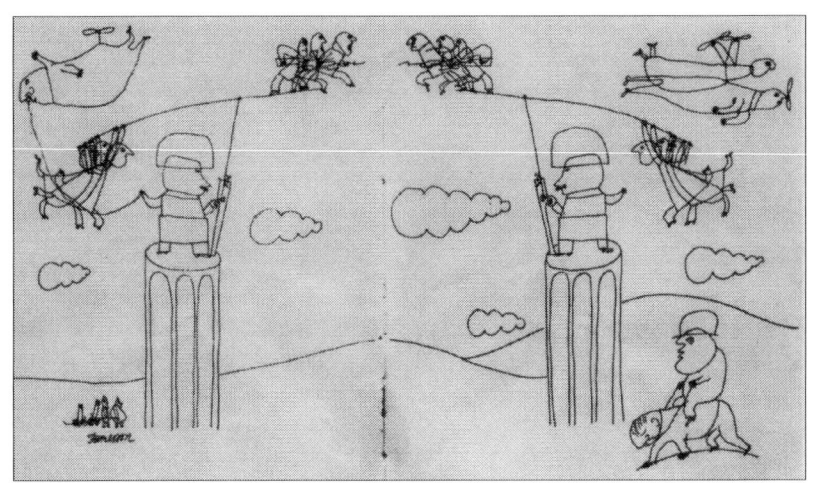

One of the pages of the pamphlet sent by Bertrand Russell to the author.

Nevertheless, that day neither mountain top nor any other safeguard could be of any avail against the wrath of Allah. They also may talk of safeguards against atomic radiations, but what safeguard is there to prove 100 percent effective against the radiations. What if there be even but one percent hazard present? Is not that one percent eventually fatal to humanity? What more could be said in this respect, you greedy seekers of wealth and power? Come on, either forsake this deadly bane of cancers and better let humankind be starved to death if no nuclear power means starvation, or else prepare yourself for the painful end. You will never be left to enjoy the fruits of nuclear energy long. It is for an exceedingly short spell of power that you risk the existence of a miserable race. Nay, the greed for wealth has blinded you that you fail to see a thundering monster greeting a few steps from your door.

Now, pray, seek the light of faith, and sober your maddening passions. Balance your life that contentment may come and open your dazed eyes to the grimmest of facts you now but faintly perceive. Balance your life between spiritual and material, and castaway this venom of nuclear energy from science and put science to the service of humanity. Make your conquest of Mother Nature subject to the Will of Allah. Put your trust in humanity and procure a sense of mutual sympathy. Live and let others live. Do not drag the world of Allah behind you into the atomic hell. Take away from your mind the thought that you will long enjoy nuclear power. Instead, you will soon find yourself under the hail of atomic bombs, but then any thought of repentance will not avail you more than naught. The rabble of this world, the poor and ignorant part of humanity, will soon learn of the havoc this nuclear energy can play with them, and their reaction is inevitable. Then the atomic bombs will not be able to save you from the curse of poor and helpless people that are dragged right from the hell of poverty into the hell of atomism.

This life is much more than most people have come to think of it. It is not merely the question of existence. There is also consideration of another life, everlasting in Heaven and fundamentally dependent on this present life. Let people, therefore, put up an earnest endeavor to better that life after which there is no death and no exit. They who can destroy the world with atomic bombs, if they think that only this is the life we live and die, and there is no more of it, they indeed are the victims of most terrible mistakes. No, but they shall see with their own eyes the Creator seated in His throne to question their deeds on earth, one to all, beginning to end, and moment to moment. Alas then! Alas for them! Poor lost souls. What shall they do to save themselves from the torture of eternal fire? I say, there might not be a Resurrection but suppose it did happen to be there, what then? Do they think their pleasure in this life or afflictions of the believers will make a whit of difference?

Nay, even if the believer lived in troubles for Allah's sake against evil and then suppose if the Resurrection did not occur, will it make a lot of difference to him that he had passed this transitory life of a few decades without ease. However, this is not reality. The believer is the happiest person on earth in that his afflictions transform into inward joy. His hope is his greatest asset. Whereas a non-believer and a skeptic can have no peace of mind, and though it may seem a paradox, yet a fact, it is. A non-believer has no peace of mind, no contentment, no joy of heart, no hope in the hereafter, even if living in palaces of gold in gardens. Let someone have a peep into his inward mind to see hell full of wriggling scorpions in the shape of material luxuries. He has not known the joy of faith, which is a lot of believers only. Peace be with all of you, brethren. Fellow human-beings! Believe me. A believer can create gardens and turn this whole world into a garden of bliss, a genuine material garden, with all these fruit-bearing trees without feeling any necessity for recourse to hateful things like nuclear energy and living miraculously both, within and without the garden.

Nuclear energy is destructive irrespective of its mode of use, whether peaceful and beneficial or war and destruction. If we fail to declare this fact on top of our voice and in extreme earnestness, we may be liable to a charge of gross negligence, namely, willful concealment of facts for personal considerations. Its peaceful endowments are equally hazardous due to its pernicious radiations.

Whether for a powerhouse or an atomic bomb, every nucleon shot in the heart of an atom to generate nuclear energy is like a deadly shaft driven through the heart of people's peace and existence. It is an unfailing harbinger of a cancer-ridden world of imbecile, dull-headed, infirm, and low-browed monsters. Every nuclear reactor or any other atomic plant, even so much as single atomic fission, is a constant source of anguish and suffering. No two things are more unlike each other than atomic energy and peace. If any two things cannot coexist, they are nuclear energy and security.

Our earnest appeal is to let people eat less and curtail material necessities rather than resort to such a dangerous power source as nuclear energy. You may not heed my word now, but your children will be cursing your memory. It is not even impossible that you might yourself be cursing the day, the hour, and the moment when science discovered nuclear energy. If you allow nuclear energy generation to continue, you will have to wipe your hands off your generation. If humanity will not stop nuclear power generation after knowing its hazards, merely because it is an additional power source, humanity has indeed become mad and blind. To allow nuclear energy in some hope of artificial safeguards is as good as to swallow poison owing to an implicit trust in the efficacy of an antidote.

The world shall soon see that their safety measures against nuclear energy will come to naught. Despite most robust safeguards, cancer, leukemia, hemorrhages, unusual and unheard family troubles, unique and grievous domestic afflictions, saddest disruptions of marital fidelity, and remarkable spread of inherited and transferable forms of loathsome monstrosities will become the plague of humanity. You will see all these forms of disorders traced to atomic plants all over the world.

Thoughtful people everywhere have read the tale of wives of certain employees of an atomic plant with concern. These wives, it was told, banished their husbands for fear of getting paralyzed or begetting monsters, following a rumor of leakage of radiations from the atomic plant where their husbands worked. The name of the nuclear processing plant was Windscale (now known as Sellafield) at Whitehaven, England.

Windscale is no longer Windscale, and the Whitehaven has tarnished to Black-Hell due to the presence of an atomic plant in its vicinity. [7]

It is the first page of a lesson that humanity has to learn, or will they take the lesson when the stage of study shall have elapsed. At present, you may treat this story as a joke. However, who knows that very soon, the trail which these scared housewives have blazed may assume a universal character, and the newspapers would not be able to report every instance due to the unimaginable redundancy of cases and scarcity of space. Cruel might have been the deeds of vandals and hooligans of the past. Still, un-proportionally heinous is the cruelty of these kind-hearted and civilized destroyers of humanity in this present age through invisible radiations.

~~*~*~*~*

---

[1] However, the detailed discussion and elaboration on the topic of 'Al-Hotama' will continue in volume-2 with particular reference to the [Nuclear corroboration of 'Al-Hotama' by atomic physics], [The radiobiological corroboration of 'Al-Hotama'], and [Our corroborative comments on the points of the prophecy as explained by the original interpreters of the Quran], etc.

[2] "The Qur'an cannot be translated. … It (translation) can never take the place of the Qur'an in Arabic." Muhammad Marmaduke Pickthall, "The Meanings of the Glorious Qur'an".

[3] It reminds us of John Keats. In this regard, relevant to the author's thought, it will not be out of place; rather, it may be in the reader's interest to quote a stanza from this poet as follows.

> "Fade far away, dissolve, and quite forget
> What thou among the leaves hast never known,
> The weariness, the fever, and the fret
> Here, where men sit and hear each other groan;
> Where palsy shakes a few, sad, last grey hairs,
> Where youth grows pale, and spectre-thin, and dies;
> Where but to think is to be full of sorrow
> And leaden-eyed despairs,
> Where beauty cannot keep her lustrous eyes,
> Or new Love pine at them beyond to-morrow."
> ['Ode to a Nightingale'; by John Keats (1795–1821)]

[4] "True vision requires the forging of a 'farsighted' and 'realistic' connection between our 'present' and our 'future'." Note the 'farsighted' and 'realistic' approach of the true vision of the author displayed before

1982 and relate it with the ongoing research unveiled in 2014 as shown in the following.

[The **high beta fusion reactor** (also known as the 4th generation prototype T4) is a project being developed by a team led by Charles Chase of Lockheed Martin's Skunk Works. In October 2014, Lockheed Martin announced that they will attempt to develop a compact fusion reactor that will fit **on the back of a truck** and produce 100 MW output - enough to power a town of 80,000 people.]

(http://en.wikipedia.org/wiki/High_beta_fusion_reactor)

[5] World-renowned scientist and Nobel Prize winner Max Planck once made a remarkable comment about the structure of matter that has been widely quoted ever since:

"As a man who has devoted his whole life to the most clearheaded science, to the study of matter, I can tell you as a result of my research about the **atoms** this much: There is **no** matter as such! All matter originates and exists only by virtue of a force which brings the particles of an atom to vibration and holds this most minute solar system of the atom together. . . . We must assume behind this force the existence of a conscious and intelligent **Mind**. This **Mind** is the matrix of all matter."

[6] Please read Book-2/volume-7/part-2: [The case of the atomic energy for peace in the Court of 'Lord Justice Science'].

[7] [The Windscale Piles were shut down following a fire in Pile 1 on October 10, 1957, which destroyed the core and released an estimated 750 terabecquerels (20,000 Ci) of radioactive material into the surrounding environment, including Iodine-131, which is taken up in the human body by the thyroid. Consequently, milk and other produce from the surrounding farming areas had to be destroyed.

According to Stephanie Cooke, the British government has been "at pains over the years to play down attempts to correlate cancers with Sellafield radioactivity, particularly when it involves individuals living near the plant but not working at it." In the early 1990s, concern was raised in the U.K. about apparent clusters of Leukaemia near nuclear facilities. Detailed studies carried out by the Committee on Medical Aspects of Radiation in the Environment (COMARE) in 2003 … … … did find an excess of Leukaemia and non-Hodgkin's lymphoma (NHL) near other nuclear installations, including Sellafield, AWE Burghfield, and UKAEA Dounreay. (Wikipedia, the free Encyclopedia)]

~~*~*~*

CHAPTER-4

THE EARLY COMMENTATORS OF THE QURAN AND 'AL-HOTAMA'

The earliest commentators who have quoted the Sahabah [the companion disciples of the Holy Prophet (peace be upon him)] have described 'Al-Hotama' or the 'atomic hell' in the clearest of terms and have left nothing ambiguous. We had at the outset promised that after producing scientific corroboration of this prophecy by the practical evidence of the nuclear phenomena, we would seek the theological proof through the commentaries of these earliest, the most authentic commentators and interpreters of the Quran.

These are all the most authentic resources, but we give a few specimens that will give the reader a glimpse of the following. However, all the commentators had the next eternal atomic hell in the next eternal world in view. We, the unfortunate, are destined to see its worldly replica.

We shall produce quotations mostly that are descriptive. For, such only of the quotations as descriptive norms serve our purpose in this place. Therefore, we have quoted from the most widely acknowledged sources as listed below.

(1) 'Tafsir Abdullah Ibn-Abbas' (619-687).
(2) 'Tafsir al-Tabari' by 'Abu Jafar Muhammad Ibn-Jarir al-Tabari' (840-923).
(3) 'Tafsir al-Kabir' by 'Imam Fakhr-ud-Din Razi' (1149-1209).
(4) 'Tafsir al-Quran al-Azim (Tafsir Ibn-Kathir)' by 'Ismail Ibn-Kathir' (1301-1373).
(5) 'Tafsir al-Jalalayn' (1460-1505).

NOTE: All these commentators had in their mind the 'Hotama' in the next eternal world; hence there is no question of the death of the agonized heart.

(1) QUOTATIONS FROM 'TAFSIR ABDULLAH IBN-ABBAS'

Quran: 'Wail'.
(English translation is: 'woe'.)
Commentator: ["It implies extreme severity of torment. It means a pit, dungeon, or a cell in hell. Moreover, it also means a valley of pus and suppuration."]

Now, see if the torment and suffering brought by the atomic explosion to its victims are less severe in any way or of a different kind. Then see if the effective range of an atomic explosion is not like a pit, a dungeon, or a cell in hell? To understand this point perfectly, bring to your view a hollow cylindrical or semi-spherical range of the atomic explosion. Is not it a pit, a dungeon, or a cell in hell?

Again, see the symptoms of 'Heat-Flash' burns caused by other raging fires caused through convection after the atomic explosion and consuming entire cities. Also, imagine the symptoms of radiation sickness like leukemia, hemorrhages, nausea, vomiting, severe heart-burning, etc., in a post-atomic assault area and bring these symptoms in view against the interpretation viz. "A valley of pus and suppuration", and then see if the after-scene of an atomic explosion is not exactly "A valley of pus and suppuration". Just imagine millions of ailing bodies, burnt and bleeding, secreting pus, and exerting streams of contaminated blood, and disgorging vomit.

Quran: 'Naarullah-il-Muqadah'.
(English translation is: 'Fire of Allah kindled'.)
Commentator: ["It is a fire which eats up the whole of the body, till it reacheth the heart."]

Now, recall to your mind the effects of ionizing radiations of the atomic explosion and remember how these radiations gradually eat up the flesh of the whole body by stopping blood supplies of the body and eventually mounting above the 'heart' and killing it.

However, let this point be borne in mind that because these commentators had the next eternal world in view when commenting on 'Hotama', therefore, the heart in their commentaries must forever live and suffer agony without the relief brought about by death. Nevertheless, our subject represents the atomic hell on the transitory earth; therefore, the victim can succumb to the agony and die. Yet indeed, they who will deserve shall be cast into the eternal 'Hotama' in the next world: the heart there to suffer eternally, without experiencing death.

Quran: 'Musadah-Fi-Amad-im Mumaddadah'.
(English translation is: 'closed in on them in outstretched columns'.)
Commentator: ["Columns of fire having considerable depth."]
Quran: 'Homaza' and 'Lomaza'.
(English translation is: 'backbiter' and 'slanderer'.)
Commentator: ['Homaza' is a backbiter while 'Lomaza' is a slanderer to one's face.]

(2) QUOTATIONS FROM 'TAFSIR AL-TABARI'
Quran: 'Innaha-Alaihim-Musadah'.

(English translation is: 'It is a fire closed in on them'.)

Commentator: ["There is going to be a man in one of the departments of hell, crying perpetually for a thousand years, "O Benign Allah, O Merciful Allah!". Allah (out of Mercy) will command the angel, Gabriel, "Go, and take my servant out of the fire." Gabriel (in obedience to the command of Allah) will go but, finding the fire closed in on them, will return and say, "O Allah! The fire is closed in on them." Allah will say, "Go and open it, and take my servant out of it." The man will thus be taken out of the fire and placed outside the Paradise till Allah will cause his **hair, flesh,** and **blood** to re-appear."]

It would mean that:
(a) The fire of hell caused the **hair** of that man to fall.
(b) The fire of hell had eaten up his **flesh**.
(c) The fire of hell had dried up the springs of his **blood**.

All three conditions are identical to the case that of atomic radiations. The atomic radiations affect their victim's **hair** so much that a white patch of hair appeared amidst the jet-black hair of a little girl affected by radiations in one of the neighboring Islands of the atomic explosion test site in the Pacific Ocean. This particular patch of hair was the target of the attack of radiations and appeared like the white bull-eye. The fire of hell had eaten up the **flesh** of the radiation victims, and the **blood** springs were dried up, as the experience has explicitly proved. [1]

Quran: 'Innaha-Alaihim-Musadah-Fi-Amad-im-Mumaddadah'.
(English translation is: 'It is a fire closed in on them in outstretched columns'.)

Commentator: ["The victims are first to be put in the cylinders, and the cylinders are then to be stretched upwards."]

Now, recall to your mind the actual scene of detonation and the explosion and the subsequent gradual upward trend of the column of the atomic explosion being stretched upwards after detonation. Before the detonation, the victims are put within the area of the effective range of the explosion. Then the detonation takes place. Then the column is gradually drawn upwards to its maximum height, and the scene is complete.

Quran: 'Amad-im-Mumaddadah'.
(English translation is: 'The outstretched columns'.)

Commentator: ["They are going to be columns of fire of vast extent." Qatadah [a close companion (disciple) of the Holy Prophet (peace be upon him)] is quoted to have said, "We {the companions of the Holy Prophet (peace be upon him)} used to discuss 'Hotama' and express the opinion that they are to be columns through which the victims were to be tortured with 'fire'."]

The experience shows that the atomic explosions are columns of 'fire' and are of vast extent, and the victims are tortured through them by 'fire'.

(3) QUOTATIONS FROM 'TAFSIR AL-KABIR'

Quran: 'Al-Hotama'.

Commentator: (a) ["('Al-Hotama' is) A fire which 'grinds to powder' whatever is cast therein; a fire which crushes 'bones' and eats up 'flesh', till at last, it attacks the 'heart'."]

See that the 'bones' are crushed, and atomic radiations eat up the flesh; the 'heart' is finally attacked. It is no hidden secret now that the atomic explosion, due to its intensity of the flame and blast, 'pulverizes everything to powder' within its effective range. The fire that crushes the bones is the atomic radiation nicknamed by the scientist as 'bone-seekers' because they first attack the bones and eat up the bone marrow. Then, they render the bone marrow incapable of producing blood. Bone marrow's primary function is producing blood.

Then they attack the blood, destroy its red and white corpuscles, and render it incapable of nourishing the body. Thus, blood supply has been stopped, the 'flesh' is eaten up, and the victim has been left a mere skeleton. Thus eventually, they mount above the 'heart'. This great commentator of the Quran has, in this context, raised some extremely subtle points which he has beautifully discussed. These commentaries excite wonder.

Commentator: (b) ["...then imagine its (heart's) plight of hellfire be plunged into it (yet the strange fact is) that although the fire of hell of 'Al-Hotama' has completely overwhelmed it, yet it is not consumed thereby."]

We have seen that although it burns its victims' skin, the 'Heat-Flash' burns neither the body nor the heart.

RESEMBLANCE BETWEEN THE FUNCTION OF 'BACKBITING' AND 'HOTAMA'

Commentator: ["The backbiter eats (metaphorically) the flesh of the person whom he backbites. The fire of 'Hotama' also eats up the skin and the flesh of its victim."]

Therein is to be found an actual correspondence between the sin and the punishment. Therein also is a point to provoke our thought. Don't you see how appropriate is the link between the particular characteristics of the people of this modern age and the characteristics of nuclear energy? We have described these characteristics more than once, and perhaps the reader might have memorized them by now. For example, a point in this commentary about the eating up of the skin by 'Al-Hotama' describes a very particular fact: the 'Heat-Flash' burns the skin, and the festering skin is eaten up. A very peculiar character indeed of 'Heat-Flash', to wit:

"It never penetrates beneath the skin and burns the skin only."
These commentaries are simply outstanding.

Commentator: ["The fire enters at the sides, and afterward it reaches the breast, and at last enters the 'heart'."]

It is well-known that the 'Heat-Flash' of the atomic explosion strikes the body at the sides, the side which happens to be towards the coming 'Heat-Flash'. Then it enters the breast through the lungs and lastly affects the 'heart'. The atomic radiations adopt the same way and enter the bloodstream through that side of the body that confronts them. Then through the blood, they make their way towards the breast and the heart.

Commentator: ["The heart is an organ most sensitive of all the organs of the body. It is thus most sensitive to anguish. There is not one organ in the whole of the body which reacts to agony with such acute sensitivity. It even reacts to the least amount of anguish with great sensitivity. Then imagine its plight if hellfire is plunged into it. Yet (the strange fact is) that although the fire of hell of 'Al-Hotama' has completely overwhelmed it, yet it is not consumed thereby. For, had it been consumed (by the fire), it must have died (and hence become insensible to anguish). It would rather remain in a state which neither is death nor is yet living. The phrase, 'a fire which mounts above the hearts', means it descends into the 'heart' via the flesh. The selection of heart for this punishment is made due to its great sensibility. Also, that it is this organ that is the heart which happens to be the seat of disbelief and other untoward and heretical views."]

Says this great commentator, "The heart, despite the fire having overwhelmed it completely, is not yet burnt by fire". This fact is most conspicuous in the action of 'Heat-Flash' that is the atomic fire. Even though 'Heat-Flash' has wholly overwhelmed it and would kill the heart on the spot, yet it has not burnt it at all.

Now, the difference between the atomic hell of the next world and this present world is that, whereas in the next world, there shall be no death for the heart, in this world, it may die. Otherwise, all the remaining peculiarities are identical. Mark the method of analysis undertaken by this worthy commentator. Also, note his scientific, rational, and philosophical approach. But the real greatness of his interpretation lay in the fact that all his views emanated directly from the theological tradition and were precisely the reflection thereof and in no way overlapping, exceeding, protruding, or contradicting the source.

(4) QUOTATION FROM 'TAFSIR AL-QURAN AL-AZIM' (TAFSIR IBN-KATHIR)

Quran: 'Amad-im-Mumaddadah'.
(English translation is: 'Outstretched columns'.)
Commentator: ["Some said these columns are to be of iron. The others thought that they were to be of fire."]

The majority have been on the latter side. These columns were to be of fire. But the former opinion regarding the iron structure of the columns, we could well apply to other bombs of the conventional type. They are columns of iron filled with fire in the form of dynamite, etc. Incendiary bombs even provide a still closer resemblance.

(5) QUOTATIONS FROM 'TAFSIR AL-JALALAYN'

Quran: 'Naarullah-il-Muqadah'.
(English translation is: 'Fire of Allah kindled'.)
Commentator: ["A fire which is never extinguished."]

Now, recall to your mind that the atomic device, once detonated, can never be extinguished until it has completed its whole process that of 'Heat-Flash', 'blast', and 'radiation emission' (ionizing radiations) as already mentioned in previous pages of this book. The process of atomic explosion takes but at the most ten seconds for its completion. The other fires that are started afterward through convection may rage for a considerable time. Still, they are not the subject because they are not an original part of the atomic explosion. However, the thought of the worthy commentator was fixed on the 'Hotama' in the next eternal world so that the 'Hotama' there must remain ablaze forever. We were to be the unfortunate people to witness its representation on earth.

Quran: 'Innaha-Alaihim-Musadah-Fi-Amadim Mumaddadah'.
(English translation is: 'A fire closed in on them in outstretched columns'.).
Commentator: (a) ["The fire is going to be enkindled in cylindrical columns. The victims having been put therein, the cylinders are to be closed."]

Read this and recall to your mind the process of atomic explosion from detonation to complete development to the mushroom top. Now, this is the exact picture of the atomic explosion. The victims are, in reality, put in the 80 miles hollow cylinder, which is afterward closed by the mushroom lid. Such commentaries are excellent.

Commentator: (b) ["Al-Hotama is a fire which is never extinguished."]

The worthy commentator here had in view the atomic hell in the next world. Yet, the fire of atomic explosion in this world is also a fire that characteristically no one can extinguish until it has completed the whole explosion process. Once an atom bomb detonates, its action will only cease after the 'Heat-Flash' has appeared, the 'blast' has taken place, and the 'ionizing radiations' have liberated. All this might take about ten seconds. However, this is a transient world. Its atomic hell should also show this characteristic against the next eternal world wherein the atomic hell shall forever and incessantly burn.

(6) THE QUOTATIONS ATTRIBUTED TO THE PERSON OF THE HOLY PROPHET (PEACE BE UPON HIM) HIMSELF

(a) "Allah will send over the victims, angels equipped with 'covers of fire', and 'nails of fire', and 'columns of fire'. They will cover the doomed with 'covers of fire', and will transfix them with 'nails of fire', and will 'stretch the columns of fire upward over them'. The entire phenomenon will be made so over airtight that no trace of delight shall enter from outside, nor a trace of agony will escape from inside. Allah will forget them on His throne and will cut them off from His Mercy. The inmates of Paradise will begin to enjoy the boons of Allah. The inmates of hell will cease to cry for help, and speech will come to an end. Their speech will then be (as the sound of) inhaling and exhaling".

(Quoted from 'Tafsir al-Jalalayn')

It seems impossible to find another description of the atomic explosion more characteristic with its various characteristics and constituents more precisely than this description. The effective range of an atomic explosion is correctly like an inverted cauldron of fire; it is accurately a 'cover of fire'. The rays of ionizing radiations are alpha, beta, gamma rays, and neutrons. They are best described as 'nails of fire' transfixed, and they pierce through the body of their victims and pin them down so that they cannot escape from the field until the process of the atomic phenomena is complete. These 'stretching upward of the columns' raised by the fire-balls of atomic explosion we have more than once explained and by now in the light of practical experience the fact remains no longer a mystery to the whole vast humankind over the earth.

(b) "The angel gets hold of the victim and placing him over the knee, breaks him like a wooden stick, and then casts him into the fire."

(Quoted from 'Tafsir al-Jalalayn')

The angel placing the culprit on the knee and breaking him like a stick of wood may be compared to the 'blast' effect of the atomic bomb. To understand the thing perfectly, we first must understand the method of destruction by the 'blast'. The first effect of a blast wave on a structure is that of a gigantic hammer blow. The shock front of the blast wave reaches the rear end of the structure. Now, the structure is surrounded by the wave entirely, and the effect of blast pressure is to squeeze or crush the structure.

Let this process be carefully understood to corroborate it by the process of "placing him over the knee" and "breaking him like a wooden stick". The shock wave would place a structure between its two knees and then squeeze or crush it to pieces. The duration of the blast of a nominal atom bomb is of the order of one second, more than a hundred times what it is for a conventional bomb, while the positive pressure phase for a 20-megaton bomb is about 10 seconds. What will this monster not do with the structure in such a prolonged duration and so strong a blast?

Interestingly, the blast of a smaller bomb of nominal size will not break the person's backbone. A person's body is remarkably resistant to damage by the blast wave in the air, but more giant atom bombs by the mere blast of, say, peak pressure of the order of 200-250 lb./in^2 would cause general bodily damage of a severe kind. Hemorrhage is caused in the lungs and other places where tissue has an internal boundary surface with an air or gas cavity and eardrums burst. Victim copiously bleeds through throat and nose and bleeds within because the whole body internally has been crushed and broken.

Yet, the angels are not to be confused and confounded with the laws of Mother Nature. Angels are a separate species of rational thinking beings. In contrast, the laws of Mother Nature and natural forces are mute and work only under the control and command of the Creator, without free will to think or act.

~~*~*~*~*

[1] [EFFECTS OF RADIATIONS ON THE HUMAN BODY

(a) **Hair**: The losing of hair quickly and in clumps occurs with radiation exposure at 200 rems or higher.

(b) **Brain**: Since brain cells do not reproduce, they won't be damaged directly unless the exposure is 5,000 rems or greater. Like the heart, radiation kills nerve cells and small blood vessels, and can cause seizures and immediate death.

(c) **Thyroid**: The certain body parts are more specifically affected by exposure to different types of radiation sources. The thyroid gland is susceptible to radioactive iodine. In sufficient amounts, radioactive iodine can destroy all or part of the thyroid. By taking potassium iodide, one can reduce the effects of exposure.

(d) **Blood System**: When a person is exposed to around 100 rems, the blood's lymphocyte cell count will be reduced, leaving the victim more susceptible to infection. This is often referred to as mild radiation sickness. Early symptoms of radiation sickness mimic those of flu and may go unnoticed unless a blood count is done. According to data from Hiroshima and Nagasaki, show that symptoms may persist for up to 10 years and may also have an increased long-term risk for leukaemia and lymphoma.

(e) **Heart**: Intense exposure to radioactive material at 1,000 to 5,000 rems would do immediate damage to small blood vessels and probably cause heart failure and death directly.

(f) **Gastrointestinal Tract**: Radiation damage to the intestinal tract lining will cause nausea, bloody vomiting, and diarrhea. This occurs when the victim's exposure is 200 rems or more. The radiation will begin to destroy the cells in the body that divide rapidly. These including blood, GI tract, reproductive, and hair cells, and harm their DNA and RNA of surviving cells.

(g) **Reproductive Tract**: Because reproductive tract cells divide rapidly, these areas of the body can be damaged at rem levels as low as 200. Long-term, some radiation sickness victims will become sterile. {Unit of radiation is the rem, or roentgen equivalent in man.}

{(www.atomicarchive.com) with permission from, and special thanks to Chris Griffith}]

~~*~*~*

CHAPTER-5

THE PROMINENT POINTS OF THE PROPHETIC WARNING OF THE QURAN

In 1964, Sir Steven Runciman, the famous historian of the Byzantine Empire, delivered my letter to Late Bertrand Russell. The reply came. Besides acknowledging my letter, the envelope contained a small golden pamphlet containing only one sentence and three caricatures. As mentioned in earlier chapters, the sentence was the final verdict of Russell on humankind, stooped in utter disappointment. The caricatures depicted the whole and the sole source of man's trouble. This sentence implied manifest absolute disappointment about the end of humankind. The sentence read as follows.

"Since Adam and Eve ate the apple, man has never refrained from any folly of which he was capable."

Thus, war and mutual tyranny of men were the whole trouble of humankind. The same is the surmise of every philosopher and every scientist of this age. They think that if they avoid wars, everything would be okay, and humankind could safely enjoy the fruits of this progress. How cursory is thus their rendering of the trouble? Their sight touches merely the outer crest of the matter. Here then, we see the difference between the ken of mortals and the supernatural intelligence of the revealed Scripture. The entire crowd of the philosophical prodigies and celebrities of this age touches only the outer crust, yet both the actual cause and the effect are before their eyes.

However, fourteen centuries ago, when neither a trace of the actual cause nor a sign of the final effect was there, the Quran reached the heart of the matter and gave the exact cause and the particular effect. Read the following Prophetic warning of the Quran about the atomic hell and then realize that it has been impossible for the sages of this age to know the true nature of the Baconian philosophy and its progress before reading the word of the Quran about it.

The Quran says:

"Woe to every backbiter, defamer, who amasseth wealth (of this world) and arrangeth it (against the future). He thinketh that his wealth will render him immortal. Nay, for verily, he will be cast into the crusher ('Hotama') and what could teach thee, what the crusher ('Hotama') is? It is enkindled fire of Allah, which reaches unto the hearts. It is (a fire) closed in on them in outstretched columns."

(Quran 'Al-Homaza' 104:1-9)

Russell died in disappointment. So, would I. However, because I discovered this warning of the Quran, humankind could avoid atomic annihilation by removing the causes of the nuclear threat, which the Quran has given in such a clear, manifest way.

Let us compare the view of the modern intelligentsia with that of the Quran. According to modernists, the whole trouble is the belligerent spirit of man. If war were banned, the situation would be safe, and they could enjoy the fruits of progress. The Quran has gone deeper. It has mentioned the causes such as 'slander', 'engrossment in wealth accumulation', and a 'belief in the eternity of the wealth-increasing' progress. War only is the result thereof and a means of the use of the atomic bomb and radiation.

The modern wise men are pre-possessed with the idea of atomic war. They have utterly and entirely ignored the other side: the hazards of the atomic energy for peace and its root, the Baconian progress. This thought is a confusing one. They seem to keep the root and think to avoid the fruit. Quran has outright condemned: the 'root' that is the greed of wealth, the 'stem' that is this systematic progress, and its 'fruit' that is the atomic bomb as destructive. If, however, the wise men of this age are inwardly disappointed, then here is a hope that the Merciful Creator has kindly given man as trustworthy guidance.

A few years ago, the world was thrilled by the news of some Biblical literature found in some urns in a cave. Here is a discovery from the Quran that had stayed concealed from the eyes of humanity for fourteen hundred years, something like in an urn in a cave. This discovery is of a nature that the thrill itself would be thrilled by it. It has the light and guidance for the doomed humankind. Such light and guidance can lead humankind out of the danger of atomic conflagration toward peace, safety, and prosperity.

It is the first time in modern history that the true nature of the Baconian atomism and this Baconian progress has been revealed. Thus, all the confounding maze of universal misunderstandings about this Baconian culture has been cleared. Baconian atomism, its progress, and the achievements of modern science have been condemned due to their attached association with engrossment in pursuit of wealth acquisition. In this particular Baconian progress, humanity could not stop this quest of wealth accumulation anywhere to infinity. More, and more production is the universal cry of this age as the only remedy for present-day ills, like adding fuel to the furnace to extinguish it. The remedy rather lies in reverting to the philosophy of self-abnegation and otherworldliness.

There is no movement in this world against the atomic phenomena or the atomic bomb at present. However, if any such movement ever starts, no one can guarantee success without considering the guidelines and basic principles furnished by this warning of the Quran. Also, no attempt and endeavor will prove much fruitful in the revival of the renaissance of religion without first understanding this warning and practically adopting its guidelines. In the presence of this Baconian progress, religion has no hope of its establishment or promulgation. The revival of religion has to follow the destruction of this Baconian progress. The Islamic countries will, in time, realize the truth of this condition. Let the weary pilot bale out of this plane before it has caught fire and exploded. Have not the appeals of all celebrities failed against the atomic bombs?

Quran characterized, most precisely, the Baconian progress of modern atomism fourteen centuries ago. At that time, neither a trace of ancient Greek atomism existed, nor it would have been possible for anyone to predict its revival in any future age. It described and characterized most scientifically the atomic phenomena, giving those characteristics which distinguish it from any other phenomena, the chemical, the electrical, and gravitational. It portrayed the nuclear bomb explosion, furnished so phonetically and functionally identical name as 'Hotamic' to the 'Atomic' phenomena. It inferred from the Baconian progress the resultant appearance of nuclear bombs and atomic radiations. This accomplishment is something not within reach of a Plato or an Aristotle. These facts render the whole affair undeniably miraculous and are far beyond the ken of the human mind.

Yet the point I must lay the tremendous stress is that this atomic hell of this transient world is only the transient replica, the mere representation of that eternal atomic hell ('Hotama') of the next eternal world in the eternal life hereafter. However, the causes of the appearance of this transient atomic hell of this world and evils which, according to the Quran, render anyone liable to punishment in the eternal 'Hotama' of next never-ending world are identical. This fact is worth considering. Therefore, even if they escaped this transient threat of the transient atomic hell, those deserving will not avoid the threat of the eternal 'Hotama' of the next eternal world. This warning sounds dreadful.

This warning of the Quran is the only hope of this world. I do not know, what would have been the practical attitude of Russell and Einstein towards this warning of the Quran, but what I know for sure is that they could not have doubted or denied its marvelous truth. For, none could deny the scientific facts and the irrefutable logical argument. Indeed, it is the design of Noah's ark for this fiery deluge of atomism, and the doomed only would refuse to embark it. One blast of the atomic bomb or one attack of radiation sickness will clear the sight of this age, but the repentance then might prove futile. So also, it is the rod of Moses for the serpents of the magicians of this modern science.

Do you think that the atomic bombs will forever deter war? Will more nuclear bombs command greater force? Should every country have atomic bombs for defense? Suppose your answer is 'yes'. Then it is a logic that presages sheer madness and is a sure indication of mental bankruptcy in this Baconian age.

~~*~*~*~*

CHAPTER-6

THE EFFICACY OF THE WARNING OF THE QURAN ABOUT THE ATOMIC HELL

Iqbal wondered when he first observed in Europe the libraries bestrewn with the books written by the ancestors of the Muslims and there in his poem of lament; he quoted the verse of Ghani Kashmiri, a notable saint-poet of Kashmir:

"Behold, O Ghani! The dark misfortune of Jacob that the light of his eyes doth illuminate the eye of Dhulaikha."

I observed the same or nearly similar experience in reading the commentaries of the early authentic commentators of the Quran: like Abdullah Ibn-Abbas, al-Jalalayn (Jalal al-Din al-Mahalli and his pupil Jalal al-Din al-Suyuti), Abu Jafar Muhammad Ibn-Jarir al-Tabari, Imam Fakhr-ud-Din Razi, and Ibn-Kathir, may Allah be pleased with them all. In that, I perceived with wonder and delight that their explanations about the fire of 'Al-Hotama' could have provided food for thought to modern thinkers. Moreover, those interpretations would have guided the nuclear scientists or at least would have warned them of the peculiar terribleness of the atomic phenomena and the causes of its creation.

These commentators have not only discerned the peculiarly distinctive characteristics of the fire of 'Hotama' but also have made remarks that would be the wonder of every nuclear scientist. Thus, for instance, Imam Fakhr-ud-Din Razi says:

"The fire of 'Hotama' though it overwhelms the heart of its victim, yet it burns not the heart, for the burning of the heart implied death and death was not in the next world."

We cannot expect yet another better description of the fire of 'Hotama' and the fire of this atomic hell with the difference that the fire of this present atomic hell can kill the heart though it does not burn it. This fire is only the replica and a temporal and transient representation of the eternal 'Hotama' of the next world wherein there is no death. We may quote the example of the 'Heat-Flash' of the atomic bomb, which does not burn the heart though it overwhelms it. However, the early commentators thought of the next world only since hell is always associated with the next world.

An excellent point appears from these commentators' commentaries. The companions of the Holy Prophet (peace be upon him) had discerned the distinctive character of the fire of 'Hotama' that distinguished it from the ordinary fire. Therefore, they held discussions about the characteristics of the fire of 'Hotama' and the strange modes of punishment in 'outstretched columns' to show that the fire of 'Hotama' topic permitted discussion and investigation.

Again, the unanimous definition of the fire of 'Hotama' given by the commentators is amazingly characteristic, namely, "The fire of 'Hotama' is a fire in which whatever is cast, is ground to powder by the intensity of the heat."

This definition reminds me of a debate with Ms. Annemarie Schimmel, a German scholar of great scholarly renown. The impression of the rapidity with which she shot back this definition at me in her reply to my question years ago is still fresh in my mind. It is impossible that this Prophetic warning of the Quran about 'Hotama' should fail to impress the scientist and the non-scientist due to its miraculous features.

In 1963, the month of September, I witnessed the efficacy of this warning of the Quran. Ms. Annemarie Schimmel, a famous German scholar, delivered some lectures at the 'University of the Punjab', Lahore (Pakistan) to prove that the Quran was not the word of Allah Himself but rather the Holy Prophet of Islam (peace be upon him) was the author thereof. She was dumbstruck and indisposed when I pointed out to her this warning of the Quran and briefly explained it to her as the sure proof of the Quran's being the word of Allah only and no one else.

I visited Lahore (Pakistan) in September 1963, where I met Late Allamah Alla-ud-din Siddiqui, the then Head of the Department of Islamiat of the 'University of the Punjab'. He afterward became the vice-chancellor of the same university. He wept when he saw me. A German lady scholar, he complained to me, had flouted their beards. He told me further that she had delivered six lectures at the 'University of the Punjab' and was supposed to deliver her last seventh on Wednesday from three to five. She denied the Quran's Divine Origin and thought that the Holy Prophet (peace be upon him) was, in fact, the writer of the Holy Quran. Then he said, pointing to me, perhaps you have been fetched by Allah for this purpose, that of saving the honor of the Quran. I invite you to the lecture. Pray do come. I heard Allamah, and I thought:

"To deny Quran its Divine Origin and call it the work of the Holy Prophet (peace be upon him) meant to put a scythe to the very root of Islam, proving it to be a mere imposture."

On Wednesday, I sat in the lecture room in the left corner of the first row. About twenty Ulema (scholars) of notable standing were present there. Four of the clergy were also present. Allamah himself was in the chair. The lady arrived, and the lecture began and went on for about one hour. The lady had a long list of such mistakes as (according to her) she found in the Quran, and because it was human to err and not divine, therefore, it was apparent that the Quran was the work not of Allah but a mortal, post hoc ergo propter hoc. [1]

After about an hour (at 4'O clock), Allamah Alla-ud-din Siddiqui, who was in the chair, dragging his chair behind him, came to my left and there took his seat and sat.

I said to Allamah Alla-ud-din Siddiqui, "Sir! You have abdicated your throne."

His answer was, "Brother! I had great expectations of you, but you sit, mum. The Ulema also are sitting silent. I, being the president in the chair, have to remain neutral and can say nothing. I have, therefore, brought myself into the audience so that I may be able to say something to refute the views of the Madam and clear some mistakes on her part."

To which I asked Allamah Alla-ud-din Siddiqui, "Allamah Sahib! Is the Quran yours?"

He said, "No."

I said, "Am I the author of the Quran? Had I written that?"

His answer was, "No."

Then I said, "Allamah Sahib! To Allah belongs the Quran, and indeed, Allah is the best protector of His word. He who has revealed the Quran to the Prophet Mohammed (peace be upon him) can defend the honor of His Quran. [2] But instead, let the knowledge and the audacity of the lady be admired and appreciated."

The lady had paused. I then stood up and addressed the lady.

DIALOGUE WITH MS. ANNEMARIE SCHIMMEL

The following dialogue followed between her and me.

Yousuf Gabriel: Excuse me, Madam! By your leave, I have not had the honor of hearing your past six lectures. I do not know what you said. I am honored by my presence in this present lecture, and thereby I gather that you deny the Quran its Divine Origin because you think there are mistakes in the Quran, and you think that the Holy Prophet (peace be upon him) has been the author thereof.

Ms. Annemarie Schimmel: Yes! It is my conviction. You prove it otherwise.

Yousuf Gabriel: I am not a man of debate, Madam! Debates generally mean to churn waters. But surely, Madam! There are no mistakes in the Quran, and it is free from mistakes. Instead, you are mistaken, but there is no time to clear those mistakes you say are in the Quran. You have adopted one line to prove your point by pointing out faults and mistakes in the Quran to prove the human origin. I leave this line entirely to you and take another one. I show you something in this very Quran which no prophet, soothsayer, astrologer, and clairvoyant, in short, nobody could have ventured to say in an age in which the Quran was being revealed to the Holy Prophet (peace be upon him). None then could reveal that matter except One, the Omniscient Creator of the world, to prove that the Quran could not have been the work of anyone except Allah. Nor an alteration has ever been made in the Quran after that.

Ms. Annemarie Schimmel: What's that?

Yousuf Gabriel: The Quran characterizes the atomic hell. But pray first tell me when the Quran was revealed or according to your conviction when it was being composed by the Holy Prophet (peace be upon him) in secret?

Ms. Annemarie Schimmel: The Quran was revealed 1380 years ago.

Yousuf Gabriel: And when the atomic bomb was revealed to the world?

Ms. Annemarie Schimmel: In 1945, American bombers dropped two atomic bombs on Hiroshima and Nagasaki in Japan.

Yousuf Gabriel: The Quran was revealed 1380 years ago, while scientists made the atom bomb in 1945. Does there any distance exist, Madam, between these two dates, 1945 and 1380 years ago?

Ms. Annemarie Schimmel: Yes! Centuries are intervening between them.

Yousuf Gabriel: Then pray, Madam! Look into your conscience and say, was it possible that 1380 years ago, in a country of Bedouins famous only for ignorance, an Ummi [3] person would write his book in concealment in the city of Makkah in pure Arabic and name it the 'Quran'. In that 'Quran', he would write a chapter about the theory of modern atomism and predict the atomic bomb giving out the causes of its appearance and the essence of nuclear science, and even portraying the atomic bomb explosion. Moreover, he would reveal the causes of the appearance of the nuclear hell that is the atomic bombs and nuclear radiations by characterizing the nuclear phenomena in a purely scientific manner, all in about 36 words? Do you not consider it a miracle of the Quran?

Ms. Annemarie Schimmel: Are you in your senses? Is it possible to find the atomic science and atomic bomb in the Quran? Because the Quran was written 1380 years ago when there was no modern science in the world while atomic science appeared in the 19th century, and the atomic bomb made its appearance in 1945. Further, the Quran is not a book of science; it is a book of religion. We cannot expect the Quran to have science. I have personally read the Quran. Nor any Muslim Ulema has ever mentioned atomic science or the description of the atomic bomb in the Quran.

Yousuf Gabriel: I think I am (in my senses) Madam, for I never drink Hashish, and I have uttered nothing that might presage insanity or envisage the derangement of man's mind.

You are correct that you have read the Quran and nowhere found anything like that, or none of the Muslim Ulema (scholars) have ever mentioned such a thing to exist in the Quran. But that the Quran is not the book of science, you are mistaken. Because, if science is no more than the knowledge of those natural laws which Allah created Himself and which govern this universe, then they must naturally exist in the Quran. Since you might have read during your study that Quran has claimed to contain every example for man. Which instance in the history of humankind could be considered more extraordinary than atomic hell, which can and is now about to devour all life on earth from East to West? The Quran contains the example of the nuclear bomb, and it is a fact as you stand there and as I stand here and as the Quran exists in this world in its pristine form and purity.

In reality, you only think it impossible to find atomic science and the description of the atomic bomb in a book that appeared 1380 years ago when there was no vestige of modern science in the entire world. So far, you think that the Quran is a book of religion, and we should not expect the Quran to have science. It is a notion entirely wrong. If you have read the Quran, you certainly might have read the claim of the Quran in two places wherein the Quran says:

"We have displayed for humankind in the Quran all kinds of similitudes."

The wrath of Allah destroyed the tribes of Aad and Thamud. The Quran mentions their destruction many times. Those tribes were no more than a Mohallah (Ward) of Lahore city and were a few hundred thousand. In contrast, atomic bombs in the atomic World War meant the wholesale destruction of the entire life on earth from Tokyo to New York that no signs of life would be left anywhere. The Quran mentions the destruction of the tribes of Aad and Thamud with great zeal. Why should it not mention the wholesale destruction done by the atomic bombs that would involve all life on the entire earth? What about the Quran's claim that of displaying for humankind all kinds of similitudes? Indeed, the Quran has treated almost all of the subjects of human knowledge. Suppose no Ulema has ever mentioned the existence of atomic science and the description of the atomic bomb in the Quran. In that case, there is no wonder because this fact I discovered only a couple of years ago and have not disclosed it anywhere. You are the first person to hear it.

Ms. Annemarie Schimmel: Well! Proceed and show me where that is?

Yousuf Gabriel: Madam! Please read the chapter 'Al-Homaza', the 104th chapter of the Quran.

Ms. Annemarie Schimmel: I am not Hafiz. [4]

Yousuf Gabriel: Shall I recite it for you then myself, or fetch the copy of the Quran for evidence?

Ms. Annemarie Schimmel: You recite it. If you recite it wrong, I shall catch you. I know the Quran.

Yousuf Gabriel: I ask the protection of Allah from the snares of the devil. In the name of most Merciful, Beneficent, and Benign Allah:

"Woe unto every slanderer and backbiter who heapeth up riches (of this world) and prepareth the same (for the times to come). He thinketh that his riches will render him immortal. By no means. He shall surely be cast into 'Al-Hotama'. And what shall cause thee to understand what 'Al-Hotama' is?"

Please tell me, Madam! What is this 'Hotama'?

(The answer of Madam came back at me like a back shot that would remind me of Rutherford's experience with alpha particles he shot into the gold foil.)

Ms. Annemarie Schimmel: Your commentators write that it ('Hotama') is a sort of a hellfire in which whatever is cast is ground to powder through the intensity of its flame (the heat).

(Scientist's answer would have been, "It is a particular phenomenon in which the substance is 'atomized' due to the intensity of temperature." The Madam's rapidity and sagacity in her answer came to me as a wonder mingled with delight. I inwardly admired her remarkable display of knowledge. She had proved my point without knowing it.)

Yousuf Gabriel: You are quite right, Madam. Your answer to my question shows that you certainly have an appreciable study of the Quran. However, it is the answer of the commentators of the Quran that reveals their admirable knowledge.

This 'Hotama', Madam, is a noun derived from the root verb 'Hatama'. 'Hatama' is a word of pure Arabic origin that means 'to break'. Its second form is 'Hattama', which means 'to break with great intensity'. For example, you have a glass in your hand, and you violently strike it against the rock, and the glass explodes into pieces. The final form is 'Tahattama', which means to explode.

Just see the phonetic and functional resemblance of 'Hatama' to the word 'atom', which is of Greek origin, adopted by the scientists. Then mark the various inflections such as 'Hattama', 'Tahattama', 'Inhatama', 'Inhitaam', 'Hitaam-ud-Duniya', and 'Hitaam-iss-Safina' etc. and then see that the Quran describes the fire of 'Hotama' saying:

"It is the fire of Allah enkindled which leaps up onto the hearts. It is a fire closed in on them in outstretched columns."

We can simply see how far the terminology of the Quran in this context is correct and how far the word 'Atom' as used by the scientist is erroneous. For your information, the term 'Atom' used by the scientist is wrong. For atom means 'which cannot be broken', while the scientist himself has broken the atom into parts. On the other hand, 'Hotama', the term used by the Quran, means 'which breaks'. The Quran has used it correctly regarding the topic.

Indeed Madam! When we compare the nuclear explanations given by the scientists to those which the Quran gives, we can easily see the difference between the human mind of the scientist and the divine mind of the Quran. The difference is that of a human being and Allah. Allah says:

"What shall cause thee to understand what Al-Hotama is?"

Also, after that, Allah explains 'Al-Hotama':

"It is a kindled fire of Allah which shall mount above the hearts (of those who shall be cast therein). Verily (it shall be as) an arched vault above them, on columns of vast extent" (Quran: 104 'Al-Homaza')

These are the distinct characteristics that distinguish atomic phenomena from chemical phenomena and every other phenomenon found globally. As is given straightforwardly by the Quran, this explanation of the atomic fire is in itself a miracle of knowledge. No atomic scientist in the world could ever be competent enough to describe the characteristics of atomic phenomena in the manner described by the Quran.

The Quran says:

"Atomic fire is the fire of Allah enkindled."

No doubt, the millions of degrees of temperature seen in the atomic fire could never be expected in the chemical fire.

The Quran says:

"Hotama is a fire which mounts above the hearts."

No doubt, the atomic bomb explosion kills at first its victims by giving shock to their hearts. Further study of the subject reveals a particular attraction of atomic radiations for the heart, or something related to the heart.

The Quran says:

"Verily the atomic fire shall be as an arched vault above them".

Nobody can give a better description of the atomic bomb explosion. However, the research further takes us to the bounds which far exceed the bounds found by the modern atomic scientist.

Madam! When the atomic bomb explodes, the shock of 'Heat-Flash' hits the hearts, and blood gushes out of the nostrils, and the victim falls dead on its knees.

However, pray tell, Madam! Have you ever seen the atomic bomb explosion?

Ms. Annemarie Schimmel: No. If I had seen the atomic bomb explosion, how could I have been here? For, that indeed kills the person.
Yousuf Gabriel: Have you seen a photograph of the atomic bomb explosion?
Ms. Annemarie Schimmel: Yes. That I have.
Yousuf Gabriel: Is there any 'outstretched column' to be observed?
Ms. Annemarie Schimmel: Yes! There is the 'outstretched column', many miles high. The column of the Hiroshima bomb rose to the height of four miles.
Yousuf Gabriel: That is what the Quran has said, 'outstretched columns'. The Quran says: 'on columns of vast extent'.

The rising column of the atomic bomb explosion rises, changing various colors, indeed very magnificent to see. For your information, the column of the 20 megatons thermonuclear bomb, called the Hydrogen bomb or the Hell-bomb, rises to the height of 20 miles and has a diameter of 3 miles.

Madam! Suppose you sat on the Himalayas peak Mount Everest, Sir John Hunt, and his party conquered a few years ago. In the plain of Panipat, where contestants have fought so many battles in the past, before your eyes, you looked through a telescope, rising atomic bombs' explosions covering one thousand square miles in an arranged symmetry just as the trees grow in a garden. You would see a magnificent scene of rising columns of atomic explosions changing beautiful colors and rising to the height of 20 miles and there covered by a beautiful roof. You would think it was a magnificent palace of some great emperor or some great theater under construction. No Madam! It was 'Al-Hotama' as is described by the Quran. It is a sort of hellfire in which anything is cast is crushed into the particles of atoms.

At the beginning of the chapter, 'Al-Homaza', Quran describes the causes of the emergence of 'Hotama' and its replica in this world that may be called atomic hell. The first of these causes is 'slander and backbiting', which is the habit universally seen in this modern age of Baconian materialism. The second cause is the 'accumulation of riches', which also is the primary feature of this modern culture. The third cause is the 'belief that wealth will keep on increasing eternally'. This feature is also a recognized one of this science-guided materialism.

This belief of the people is so strong that they may be said to think that they will achieve immortality due to their wealth and that the monuments of their wealth will become immortal. To which the Quran says, "by no means". Both they and the monuments of their wealth will be plunged into the crushing 'Hotama'. These three characteristics, namely, the 'slander', the 'accumulation of wealth', and the 'complete faith in the eternity of the accumulated wealth', are the basic features of the theory of modern atomism, the Baconian philosophy of 'fruit' and 'utility'.

The debate ended with the fall of Madam on the chair. She fell on the chair confounded and indisposed at hearing from me to explain this prophecy as proof of the 'Divine Origin of the Quran'. There is a difference between sitting in the chair and falling on the chair. She collapsed to her chair and appeared visibly indisposed. Lady virtually appeared to have succumbed to the debate. She had received a severe shock. Her mission had failed, and her loss was immense. The debate had proved her life-long study of the Quran as erroneous in a matter of moment. She received an answer that convinced her of the argument's truth and had explicitly falsified her personal view. In reality, she was converted to Islam at that very moment because she had seen a straightforward truth of the 'Divine Origin of the Quran', which she had intended to destroy. [5]

She departed, and as far as my knowledge goes, she never returned to Pakistan for ten years after that. And when she came, her topic was not the human origin of the Quran. On the other hand, she had written the most excellent books on Iqbal, Sultan Bahu, Ameer Khosrau, Islamic calligraphy, and other Sufi Saints of Islam. My overall conceit of her is one of gratitude. Not all the Ulema of Islam could have rendered me the service which she was suitable to do. Howsoever my discourse had impressed Ulema, they could not provide a verdict as confident and a proof of the validity of my discovery of 'Hotama' as sure, as did scholarly lady falling in the chair, and cessation of the topic of the origin of the Quran after that. It might come as a surprise to most that at that time, after about three years of my discovery of the Quran's prediction of atomic hell, I did not even know the structure of the atom, nor had I seen a book on nuclear physics.

Such has been the guidance in my course as, not a word, not a point, not a thought, more or less was granted to me than was necessary for my mission at a particular point of my course. Noteworthy is the sequence of events in my lengthy course. After 1971, the knowledge of atomic physics and Radiobiology burst upon me. Books were supplied to me in the strangest of coincidences so that now the state is different. Poor Schimmel is now left miles behind. Einstein and Russell are needed to listen to the case and read wonders. Einstein would not be ashamed to sit with me. Perhaps I would suggest specific guidelines in his subject to save him from considerably unnecessary trouble and toil.

Afterward, the Ulema (scholars) present in the lecture who were the primary audience of my debate with Ms. Annemarie Schimmel, highly pleased with my demonstration, asked Allamah Alla-ud-din Siddiqui about me. For, they did not know me due to the reason that I had always struggled in seclusion.

And it was in response to their inquiry that Allamah spoke about me those memorable words, namely, that:

"Respectable Ulema! Allah has created this man in the Muslim nation by chance. If this nation fails to receive and benefit that intellectual light of knowledge and the light and understanding of the Quran which Allah has bestowed on him, Allah will never forgive this nation on the Day of Judgment. Another one like him will not appear in this nation."

The efficacy of this warning of the Quran is unfailing since this warning about the atomic hell is a miracle most manifest. Neither a scientist nor philosopher can doubt or deny it with reason. It has expelled the notion of the denial of miraculous and supernatural by science, and not all the works of the votaries of Baconian philosophy combined could withstand it. Nor all the stockpiles of atomic bombs in the world could withstand its powerful neutralizing effect. As the only direction to avoid the atomic ruin and the last hope of humankind, it has appeared so that humankind destined to meet a doom preordained only might miss it or neglect it. My conviction is that it will save this world from atomic ruin. Insha-Allah (God willing).

~~*~*~*~*

---

[1] **Post hoc ergo propter hoc:** Latin for "after this, therefore because of this" is a logical fallacy (of the questionable cause variety) which states, "Since that event followed this one, that event must have been caused by this one." We often shorten it to 'post hoc' and sometimes refer it to as 'false cause', 'coincidental correlation', or 'correlation not causation'.

'Post hoc' is a particularly tempting error because temporal sequence appears to be integral to causality. The fallacy lies in concluding based solely on the order of events rather than considering other factors that might rule out the connection.

[2] "Lo! We, even We, reveal the Reminder, and lo! We verily are its Guardian."

(Quran 15:9)

[3] **Ummi** is an unlettered or illiterate person. Here, the word refers to the person of Muhammad (peace be upon him), who was admittedly a person who never had read any book nor had held a pen in his hand to write.

[4] **Hafiz** means a person who has memorized the Quran and can repeat the Quran from memory.

[5] (a) Ms. Annemarie Schimmel's tombstone (in Bonn, Germany) is carved with a saying in Arabic narrated from Ali Ibn-Abi Talib [the cousin and son-in-law of Islamic Prophet Muhammad (peace be upon him) and fourth Caliph of the Islamic Caliphate] as follows.

"People are asleep; only when they die will they be awakened."

(b) ["Throughout her life, Ms. Annemarie Schimmel felt a deep bond with the Islamic religion and its cultures. She was often asked by both Muslims and non-Muslims alike 'whether she was a Muslim or not'. In such cases, she preferred to give an evasive answer, saying, for example, that only those who are not sure whether they are good Muslims or not can really be good Muslims. She loved Islam, but only as long as she did not have to belong to it. Perhaps it was the effort of maintaining this balancing act that was one of the driving forces behind her incredible productivity.

The burial: It was Ms. Annemarie Schimmel's request that the 'first Sura of the Koran' be recited over her coffin as a sign of reconciliation between the religions that went beyond her death. Sheikh Ahmed Zaki Yamani, a long-term confidant of Ms. Annemarie Schimmel and chairman of the London-based Al-Furqan Foundation to which she was an advisor, recited the Fatiha at the close of the Protestant service held in the Kreuzkirche in Bonn on February 4, 2003."]

["Searching for the Inner Life of Islam" by Stefan Wild (Professor for Semitic Philology and Islamic Studies at the University of Bonn)/http://en.qantara.de]

~~*~*~*

CHAPTER-7

THE CHARACTERISTICS OF THOSE DOOMED TO ATOMIC HELL

From science, now, we diverge to enter the field of philosophy to discuss the characteristics attributed by the Quran to those atomic-hell-bound people. These characteristics are mainly responsible for the resultant emergence of atomic hell. They have guided the primary motives behind the scientific discoveries and inventions and led them onto such paths as culminated in their natural destination, the nuclear hell.

The Quran elaborated these characteristics at the beginning of the text of its prophecy. However, we have purposely deferred them to the end of our discussion of the nuclear phenomena. The purpose was to familiarize the readers first with all the necessary details of the actual phenomena. Perhaps they might sufficiently understand the nature of such characteristics responsible for the emergence of such dire consequences. They had engendered so universally ignominious a ruin of all humankind that in the absence of these horrors might merely seem ordinary matters of routine.

The emergence of nuclear energy and the subsequent appearance of its crowning glory, its golden fruit, the atomic bomb, should not be taken as something 'accidental' or the product of mere blind 'chance'. There happens to be nothing of haphazard nature in it throughout its development. Rather a conspicuous process, continual and consequential, is to be traced in its gradual progress from the beginning to its end. Only two occurrences present blind chance or hazards throughout the long history of atomism over twenty-five centuries. One of these instances is the accidental discovery of X-rays by German physicist Roentgen in 1895. The other one is French physicist Becquerel's haphazard choice of Uranium Nitrate (as the substance of investigation by a single good fortune, as someone delighted with its subsequent success might tell) while seeking a possible connection between phosphorescence and X-rays. These events led unexpectedly to the discovery of radioactivity in 1896.

However, was this all the result of a chance play? The philosopher who would think of the 'accidental' creation of the earth and this life as the product of blind play of 'chance' might also say so regarding the two chance-like instances mentioned above. [1] However, we see in this case, the element of chance is no more involved than chance guidance of a hawk's flight towards a pigeon or a spying dog's direction towards the hideout of a thief. Why not, we ask, chance led Mr. Roentgen or Mr. Becquerel to do something which did not possess the pernicious attributes which nuclear energy did possess. For, that would have meant the complete negation of our theory regarding the primary connection between the three untoward requisite characteristics prevailing amongst humanity and the atomic hell.

The atomic bomb, no doubt, is the fruit of the tree of atomism that Democritus planted in 500 BC, or we could say it is the egg of the hen of atomism that Dalton reared in the 19th century AD. From the first conception to actual laying, the whole history of this egg, with utmost accuracy and indeed much amusement, we can trace in the research and discoveries of atomists from Dalton to Oppenheimer. After its first appearance 2500 years ago, the conditions remained uncongenial to atomism for a long time. So, it remained quelled and suppressed. But when in time centuries later the circumstances changed and the conditions became suitable to its growth, it flourished and blossomed and fruited. As long as faith remained the dominating power in human affairs, atomism had no chance. But as the power of faith flattened and materialism got hold of the human mind, 'wealth accumulation' in an atmosphere of 'wealth worship' and 'backbiting' and 'slander' against faith became the universal vogue, atomism assumed utmost popularity. It led the whole vast field of affairs to a logical end.

As enumerated by the Quran in this prophecy or a warning, three characteristics are responsible for producing atomic hell. In the reformation of these characteristics, humankind could avert the danger of atomic conflagration. These characteristics are as follows.

(1) The Quran says:
"Woe unto every slandering traducer."
The accusation implies a calumnious temperament given to 'slander' and 'backbiting'. This temperament in modern times is not only apparent in people's general character individually and collectively, but it offers a very queer study when particularly its modernized activity against faith is subjected to our view. This field offers a fascinating and instructive study, which unfortunately has received not the attention it indeed deserved. In this work, we will try to do some justice to it. It is quite a new thing and perhaps may be found of some interest, mainly because it has been judged in the light of

the Quran and against a philosophy that has hitherto not been shown in this particular way.

(2) The Quran further says:
"Who heapeth up the wealth (of this world), and arrangeth it."
This heaping up of wealth and arranging it for the future implies a complete absorption in the bodily affairs of a material world without any consideration of the spiritual side or the next world in Heaven.

(3) The Quran further says:
"He thinketh that his wealth shall render him immortal."
It indicates the tendency of excessive and undue confidence in the potency of wealth, amounting to faith in it, a faith in its ability to bestow immortality on its possessors, a quality indeed attributable only to Allah. Such a belief implied a denial of Resurrection, which could only be possible after death. Therefore, it is unthinkable if people existed in a state of immortality, denying Allah's final Judgment and life in Heaven.

Now, the habit of backbiting and slander invariably would produce mutual mistrust and distrust among people both individually and collectively. Wholesale engrossment in the accumulation of wealth and the world's affairs leaves neither mind nor time for the remembrance of either Allah or the otherworld. Complete faith in the omnipotence of wealth is tantamount to a complete disregard of Allah, the Giver of wealth, for people, like the legendary Qaroon (Korah), consider their wealth as the result of their ability. Again, a notion of immortality achieved by wealth within this transitory world, as stated above, implied a denial of the Resurrection, Judgment, next life in Heaven, and all.

All these different qualities and characteristics and various traits, we are so sorry to observe, exist in enormous, instead, in alarming proportions in this present modern age. They have come to manifest themselves in colors so very conspicuous compared to all the past ages that we would perhaps, with quite a plausibility, characterize them as the distinctive features of this present age. Moreover, how regrettable would have seemed this state of affairs if the fact would come to people's knowledge that in the absence of these three peculiar characteristics, the Quran has enumerated as the causes of the emergence of atomic hell, the atomic hell could not have created.

Firstly, the people of America were never so callous-minded, cruel, or utterly devoid of human considerations as to build up such a monster as the atomic bomb; had the fear not guided them that Germany was possibly already engaged in the field. If it succeeded, the consequences would be catastrophic for the allies. Moreover, they couldn't have built the monster of a still more outstanding caliber in the form of Hydrogen or Hell bomb had the incontrovertible evidence that the Soviet Union had detonated a fission device not prompted them.

Hence, the fear of losing the contest was the primary cause for their advancement toward the Hell bomb. Nor do we believe that Russians would have manufactured so grisly a terror as the atomic bomb merely to destroy fellow human beings had they not seen the two dropped on Hiroshima and Nagasaki. They thought it was essential to break the monopoly of the U.S.A. in the nuclear field. All this is the work of 'mistrust' and 'distrust'; these twins happen to be the offspring of 'lady Backbiting' and 'Mr. Slander esquire'.

Secondly, without the colossal scientific and industrial setup and the unbelievably vast accumulation of American wealth, so costly a demon as the atomic bomb could not possibly have been manufactured. All the wealth of the emperors of a pre-modern generation united could not perhaps have sufficed to build up a single atomic bomb.

Thirdly, it is due merely to their faith in deathless attributes of wealth that the present-day human race is embracing the deathly nuclear energy with the confidence of a snake-charmer despite their knowledge of its sure fatality.

Indeed, these three characteristics, which the Quran has given out as the cause of nuclear energy, have, like an inebriating drug, made modern humankind blind to the deadly effects of nuclear power, and they shall remain so as long as these characteristics persist. Then either they shall cast them away and will avert the hazard, or they shall in the same state of drunkenness plunge themselves into the flames of atomic hell. Also, unfortunately, the crux of the matter is that advising them today or giving them warnings of atomic danger is like advising against the drunkenness of a person who happens to be in a state of drunkenness. A danger sign with a skull and cross-bones on a road corner means nothing to a motor driver raving in a state of drunkenness and singing, "de-lara-ra, ho, hiccoo, hic".

This habit of backbiting and slander in our modern propagandistic age is no hidden secret. We witness everyone engaged in backbiting and slandering every other person. The practice has assumed a universal modern, sophisticated art and has become a part of our culture. And in the guise of this well-developed art, the individual is engaged against the individual, nation against nation, sect against sect, creed against creed, cult against the cult. Backbiting, slandering, and the main motive behind all this is exclusively worldly greed.

GABRIEL'S EXTINGUISHING THE ATOMIC HELL SERIES

We observe it with due regret that science itself has also been involved and made the instrument of backbiting. Here, neither we are summing up the extent of guilt of oppressive Church (as writers themselves reflect), nor we are tempted to attempt an assessment of the justification of retaliative tendencies of the votaries of science against the Church at the time of the Renaissance of the West and the birth of modern science. This topic is very delicate, warrants fuller treatment and an extremely cautious approach, and is out of our scope in this present work. We will only content ourselves by saying that this science-religion conflict, whatever its causes are, has been an unfortunate affair for the whole of humankind.

Let us skip and leave all irrelevant discussions out at present. Somehow from Galileo's astronomy to Darwin's biology, and from Newton's gravity to Einstein's relativity, there has not been a discovery in the whole field of modern science that did not emerge as the subject of a science-religion controversy as a grave conflict.

Later on, a school arose amidst the scientists who made it their business to deny the doctrines of the faith on the dint of the ascertained facts, hypotheses, or propositions. The predisposition of the mind seems to play a very decisive role in this philosophy in question. However, it has provided us with a philosophy that we can name the most typical of modern backbiting and slander because this is the backbiting against faith. It has been employed on the grounds of modern science. We shall put the merit of such philosophy to the test at a proper place later on in this book. We have no mind here, as we have said, to give our judgment in this Science-Church conflict.

However, so much only we shall say that the votaries of science ought to have put up an endeavor with enthusiasm equal to their gusto in science to do thorough research in religion at a time when they had found themselves able and were in a position to do so. Thereby, they ought to have reformed religion instead of strangling it to death to eliminate this supposed embarrassment. In the absence of the controlling authority of faith, their science consequently came to play havoc with their own and with all of the remaining humanity's lives. Material progress they have indeed made to an unusual degree, but alas! To what end?

Thus, the Quran has given out the causes of the atomic bomb's appearance as slander, backbiting, complete engrossment in wealth accumulation, and undue confidence in wealth amounting to worship. Now, it hardly needs the discerning eye of Socrates to know that all the three characteristics are the most peculiar and particular features of this modern materialistic age of propaganda, wealth accumulation, and wealth worship.

Remember that this prophecy of the Quran is only a warning. Hence, if we remove the causes, the danger must automatically disappear. The scientist has neither succeeded hitherto in producing any neutralizer of atomic explosion nor has he been able to find any radiation sickness treatment. So has the strategist found himself quite at a loss to find any ways of safety or defense against nuclear warfare. Treaties and agreements will prove, but singed hair and the only hope for humankind has appeared in this warning of the Quran.

A Scripture has at last risen to the occasion to save humanity and to vouchsafe glory to the world of Allah in His last declared Will to the whole humankind. It is a living miracle of the Quran and the last hope of humanity. Everyone may understand the topic, but critical appreciation is reserved for the elites only, as they possess the versatile genius of the highest order.

~~*~*~*

---

[1] Reference is here given to 'The Mysterious Universe' by Sir James Jeans, which is discussed in detail in Book-2/volume-6: [Quran versus the philosophy of the 'Unscientific Scientist Philosopher'].

~~*~*~*

CHAPTER-8

THE ATOMIC BOMB IS THE WRATH OF ALLAH AND NOT A WEAPON

Whither this world goeth? What it wanteth to do? Where doth it stand now? Einstein recorded his impressions of this world in 'The World As I See It'. What these impressions were, I am not aware though I see this world myself and find it very distracting. [1]

The overall picture is one of confusion mingled with confusion and confusion heaped upon confusion. It is confusion intermingled with anarchy, and anarchy intermingled with falsity. I thought of myself as one dead set against the toxic philosophy of Darwinian evolution. But when I see the state of humankind today, thanks to the inebriating influence of Baconian rationalism, that lunatic philosophy of man's base ape-like origin appears to find some countenance in the behavior of this present-day humankind. Howsoever the philosophy of man's base ape-like origin might have been based on error and doubt regarding humanity in general, yet as far as this Baconian humankind of this Baconian age is concerned, Darwin's eye appears to have observed the spectacle sufficiently correctly. With a perceptible disgust, Darwin's mind might have imagined the modern human race identical to a species of intelligent anthropoids tending on the way to the conversion from the phase of anthropomorphic humanity to the supreme godhead. However, cursed be the science-guided process of this Baconian progress that approached its end in destroying life within just three centuries, breaking the Darwinian dream into pieces.

It is painful to observe that this humankind, not even in its ancient stages of dark superstition, displayed such utter lack of sense and sensibility like today in this age of knowledge, science, enlightenment, and advancement. It is well-known that no protection exists either against the atomic bomb or atomic radiation. It is also well-known that there are no signs of protection in view. Again, it is well-known that humanity cannot forever avoid atomic war in the presence of stockpiles and reactors. Known also is that atomic war meant wholesale destruction of life on earth and that anyone could not survive and enjoy the honor of a victory. Yet, instead of banning the use of atomic energy and atomic bombs, the entire endeavor is being directed toward building the atomic reactors and atomic bombs, and worse still is the optimism about the discovery someday of some remedy.

Moreover, indeed those who survived in an atomic war would envy the death of those who were fortunate enough to meet death. Yet countries are vigorously engaged in building more and more atomic weapons and improvising on the existing specimens. Again, neither the follies of those countries which themselves are engaged in building atomic reactors and atomic bombs and yet deny this right to others in the name of proliferation are understandable nor explicable the follies of those countries which have no nuclear power but are endeavoring to approach that status. What if they add a few more atomic bombs to the existing number of eight thousand? The number existing is quite enough to destroy everyone on earth. The world indeed has gone crazy. An old American stamped the earth and asserted that America could not be destroyed. Who could tell him that America could be destroyed before he raised his foot to stamp the earth a second time? … Nevertheless, either to Heaven or Hell, I want to tell you that the atomic bomb is neither a weapon of war nor defense. According to the scientist, it is a means of wholesale destruction of life on earth, while according to the Quran, it is the atomic hell. It is the divine vengeance, the wrath of Allah enkindled. The Quran no doubt has enjoined on the Muslims to keep weapons in readiness to awe the enemies, but they need first to decide whether they could include atomic bombs in the category of weapons? It is the fundamental question of policy, crucial and remarkably far-reaching in consequence. It is just like to think before you leap into the well of the hell, the Baconian hell, the atomic hell, the nuclear hell.

~~*~*~*

---

[1] Not pretty sure, but it looks that the author in his lifetime could not thoroughly study Einstein's book referred to as 'The World As I See It'. However, the following extract (of Einstein) included here later from his book will be of great interest to the reader regarding Einstein's views about **wealth** and **wealth-accumulation**, which are in total conformity with that given by the Bible and the Quran:

"I am absolutely convinced that no **wealth** in the world can help humanity forward, even in the hands of the most devoted worker in this cause. The example of great and pure characters is the only thing that can produce fine ideas and noble deeds. Money only appeals to selfishness and always tempts its owners irresistibly to abuse it. Can anyone imagine Moses, Jesus, or Gandhi armed with the money-bags of Carnegie?" (Albert Einstein: 'The World As I See It': P-21)

~~*~*~*

CHAPTER-9

ACCUMULATION OF WEALTH AND WEALTH WORSHIP

According to the Quran, the qualities number two and three of that atomic-hell-bound are 'systematic accumulation of wealth' and 'wealth worship'. Now, none need borrow the judgment of either Bacon or Macaulay to realize that this quality of engrossment in the accumulation of wealth and indeed in alarming proportions is the fundamental characteristic of this modern age of outstanding and all-pervading materialism. A strange fact that can delude nobody is that the very existence of anyone in this age is only possible if he has wealth. This queer trait is due to a particular setup of a materialistic age's social and economic system. This system necessarily has resulted in the appearance of bonds, insurance, banks, saving certificates, passbooks, saving accounts, lotteries, and scores of other methods of accumulating wealth both on an individual and collective basis. If we raised someone of pre-modern age from his grave by a miracle, he would find no words to express his surprise to see so many modes of wealth accumulation tampered with such an acute sense of panic for wealth everywhere.

The Baconian slogan that is, "On to the conquest of the realm of Mother Nature" has in truth turned out to be, "On to the accumulation of wealth through wealth worship" by humankind in general: wealth as the heart, the soul, the body, the deity, and as the goddess. Yes, but alas! A false heart, a false soul, a false body, a false deity, and a false goddess. Humankind dived into the desert of wealth, closing their eyes from everything else, till at last, they have appeared as a picture of misery panting in anxiety, with tongues lolling and eyes startling out of sockets. The more they accumulate, the hungrier they feel for accumulation. So overwhelming is their thirst for wealth that, for its sake, people all over the world are recklessly engaged in enkindling atomic furnaces to burn themselves, their children, their near ones, and dear ones. They are even determined and prepared to consume the whole of humankind in atomic kilns. They need wealth, and they must get it anyhow, anyway. This order is that of this materialistic setup.

In ancient times, some people, indeed very few, have destroyed their children for fear of poverty. Their mention even today saddens the hearts. One essentially shudders to hear such a story. But today, not of course for fear of poverty but generally for acquiring more wealth, this humanity of our times, this civilized generation of human history, is fast preparing to hurl their children in millions and along with their children, the children of all humankind into nuclear burning fires and blazing pyres alive. The inhabitants of the modern age are enlightened, knowledgeable, and civilized. But, on the other hand, they are worse than the ignorant barbaric and rustic savages of the past at whose very mention we proudly sneer, scoff, and frown in utter contempt. The people of this modern, materialistic, and deluded race are the worshippers of wealth, and the adorers of riches, who think they shall forever progress and their bank balances will endlessly swell. They think that they shall never die, forgetting the fuel they add to the enormous explosive pyres in truckloads continually and wanting a slip to fall into the nuclear flames. It is a mad generation of maniacs burning in the flames of mutual hatred, envy, and selfishness to the degree that well justifies their ruin by raining atom bombs and a hail of atomic missiles and plaguing radiations.

In the hope of Allah's Mercy, I will implore them to avail the only chance left for them and now let them think at least for the sake of their children if at all a little parental affection is still left in their hardened hearts and stony bosoms. Or else let these wise people feel the earth beneath their feet sinking into the burning nuclear hell below. The bewitching sorceress, the goddess of wealth, is sitting most conspicuously in her shrine within every human heart. Humans assumed such unity of sentiment never once in history as they have in the adoration of wealth these days. Not even one Allah ever achieved such universal popularity as this wealth has. The death, otherworld, or bliss of poverty is never mentioned, and everyone is worriedly wheezing over the thought of more. Yet, wealth has not conquered death. It shall never be. It may come any moment, and it certainly shall come. If death remains unconquered, then who could avert the final Judgment and thence the otherworld?

Remember that unless the three characteristics pointed out by the Quran are not eradicated, the extinguished torch of faith is not re-enkindled, and Allah hasn't been reinstated in His place: no power on earth, treaties, entreaties, wishful thinking, and policies of balanced war strengths can save humankind from the dreadful doom, that is, a terrible nuclear war. The wealth then but enhances the destruction. Destiny will open the forgotten gate of death, and death will rush out in torrents. But alas! To what advantage at that juncture when the Providence has spun the destinies, and the die is finally cast? Will, you not pay attention then to the advice of your inner conscience, or are you certainly doomed, you wealth diggers, wealth accumulators, and wealth worshippers? Now, hear O miserable soul! The cry of the newborn child and interpret what it says. It says:

"O! How am I going to cope with these problems of tyrannical necessities of life?"

O thou poor tiny babe that worried about necessities of life, I pray you: open your innocent eyes and see thy parents and the parents of millions of other petite babes like thee all over the world, dancing around their goddess of wealth, and adding all the while fuel to the worldwide kiln, and if thou couldst see the furious tongues of flames emerging like tongues of fiery snakes impatiently to devour all the babes like you and the elders along with them, and who will hurl you in it but your parents themselves with their own hands and will jump themselves along with you into the depths of that burning hell of atomism. Yes, and alas! I wish I could make you understand what I say to you, O, innocent petite babe. It is wealth that has made this hell possible.

Now, at least there should be an economic system introduced based on the sentiments of equality, equity, and generosity that perhaps the burning pains of the human heart are mollified a little. Because most of humankind's troubles today could well be traced to economic disparity and greed for more, never-ending more.

Indeed, in their belief in the never-ending cycle of their material progress and their ever-linking five-yearly plans to infinity, could be traced their notion of immortality. Without any fear of death, loss, or failure, they move on their path of the ever-developing economy.
It is just as the Quran says:

"He thinketh that he shall forever remain rich and wealthy."
Nevertheless, blessed be the word of the Quran, it further says:

"Nay, but he shall be cast into 'Al-Hotama' (along with his riches)."

Let people, therefore, pause for a while and reflect that perhaps they may be saved. Perhaps folks may escape the atomic doom, a dreadful aspect indeed.

QURAN AND THE 'ACCUMULATION OF WEALTH'

(1) "And let not those who 'hoard up' that which Allah hath bestowed upon them of His bounty think that it is better for them. Nay, it is worse for them. That which they hoard will be their collar on the Day of Resurrection. Allah's is the heritage of the heavens and the earth, and Allah is Informed of what ye do." (Quran 3:180)

(2) "They who 'hoard up' gold and silver and spend it not in the way of Allah, unto them give tidings (O Muhammad) of a painful doom on

the day when it will (all) be heated in the fire of hell, and their foreheads and their flanks and their backs will be branded therewith (and it will be said unto them): Here is that which ye hoarded for yourselves. Now taste of what ye used to hoard." (Quran 9:34-35)

Now, please read the above-quoted signs of the Quran and see if you find any justification for the opinion of those who might accuse Islam of worldly trends. Yet, there is not much to wonder in their opinion. However, the wonder is excited by the enormousness of the properties of followers of Islam and the Quran.

The Prophet of Islam (peace be upon him) is said to have given in charity the only two gold coins in his household at the moment of his death, saying:

"Mohammed would not like to meet his Lord in a state that two gold coins be in his possession."

(3) Usury is the greatest abomination in the sight of the Quran.
"Those who swallow usury cannot rise, save as he ariseth whom the devil hath prostrated by (his) touch. That is because they say: Trade is just like usury, whereas Allah permitteth trading and forbiddeth usury. He unto whom an admonition from his Lord cometh, and (he) refraineth (in obedience thereto), he shall keep (the profits of) that which is past, and his affair (henceforth) is with Allah. As for him who returneth (to usury) such are rightful owners of the fire. They will abide therein." (Quran 2:275)

(4) When men forget about faith, their success in progress might be easy and complete.
"Then, when they forgot that whereof they had been reminded, We opened unto them the gates of all things till, even as they were rejoicing in that which they were given, We seized them unawares, and lo! They were dumbfounded." (Quran 6:44)

WEALTH WORSHIP

(1) "Serve Allah. Ascribe nothing as partner unto Him." (Quran 4:36)
(2) Worship not wealth but Giver of wealth.
"And of His portents are the night and the day and the sun and the moon. Adore not the sun nor the moon; but adore Allah Who created them, if it is in truth Him whom ye worship."

(Quran 41:37)

(3) "Yet of humankind are some who take unto themselves objects of worship which they set as rivals to Allah, loving them with love like (that which is the due) of Allah (only)!" (Quran 2:165)

~~*~*~*~*

CHAPTER-10

HOW TO AVERT THE ATOMIC DANGER IN THE LIGHT OF THE QURAN

Blame neither a nation nor any individual for the appearance of this evil doom, the atomic bomb. Instead, curse that particular setup, which through natural causes eventually brought about the inevitable: this resultant form of a lengthy and logical process that is an all-consuming and unrelenting conflagration of nuclear giants.

O, how amiable, how sophisticated a name, this nuclear energy; yet so harsh in action, so savage indeed, apt retribution for so soft-spoken a generation, so far removed from pity, mercy, lenity, pathos, seemingly dulcet but indeed morose as if duped into the act of 'danse-macabre'. [1]

I could but write this work and have poured the blood of my heart into it, but will they listen? Will they pay some heed? Will they pause to consider in a world of dizzied minds and nodding heads and rolling eyes? All engrossed in thoughts of wealth, more wealth, whole wealth, nothing but wealth.

It is justly said that to him who devotes his life to science, nothing could give more pleasure than making discoveries, but his cup of joy is complete only when the results of his studies find practical application. However, we are sorry to be obliged to add something to this undeniable truth. Whoever unlucky has been engaged in making discoveries in nuclear science, anything that would fill his cup if he would survive the practical application of his findings, could not have been other than sorrow and regret. Moreover, the applause he would receive for his remarkable services would be the shrieks of burning victims and heart-rending cries of miserable people suffering from painful cancers and lying in some inhospitable hospital.

This tiger of atomism has now been let loose. But who will put it back into the cage?

A tiger, they say, was once caught in a trap. The tiger rolled, bit with rage and grief, and tried to get out but in vain. Finally, a poor simple Brahman passed by, and the tiger cried, "Let me out of this cage! O pious one."

"Nay, my friend," replied the Brahman mildly. "You would probably eat me if I did."

"Nay, trust me that shall I not," said the tiger. "On the contrary, I shall be forever grateful and serve you as a slave."

Now, when the tiger sighed and wept bitterly, the pious Brahman's heart softened, and at last, he consented to open the door of the cage. Popped out the tiger and, seeing the poor man, cried, "What a fool you are? What is to prevent my eating you now, for after being cooped up so long, I am just intolerably hungry?"

In vain, the Brahman pleaded for his life. The most he could get was a promise to be allied by the decision of the first animal he chose to question as to the justice of the tiger's action. As he went on his way, the Brahman met a jackal, who called out, "Why? What's the matter, Mr. Brahman? You look as miserable as fish out of water."

The Brahman told him all that had taken place.

"How very confusing?" said the jackal when Brahman revealed to him the story. "Would you mind telling me over again? For everything has gone so mixed up."

The Brahman told him all over again, but the jackal shook his head as if he were still unable to understand.

"It is very odd," said he sadly. "But the tale seems to go in at one ear and out at the other. Then, finally, I will go to the place where it all happened. And then perhaps I will be able to give a judgment."

So, they returned to the cage, besides which the tiger was still waiting for Brahman sharpening his teeth and claws.

"You have been a long time," growled the savage beast. "But let us begin our dinner."

"Our dinner," thought the wretched Brahman as his knees knocked together with fright. What an unhappy way of speaking.

"Give me five minutes, my Lord," he pleaded, "so that I may explain the matter to the jackal here who is somewhat slow in his wits."

The tiger consented, and the Brahman told the whole story again, not missing a single detail and spinning as long a yarn as possible.

"Oh, my poor brain," cried the jackal, wringing his paws. "Let me see how it all began. You were in the cage, and the tiger came walking by...."

"Pooh," interrupted the tiger. "What a fool you are. I was in the cage."

"Oh, of course," cried the jackal pretending to tremble with fright. "Yes, I was in the cage. ... No, I was not. ... dear. ... dear. Where are my wits? Let me see. The tiger was in the Brahman, and the cage came walking by. No, that's not it either. Well, do not mind me but begin your dinner, for I shall never understand."

"Yes, you shall," returned the tiger in a rage at the jackal's stupidity. "I will make you understand. Look here. I was in the cage. Do you understand?"

"Yes! Please, my Lord, how did you get in? How? Why? In the usual way, of course, O, dear! I, my head, is going to whirl again. Please do not be angry, my Lord, but what is the usual way?"

At this, the tiger lost all patience and jumped into the cage and cried, "This way. Now, do you understand how it happened?"

"Perfectly," grinned the jackal as he cleverly shut the door. "And if you'll permit me to say so, I think the matters will remain as they were."

We heard that this story ends here. However, things developed further. A fierce quarrel broke out among the beasts of the jungle. The weaker party approached the caged tiger in the hope of getting help from the mighty king of the beasts, and after some conversation, they opened the cage on their own accord without even the sulky tiger having asked for it. So rushed out the wretched beast, and they say that the first thing he did was tear these envoys of the beasts and devour them up, flesh and bone. The remaining beasts of the jungle became his prey soon after.

Humanity, but instead, the survivors of the atomic conflagration amongst humanity, will realize the truth of this story one day. And some aged grandpa may relate it to his monstrous little brood around him.

Nixons and Brezniefs are endeavoring hard to keep this atomic tiger caged, just as Eisenhowers and Khursheves have done before them, and their successors will do the same in future times. But will they, despite their genuine attempts and sincere efforts, be able, like the jackal, to imprison this furious monster into its cage forever when the devil moves free to dab the wall with syrupy fingers everywhere? Suppose they succeed for a while in their endeavor. Even then, who will stop the emission of venomous rays which the atomic tiger, i.e., nuclear reactor, perpetually breathes out of the cage?

The history of the human mind reveals a constant struggle between an inherent love of pleasure and hatred of pain but a weighty thought of eternity against transitoriness of things has often permeated the most extraordinary human minds throughout the long history of humankind. Such minds have sacrificed the transitory pleasures to seek eternity of pleasure and have chosen to bear the transitory pains patiently. Permanent, unmixed, and eternal bliss was their goal. They considered temporary pleasures of this transitory world as a source of eternal pains eventually. While on the contrary, they deemed fleeting pains of this short-lived world a source of eternal pleasure eventually.

Excessive food and drink resulted in gastric troubles; a day-long fast was rewarded with pleasantness in the evening feast. Similarly, a constant reminder of the evils of worldly greed was forever present to sober the excessive desire for worldly things, and people generally achieved a sort of moderate behavior. The death and the deceitful nature of this life were forever present before the eye of their mind.

They used to teach such a philosophy in every temple, mosque, monastery, hermitage, nursery, or cavern throughout the world as far as the recorded history of man can take us back into antiquity. The mind was to be preferred to matter, and the soul deserved more consideration than the body. People thought of this world as a deceitful provision against the eternal life in Heaven. They bore calamities and vicissitudes with patience. Humanity moved on the path of morality and spiritualism, gradually progressing until these qualities reached a point that seemed like a zenith.

Then started a decline. People began to abuse faith. Falsity arose in the garb of truth, and the devil engaged in the guise of a saint. Selfish motives expelled the light of sincerity. The cleverer sort played upon the superstition of ignorant masses. Gradually the situation worsened till it could worsen no more. The very name of religion struck a terror in the minds of people.

Then appeared a balanced religion which removed all taint of superstition and undesirable part of the superstitious dread. It allotted proper places to matter and mind, body and soul, this world, and the otherworld. The things assumed a happy appearance once more.

This state of affairs persisted for a long time, but things finally worsened, and another phase appeared. Folks started suspecting faith as a mere hoax. The whole atmosphere became so overcast with doubt, mistrust, and suspicion that man's eyes saw nothing but pretentious attitudes, feigned piety, concealed falsehood, cloaked ignorance, pretexted tyranny, everywhere and every way.

People considered faith an obstacle in their way to the feast of Mother Nature. They believed it to be mere superstition, foul play, and a wall against their path to progress. Religion became a word of reproach. The thoughts of mercy, charity, and moral fortitude waned and also dwindled the hope in Heaven. At the time of humankind's start, a dispute had emerged between the mind and the matter. Previously, it had always been decided in favor of the mind. However, this argument started afresh. But this time, it terminated in the complete victory of matter over mind, body over soul, and this world over next world.

Humanity considered faith a cumbersome burden and assumed the conquest of the realm of Mother Nature. However, initially, with some thought of faith, materialism excluded the faith gradually from the thoughts and reigned supreme. Thus, life was once again unbalanced though this time not towards spiritualism but materialism. Therefore, humankind could not escape the consequences of unbalance and found itself standing on the brink of atomic hell, ready to be plunged into it at any moment.

Once again, a balanced life is the dire necessity of the world if this dreadful doom needs to be averted. An essential compromise between these old adversaries that is mind and matter is the need of the hour; since both are indispensable, and humankind could discard none of these. Yet, they have different places and ought to be justly placed. The mind is to be the leader, but it is to be led by faith in turn. The body is to be fed and prepared for good works. In that case, sleep and rest shall also be deemed part of work since these prepare the body for further work, and every act of kindness shall be deemed a charity. To smile in an afflicted brother's face or lead a blind person on to his way are considered equally works of charity. A constant struggle should be made against the evil of every kind: like an act of felony, fraud, or tyranny.

Let justice, equity, and equality be the rule, and let universal fraternity and brotherhood prevail. Let men be judged by worth and not by substance, and let every deed reflect the thought of the Day of Judgment. Honorable in the Judgment of Allah is he who fears Allah more and leads a life of righteousness. This life is but transient, and this world is but a temporary abode. Man's natural home is in Heaven whence he came. Those who have made this earth their permanent abode, have subjected themselves to severe consequences. Their progress has provided deceit. Their light is not light but darkness visible to discover sights of woe, regions of sorrow, doleful shades, where peace and rest can never dwell, hope never comes.

Humanity today needs a faith of a balanced kind. A life balanced between the mind and matter, body and soul, material and spiritual, terrestrial, and celestial, this world and the otherworld so that mind and not matter shall lead; the matter is but a servant of the mind. The soul and not the body shall lead; the body is but a servant of the soul. The otherworld and not this world shall lead. This world is but a sowing field and life a season for sowing that humanity shall reap in the otherworld, all being led by faith in Allah and His angels, Scriptures, apostles, and Resurrection.

Let the body be allowed food and apparel and other reasonable necessities of life because it serves the cause of good against evil. Let men live in society and work their way to the paradisiacal bliss of Heaven under the Sovereignty of one Allah over this globe under the canopy of the heavens. Let wealth be deposed from its usurped godhead and brought to its actual place that of necessity, and let folks spend it on good works and needy people. Let religion be generalized and brought within reach of everyone. Let everyone be allowed the necessities of life but let not the spirit of self-abnegation and self-sacrifice be allowed to die out. Let the feelings of spiritual values always be the primary consideration.

Let people live within this world and society, yet attached only outwardly but detached inwardly and attached to Allah and the next world. Let people live like soldiers by day and hermits by night and lead an unbiased life. Let them be moderate in everything and avoid extremities of every kind, an average mark only since too lofty ideals are for a few selected and are fraught with great dangers. Let the acquirement of knowledge be made compulsory, but at the same time let it be made subservient to faith, or else it may turn perilous. Our modern knowledge is one such example and needs this treatment. In the absence of faith, modern knowledge has enkindled a hell of a kind unknown to the ancient people of the past ignorant ages. It has assumed the form of blood-curdling terror, a horrible grisly, a fright with fiery tongues and flaming breath which consumes human beings to a distance of hundreds of miles and is called the demon Atumbumb. A religion with such features described can bring peace and contentment to distressed humanity and naturally avert the atomic danger.

AN AMULET TO WARD OFF THE ATOMIC EVIL

In the following, we present a code formulated from the Quran. We will call this code an amulet to ward off the atomic evil from humankind and scare away the 'Giant Atumbumb'. Suppose humanity adopts this code and wears the amulet. In that case, this amulet shall exorcise every apparition, ghost, vampire, witch of greed, felony, injustice, tyranny, and every other evil spirit out of this modern race. Besides revival of an atmosphere of mutual goodwill, sympathy, trust, and a sense of universal brotherhood that comes in the wake, the destruction of such evils as disease, poverty, and ignorance also is guaranteed.

Millions of hearts all over the world throbbing together in perfect unison, sweet harmony, and affable concord in a world full of love and sympathy resulting from a transformation of hearts so strange that hearts filled with hatred and distrust today and deserving destruction of at least this world of Allah through a rain of atomic hail and deadly missiles, would feel tomorrow a tinge of mercy and revival of hope and charitable sentiments. This gloomy earth and these scowling skies would smile once more on a panic-stricken human race.

Lastly, let no one delude himself into a belief that after the atomic bomb, this representation of certain untoward tendencies of deluded humankind, has made its appearance in the world, either caution or prudence on the part of ill-fated humankind amidst a world of unforeseen and unpredictable circumstances, unavoidable variations and thousands of undercurrents viciously converging towards infinite points of probable collisions, might perhaps succeed in retaining a hold on this most treacherous of all monsters to the last: nay, even for a very long duration unless the fundamental causes of the emergence of the atomic bomb, as stated by the Quran, are removed. No doubt, when a single nuclear bomb has once been detonated and dropped on any human habitation, any hope of existence, either of civilization or humanity or health amidst the vengeful cannonade of atomic bombs, ought to be considered as futile.

The name of the atomic bomb is indeed terrible. The very mention of this name strikes terror in the heart of flawed helpless humanity. But worse is another face of nuclear energy, a facet that I might have repeated a hundred times in this work. And which I would never feel tired of repeating as long as I live and breathe, quite unmindful of the charge of unnecessary repetition, namely, the lethal effect of the inherent and inescapable ionizing radiations of nuclear energy generated for war or peaceful purposes. I observe a general tendency in humanity's responsible guides with much heartfelt grief, which can move any sincere-hearted person to genuine resentment. This tendency is to underestimate the radiological hazard of atomic radiation on the plea of obtaining much-needed power from nuclear energy. Of course, it will be with a guilty conscience if I skip this fundamental reality without declaring it at the top of my voice to the whole human species.

I honestly believe that there isn't one individual couple in this vast world of Allah that might not prefer to see their innocent children half hungry or barefooted to expose them to radiation and see them lepers or cancer-ridden monsters. The miserable plight of their children will be cutting at the very heartstrings of wretched parents who would, but helpless by a sigh, curse the day when humankind discovered this epidemical blight of nuclear energy. Alas for unfortunate, ill-starred, and ill-advised humanity.

Suppose faith is prescribed as a remedy for humanity's ills today, and the divine Scriptures are referred to in search of treatment. In that case, the Quran indeed occupies a place of honor amongst these celestial guides of the human race. Also, if a patient can condescend to receive the treatment from a doctor in whose particular faith he does not believe, then why anyone who does not believe in a Scripture should refuse to benefit by the guidance that such a Scripture may effectually offer without obligation. Why should a thirsty man refuse to drink from a spring just because the spring did not exist inside the territory of his native country? During my lifelong study of Scriptures, I have found Quran always to contain a piece of great advice. Suppose it has guided humanity in the past ages of simple problems and has furnished them with satisfactory answers for their simple problems. In that case, it has the necessary light to guide present-day humanity and provide answers to their complex problems.

I have often watched the very signs (verses) of the Quran with amazement, which in antiquity had provided answers to straightforward questions particular to those simple ages. The same emblems (verses) achieve a transformation in some strange, mysterious way to give detailed and appropriate answers to typically modern problems of a highly complex nature. Current circumstances raise these issues of complex nature bearing the stamp of present complexity and are particularly characteristic of the contemporary environment. I have found with astonishment these signs adopting a stylish appearance in a modern atmosphere. Coming from different directions, like flocks of birds in flight from Eden, they converge to a particular objective. There, they would first identify with the point of discussion, its object, and subject through an apt allusion, an appropriate hint, or a suggestive reflection. Then they discuss the actual problem in a few judged words in a brief, concise manner, yet clear and surprisingly comprehensive in detail. After assessing the essence of the absolute truth, they would finally depart with some weighty aphorism or a piece of heart-touching advice. The clouds suddenly appear in the sky with lightning and thunder, and the rain pours in buckets leaving the azure sky bright and clear. Details are sometimes described with exact minuteness, precise bearing on the problem, and an unmistakable identity with the issue in question. It seems as if the verse had been revealed against a question put to an Oracle for the reply.

A LIGHT-HOUSE WITH SEVENTY CANDLES

Now, we produce the codified amulet derived from the Quran. It can be likened to a celestial, seven-sided beacon of light with seventy candles with some aptness. The lighthouse is molded into a brilliant crown to outshine the sparkle of the orient sun and suppress the blinding dazzle, the deafening thunder, and the stunning blast of the thermonuclear destroyer of this world of Allah.

The scientist, it seems, will never be able to invent a neutralizer for the atomic bomb. The politicians, it seems, will never be able to guarantee a 'No-Atomic-War' pact forever. Still, the amulet prepared by the Quran is, without a doubt, a sure redeemer of humanity from the clutches of this atomic monster. The Quran has predicted the danger of atomic conflagration and prescribes this unparalleled danger to humankind. It is definitely by applying the method which the Quran has shown that humanity can avert this disaster.

It is not only the nuclear dread that humankind would eradicate if this code presented by the Quran is abided by, but surely the long-lost joy, peace, and contentment of humankind will return once more in a distressed world. Therefore, let not the present-day sailors of the whirling boat of humanity refuse the sails and magnetic compass offered by the Quran in so dark a night and so enraged the ocean. Perhaps the ship may emerge from this dangerous situation and move onward on its voyage to its destination in peace and safety.

THE SEVEN SIDES OF THE BEACON

The seven sides of the beacon are as follows.

(1) It is the face of the beacon. It bears an inscription relating to the Guidance and Mercy of Allah, that is, the Quran.
(2) It is about this world.
(3) It is about the otherworld.
(4) This life is a trial.
(5) It is the reasonable necessities of life allowed to a reasonable extent and on condition.
(6) It is the principles of Economics of the Quran.
(7) It is faith.

Adopting this code, the habits of slander and backbiting, exclusive engrossment in the accumulation of wealth, and wealth worship will vanish. Along with it, the threat of atom bombs and nuclear energy will vanish. The signs which we have quoted are not a random selection. Instead, every sign has a direct and exact bearing on the modern age and its modern problems. Space and time do not permit us to give explanations. Therefore, let the readers at their own try to find the peculiarities of this nature.

THE SPIRIT OF THE AMULET

"Our Lord! Give unto us in the world that which is good and in the Hereafter that which is good and guard us against the doom of fire."

(Quran 2:201)

THE OUTER INSCRIPTION OF THE BEACON

"Allah is the Light of the heavens and the earth. The similitude of His Light is as a niche wherein a lamp is. The lamp is in a glass. The glass is, as it were, a shining star. (This lamp is) kindled from a blessed tree, an olive neither of the East nor the West, whose oil would almost glow forth (of itself) though no fire touched it. Light upon Light, Allah guideth unto His Light whom He will. And Allah speaketh to humankind in allegories, for Allah is the knower of all things." (Quran 24:35)

SIDE 1: **THE FACE OF THE BEACON**

Candle 1: "O humankind! There hath come unto you an exhortation from your Lord, a balm for that which is in the breasts, guidance, and a mercy for believers. Say: In the bounty of Allah and His mercy: therein let them rejoice. It is better than what they hoard." (Quran 10:57-58)

SIDE 2: **THIS WORLD**

Candle 2: "Know that the life of this world is only a play, and idle talk, and pageantry, and boasting among you, and rivalry in respect of wealth and children; as the likeness of vegetation after rain, whereof the growth is pleasing to the husbandman, but afterward it drieth up and thou seest it turning yellow then it becometh straw. And in the Hereafter, there is grievous punishment and (also) forgiveness from Allah and His good pleasure, whereas the life of the world is but a matter of illusion. Race one with another for forgiveness from your Lord and a Garden whereof the breadth is as the breadth of the heavens and the earth, which is in store for those who believe in Allah and His messengers. Such is the bounty of Allah, which He bestoweth upon whom He will, and Allah is of infinite bounty."

(Quran 57:20-21)

Candle 3: "Beautified for humankind is the love of the joys (that come) from women and offspring, and stored-up heaps of gold and silver, and horses branded (with their mark), and cattle and land. That is the comfort of the life of the world. Allah! With Him is a more excellent abode."

(Quran 3:14)

Candle 4: "Whoso desireth the reward of the world, (let him know that) with Allah is the reward of the world and the Hereafter. Allah is ever Hearer, Seer."

(Quran 4:134)

Candle 5: "Whoso desireth the harvest of the Hereafter, We give him increase in its harvest. And whoso desireth the harvest of the world, We give him thereof, and he hath no portion in the Hereafter."

(Quran 42:20)

Candle 6: "Whoso desireth the life of the world and its pomp, We shall repay them their deeds herein, and therein they will not be wronged. Those are they for whom is naught in the Hereafter save the fire. (All) that they 'contrive' here is vain and (all) that they are wont to do 'fruitless'."

(Quran 11:15-16)

Read the above-quoted sign with care. It precisely describes the state of the modern materialistic age. Humankind moved on the path of material progress and has got a good reward in the struggle. However, because they forgot Resurrection and the next world in Heaven, they have found themselves face-to-face with a raging fire of atomic hell even in this world, and who knows their lot in the world which is hereafter?

The two terms used in the above-quoted sign, the 'contrivance' and 'fruits', are fascinating. These are the two very same terms that are the essence of the Baconian philosophy and frequently used in Bacon's writings, namely, 'contriving' the methods of experimentation and seeking the 'fruit'. Hence the philosophy of Bacon is aptly known as the philosophy of 'utility' and 'fruit'.

Bacon himself very sagaciously had tried to balance his philosophy between the material and the spiritual. Still, unfortunately, his followers soon discarded the spiritual side and were entirely inclined towards immediate material gains. As a result, the fruit was tainted. The first few bites were sweet enough, whiffs quite inebriating, and swings exhilarating, but then a taint of sourness spread throughout. The sweet taste of the fruit vanished. Inebriation changed into dizziness, and the pleasant glide of the swing assumed frightfully impetuous whirl. Heart-burning spread like an epidemic. Discontent and frustration increased in exact proportion to the fruit's increase, so the Quran says much appropriately.

Candle 7: "Such are those who buy the life of the world at the price of the Hereafter: Their punishment will not be lightened, neither will they have support."

(Quran 2:86)

Candle 8:
They will never be satisfied.
"Unto Him is the real prayer. Those, unto whom they pray beside Allah respond to them not at all, save as (if the response to) one who stretcheth

forth his hands toward water (asking) that it may come unto his mouth, and it will never reach it. The prayer of disbelievers goeth (far) astray."

(Quran 13:14)

Candle 9:
They will be punished with the wealth they hoarded.
"So let not their riches nor do their children please thee (O Muhammad). Allah thereby intendeth but to punish them in the life of the world and that their souls shall pass away while they are disbelievers."

(Quran 9:55)

Candle 10: "Then, when they forgot that whereof they had been reminded, We opened unto them the gates of all things till, even as they were rejoicing in that which they were given, We seized them unawares, and lo! They were dumbfounded."

(Quran 6:44)

In reality, this is the case of the modern age of progress and atomic hell.

Candle 11: "Every soul will taste of death. And ye will be paid on the Day of Resurrection only that which ye have fairly earned. Whoso is removed from the fire and is made to enter Paradise; he indeed is triumphant. The life of this world is but the comfort of illusion."

(Quran 3:185)

SIDE 3: **THE OTHERWORLD**

Candle 12: "Now have ye come unto Us solitary as We did create you at first, and ye have left behind you all that We bestowed upon you, and We behold not with you those your intercessors, of whom ye claimed that they possessed a share in you. Now is the bond between you severed and that which ye presumed hath failed you."

(Quran 6:94)

Candle 13: "And the abode of the Hereafter is better, for those who ward off (evil)."

(Quran 7:169)

Candle 14: "As for man, whenever his Lord trieth him by honoring him, and is gracious unto him, he saith: My Lord honoreth me. But whenever He trieth him by straitening his means of life, he saith: My Lord despiseth me. Nay, but ye (for your part) honor not the orphan and urge not to feed the poor, and ye devour heritages with devouring greed and love wealth with abounding love. Nay, but when the earth is ground to atoms, grinding, grinding, and thy Lord shall come with angels, rank on rank, and hell is brought near that day; on that day man will remember, but how will the remembrance (then avail him)? He will say: Ah, would that I had sent before me (some provision) for my life! None punisheth as

He will punish on that day! None bindeth as He then will bind. But ah! Thou soul at peace! Return unto thy Lord, content in His good pleasure! Enter thou among My bondmen! Enter thou My Garden!"

(Quran 89:15-30)

SIDE 4: **THIS LIFE IS A TRIAL**

Candle 15: "Who (Allah) hath created life and death that He may try you, which of you is best in conduct; and He is the Mighty, Forgiving."

(Quran 67:2)

Candle 16: "It is He who hath placed you as viceroys of the earth and hath exalted some of you in rank above others, that He may try you by (the test of) that which He hath given you. Lo! Thy Lord is swift in prosecution, and lo! He is Forgiving, Merciful."

(Quran 6:165)

Candle 17: "Lo! We have placed all that is in the earth as an ornament thereof that we may try them: which of them is best in conduct."

(Quran 18:7)

Candle 18: "Had Allah willed, He could have made you one community. But that He may try you by that which He hath given you (He hath made you as ye are)."

(Quran 5:48)

Candle 19: "I created the Jinn and humankind only that they might worship Me."

(Quran 51:56)

Candle 20: "And were it not that humankind would have become one community (through the love of riches), We might well have appointed, for those who disbelieve in the Beneficent, roofs of silver for their houses and stairs (of silver) whereby to mount and for their houses doors (of silver) and couches of silver whereon to recline, and ornaments of gold. Yet all that would have been but a provision of the life of the world. And the Hereafter with your Lord would have been for those who keep from evil."

(Quran 43:33-35)

Candle 21: "Your wealth and your children are only a temptation, whereas Allah! With Him is an immense reward."

(Quran 64:15)

Candle 22: "Say (O Muhammad): Lo! My Lord enlargeth the provision for whom He will and narroweth it (for whom He will). But most of the humankind knows not. And it is neither your wealth nor your children that will bring you near unto Us, but he who believeth and doeth good (he draweth near). As for such, theirs will be twofold reward for what they did, and they will dwell securely in lofty halls."

(Quran 34:36-37)

Candle 23: "O humankind! Lo! We have created you male and female and have made you nations and tribes that ye may know one another. Lo! The noblest of you, in the sight of Allah, is the best in conduct. Lo! Allah is Knower, Aware."

(Quran 49:13)

Candle 24: "(This lamp is found) in houses which Allah hath allowed to be exalted and that His name shall be remembered therein. Therein do offer praise to Him at morn and evening. Men whom neither merchandise nor sale beguileth from the remembrance of Allah and constancy in prayer and paying to the poor their due; who fear a day when hearts and eyeballs will be overturned."

(Quran 24:36-37)

Candle 25: "O! Ye who believe! Let not your wealth nor do your children distract you from the remembrance of Allah. Those who do so, they are the losers."

(Quran 63:9)

Candle 26: "Yet of mankind are some who take unto themselves (objects of worship which they set as) rivals to Allah, loving them with love like (that which is the due) of Allah (only) - those who believe are stauncher in their love for Allah - Oh, that those who do evil had but known, (on the day) when they behold the doom, that power belongeth wholly to Allah, and that Allah is severe in punishment!"

(Quran 2:165)

Of the objects we could set as the rival of Allah, one may mention wealth, which folks these days adore with the adoration due only to Allah.

Candle 27:

(a) "Allah enlargeth the provision for whom He will of His slaves and straiteneth it (for whom He will)."

(Quran 28:82)

(b) "And if Allah were to enlarge the provision for His slaves, they would surely rebel in the earth, but He sendeth down by measure as He willeth. Lo! He is Informed, a Seer of His bondmen."

(Quran 42:27)

Candle 28: "Vie one with another in good works. Unto Allah, ye will all return, and He will then inform you of that wherein ye differ."

(Quran 5:48)

Candle 29: "For all, there will be ranks from what they did. Thy Lord is not unaware of what they do." (Quran 6:132)

SIDE 5: **REASONABLE NECESSITIES OF LIFE ALLOWED TO SOME REASONABLE EXTENT AND ON CONDITION**

Candle 30: "Eat and drink of that which Allah hath provided, and do not act corruptly, making mischief in the earth."

(Quran 2:60)

Candle 31: "O humankind! Eat of that which is lawful and wholesome in the earth, and follow not the footsteps of the devil. Lo! He is an open enemy for you."

(Quran 2:168)

Candle 32: "Eat of that which Allah hath bestowed on you as food lawful and good, and keep your duty to Allah in Whom ye are believers."

(Quran 5:88)

Candle 33: "O ye who believe! Forbid not the good things which Allah hath made lawful for you, and transgress not. Lo! Allah loveth not transgressors."

(Quran 5:87)

Candle 34: "He hath forbidden you only carrion, and blood, and swine flesh, and that which hath been immolated to (the name of) any other than Allah. But he who is driven by necessity, neither craving nor transgressing, it is no sin for him. Lo! Allah is Forgiving, Merciful."

(Quran 2:173)

Candle 35: "Eat of that over which the name of Allah hath been mentioned if ye are believers in His revelations."

(Quran 6:118)

Candle 36: "O ye who believe! Strong drink and games of chance and idols and divining arrows are only an infamy of Satan's handiwork. Leave it aside so that ye may succeed. Satan seeketh only to cast among you enmity and hatred employing strong drink and games of chance and to turn you from the remembrance of Allah and (His) worship. Will ye then have done?"

(Quran 5:90-91)

Candle 37: "And there is not a beast in the earth but the sustenance thereof dependeth on Allah. He knoweth its habitation and its repository. All is in a clear record."

(Quran 11:6)

Candle 38: "O Children of Adam! Look to your adornment at every place of worship, and eat and drink, but be not prodigal. Lo! He loveth not the prodigals."

(Quran 7:31)

Candle 39: "Say: Who hath forbidden the adornment of Allah which He hath brought forth for His bondmen and the good things of His providing? Say: Such, on the Day of Resurrection, will be only for those who believed during the life of the world. Thus, do We detail Our revelations for people who know. Say My Lord forbiddeth only indecencies, such of them as are apparent and such as are within, and sin and wrongful oppression, and that ye associate with Allah that for which no warrant hath been revealed, and that ye tell concerning Allah that which ye know not."

(Quran 7:32-33)

Candle 40: "Allah is He Who created the heavens and the earth, and causeth water to descend from the sky, thereby producing fruits as food for you, and maketh the ships to be of service unto you, that they may run upon the sea at His command, and hath made of service unto you the rivers; and maketh the sun and the moon, constant in their courses, to be of service unto you, and hath made of service unto you the night and the day. And He giveth you of all ye ask of Him, and if ye would count the bounty of Allah ye cannot reckon it. Lo! Man is verily a wrong-doer, an ingrate."

(Quran 14:32-34)

Candle 41: "Then We caused Our messengers to follow in their footsteps; and We caused Jesus, son of Mary, to follow, and gave him the Gospel, and placed compassion and mercy in the hearts of those who followed him. But monasticism they invented. We ordained it not for them. Only seeking Allah's pleasure, and they observed it not with right observance. So, We give those of them who believe their reward, but many of them are evil livers." (Quran 57:27)

SIDE 6: **QURAN'S ECONOMIC PRINCIPLES**

Candle 42: "Lo! Allah enjoineth justice and kindness, and giving to kinsfolk, and forbiddeth lewdness and abomination and wickedness. He exhorteth you so that ye may take heed."

(Quran 16:90)

Candle 43: "O! Ye who believe! Squander not your wealth among yourselves in vanity, except it be a trade by mutual consent, and kill not one another. Lo! Allah is ever Merciful unto you."

(Quran 4:29)

Candle 44: "Eat ye of the fruit thereof when it fruiteth, and pay the due thereof upon the harvest day, and be not prodigal. Lo! Allah loveth not the prodigals."

(Quran 6:141)

Candle 45: "Establish worship, pay the poor-due, and bow your heads with those who bow (in worship)."

(Quran 2:43)

Candle 46:
Following is the Keynote of the Islamic Economic System.
"And they ask thee what they ought to spend. Say that which is superfluous. Thus, Allah maketh plain to you (His) revelations that haply ye may reflect."

(Quran 2:219)

That is, prefer the next world and spend most in the name of Allah, and the same you will get paid in that eternal life.

Candle 47:
Following is the fundamental of the Islamic Socio-Economic System.
"That which Allah giveth as spoil unto His messenger from the people of the townships, it is for Allah and His messenger and the near of kin and the orphans and the needy and the wayfarer, that it become not a commodity between the rich among you."

(Quran 59:7)

Wealth should not merely make a circuit between the wealthy among you, lest (the riches) be (forever divided) in a circle among such of you as are rich. The Quran commands a reasonable division of wealth: A few excessively rich and others extremely poor is not the ideal of the Quran; rational equality in this matter is sought.

Candle 48: "The likeness of those who spend their wealth in Allah's way is as the likeness of a grain which groweth seven ears, in every ear a hundred grains. Allah giveth increase manifold to whom He will. Allah is All-Embracing, All-Knowing."

(Quran 2:261)

Candle 49:
Following is the basis of the Islamic Economic System. Allah is the actual owner and inheritor.
"And let not those who hoard up that which Allah hath bestowed upon them of His bounty think that it is better for them. Nay, it is worse for them. That which they hoard will be their collar on the Day of Resurrection. Allah's is the heritage of the heavens and the earth, and Allah is Informed of what ye do."

(Quran 3:180)

Candle 50: "Greed hath been made present in the minds (of men)."

(Quran 4:128)

Candle 51:
(a) "And whoso is saved from his (own) avarice - such are they who are successful."
(Quran 59:9)

(b) "So, keep your duty to Allah as best ye can, and listen, and obey, and spend; that is better for your souls. And whoso is saved from his (own) greed; such are successful."
(Quran 64:16)

Candle 52: "Lo! Ye are those who are called to spend in the way of Allah, yet among you, some hoard. And as for him who hoardeth, he hoardeth only from his soul. And Allah is the Rich, and ye are the poor. And if ye turn away, He will exchange you for some other folk, and they will not be the likes of you."
(Quran 47:38)

Candle 53: "Allah hath blighted usury and made almsgiving fruitful. Allah loveth not the impious and guilty."
(Quran 2:276)

Candle 54: "And how many an animal there is that beareth not its (own) provision! Allah provideth for it and you. He is the Hearer, the Knower."
(Quran 29:60)

Candle 55: "They who hoard up gold and silver and spend it not in the way of Allah, unto them give tidings (O Muhammad) of a painful doom, on the day when it will (all) be heated in the fire of hell, and their foreheads and their flanks and their backs will be branded therewith (and it will be said unto them): Here is that which ye hoarded for yourselves. Now taste of what ye used to hoard."
(Quran 9:34-35)

Candle 56: "As for those who disbelieve, lo! If all that is in the earth were theirs, and as much again therewith, to ransom them from the doom on the Day of Resurrection, it would not be accepted from them. Theirs will be a painful doom."
(Quran 5:36)

Candle 57: "Lo! Those who keep from evil will dwell amid gardens and water springs. Taking that which their Lord giveth them; for lo! Aforetime they were doers of good; they used to sleep but tittle of the night and ere the dawning of each day would seek forgiveness, and in their wealth the beggar the outcast had due share."
(Quran 51:15-19)

Candle 58: "Those who swallow usury cannot rise, save as he ariseth whom the devil hath prostrated by (his) touch. That is because they say: Trade is just like usury, whereas Allah permitteth trading and forbiddeth usury. He unto whom an admonition from his Lord cometh, and (he) refraineth (in obedience thereto), he shall keep (the profits of) that which is past, and his affair (henceforth) is with Allah. As for him who returneth (to usury) such are rightful owners of the fire. They will abide therein."

(Quran 2:275)

Candle 59: "O! Ye who believe! Observe your duty to Allah, and give up what remaineth (due to you) from usury if ye are (in truth) believers. And if ye do not, then be warned of war (against you) from Allah and His messenger. And if ye repent, then ye have your principal (without interest). Wrong not, and ye shall not be wronged."

(Quran 2:278-279)

Candle 60: "Allah hath blighted usury and made almsgiving fruitful. Allah loveth not the impious and guilty." (Quran 2:276)

Candle 61: "That which ye give in usury so that it may increase on (other) people's property hath no increase with Allah; but that which ye give in charity, seeking Allah's Countenance, hath increase manifold."

(Quran 30:39)

Candle 62: "But as for him who is given his record (on the day of Resurrection) in his left hand, he will say: Oh, would that I had not been given my book, and knew not what my reckoning! Oh, would that it had been death! My wealth hath not availed me; my power hath gone from me. (It would be said): Take him and fetter him, and then expose him to hell-fire, and then insert him in a chain whereof the length is seventy cubits. Lo! He used not to believe in Allah the Tremendous and urged not on the feeding of the wretched, therefore hath he no lover here this day, nor any food save filth, which none but sinners eat."

(Quran 69:25-37)

SIDE 7: **FAITH**

Candle 63: "O humankind Worship your Lord, Who hath created you and those before you, so that ye may ward off (evil). Who hath appointed the earth a resting place for you and the sky a canopy; and causeth water to pour down from the sky, thereby producing fruits as food for you. And do not set up rivals to Allah when ye know (better). And if ye are in doubt concerning what We reveal unto Our slave, then produce a surah of the like thereof, and call your witnesses besides Allah if ye are truthful. And if ye do it not and ye can never do it, then guard yourselves against the fire prepared for disbelievers, whose fuel is of men and stones."

(Quran 2:21-24)

Candle 64: "Lo! those who believe (in that which is revealed unto thee, Muhammad), and those who are Jews, and Christians, and Sabaeans, whoever believeth in Allah and the Last Day and doeth right, surely their reward is with their Lord, and there shall no fear come upon them neither shall they grieve." (Quran 2:62)

Candle 65: "And serve Allah. Ascribe no thing as partner unto Him. (Show) kindness unto parents, and near kindred, and orphans, and the needy, and into the neighbor who is of kin (unto you) and the neighbor who is not of kin and the fellow traveler and the wayfarer and (the slaves) whom your right hands possess. Lo! Allah loveth not such as are proud and boastful." (Quran 4:36)

Candle 66: "O ye who believe; believe in Allah and His messenger and the Scripture which He hath revealed unto His messenger and the Scripture which He revealed aforetime. Whoso disbelieveth in Allah and His angels and His Scriptures and His messengers and the Last Day, he verily hath wandered far astray." (Quran 4:136)

Candle 67:
Sincerity should be the motto and the motive.
"It is not righteousness that ye turn your faces to the East and the West, but righteous is he who believeth in Allah and the Last Day and the angels and the Scriptures and the Prophets; and giveth his wealth, for love of Him, to kinsfolk, and orphans and the needy and the wayfarer and to those who ask, and to set slaves free; and observeth proper worship and payeth the poor, due; and those who keep their treaty when they make one, and the patient in tribulation and adversity and time of stress. Such are they who are sincere. Such are the Allah-fearing."

(Quran 2:177)

Candle 68: "Say: In the bounty of Allah and His Mercy: therein let them rejoice. It is better than what they hoard." (Quran 10:58)

Candle 69: "Lo! Verily the friends of Allah are (those) on whom fear (cometh) not, nor do they grieve. Those who believe and keep their duty (to Allah); theirs are good tidings in the life of the world and the Hereafter. There is no changing the words of Allah that is the Supreme Triumph." (Quran 10:62-64)

Candle 70: "[(On that Day) (of Resurrection)] neither the riches nor the progeny of those, who disbelieve will aught avail them with Allah. They will be fuel for the fire." (Quran 3:10)

~~*~*~*~*

---

[1] **danse-macabre**: The dance of death.

~~*~*~*~*

CHAPTER-11
THE CONCLUDING WORD

To whatever creed, color, caste, religion, or faith you may belong to, the atomic bomb will not discern and burn all alike white, yellow, dark, or brown. All human beings are equal prey of nuclear energy, and all have a common cause against this greatest of all enemies of humankind. If it were the question of death only, the case would have been quite different. You could easily make a bonfire of this world, but it is not so. It means a painful existence, also more painful than any human mind can imagine. You have all to see with your own eyes your next generation of cancer-ridden, dull-eyed, pitiable monsters. Above all else, how the sons of Adam would face with embarrassment the devil that had shown great displeasure at making a lowly anthropoid of mold and refused the explicit command of the Creator to bow before Adam and thus incurred the wrath of Allah? You may think at this present time of skeptic thoughts such things as fantastic, but you shall realize their truth in due course, perhaps soon when you wake up from your deep slumber.

Let the scientist remember that the first detonation of an atomic bomb in war shall prove the first and the last fatal blow to science and their philosophy, as quoted in this work. Science and philosophy have prepared the way for atomic warfare. Let the scientist again not forget his honest role regarding the matters of science as in the past. He should tell the whole world plainly and selflessly that nuclear energy is dangerous due to its inherent ionizing radiations: deadly, detrimental, and toxic to the existence of humanity. Let him picture a world of cancer-ridden, impotent, and miserable monsters to his fellow human beings who have come to place trust in him. Let the scientists clear their conscience by telling innocent humanity that nuclear energy is dangerous whether used in the name of peace or war.

Otherwise, **O scientists**! You will rightly deserve the epithets far worse than the victimized Christian community had coined for the tyrannical priests. Indeed, signs are that your atrocities of nature shall prove far worse than those of the Papal origin. Nay, but your cruelty will far exceed all the cruelty of all sorts of felons in the whole history of humankind united. The advantages of power that nuclear energy may bring to humankind are a mere triviality against the harms inherent in this power. On the other hand, you may honestly contradict my word, but pray do not fall into the excessive categorization of 'permissible' and 'lethal' doses. Every nucleon shot into the heart of an atom is lethal eventually. Therefore, you will never succeed despite your strenuous efforts in finding any means to neutralize the ill effects of atomic fission.

O, political leaders of nations! You cannot assume yourself as ignorant or unaware of the hazards that are incident on nuclear energy. You very well know that your country has no chance to escape its ruinous consequences in the case of atomic warfare. You have by now realized that the possession of atomic bombs can no longer be expected to create a wall of terror around your country against your foes, nor it is to remain for long a title of special prestige or a sign of exceptional power.

However, in dismay, you will soon see that the non-atomic people and the atomic-people that are whole vast humankind will gradually develop a bitter hatred of nuclear energy. This hate will be in proportion to their fast-increasing knowledge of the detrimental effects thereof in time of peace and a hail of retaliative atom bombs in case of war. Why not then realize the grim truth in time and be saved? Do you people feel no compassion for your people and wretched, miserable, and worry-ridden humankind of this materialistic age? Why not then live in peace and free from the constant threat of nuclear war and move towards the ultimate destination on the path of peace, love, sympathy, and prosperity like good fellow human beings and fellow sufferers of the afflictions of this life on earth. On the contrary, are you sworn to destroy humankind along with your people: nay, even yourselves and your children. Do you not realize that no 'No-Atomic-War' pact could be reliable? Is it delightful to take the blood of a whole world on your head? Will you sit for a while alone and think?

I have to say a word to the **religious leaders** too. I know you are equally dependent on the oppressive needs of life. Still, your peculiar duty towards humanity and your particular situation demand more sacrifice of your desires than anybody else. Will you not recognize the situation's urgency and not prove faithful to the salt and worthy of a particular place you hold amongst humanity? Forget about petty little prejudices and other tiny considerations and rise to the occasion to adopt a pure and crystal-clear faith and a generous, sympathetic, and cordial disposition? Act wisely and selflessly according to the demands of the occasion, in all love for Him in whose name you work. Show affection for His poor creatures who are now dragged helplessly and whipped mercilessly by cruel circumstances towards a horrible doom in utter darkness. This way, perhaps humanity may be saved, and with it the civilization that once held such esteem.

Man, since the birth of humanity, has kept up an un-interrupted endeavor towards building a civilization through a path of sweat and tears, trial and turmoil and ordeal, struggling incessantly generation after generation, century after century, rising step by step, age after age, till the fruit of such endless labor came to be inherited by the modern age. It was a most solemn duty of the inhabitants of the modern age to keep up the standard of that civilization which they had received as a solemn trust from previous eras. Nay, they were even expected to add something to the existing luster and bequeath it further to future generations.

But, unfortunately, darkness has appeared in certain other features despite their exertions and genuine efforts at enlightenment and great strides in particular crucial factors of civilization. Consequently, the beauty of bright aspects that were the characteristic beauty of civilization and the glory of this age were tainted. Hence, instead of giving peace and life, this fascinating civilization has become the most dangerous hazard to modern humanity's mind and body. It has come to threaten with unfailing certainty the very existence of the human species, nay, but every species that now exist on earth. Yet the strangest thing, despite their knowledge of these facts, is that no single soul ever stirs or even speaks a word. They all go towards the burning hell, dumb, deaf, and blind, spellbound.

Now, chalk out a process to avoid the atomic hell. It is not challenging if men sincerely want to avoid this danger. Enkindle the extinguished torch of faith. Develop the fear of Allah and the remembrance of the Day of Judgment in Heaven. It is all something but natural to man. Let the wealth be deposed from its godhead and bring it down to its proper place, as means and the necessity to better the life in Heaven, the eternal life. Subject every affair of the world to the thought of the otherworld. There are peace, contentment, and joy in it. Let people enjoy the feast of this world but only to prepare for the service of Allah and humanity. Knowledge, power, wealth, science, and the world are nothing in themselves. It is their use and the intent behind it that matters. Achieve progress in science, not to destroy but to build. Know that this life is only transient, a short journey. You can never become immortal. [1] Take away this maddening greed and dwell serenely.

Let this world be a garden of peace and not a hell ablaze. Turn your science to better use, that is, to peaceful use. Let your science turn this abode into a garden of peace, plenty, and prosperity, and let not science ever set your house on fire. Know that the use and intent rule, which applies to power, science, knowledge, and wealth, does not apply to nuclear power, the atomic power as you call it. It is the only exception to the rule. It stands beyond the bounds of the reconcilement, whether used for peace or war. It is forever dangerous. It is never at peace with the environment. It has only one face, and that is of death. Its generation means wholesale destruction inevitably.

Therefore, abjure the habit of backbiting, slander, and complete engrossment in the accumulation of riches that is excessive greed and the deification of wealth so that the atomic power is dissolved in the sun's rays and disappeared like the mist. Let people's lives balance matter and mind, material and spiritual, wealth and contentment, this world, and the otherworld. Eat that you be able to serve Allah and fellow human beings. Wear that you may protect yourself from cold and heat.

Acquire the wealth that you spend on those needier. Be generous, hospitable, soft-spoken, and truthful but stand against evil resolutely. Judge not people based on blood, color, or substance but personal merit only. The fear of Allah and the love of good should be the judgment criteria. Let the sense of equality prevail among you, and let there be strict economic and social justice. Know that this economic and social injustice is the source of a hundred and more troubles and is responsible for most human misery today and always. Never forget that terrible times are ahead for humanity. Let now the senseless, over-dazed, and dizzy race of drunken dupes of wealth, get a little sober and think and look up towards the horizons and carefully see what's ahead. Now, if you have looked up and seen the dreadful spectacle, then sit back to think once for all that the verdict of the time is as follows.

"Let humankind either ban the nuclear power or else prepare to die a most ignominious death following a most miserable existence."

Moreover, unless the banishment of characteristics responsible for the emergence of nuclear power is affected, you can never banish nuclear power. Awake, therefore, and dissolve not the creed built in the 'heart' of things before a twinkling 'atomy'. Wordsworth said this, and you will find it prefixed to 'God and the Atom' of Ronald Arbuthnott Knox, who knocks in his book on the hearts of men. But will they open the door of their heart, "To let a breeze in their heart of hearts."?

The essence of the Christian religion is a negation of slander and backbiting, renunciation of the world, and an intense hatred of wealth. Still, it is surprising to see the Christians so deeply involved in so gross a materialism.

A point may arise in many a mind during their perusal of this work. People with those particular characteristics that the Quran has given out as the cause of the emergence of the atom bomb might, with justice, become victims of atomic conflagration. Still, those innocents of these qualities will also see the same doom as those guilty. Why should they be punished for what they have not done?

The answer to this very genuine question is that you might not find in today's whole world many whom you might entirely regard as innocent of those qualities. The wind has blown throughout the world. Suppose there be some or many such souls, and it is wished there be many because they are the hope of humankind's future on earth. In that case, they will also share the punishment with guilty ones because of their restraint, silence, and cowardly or insensible compromise with the circumstances. Let them rise against the hazard and do whatever is possible for them to do to avert the danger. According to Islamic ideology, they are to be deemed partners in the guilt if they do not exert to the best of their power, might, and influence against the danger.

Nevertheless, if, despite their genuine endeavors, they fail and become the victims of a conflagration brought on them by the guilt of others, then, of course, they will be reimbursed in the next world by Almighty Allah. Unfortunately, however, the situation in the world shows not even a single person amongst millions that might know anything about the reality of nuclear energy or the effects of radiation. Unfortunately, though, the gloomy clouds of atomic calamity scowl on the horizon of unwary humankind to consume them any moment. Therefore, a voice against the dangers of nuclear energy we still expect to hear. Once, such a voice appeared that of Late Bertrand Russell, who sounded an alarm reasonably loud. However, one sentence that reflects the essence of his experience now lies before me, as given in the following: "Since Adam and Eve ate the apple, man has never refrained from any folly of which he was capable."

~~*~*~*

[1] With the help of colossal wealth accumulated by this age, they (the scientists) are still trying to <u>fight death</u> through projects like **Silicon immortality**. The excerpts from a most recent report published by B.B.C. on December 27, 2014, on their website are reproduced here for the reader's knowledge as follows. ... "I think the development of full <u>artificial intelligence</u> [A.I.] could spell the end of the human race." Professor Stephen Hawking's verdict on A.I. in a recent B.B.C. interview wasn't exactly good news for the rest of us. "Once humans develop A.I. it will take off on its own and redesign itself at an ever-increasing rate. Humans, who are limited by slow biological evolution, couldn't compete and would be superseded," he said. ... Machines can already "outlive" the humble human many times over, according to tech editor, investor,

and author Michael S Malone who grew up in Silicon Valley. "Every living thing has one billion heartbeats in its lifetime," he told the B.B.C. "The modern microprocessor goes through the equivalent of 5-10 billion operations per second. These devices are essentially immortal. Just in the time you own your phone, the micro-processor is going through almost all of human existence in terms of digital heartbeats." So might machines contain the secret of eternal life? Mr. Malone is fearful.

SILICON IMMORTALITY: If Moore's Law - the doubling of transistors per square inch on integrated circuits every year, coined by Intel co-founder Gordon Moore - continues, the computers of 2030 will have as much power as the human brain, he believes. "Then you get into this world of Ray Kurzweil [Google's director of engineering] - the singularity - at a certain point we will just map our brains into a computer, and that will give us a kind of silicon immortality," he reasons. "I wonder if the first person who maps their brain into a computer if the first message they send back will be "pull the plug"." ... "What happens to consciousness, to selfhood, when your brain leaves your body and inhabits a silicon-based machine in the corner? What are you? Are you human? What happens if you can live forever but have no physical self?" There are worrying precedents for what happens when man swaps some of his biological parts for the computer or mechanical equivalents.

FIGHTING FATE: So perhaps we are not emotionally ready to make that leap into the machine - but Mr. Clark's experience has not deterred some of Silicon Valley's heavyweights from fighting back against mortality. "We have this strange combination of acceptance and denial - I would prefer our mode was more one of fighting ... Fighting death, fighting decline," serial tech entrepreneur and investor Peter Thiel told the B.B.C. "It's true that death may be natural, but it's also natural that we should fight death." But let's not forget that nature itself has a habit of fighting back. ... In 1859 the biggest solar storm on record took place. Called the Carrington Event after astronomer Richard Carrington, the solar flare was so powerful that there were reports of telegraph pole wires melting and causing fires. It is not known how regularly flares of this size occur or if there will be another - but the consequences for 21st century Earth would be utterly life-changing. "If we had one now, it would take out every chip in the world," says Michael Malone. "If that happened, civilization would sort of stop." (www.bbc.com)

~~*~*~*

VOLUME-2

THE QURAN PREDICTS AND CHARACTERIZES THE TECHNICAL KNOWLEDGE OF NUCLEAR SCIENCE

TABLE OF CONTENTS

VOLUME-2

WARNING 263

Chapter-1
Introductory 265

Chapter-2
Nuclear corroboration of 'Al-Hotama' by atomic physics 363

Chapter-3
The radiobiological corroboration of 'Al-Hotama' 446

Chapter-4
Our corroborative comments on the points of the
prophecy as explained by the original interpreters of the Quran 509

Chapter-5
The Quran phenomenally characterizes
the atomic hell and averts it; A summary 569

Chapter-6
Application of the Quran's characterization
of the atomic phenomena to the electric phenomena 575

Chapter-7
Quran and science of meteorology:
Quran treats the phenomena of 'rain' and 'hail' 577

WARNING

I wrote 'Gabriel's Extinguishing the Atomic Hell Series' from 1972 to 1982. This present volume, I wrote in 1978. Moreover, in 1982, after completing my work, I became ill, which I am still. I pray to Allah, let this guidance reach humankind.

Let no one dare treat the subject of the Quran versus science until he has attained perfection in science with the perfect knowledge of its present situation and future possibilities and trends. It is an ever-changing subject, and the writer must differentiate the eternally proven facts from the mere theories and hypotheses. The slightest slip of the interpreter of the Quran might result in grievous damage to the integrity of Scripture and the ruin of the interpreter himself. Deep knowledge of the mind of the Quran, abounding grace, and mercy of Allah also are the pre-requisites for such an enterprise. While the mastery of science is no easy task, a genius coupled with the life-long struggle in the field is essential. Even the acquaintance with the mind of the Quran and the world of knowledge contained miraculously in the Quran is not an easy matter. Many an interpreter of the Quran in this modern age that have treated the subject of science and the Quran have blundered with fatal consequences to the integrity of the Quran itself despite their genuine sincerity and exceeding desire to bring glory to Allah's word.

Nevertheless, it is a matter of absolute gratification that the works of such authors have been in vernacular languages, and none of them crossed the international borders to afford an opportunity of criticism to the knowing eye of the scientists and the scholars of international caliber. The caution equally applies to this work of mine. However, this is the fruit of more than forty years' incessant toil, labor, and struggle in every field of knowledge and indeed much sacrifice. Every word of this work I have written in the light of my great responsibility. Moreover, every thought and every point I have weighed with utmost care. Yet if anywhere I have erred or slipped, I ask for forgiveness from Allah. May Allah forgive me, for my intention eternally has been genuine and sincere.

Throughout, I had envisioned this work, not for a few elites but every class of people. Hence, I have endeavored to explain things so that the non-scientist world should also read and understand them with the utmost facility. Of course, no prior knowledge of science has been assumed in the reader to read and perfectly understand this work. However, the scientific world might find it interesting and its points impressive due to the controversial nature of the subject and the burning novelty of the theme.

YOUSUF GABRIEL
February 3, 1978.

~~*~*~*~*

THE TEXT OF THE PROPHECY OF THE QURAN ABOUT 'AL-HOTAMA' (THE HELL OF THE 'HOTAMA') THAT IS THE 'ATOMIC HELL'

"Woe to every backbiter, defamer, who accumulateth wealth (of this world) and arrangeth it (against the future). He thinketh surely that his wealth shall render him immortal. Nay, for verily he shall be cast into 'Al-Hotama'. And what shall teach thee what 'Al-Hotama' is? It is Allah's enkindled fire, which rises unto the hearts; it is (a fire) closed in on them, in outstretched columns".

(Quran: 104 'Al-Homaza')

~~*~*~*~*

CHAPTER-1

INTRODUCTORY

Never in its history was humankind exposed to so grievous a threat to either its peace and prosperity or existence as it is in the present age due to the appearance and development of atomic fire. The threat of atomic devastation means not only the extermination of peace, prosperity, civilization, and all in an atmosphere of untold miseries and innumerable afflictions. However, it even amounts to the complete extinction of life on earth. This earth may be rendered uninhabitable for millions of years to come due to the universal dispersal of radioactive substances in the form of fission products by atomic explosions or radioactive substances salvaged as residue from the nuclear reactors.

Any moment, there is a possibility that a hail of nuclear bombs might consume the world in a matter of days, hours, or even minutes despite all the futile efforts of humankind to avoid such war. The course of atomic energy for peace generally considered and recommended as safe and harmless would prove hazardous in the long run. Indeed, the so-called atomic energy for peace will eventually prove destructive, perhaps even more damaging than the hail of the nuclear bombs of the nuclear war. No amount of wishful thinking and dreaming or behavior like an ostrich will ever change the disastrous results. Nay, in a way, the atomic war may prove an experience less harmful than atomic energy for peace.

The first war of atomic bombs may teach humankind a lesson and destroy this modern world's mechanical means and methods and save it from the future threat of atomic devastation. However, such a war has to be small to leave some chance of living on earth. We may not make any predictions in this respect beforehand, and there is no joy of a lesson received as a result of an atomic war. On the other hand, the destruction wrought by the atomic energy for peace will be final without leaving any chance for life on earth to survive. The results of nuclear energy for peace will appear on a long-term basis. They will appear after they have secretly and wholly undermined the health of populations, and the sickness at that time will be in a state past cure. Although the present humankind cannot understand the true nature of the atomic phenomena, the Quran warned about this curse fourteen hundred years ago, defining and describing the atomic hell and assigning the natural causes of its emergence. This warning of the Quran constitutes the subject of this series of volumes.

That a religious Scripture should prophesy about the atomic bomb may come as no little surprise to humankind. The prophecy describes nuclear phenomena' peculiar and distinctive features, unfolding and differentiating its characteristics from other phenomena, e.g., chemical or electrical. It explains the nuclear phenomena in a most scientific method, astonishingly concise and strangely mysterious yet in the clearest of terms, all within only fourteen words. Moreover, the scene is set fourteen hundred years ago in an age entirely innocent of science and in a country famed then for ignorance. Only the knowledgeable scientist could appreciate these facts, which would undoubtedly leave every knowing scientist stunned with wonder.

The prophecy in assigning the causes to the emergence of 'Al-Hotama' displays all the various doctrinal aspects of modern atomistic materialism, social, ethical, and economical, all in eighteen words. It should appear to every genuine philosopher nothing less than an astounding marvel. Again, causes assigned to such a startling consequence as the appearance of the atomic hell within this very world is a fact so extraordinary that it should throw the mind of every single philosopher and scholar into sporadic convulsions. Nor even the share of surprise of the Muslims themselves, followers of the Quran itself, will be any the less astonishing in the recent discovery of the prophecy. The discovery of the prophecy to those that have for ages perused, recited, translated, preached, and interpreted will appear indeed startling. I thank Allah for having led me to this so unique, so important discovery.

Whereas we reserve the office of the critical appreciation of the philosophical side of prophecy for philosophers, critical appreciation of the scientific side of the prophecy we earmark for scientists.

Suppose the philosopher finds himself engrossed in the startling discovery of the mysterious connection between the three habits of 'slander', 'wealth accumulation', and 'wealth adoration', and the emergence of the atomic bomb. In that case, the scientist's mind will find it difficult to relieve itself of the surprise at the difficulty of such a prediction, in so remote an antiquity and the scientific description of so intricate and complex a subject of modern science in an age of no science. Indeed, they only will be able to truly appreciate the superb characterization and subtle differentiation of the fire of 'Al-Hotama'. The Quran has minutely discerned, accurately described, and miraculously linked this fire of 'Al-Hotama' to the causes of its appearance. Hence, the Quran has well initiated this notion in subtle mysteries of science. It possesses a thorough knowledge, and Allah has endued it with keen insight in such matters.

Again, they amongst even the scientists who stand in a preferable position will more precisely appreciate the actual difficulty and true worth of such a prediction. These scientists have themselves advanced the theories in nuclear science and have had a share in the discoveries and the development of atomic science. Because they know the difficulty of advancing theories in nuclear science, they are also familiar with the plight of their ideas in due course that could judge the supreme worth of a notion (that of the Quran) in the light of their personal experience. This notion of the Quran stood and would forever stand as fixed, infallible, unchangeable, and all-pervasive in its own superior right and remote merit.

There may be thousands of scientists in the world today able to comprehend and appreciate this prophecy of the Quran. Yet, it is for the caliber of Curie, Rutherford, Chadwick, Niels Bohr, Hahn, Strassman, Douglas Lea, Crowther, Muller, and Einstein to judge, evaluate and assess the true extent of its scientific sublimity and its superhuman, transcendent merit. Great Einstein himself, in his now-famous letter to Roosevelt about the realization of the fission chain reaction, could but assume a mere possibility of utilizing the phenomenon of Uranium fission for the construction of a powerful bomb of a new type. Yet, the tone of the Quran about the emergence of 'Al-Hotama' conditional to the presence of causes is one of steadfast certainty.

Einstein, in his letter, hinted at only a possibility of a powerful bomb. On the other hand, the Quran has exhausted the whole subject of atomic phenomena and atomic philosophy with astonishing accuracy and doubtless variety. Einstein had the whole scientific multitude of facts inherited through several centuries of research and knew the latest investigations of nuclear science. In contrast, Quran spoke in an age when even the mention of any modern achievements of science would have made people jeer at it as sheer nonsense of lunatic bluffer. We lament Einstein's death as unfortunate and untimely. Because his death a few years ago deprived him of the wonders of a prophecy that would have out-shadowed all the most incredible wonders that he had experienced in his career as a top-ranking physicist.

All astonishing discoveries he made as a theorist of unique ability in the field of physics would merely have faded out before the blinding dazzle of the discovery of the Quran. To Einstein, this prophecy would have appeared as a vision, marvel, and miracle. What wonders his curious, imaginative, and sensitive mind would not have beheld in the prophecy? What revealing views, lights, visions, and images would not have wavered before the mercuric eye of his perspicacious mind? What new trains of thought would not have started in a mind that excelled in ingenuity most of the contemporaries and the predecessors and successors in the field? No doubt it is with a genuine humility that a man of the understanding of Einstein would have gradually learned a look at the inconceivable transcendence of the Scripture's superhuman vision compared to the human ken.

Enrico Fermi was the discoverer of the fission chain reaction; Robert Oppenheimer, the designer of the first-ever, made atomic bomb; and Edward Teller, the maker of the first Hydrogen bomb. None of them could predict the success of their experiment a moment before the actual result had appeared. Einstein himself had to wait for forty years for decisive proof of his theory of Equivalence (of the mass and energy) till the atomic storm burst to accomplish the destruction of Hiroshima and Nagasaki. It is the measure of the difficulty of nuclear science, and it bears not in any way the inability of these eminent scientists. The subject itself is far too complex and intricate and highly subtle, delusive next only to metaphysics. Mark, then in comparison, the unimaginably keen insight, unbelievably amazing farsighted and unusually audacious exactness, brevity, and authority of the revelation. It is hard to believe that in so few words, all the essential principles of so vast a subject comprising several volumes could be so dexterously exhausted as has been done by the Quran and which anyone could see most manifestly.

The complexity, intricacy, subtlety, delusiveness, and mystery of the subject of nuclear science are unique and uniquely proverbial. According to the atomists and Radiobiologists of supreme ability, it is baffling, deceptive, and defiant. However, the miraculous vision of the Quran has penetrated all the various series of veils that hide the secret from human eyes to deep-most regions of the atomic nucleus that is the 'heart' of the atom, the basic building block of the creation of the universe. This fact constitutes a miracle which, strangely enough, has appeared in this age of no miracles. This miracle no man howsoever skeptic, but with a knowledge of the subject of nuclear science, will deny.

We will treat a miracle that will impress the recognized skeptics' minds about the possibility of miracles in this world. It will provide irrefutable proof of the Divine Origin of the Scripture that of the Quran. None shall hereafter ever be able to deny the Divine Origin of the Quran, for no mortal of whatever merit could ever have ventured to make such a prophecy as the Quran has. None shall ever be able to deny the miraculous nature of such a marvel as the Quran in this twentieth century has displayed within this age of exceptional knowledge and science. In a bygone age, when none in the world could even dream of the nuclear notion of the structure of matter, the Quran discussed atomism from a nuclear viewpoint as distinct from a chemical standpoint. It is in itself a fact that would seldom fail to excite the wonder of every discerning scientist of this age and would hardly fail to impress the divine supremacy of the Scripture on his human mind.

In any era, or when the Quran made such a prophecy, a soothsayer, clairvoyant, or astrologer couldn't make a prophecy of this nature. The description and definition of the nuclear phenomena scientifically were simply beyond the scope of any astrologer, soothsayer, or clairvoyant. With a vision that could penetrate the atom's minutest regions and keep in view the whole future to the modern atomic age and the entire past to the age of Democritus in remote antiquity, only the Omniscient mind of Allah could have achieved the wonder of making such prophecy. In a philosophical sequence, assigning ethical causes to the consequent appearance of effects in the form of 'Al-Hotama' was yet added difficulty for the astrologer, the soothsayer, or the clairvoyant. It is not his office to link the moral and economic causes logically to the appearance of the ultimate phenomena. And yet, again, not even a philosopher could have been expected to make such a prophecy. By way of the Quran concluded, which eminent philosopher of that or any other age could have inferred from causes, so startling an effect as the appearance of the atomic bomb and nuclear hell.

Socrates, Plato, and Aristotle, some of the greatest of the thinking minds that humankind has produced, were contemporary with Democritus, the founder of the theory of atomism. All the three were reputedly the most redoubtable antagonists of atomism. It could not have been without a philosophical reason that these greatest philosophers had opposed the theory of atomism. They indeed must have contemplated the harms and ill-effects of the theory, which they so vehemently opposed. Yet which of them has left on record the type of future ill-effects that theory may have on humankind? Which of them could have inferred from the worldly love and the hedonistic features of atomism the resultant appearance of the atomic bomb or the atomic energy? If this is considered a far-fetched inference, which of them could have scientifically explained the nuclear phenomena? Which of them could have coined a term like 'Hotama' so far-reaching and at the same time bearing such class resemblance to the word 'atomism', both phonetically and functionally? All these greatest philosophers in this respect appear like little lisping innocent children engrossed in the transcendent brilliance of the superb intellect and sublime wisdom of the Quran.

In an age in which the world had forgotten the idea of atomism itself, the Quran undertook the task of revealing atomism a millennium after the great Greek philosophers like Socrates, Plato, and Aristotle. It took up the long-relinquished theme and treated it philosophically and scientifically to its far distant and surprisingly logical end. It did all this by defining 'Al-Hotama', describing all the characteristic features of the fire of 'Al-Hotama', portraying the form of the atomic explosion distinctly, and assigning the philosophical causes to the consequential appearance of 'Al-Hotama'. The assigning of such causes as 'slander' and 'wealth worship' to the appearance of the atomic bomb is far beyond the human ken and needs a divine vision. Which philosopher of today shall be able to repress his wonder at so startling a link between such causes and a result, so truthfully established by the Quran? To Bertrand Russell, it might have appeared as something too astonishing, nothing short of a miracle.

Thus, the vast distance lies between the ken of the greatest of the human intellects and the celestial cognizance of the divine revelation, and it is in this age so famed for excellent knowledge and great science that the incomparable ascendancy of the Quran has ultimately obtained the proof. Suppose we associate the knowledge of this knowledgeable age with the moon. In that case, we may compare the knowledge of the Quran to the dazzling brilliance of the sun or a galaxy of distant luminous stars that could be seen visibly shining always and everywhere.

Suppose a miracle makes alive the intellectual celebrities of whole human history as Socrates, Plato, Aristotle, Galenus, Heraclitus, Hipparchus, Eratosthenes, Archimedes, Zeno, and Xenophon, and hundreds of thousands of others that ever existed in any age on earth with a reputation for knowledge or wisdom. Someone describes and explains this prophecy of the Quran to them. In that case, it is simply beyond the power of an average human mind to imagine their plight, the extent of their wonder, and amazement or the depth of their trance, nothing whatsoever would disturb their engrossment.

With what a glint of wonder and surprise in their penetrating eyes and absorption of their influential minds, they would listen to the marvels of the prophecy: its revealing logic, startling inference, simple and yet all assuming description, the brevity, and precision of its expression, its masterly terms, and authoritative tones? With what rapture they would behold, the whole philosophy of atomism exposed in the minutest detail to the dazzling brilliance of the Omniscient sun of the Quran? With what fascination and awe would they watch the blinding dazzle, the ear-piercing thunder, the sky-high column, and the covering mushroom of the atomic explosions of Hiroshima and Nagasaki? With what dread would they have witnessed the dire spectacle of the nuclear hell ablaze in the cities worldwide? With what horror they would have beheld the horrific scene of millions of human beings, men, women, and children being roasted alive in flaming fires along with humbles and brutes, the cities tossed about, buildings being reduced to dust and shot into space? In short, they would see an absolute hell enkindled as the ultimate consequence of the theory of atomism.

Last but not least, with what fascination would Socrates, Plato, and Aristotle have seen the result of the theory of their countryman, contemporary, and antagonist, Democritus? This theory of Democritus they had dreaded and vehemently opposed twenty-five centuries ago and had cast all their influence in the scale against it due to its ill-beseeming and dangerous features. The added interest, however, in this respect is reserved for Bertrand Russell and Einstein. Description of the fire of 'Al-Hotama' by the Quran is superb enough to throw the mind of a modern knowing scientist into convulsions due to his knowledge of the subject.

The so-called rational criticism of the modern atomistic age has condemned the Old and the New Testaments. Indeed, it has also charged every other Scripture that has contained the miraculous element. It accused the Scriptures of being fantastic and legendary, doubtable in origin, incompatible with reason, mutually inconsistent, self-contradictory, replete with later forgeries, etc. Of the numerous reasons for this attitude, the main one is the miraculous and supernatural element in the Scriptures.

We may trace the origin of this particular attitude to a denial of the miraculous and supernatural by modern science. The votaries of science deny the existence of miraculous and supernatural because modern science denies such a possibility. Science has denied such a possibility because it has hitherto been and will forever remain outside its scope. According to the followers of science, the miraculous and the supernatural's presence is to stand outside the province of scientific reason. According to them, the non-scientific explanation is set aside as unacceptable by astronomers, physicians, or geologists and not accepted without inquiry by the historian. To the rational inquirer, according to them, a straightforward reason settles the question; namely, there is no room for belief in things of which the world can offer no experimental trace. Science alone, according to them, seeks after the pure truth.

Science alone supports the truth by convincing reasons and subjects the methods of her convictions to a severe examination.

Although the miraculous and supernatural element is a fact, the Scriptures have stood mute against the objections of the votaries of science and have not been able to advance any scientific proof but instead have depended on the credulity and implicit faith of men.

At last, we see the Quran, a revealed Scripture to show the votaries of science a miracle that science itself cannot deny and is forced to accept the possibility of miraculous and supernatural. The Quran grants these votaries of science in their peculiar scientific method of judging the truth and then displays a miracle in their specific field of science. The Quran herein has accepted their peculiar postulates, their particular conditions, and their specific methods. It presents its prophecy about the atomic bomb on scientific lines in vogue in the realm of science. It is well-known that the Quran preferred the manifest works of Allah to the miracles granted to the Prophets. It has also declared itself a standing miracle for all ages and proved its worth as a standing miracle in this prophecy of the atomic bomb. This prophecy is a kind of a miracle that none of the knowing votaries of science will ever be able to deny. It will go straight into the heart of every just and generous scientist. The Quran, at last, has risen as a champion of the Scriptures, and it has espoused their cause most convincingly and admirably.

We can rightly name the behavior of the Quran in this prophecy as 'Scientifico-Supernatural'. It has produced a miracle in the very heart of modern science in a way that it would prove to be an eye-opener to anyone who has concluded that the miracles of the ancient Prophets were but a pious fraud. It is a great fallacy to deny the existence of miraculous or supernatural because of the incompatibility of such phenomena with modern science. Due to its specific shortcomings, if this modern science cannot find experimental proof of supernatural things, it would not mean that the supernatural could not exist. We cannot accept the denial by the blind of the presence of the sun as truth. This modern science entirely and exclusively has its dependence on the five senses alone. Beyond the scope of the five senses, modern science can see nothing, hear nothing, touch nothing, and neither smell nor taste anything.

Now that science has reached a particular stage in its advancement, its shortcomings and limitations have come to light to frustrate its voters' infinite hopes and expectations. As far as the material world, the actual field of science is concerned, science could no more than lisp, but as far as the spiritual world, which certainly exists, is concerned, science turns utterly dumb, deaf, and blind. Therefore, to deny the existence of the spiritual, the Resurrection, the Judgment, and the life in Heaven merely because modern science cannot prove or attest to it is a fallacy that could and would subject this world to destruction despite all the discoveries and facilities of science. It is an error of grievous nature and more far-reaching consequences than it is generally understood these days. However, some leading scientists have realized the shortcomings of the science and undue and exaggerated confidence of its votaries. Therefore, the previous wave of enthusiasm is now gradually decreasing.

The scientist will indeed be able to comprehend and appreciate the scientific side of the prophecy of the Quran about the atomic bomb. So also, will the philosopher be able to discern the philosophical and logical inference drawn by the prophecy from the fundamental causes. Yet, the actual critical appreciation of the entire prophecy in its completeness places unusual and exceptional demands on the intellect. It entails excellent versatility besides a thorough understanding of diverse subjects and variant branches of knowledge, generally not combined in a single person in this age.

The knowledge of science and religion, for instance, could seldom be found these days united in a single individual. The scientist usually does not know much about religion, while the theologian is generally unacquainted with modern science. Nay, even the scientist could hardly be expected to know about all the various branches of science. Because the knowledge of science these days has expanded to such an extent that no one can master every branch or even several branches of scientific knowledge within a single life-span. A physicist who has spent all his life pursuing his particular subject might know little about the latest advancements in the topic of chemistry.

A perfect comprehension of this prophecy necessitates knowledge of the Arabic language and the mind of the Quran, and the understanding of nuclear science, in the highest order. The most authentic and original commentaries among the interpreters of the Quran in the Arabic language should be deemed an aid and asset in the proper appreciation of the topic. The original text of the Quran is essential. The mere translation in a language, howsoever excellent, will not do, for a translation of the Quran in any language appears as the slaughtered animal in the form of meat in the shop. In contrast, the original breathes like a living one in its stable, comprising the whole universe and the spiritual Heaven.

The original text of the Quran is essential. It furnishes the reader with various meanings and shades of meanings of a word and can lead the inquiry into fresh discoveries. Conversely, even the best of translations could give at a time but one of the various meanings and, therefore, cannot be of much avail in leading the reader to new fields and new objects of discovery. The Quran is miraculously kaleidoscopic in composition and changes its face in relation to the particular age, just as the sunflower changes the direction of its look toward the sun in its passage through the sky.

The question of mere comprehension of this prophecy is far different from its critical appreciation. Whereas its mere comprehension is within reach of millions, its genuine critical appreciation will find but a few worthy ones in the whole of the world, for how many today exist on earth who would fulfill all the various conditions mentioned above. There are many great theologians in the world of Islam. There are numerous scientists of note in scientifically advanced countries. But who at once possesses a scientific genius of higher-order and a mastery of the subject of the Quran?

Being the author of this present work, if I would seek after a critic who could bestow a just and comprehensive review on this work, I will perhaps be obliged to search through every nook and cranny of this world to find such a one. Again, if the hand of luck would guide the inquisitive author to such a prodigy of knowledge, who knows what shall be the attitude of such a one concerning the work, judging from the personal engrossment of highly learned men in this age of no leisure and the formidable nature of this work itself.

A few luminaries could perhaps undertake such a task with any natural justice in the advanced countries and fewer still in the backward ones. A few, even among those few, may find them capable of inclining their ear toward truth, a bitter truth, and perhaps opposed to the prior disposition of their mind. Also, a tinge of justice and the light of faith are essential for a critical appreciation of such work.

However, the author has nothing but an earnest desire to proclaim the truth: a pure fact in the manner of the friendliest sentiment and heartfelt human sympathy for fellow human beings all over the earth irrespective of caste, color, or creed, lest someone say, alas! Nobody told us. Perhaps we had heeded the warning. Maybe we had listened to advice and had been saved from a miserable life and so painful an end.

Nevertheless, it is genuine gratitude that although the critical appreciation of the theme we reserve for a few elites, the general obligation is within reach of every man with moderate knowledge and average intellect everywhere in the world. Moreover, it is far easier to follow this prophecy than, for instance, the evolution of Darwin in the

'Origin of Species', which appears as difficult to most, even to the learned scholars among the followers of Darwin himself.

We can never doubt the honesty, integrity, sincerity, and ability of the community of modern scientists in the face of the most irrefutable proofs that sparkle like the stars in heaven on a starlit night. Fortunately for humankind, this prophecy of the Quran should be decided in the light of science's hard and fast facts. Provided there is a requisite amount of scientific knowledge; there is no difficulty judging the truth. However, the hypnotic charm of three evils, which the prophecy enumerated as the fundamental causes of the emergence of 'Al-Hotama' (the atomic hell), might veil the sight of humankind against this warning of the Quran. Yet if this humankind is not highly unlucky in this respect and the atomic doom is not inevitable, this timely warning of a Scripture may well be availed. Suppose the ignominious doom of this present humankind is not pre-ordained and has not wholly blinded the human eye. In that case, instantaneous and unanimous recognition of this warning of Merciful Creator will impress the grateful heart of humanity all over the world, and soon a universal revolution will set in.

The severity of the tyrannical necessities of life and a relentless urge of greed for more and dread of poverty in the present unethical hedonistic age of atomistic materialism seem to have numbed the senses of humankind, including those of the scientists and philosophers. In the prevalent heat of current crushing circumstances, humanity may ignore the warning of the prophecy. Hence, it may ruin present-day life and life hereafter. On the other hand, suppose it is in the destiny of humankind to live in peace and prosperity by avoiding the atomic hazards of every kind. Then, humanity must accord a ready welcome to this most timely warning of the Scripture and follow its advice precisely. Dazed by the hypnotic charm of the atomistic philosophy, the scientist will be awakened from his torpor, realizing that the atomic energy was but a kind of 'damnosa hereditas'. [1] And he will deem it right to rise to the occasion to assume his great responsibility toward fellow humans.

The Quran has worked a wonder that it has couched all the technical knowledge of nuclear science in a language that seemed quite ordinarily intelligible to even the rudest of its readers. The expression wonders that this straightforward language of the prophecy contained and encompassed the essence of all that nuclear science that the scientist has hitherto discovered. The description and definition of the fire of 'Hotama' given by the prophecy in the simplest terms could now lend itself most adequately to the most technically scientific expression of modern nuclear science.

The treatment of the nuclear subject in the Quran in a modern scientific language would have appeared to the first audience of the Quran, the Arabs of the seventh century, as a mere unintelligible gibberish. It might have appeared as deceptive jugglery of baffling terms to describe the subtleties of the nuclear characteristics of nuclear phenomena in scientific expressions and formulae to the hostile ears. All of it would have been to pour in the ears of the simple primitive listeners an assortment of hallucinatory incantations of a frizzing spirit.

Following are the most straightforward terms used in nuclear science: 'nuclear', 'thermonuclear', 'irradiations', 'dazzling Heat-Flash', 'deafening thunder', 'earth-shaking blast', 'heaven-high columns of three miles diameter', 'million-degree temperatures', 'collapsing cities', 'submerging islands', 'radio-logical hazards', 'mass-energy equivalencies', etc. It is not difficult to imagine that mentioning the terms as these would have caused primitive auditors of the Quran to stop their ears. In case they had not yet believed in the Holy Prophet (peace be upon him), giggling in scornful panic, they might have run away before the incomprehensible tirade of abracadabra. But the believers in such a situation would have maintained silence out of respect. But, they would not have missed embarrassment by the unintelligibility and doubtfulness of such terms and the jeers of opponents of an emerging religion.

How could the primitive listeners of the Quran be expected to understand the most complex of the terms and the formulae of nuclear science as are met within the textbooks of atomic physics these days that perplex even the minds of the most outstanding nuclear scientists themselves? To describe the nuclear bomb explosion phenomenon to the first innocent listeners of the Quran in the seventh century within the confines of Arabia would have seemed like an incredible piece of mythical foolery and hyperbolic nonsense. It would have been unbelievable, even to the most intelligent among the people, not only of Arabian origin but even those belonging to the most civilized and educated people of that age. While to the opponents of Islam among the Arabians, the fact would have furnished an occasion for most effective ridicule so detrimental to the rising religion. Further, say, after describing all the disastrous, world-shaking, and city-consuming phenomena of nuclear fire, you told them that all this would happen through the fission of merely a nucleus of a tiny, invisible atom. It would have meant to invite a storm of derision from the unbelievers and to cast indelible doubts in the hearts of the nascent believers.

When Allah revealed the Quran, the terms, and expressions of the nuclear science that in today's age of knowledge are taken as the expressions of the most profound visions of the human mind, then would have been taken by the people as a sheer hocus-pocus of disgusting delirium. Suppose the Quran had used the terms and expressions of current nuclear science to pronounce the prophecy. Also, the Holy Prophet (peace be upon him) preached an unseen Allah against the venerable idols of Makkah's infidels' false gods. Alas then! Just by dint of his stand against the gods of the infidels, all this would have most effectively countenanced the incredible charge of lunacy that the hostile miscreants used to level against the consecrated person of the Holy Prophet (peace be upon him) to defame him.

The narrative of the nocturnal journey to the heavens by the Prophet (peace be upon him) caused a tremendous seductive tumult in the city. Consequently, both the Prophet (peace be upon him) and his disciples were subjected to a depressing assault of frantic jeers from every side, and Islam incurred the loss of some believers. Therefore, the matter-of-fact descriptions of the nuclear phenomena and the incomprehensible expressions of atomic science might have done graver damage to the body of Islam. It even might have jeopardized the very existence of the then-nascent religion within the confines of Arabia. The Quran then was obliged to be content with merely telling those who called the Prophet (peace be upon him) a mad man that he was not mad, and that the Quran revealed to him was the miraculous compendium of knowledge. It was not for the ignorant and crude opponents of the Holy Prophet (peace be upon him) amongst the Arabians to judge the limits of that universal knowledge which the Quran had contained. But instead, it was for the most suitable stage of development to verify the claim of knowledge in the Quran. It was in its destiny that this modern technological age, so justly famous for the scientific facts, should have proved it.

It is now at last that the occasion of proving the knowledge of the Quran has arrived. The topmost scientists and the leading philosophers, all the most learned in this present age, may be called upon to judge the truth themselves. And then vindicate the academic honor of the Quran to prove the absurdity of the charge of ancient ignorant antagonists who used to call it a mere hodge-podge or a collection of mere old fables. As far as the state of the Quran from the viewpoint of knowledge and science is concerned, it is the duty incumbent on those in this age that have actual knowledge to subject it to scrutiny, for it is recognized champion of knowledge and hence the champion of this age of knowledge and science. Therefore, its study will never disappoint any knowledge-seeking or knowledgeable reader.

On the contrary, it will certainly reward him with a plentiful harvest in the fields that will never be exhausted and be found forever abloom and blossoming out into ever-fresh flowers and fruits infinitely. No sooner the contents of a passage are harvested with a thought that no more remained to put a sickle to than a fresh harvest appeared in the very same passage ripe for harvesting. This marvel happens to be indeed a strangely miraculous feature of the contents of the Quran. This feature of the inexhaustibility of the Quran is simply incomprehensible to the human mind.

Let us revert to our point. What if Quran had ventured to express nuclear phenomena contained in the prophecy, or besides that any other complex scientific phenomena to be discovered in the modern age, precisely in scientific jargon to be found in science textbooks these days? It would have been incomprehensible to its first auditors, nay even to all the pre-modern readers of the Quran. Moreover, it would have easily lent itself to the mockery of its first listeners and would thus have risked the very existence of the then-nascent faith.

To talk in scientific jargon of this modern age to a people in the seventh century or even in the seventeenth century and tell them about such unbelievable novelties as railways, airplanes, gramophones, radios, televisions, submarines, armored ships, motor cars, X-ray plants, and Moon-and-Mars reaching rockets, would have meant to conjure up things incredibly fabulous before the eyes of the astonished crowds much too bewildered to believe their ears. We are familiar with these spectacles of this age but revive all the pre-modern humankind and let them behold these things in this present-day world and then imagine their surprise and panic. Yet it was the office of the Quran in its capacity as the last declared Will of the Creator to humankind, to foresee and warn against the peculiarly atomistic features of a future age. However, the Quran succeeded with fantastic talent in solving the formidable complexity of the expression about the descriptions of the scientific phenomena of the modern age.

It will be read with surprise that the Quran has, besides this phenomenon, mentioned the basic principles of the laws of Mother Nature even more than modern science has hitherto discovered. However, let there be no misunderstanding that the Quran, by dint of its interest in natural laws, also endorses the use of such laws as is extant in this age in the line of atomistic materialism. Thus, though the Quran has an antagonistic view in this respect, it has an everlasting store of scientific knowledge for the scientist, all couched in the most straightforward language.

GABRIEL'S EXTINGUISHING THE ATOMIC HELL SERIES

As far as the prophecy under discussion is concerned, despite the formidable scientific material contained in it, it has satisfied the intellect of every reader of every age. The queer features of the fire of 'Al-Hotama' evoked a good deal of curiosity amongst the disciples of the Holy Prophet (peace be upon him) and later on amongst the early interpreters of the Quran. Thought-provoking discussions arose amongst these interpreters of the Quran just as, before them, had arisen amongst the disciples of the Holy Prophet (peace be upon him). Nevertheless, to the average reader, the whole affair appeared but usual. To him, 'Al-Hotama' was but a hell whose fire did 'leap up over the hearts' and was 'closed in on them in outstretched columns'. All this was to take place in the next world on the Day of Judgment just as any other kind of hell was, little knowing, what formidable facts of nuclear phenomena were with what exactitude represented by these simple expressions they thought to be quite as commonplace.

Moreover, the original commentators of the Quran have said amazing things regarding the fire of 'Al-Hotama', and their treatment of the topic, judging from the age in which they had lived, seems undoubtedly marvelous. All the same, the proper appreciation of this strange fire was reserved for us, the unfortunate inhabitants of this age of modern atomism. It was for us to know the crushing characteristics of the fire of atomic hell and how 'it rises unto the hearts', and how 'it is closed in on them in outstretched columns'. This description is the distinguishing narrative of 'Al-Hotama' as is given by the Quran.

Now, try to think for yourself, how much of the nuclear science can you find these few words to embrace. Then, after you've read this work (Book-1 & Book-2), recall to your mind this present moment to find how well you had recognized the nuclear science in this description of 'Al-Hotama' by the Quran in these few words. Therein lay a miracle of the Quran, and it is a miraculous description. There is no doubt about it that you indeed will find yourself in agreement with this claim by the time you have finished these books. Within a few words of prophecy, you shall see all the phenomena of nuclear science that hitherto science has encompassed and even more that it has not discovered yet.

For some time after the revelation of this prophecy about the 'Homaza Lomaza' (backbiter, defamer), the general notion was that the revelation leveled the threat against the particular person of one or several recognized rivals of the Holy Prophet (peace be upon him) himself. Also, the definition of condemned embraced any individual who was habitually endued with the evils enumerated and accordingly fulfilled the conditions assigned by the prophecy to justify the punishment of the fire of 'Al-Hotama' strangely enough, irrespective of the factor of faith. It was supposed that all notorious calumniators of the Holy Prophet (peace be upon him) like Akhnas Ibn-Shuraiq, Walid Ibn-Mughayyirrah, Umayyah Ibn-Khalaf, Jamil Ibn-Amir Jamaee, and Aass Ibn-Vile, either individually or severally, be there named as the object of this denunciation.

Nevertheless, gradually the opinion changed through genuine ratifications by the early, authentic interpreters of the Quran. The disciples of the Holy Prophet (peace be upon him) provided authentic evidence about the prophecy. In the early days, in the light of that reliable indication and the exact purport of the word of the warning itself, the leading interpreters of the Quran confirmed and agreed that the Quran did not mean the rebuke against any particular person or several persons by name. Instead, on the other hand, it had a general purport and universal application. Enlightening discussions and revealing hints are frequently to be met within the interpretations of the prophecy by these early, original, and authentic interpreters touching the characteristics of the fire of 'Al-Hotama' and the characteristic causes of its emergence; hints realistic enough to start into the mind of the investigator of nuclear science and the pursuer of the modern philosophy, trains of such thoughts as may lead to the actual recognition of superb facts.

Yet, clear-cut appreciation of the wonders of Prophetic characterization of the nuclear phenomena was reserved for us, the unfortunates of this nuclear age in the presence of atomic energy and the atomic bomb. Now, all the characteristic features and corroborative exhibits of the replica of 'Al-Hotama', including a life-like portrait of the column-raising explosion of the atomic bomb, emerged within this very world before our very eyes. It afforded direct scrutiny and evident proof of the validity of the prophecy. Also, it provided a vivid spectacle of the consequential and logical result of the philosophy of modern atomistic materialism as a miracle of vindictive justice. This retributive justice is so terrible that some people have come to think of it as the actual event of doomsday. That means the global destruction of this world before enacting the justice of the Last Judgment mentioned in the Scriptures. However, it is not like that. For, the disintegration of the earth through nuclear doomsday before the Last Judgment means utter destruction of the entire world on the globe without any justice of the Last Judgment.

In contrast, the global obliteration of life on earth through atomic fire will not affect the basic structure of this earth. However, it may impair its capability of producing life due to the worldwide dispersal of radioactive material. It will not touch the rest of the universe. But will work destruction and inflict misery differently on the individuals and populations. It may happen in a series of atomic wars of various magnitudes or through the atomic radiation of the atomic energy for peace. Or maybe, the nuclear wars or the atomic radiation of the atomic energy for peace, both will be responsible for it. In a period of unspecific length, it may ultimately affect the extinction of life on earth, following a miserable existence of its inhabitants. Thus, it would pose as a replica of doomsday on earth, just as the atomic-hell is the replica of 'Al-Hotama'. Hence, it may not at all be the means of bringing about the final disintegration mentioned in the Scriptures. That might happen later. When will it happen? None but the Omniscient Allah knows only.

Every reader of the Quran perused the words and terms of the prophecy in their simple attire over time through centuries without ever suspecting a whit of anything uncommon or suggestive of something unusual. Yet, the very same words and the warning phrases suddenly became alive like the miraculous rod of Moses at the appearance of the atomic explosions of Hiroshima and Nagasaki and, assuming a mercuric attitude in a kaleidoscopic manner, reflected and described the nuclear phenomena in a mysterious yet straightforward way. All the characteristics of the prophecy sprang into a scintillating galaxy of facts and pictures that clearly described the whole theme of the nuclear science of this modern age. In a dreamy moonlit night could be seen a worldwide arena full of spectators in the realm of the atomistic pharaoh, the atomic magicians having thrown their ropes and rods in the arena that seem to wriggle in a serpentine motion under the influence of scientific magic as a challenge of a contest to Moses. Like the Rod of Moses, the prophecy of the Quran has cast itself among the wriggling serpents. It transforms itself into a substantial miraculous python that will swallow all the serpentine apparitions in the arena.

In history, magicians in the court of Pharaoh prostrated before the God of Moses, the God of all creatures. Time only shall reveal whether it is in the destiny of the atomic magicians of the present modern age to recognize the truth of this prophecy and throw themselves prostrate before the Revealer of this prophecy or not? But regarding the prophecy in question, the scientist carefully perusing this interpretation of the prophecy, in his sight, will find the validity of this simile well-justified.

No doubt, any scientist who happens to read this work will, for the rest of life, find his mind prepossessed by the sound of the words of the prophecy. Any time his eye shall fall on a portrait of the atomic bomb explosion in a book, the portrait of the nuclear column sketched by the words of the prophecy shall instantly appear in his mind as a reminder. Any time he has read or thought of any nuclear phenomena, he will find the relative description of the prophecy always present in accompaniment. The words of the prophecy have for centuries appeared in the Quran without any scientific significance. The very same verses of the warning, at last, have come to tax and even outstrip the greatest of the scientific intellects of this age of science and lead their mind to regions where nothing but illusions remain for the human intelligence. What do you call it if not a miracle in itself?

There seems a slight possibility that man will ever be able to exhaust all that knowledge that the prophecy miraculously contained in these few simple words, no matter how far he may become advanced in his nuclear knowledge with time. If a man endeavors to infinity in the field of nuclear science, the latest results of his research, he shall find within these few words of the prophecy.

Such is the miraculous nature of these words that they shall keep on multiplying the shades of their meanings and constantly expanding to encompass all novel discoveries ever to be made by man in the field of nuclear science. Hence, the further the scientists go into nuclear science, the greater their appreciation of this prophecy. These things may appear as strange, indeed quite incomprehensible at the stage of this work, but their truth shall appear most manifestly to every genuine reader after he has brought the study of this work to completion.

The Quran has more than once claimed in unambiguous terms that it has contained every example for humankind. No one could safely venture at such a claim on behalf of even the largest libraries of the world containing hundreds of thousands of volumes. It is by nature the most challenging a claim in itself, a claim to a miracle indeed of a very unusual kind. It is a claim to a miracle at which every miracle ever recorded in history would gaze in surprise. However, this miracle could be put to the proof in the present age of knowledge and science on the grounds of science and knowledge because this is an age in which wisdom and science have assumed the high most pinnacles humanly possible. All knowledge of pre-modern ages might seem but trifle against what humanity has accumulated in the present period.

Judging from the nature and the magnitude of the impending threat of nuclear devastation, it is pretty clear that humankind now confronts a problem of nature as grievous as it is impossible to find another precedent in whole human history. It is a problem next only to the final disintegration of this world preceding the enactment of the Final Judgment. What problem then would be worth mentioning more than the problem of this prospective destroyer of the creation of Allah on earth? Furthermore, the Quran has mentioned the destruction of past froward tribes and their habitations through divine vengeance and even particular modes of destruction. So then, how could the mention of possible universal destruction by the atomic bombs and nuclear radiation be expected to be ignored?

The Quran has openly discerned and accordingly described the possibility of the terrific destruction and the impending calamity of nuclear origin. It has described the whole atomic phenomena minutely and comprehensively and has elucidated the original causes of the resultant catastrophe. It has provided humankind with invaluable and infallible guidance to avoid nuclear calamity by removing the fundamental causes that the prophecy has most succinctly enumerated.

Now, this humankind stands seemingly and inescapably involved in the impending nuclear cataclysm. The only guide to escape the ruin in the eleventh hour lay in the warning which the most Merciful and Benign Allah so kindly placed in His Quran fourteen centuries ago. Hence, perhaps His creatures might benefit by it in the moment of their difficulty to avoid the most grievous doom that ever befell the populations of any age since the appearance of man on earth.

It is a matter of genuine gratitude that the prophecy about 'Al-Hotama' is in the form of a warning, and it is not a decree pre-ordained. The Quran has given out the punishment of 'Al-Hotama' as conditional resulting from three evils: 'slander', 'complete engrossment in pursuing wealth', and 'confidence in its immortalizing powers'. The removal of these causes meant the consequential removal of the substantial hazard. The causes in question, however, and very unfortunately, encompass the entire world of today and no doubt very overwhelmingly. The atomism, which essentially is the creed of this present world, is a creed in which this world figures as eternal abode: its wealth as a worshipful deity; Democritus, the founder of atomism, as the patriarch; materialism as faith; science as the scripture; scientist as the sage, saint and the divine in a realm in which the attitude of criticism moves as the spirit. It is a realm in which this world alone is the object of man's achievement, an object to be achieved through the conquest of the forces of Mother Nature for material progress meant to benefit humankind in general. The enlargement of man's dominion over Mother Nature is the purpose of man's existence on earth. Nothing exists beyond the scope of the five senses. Hence, people consider any thought of a spiritual world, spiritual values or Resurrection, Judgment, and life in Heaven, no more than a mere illusion and the product of sheer superstition.

All this undoubtedly is the exact antithesis of the doctrine of any true faith ever preached in any pre-modern age on earth in the whole of human history. The causes given out by the prophecy of the Quran about 'Al-Hotama', namely, 'slander', 'wealth worship', and a 'notion of forever living in this world', could well be judged as the necessary outcome of the philosophy of atomism. Hence, it is that these evils prevail in this age of atomistic materialism. The warning of the prophecy thus could be seen to issue against this modern creed of atomism. Be it clear from the outset that wherever we have used the term 'modern age' in this work, we always have used it purely and exclusively about its atomistically worldly aspect. Faith still seems to breathe and claim the allegiance of millions globally, even maintaining influence in essential matters. Yet, the suppressing prevalence of atomistic materialism has a universal sway everywhere. Faith may again emerge as an authoritative power in this world, but the case is different at present.

As mentioned before, the reader should always view our citing of the 'modern age' as a purely atomistic aspect. Also, this modern age appears as an antithesis of every pre-modern age due to this atomistic aspect. In this respect, we may divide human history into two distinct parts that stood against each other in distinct and direct opposition. The pre-modern ages combined constitute one of these parts, while this modern age constitutes the other due to its atomistic aspect. In the pre-modern ages, the factor of spiritualism predominates, while pure materialism leads the modern age. In the former, the torrents of genius, intellect, and inspiration generally moved within the spiritual sphere; in contrast, the sphere of materialism is mainly the field of mental activities in the latter.

In the former, the world's eye was like that of Plato in Raphael's cartoon of the school of Athens pointed upward toward Heaven, while in the latter, it is like that of Aristotle (in the same cartoon) pointed downward toward earth though in a manner far at variance with that of Aristotle. Men in the former looked upward in an endeavor to behold the majesty of the Creator, conversed with Him, and received His supernatural revelations containing His divine Will, the purpose of their creation, and the light and guidance in life. In contrast, men in the latter consulted the natural genius to conquer the forces of Mother Nature for material benefits and enlarge their dominion in the realm of Mother Nature. In the former, they contemplated the works of Allah to glorify Him, while in the latter, they contemplated the works of Allah for material exploitation. In the former, souls, spirits, angels, and cherubic beings were cherished, sought, viewed, and conversed with, while physical, chemical, and psychological behaviors are observed and recorded in the latter.

People's lives in the former were considered a trial, the purpose of attaining a better life in Heaven. In contrast, in the latter, their life and indeed the whole creation is given out as the result of a mere 'accident' and the product of mere 'chance' with no question whatsoever of a purpose or Resurrection, their only practical being the maintenance of life in search of physical comfort. Such a surmise may surely come as a surprise to millions who have explicit and implicit faith, and their faith condemns all these factors attributed to the modern age. However, the reality is that all these various factors attributed to the modern age are the distinctive characteristics of the philosophy of atomism, and any discerning eye could visibly see them as prevalent in this modern age.

The hell of 'Al-Hotama' has generally been regarded as appearing not in this same world but the next world, like any other type of hell. Yet, as per the prophecy, the causes that rendered someone liable to the punishment of 'Al-Hotama' are so precise, and anyone could view with such clarity their universal prevalence in this present age that it is hard to miss the possibility of the result of the process appearing within this very world. It is not the Quran alone that has affected the condemnation of these three evils responsible for the punishment through 'Al-Hotama' fire. Even the Bible and every other true Scripture has severely condemned the evils in question. However, the credit of miraculously associating these evils with Al-Hotama's appearance goes to the Quran. These evils have been present in the world from the very beginning. Yet, they gained a particular momentum collectively with the advent of modern materialism so that within a period of but a few centuries, the result in the form of the atomic hell appeared before the very eyes of a miserable science-guided, machine-ridden world.

Allah has never destroyed a people before sending them a warner lest they say no one warned them. Here now then is a warning of Allah in the most manifest of terms and indeed in a most miraculous manner which, if heeded to, will undoubtedly lead this humankind out of the impending catastrophe of the atomic hell and save them from the most painful and equally disgraceful doom. Judging from prevailing circumstances of the world at present, know that there is no power, other than this warning, under this blue sky and above this mild earth, to save this humankind from the ignoble ruin through nuclear devastation. Yet, it could be of any avail only if folks abide by its conditions and duly remove natural causes of the trouble. Therefore, any ray of hope left is in the guidance of this warning by Allah for this present humankind. If, however, this warning will be ignored by humankind, it shall assume the form of a decree, and this world shall, there can be no doubt, see the atomic hell ablaze, and this humankind shall see itself consumed by the flames thereof. This world of today is a world of confusion. Hence, it is high time that people clear all confusion from their minds and view things as they indeed are. Therefore, no one could treat 'No-War-Agreements' as final. Such agreements will prove no better than the singed hair when the moment arrives.

However, the prophecy's warning entails the necessity of a complete revolution of outlook and a revolution as universal and as dynamic as the economic setup and the social culture, which is extant in the world. Humanity shall have to mold the whole outlook and see the things in that light. For instance, while judging the adoption of atomic energy for peace, the point of engrossment in pursuit of wealth has to be viewed. If the adoption of nuclear energy tended to support the factor of engrossment in the pursuit of wealth, its material benefit was to be ignored. It was to be rejected as an aid to the cause of the appearance of the atomic hell. This fact may, in the present circumstances, and the prevailing setup of the world seem impracticable, even perhaps absurd under the influence of atomism. However, its worthiness and applicability might well be comprehended when atomic bombs begin to rain from the heavens over the heads of stunned people, or the earth becomes a massive asylum of an infirm, ailing, miserable race perishing in radiation epidemic of atomic energy for peace.

Quite the reverse, a possibility may be considered that is not entirely out of the question. In the light of the knowledge of pros and cons of atomic energy by weighing the hazards indeed incident on it as against the material advantages that accrue from there, this same humankind may become serene enough to avoid this hazard in time. In that way, humanity can prevent everything certainly that in any way tended to promote the atomic threat in the world.

If that happens, they will dread the atomic radiations no less than they at present dread deadly vipers, or their forefathers in ancient times had dreaded the invisible ghosts in the darkness of the night. Nay, it is not only the atomic radiations that they will dread but also the habit of slandering and the engrossment in the pursuit of wealth, and this world itself shall appear in their eyes as an object of great horror. Yet all that we may say about warning this generation against the hazards of atomic energy may appear like dreamy hallucinations of an unrealistic visionary. Because humankind waves like a senseless drunkard intoxicated by the love of wealth and bereft of all judgment, not hesitant even to lay its hands on the deadly adder of the atomic energy.

However, an atomic raid or the first flaying of the radiation epidemic might exorcise the atomic devil out of them and open their eyes to their grievous folly. Yet, alas for humankind, for once the atomic energy has prevailed, then there will be no way out of it. Under the scientific truth, we say that there is no tracing the steps back out of the atomic labyrinth, nor there is an exit ever to emerge from it. Don't consider all this as a mere fanciful talk of a moody philosopher. Once the atomic energy for peace has ultimately prevailed globally, humankind will be permanently, irredeemably, and eternally lost by then. Read works of the knowing scientists on Radiobiology. Then make a peculiar judgment to disapprove of Darwin's opinion about man's origin.

An extremely meager margin from consideration in the adoption of the course of atomic energy is left. A step further, and this world will plunge into the burning pit of nuclear hell. There is an ancient saying, "think before you leap." If this saying ever had validity at any stage of human history, it is now in the case of this leap that this world will take into the hell of atomic energy for peace. Once plunged, it is forever plunged.

Hell has traditionally been associated with the next world, and naturally, the interpretation of the prophecy about the hell of 'Al-Hotama' hitherto has assumed the established line. No one could ever have thought of a hell appearing in this very world. Yet, if hell predicted by the Quran would appear even in world and life, and before the eyes of people, then what a miracle on the part of Scripture it would be? And how impressive the word of the Quran would become if it has said respecting the things that seem difficult to believe: the Resurrection, Judgment, and the life in Heaven.

Let it be known from the outset that the atomic hell of this present world is the mere transient replica of the eternal 'Al-Hotama' of the next eternal world and the appearance of 'Al-Hotama' in the next world is a certainty. However, a strong argument exists to support the view of 'Al-Hotama' appearing in this very world. It is not unreasonable to assume the necessity of the appearance of the representation of the fire of 'Al-Hotama' within this world. Ordinary fire represents the hellfire of the next world. Paradise of the next world finds its representation in the shape of gardens, rivers, and other objects of felicity.

These signs are produced within the world to acquaint people with their nature in the next eternal world, lest someone say on the Day of Judgment:

"O, Allah! We had never known in the world what hellfire or the paradisiacal bliss was. Had we known their true nature, we perhaps had exerted to save ourselves from the eternal torture of the hell-fire and made endeavors to attain the eternal bliss of Paradise".

The base of this argument would be on reason. We could say the same regarding the 'Al-Hotama' fire, characteristically different from the ordinary fire.

As far as the hell of 'Al-Hotama' is concerned, it is also fire and described by the Quran as fundamentally a fire. Even though the fire of 'Al-Hotama' is a different kind of fire, since it is the fire of nuclear and not chemical nature, it is fire enough to remind one of the hell-fire of the next world. Therefore, no pretext being unacquainted with the particular fire of the hell of 'Al-Hotama' on anyone's part could justly carry any weight on the Day of Judgment. However, how 'Al-Hotama' came to appear in the form of its terrestrial replica within this world is the question. Moreover, it is a question of great importance. While seeking an answer to it, it has to be recalled to one's mind that all the material ingredients that could combine to produce the atomic fire together with the principles and laws that governed the process of producing the atomic fire did exist in this world since its birth.

Nevertheless, they lay dormant till the requisite moral, religious, philosophical, and scientific conditions were ripe for the appearance of the nuclear fire. Also, the Quran's given evils as causes of appearances of the fire of 'Al-Hotama' were extant in the world for long ages. However, every pre-modern age was under the strong influence of religion. The philosophy of religion extremely discouraged all the articles that constituted the cause of the appearance of the atomic fire. So strong indeed was the influence of faith in the pre-modern ages that 'slander', 'love of this world', engrossment in 'wealth-accumulation' as the object of one's life, and the 'wealth worship' which are the supposed causes of the punishment by the fire of 'Al-Hotama', were generally shunned as evils.

Such indeed was a dread of unseen hell of the next world that the people feared its very mention in their imagination. They feared far more than the obstinate and hard-headed population of the current times care for the presence of the atomic hell ablaze before their very eyes in a tangible form. These modernists entertain a very faint fear of the atomic hell. On the contrary, they are endeavoring to enkindle the same nuclear hell to the best of their ability. Moreover, they are toiling hard in gathering the requisite fuel, piling up their stockpiles higher and ever higher. Unluckily, they know very well that these stockpiles were but the atomic pyres in which the friend and the foe, including themselves, their children, and the children of their children, were to be sooner or later consumed.

It is well-known that every single true religion in this world has vehemently opposed the habits which the Quran has given out as the causes that resulted in the liability to the punishment in the fire of 'Al-Hotama'. As far as generations before the revelation of the prophecy about 'Al-Hotama' are concerned, the hold of faith being strong in those ages, its denunciations against such evils proved to be of considerable efficacy. In contrast, people of the current era, due to the influence of the philosophy of modern atomism, severely blinded by the dazzle of the three evils in the absence of the conflicting influence of faith, are moving into atomic hell like a mighty horde of drunkards intoxicated by the spirit of greed and excessive love of wealth and world.

The present humanity is entirely under the influence of the philosophy of modern atomism. According to this philosophy, the material world alone figures as the world, and the attainment of the material objects is the sole object of man's life. Whereas no consideration whatsoever of any moral or spiritual values, Resurrection, Judgment, or life in Heaven exists there as could be attested by any student of that philosophy. The conquest of the material forces of Mother Nature and the infinite increase in man's dominion through continued scientific inquiry and research to obtain physical comforts and material facilities for humankind, in general, is the sole aim of the modern philosophy of atomism. We can read this passion in the writings of the advocates of atomism and observe it in this present age's realistic view.

Although faith too could be discerned as a conspicuous entity, in cases even a prominent entity with millions of its followers, closer scrutiny reveals that it is the material necessity and not the self-abnegating religion that holds the sway over man's mind. Whenever faith and material necessity come into conflict, generally, the faith suffers defeat.

They who still have not assigned a secondary place to faith as a merely private matter have tried to compromise between the material necessity and faith. They have tried to relieve conscience by assuming on the authority of their Scriptures that their faith allowed the necessities of life. They little realized the difference between procurement of necessities of life for existence in an atmosphere of faith and wholesale engrossment in material pursuits at the cost of faith in a world in which wealth figures as the sole deity and the contemplation of the works of Allah means material utility instead of the glorification of the Creator.

At the same time, 'criticism' has assumed the form of 'slander'. Engrossment in wealth accumulation, and hope of forever living in this world with ever-increasing riches regarded as evils in the pre-modern ages due to the influence of faith, have emerged as the fundamental principles and the basic pillars of this science-guided, machine-ridden age of the philosophy of the atomistic materialism. The West adopted this philosophy at the beginning of the Renaissance. It gradually spread all over the world. Until today, we see every nation on earth engrossed in wealth accumulation and engaged in an endeavor to attain self-sufficiency in the material field.

Moreover, we can see well that this age has adopted the universal character of the 'Homaza Lomaza', the 'slandering wealth-accumulator', as described by the prophecy of the Quran. It is hard to deny that the character of 'Homaza Lomaza' did not exist in those pre-modern ages, nor could it be assumed that there are no exceptions to the rule in this present age. So many could be found even today free from the evils of slander and greed of wealth. Yet, these evils are the collective characteristics of this modern age of atomistic materialism. On the other hand, the slandering wealth-lovers in the pre-modern eras existed individually in a general atmosphere of faith with its prevailing philosophy of world-hatred and self-abandonment, spiritual and moral values, and considerations for the next celestial world. In those ages, we could liken the characters like the 'Homaza Lomaza' being individual and sporadic to scattered icebergs of various categories, and diverse denominations in an ocean kept warm by faith. Or, more appropriately, we could compare them to sporadic meteorites shooting in space and kept calm by the influence of religion. Thus, the atomic hell could not have been enkindled in that situation, and nuclear energy lay secretly dormant in the world.

But came the age of atomistic materialism, and the character of 'Homaza Lomaza' became a general and universal feature. The world's space became congested with the so-called meteorites of combined slander and greed, and the earth seemed like an atomic oven ready to blaze up in the form of nuclear hell of nuclear bombs and radiations to consume this entire world. This atomic hell appeared due to a most logical and scientific process beginning with the atom to end in the atomic bomb. We could correctly sum up this process and accurately calculate the duration by considering all the necessary factors.

With all characteristic circumstances and atmosphere, suppose this modern age commenced with the appearance of the theory of atomism in the times of Democritus, the founder of this theory (5th century BC). Then, the role of Jesus Christ five centuries later might have been a matter of guess. Was he ordained to fight against atomistic materialism, science, the atomic bombs, and radiations or teach the atomic wreck survivors the correct ways of passing life on earth and patience in their post-atomic miseries? The historian could assign the correct dates to the events of that ancient atomic age relative to those appearing in this present atomic age. Thus, the dates of the discovery of atomic energy, the construction of the atomic bomb and the Hydrogen bomb, and the neutron bomb in the old atomic age could well be estimated and recorded.

The true destiny of this present age, however, is still dubious. The atomic war may destroy it. But, on the other hand, it may avoid the atomic war and be destroyed through atomic energy's atomic radiation for peace. Alternatively, it may be so fortunate to avoid atomic destruction by removing the primary causes of the trouble.

Minute scrutiny reveals an exact identity between the causes of punishment by the 'Hotama' and those prevailing in this age. We could say the same about the characteristics of the fire of 'Al-Hotama' and the atomic fire. Indeed, exact identity exists between the two, both phenomenally and functionally. Whoever knows the atomic phenomena could hardly miss this fantastic identity between the two. Moreover, any man endowed with an average power of observation will never miss the prevalence of three evils, causes of the emergence of the atomic hell in the present world, or the clear identity existing between these prevalent evils and those mentioned by the prophecy as the causes of the appearance of 'Al-Hotama'.

Traditionally, the idea of hell has been associated with the next world. Naturally, a mention of the appearance of hell within the world may appear as a fact indeed quaint. The next world is generally considered something far remote in oblivion; the thought of appearing the hell therein might provide a source of solace in Heaven to bask in the lulling thought of the remoteness of the event and provide a cause for an attitude of despair and forgetfulness. But when one remembers that the process of divine retribution is inherent in the very nature of the creation beginning with it and clearly functioning in a universal, all-pervading, and unfailing manner whether man comprehends it or not, nor ending with it but moving further into the next world through the bridge of death, there remains little reason to doubt the appearance of the result when the requisite factors of a particular process have been duly accomplished. The destruction of the froward tribes of 'Aad' and 'Thamud', 'Sodom' and 'Gomorrah', through the Creator's supernatural

Will, are the instances of heavenly punishment. When such precedents of divine vengeance occurred in this very world are considered, no particular reason remains for doubt in the possibility of the appearance of the wrath of the Creator in the form of hell in this same world without danger of damaging the notion of the appearance of hell in next world. The Quran has cited many an example in this respect.

For instance, the Quran says:

"The Reality! What is Reality? Ah, what will convey unto thee what the reality is! (The tribes of) Thamud and A'ad disbelieved in the judgment to come. As for Thamud, they were destroyed by lightning. And as for A'ad, they were destroyed by a fierce roaring wind, which He imposed on them for seven long nights and eight long days so that thou mightest have seen men lying overthrown, as they were hollow trunks of palm-trees. Canst thou (O Muhammad) see any remnant of them? And Pharaoh and those before him, and the communities that were destroyed, brought error, and they disobeyed the messenger of their Lord, therefore did He grip them with a tightening grip. Lo! When the waters rose, We carried you upon the ship that We might make it a memorial for you, and that remembering ears (that heard the story) might remember."

(Quran 69:1-12)

Clearly, in the light of this revelation of the Holy Quran, we know that the chastisement of the froward tribes and communities happened through divine vengeance within this same world, though they shall get condemned in the next world also. But is there any comparison between the destruction of those tribes comprising a few hundred thousand souls at the most and the wholesale destruction of entire humankind by atomic hell in this age? What if nuclear bombs and radiation have wreaked the complete devastation of humanity, and the world as a whole or a considerable part of it turns to ruins?

It may reasonably be said:

"This humankind ignored the injunctions of faith. They forgot their eternal abode in Heaven, falling headlong into this world, engrossing them entirely in the pursuit of the accumulation of wealth. They brought on their head wholesale destruction wrought by their own hands and consumed by the same atomic bombs they had with their own hands prepared and which their minds had devised. See how they now lie in heaps among the ruins of their tall buildings and see how all their wealth and property, so dear to them in their life and for whose sake they even had not scrupled to build the dreadful atomic bombs, are scattered in heaps of ruin all consumed.

But alas for them. For, it is not all. Three evils, for which they have incurred a miserable death and dejected destruction in this world and the next world, have been figured in the Quran as the causes that rendered people liable to punishment of fire of the eternal 'Al-Hotama' in the next endless world. This world certainly shall appear to the astonishment of many. They thus have not only ruined their life within this world but have further ruined their prospect in the next eternal life in Heaven."

What difference exists between the destruction of froward tribes of past ages and the impending wholesale doom of the modern era? The divine vengeance of Allah destroyed those tribes. The Providence supernaturally raised cataclysms in natural phenomena in the case of the ancients. Whereas, in this present age, the cataclysm which people will themselves raise with their own hands for demolition will bring about the wholesale destruction of humankind.

The text of the prophecy clearly describes 'Al-Hotama' as a fire possessed of specific characteristics and features. We can most clearly identify these characteristics and the features with those of atomic energy and its radiations. The text of the prophecy has contained the explanation of certain evils as the causes of punishment in 'Al-Hotama'. We can unmistakably see the very same evils as the cause of the emergence of the atomic hell that is the atomic energy with its atomic bombs and atomic radiations within this very world in this age. How then someone can doubt the appearance of the replica of 'Al-Hotama' in this very world. The purport of the text of prophecy further supports the idea of fire of 'Al-Hotama' appearing within this world and the life-tenure of the 'slandering wealth accumulator'. According to the warning, the slandering wealth accumulator has a notion of forever living in this world based on his wealth.

The words of the prophecy are:

"He thinketh surely that his wealth shall render him immortal."

However, instantly comes up the negation of his notion by the prophecy. Then, as if in a retort, prophecy proceeds to negate his notion of forever living in this world by words:

"Nay, for verily he shall be cast into 'Al-Hotama'."

When we know the meanings of 'Al-Hotama', we at once realize the significance of this retort of the prophecy, for 'Al-Hotama' means a 'crusher'. To wit, that the slandering wealth accumulator who thinks that he shall forever live in this world on the dint of his wealth shall be cast into the fiery crusher to be crushed so that he might himself see the negation of his false notion.

Therefore, we can take the retort of the prophecy to mean that:

"You think that you shall forever live in this world on the dint of your wealth. Nay, but you shall be cast into the fiery crusher of 'Al-Hotama' to be crushed, aye, you and your wealth as well, in which you had put so undue a confidence."

No doubt some of the early authentic reciters of the Quran in an authoritative and recognized reading had read the original word 'Layunbazanna' ('shall undoubtedly be cast into') in dual form as 'Layunbazaanne' ('both he and his wealth shall be cast into'). If casting one's wealth is meant to torture and pain, then the loss of wealth is undoubtedly painful within this material world where material wealth is much prized by people. While in the next world, the material wealth may be of little use and loss of little pain to the loser.

Further, suppose the word of the prophecy would with such reality appear even within this world. In that case, indeed, the fact is likely to bestow a particular authenticity on the word of the Quran and lend a countenance to other doctrines contained therein, more challenging to believe, e.g., the Resurrection, the Judgment, and the life in Heaven. If a hell mentioned by the Quran could appear within this world, then certainly the appearance of the hell in the next world as stated by the Quran must be a truth exceptionally veritable. As proclaimed by the Quran, within this very world, the appearance of hell is a miracle of prediction, of anticipation and logical truth, and a true embodiment of certainty, inevitable and undeniable.

The negative retort of the warning to slandering wealth-accumulators' notion of forever living in the world on the dint of their wealth may be accomplished in this world and life-span by casting them and their wealth right into the fire of 'Al-Hotama'. In that case, what more significant proof of the truth of the prophecy do they expect? Never in whole human history was man confronted with such a grievous threat as that of the atomic hell. Not once was wrought such a miracle of prediction and warning as this prophecy of the Quran. And by no means indeed, humanity shall be more unfortunate than to neglect this warning and incur the wrath of Allah in the form of the fire of the atomic hell within this world.

However, let the eternal 'Al-Hotama' of the next eternal world be not lost sight of, for the thought of the 'Al-Hotama' of the next world would imply a belief in the next world. The belief in the next world would save humanity from this present atomic hell since such a belief would reduce their love of this world and its wealth. So, the reduction in the love of wealth would automatically cause the danger and the means of the impeding atomic hell to disappear.

We have explained that atomic hell is a destructive phenomenon. We can take it on a par with destruction modes applied in the annihilation of froward tribes and communities of the ancient past ages. So, let us resume the above-quoted text of the Quran to realize the distinction which the Quran manifestly attempts to make between the destruction of a people within this world and the eternal punishment of the next endless world.

The Quran continues to say:

"And when the trumpet shall sound one blast, and the earth with the mountains shall be lifted upward and crushed with one crash, then, on that day will the Event befall. And the heaven will split asunder, for that day it will be frail. And the angels will be on the sides thereof, and eight will uphold the Throne of their Lord that day, above them. On that day, ye will be exposed; not a secret of you will be hidden. Then, as for him who is given his record in his right hand, he will say: Take, read my book! Surely I knew that I should have to meet my reckoning. Then he will be in a blissful state in a high Garden whereof the clusters are in easy reach. (And it will be said unto those therein): Eat and drink at ease for that which ye sent on before you in past days. But as for him who is given his record in his left hand, he will say: Oh, would that I had not been given my book and knew not what my reckoning! Oh, would that it had been death! My wealth hath not availed me; my power hath gone from me. (It will be said): Take him and fetter him and then expose him to hellfire and then insert him in a chain whereof the length is seventy cubits. Lo! He used not to believe in Allah the Tremendous, and urged not on the feeding of the wretched, therefore hath he no lover here this day, nor any food save filth which none but sinners eat."

(Quran 69:13-37)

Now, herein has been the description of Paradise and the hell of the next world. Mark that this shall happen after the disintegration of this universe, and there will be no death there, which means eternity as against the transiency of this present world marked by death.

In the Quran, illusions exist that indicate the possibility of the signs of the hell of the next world itself appearing within this material world. Thus, for example, Allah's challenge appears in the Quran to the opponents of faith as follows.

"Then let him call upon his henchmen! We will call the guards of hell."

(Quran 96:17-18)

The complete text of this challenge is as follows.

"Is he then unaware that Allah seeth? Nay, but if he ceases not, We will seize him by the forelock; the lying, sinful forelock. Then let him call upon his henchmen! We will call the guards of hell. Nay! Obey not thou him. But prostrate thyself, and draw near (unto Allah)."

(Quran 96:14-19)

All the commentators of the Quran agree that these verses placed such a challenge to Abu Jahl, the great adversary of Mohammed, the Holy Prophet (peace be upon him). All the interpreters explain that Abu Jahl had threatened that if he ever caught Mohammed (peace be upon him) in the act of adoration, he would (Allah forbid) set his foot on Prophet's neck. However, when Abu Jahl saw the Prophet (peace be upon him) in the act of adoration and approached near him to execute his threat, he turned suddenly back in fright. When people asked what the matter was, he confessed that he beheld a ditch of fire between him and the person of the Prophet (peace be upon him) and a terrible appearance of winged troops to defend the Prophet (peace be upon him). When the folks asked the Prophet (peace be upon him) of the matter, he solemnly said that had Abu Jahl advanced a step further; the angels would have torn him to pieces. Thus, commentators of the Quran say that Abu Jahl saw merely a glimpse of hell of the next world in advance within the world.

The incident indeed furnishes the possibility of hell of the next world appearing within this very world beyond any doubt. We can apply this principle to the case of 'Al-Hotama' appearing within this very world in the form of atomic hell of atomic bombs and atomic radiations, and heart-burning. However, as far as the role of atomic hell in the destruction of life and property is concerned, a little difficulty arises in identifying the modes of the demolition in past ages of the froward tribes and communities destroyed using a divine vengeance.

Thus, on the one hand, the atomic hell of this world shows characteristics of 'Al-Hotama' of the next world to qualify it for the appellation of hell. On the other hand, its destructive capacities are conspicuous enough to bring it on a par with the supernaturally-raised damaging cataclysms of the by-gone ages that had destroyed the froward tribes by dint of divine vengeance.

There might be differences in quality and quantity. Still, on the whole, atomic hell is the prospective destroyer of the entire world and a harbinger of the universal miseries of unprecedented categories and unspeakable severity. It leaves all the supernaturally raised cataclysms of history far behind to the extent that they could hardly sustain its comparison in quality or magnitude. In the past, the wrath of Allah punished and destroyed victims of cataclysms to let people comprehend the truth of the next world.

Just as the Quran has said:

"Even thus is the grasp of thy Lord when he graspeth the townships while they are doing wrong. Lo! His grasp is painful, very strong. Lo! Herein verily, there is a portent for those who fear the doom of the Hereafter. That is a day unto which humankind will be gathered, and that is a day that will be witnessed. And We defer it only as a term already reckoned."

(Quran 11:102-104)

We have been at pains to prove the plausibility of 'Al-Hotama' appearance in this world since the general trend has been to associate it with the next world. However, if the text of prophecy is strictly adhered to, nothing but the cause and effect of a process could be seen, not mentioning a period or world.

If the argument to prove its appearance within this world is necessary, it is equally essential to confirm its appearance in the next world. But if the actual appearance of the atomic hell in this world has provided proof, its appearance in the next world is supported by equally convincing arguments; as a rule, the people perishing through divine vengeance in this world must be subjected to punishment in the next world. They, who were subjected in the current world to the retribution of atomic hell because of certain evils, should in the next world as well be subjected to the punishment in 'Al-Hotama', promised due to the same vices.

Death, suffering, and the loss of wealth in this world are the lot even of the most pious of men; therefore, the real punishment for the wicked is the punishment that embraces the idea of eternity. The punishment in this world, being transient due to the transient nature, passes away and is forgotten with death, and the eternity of punishment is the absolute ideal of punishment. Therefore, the wicked should be subjected to eternal punishment to realize the true ideal. Convincing arguments of this fact are available. In this respect, the authority of the authentic interpreters of the Quran was enough as a most irrefutable argument to favor belief in the appearance of 'Al-Hotama' in the next world. They were the most pious among men and had a proper understanding of the mind of the Quran. They were the embodiments of truth. Their talent and ability are beyond any doubt.

Against all these identical points between the atomic hell of this world and 'Al-Hotama' of the next world, there is a point of difference: that in case of 'Al-Hotama' of the next world, only those found guilty will be cast into it, while in the case of the atomic hell of this world, there exists the possibility of some undeserving to share the doom with those deserving. However, they (unworthy) may be well compensated for their affliction in the next world to a more significant advantage since the misery in this world was transient. In contrast, their reward in the next world would be eternal. They, however, may be accused of assuming reticence and not opposing the development of the causes and the effects of the atomic hell in the world and may be subjected to some sort of punishment, quite properly the punishment of 'Al-Hotama'.

You may raise a question as to why the prophecy about the atomic hell was not discovered and expounded before the actual appearance of the atomic hell itself? This question evokes a world of arguments and discussion for answering it. In reality, the subject of prophecy had been such as could not possibly have been divulged or explained, nor could it be understood if described before the actual appearance of the atomic bomb or the development of nuclear energy to a particular stage. The course of discovery and even progress of nuclear power to the point of appearance of a nuclear bomb had provided a little scope of anticipation of the next step during progression. The discoverers of the atomic phenomena themselves remained dark to the last stage. Again if, on the one hand, the scientists were primarily ignorant of the Quran, on the other hand, they who knew the Quran were ignorant in science. Therefore, the possibility of having a knowledgeable person who mastered both subjects simultaneously to comprehend the purport of the prophecy was excluded.

Judging from the nature of the subject and the course of the discovery and the development of the atomic phenomena and several other relative factors, it appears that if the divulgence of the prophecy was impossible before the atomic age, its realization during the development of the atomic phenomena was no less complicated. Nay, even the divulgence of the prophecy's secret after the atomic bomb's manifest appearance must be referred merely to the grace of Allah Almighty, the Benign Allah. Yet, suppose if someone at a stage before the complete development of atomic phenomena advanced prophecy of the Quran as an indicator of nuclear hell, who would have understood or believed the hint in the world? It was only in the face of the complete information about the atomic fire and the atomic bomb that the corroboration of the subject could perhaps be undertaken or understood. Instead, it was probable that some attempt before the actual appearance of the atomic bomb would have been laughed at scornfully and rejected by the most knowledgeable persons, even by the atomists.

GABRIEL'S EXTINGUISHING THE ATOMIC HELL SERIES

In a world flushed with the hopes in the possibilities of significant advancement and material advantages available through the great discovery of a new type of energy, let us see how far humankind will avail this warning of the Quran in the eleventh hour, standing on the brink of wholesale destruction.

Most Western philosophers never felt easy with gradual suppression of mind by matter in the notorious mind-matter conflict commencing with adopting the philosophy of modern atomism by the West. Those thinkers have constantly endeavored to reinstate the mind in its proper place and have hated and struggled against modern materialism. Yet, none ever linked the causes as slander, the greed of wealth, etc., to the appearance of the atomic hell in the world.

The whole credit thereof in producing so startling a link goes exclusively to the supernatural vision of the Quran. The efforts of these philosophers apparently failed, the mind gradually sank into oblivion, matter triumphed, and materialism prevailed till its effects appeared in the form of the atomic hell. We see the disappointment of the genuine philosopher in its climax in the verdict of late Bertrand Russell, namely:

"Since Adam and Eve ate the apple, man has never refrained from any folly of which he was capable."

This very realistic and terrific verdict appears in the form of a pamphlet in golden color issued on 18th May 1962, captioned as, 'History of the world in epitome'. Russell was so kind as to send one copy of the pamphlet to me in response to my lengthy letter to him, hoping that I might enjoy the same. The whole affair was reminiscent of deep despair, the sad and saddening surmise of a keen philosophical career extending for about fourscore years spent in constant study and observation. Nevertheless, the weighty sentence spread over the pamphlet pages contained two very meaningful cartoons interposed between the sentence clauses at proper places. In one of these cartoons could be seen an outline of Adam and Eve in caricature, sitting face-to-face, each holding a half piece of an apple in readiness before partaking of it, but engrossed in musing upon the undisclosed effects of strange fruit; faces, both of the husband and wife reflect the anticipation and the apprehensions of the impact of venture according to their male and female nature respectively.

These, at least, were my musings upon the features of the cartoon. Whether the cartoonist had these thoughts in mind to guide his hand accordingly or not is known only to the artist that drew the cartoon. The head of a subtle snake was shown peeping on the side of Adam, stretching out its forked tongue, its mouth reflecting a sense of clandestine crookedness, its eye narrowed in some sinister expectations as of a plotter at the beginning of his carefully laid plot. Its serpentine body entwined around the pole of the partition that stood between Adam and Eve.

In the second cartoon, two towers faced each other, and on each one stood a warlord, in mutual confrontation, holding a weapon of war in his hand. At the same time, each with the other hand was flying a long line of toy fighter planes and certain other toy weapons above and behind his head like a balloon seller. All this signified war and fighting as the main occupation of humankind.

Below the cartoon, a hatted man was riding a hatless man in the manner of a donkey and holding the ridden man through bridles to signify tyranny as the business of man. The bridle hinted at the means and ways of affecting the tyranny. Thus, it is evident that it is the perpetual and inherent greed for wealth and power and the practice of mutual tyranny that Russell has considered the cause of the end of man through the atomic destruction. Thus, it is that we can see that the verdict of Russell coincides with that of the Quran. Russell has given the greed for wealth and tyranny as the cause of the atomic devastation of man. While, the Quran has given slander, wealth-accumulation, and the notion of forever living in the present world as causes of punishment in the fire of 'Al-Hotama'.

Russell, however, has furnished us with yet another instance of a comparison between the human intellect, howsoever great it might be, and the supernatural revelation of a Scripture. Russell undeniably has been the most outstanding intellect of his time and one of the greatest thinkers this world has ever produced. Yet, what comparison his sentence has to the prophecy of the Quran about the atomic bomb in reality. There exists hardly any reason for bringing the two into contrast.

Russell gave his sentence in full view of the manifestation of the fundamental causes of the atomic bomb. Whereas the prophecy of the Quran depicted and described the entire Philosophico-Scientific phenomena with all the primary causes fourteen hundred years ago. In that era and atmosphere, no human intellect could dream of the atom bomb or see any link between the causes ('slander', 'wealth-accumulation' and 'notion of forever living in this world') and appearance of the atom bomb, as the Quran has done. Even as strong as Socrates, Plato, Darwin, Bacon, Russell, or combined, human intellect could not have made such a feat possible.

The scientific definition and the description of the fire of 'Al-Hotama' is in itself a miracle of the rarest kind and far beyond the scope of any human intellect and would not have been possible for any human being before the appearance of the atomic bomb. At the same time, the Quran treated this subject in advance and the clearest of terms. Undoubtedly, the Omniscient Wisdom of Allah only could have achieved a treat like that. Russell's sentence quoted above is the expression of just observation and no more than a commentary on the existing situation of the world in the light of the current circumstances. Anyone could see that the present race of armaments started due to greed for power and wealth. The atomic bomb will bring about the end of this world since all these factors are currently present before the very eyes of humanity.

However, to link the three evils with the appearance of the atomic hell fourteen centuries ago in the past is something that defies human intelligence. Again, the sentence of Russell is but a bare remark on the history-long practice of human tyranny and greed of power with the expected end of humankind in the atomic war. In contrast, the prophecy of the Quran treated the whole Philosophico-Scientific process involved in that concerning the philosophy of ancient and modern atomism. It furnished the real essence thereof in a miraculous manner and describing wonderfully the characteristics and the features of the fire of 'Al-Hotama', the phenomena of the generation of the atomic energy: the fire, the blast, the radiation, and all the basic principles from the beginning of the nuclear process to its ultimate end.

The strangeness of the truth of the connection existing between the causes, that is, the three evils and the resultant emergence of the atomic hell, is sure to make a miraculous effect on the mind of humankind. Suppose it is not in the destiny of humankind to be broiled in the fire of the atomic bombs or subjected to a slow rot through harmful radiations. In that case, this warning of the Quran will not go unheeded by humankind due to its miraculous nature. Once humanity is determined, it may not be difficult to eradicate the Quran's precisely and effectively given causes to avoid the devastating threat of atomic bombs and radiation.

Thus, we see another difference between the sentence of Russell and the prophecy. Whereas Russell gave a verdict of disappointment and dismay, the Quran has sounded the warning and has given out causes to be rooted out. Hence, the Quran has engendered hope for humankind. Humanity can yet live in peace and prosperity by removing the roots of the appearance of the atomic hell. The difference in the sentence of Russell and the prophecy is subtle enough. Yet, it is not such as may be out of the scope of the average intelligence of a person. Russell concluded his verdict from practical factors. In contrast, the Quran revealed prophecy long ago when anyone could even dream of any signs of such factors in the world.

Russell has read the signs of the present circumstances and made his remark without establishing any Philosophico-Scientific origin of the appearance of the atomic bomb in people's greed for wealth and power. He has had no idea of tracing the emergence of the atomic bomb to its original causes; the 'slander', the 'wealth accumulation', and the 'notion of forever living in this world'. Russell only observed the practice of mutual tyranny among humankind and their tendency toward war. He saw the atomic bomb in appearance and knew that human greed for power and tendency toward war would engender the danger of war.

It was, however, for the Quran to trace the appearance of the atomic hell to its various original types of causes beforehand and thus record a miracle of Philosophico-Scientific insight that no mortal could ever have thought. None of Adam's children, howsoever wise, could ever have dreamed the link which the Quran established between the three evils, the atomic hell, and the description of the fire of 'Al-Hotama' which it so scientifically made in an age of no science.

It is a miracle to see that the description of the fire of 'Al-Hotama' is scientifically identical to the nuclear fire. Our amazement is further enhanced when we see that the three evils, which the Quran has given as the causes of the emergence of the atomic hell, are precisely the characteristic features of the philosophy of atomism: both ancient and modern. Moreover, these three evils are extant in the same era, producing the nuclear bomb. Thereby we understand how accurately the Quran traced the future history of humankind from the beginning of the modern age to its end in the atomic wars or the atomic radiations of atomic energy for peace.

We can at most take Russell's sentence as the last vanishing groan of a heart dying of dismay. On the other hand, the Quran's sentence sounds like the clarion call of hope with a force that might shake the earth to rid the stupor of this present humankind. It will lead them away from the threat of atomic devastation unto the path of absolute peace and real prosperity towards their ultimate destination.

However, how we miss gentle and intelligent Russell, whose importune death has robbed him of the wonder and satisfaction, he would have derived from the description of this prophecy of the Quran. How would this prophecy have revived his belief in the possibility of miracles in this age of no miracles? How would he have shuddered to call himself a man with no religion? How would the prophecy have affected him like physic in his deadly ailment of dismay, and how the light of hope would have shown afresh in his eyes? Indeed, he would have felt a new man with a new vision, provided Allah indeed had so willed. Nevertheless, he missed this life-giving elixir. Alas for him. However, there might be others yet alive to avail themselves of this golden chance and realize that the gold they accumulated was trash while the real treasure lay in this prophecy.

No doubt, the thought of the atomic bomb is diffused with universal fear. We would hardly expect a voice to meet with any opposition, even in countries foremost in developing their stockpiles, against the atomic war or demand for banishing nuclear bombs. However, it is uncertain that even the sincerest efforts opposing the risk of atomic war will ever succeed. Moreover, the actual accomplishment in 'No-Atomic-War' agreements or campaigns to abolish nuclear weapons will not guarantee to avoid any atomic war in the present circumstances.

Not the agreements, but rather the removal of the fundamental causes of the atomic war could perhaps ensure safety from the necessities of the atomic war. Even how severely someone condemns the nuclear war or fiercely criticizes the nuclear bomb, because of the dread associated with the atomic bomb's name, there is the slightest chance of incurring the displeasure of those countries whose pride and supremacy are rooted in having super bombs. Nevertheless, remember that no efforts will be of any avail in banishing the atomic war from the world unless humanity removes the evils which the Quran has given out as the fundamental causes of the emergence of the atomic hell.

Moreover, what is the good of banishing atomic war? For, if humankind defers atomic war for the time being or forever, nuclear energy for peace is there to assume the role of the nuclear destruction of this world. Atomists are consoling humankind to have obtained a particular isotope of Uranium used only for peaceful purposes of atomic energy. They cannot use it to construct nuclear weapons. Also, people of a continent could obtain atomic security for a particular part of that continent in the world atomic war. These are childish things. Suppose any statement of any scientist today regarding atomic energy is worth any consideration. In that case, he should declare that he has been successful in obtaining a fissile material that generates atomic energy without at the same time producing atomic radiations. Scientifically speaking, this achievement seems almost impossible.

Furthermore, the only security against the wholesale destruction of the atomic war, which could be worth considering, is that this whole earth should be declared free from the danger of the atomic war. A part of a lake could not be kept free from pollution unless you purge the whole of the lake. It is with complete safety, as we have said that anyone could rail at the atomic bomb, but it is not at all safe to open one's tongue against the atomic energy for peace. Presently humankind shows mental bankruptcy in the whirlwind of the present atomistic materialism. Indeed, the oppressive necessities of life have so utterly rendered purblind the vision of present-day humanity that whoso utters a word against the hazards of atomic energy for peace is supposed their most dangerous foe. It is because this adversary snatches away from their hungry mouth the nutrition pill. Whether the pill has poison is not considered presently in these pressing circumstances.

They also need atomic energy for defense purposes. Their enemies have the atomic energy for making atomic weapons. Why should they not? The hazards of atomic energy for peace are not hidden secrets now, but this world seems to be determined to face the hazards. Hazards or no hazards, nations must have the energy potential of atomic energy. The world has overlooked the entire grievous hazards incident on it. However, it could be hard to find a parallel of more appropriate behavior like an ostrich than humanity's present neglect of danger in adopting atomic energy in all human history.

In clear-cut contradiction to the dictates of science, the world leader of the scientific opinion (scientist) recommends using nuclear power for peace and gives hope to the world of someday finding protection against atomic radiation and discovering some sure cure for radiation sickness. No universal protection against radiation exists, and there is a slight possibility that humankind shall ever achieve such a feat. No sure cure for radiation sickness exists at present, and there is none in sight as yet. And, judging from the nature of the experiment involved, the matter seems like a remote possibility. The crux of the problem is that the scientist may never achieve universal protection against radiation or a sure cure for radiation sickness despite all his hopes and consolations.

The most dangerous of all the effects of atomic radiation is the 'genetic effects'. Even the smallest dose rate can produce these effects. These effects move insidiously through generations and are cumulative. They manifest themselves in any future generation in the form of abnormal births. That further are inheritable so that the monsters beget monsters and the kinds of monstrosity multiply through marriage. Gradually, this world might become the abode of chimeras of infinite types; humans, animals, and plants. Therefore, the act of recommending the use of atomic energy for peace on the scientist's part, despite our genuine regard for him, is unscientific and criminal to the extent of a justification of legal prosecution. It is just like someone ministers poison to the whole of the innocent humankind in false hopes of finding an antidote someday, sometime, somehow.

It can be well observed that the hypnotic effect of three evils given by the prophecy of the Quran as the cause of the appearance of the atomic bomb has blinded the scientist along with all the rest of the blinded humankind. The force that has been able to bend the mind of the most unrelenting community of scientists has driven them to a state where they defy the principle of the actual science by indulging in mere hope in tomorrow must essentially be a force far too inexorable. Scientist recommends using atomic energy for peace. He is pretty aware that no universal protection against radiation and no assured cure for radiation sickness exists. He knows that the genetic effects of radiation are insidious and inheritable. He recognizes that these genetic effects are a cause sure enough for turning entire humankind into a herd of abominable chimeras in the future. Despite all this knowledge, ask him why he is so enthusiastic about recommending atomic energy for peace? Wait for his answer. When it comes, see the trace of any justification in case you are acquainted with the subject of nuclear science.

Moreover, if you are satisfied with the answer, sit awhile in solitude, and try to find out how far the effect of three evils that the Quran has given out as the cause of the emergence of the atomic hell have tarnished your sight. Peace is no magical formula for chanting, nor only would the act of attaching the label of peace to the name of the atomic energy in any way render humankind immune from the ill-effects of radiations. Nor is it wise to think that as long as atomic energy in any form exists globally, the danger of atomic war could be affected anyway. Suppose, after adopting the atomic energy for peace, if for a moment the seeming improbability of someday discovering the universal protection against radiations and finding some assured cure for radiation sickness is assumed as a probability. In that case, does not the scientist know that: the genetic effects of radiations are irreversible, irreparable, inheritable, and multiplicative? Therefore, after a particular stage of development of atomic energy for peace, the discoveries of the scientists in this respect might prove useless. Will then the responsible scientist give some little thought to this point before taking the hazardous leap into the zones of the atomic hell?

How the atomic fire is enticing this generation into the trap reminds one of the legendary beguiling Sirens. Like the three Gorgon sisters, [2] slander, greed, and wealth adoration have petrified the human mind to blindness and deafness regarding the hazards of atomic energy. The unpleasantness of any warning, howsoever scientifically convincing, is quite apparent. Unbelievably absorbed at present seems the scientific community despite all their knowledge of their own discovered hazards of atomic energy. Any attempt to condemn nuclear energy for peace would seem to some of them to negate the basic methodology of science, that is, the negation of the fact that we can use science for construction and destruction. They might suspect the loss of the otherwise firm grip on the part of the author befitting in seriousness the grave nature of the subject, who, after great deliberation, has assumed the atomic energy as a natural exception to the general rule of the basic methodology of science. Atomic energy, according to him, is only meant for destruction, and the thought of construction is a mere delusion, a mere means of enticement into destruction.

We invite the scientist to investigate the truth of this fact in the findings of the top scientists themselves that will, without any fundamental ambiguity, show atomic energy as a clear exception to the basic methodology of science. We can witness the constructive propensities of atomic phenomena as a mere allurement, and its ruinous disadvantages would ultimately swallow the initial advantages derived from it. The definitive outcome of atomic energy will be wholesale destruction, infinite and boundless, insidious, open, cumulative, and multiplicative. The present notion of utility entertained by humankind will eventually prove a fascinating charm to entice them into the abysmal furnace of invisible, insidious, and obnoxious radiations if, by chance, they have avoided their destruction through the hail of the atomic bombs. This generation's dizzy-minded scientist may fail to realize these realities in the passion of progress despite his knowledge. However, the distressed and cancer-ridden community of the scientists in some future generations will undoubtedly understand these realities well. Moreover, the scientists will be shocked at their predecessors' unconsciousness and will curse them in extreme helplessness, lamenting their insensibility in a matter so highly grave and so disastrously grim.

However, this present generation of scientists and non-scientists may have the only consolation that this present generation may pass away unscathed if no atomic war intervenes. Still, there can be no doubt that they will undoubtedly bequeath the undisclosed effects of the atomic radiation to the next generation. They will talk of the rules of the scientific methodology and fail to observe the anxiety in the face of the science itself due to the hazards of atomic energy. They miss the palpitations of its heart and are deaf to the shrill cries of pain and fear its much-frightened spirit is emitting at present.

The existence of atomic energy is a hazard to the existence of science itself. With one worldwide atomic war, science, along with this entire world, will be wiped out of existence. If, however, the atomic war is deferred to such a time as the atomic radiations of the atomic energy for peace have the opportunity to destroy humankind: then science too will go to its grave along with humanity. They, who are confident in the serenity of humankind in avoiding the atomic war endlessly, overlook only the inherent bellicosity and fierceness of man and the compelling forces of the circumstances. They only forget the destiny of the appeals of the eminent scientists against the atomic bombs. Though many of them are great, the scientists themselves are playing blind to the hazards of atomic energy for peace.

Indeed, nothing could have been more straightforward than altogether omitting this most misunderstood of all the topics, that of the atomic energy for peace: mainly as I see that all the world is raving its throat hoarse to get the nuclear reactors. Countries, communities, and nations of the East and the West today seem in a feverish mood to obtain the means of generating the atomic energy and will not hesitate to pawn their integrity, solemnity, nay even their very existence unknowingly to receive a nuclear reactor or a reprocessing plant.

Compelled by the acute necessity of energy and by dint of competitive spirit due to the nuclear advancement of rival countries, the heads of the states and the political leaders are endeavoring to the best of their ability to equip their countries with atomic reactors rapidly. Thus, quite unintentionally, they indeed are plunging their homelands and people right into nuclear hell. They are doing this, little realizing in the heat of their endeavor that they are contributing their share to the worldwide pile of nuclear fuel increasing every day. This process of piling-up of atomic energy will finally adopt such an alarming magnitude as one day it will instantly flare up and consume this world including their dear homeland: for whose welfare, well-being, integrity, solemnity, peace, plenty, and prosperity, they had so strenuously and sincerely exerted in obtaining the means of atomic energy.

The topic of nuclear energy is the most mysterious and deluding of all the subjects of knowledge that humanity has ever learned. Unfortunately though, and quite obviously all the heads of states (excepting Jimmy Carter, the present President of America) and all high dignitaries holding authority in policy matters of the various communities of the world, stand today in dire need of a complete initiation into the mysteries of the subject of the atomic energy. These dignitaries grasp the future fortunes of humanity globally and this whole creation of Allah. Unless these celebrities understand the scientific consequences of adopting atomic energy entirely, they are bound to be misled by the label of 'peace' attached to nuclear energy. They will take all humanity with them right into the atomic hell from where there is no outlet.

The only exception to the rule of universal ignorance of the states' heads worldwide in atomic energy matters is Jimmy Carter, the present President of America. But woe upon woe, we see him standing on board of the nuclear submarines of his country in very exhilarating and jubilant airs teeming with a sense of genuine pride in an achievement that signified the superiority of his nation in the nuclear field.

Nuclear energy is the most desired object and the utmost necessity presently. The world is determined to adopt atomic energy at any cost. It would at present behold with unpleasantness any view that favored an opinion adverse to the adoption of nuclear energy. The scientist community, blindfolded by the Economico-Political pressure, could be seen playing the blindman's buff with the truant radiations unsuccessfully and echoing the recommendation of adopting the atomic energy in the hope of one day catching the vagrant radiations and putting them to scientific subjugation.

If such be the state of affairs, the best indeed of all the possible courses open to me would have been to omit the very mention of the subject of atomic energy entirely. Is it not better to pocket all the praise and admiration and gratitude of humanity by condemning the military aspects of atomic energy and save oneself from the inconvenience of confrontation and controversy and all the rest of the unpleasant consequences of opposing the popular view simply by omitting the very mention of the topic of the atomic energy for peace?

Moreover, I assure the reader that I would have sidetracked the whole topic of atomic energy for peace without arousing any suspicion in the reader's mind regarding the omission. None in the world knew anything about the theme I held under treatment; nay, none indeed could have even dreamed of it. Did I not know that part of my theme concerned exclusively with the opposition of the military use of atomic energy was sure to fetch admiration and gratitude of humankind, perhaps even medals, and noble prizes as a testimony of the universal regard for my services for humanity? Instead, I forsook every thought of a reward and renounced every desire of praise, admiration, even gratitude. I willingly yielded myself to the much-expected wave of universal bitterness, ire, ill-feeling, even enmity of my fellow human beings merely for the sake of my truthful duty towards those for whom I entertained the deepest sympathies in the heart of my hearts.

Did I not know the helplessness of present-day humankind? Yes, I knew it. Was I ignorant of their miserable plight? No, I was not. Did I neglect in pure indifference the extreme demand of their need for energy? No, I never neglected it. Did not my heart bleed over the painful afflictions of my fellow humans? Yes, of course. How could it be otherwise?

But, on the other hand, could I be deemed in any way unaware of the inconvenience to which the mind of a troubled generation this dire cry would put in these urgent circumstances? Nay, but with heartfelt apology brethren, let me implore your conscience that the pangs of my inner conscience have been far too severe. They did not allow the expedient of my reluctance to hold its sway in full view of a maddening perspective of the annoying consequences of adopting atomic energy. As a result, I find myself quite out of myself. I see myself set before a spectacle of a world turned into hell: the atomic hell in which this whole world is burning midst a din of heart-splitting wails and blood-curdling groans in the extremity of tortures and torments that are enough to move a plaint-hearted spectator.

If such be the state of my mind, and if such be the spectacle which I find before my eyes in the perpetual display, then tell me, brother human, if you honestly could find a heart to criticize me or to blame me if I cry:

"Let the truth be told in its entirety and let the truth appear like the truth, the whole truth, and nothing but the truth, Allah willing indeed."

Whip, rack, bastinado, even gallows are preferable for the sake of truth to the crowns and wreaths of glory received by concealing the truth or a part thereof. You can gag a man, stop his mouth, kill his body, but you cannot keep his soul from crying. Even the mold of his remains in the grave shall cry the truth for whose sake he sacrificed his life. So will scream the dust of my body too:

"Adopt not the atomic energy O, man, for it is not energy. It is the wrath of Allah enkindled against a transgressing generation. It has neither peace nor prosperity, but it rather is a hell, the atomic hell ablaze to consume you and your future generations. Cease, therefore, and repent that perhaps Allah may yet save you."

But rest assured, my dear reader, that I have based this my theme neither on mere emotions nor mere theological dictates and doctrines. Moreover, it is never a mere burst of uncontrolled feelings, but rather the whole argument pedestals on the recognized facts of most modern science that have been discovered and authenticated by those recognized as the leading and the genuine among the community of scientists. This fact shall all the renowned scientists of the world testify and will surely attest that there happens to be not one fact that is a whit in contradiction to the ascertained facts of science.

Nevertheless, O, Allah in whose name I have endeavored to speak the truth to my fellow humans, pray, I implore you to save me from the baseless doubt, unqualified vagary, and the tormenting echo of the shallow knowledge. I have not much reason to complain, yet that type of misunderstanding is worse than the pangs of death itself. It is torture exceedingly mortifying to hear a baseless objection from a tongue that does without sure knowledge echo the half-understood strains that would enter my ears like a jet of hot acid. The quotations of the authorities that are not adequately understood even by themselves quoted to support their objection sound worse than the tormenting noise of a trumpet raised by a learning trumpeter in practice. However, nothing but sympathy is there in my mind regarding all such fellows, for they do not know what they say in earnest zeal. However, their argument is generally frail, their facts are immature, and their knowledge is usually always trivial.

I solemnly believe that every true scientist will discern in my voice the faithful echo of the voice of his inner mind and heart which he finds himself unable to emit due to the prohibitive exigencies of the prevailing circumstances in this world of today. We may well imagine the heart of every genuine scientist caught in the dread of the ruinous hazards of the atomic radiations, which he knows to be inherent in the very nature of the atomic energy and accepting no control hitherto. Anyone can undoubtedly envision the mind of every genuine scientist in a state of dissatisfaction over the uncertain and dangerous state of the subject of atomic energy. Therefore, we could expect every genuine scientist to be only too happy to see the opponent of the adoption of atomic energy for peace.

Conversely, compared to even the honest scientist, the adversary of the adoption of nuclear power for peace is at least at liberty to discard every consideration for the sake of truth and expresses the echo of his inward conscience through his voice. Alas for the sincere scientist whose heart cries inwardly at the expected havocs of the atomic energy but caught in the cruel grip of the economic [3] and political vice, can but stare mutely: tongue-tied under the perpetual torture of the painful pricks of conscience, or is even forced against his will to offer his cooperation in the development of the deadly bane. The heart of every intelligent scientist who knows the consequences of the venture cries when he finds himself forced to issue his recommendation of the adoption of atomic energy. Alas for them, those find themselves helpless to voice the cry of their own inner heart.

Dear reader! Pardon me for all inconvenience which my quaint startling views would cause you at the outset, disturbing the equilibrium of your mind and destroying the existing setup of your previous opinions about the atomic energy: the ideas which hitherto you had considered as established. I am not ignorant of the first effect which my views are going to make on your mind. We can compare the affair to the effect of a sledgehammer in a glass shop.

However, the first effects over your mind will gradually learn to assimilate the bitter physic. None is to be blamed, for the subject of atomic phenomena is far too complex, the knowledge available, scanty, and the necessity of energy extreme. A few only in the world could claim mastery therein; the rest have to depend on fragmented and inadequate knowledge.

After long thought and deep deliberation, I have decided to adopt the course of the whole truth. Thus, after a well-judged decision, I have included the topic of atomic energy for peace in this work. In the treatment of the subject, I have neither flinched from unpleasant reactions of the world nor ever for once thought of remorse for not having side-tracked the topic of atomic energy for peace has touched my heart. I did it despite the knowledge that by so doing, it could neither in any way damage the central theme of my work nor the discrepancy of any kind whatsoever would be discernible to the eye of even the most competent critic in the whole world.

How easily the provocative obsequies emanating from the condemned pyre of an element so dear to the heart of humankind at large, even if in reality so grievously hurtful, could have been evaded, and the mouth of colic controversy so effectively shut? Furthermore, how much labor and painstaking could have been saved by just assuming a reticence about the much perplexing topic of atomic energy for peace? Besides that, what plausible expectations I could not have received of plumes, laurels, and panegyrics? But alas! In reality, all these praises would have been laments and censures.

Such indeed is the despotism of the conscience. We must tell the truth about atomic energy for peace. However, has not the scientist himself manifestly told the truth? The credit for every discovery goes to those amongst the scientists who have discovered the hazards of atomic energy. For me, it is no more than to arrange those discoveries in an array before the world. I have only cared to segregate the portion of mere wishful thinking, vague hopes, and expectations about the discoveries of some universal protection against radiation and some sure cure for radiation sickness from pure scientific facts. I have based my study on the hard and fast facts of the subject. Judging from the nature of atomic energy, I have endeavored to show that any consideration of hopes in discoveries that are yet in the womb of the future is unscientific and fatal. For, by the time the findings may come, the radiations might have done their work secretly and openly, resulting in irreparable loss or even wholesale destruction of humankind.

Again, there is the possibility that the discoveries so expected may never come. We have to assess the extent of possibility and realization of the future hopes in expected discoveries in the light of the nature of particular intricacies of the subject of nuclear science. Due to inaccessible littleness, nuclear reactions within the atom's subatomic regions are of a misleading unreachable nature. That is why the scientists' hopes in the discoveries of some universal protection of humankind against radiation and some sure cure for radiation sickness may appear if not utterly impossible, at least nearly impossible. The difficulties in achieving some sure, universal control of radiation or procuring some sure cure for the radiation sickness appear almost impossible. The nuclear reactions derange the basic atomic structure of the atom. While rearranging this deranged structure to its original form has neither hitherto been found to be possible, nor is there any sure hope that atomists shall ever accomplish the feat in the future.

Nor is it in any way possible to shield every single individual in the world against the radiations. The people could only be protected from radiations completely and materially, covering the source of radiations. There is every possibility of radiation leakage from the sources. Also, there is a possibility of the explosion of the origin of atomic energy. Then, can anybody boast that covering the sources of radiation is enough? Besides, does the future state of the affair deserve to be disregarded when the reactors shall scatter over the earth, and the redundancy of atomic mishaps amidst unprotected humankind shall become a universal feature? [4] To pin one's hopes on any future discoveries in this respect and venture to adopt atomic energy for peace merely by dint of such far-fetched hopes is dangerous and misleading. Also, this attitude is against the dictates of science itself. Science cries aloud against such disregard. Alas! Humanity at present has ignored these cries of science in the dint of the demands of energy.

Future discoveries may or may not come. Even if they come, they might come at a stage when the radiations have secretly or even openly undermined the health of this humankind. Do they forget that the genetic effects of radiations are secret, heritable, multiplicative, and can turn this whole humankind into a herd of chimeras of various kinds and miscellaneous categories? Moreover, the genetic effects of radiation are irreparable and irreversible. Do they not understand what the terms irreparable and irreversible mean? Conversely, are they blinded by the heat of the necessity of energy so much so that they will not hesitate to swallow this nutritious venom?

Let us postpone the adoption of atomic energy for peace until science discovers universal protection against radiation. Such findings should provide some sure cure for radiation sickness and ensure every individual with protection in this world against radiation effects through radiation-proof dress. This demand is indeed in exact conformity to the dictates of science. Unless science makes it happen, let every scientist who recommends using atomic energy for peace know that he stands guilty in the sight of science as a defaulter and liable to impeachment. Yet, by the attitude of the generality of scientists of our times, it appears that they are in a mood to change entire humankind into a race of guinea pigs in a worldwide laboratory of nuclear science.

Nevertheless, remember that once their experiment in such a laboratory begins, then judging from the nature of the experiment, there is no way back, and there is no possibility of tracing the steps back towards safety. Like an epidemic, the effects of radiation will spread globally, and humankind will never attain its pre-nuclear age health. Therefore, it seems reasonable that the authorities must underline every paragraph in a nuclear science book with the following sentence.

"Let us postpone the adoption of the atomic energy till universal and sure protection against the radiations and sure cure for radiation sickness have been discovered."

Again, what a greater fallacy could we see in the whole history of science than that of the scientists who consider sacrificing a certain proportion of humankind to radiations worthwhile and reasonable in the zeal of energy in the present perspective of sheer necessity? They believe it is not in any way disastrous to humanity as a whole. They ignore the fact that they have neither means to check the amount of the genetic load of an individual or a population at a particular time nor have any means to check the effects thereof if they became manifest at any time. Once the effects of radiation have appeared in a specific population, the other folks might begin to show the impacts like rabbits in an epidemic till the whole of humankind has perished. Alternatively, shall we be suspected of being a little too unscientific in this respect, or will this statement be considered a specimen of the alarmist view? Yet, can we stop this humankind if they are determined to swallow the poison they so urgently need for their nutrition? However, we must warn them to the end.

Will then the people of this world try to understand the point which means their death and life? Is it impossible to postpone the atomic energy program until science has brought the subject under complete command and control, or are they determined to ride the unbridled python in the dark? This matter warrants a very rigid and very matter-of-fact attitude on the part of the scientist and everyone who bears a share in the adoption and development of atomic energy in the world. The scientist must cast away every illusive hope and expectation in this matter and adopt a very scientific attitude.

Another point that deserves equal attention is that in the future, atomic energy in the world shall be in a full-fledged state having a universal prevalence, and not at all in the present perspective when nuclear power is next only to nothing. Hence, humankind ought to make the opinion in this matter in a future viewpoint. Try to imagine a world in the future when no place on earth shall be found free from the sign 'HOT", which signifies the den of the murderous witch that is radiation. Therefore, the tremendous stress on the point of the atomic energy for peace is necessary. Because the first leap in this nuclear hell shall prove to be the last, and the world shall go down in the ditch without any hope of ever emerging from it. The genetic effects of radiations are irreparable, irreversible, inheritable, and cumulative.

The real tragedy is that once atomic energy is adopted, a stage may soon arrive when radiations undermine populations' health due to their insidious, heritable, cumulative, and multiplicative effects. This damage to the health may be to the extent that even the banishment of atomic energy would be of little avail. In that case, humankind, all the same, would come to everlasting grief that may end only in the partial or complete demolition of life after indeed an excruciating and miserable existence on earth. Since even minor radiation damage, in the beginning, may multiply like an epidemic that has no cure, neither could it be prevented from spreading.

The genetic effects of radiations, a well-established fact, do move insidiously and secretly through successive generations entirely undetectable till they manifest themselves in some generation in the form of abnormal birth. The genes mutated by radiation, known as recessive, are continually transmitted to future generations without even the parents' knowledge. There are no scientific means to discover, cure, or rid them. They keep on moving through generations surreptitiously till they manifest their existence in abnormal birth to the great misfortune of the parents, the individual itself, and indeed the humankind in general, for such abnormal persons beget abnormal children. Because these abnormalities multiply through marriage, there is every likelihood that these genetic effects of radiations may eventually change a substantial part of humankind into promiscuous herds of chequered chimeras.

Consequently, genetic mutations might transform various species, men, and other creatures into unrecognizable and hideous creatures. Humanity should realize the difficulty of this matter by the facts regarding the genetic effects of radiations. Any means cannot detect the genetic effects of radiations. None today can tell how much genetic load a specific person or humankind, in general, is carrying and that there is absolutely no treatment of the genetic damage of radiations. There exists no means of detection, nor does there exist any cure for such a sickness.

Moreover, there is a solid reason to assume by judging the nature of the subject that there is hardly any possibility that science shall ever find any means of discovering the genetic effects of radiation or any cure for them. Hopes of the optimistic scientists may remain extant in this respect, but their hopes in this most hopeless of all matters shall cause the real tragedy. In this particular respect, the scientist's behavior, judging from the factual realities, seems sure to exceed far the superstitious attitude of the ancient people of the darkest ages of the worshippers of malignant spirits. They seem to have deserted the hard-headed track of science entirely. How could a scientist reconcile his mind to the idea of recommending the adoption of atomic energy for peace if this is the situation?

Humankind could easily suffer the most inhuman atrocities inflicted through conventional weapons. But it is not the case for the hazards of atomic energy imposed on humanity. Even one couple of human beings left in this world after the war with the traditional phenomenal weapons may propagate in the world safe for living. Therefore, it would be considered far less dangerous for humankind than the adoption of atomic energy in its present unsafe state.

In contrast, the effects of atomic energy's atomic radiation for peace will change this world into one incapable of providing a safe and healthy living to its inhabitants for millions of years. No doubt, the statement may sound as highly hyperbolical, perhaps even fantastic, and far exceeding in alarm all the most alarmist views. Yet even if it so appears, let its credit go to the scientist himself responsible for all the discoveries on which such a statement could be most scientifically based. Even though possessed of all knowledge on nuclear science, a scientist may find any hyperbolic or alarmist views in these statements. He stands in dire need of searching his mind in the light of atomic knowledge, for the fire of 'Al-Hotama' rises unto the hearts according to the Quran. But, unfortunately, the heart of such a scientist might have been blurred by the encompassing envelope of the fire of atomic hell, so he finds himself unable to discern the truth in the statements in question.

The only consolation which the present generation can have is in the possibility that this present generation may only transmit the harmful effects of radiation to the next generation. In contrast, the present generation itself may seemingly go unhurt. However, alas for the blinding influence of the fast approaching and dreadful doom. The nuclear octopus shall never leave its victim, this humankind, till it has devoured it ultimately.

The safeguards against the atomic radiation on which this generation depends are all, as it is no hidden secret, not fool-proof or hundred percent certain. But, of course, they are pretty insufficient to allow such a leap into the atomic hell to adopt nuclear energy for peace. Woe to this humankind, the atomic energy for peace, despite its label of 'peace', may, in case humankind infinitely avoids the atomic war, prove eventually at least as disastrous as the atomic war if not more. Every scientist knows that it is not enough to cover the atomic reactors materially, for there is every possibility of occasional leakage of radiations. It is impossible to cover every individual of humankind materially for protection against radiation. So, it is amongst the scattered and unprotected humankind that the radiations in the atomic age shall play the universal vagrancy.

Some scientists speak of sacrificing a specific portion of the population to the effects of radiation to obtain the benefits of atomic energy. Yet, none can tell how much the population is carrying a genetic load? Nor can they state how much genetic load a person is having at some specific time? So, where is the judgment criterion to know that the proportion of the population involved in the genetic effects of radiation has reached the level where we have to stop it to assess the ratio of the population that we can safely sacrifice to atomic energy? Moreover, suppose they find the means of judging this fact, how can they stop the proportion on a particular point? No, but the whole thing is wrapped in utter darkness, and the arrows are being shot blindly in every direction haphazardly. Thus, the following questions raise another humanitarian aspect.

"Why should even the most minor proportion of humankind be subjected to radiation hazards to benefit from atomic energy? Why then is the cumulative and multiplicative factor of radio-genetic hazards neglected? On what horns of the dilemma, the poor scientist is caught, and what a fiery cobra he has conjured up to his own as well as humanity's great misfortune, and none knows to what terrible disaster this scientific fee-faw-fum will eventually lead this unfortunate humankind?"

It is not humankind alone that has a reason to lament the adoption of atomic energy for war or peace. Still, science is in a state of mourning for the hazard to its existence that is incident on the atomic energy. Science at present stands trembling before the dreadful offspring of the dame atomic energy, the atomic bomb. It hides her face from the poisonous breath of the fiery field that is the atomic radiation. We can never expect science to be the victim of mere hallucinations and reckon the fears of science as most scientific and well-judged in this respect.

So also, could be said of the scientist, the authoritative interpreter, and propagator of science. The poor fellow seems naturally forced under the unbearable stress of the existing circumstances of the much needy humankind to bend his views regarding nuclear energy and depart from the unbending path of science. In granting permission to adopt atomic energy, the scientist may resort to the excuse of the lesser evil, though alas, a lesser evil it certainly is not. Indeed, it is the greatest evil that ever appeared on this earth in the whole history of humankind. It is the saddest of all the sad issues, and sadder still is the scientist's connivance in this matter. The demon and its dame: the damned atomic bomb and the damnable witch, the atomic energy, emerging from the bosom of science confront the humankind glaring with fiery eyes and shaking fatal trident, threaten to consume the world, including science and scientist. In the case of atomic energy for peace, its benefits may, in the beginning, perhaps to several generations, be sweet indeed, but eventually and with utmost certainty, nothing but misery shall be a lot of radiation-ridden humankind.

"Today you shall wed Sorrow,
And Repentance will come tomorrow."

('The Pilgrim'; by John Fletcher (1621): Act-4/Scene-2/Page-301) However, alas! No repentance in the atomic energy for peace will be of any avail. On the contrary, the multiplicative retribution shall certainly be exacted until this humankind, turned into chimeras, gradually becomes extinct and leaves earth as a barren and abandoned wilderness behind as a memorial of the follies of a race created in the image of the Creator Himself. But who shall speak on behalf of dumb mutes, the poor victims of man's deeds?

The scientist has been regarded with reverence, even as a great benefactor by humankind since the advent of this modern science-guided and mechanical age, due indeed to his honesty, integrity, sincerity, and ability in the matter of science, and due in particular to the excellent services rendered by him to humankind in providing the facilities of science in obtaining material comfort and wealth of the world. But, in due course, due to the unbearable and untold miseries brought about by the discoveries of science in general and by the discovery of atomic energy in particular: yea, the very same scientist will be looked upon by a generation of humankind sizzling in the heat of the nuclear hell of the atomic age, as the greatest enemy of humanity, and most malicious of all the numerous hosts of seducers that have ever appeared on earth in whole human history.

The reason for this blindness of the scientist in neglecting all the hazards of the atomic energy despite his knowledge, and recommending its use for peaceful purposes, could be attributed to the worldwide hypnotic effect of the three evils: namely, slander, wealth-accumulation, and a belief in the power of wealth to make immortal. These three evils that produce particularly oppressive economic circumstances throughout the world have created a universal atmosphere in which the hard-headed scientist too has been drowned and obliged to assume a most unscientific attitude regarding atomic energy. There could be no other reason for the scientist's attitude except that he too has been stupefied by all-pervading effects of three evils. A scientist from whose mind, even today these effects are expelled for a moment, will himself wonder at the quaint attitude of the scientists regarding atomic energy.

It is for scientists now to know the exceptional nature of nuclear energy in the realm of science. It is an essential point ever risen in the whole history of modern science and one deserving the utmost attention of the scientist. Scientists should also know that the margin now left for thought regarding atomic energy is too meager, and instant action is warranted. It is most expedient now that the scientist must contemplate the problem in seclusion and view the whole very thoughtfully, very disinterestedly, weighing all the pros and cons of the dilemma carefully.

Should not the scientist consult the very findings which he has put before the world and judge in their light whether there are any possibilities of some future discoveries to resolve the issue of protection against radiation? If yes, will they afford universal protection to the whole of humankind individually, or may guarantee any sure cure for radiation sickness, or provide any means of detecting or treating the mutated genes? Then he may see in the light of his cautious scrutiny if the atomic energy, even for peace, were not like an issue that would appear as a sort of 'damnosa hereditas', nay rather an inheritance ultimately ruinous to all humankind.

Suppose such would be the case, and it indeed is such a one. In that case, it is incumbent on the scientist to properly consider this most catastrophic of all human problems. He should endeavor to the best of his ability to cast away the hypnotic spell of the three evils in the light of the scientific light of the well-established facts because this world is on the extreme verge of wholesale destruction. The margin for thought now left is so narrow: that one step further into the atomic energy, and the world goes down into the burning ditch of nuclear hell without any hope of ever coming out of it in the future. The responsibility, indeed, most of it, falls on no one else but the scientist himself.

None in history ever was so precarious a situation as the scientist of this age today is in this matter of the adoption of atomic energy. Therefore, let the scientist beware and wake up from his long stupor and face the fact resolutely, lest the miserable humankind segregates him as the curse, the scourge, and the seducer of humankind. Let this modern world now, instead of labeling the people with the epithets like the fanatic, the bigot, and backward, see their minds' state and cease calling the people superstitious. This modern superstition of the modern scientific age seems to have far surpassed the superstition of those ancient people whom the modernists have long sneered with contempt.

Indeed, the case of atomic energy has shattered all the claims of this modern age to rationalism and hardheadedness. Their thought is not the people's views famed for their rational and scientific outlook compared to the people of the pre-modern ages. Neither modernists nor any skeptic has the right any longer to look down on the superstitious behavior of the people of past ignorant ages. Howsoever ignorant and superstitious the ancient people might have been, we have never expected them to think in such terms as world consuming atomic bombs and globally prevailing deadly radiations, as the people of civilized and learned age at present do. And how sad seems the situation when regarded enthusiastic in comparison.

It is high time now that the scientists search their minds, follow the voice of their conscience, and declare that science must provide every individual human being and every individual beast on earth with sure means of protection against the inherent radiations. Scientists must find some sure cure for radiation sickness. They must discover some means of finding the recessive gene in individuals, curing it, and checking its inheritable effects. First of all, scientists must succeed in achieving all these accomplishments in the realm of nuclear science. Until then, any amount of atomic energy, however small, should neither be recommended by any conscientious scientist on the face of this earth nor scientist should cooperate in the adoption or development of atomic energy anywhere, whatever be the personal consequences. In such a situation of the world, and at a nascent stage of discovery and development of nuclear energy, recommending the adoption of atomic power for peace is an act in no way different from ministering a deadly poison to a hungry person like food, in the hope of one day discovering some effective antidote.

The event brings added sorrow if the poison in the case mentioned above is ministered by a well-qualified and authoritative doctor, knowing that no antidote for that poison existed. Be not surprised, dear reader! And don't have the slightest doubt about the fact that the act of recommending the use of atomic energy for peace at the present stage of nuclear power is not a whit at variance with the action of ministering deadly poison to the entire humankind, having no antidote, in the hope of someday to discover a cure.

Indeed, no universal protection against atomic radiation exists at present, and yet science has found no sure cure for radiation sickness. None is yet in sight. And none might ever come due to the difficulty of approaching the tiniest regions in which the nuclear reactions occur and tackling the atomic particles with deceptive minuteness. However, the fact further enhances the sadness of the affair that recommendations should come from scientists who know all facts and have even discovered and authenticated such discoveries themselves. What else will you call this then, if not the blinding influence of a dreadful doom to befall this humankind due to the effects of the three evils that so overwhelmingly prevail at present all over the world? In history, humankind neither confronted such a critical problem nor stood on the horns of such a perplexing dilemma.

If then atomic energy is adopted at its present stage of development, it shall jeopardize the existence of science itself and that of humankind. It is most likely that atomic energy will destroy both science and humankind sooner or later.

Late Bertrand Russell wrote me the following sentence.

"Since Adam and Eve ate the apple, man has never refrained from any folly of which he was capable."

To this statement could be added the following.

"But man's last and greatest folly had been the adoption of the atomic energy before achieving any control over the atomic radiations. So, he rode an unbridled fiery horse that dashed him against the igneous rocks and brought about his complete ruin."

The subject of atomic energy for peace might indeed be a very subtle one, but what subtlety is there in the subject of atomic bombs? It is not difficult to realize by anyone of average intellect that the atomic bomb is not a weapon of war or defense. Instead, it is a sure means of complete annihilation and wholesale destruction of this world. The atomic bombs will certainly roast alive all the people and their children before their very eyes, their beasts, and birds too, their friend and their foe. Yet how little they seem to realize, who are engaged in making the atomic bombs these days, that it is not only for their enemies but also for their kith and kin compatriots that they are producing these monsters of destruction. They seem to forget enthusiastically the certainty of retaliative action of enemies engaged in a similar initiative.

Thus, the people of one atomic power make the atom bombs like an invitation to the atomic bombs of another power. The people of the modern world have accumulated wealth with an arduous struggle and have a love and necessity for their wealth. However, it is surprising that the same folks ignore that the atomic bomb destroys all property and wealth. Even one single nuclear war is likely to bring the fruits of all their incessant labor and gruesome toil of centuries to naught, in a matter of days, hours, or even in seconds. Nevertheless! Alas for them. Why are they so over-solicitous in the manufacture of their atomic weapons? Do they think that they are preparing these weapons to defend the wealth of their country? How little do they realize then that they are making these monsters inviting simultaneously similar monsters which their rivals are preparing to ensure the destruction of all their accumulated wealth and possessed property?

Judging from the enthusiasm and gusto of present humankind in material progress and the extreme intensity of their prepossessed minds, we may not consider out of place the apprehensions about the possibility of their neglecting this warning of the Quran. The dizziness of their mind may prove too thick a veil to allow the light of the warning of the Scripture to reveal the consequences of the exclusive material progress. Yet, a relationship between the atomistic character of the present age and resultant atomic sufferings will not be missed even by eye deprived of sight because of the influence of three evils mentioned by the Quran as a cause of the emergence of 'Al-Hotama'.

However, the passage of time, along with the gradual development of the atomic age, will, if, on the one hand, make such a correspondence clearer and more transparent, it would, on the other hand, dim the discerning sight of the inmates of that age. Such indeed is the justice of the whole affair. Suchlike appropriateness exists between the character and the retribution in the case of the atomic catastrophe that not the slightest cause for any complaint could appear to find any justification. But pity the eye which can see and constantly tortured at the sight of distressed humanity chained by the necessities of life that are dragging the human race over the scorching sands and thorny bushes of the atomic miseries toward the all-consuming atomic hell: men, women, children, and all to be blown up or roasted alive in the nuclear bomb explosions and pierced through by the swarms of the deadly poisonous needles of atomic radiations to their ultimate extinction.

Nevertheless, it is hard for anyone to describe the atomic hell or to express the horrors thereof in words, no matter how exclusively great one's talent for expression might happen to be. Try to see how piteously the chains of three evils are dragging present humankind over rugged paths: these evils are the slander, the greed for wealth, and the atomistic thought of forever living in this world? In what a stunning state, how heavily panting, and how profusely perspiring they are being drawn over atomic shambles to be roasted in the atomic oven till completely consumed and reduced to black soot and grey ashes and blown away in every direction as the memories of a past creation?

The tyrannical necessities of life are making dizzy the present humankind. It is moving on the mirage-like path of self-sufficiency through constant economic and industrial progress. This spectacle is sad enough to drive any person to tears who still has a vestige of feelings for fellow humans left in his heart despite all-pervading selfishness in this present age fostered by the philosophy of atomistic materialism.

Most scientists could have claimed a share in discovering atomic energy or its initial development into nuclear weapons. They might, by now, have left this transient world forever, neither taking their wealth with them nor leaving behind any memories of peace and content in the world. Those amongst them who are yet alive to enjoy an outstanding reputation as the great benefactors of this humankind must sooner or later follow the suit of their former colleagues to prove the vanity of the life of this world, leaving behind them the epidemic spread of the effects of their nuclear discoveries. Their death and inevitable departure from this world prove the fact that neither their accumulated wealth, nor their great discoveries, nor even their belief in the possible attainment of immortality through scientific experimentation could have rendered them immortal. Therefore, it is in the fitness of the things that let the scientists first achieve the feat of attaining immortality before posing at the world the fatal trident of the atomic energy either for war or for peace.

Indeed, atomists have left a name in the world, but certainly, the blast of the atomic bombs or the deadly effects of atomic radiation will blot their name from the world. There, however, might appear an intervening period between the adoption of atomic energy and the final extinction of humankind by the atomic conflagration when the extreme miseries of the atomic nature would submerge under their weight the excellent material services rendered by the scientists to humanity. Then, people will remember these benefactors of humankind as the greatest enemies of humanity. Alas! To numerous persons at present, these things may appear visionary and impractical in this world of today; instead, merely the hallucinatory outcries of a soul turned cynic. We could indeed expect not a different opinion from the minds that think about scientific progress in terms of infinity.

Only those unfortunate people will better know the accurate assessment of atomic energy and the respective merit of its discovery which will find themselves involved in the hail of the nuclear bombs. Or, in the case of nuclear power for peace, they will find themselves forever trapped in the worldwide hot pit of atomic radiation. To them, indeed, atomic energy and discoverers will appear in a light quite different from those who at present entertain the hopes in the un-surpassing excellence of the energy potential of nuclear power and rejoice in the expected benefits derived from there. To them, it is that the present-day scientific benefactor of humankind will appear in the guise of the originator of atomic hell and the author of all their intolerable miseries. To them, all the priestly tyrannies and the princely atrocities ever perpetrated on people in any past ages combined will appear but as a trifle compared to the scientist's single atrocity that of discovering the atomic energy.

In contrast, they will themselves consume all the past services rendered to humankind in the flames of the miseries of atomic explosions and radiations of nuclear energy for peace. To them, therefore, the scientist shall never be a benefactor but rather a fiendish originator of the atomic hell, the horrible author of all their untold and endless miseries, an accursed seducer in league with the devil. This epithet in history was generally assigned to him by every faithful Christian. Just imagine the difference.

At the beginning of the Renaissance of the West, the inquisition cast Bruno alive into the flames. This act threw the minds of the whole of humankind into convulsions. The world shuddered at the atrocity so inhuman. But, it is not one priest only. Now it is the whole of humanity involved: men, women, children, beasts, brutes, and birds that are going to be cast into the flames of the atomic hell of atomic bombs or the radiation hell of the nuclear energy for peace, to be broiled in fire or to be subjected to the fiery stings of the deadly invisible radiations of the atomic energy for peace without causing so much as a ripple in the mind of this so very civilized and enlightened age, so very proud of its civilization, enlightenment, knowledge, and science.

Then, when the miseries of atomic energy come to prevail among humankind, the scientist will himself be among the rest to taste the effects of his discovery and will presumably be among the most miserable. A scientist covered with cancers, warts, cysts, and running ulcers will then offer a spectacle worthy of pity. Still, perhaps it is not with pity but with hatred that the miserable humanity shall regard him.

It is hard indeed to portray the picture of horror that the scientist shall then be. He will be a grievous reminder of the folly of the previous generations of scientists, which relaxed in consolation that their age might pass away unharmed from the dangers of atomic fire and expected to discover some remedy someday for the bane of nuclear radiation. They discarded the probability of nuclear war because of their faith in the serenity of the political sense of humanity. They always ignored the possibility that someday to the great chagrin of both the scientists and the non-scientists, the raging demons of atomism assuming the form of the atomic bombs might pounce upon the miserable humankind with dire yells, heart-rending shrieks, and ear-piercing thunders in a fiery storm to consume this world: bone, flesh, hair, and all, leaving it in a state so pell-mell that destruction to be wrought by all the legendary gods of Olympus together with all the colossal giants of ancient myth would seem only a trifle in comparison. Nor had those scientists of the first atomic energy generation ever tried to imagine the accurate picture of that misery that humankind in the atomic age of the atomic energy for peace would ultimately present to the spectator's view.

A worldwide hail of atomic bombs descending from the sky, with their hearts burning with fury, could only be left to the individual imaginings so that everyone could form the picture of the view according to one's mental capacity. We can imagine the modern Northumberland in desperateness crying at the approach of the blinding thunders of the crushing volleys of the supergiants.

> "Now bind my brows with iron; and approach
> The rugged'st hour that time and spite dare bring
> To frown upon the enraged Northumberland!
> Let heaven kiss earth! Now let not Nature's hand
> Keep the wild flood confined! Let order die!
> And let this world no longer be a stage
> To feed contention in a lingering act;
> But let one spirit of the first-born Cain
> Reign in all bosoms, that, each heart being set
> On bloody courses, the rude scene may end,
> And darkness be the burier of the dead!"

('King Henry-IV'; by Shakespeare, Part-2/Act-I/Scene-I)
The miserable state of humankind of the radiation-ridden atomic age of the atomic energy for peace needs a subtler faculty of expression to portray in words.

Almost everyone today regards the progress of science in terms of infinity, to wit, that the progress of science will go on infinitely and forever. We see the monuments of the progress of science these days dispersed all over the earth in the form of massive factories, colossal buildings, long bridges, stately railways, spacious airports, and scores of other such like installations functioning in a universal and reliable economic and industrial setup. Because of the strength and multitudes of these impressive monuments, the aspect of the scientific progress is considered everlasting: yet, at the same time is ignored the destructive power and redundancy of modern armaments, notably nuclear weapons.

It is a matter of seconds, minutes, or at the most days, or like the old saying is, in the twinkling of an eye that all worldly monumental paraphernalia could disappear as if by the touch of a magic wand under a hail of atomic bombs. Or in case the nuclear war is deferred, the effects of the radiations of nuclear energy for peace would ultimately bring these monuments along with humankind to naught due to a systematic decay. Astonishing indeed is the non-realization of this fact, but more surprising still is the indifference of such lovers of wealth and property to the destruction of wealth and property involved in the hazards of atomic energy for war and peace. Despite all the knowledge and wisdom extant in the present age, to what other reason we can attribute such a peculiar attitude of the current generation except to the magical influence of a grievous doom engendered by the blinding effect of the three evils that so overwhelmingly predominate this present age. It seems surprising to witness folks of current age engrossed in business day in day out.

Nevertheless, they do this with ever-increasing enthusiasm as there existed no threat in the world to their business or life by any sources. Also, they think to continue forever advancing on the path of progress until they have conquered all the forces of the universe and become the sole masters of this world. It has something more than amusing in it to observe their indifference to all the most impending dangers to their wealth, health, life, and existence.

One wonders, why are they taking all these pains, and for what? In but a few moments, all their accumulated toil of centuries might vanish before their blinking eyes, and they might themselves form a part of the heaps dispersed all over the earth. If "Uneasy lies the head that wears a crown", [5] then even more uneasy lies the head that contemplates the subjection of the atomic energy to their service. Humankind may, with success, avoid the atomic war for some time or even for a long time, but it is hard to believe that it shall forever banish the atomic war from this earth. The nature of man and the necessity of circumstances speak against eternal peace and no war. In any form on this earth, the presence of atomic energy would always furnish a ready and slippery side-shift towards the atomic weapons.

Yet if humanity would banish the atomic war forever from this world, the atomic energy for peace, an equally destructive agency, is there to take the toil and produce results identical to those produced by the atomic bombs. Suppose they keep successfully fleeing from the fiery lion of the atomic bomb. In that case, they will not escape the formidable jaws of the atomic crocodile of the atomic energy for peace. At this stage, everybody must understand that it should not be the ratification of the 'No-Atomic-War' pacts of the atomic powers that will remove the threat of the atomic destruction of the world. Instead, it essentially is removing the primary causes of the appearance of atomic energy and the atomic bombs that could sternly achieve this objective. The whole inhabitants of the globe are trudging in chains and scuffling along the path of progress, eventually to be hurled over cliffs down to the bottomless pits of the hell of atomic fire, that is, the nuclear bombs and nuclear radiations. How painful is it to see that the present-day knowledgeable nuclear age sages should miss such a miserable sight of the entire people of the earth? A discerning eye could see the chains and the driving force consisting of the three evils.

Today, even the sensible people of this generation are incapable of discerning the reality of this current atomic tragedy as the Quran has done. Everyone who can wield his pen or move his tongue in this matter is busily beating the drum of progress and self-sufficiency, and we witness a world of chins, jaws, eyes, and tongues wagging in a fuming atmosphere lit by the hope of progress. It is hard to believe that this humanity in such circumstances as do currently prevail in this world will find itself able to appreciate or pay much heed to a type of work we now propose to produce in these books.

This present generation may pass away unscathed by the effects of atomic energy. Still, it will not be so with some future generation that will find itself trapped in the atomic hell of radiation or might have fallen into the cruel grip of the atomic war. You, folks of this present generation that have a possibility of passing unscathed by the ill-effects of the atomic radiations, might ignore the guidance offered by these books of mine. Still, indeed, some future generation of humankind might need the advice contained therein. For sure, you will bequeath to them secretly the effects of the radiation. They, miserably caught in the fiery dungeon of the atomic radiations, will in their relentless endeavor to emerge from that miserable dungeon seek the knowledge and guidance contained in books of this type.

Remember that only you will be responsible for the imprisonment of your future generations in that atomic hell. O, you callous-minded and selfish people of this generation! Are you so determined to leave the legacy of suffering to your grandchildren to gratify your present lust? Do you find yourself unable to do anything to relieve them of their torture in this respect? If yes, then at least, for Allah's sake, do one thing for them. That may mean a great favor to those tormented people in their acute misery, and it is as follows.

Let you preserve these books of mine for them. So that they might find some guidance from these in their strenuous efforts to come out of the tormenting ditch of miseries in which they shall find themselves tumbled. Unfortunately, it would happen to them not due to their fault but because of the selfishness of their inconsiderate predecessors, their loving grandparents.

They may at least find some consolation and hope amidst numerous curses and afflictions that shall have surrounded them. Today in this world, none would find any interest in writing a work of this nature. Nor is there any hope that someone in the declining religious sentiment and increasing atomic intoxication in the future will be inclined to produce a work of this kind. Who will subject himself to so torturous and presumably so unpopular an ordeal? Believe me then, in faith; this might be the last ray of hope for humankind drawn unto the brink of wholesale destruction.

However, my appeal for preserving this work for future generations would lose its uniqueness in another request of Professor C. H. Waddington to join with mine like Gemini the Twins. Waddington's appeal has been as follows.

"Even if we cannot discover a cure for the ills that we may be inflicting on future generations, we ought at least to take the trouble to find out so that we can decide how far we shall go in running up biological debts which our descendants will have to pay."

Now, join my appeal with it as follows.

"Even if we cannot utilize the guidance contained in these books due to our present adverse circumstances, we ought at least to take trouble in passing it over to our future generations. So, they might need the light contained in it and might also find themselves willing enough to put it to utility in their endeavor to emerge from the tormenting pit in which they shall find themselves fallen as a result of our present follies."

Humankind today is in the overwhelming grip of the horrible demon of atomism in a world that is fast changing into an atomic hell. A storm of sizzling passions is raging all over the earth. Nations rave madly about pursuing wealth and the necessities of life like over-pressed hosts of raging menaces in quest of self-sufficiency. Nothing else whatsoever is at present to their liking. Not a mind in this world today is left to cater to any consideration other than material wealth. We can see today's entire humankind hankering after the books that might contain some method, some device, and some contrivance of making some money. People eagerly seek any book, booklet, or pamphlet containing some lesson from which some material benefit might accrue, and they anxiously devour its contents to get some idea of 'money-making'.

The author of a tiny pamphlet or an article to contain a method of generating radiation-free atomic energy would instantly find himself revered as the greatest ever benefactor of all history. However, who, on the other hand, shall ever like to read a book that would endeavor to snatch from their hands so excellent a potential as that of nuclear energy and would try to extinguish the spirit of so urgent an enterprise in the heart of this present hard-pressed and power-hungry humankind?

To commit a folly as outstanding or perhaps even more incredible than anyone did ever commit in the history of humankind by interposing oneself between people and their material interests, and then to expect any instantaneous popularity is folly itself of a most glaring category. It takes at least some time before the truth is understood and appreciated. The truth, however, regarding the atomic energy in these present times is a truth of the rarest kind and one too hard to appreciate. A man dying of thirst and eagerly holding a cup of cool refreshing water to his lips will not find himself in a mood either to be dissuaded by entreaties or by threats to part with that cup of water in which he thought was his life. Even though the water contained poison without his knowledge, a fact which the dissuading person only knew. However, suppose there would not be any other water available, as it may sometimes happen in a desert. In that case, likely, the person dying of thirst would not cease even from drinking the only accessible cup of water even if he knew that it contained a deadly poison.

Such indeed is the ill-luck of the author of a book like this, for his case is in no way different from the man who endeavored to dissuade the thirsty man mentioned above from drinking the cup of water, for it contained deadly poison. My case as an author is a unique one. There can be no doubt that an author, who has the inopportune audacity to produce such books as these, deserves punishment. Deservedly, he should be whipped, scourged, thrown into prison, and hanged, then bastinadoed and mercilessly lashed, for he seems to have no mercy in him. People are engaged in hot pursuit and burning rivalry to attain self-sufficiency, which means the question of life and death for them. Can someone tell such miserable inhabitants of the world at present to turn away from this crucial race in which they all are engaged? It will be undoubtedly an act of unambiguous callousness on the part of anyone who, in the zeal of doing his duty to his fellow humans, seems to forget their present necessity of exertion for material progress. Yet, there might not be a shortage of persons in this world who might read these books and say:

"Here are the books, the elixir, the remedy of all our ills, and a guarantee for peace and prosperity."

Do whatever they like with such unruly and troublesome an author, and so incredibly indiscreet a person whose sole business seems to disturb the equilibrium of peace and disrupt the entire system of this world; their action shall find grounds for justification. They would be well-justified to whatever extent they go in executing his punishment. It seems in the exact fitness of the things that his utter existence is wiped out from the earth, and it is compatible with justice that he is deprived of his right to exist in this age of progress.

But alas, who will then there be to mourn their painful destruction when in their hot pursuit of atomic power, they shall come to grief and find themselves helplessly encompassed by a blazing, worldwide atomic hell. And who will then there be to weep over their miseries when they shall find themselves in hell, wherein they shall find themselves subjected to the torturous stings of fiery snakes and shall be constantly lashed with lashes over-grown with fiery scorpions? Therein they shall be in a state in which they shall neither be living nor shall they be dead.

To many at present, all this may seem no more than mere bursts of foolish emotions; mere high-flown, hollow, and meaningless rhetoric, but they indeed whose lot it shall be to see the truth shall also discern the fact of these void emotions and vain expressions. Nevertheless, alas for them then, for no degree of repentance or any amount of penance shall prove of any avail to them in their misery. Such indeed is the particularity of the genetic damage done by nuclear radiation. It is a sort of damage that, once done, is forever done, and no one can produce chemical damage as a match for it.

The author does not believe that humankind shall judge death against him for speaking the truth and taking a course counter to their material ambitions regarding atomic energy. Humanity is engaged in universal atomic suicide by building nuclear reactors and replenishing their stockpiles of atomic bombs. Yet, how strange, if same humankind should declare the sentence of death against a man who has committed no offense except speaking the truth about their suicidal attitude, and exposing the exact situation to their eyes, and has done so merely to clear his burdened conscience.

However, do not the atomic reactors and stockpiles imply death and destruction? Do they not yet realize that the atomic bomb is not a weapon of defense or war? Instead, it is the omen of complete eradication of life on earth. Thus, the atomic reactors and the reprocessing plants are more of misery and destruction than energy potential. Further, nuclear energy is the mother of these twin brothers, the atomic reactor, and the atomic bomb, and building these is suicidal.

The author is grieved to the depth of heart to see the world engaged in the act of committing atomic suicide universally under the stress of the need for energy and will, therefore, never think of budging so much as a hair's breadth from the principled stand for consideration just of popularity or rewards. However, in the heart of hearts, he earnestly covets a reward that humankind, having heeded the warning issued in these books and the guidance provided therein, is saved from dreadful doom, and has attained to the path of absolute peace and real prosperity. Also, he is remembered with love and reverence after he has departed this world. He would nonetheless consider it a sufficient reward for all his pains if even a single soul in this world is convinced of the truth of these books and would shed a tear in solitude. And it says sighing:

"Blessed be the soul that said these things and expounded this truth in a thundering tempest against the raging desires of an impassioned humanity."

Think not that author is disappointed to the point of petrifaction regarding the future of humankind in the present mortifying state of the affair. But howsoever remote the possibility of reducing this roaring storm of the atomic energy might seem in these present circumstances, another case, that the truth should dawn on the mind of humankind any time before the die is essentially cast, could not be entirely excluded. Opinions might be molded, views might receive a change, and revolutions might set in. The case of atomic energy is no longer a mystery; its hazards are too glaring to be missed. On the other hand, the terror of the miseries created by atomic energy might terrify humankind to the inspiration of the truth and inspire them to have the courage necessary to keep a tight rein on the passion of greed and teach them the necessity of being content with less.

The author's part in this has been to point to the snare and raise a hue and cry, that perhaps they might be startled out of their engrossment and discern the hazards ahead. Nor is the author so devoid of hope in Allah the Almighty to deprive His creatures of His Mercy. The most Merciful Allah is all-powerful, and His Mercy and His Grace find no bounds. He has the power to change even the very hearts of men. There exists no possibility, which is not possible for Him. He has worked miracles in the past and can still perform the same even in this era. Out of His Mercy, He can save His creatures from the dreadful doom that now awaits them.

O, Merciful Allah! Bless this humankind with a heart that craves only for that which is undoubtedly helpful and desirable, and bestow on them a sight that discerns the things aright. O, benign Allah! Indeed, some of us justly deserve the punishment of the fire of atomic hell in this world and that of 'Al-Hotama' in next world, yet look not toward our faults, instead look toward your Mercy, and save us from painful doom, we with our own hands now prepare. Bestow on us sense and spirit that we may avoid this ruinous pit that now falls in our way.

O, Allah! Numerous transgressing communities in the past incurred your wrath and met their doom and destroyed their prospect in this world and the next eternal world and incurred eternal damnation. Save us, O, Allah! From that doom, and guide us aright lest we be destroyed by the atomic bombs and atomic radiations in this world while in the next world our lot be with those cast into the hell of 'Hotama' to taste everlasting affliction. If your laws, O, Allah, be inexorable; pray, change our hearts so that our deeds may save us from the just sentence of nemesis. Yet it is not justice that we ask of you, but instead your Pity and your Mercy it is that we seek. Grant O, Allah! In you, we place our trust, and in your ways, we do move, and it is in your Mercy that we take refuge. Guide us on the right path and save us from calamities. Aameen.

Fellow humans! This work of mine is the boiling cup full of my heart's blood and a piercing cry of my agonized soul. My heartfelt conviction is that this shall not go in vain, and all this painstaking of mine shall be entertained with whole-hearted gratitude by this present and the future generations of humankind. This world might, despite all the oppressive heat of the economic necessity, may not yet be so devoid of grace as to overlook blindly the light that would pierce the darkest corners of the human mind.

Yet, the urge of material necessity may prevail against this light, and humankind neglected the truth. In that case, my recourse is to the Mercy of the Merciful Allah who has the power to lead us aright and lend us His Grace and bestow on us His Mercy, for His Grace is unlimited, and His Mercy finds no bounds. If, however, this humankind is destined to be consumed by the flames of the atomic hell, then there appears to be not the slightest reason for complaint, for it shall be precisely consistent with justice. The deserving shall get the reward they deserve. Alas, if somebody could have shown this present humankind a true mirror of its present activities, thoughts, trends, tendencies, habits, inclinations, behavior, demeanor, and the overall picture of its life on earth.

Try not to be curious about who I am, what I am, where I am, or whence I am. Sympathy is my heart, sincerity is my soul, affection is my body, and the truth is my pursuit. Seek the truth in whatever I have offered: weigh and judge it. Use reason and discuss it.

The demon that might have duped you would try to blur your sight and misguide you and create misunderstandings and doubts in your mind. Nevertheless, pray beware of the demon that would lead you to your destruction both ways. If I were a voice, I would have proclaimed throughout this world that their wholesale destruction through the atomic bombs and atomic radiations was nigh at hand. And if I were a ray of the sun, I would have brightened their eyes to the fact that people who deserved the punishment of the atomic hell of this transient world qualify themselves for the eternal flames of 'Al-Hotama' of the next endless world. Moreover, no misfortune is more significant than one's inability to judge the certainty of the Resurrection, Judgment, and the life in Heaven. Let them, therefore, fear retribution, fear nemesis, fear Resurrection, fear Judgment, and discern the transitoriness of this temporary life on this temporary earth. Who likes to avoid the eternal affliction and rejoice in eternal bliss?

O, poor, distressed, and highly miserable humankind of this age! How fiercely this exigency of energy has afflicted you with madness and has made you the victim of a ruinous misunderstanding regarding the use of atomic energy. With what earnestness of my heart do I wish you had known that the favorable attitude of these among scientists presently regarding the adaptability of the atomic energy is falsely consoling, wrongly optimistic, erroneously misleading, and in strict defiance to the statutes of science.

The opinion of the scientist these days bears an authenticity comparable to the article of faith. Unfortunately, your outlook regarding the feasibility of the utility of atomic energy irrespective of hazards involved, O, dear reader, has been framed in agreement with that of the scientist's recommended prevailing opinion. Because of the opinion under scientist's influence, your notion of the harmless utility of atomic energy potential is likely to receive shocks and blows after blows during your perusal of these books. Indeed, by the time you have reached the end of this work, you may find yourself at a loss how to gather the smithereens of the shattered notions and piece them up again.

Unless, O, dear reader, you possess a knowledge of the subjects of nuclear science and Radiobiology, at least to the level of a nuclear scientist reasonably conversant with his subject, if not to that of men like Einstein and Muller: there is every likelihood of your suspecting the author (that is me) of falsity, exaggeration, ill-treatment, even ignorance, nay besides that even fanaticism. It may be hard for you to reconcile your mind to the strangeness and doubtfulness of the views of a single person worldwide. That man appears in conflict with all the scientists, whose word world takes authority and whose integrity and authenticity accepts without any doubt. Herein is the crux of the whole matter.

Few in this world might claim to have a greater appreciation of the scientist's ability, integrity, honesty, and sincerity than my humble self. No doubt, I have always felt a sense of admiration and gratitude for the scientist for his services to humankind in a worldly way. However, I proclaim even on the drumbeat that scientist in the dilemma of atomic energy is the victim of a seducing devil. In recommending the use of nuclear power merely in his hopes of future protective discoveries against radiation, he is committing a folly that shall destroy all his past services.

Neither any mortal could claim Omniscience nor immunity from committing an error. But let my dear reader! Be assured after my confession that within theological, philosophical, or scientific facts presented in these books, you will notice neither a whit of misstatement nor a jot in contradiction to established and authentic truths. The whole work has been written based on the principle of entire truth without any vestige of prejudice or shade of bias. Yet, when I see my fellow human beings entangled in a catastrophic misunderstanding and pursuing the paths that openly lead to ruin, my heart cries and would not be comforted. When I see their painful doom, I shudder. What if my fears were justified and my judgment proved true? How miserable and ruinous will be your doom and deep your sorrows at not paying heed to the warning of a friend? What will you do then? Alas, for me, if every pore in my body would turn into a tongue, all these various tongues would then cry against the path that you at the present tread.

My dear reader, you are engrossed in your worldly pursuits. How little do you know the difference between disasters that happened to me and that which will occur to humanity? Whether the calamity which will befall humankind against which I shriek or the catastrophe which has occurred to me in undertaking this ordeal of crying against your doom is direr? For, I have suffered during this gruesome and bloodcurdling ordeal nothing less than that which erring humankind will suffer when their atomic doom befalls them. I am the first victim of atomic hell. Alas, but my sufferings, sorrows, and afflictions fall far beyond the imagination, or the concern of a generation insensibly lost in their material pursuits.

Lastly, my dear reader! You will be staggered at my views. Remember that I base my conflict with the scientist, not on scientific facts. My difference with him arises only at his recommendation of using atomic energy against the very facts of science that he has himself discovered and pronounced as the proven facts. This problem has reached such a turning point where it is facts of science and not scientists' formulated opinions that ought to consider, for it is both in the interest of the scientists and humankind in general.

Humankind today stands in dire need of the propagation of the knowledge of nuclear science. Unless humankind knows the subject's reality, it is hard for them to decide the matter correctly. Yet, time shall prove which of the services is greater: whether to teach people the subject of nuclear science to adopt the atomic energy or make them aware of its hazards, thereby warning them that they may avoid the ruinous course. Of the readers of these books of mine, the scientist has the most significant reason for entertaining the feelings of heartfelt gratitude for me. It may come as something very strange to the world that the scientists should see the logic in my view and recognize it with gratitude and cry with one voice as follows.

"Down with atomic energy, the ruin of humankind."

This work has to be read and judged on the basis exclusively of science is a fact which I shall forever own. But, unfortunately, the current atmosphere is steeped in materialism and is decidedly more favorable to a philosophy that favors materialism. Therefore, the fact that people will read it in suchlike an atmosphere is harmful to the philosophy presented in my books. Besides, because the influence of materialism in today's world is exceptionally vehement, there is a possibility that humanity will discard the facts of these books with indifference and the warning of the Quran ignored to the ultimate destruction of this world. Therefore, humankind should consider the divine authority of the Quran and the miraculous nature of prophecy to make up for this loss.

Suppose the hand of fate has not predestined this humankind to wholesale destruction through atomic bombs and atomic radiations. In that case, it could be noticeably seen and with reason be believed that the miraculous nature of the prophecy of the Quran owns more than sufficient force to counterweight the overwhelming effect of the materialism of this age. Therefore, it deserves respect much more than all the writers who write in favor of materialism.

Some people entertain a belief that materialism is hereafter to exist as the eternal culture of this world. Several others think that the age of religion is over. Various others fancy that the God of the world is now dead, and the Scriptures are now outmoded. Indeed, they all happen to be the victims of mistaken notions, unfortunately. Materialism is not going to exist eternally. The age of religion is not past. God is not dead. The Quran shall never be outmoded. Let not the inebriated superpowers of these days think when they declare that they can destroy this world so many times with their existing stockpiles that the Allah of the world does not hear what they say. Allah hears them well, and if He is so inclined to save His creatures from this destruction, He shall find no difficulty in achieving His wish. His Will be done. However, it is not Allah; instead, the people of this age themselves are bent on their destruction.

The boast of these superpowers about their ability to destroy the world is not a whit better than the boast of a person resolved to commit suicide, and he vaunts about his courage in his act. It is not the boast of the superpowers, but it, in reality, is the wail of the spirit of the three evils, the three vices responsible for the emergence of the atomic hell as given out by the prophecy of the Quran. Let not humankind now continue to slumber since the period of joking with Mother Nature has ended. It now appears with a dreadful retort like atomic bombs and atomic radiations to destroy misguided humanity that aspired to conquer the forces of Mother Nature for material well-being. Faith alone can now save this world from the frightful reprisal of the much wronged and much-exasperated Mother Nature.

Whatever the merits or demerits of this modern age of science, one thing that appears as its most distinctive mark is that this same age provides a matter of infallible judgment to prove the Origin of the Quran as Divine. For fourteen centuries since the appearance of the Quran, its votaries have been giving it out as a work of Divine Origin, instead, the word of Allah Himself, while the non-Muslims have during all these centuries been considering it out as the work of the Prophet (peace be upon him) himself.

The point of this controversy in itself is one of great importance. Since if the Quran be not the word of Allah but is instead the work of the Prophet (peace be upon him) himself then (Allah forbid) the Prophet (peace be upon him) appears to be a liar; a fact which itself renders the whole affair of Islam a mere hoax. The non-Muslims simply have not been able to believe that the Arabian Prophet (peace be upon him) could have received the revelation of Allah. Among them, some have in their writings lavished praises and extolled the merits of the Quran. They could believe that Allah could condescend to talk in person with Moses on Mount Sinai. However, they have found themselves unable to entertain a belief that Allah would reveal His word to the Arabian Prophet (peace be upon him).

Howsoever great and howsoever convincing had been the arguments of the votaries of the Quran to prove the Divine Origin of that book, none has been able to clear the doubt completely. So, the controversy has raged all these centuries without any final decision. But, at last, as the world stands at the brink of atomic desolation, it is by discoveries of modern science that the point of this controversy could be settled forever, certainly in favor of the Divine Origin of Quran.

Quran challenged humanity and Jinn to conjointly produce a chapter or even a single verse similar to the Quran. This challenge did not go unaccepted at a time when Arabia was replete with the most extraordinary wits and geniuses in the field of poetry and oratory. However, every effort failed, even in the eyes of the author himself. No genius for fourteen centuries has been able to parody the Quran. Although hundreds of geniuses of excellent caliber have risen in various countries during this period, none even in Arabia could have undertaken to write in the style of the Quran. However, as is apparent, the fact could not convince the doubtful person of the Divine Origin of the Quran.

The fulfillment of the seemingly impossible prophecy of the Quran regarding the victory of conquered Romans over victorious Persians in the Persia-Greek war could have offered yet another convincing proof of the Divine Origin of the Quran. Yet, that argument too failed to bring conviction. However, who will now refute the argument of producing the modern discoveries of science in the Quran, a book revealed in an age of no science. The fact, at last, appears to offer irrefutable proof of the Divine Origin of the Quran. Howsoever great, no human genius could have included in his writings the scientific facts that were to be discovered only after a period of above thirteen centuries and were unknown to anyone when Allah revealed the Quran.

Supposing some uncommonly great genius had appeared in any pre-modern age to undertake the parody of the Quran and had successfully produced a work judged as equal or even superior in merit and had furnished a topic of heated controversy. The judge of modern science could have settled that controversy. The decision would have gone in favor of the Quran since no human intellect could have included the discoveries of the facts of modern science in any pre-modern writings. We could have only judged the performance on literary or philosophical merit. Therefore, the absence of scientific facts would have excluded such a parody from the honor of Divine Origin compared to the Quran.

We only have supposed this fact, and indeed no one could produce a book like the Quran even from the literary point of view. The literary excellence of the Quran is beyond the approach of any mortal; howsoever great his genius might have been. This point ought not to be judged from the translations. It is not for nothing that the sound of the Quran melts the flinty hearts and causes the gravest of creatures to cry and sob like bereaved children, and the Quran achieves this not by reciting some tragic tale but by reminding hard and fast facts and realities. In this respect, whoever comprehends the original text is fortunate only.

We here produce another very famous prophecy from the prophecies of the Quran, alluded to in the previous pages. We describe this other prophecy to compare the two prophecies, namely, this one which is about the victory of the conquered Romans over the victorious Persians, and the other one about 'Al-Hotama', which is the actual theme of this work in comparison, and making a differentiation between the two kinds.

YOUSUF GABRIEL

PROPHECY OF THE QURAN ABOUT THE VICTORY OF THE CONQUERED ROMANS OVER THE VICTORIOUS PERSIANS

Following is the prophecy in question.

"Alif. Lam. Mim. The Romans (Greeks) have been defeated (by the Persians) in the nearer land, and they, after their defeat, will be victorious within ten years (Quran here uses a term 'Bidhe' which means a period between three and nine years while the tenth year could also be included). Allah's is the command in the former case, and in the latter and in that day, believers will rejoice in Allah's help to victory. He helpeth to victory whom He will. He is the Mighty, the Merciful. It is a promise of Allah. Allah faileth not His promise, but most of the humankind knows not (the integrity of Allah). They know only some (outward) appearance of the world's life and are heedless of the Hereafter. Have they not pondered upon themselves that Allah created not the heavens and the earth, and that which is between them, save with truth and for a destined end (had set them for a determined period)? But truly, many of humankind are disbelievers in the meeting with their Lord (at the Resurrection). Have they not traveled in the land and seen the nature of the consequence for those who were before them? They were stronger than these in power, and they dug the earth and built upon it more than these have built. Messengers of their own came unto them with clear proofs (of Allah's Sovereignty). Surely Allah wronged them not, but they did wrong themselves."

(Quran 30:1-9)

The letters 'Alif', 'Lam', and 'Mim' prefixed to this chapter are the abbreviations whose purport none, but Allah knows. Several chapters of the Quran begin with such abbreviations, and none but Allah knows their real purport. Guesses, however, have been made by some.

This prophecy is nothing short of a miracle. It appeared when the infidels of Makkah relentlessly persecuted the small band of the Prophet's followers (peace be upon him) in Makkah in the earliest days of Islam. The tempo of persecution had increased to alarming proportions with the continuous news of the victories of Persia over Rome in the Persia-Greek war. The infidels of Makkah entertained the notion that Persians were idol worshippers just like themselves, and they were defeating the Romans who, like the Muslims, worshipped one God. Therefore, they, too, being idolaters like the Persians, would become victorious against the Muslims who worshiped Allah, similar to the Romans.

This notion gave them great daring, and their persecutions of the Muslims crossed all bounds. The prophecy appeared in such circumstances. It foretold not only the victory of the then vanquished Romans over the Persians but also, in the same breath, predicted the victory of the Muslims over the infidels of Makkah on the very same juncture of the victory of the Romans. The prophecy, being very improbable, was turned to be ridiculed by some of the infidels, and one of them even laid a wager of hundred camels with Hazrat Abu Bakar (Razi Allah ho taa'la unho), a devout Muslim. The prophecy, however, proved true, and Hazrat Abu Bakar (Razi Allah ho taa'la unho) won the wager.

Quran revealed this prophecy in about the twelfth year of the twenty-two-year-long Persian-Greek war. At that time, the Roman Empire had lost Syria, Jerusalem, Egypt, etc. It was confined to the walls of Constantinople, which too was besieged by the victorious armies of Khosrau II Pervaiz, the king of Persia (550–628). The day of Constantinople's fall would have meant the last day of the Roman Empire. Khosrau Pervaiz, the grandson of great Naushirwan, carried on a terrible war against the Romans in an uninterrupted course of twenty-two years; beginning with the year 602 to avenge the death of the Roman Emperor Flavius Mauricius Tiberius Augustus (Maurice), his benefactor and father-in-law, the father of Khosrau's first wife, Flavia Miriamne. This Khosrau Pervaiz was later married to Sirin or Shirin, the famous 'Shirin-Farhad' romance heroine. Maurice had been deposed and caused to be slain by Flavius Phocas Augustus, a simple and obscure centurion. The latter turned into Emperor of Rome. He, in turn, was beheaded by Heraclius, the son of the Heraclius the Elder, the exarch of Africa. The Roman people entreated this Heraclius to assume the throne. After some hesitation, he accepted the offer utterly ignorant of the fact, to what unique honor the hand of destiny was thus leading him.

As the best authorities confirm, the Quran revealed this prediction at Makkah in the twelfth year of the Persian-Greek war. It was about 615 AD or 616 AD (the sixth or seventh year before the Hijra). The Romans did not have the most negligible probability of retrieving their losses, much less to distress the Persians. The various authorities unanimously agreed that no prophecy could have been more distant from its accomplishment when the Quran ventured this prediction. Conquest of the king of Persia had then reached as far as sea-coast of Pontus, the city of Ancyra, and the Isle of Rhodes. Indeed, if he had possessed any maritime power, his boundless ambition, according to Western historians, would have spread slavery and dissolution over the provinces of Europe. Judging from the fierceness with which the Persian king pursued his war against the Romans, there appears to be no reason to doubt the fears of these historians. The Persians grievously defeated the Romans.

The king of Persia was scornfully triumphant when the Quran had the audacity of venturing at the prediction of a complete reversal of their relative circumstances. Consequently, the imperious reply of contemptuous and victorious Khosrau to his General Sain (Shahin), who had undertaken the liberty of bringing a Roman embassy in his company to beg peace of the Persian king, was as follows.

"It is not an embassy; it is the person of Heraclius, bound in chains that you should have brought to the foot of my throne. I will never give peace to the Emperor of Rome till he has abjured his crucified God and embraced the worship of the sun."

The unfortunate General was flayed alive for his sole offense of mistaking his sovereign's mind while the Roman ambassadors were separately and vigorously confined.

The Malignant Umayyah Ibn-Khalaf was one of the most confirmed foes of the Prophet (peace be upon him) who turned this divine prophecy of the Quran to ridicule. On the other hand, Hazrat Abu Bakar (Razi Allah ho taa'la unho) was a devout Muslim and the first Caliph of Islam afterward. In Persia, the imperious Khosrau, the relentless foe of the Romans, imprisoned the members of the Roman embassy violating the law of nations and the faith of an express stipulation. At the same time in Makkah, Umayyah Ibn-Khalaf laid a wager of a hundred camels with Hazrat Abu Bakar (Razi Allah ho taa'la unho), stipulating nine years. The Quran used the term 'Bidhe' to fulfill the prophecy, which means a period between three and nine years, while the tenth year could also be included.

Romans could at that time offer little resistance, for, besides the onslaught of the formidable armies of Persia, they also were harassed by the hosts of Avars and Slavs. [6] Further, the internal disputes made their misery complete. However, things began to change after the delivery of the prophecy of the Quran as if by a miracle. The Roman Emperor, that slothful Heraclius miraculously turning into an energetic lion, began to gain victories after having sustained defeats for the past twelve years. Gaining victory after victory, achieving conquest after conquest, and enjoying a continued series of good fortune, Heraclius advanced even into Persian territory to the final deposition and death of Khosrau.

In 624, he advanced into northern Media (north-western Iran and south-east Turkey), where he destroyed the grand fire temple of

Goudzak. Later, the cross carried away by the forces of Khosrau from Jerusalem was restituted to the Holy Sepulchre. Heraclius performed pilgrimage in Jerusalem, discreet patriarch verified the identity of the holy relic, and this ceremony has been commemorated by the annual festival of the exaltation of the cross.

Associated with this service in Jerusalem, in Makkah could be seen another service that testified the victory of conquered Romans over triumphant Persians and thus signified the fulfillment of the prophecy of the Quran. Hazrat Abu Bakar (Razi Allah ho taa'la unho) received a hundred camels from the heirs of Umayyah Ibn-Khalaf, with whom he had laid a wager nine years ago. Umayyah Ibn-Khalaf had died in the third year of Hijra of a wound he had received in the battle of Uhud. Therefore, Hazrat Abu Bakar (Razi Allah ho taa'la unho) triumphantly led the train of hundred camels from Makkah to the mosque of the Holy Prophet (peace be upon him) in Medina and there distributed the whole lot among the poor and the needy immediately by the command of the Prophet (peace be upon him).

The credit of victory of Roman armies in this war is attributed nearly by every historian of that age to the personal merit of Heraclius, the Roman Emperor. Indeed, after Providence turned the scales in their favor, there can be no doubt that Heraclius personally achieved all the victories of Roman armies. His inspiring example, unique bravery, and utmost skill in every battle resulted in the victory against a long triumphant and formidable foe. But did not Romans sustain the defeats for about twelve years before these victories, also in the tenure of Heraclius himself, who then had all the time watched the constant dissolution of the Roman Empire as an idle spectator of the calamities of people?

A change appeared in the character of Heraclius instantly with the appearance of the prophecy of the Quran. It strikes as an instance of a very unusual kind in the whole history up to the mind of the modern historian. How a man, known only for sloth and pleasure, suddenly changed into a lion and hero as if by the touch of a magic wand, presently endued with qualities that out-shadowed the fame of heroes of the caliber of Alexander the Great?

Historians have noticed this change, but none so far has linked it to the agency of the prophecy under discussion. This change in the character of Heraclius has astonished Edward Gibbon. After complaining about the neglect of Byzantine historians in revealing the causes of his slumber and vigilance, he has proceeded to make some reasonable conjectures of his own.

Says he:

"Of the characters conspicuous in history, that of Heraclius is one of the most extraordinary and inconsistent. In the first and last years of a long reign, the emperor appears to be the slave of sloth, of pleasure, or superstition, the careless and impotent spectator of the public calamities. But 'the languid mists of the morning' and 'evening' are separated by the brightness of 'the meridian sun': The Arcadius of the palace arose the Caesar of the camp, and the honour of Rome and Heraclius was gloriously retrieved by the exploits and trophies of six adventurous campaigns."

('The History of the Decline and Fall of the Roman Empire'; by Edward Gibbon, Vol-5/Page-91)

After the appearance of the prophecy of the Quran, 'the meridian sun' in Heraclius's life appeared to dispel 'the languid mists of the morning' of his sovereignty. It was again soon after the proclaimed object of the prophecy had been achieved that 'the meridian sun' instantly disappeared. Once again, 'the languid mists of the evening' appeared in the life of the very same Heraclius quite naturally. The effect of the prophecy transformed the very nature of Heraclius. The iron was changed into a temporary electromagnet by the current of electricity. Yet, no sooner the current was removed than the temporary electromagnet had lost its borrowed magnetic quality, and it became a simple piece of iron again.

Discussing the causes of such a change in the character of Heraclius, Gibbon continues to write as follows.

"It was the duty of the Byzantine historians to have revealed the causes of his 'slumber' and 'vigilance'. At this distance we can only conjecture that he was endowed with more personal courage than political resolution; that he was detained by the charms and perhaps the arts of his niece Martina, with whom, after the death of Eudocia, he contracted an incestuous marriage; and that he yielded to the base advice of the counsellors, who urged as a fundamental law, that the life of the emperor should never be exposed in the field. Perhaps he was awakened by the last insolent demand (the annual tribute of a thousand virgins) of the Persian conqueror."

(Ibid: Page-91)

These conjectures of Gibbon undoubtedly would have carried considerable weight in the absence of the factor of the prophecy. However, then, there existed the possibility of an assumption that no change whatsoever had appeared in the character of Heraclius and that the Roman Empire was utterly lost to ratify the resolution of the unrelenting and determined Persian conqueror. What guarantee could have been there for so radical and abrupt a change in the character of a man who for twelve years had seen dreadful calamity approaching and was not capable of moving out of the slush and sloth? What if he had continued in sloth for a little while more till the last besieged city of Roman Empire, Constantinople, had fallen to announce the end of the Empire?

The point of the prophecy has interposed itself in this matter so that anyone could not simply take it away. It appears genuine justification in surmising that amid all conjectures of historians about causes of change in the character of Heraclius, the factor of this prophecy seems similar to the sun; in whose light stars, howsoever shining in the darkness of night, disappear even from the sight of keenest of eyes. Had not divine will be moved into action with the revelation of prophecy, there was a possibility that slumbering Heraclius might have persisted in his slumber a little while more to allow the fall of Constantinople to proclaim to the world the end of the Roman Empire. Then none had the occasion of making conjectures at the causes of the change in the character of Heraclius. Instead, the causes of his failure would have been the object of investigation for the future historian.

Gibbon hinted at the depressed state of Roman affairs when Heraclius assumed the spirit of a hero. Then he recorded fantastic effects of change in the character of Heraclius and the uniqueness of initiative achieved by him for the deliverance of Empire in the following words.

"At the moment when Heraclius assumed the spirit of a hero, the only hopes of the Romans were drawn from the vicissitudes of fortune, which might threaten the proud prosperity of Khosrau, and must be favourable to those who had attained the lowest period of depression. ... Two days after the festival of Easter, the emperor, exchanging his purple for the simple garb of a penitent and warrior, gave the signal of his departure. ... Whatever hardships the emperor imposed on the troops, he inflicted with equal severity on himself; their labour, their diet, their sleep were measured by the inflexible rules of discipline; and, without despising the enemy, they were thought to repose an implicit confidence in their own valour and the wisdom of their leader. ... The spirit of their chief was first displayed in a storm; and even the eunuchs of his train were excited to suffer and to work by the example of their master. ... Since the days of Scipio and Hannibal, no bolder enterprise has been attempted than that which Heraclius achieved for the deliverance of the empire. ... He again ascended his throne to receive the congratulations of the ambassadors of France and India: and the fame of Moses, Alexander, and Hercules, was eclipsed in the popular estimation by the superior merit and glory of the great Heraclius. Yet the deliverer of the east was indigent and feeble."

(Ibid: Pages 92-112)

With reason and justice, we can argue that the spirit which raised Heraclius to such heights in the estimations of his countrymen as to surpass the prodigies like Moses, Alexander, and Hercules, was a clear manifestation of the miraculous Will of God. As the determined acquitter of the cause of Islam, this Will of God disregarded the notion of the infidels of Makkah with divine audacity. Moreover, the same spirit proved the truth of God's word in the victory of the conquered Romans and the defeat of the proud infidels of Makkah. It frustrated their every design against the seemingly weak and helpless Muslims.

History tells us that Romans did gain but a temporary triumph by these exploits and victory. Only eight years after their victory over the Persians, all the provinces they had retrieved lost to the Muslims. No sooner the Persian war finished than Heraclius, the hero of that war, relapsed into his previous state of 'sloth' and 'pleasure', as if the spirit infused in him by the word of the prophecy had left him to himself. In the post-Persia-Greek war years of the life of Heraclius, we see nothing of the heroic liberator of the Roman Empire. There was nothing in him at all that is worth mentioning.

According to Gibbon, Heraclius, after the accomplishment of his enterprise and the deliverance of Roman Empire, was but an "Aged husband too feeble to withstand the arts of conjugal allurements."

(Ibid: Page-207)

Our thoughts, however, are directed through the heroic exploits of Heraclius to the prophecy of the Quran. For, had the prediction failed, destiny had sealed the doom of Islam with the defeat of the Roman Empire, and the course of the world's future history would have been different. Every author recognized worldwide that at the time Quran ventured this prophecy, the victory of Romans over Persians was a sheer improbability. Every Muslim writer has universally attributed the achievement of unlikelihood to the prophecy's effect. This point is worth observation.

Nevertheless, perhaps quite logically, the affair of the Muslims versus the infidels' conflict in Arabia about the prophecy could be observed as overshadowed by the affair of the Romans. We notice that the second part of the prophecy consists of the good tidings for the Muslims, and therein Allah, in whose hands every affair rests, has promised aid.

The case of Muslims against Arabian infidels was far worse than that of the Romans versus the Persians. The victory of Muslims over infidels of Makkah and after those over infidels of entire Arabia was far more improbable than the victory of the conquered Romans over the victorious Persians.

Naturally, the second part of the prophecy about the victory of Muslims assumes, if not greater, at least as much importance as the first part of the prophecy concerned with the triumph of Romans. Howsoever worse the plight of the Romans or near the point of collapse the Roman empire had then been; the contest was between two rivals and equally powerful states that could be likened to two mighty elephants of equal stature, though one of them was about to fall. Yet, before its fall, it might muster up courage and strength enough to throw the other down. Even the last city, Constantinople, was about to fall; Heraclius's forces against Persians were of the same caliber and category as those of the Persians.

However, in the case of the Muslims versus the infidels' conflict, the ratios are quite different, and the disparity is incredibly significant. Here the contest was not between two elephants but rather a netted fish was to struggle with an octopus. Here a little, persecuted, oppressed, and a poverty-stricken band of Muslims against numerous potent hosts, mighty chiefs, and great warlords of entire Arabia had to fight in a continual series of battles until finally they utterly defeated the opponents.

Unable to sustain themselves in Makkah against a formidable foe, they were obliged to flee in search of refuge. The escape of the Prophet (peace be upon him) unhurt from Makkah is a miracle itself. He left his house when forty of the assassins had besieged his little house with intent to kill him. For three days, the Prophet (peace be upon him) laid concealed in a cave on his way to Medina but three miles from Makkah. The search parties combed everywhere. Finally, one of these parties reached the cave and almost peeped within. However, the spider's net stretched over the cave's mouth, and the eggs that a dove had laid there deceived the party.

The Quran has attested this fact, and anyone could not doubt the testimony of the Quran in this matter. Herein indeed was the aid of Allah, which He promised in the prophecy. The Prophet (peace be upon him) reached Medina sound and safe.

Every battle waged between the Muslims and the infidels of Arabia from the 'Battle of Badr' to 'Battle of the Trench' ('Ghazwah al-

Khandaq') was the battle not between two armies but rather the fight was between a single dove and a host of Hawks.

Yet, it was due to the promised aid of Allah that the dove always had the upper hand and a decisive victory. None of these victories anyone could have attributed to material factors. The death of the Prophet (peace be upon him) or defeat in any of these battles would have decided the issue forever. The blood-thirsty enemies of Muslims would have torn them to pieces and continued worshiping their idols, but Allah had to fulfill the second part of the prophecy.

The prophecy after predicting the victory of Romans had continued to say as follows.

"In that day, believers (Muslims) will rejoice in Allah's help to victory. He helpeth to victory whom He will. He is the Mighty, the Merciful. It is a promise of Allah."

On their way back home in Medina from the victory of 'Badr', the first battle fought between the Muslims and the aggressor infidels of Makkah; the Muslims received the news of the victory of the Romans.

A diverse crowd of 313 young and old Muslims, including children, starving and scantily armed, defeated a well-equipped force of a thousand stalwarts of Makkah at 'Badr'. A group of 700 Muslims got a victory against a formidable force consisting of 3000 warriors of Makkah at 'Uhud'. Just a few hundred fighting Muslim citizens during the siege of Medina prevented the city's downfall and compelled a besieging force of 10,000 infidels from Makkah to retreat in the 'Battle of the Trench' ('Ghazwah al-Khandaq').

Indeed, these events could, with much credibility, be attributed to the aid of Allah promised in the prophecy. The survival and the victory of the few weak, harassed, persecuted, victimized, and pursued Muslims at that time could hardly be regarded as less than a miracle.

It has been a remarkable prophecy in its own right, and the Muslims have justly celebrated it as a clear proof of the Divine Origin of the Quran. People generally acclaim its utter fulfillment, though they seldom consider the dire consequences of its failure. There can be no doubt that if this prophecy had failed, it would have wrecked the whole prospect of the Quran and Islam. In venturing a prophecy like this against such odds with little probability of fulfillment, the Quran certainly had taken a significant risk. Nine years is but a short period, and the result was soon to decide the whole affair for or against the venturing authority. They might not have to wait for nine years.

For, perhaps the fall of Constantinople a year, a month, or even a day after the declaration of prophecy would have, if on the one hand marked the last day of the Roman Empire, it would have on the other hand, and at the same time, sealed the doom of the Quran and Islam forever. It would have grievously damaged the reputation of the Quran tainted by the failure of the prophecy to sustain people's faith in it. This fact inevitably would have caused the vanishing of Islam amid the incurable doubts of the believers and the indefensible taunts of opponents. No trick or dexterity even of the rarest kind could have succeeded in explaining away so apparent a failure of so clear a prophecy within so short a time. It would have doomed every endeavor in retaining the heart of even the most devout among believers to a most miserable failure.

John Medows Rodwell (1808–1900), a famous non-Muslim Islamic scholar and English translator of the Quran in the nineteenth century, has recorded a suspicion of his own, considering the possibility of a pre-arranged linguistic trick played to prove the prophecy true in either event.

Rodwell, in a footnote of his translation of the Quran, writes as follows.

"The Mohammedans appeal to this passage as a clear proof of the inspiration of their Prophet. But it should be borne in mind that the vowel points of the consonants of the Arabic word for defeated in verse 1, not being originally written, and depending entirely on the speaker or reader, would make the prophecy true in either event, according to as the verb received an active or passive sense in pronunciation. The whole passage was probably constructed with the view of its proving true in any event."

('The Koran'; by John Medows Rodwell, Page-210, J. M. Dent, and Sons Ltd. 1950 Edition)

It is a grievous charge. Rodwell has shot a poisonous arrow at the very heart of a Scripture that has claimed a Divine Origin. Whether the charge has any grounds or not, it has meant with one stroke to pull down the entire structure of religion and has endeavored to uproot its very basis.

Suppose the suspicion of Rodwell has some basis. In that case, it shows the Quran (Allah forbid) simply a hoax, Islam a deception, the Holy Prophet of Islam (peace be upon him), the author of the Quran, and a swindler, his contemporary followers the base accomplices in the worst kind of a fraud ever practiced in the history of faith, while the followers of Islam during all these fourteen centuries, the misguided victims of a grievous deception.

Suppose anyone had expended volumes in lavishing praises on the Prophet (peace be upon him), Islam, and the Quran, yet had brought the lengthy eulogy to an end with a remark such as Rodwell has made. In that case, he would have turned all the sweetness of the praises into bitter poison. The spirit of the whole affair, including the eulogy, would have turned into the darkest calumny.

If this charge of swindling against the Prophet of Islam (peace be upon him) be furnished with proof to countenance it, then therein appears something as fatal as the actual failure of the prophecy itself. The failure of the prophecy indeed would have been far better than this grievous charge. A book that has claimed a Divine Origin ought, as a rule, be free from every error, not to speak of fraud of such malicious nature. This charge, therefore, deserves a thorough examination.

The original Arabic text of the subject prophecy is as follows.

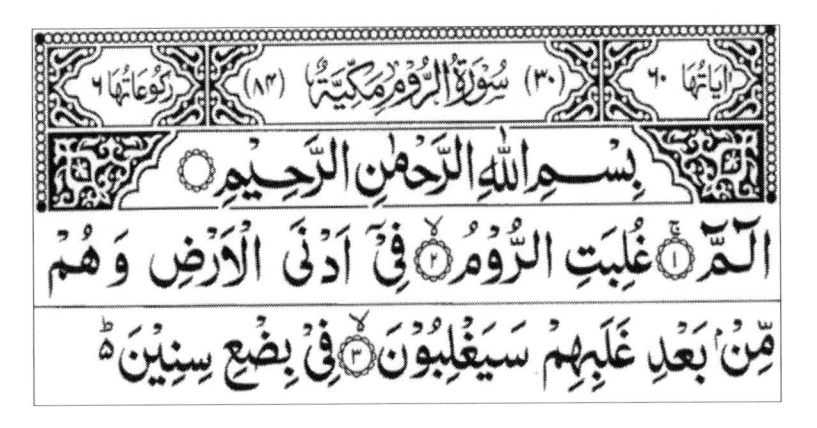

بِسْمِ اللَّهِ الرَّحْمَٰنِ الرَّحِيمِ

الٓمٓ ۝ غُلِبَتِ الرُّومُ ۝ فِىٓ أَدْنَى الْأَرْضِ وَهُم مِّنۢ بَعْدِ غَلَبِهِمْ سَيَغْلِبُونَ ۝ فِى بِضْعِ سِنِينَ ۝

The original Roman-Arabic text of the prophecy is as follows.
"Ghulebat-il-Rum Fi Adna-al-Ardhe Wa Hum Min Baade Ghalabihim Say<u>a</u>ghlibun".
The original English rendering of the prophecy is as follows.
"The Romans (Greeks) have been defeated in a land hard by, but after their defeat, they shall <u>defeat their foes</u> (will be victorious)."

The Arabic word for 'defeat' is derived from the root verb 'Ghalaba', which means 'to defeat', the active voice. When the two vowels of this word 'Ghalaba' that is the first 'a' and the second 'a' are substituted by the vowels 'u' and 'e' respectively to read as 'Gh<u>u</u>l<u>e</u>ba', this word assumes the passive voice and then means 'to be defeated'.

Thus, Rodwell meant that it could show Romans both as defeated or the defeaters by using these vowels just the occasion demanded. That means, if the Persians ultimately defeated the Romans, it could show them as such, and in case of Romans assumed victory, it could also show them as such by changing the voice of the word 'defeat'.

Moreover, because the vowel points were not fixed in <u>writing</u> when Allah revealed the Quran, Rodwell presumed the possibility of an etymological trick of this kind. However, Rodwell overlooked that the <u>spoken</u> word also necessarily indicated the vowel points' sound, negating the possibility of such a trick.

Thus, if the suggestion of Rodwell is considered, in case Romans were ultimately defeated, the words of the prophecy, by the trick of vowel points, would have been as follows.

"Ghulebat-il-Rum Fi Adna-al-Ardhe Wa Hum Min Baade Ghalabihim Say<u>u</u>ghlibun".
That means as follows.

"The Romans (Greeks) have been defeated in a land hard by; but after their defeat, they shall <u>be defeated by their foes</u>."

Now, this is the actual form which could have been accomplished as a result of changing the vowel point '<u>a</u>' in the second word for 'defeat' by the vowel point '<u>u</u>' to endow it with the passive form, and this same would have been the trick to which Rodwell has pointed.

It is hardly necessary to point to any intelligent person the absurdity of such a sentence, given as follows.

"The Romans (Greeks) have been defeated in a land hard by, but after their defeat, they shall <u>be defeated by their foes</u>."

See if such a sentence could make any sense anyway. And it is the only second word for 'defeat' that could undergo a change of the vowel point. Because the first word for 'defeated' could no way be changed since Romans at the time of the prophecy were being 'defeated' and could in no way be shown 'victorious', and this is the gist of the suspicion of Rodwell. Therefore, instead of acting in the manner of Jesting Pilate, had he taken a little trouble to tabulate the various forms possibly achievable through the change of the voice of the word 'defeated' in this instance, he would have been saved from this posthumous embarrassment.

Following is given a table of all possible forms which one can get by inversion of the voice of word for 'defeated'.

S. No.	SENTENCES & VOICE
1.	"The Greeks have defeated their foes **(active)**, but afterward, they shall defeat their foes **(active)**."
2.	"The Greeks have defeated their foes **(active)**, but afterward, they shall be defeated by their foes **(passive)**."
3.	"The Greeks have been defeated by their foes **(passive)**, but after their defeat, they shall be defeated by their foes **(passive)**."
4.	"The Greeks have been defeated by their foes **(passive)**, but after their defeat, they shall defeat their foes **(active)**."

Read and perceive all these four forms. The first and second are out of the question because Greeks were not defeating at the time of prophecy. The absurdity of the third is obvious; the defeat of the already defeated Greeks makes little sense. Now, it remains the only fourth one that makes sense, and indeed we find it in the text of the prophecy. It seems that it was the third one that gave birth to the presumption of Rodwell.

Let not the reader be puzzled by the words 'Greeks' and 'Romans', for both the 'Greeks' and the 'Romans' mean the same thing in this instance. The Greeks were then the subjects of the Constantinopolitan Empire. The actual word used in the Quran is 'Rum', or 'Room', which is the name given by the Arabs to the Romans and other Europeans.

If we leave all these syntactic subtleties aside, the common sense itself is enough to point to the absurdity of the remarks of Rodwell.

Suppose the people of that time when the Persia-Greek war was in progress heard a proclamation that for some reason stopped after saying:

"The Greeks were being defeated by Persians, but ...."

What then would have been the expectation of the listeners after the word 'but'? Would they expect to hear the words as follows?

".... they are now defeated"?

Nay, but they would expect the words as follows.

"…. they now have defeated their foes."

Indeed, we regret to say that our treatment of the suspicion of Rodwell in this matter would reward us with many wonders but slight improvement. One fails to see any surprising flash of ingenuity in Rodwell's remark, yet it is exceedingly dangerous.

Rodwell imagined the matter as if it were the case of some lottery and not a prophecy revealed and made public as if the contents of the prophecy were kept secret for nine years and were read to the audience with the voice of the word 'defeated', changed as would suit the occasion. This thing was impossible.

However, suppose it was the situation, what worth would have been of such prophecy by the judgment of the folks? Moreover, the possibility of the etymological trick, which Rodwell has pointed out, was quite out of the question technically. No one could have played such tricks, as has already been shown in all the achievable forms. Yet, anyone could not have treated the event like a lottery.

Then, by what means Rodwell could feign himself ignorant of the atmosphere of vigilant hostility, opposition, strife, hatred, faction, and seduction in which the Quran revealed the prophecy. It could not have been a prediction secretly sealed and deposited in a secret receptacle without the knowledge of anyone but the Prophet (peace be upon him) himself.

Instead, it was essential to be made public. And it was made public and remained an issue of mutual discussion between the Prophet's (peace be upon him) followers themselves and existed as the subject of much-heated controversy for years between the believers and their opponents.

What if the Holy Prophet (peace be upon him), when the news of the victory of the Romans reached Medina, had come out with the prophecy telling people that the prophecy was revealed to him nine years ago in Makkah? Who then, whether of his followers or others, had taken the prophecy as the prophecy?

On the other hand, suppose the Prophet (peace be upon him) for once even declared the prophecy at the time of its revelation nine years before its fulfillment. In that case, every possibility of some etymological trick was instantly ruled out, for he did not issue the prophecy in the <u>written</u> form, but instead, he <u>spoke</u> it with his mouth. Moreover, in doing so, he could use but <u>one form</u>. He could pronounce a word either in the <u>active</u> or in the <u>passive</u> voice. Thus, the hearers would have taken and remembered, and no possibility of reversion there remained. This fact Rodwell did himself know very well. He knew that the revelation of the Quran was <u>spoken</u> by the Prophet (peace be upon him) and not issued in the <u>written</u> form in the first instance. In his translation of the Quran, he writes as follows.

"And of all the Surahs (chapters), it must be remarked that they were intended not for 'readers' but for 'hearers' --- that they were all promulgated by public recital."

('The Koran'; by John Medows Rodwell, Preface, Page-4, J. M. Dent, and Sons Ltd. 1950 Edition)

Further, referring to George Sale's 'Preliminary Discourse' to Sale's translation of the Quran, Rodwell writes as follows.

"But to Sale's 'Preliminary Discourse' the reader is referred, as to a storehouse of valuable information."

('The Koran'; by John Medows Rodwell, Preface, Page-17, J. M. Dent, and Sons Ltd. 1950 Edition)

George Sale writes as follows.

"After the new revealed passages had been from the Prophet's mouth taken down in writing by his scribe, they were published to his followers, several of whom took copies for their private use, but the far greater number got them by heart. The originals, when returned, were put promiscuously into a chest."

('The Koran'; by George Sale, 'A Preliminary Discourse', Page-51) Therefore, it is clear that the Prophet (peace be upon him) had spoken the words of the prophecy by mouth. Thus, by so doing, he could naturally have uttered but one version of the prophecy that he either could have said, that "the Greeks shall ultimately be victorious", or that "they shall be defeated". He couldn't utter two versions simultaneously. The scribe, too, would have taken down the only version spoken by the Prophet (peace be upon him). Copies for personal use, too, would have been taken according to the first copy, and the version taken by heart would have been identical with the original.

Therefore, it isn't easy to understand how all the heterogeneous crowd could reconcile to the idea of a gigantic imposture. All the Prophet's (peace be upon him) followers mingled frequently, discussed the matter, recited the portions of the Quran, and could have only one decisive version. Yet, these are all suppositions that we are obliged to discuss for merely the supposition's sake. Otherwise, anyone could understand that they could have advertised only one version of the prophecy contained in the Quran.

The victory of the Greeks could be predicted and published after mentioning their defeat at the hands of foes. After mentioning their current defeat, the prediction of their ultimate and final defeat would have given no meaning to the Prophet's (peace be upon him) followers, and nothing but great confusion would have resulted from the ventures.

It is surprising to observe that a man of Rodwell's learning and intelligence, despite his knowledge of the entire situation at the time of the prophecy, should have recourse to such improbability. It is absurd that such a discovery should come from a stranger (Rodwell) after the lapse of centuries. Whereas the hostile critics of the Prophet (peace be upon him) in Arabia, whose mother tongue was Arabic, should miss the trick that would have provided them with a most significant cause for his (Prophet's) downfall. Yet, they not only kept mum over the whole affair but unquestionably paid the wager.

Another precious point this prophecy has proved is that the Quran had not been the Prophet's (peace be upon him) work, but rather its claim to be the word of Allah was a truth. It is hard to believe that any person, not to speak of the Prophet (peace be upon him), in a situation just he and his religion at that time, could have dared to make so improbable a prophecy against such odds. The failure of this prediction was sure to ruin all his prospects as Prophet. It would have wrecked his plan, design, and all, while the loss of such a prophecy seemed almost inevitable.

There was no particular demand on him to make such a prophecy, nor did there appear to be some immediate necessity. It also could well be guessed that it was due to his explicit faith in the revelation that he did not hesitate to publish seemingly such improbable a prophecy. The fact furnishes prodigious proof of his faith in the truth of the revelation that came to him from the supernatural world, for indeed this was a prophecy which seemingly did overrule human judgment.

No doubt the Prophet's (peace be upon him) opponents were elated by the news of the defeats of the Romans and had acquired thereby a great daring. Yet, suppose Prophet (peace be upon him) had been in danger of his followers torn to pieces by the opponents due to the latter's delight by the news of the defeats of Romans. In that case, in his proper senses, he would barely have been expected to venture so improbable and so hazardous a prophecy that mounted to willful and all-out suicide. The fall of Constantinople, a day after the revelation of prophecy, would soon have left Prophet (peace be upon him) bereaved of his followers and at the mercy of his enemies.

The slander of Rodwell reminds one of a parallel in the Shakespeare-Bacon controversy in Great Britain. A mere whisper based on some silly cipher raised a tempest in a teacup. This storm raged to the point of depriving Shakespeare very nearly of credit as the author of his famous works that had gone in his name till then. This controversy had almost transferred the honor of Shakespeare to Francis Bacon, the illustrious Lord Chancellor of the English exchequer, the renowned philosopher, and the celebrated author of the 'Novum Organum'.

The controversy raged for some time between the Shakespeareans and the Baconians. Baconians could not believe that a person so illiterate as Shakespeare could perhaps have produced works of such intellectual caliber. Because someone had found some cipher somewhere from which it could dimly suggest that Bacon, in reality, wrote Shakespeare's works. It came as the basis of the belief, and controversy soon ensued. Judging from the achievement of Bacon's mind, it was pretty easy for them to believe that intellect of that caliber could have been considered the author of such magnificent works with much plausibility. Their answer to the question as to why then Bacon had not published these works in his name was that it was below the dignity of so great a person as Francis Bacon to associate his name with works of dramatic nature.

It has been an exciting controversy, and we can refer any interested reader to an article of Henry Irving appearing in the preface of "The Complete Works of Shakespeare" (Odhams Press Limited, Long Acre, London, W. C. 2 1923). However, the dispute finally fell against Baconians because of the argument's lack of proof and unreasonableness.

The time, it is said, is the most outstanding judge, and so indeed it is. Suppose we read Shakespeare's 'King Lear' after seeing the picture of the age of the atomic hell as we shall describe it in this present work of ours. In that case, we hardly miss a representation, a very faint one, though, compared to the picture of the atomic hell of the age of atomic energy in 'King Lear'.

Therein we find that miserable age pictured and meet most of the characters and the scenery, and therein we trace the features of the atomic age. Francis Bacon was the author of the 'Novum Organum' and the pioneer advocate of atomistic materialism of this modern age. The result of Bacon's philosophy appears in this world in the form of the atomic hell itself. How could he have produced work like 'King Lear' in which the age of the nuclear hell resulting from the 'Novum Organum' the author has pictured with an astonishing resemblance?

The 'Novum Organum' and 'King Lear' run counter to each other. Could then Bacon have been expected to produce the antithesis of his advocated philosophy, or did he, in doing so, realize that he then produced the unfortunate result thereof, are the questions that quite naturally arise. If then Bacon, while producing 'King Lear', knowingly had described the ultimate result of his philosophy, indeed an unfortunate result, then it was an extraordinary genius at work, the like of which no one saw in the whole history of the human mind.

However, suppose he advocated a philosophy whose results he had depicted in 'King Lear' and still insisted on promoting his philosophy. Then he would have found himself most anxious to disown the ownership of 'King Lear', dreading the epithet to be deservedly conferred on him by humankind. A man of humble pretensions like Shakespeare could, without any such apprehension, stick to the claim of the ownership of work like 'King Lear'.

In pious zeal for the sake of their religion, the critics of the modern age have tried to disparage Quran in misguided enthusiasm and mistaking the actual foe of their faith, which was not the Quran. Instead, the philosophy of atomistic materialism was the foe that devoured their religion, whatever religion theirs' was. They can now stand up and see what this foe has done to their dear religion and can estimate how much antipathy it deserved from them. They spent all their strength in finding faults with Quran.

Instead, trying to read and understand, they certainly would have realized what capacity this book had in challenging their real foe of the philosophy of atomistic materialism. Those critics would have discovered how discreetly the Quran had discerned and described the age of this philosophy. They would have learned what remedies it had offered for the wrongs this philosophy had done to the world. The Quran rises as the champion of true faith, and it contains all the light necessary to lead this world out of the pits of the atomic hell in which the atomistic philosophy has cast it already and shall drive it lower and lower with time.

We have sufficiently explained the prophecy about the victory of Romans. Let us turn to the main object of citing this prophecy about Romans in this context: namely, differentiation between two predictions; the one about the victory of Romans and the other about 'Al-Hotama'.

The prophecy about the triumph of Romans is but a piece of news about some future event. There exists the possibility of such a venture by a soothsayer or an astrologer. We speak here only of the possibility of such a venture, for the astrologer's or the soothsayer's knowledge is based not on certainty and more or less is a sort of a conjecture. At the same time, the world of the Scripture emanates from the very source of divinity, and it pedestals on sure knowledge.

Therefore, we cannot view the two origins of the astrologer and the Scripture in comparison. However, the prophecy of the victory of Romans was of the nature of mere news of an event. If two astrologers simultaneously prophesied in radical opposition to each other, one of them at least would prove correct in his word. If, for instance, one of them had said that the Persians would defeat the Romans while the other had said that the Romans would be victorious, the latter would be proved correct in his prophecy, though only in a random utterance. The failure of the word of soothsayer or astrologer would have been of little consequence.

However, there are instances in history when the disqualification of his prophecy cost the astrologer his head. Still, the prediction of the Quran about the victory of Romans or any other forecast so conspicuously failed before the very eyes of people would have wrecked the whole prospect of Islam immediately.

The case of the prophecy about 'Al-Hotama', however, is quite different. It is not a decree pre-ordained, but instead, it is fundamentally conditional. Romans were to achieve victory, and Providence imposed no conditions. Providence had decreed their victory while the punishment in 'Al-Hotama' is conditional to the act of 'slander' and 'wealth accumulation' etc. If any persons showed such and such characteristics, would be cast into 'Al-Hotama'. In case, however, when such acts as 'slander' and 'wealth accumulation' were there, the punishment in 'Al-Hotama' would be taken as the inevitable decree.

The prophecy of 'Al-Hotama' is more than a piece of news; it deals with a Philosophico-Scientific problem. It is the scientific answer to an Ethico-Economic problem that the prophecy has described therein. It has linked the causes like 'slander', 'wealth accumulation', and 'notion of forever living in the world' to their consequence: the fire of 'Al-Hotama'. It has scientifically described the fire of 'Al-Hotama'. These things, namely, the philosophico-logical treatment of the matter and the scientific description of 'Al-Hotama', are beyond the scope of any astrologer, soothsayer, etc.

When we have known well the fundamental difference between these two prophecies of the Quran, we can feel yet another difference therein. It happens to be a point of great momentous import to this present humankind. Whereas the failure of the prophecy of the Quran regarding the victory of Romans would have wrecked the prospect of the religion of Islam, the inability of present humankind to pay heed to this prophecy about 'Al-Hotama' will ruin the whole outlook of the entire humanity.

Now, I would like to say a word or two as humble advice to every aspirant to the dangerous office of the scientific corroboration of the Quran. It is a mighty sword, and it is too dangerous to tamper with it. Unusual patience and perseverance are the pre-requisites of so tremendous and hazardous an undertaking, and unusually great demands on intellect, insight, and sagacity are thereby employed. One has to match the heart's desire with the pre-requisite qualifications of a nature rare and versatile. For it is a path in which even angels fear to tread, and a casual slip or a false step in the endless maze of science would throw the reputation of the Quran itself in Jeopardy. It may render the Quran (Allah forbid) a laughingstock despite all the sincerity of one's heart. We don't deter any person from doing work of authentication.

On the contrary, corroboration would be genuinely beneficial in introducing Quran's teachings to seek answers to the problems of the current age, in the light of the Quran, and understand the mind of the Quran about characteristics of the present era. This age being mainly the age of science, the scientific aspect of the Quran deserves to be divulged and illustrated. The theological aspect thereof might not interest the people of the modern age till the scientific qualifications of the Quran are impressed upon the minds of the people.

However, it is not an easy task. The prayers of anyone engaged in such a task should always be, O, Allah! Guide me aright, and bless me with the proper understanding. Teach me the factual mind of the Quran and bestow on me all the necessary knowledge and cause the light of faith to shine in my heart. The prospective attester has to be endowed with sagacity besides extreme patience and perseverance to judge the time ripe for the commencement of such work after a long ordeal of study and pursuit of knowledge. The universality and versatility of a mind aspiring to undertake this task must be almost unique.

In short, one has to know all about the Quran and science, which is no exaggeration. Without such an achievement, it is difficult to do justice to such a subject. The Quran is not a mere stream. It instead is an ocean inexhaustible and unfathomable in itself. So also, in a way, is modern science. A genius of understanding the Quran and equally a genius in modern science is necessary to the theme. Today, it is hard to find a prodigy of knowledge equally conversant with religion and science in this world. He who knows religion is ignorant of science, and he who knows science is ignorant of religion while the subject of corroboration demands both.

Moreover, where is the time? A cursory knowledge of the Quran demands the study of an entire life, and so does science. A great mind might pass all life in reading even one branch of science and yet might not claim the mastery. Also, science has innumerable branches. Again, science is a constantly advancing and changing subject. One, therefore, is required to know science exceptionally well. He must know its present situation and future tendencies and discern its propensities, limitations, and shortcomings. He should distinguish between the recognized facts and the mere hypotheses, and their various categories have to be kept in mind. He must separately judge every theory of science and subject it to minute scrutiny.

Sir James Jeans was such one, for he has given ample proofs of his admirable conversance with the subject of science. He could set every theory of science in its proper perspective and knew well the shortcomings and the limitations of science. It is not creditable to science to treat its solar theory of the creation of earth stripped of all ifs and buts, and perhaps with which history is replete due to the uncertain nature of the conjecture. Nor is it creditable to the Quran to show it endorsing one science theory today and shifting tomorrow to follow the science if the scientist rejects the same theory on the proof.

A corroborator must discern possible pits on this verification path and know all the sciences. The possibility, however, of committing the most grievous and far-reaching errors is to be feared in someone devoid of the understanding of the actual mind of the Quran. Such a man may delude into the belief that the material achievements of modern science are the actual accomplishment of the very primary aim and the object of the mind of the Quran. He may think as if the Quran not only disregarded the money-oriented aspect of the material achievements of modern science but did as well enjoin in its teachings the worldly pursuits that are thoroughly bound with this modern materialism at the cost of faith and the element of spiritual.

May Allah bless everyone who endeavors to serve the cause of His Quran with accurate insight and show him the natural mind of the Quran. And give him the proper knowledge of this modern age and present the correct picture of contemporary atomistic materialism before his mind and bestow on him real wisdom in seeking the answers of the Quran to the intricate problems of this present age. In his sincere but misguided zeal, lest he mars the whole aspect and do grievous damage with most far-reaching effects and prove a misleader of humankind instead of a guide and throw this world in the burning pit of hell.

These efforts may prove fruitless with humankind, but mine is, to tell the truth only lest they say someone did not tell them. This present greedy, ignorant, and selfish generation has enough reason not to pay heed to my warning in that it has little to fear from the ill-effects of atomic energy and has every hope of reaping the material benefits thereof. However, some future generations shall have to pay the accumulated debt; and people now appear not to take care of that debt.

This warning of the Quran about 'Al-Hotama' has existed in the Quran since its revelation. I found this warning applicable to worldly atomic hell according to the characterization of phenomena and the causes of the appearance of the phenomena. The discovery is my own. None in the world knew it. Also, the entire work in this respect is my own. It has been a formidable task, and I could not have accomplished it without the Grace and Mercy of Allah. In this world of Allah, I stand alone, indeed my Allah on my side. His help that I seek, and it is He that will help me in this ordeal. Would to Allah, the truth prevails. Aameen.

~~*~*~*

[1] **Damnosa hereditas** is a Latin Phrase that means: 'An accursed inheritance or gift which brings more harm than benefit; a harmful or burdensome inheritance; Inheritance of damnation, ruinous legacy'.

[2] In Greek Mythology, **Gorgons** are three female monsters (viz. Medusa, Euryale, and Stheno) covered with impenetrable scales, hair of living snakes, hands made of brass, sharp fangs, and a beard. They turned into stone everything upon which they cast a look.

[3] **"Scientists are economic prisoners"** with **"money-based goals"**.
(Dr. Rosalie Bertell)

[4] (A) Recall to your mind the explosion of the **Chernobyl** nuclear reactor (U.S.S.R.) and think about the aftermath of nuclear radiation. The author completed this 'Gabriel's Extinguishing the Atomic Hell Series' of 09 volumes (warning against such nuclear hazards) in 1982 and just after four years on April 26, 1986, the world's worst nuclear accident with the explosion of 'Chernobyl Nuclear Reactor' took place and spread the flood of nuclear radiations all around. The effects of radiation discharged on the inhabitants and newly born abnormal babies are now no hidden secret to the world. Still, these effects are in action after so long a time.

"The explosion at the Chernobyl power plant in northern Ukraine sent 190 tons of radioactive Uranium and Graphite into the air. 600,000 'liquidators' were conscripted for the cleanup and were exposed to massive doses of radiation. Since the accident, over 13000 liquidators have died. The people of Chernobyl were exposed to radiation 90 times greater than from the explosion of the atomic bomb at Hiroshima. Over 400,000 people were evacuated. More than 2000 villages in the area were demolished. None were more affected than the children of Chernobyl."

(A quotation from the 'Chernobyl Heart' video)

(B) CHERNOBYL 'SHOWS INSECT DECLINE'
By Victoria Gill, Science reporter, BBC News, Wednesday, March 18, 2009

GHOST ZONE

Two decades after the explosion at the Chernobyl nuclear power plant, radiation is still causing a reduction in the number of insects and spiders.
--- According to researchers working in the exclusion zone surrounding Chernobyl, there is a "strong signal of decline associated with the contamination". --- The team found that bumblebees, butterflies, grasshoppers, dragonflies, and spiders were affected.
--- The two researchers previously published findings that low-level radiation in the area has a negative impact on bird populations.

(http://news.bbc.co.uk)

(C) CHERNOBYL BIRDS ARE SMALL-BRAINED
By Matt Walker, Saturday, February 5, 2011
Birds living around the site of the Chernobyl nuclear accident have 5% smaller brains, an effect directly linked to lingering background radiation.
--- Mammals were declining in the exclusion zone surrounding the nuclear power plant.
--- Insect diversity has also fallen, and previously, the same researchers found a way to predict which species there were likely to be most severely damaged by radioactive contamination by evaluating how often they renewed parts of their DNA.

After controlling for the differences between species, they found that the birds had brains 5% smaller on average compared with birds not exposed to background radiation.
--- Chernobyl is largely human-free but still contaminated with radiation.
--- Background radiation could be having an even more pronounced effect on other organs within the birds.
--- However, if that were the case, the scientists say they would expect to see pronounced changes to the size and shape of other parts of the birds' bodies.

(http://news.bbc.co.uk)

(D) SOME EXCERPTS FROM THE LATEST UPDATE ON MARCH 18, 2015, BY B.B.C.

<u>CHERNOBYL</u>: CONTAINING THE WORLD'S WORST NUCLEAR ACCIDENT

Our science editor David Shukman inspects the colossal dome being constructed to house the crippled Chernobyl nuclear power station.

--- Rising above the scene of the world's worst nuclear accident is the spectacular sight of the largest moveable structure ever created on land.

--- The project is to build what is called a <u>New Safe Confinement</u> – in effect, 'a giant cover', 'a kind of dome', 'to fit over the building that houses the reactor that exploded on April 26, 1986'.

--- <u>The radiation immediately above the reactor is still far too intense for the new enclosure to be built exactly where it is needed</u> – anyone working there can only stay very briefly.

--- When complete, it will weigh an extraordinary 31,000 tons.

"Until this project is in place, we will not be safe," Vince Novak, who runs the nuclear safety department of the European Bank for Reconstruction and Development, said during a media visit to the site. "The ultimate objective is to protect the environment, contain the threat and deal with the radioactive material inside."

DANGEROUS MIX

This material is a nightmare mix of more than '100 tons of uranium', 'one ton of plutonium', and other highly radioactive elements formed into a previously-unseen lava-like mass.

--- Added to that are several thousand tons of sand and boron dropped on to the site by emergency workers at the time.

--- <u>Vast quantities of radioactive liquids and dust are also present inside a reactor building that has itself long been in danger of collapse</u>.

--- The reactor building itself is unsafe and is at risk of collapse.

--- The goal is not merely to enclose the damaged reactor and isolate it from the corrosive effects of the weather - but also to create a space in which to start the job of dismantling the most hazardous components.

Suspended from the apex of the structure will be remotely operated cranes designed to tackle <u>tasks too hazardous for human beings</u>. During the assembly phase, the radiation risk has been minimized by the construction of a protective wall right besides the reactor building. This means the workforce at the assembly site receives minimal doses of radiation.

The man in charge of the project's management, Ron Hink, joked that he probably gets a higher dose while flying home to Kentucky.

--- But he acknowledges <u>a greater risk during a crucial stage of the forthcoming operation to install the new structure</u>.
--- The hope is to have the new structure in place and fully commissioned by November 2017. --- If that is achieved, it would be 31 years since the disaster itself – but should provide protection for at least a <u>century</u>.

(www.bbc.com)

Now, everything is self-explanatory here. Until 2015, even 29 years have passed, but the radiations are still lurking in search of prey. This dome "should provide protection for at least a century". What will happen then after "a century"? We advise the reader to remember this **Encompassing Feature** of radiations discussed throughout while studying this work.

Moreover, most recently, on March 11, 2011, after a severe earthquake, Tsunami hit the Japanese nuclear reactors at **'Fukushima Nuclear Plant'**. Their cooling system failed to melt the reactors' fuel rods and spread nuclear radiation all around, endangering the inhabitants' lives in the vicinity. This accident happened not far away in the hidden history of the world.

Mother Nature will always react and resist every effort of humankind to have Baconian dominion over Mother Nature. Such a chain of accidents will continue to happen worldwide wherever these <u>satanic reactors</u> are installed. Are these accidents not enough to open the eyes of the people of the world yet?

[5] **"Uneasy lies the head that wears a crown."**
('King Henry-IV'; by Shakespeare, Part-2/Act-III/Scene-I)
It means that the head that wears the crown sleeps uneasily. A person with significant responsibilities, such as a king, is constantly worried and therefore doesn't sleep soundly.

[6] **Avars:** A Caucasian or eastern European member whose empire, centered in southern Hungary and extending widely between the Elbe and Dneiper Rivers, reached its peak in the late sixth and early seventh centuries.

Slavs: A member of one of the Slavic-speaking peoples of Eastern Europe.

~~*~*~*

CHAPTER-2

NUCLEAR CORROBORATION OF 'AL-HOTAMA' BY ATOMIC PHYSICS

~~*~*~*~*

PART-1
THE THEORY OF NUCLEAR PHYSICS

THE NEED FOR ACQUAINTANCE WITH ATOMIC THEORY

To understand the actual corroboration of the characteristics of the fire of 'Al-Hotama' by the facts of nuclear science, the non-scientist reader needs some prior acquaintance with the theory of nuclear physics. To achieve this end, we have included a brief but to-the-point treatment of nuclear physics theory. However, the book's contents could well be understood and fully comprehended by even those presumed not to know the theory of nuclear science, though better appreciation is reserved only for those who know that theory most.

We have purposely deferred the first part of the prophecy, comprising causes of the emergence of fire of 'Al-Hotama', to a later chapter in which we will examine the views of the interpreters of the Quran. In the following, a careful perusal of this part of the present chapter dealing with nuclear physics theory will benefit the non-scientist reader. The reader will find it highly advantageous to ensure a far better appreciation of the subsequent treatment of the subject and afford the much-added interest.

THE WORLD OF ATOMS

Within this rippling, four-dimensional, bubble-like universe of outward appearance, there exists the scintillating world of tiny, invisible atoms in billions of billions; each atom with its electrons revolving about it like tiny planets with almost invisible rapidity and the whole atmosphere steeped in such breathless silence as even the inaudible wheezing within one's ears might sound like the tumult of a furiously raging tornado. At the same time, the soft inner heartbeats of one's heart might appear like the thundering beats of a frightening drum.

THE DISCOVERY OF ATOMIC ENERGY IS OF RECENT ORIGIN

Man has long since used gravitational energy (flowing water) and the energy produced in burning wood and charcoal. This energy is chemical energy and essentially electrical in origin. Atomic energy, also called nuclear energy, roughly a million times more powerful than any chemical process and derived from the nucleus of an atom, is a discovery comparatively of recent origin.

ATOM

The matter is composed of atoms. Atoms pervade the whole field of science, yet none hitherto has seen the atom. No microscope or electroscope can show it, for it is too small, and it has to be enlarged thousands of times to make it visible. A hundred million atoms can be placed side by side at a distance of half an inch. Suppose you want to count the number of atoms in your thumb; then you have to multiply 10000 by a million, further multiplied by a million, and again multiplied by a million, and so forth. Your surprise at the enormousness of this number is genuine. What if your bank manager would tell you to count dollar notes equal in number to the atoms in your thumb? You will have the dollar notes as a prize. But at that time, have no joy in the offer, for you will take millions of millions of years to count, and by the time you have finished your counting, this world may have perished long since. Imagination itself is unable to view the mystery. Similarly incredible is the magnitude of destruction wrought by this tiny little, imperceptible atom called the 'basic building block of the universe'. Great are the works of Allah; how fascinating.

A question naturally arises, how then are all these facts known about this atom when nobody has ever seen it? The answer to this question is that all the observations of the atomists in this respect are indirect. Extra sensitive photographic plates, magnetic fields, cloud chambers, etc., are the means that help trace the signs of the sub-atomic parts of the atom.

THE STRUCTURE OF THE ATOM

Scientists generally picture an atom as a vacuous sphere with its nucleus somewhere in the center and electrons revolving around the nucleus.

THE NUCLEUS OF THE ATOM

The nucleus of an atom consists of protons and neutrons, but just the hydrogen atom contains only one proton and has no neutrons. Different atoms have a different number of protons and neutrons in their nuclei. The protons (positive) and electrons (negative) mutually neutralize each other, and thus the atom attains its equilibrium. A neutron is slightly heavier (one part in 750) than a proton, while the mass of a proton is 1836.2 times the mass of an electron.

THE ATOMIC NUMBER AND THE ATOMIC WEIGHT

Every element has its 'atomic number' (Z) and 'atomic weight' (A). The atomic number is the number of protons that is the number of positive charges in an atom. Atomic weight or the mass number of an atom is the number of protons and neutrons added together. For example, the atomic number of Chlorine is 17, and the atomic weight of Chlorine is 35, which means that its atom has 18 neutrons in its nucleus to make the mass number or the atomic weight as 35 by the addition of 17 protons to 18 neutrons.

THE ELEMENTS

An element is a substance that cannot be decomposed into or built up from simpler substances. For instance, Chlorine is an element and has a particular atomic structure of its atom. The total number of elements hitherto known is 103. Those up to atomic number (Z) 92, we find naturally, while from (Z) 93 to (Z) 103 have been synthetically formed. The atomic numbers from 83 to 92 are all radioactive, and so are the synthetically formed atomic numbers from 93 to 103.

ISOTOPES AND ATOMIC WEIGHT

Suppose two atoms have the same number of protons in their nuclei but have different neutrons. In that case, they are the isotopes of the same element because the number of protons decides the element's name. The number of protons is the number of positive charges in the atom's nucleus. Therefore, isotopes of an element are atoms with the same atomic number but different atomic weights. An example is the isotopes of Chlorine. The atomic number of the atom of Chlorine is 17, and its atomic weight is 35. However, a Chlorine atom may have an atomic weight of 37 also. The former has 18 neutrons, while the latter has 20 neutrons in the nucleus, and both are Chlorine atoms because both have the same charge, that is, the same number of protons.

What is the atomic weight? The atomic weight is the mass of its 'weighted average' atom in atomic mass units. The values of the atomic weights are relative, not absolute. One element is selected as the standard arbitrarily, and others are measured relative to this standard. For example, Bismuth consists of 83 protons and 126 neutrons. Bismuth thus has a total of 209 nucleons in its nucleus.

If we take Hydrogen with one nucleon in its nucleus as the standard, then bismuth is 209 times larger than the standard and, therefore, has 209 as its atomic weight. At first, the lightest of all the atoms, the Hydrogen, was chosen quite logically as the standard and assigned a relative value of precisely one. The atomic weights of other elements were measured relative to that of Hydrogen. Later on, scientists adopted Oxygen (16) and then, in 1961, carbon (C-12) as the standard for various reasons. Most elements are mixtures of isotopes. Their atomic weight, therefore, is the average mass of the isotopes of the elements. For example, the atomic weight of Tin is 118.70. This number is the mean mass number of its eleven isotopes, which, taken in their abundance order, are 120, 118, 116, 124, 119, 117, 122, 121, 112, 114, and 115.

SYMBOLS OF ELEMENTS

Elements have been allotted symbols for the sake of convenience. Hydrogen, for example, is written as 'H', Oxygen as 'O', and Uranium as 'U', and so forth. We give a few examples of elements' atomic numbers, atomic weights, symbols, etc.

Atomic No.	Atomic Weight	Element	Symbol
1	1.008	Hydrogen	H
2	4.002602	Helium	He
6	12.011	Carbon	C
8	15.999	Oxygen	O
92	238.02891	Uranium	U
94	244	Plutonium	Pu
103	262	Lawrencium	Lr (formerly Lw)

ELECTRON SHELLS

The number of electrons is always equal to the number of protons existing in the nucleus of an atom. Electrons keep continually revolving around the atom's nucleus with the speed of a thousand billion rounds per second in different orbits. They are arranged in various shells and spin in definite orbits. Atoms of one element have the same number of electrons and have identical electron shells.

The most significant number of shells is 7. We symbolize these as K, L, M, N, O, P, and Q. Different shells have different energy levels of electrons. Hydrogen has only one electron in the K shell, while Uranium 92 has 92 electrons distributed in its seven shells.

We determine the chemical properties of an atom by the number of electrons in its outermost shell. All the atoms strive to obtain the octet that is eight electrons in their outermost shell. They can do this by gaining electrons from other atoms or yielding their own few that they might have in their outer shell to some other atom with a higher number of electrons in its outer shell. Atoms strive to gain the octet in their outer shell because they are most secure and stable if they have eight electrons in their outer shell. Hydrogen and Helium, however, are two exceptions to this rule. They are pretty stable if they have two electrons.

MOLECULES

Atoms are seldom found alone in nature. They generally exist in combination with the atoms of some other element. This combined formation of atoms is called a molecule. Atoms of certain elements join with other atoms of the same element as a molecule, e.g., Hydrogen atoms.

IONS

We define Ion as a charged atom or a group of charged atoms. The charged atom means an atom having lost an electron, thus assuming a positive charge or assuming the negative charge by gaining an electron. Electrons and protons are equal in number in an atom. Electrons have a negative charge while protons have a positive charge, and thus, neutralizing each other by opposite charges, they maintain the equilibrium of the atom.

Even when one electron of an atom is lost, the negative charge of the atom is decreased, and consequently, the positive charge of the atom increases. The atom then is called a positively charged atom. On the contrary, if the atom has gained an electron, the negative charge on the atom is increased, and the atom is, therefore, called a negatively charged atom. These negatively or positively charged atoms are called ions.

FREE RADICALS

Free radicals are ions but of a particular kind. These are highly reactive and do not happen to have an octet in their outer shell. Suppose we call the negatively or positively charged atoms as ions because the meaning of the word 'ion' is a 'wanderer'.

In that case, free radicals could with appropriateness justify the appellation of 'lunatic pirates' since they rush about in mad pursuit of other atoms in an endeavor to gain their lost electron to compensate their loss or to lose their excess electron to some other atom.

ATOMIC ENERGY

That so little a thing as an atom should generate such a tremendous amount of energy as it does is indeed surprising. We generate atomic energy by fission and fusion processes. In the fission process, we knock out particles from the nucleus of an atom, and the nucleus divides into various nuclei, and this process liberates energy. In the fusion process, we crush the nuclei of atoms into the nuclei of other atoms, which also releases energy. We will describe both of these processes later.

How could so tiny an atom generate so much energy? It is because the process takes place within the nucleus of the atom. The nucleus is the heart of the atom: the basic building block of the original structure of the universe. It suffers a derangement of its natural structure in a way that implies death to its very existence. The death blow to the nucleus (heart) of the atom excites it to exert all that force in it to defend its life. The atomic that is the nuclear energy shot out by the atom is thus all the amount of energy that an atom naturally could have contained. It is all the energy that it possibly can produce to save its existence.

We can give out the atomic energy as the frantic outcry of wronged Mother Nature emitted like a grievous protest against man's encroachment on its basic, original structure, the nucleus (heart). Man, therefore, should be prepared to bear the severe reprisals of the enraged Mother Nature for this gross outrage.

However, in the chemical processes, the nucleus (heart) of the atom is not touched, and the essential, original structure of matter remains unchanged. Though it liberates the energy yet because the heart is not touched, the cry of Mother Nature is not as wild, and hence the amount of energy liberated is relatively not as tremendous.

BINDING ENERGY

All atoms except for Hydrogen have more than one proton in their nucleus. Now, the protons have a positive charge, and so have the protons enclosed within a single nucleus, and we know that like charges always repel each other. How is it then that all nuclei protons with similar charges stay bound together within the nucleus? There certainly must be some binding force that keeps them bound together so closely packed. When the atom's nucleus breaks, this binding force, whatever it is, is released as energy and hence the appellation of binding energy.

PACKING LOSS AND PACKING FACTOR

The nucleus of an atom is composed of protons and neutrons. We know that the atomic weight of an atom is the weight of all its protons and neutrons added together. The atomic weight of an atom thus must naturally be expected to be the combined weight of the protons and the neutrons contained in its nucleus, but this essentially is not the case.

Accurate determination of the masses of isotopes reveals a difference. For example, Helium ($2He^4$) turned out to be 4.00280, while it has 2 protons and 2 neutrons that are 4 in all. The calculations show that the mass of 2 protons 2.01516 plus the mass of 2 neutrons 2.01786 is 4.03302. It is 0.03022 more than the mass of the Helium atom, which is 4. 00280. We have to account for this deficit for debit. Where has this mass gone? We cannot say that the mass is lost. Nothing can be lost. Here the particular theory of relativity advanced by Einstein comes to our aid. We understand that mass and energy are inter-convertible. The loss of mass means its conversion to energy in a relative proportion by the history-famous Einstein equation, i.e., $E=MC^2$.

Instead of going into minute technicalities, let us try to understand it by a most straightforward example. The simplest example to make this point (of binding energy) clear is a wrapped package bound with a tightly drawn elastic strip. Cut the strip and see how it jumps upward and then shrinks. Every little boy who ever had a chance to play with a rubber catapult has seen this experiment repeated every time he drew the rubber strips, let them go, and sent the stone flying at the bird. The honor, however, of applying this principle to atomic energy was reserved for Einstein.

What joyful hopes would not have filled the hearts of the scientists worldwide in the possibility of changing all mass of this universe to energy in the light of this history-famous equation of Einstein? There, at last, was the possibility of a utopia in view: energy, energy, everywhere energy. At last, the scientific interpretation of the saying of Leibniz, namely, "The best of all possible worlds", was in sight. However, alas! The equation was tested with certainty in Hiroshima and Nagasaki, while the dream of converting mass into energy was a false hope. Only Uranium could have been used to generate atomic energy for practical purposes.

The loss of mass forming a nucleus from protons and neutrons is known as its 'packing loss'. The idea is that the protons and neutrons are packed very tightly in the nucleus. The packing loss of an element per unit of atomic mass is secured by dividing its packing loss by the number of units (protons and neutrons) in its nucleus and is called the 'packing factor' of the element. Hydrogen has a packing factor of 0 (zero) because its nucleus is just a single proton. We secure the value of any other element by subtracting its actual atomic weight from the sum of weights of protons and neutrons in its nucleus. This result gives the packing loss, dividing by the number of protons and neutrons in the nucleus, giving the packing factor. For example, Krypton 78 has 36 protons and 42 neutrons in its nucleus.

36 protons = 36 x 1.0076 = 36.2736
42 neutrons = 42 x 1.0089 = 42.3738
======================

Sum = 78.6474
The atomic weight of Krypton 78=77.9262
Packing loss=0.7212
Packing Factor = referred to Hydrogen 0.0091, or 91 parts per 10,000. Krypton 78 has lost 91 parts per 10,000 for each of 78 protons and neutrons entering into the structure of its nucleus. It must be a stable nucleus indeed.

GENERATION OF ATOMIC ENERGY

FISSION AND FUSION

There are two processes of generating atomic energy, namely, fission and fusion. In the fission process, we disintegrate a nuclide (proton or neutron of a nucleus). In the fusion process, a nuclide of one atom has to combine with the nuclide of another atom to generate energy. A nuclide having a mass number greater than about 56 has to disintegrate in fission to generate energy. In contrast, a nuclide below 56 has to combine with a particle to generate energy in the fusion process. The fission of Uranium-235 is an outstanding example of the release of nuclear energy by disintegration (fission). In contrast, the fusion of Hydrogen-1 with other Hydrogen atoms is an example of releasing energy through nuclear combination (fusion).

FISSION

If we direct a stream of protons against a film of alkali metal, Lithium ($3Li^7$), alpha particles emerge, traveling at a very high velocity. For each proton that hits a Lithium nucleus, two alpha particles appear. An alpha particle is the nucleus of Helium ($2HE^4$) without electrons. Proton is the nucleus of Hydrogen ($1H^1$) without electrons. Together, Proton and Lithium ($3Li^7$) are changed into 2 Helium nuclei, each with mass 4 and charge 2. These added together would contain 4 protons and 4 neutrons to make mass number 8 instead of Lithium ($3Li^7$). The two Helium nuclei fly apart excessively as if considerable energy were released to adjust the unstable nucleus. After each collision, two particles are released with a combined energy of 27.2 millionths of an Erg for each Lithium atom. Scientifically speaking, the resultant energy for each atom proves exactly Einstein's equation ($E=MC^2$) of mass and energy.

The experiment above-quoted helps to understand the process of fission. Lithium in the above-quoted experiment broke into two equal Helium nuclei. The process is called 'fission', 'atomic fission', or more appropriately 'nuclear fission'. Physicists adapted the term fission from biology. When a cell divides to produce two identical daughter cells in biology, the process is called fission. It is also said that the atomists adapted the term fission from botany, wherein the plant cell divides into two daughter cells.

The interesting point from the above-quoted fission experiment has appeared: when a proton and a Lithium nucleus collide, the result is two Helium nuclei and considerable energy. The atomic energy is there but not for technically valuable purposes.

NOTE: [(**MeV**: Mega-electron volts) or (**mev**: million electron volts) = 10^6 electron volts]

Generally speaking, any heavy nucleus can undergo fission if the excitation energy is abundant enough, e.g., fission in gold occurs for neutron energy of about 100 MeV. But, it may prove a costly affair and useless for practical purposes. Uranium, however, of all the elements proved to be the most functional element for fission. One of its isotopes, Uranium-235, was found to automatically fission in the presence of a slow neutron, releasing a tremendous amount of energy, namely, 200 MeV for a single fission atom.

In other words, if all the atoms in one gram of Uranium-235 were to undergo fission, the energy released would be equivalent to that set free in the explosion of 20 tons of TNT. If all the atoms in a pound of Uranium-235 pass through the process of fission, the energy released would be over 400 billion ergs, or in standard units 12,000,000 kilowatt-hours. It would explode in a fraction of a second with the force of 10,000 tons of TNT. It means that pound-for-pound Uranium-235 could yield an explosive force 20,000,000 times more powerful than TNT.

This resultant force is the cause of that temptation that could make even the most serene of men of the present power-hungry generation blind to all those severe hazards that are incident on the atomic energy.

FISSION OF URANIUM-235 AND FISSION CHAIN REACTION

It is essential to understand the fission process in nuclear science, most significant but not very difficult to understand in its over-simplified form. This fission and the subsequent fission chain reaction have made the generation of atomic energy possible. The fission process is vital from our particular point of view too, and basically, it is described as follows.

We shoot a slow neutron into a lump of Uranium-235. The neutron attacks the nucleus of one Uranium-235 atom and knocks out two neutrons from it. The knocked-out neutrons further attack an atom each, and each knocks out two neutrons from the atom thus attacked.

The four knocked-out neutrons further attack an atom each, and each knocks out two neutrons from the atom thus attacked, and so forth; the process of doubling continues till the entire mass of Uranium-235 has gone through fission. Every Uranium-235 atom, which fissions, divides into two daughter nuclei, e.g., Krypton (36 Kr^{92}) and Barium (56 Ba^{141}), and energy is released.

The atomic weight of Krypton and Barium added together is a little less than that of Uranium-235. The loss occurred in mass has been converted into energy, which is a tremendous amount of 200 MeV per fission. The continued process of fission is called the 'fission chain reaction'. Note that the atomic energy is generated in the atom's nucleus and, more appropriately, we call it nuclear energy. No chemical energy process could ever touch the atom's nucleus. This feature is particularly distinctive in that it distinguishes the two processes: atomic and chemical energy generation.

THE ATOMIC REACTOR

The atomic reactor these days is a much-prized gift. This radio elephant is yearned after by most of the countries of the world these days. It will be no exaggeration to say that some of the countries are dying for the atomic reactor. The reactors could be of several kinds, such as converter reactors and research reactors, etc. However, the general purpose of a reactor is to convert Uranium-238 (natural Uranium) into Plutonium-239.

The first successful reactor was made by Fermi on the fateful day of December 2, 1942, in a squash court under the west stand of Stagg Field, the stadium of the University of Chicago.

An inscription on a plaque on the wall of its building read:

"On December 2, 1942, man achieved here the first self-sustaining chain reaction and thereby initiated the controlled release of nuclear energy."

The inscription has lately been torn down. However, we may suggest that the same writing with added words on the other side of the plaque be inscribed as given in the following.

"...To the ultimate ruin of humankind and a general annihilation of life on earth."

The atomic reactor is merely a lattice pile consisting of layers of Graphite bricks interspersed with lumps of Uranium or Uranium-oxide.

From some neutron source, we shoot neutrons into Uranium-238 (natural Uranium). Uranium-238 is converted into Neptunium and finally into Plutonium-239 with the emission of radioactivity. In other words, a pile is an atomic factory to convert Uranium-238 into

Plutonium-239. The reactor converts Uranium to Plutonium in a controlled process of fission chain reaction.

Because it is challenging to separate Uranium-235 from natural Uranium-238, Uranium conversion into Plutonium seemed like a God-sent opportunity to a doomed race. Plutonium is as fissionable as Uranium-235 and can be had very simply in reactors in sufficient quantities.

Removable rods of cadmium are inserted in various parts of the lattice pile to regulate the multiplication factor. If every neutron knocks out one neutron in the fission process, then this factor is 1.00. In that case, it builds a chain reaction. If less than 1.00, then a chain reaction is not possible.

If, on the other hand, the multiplication factor is more than 1.00, then an explosion may occur. The multiplication factor 1.00 simply means that the number of neutrons in one generation equals the number of the preceding generation.

Moderating rods absorb neutrons and slow down the process. If we withdraw them, the process speeds up, and the reactor goes out of control. If they are inserted deeper, the process may come to a standstill.

ATOMIC BOMB

Unlike the reactor, which uses Uranium-238, the atomic bomb requires pure Uranium-235 or Plutonium-239. Both of these are highly fissionable elements, and there is nothing to absorb the neutrons except the atoms that fission and produce more neutrons. All the neutrons that remain in the lump will result in fission. The multiplication factor of the atomic bomb is 2 as against 1 in the reactor. It means that every neutron ejects 2 neutrons from the Uranium or the Plutonium atom. Therefore, each neutron generation will result in twice the number of splitting atoms produced by the preceding generation. The first atom that fissioned produces 2 effective neutrons, which are absorbed by 2 atoms that fission and produce 2 neutrons, each making 4 neutrons. Each of these is absorbed by an atom that fissions with a total result of 8 neutrons available. Thus, the generations of splitting atoms number 1, 2, 4, 8, 16, 32, 64, 128, and so forth.

Such a reproductive series increases at a fantastic rate. The tenth generation is 1024; the twentieth is over million, thirtieth over a billion, and sixtieth over a billion of billion, and ninetieth over a billion of billions of billion. Suppose each neutron generation lasts one-millionth of a second, then in ninety generations or 90-millionth of a second, over a billion of billions of billion atoms will have fission. In the minutest fraction of a second, the whole mass of material will have fission and release the energy. The fissile material thus goes off with a tremendous blast like the bomb. The atomic reactor may also occasionally go out of control, and the multiplication factor may rise to such a ratio that the blast may occur.

RADIOACTIVITY

Radioactivity is the primary root from which the whole subject of nuclear science sprang. Neither the atomic energy nor the atomic bomb would have appeared if the scientists had not discovered radioactivity accidentally. What is radioactivity? Radioactivity is a peculiar quality of spontaneous disintegration peculiar to radioactive substances. It is the condition of substances that atomic nuclei of which are perceptibly disintegrating with the emission of alpha particles, and or beta particles, and or gamma rays. It simply means that certain substances keep on disintegrating by spontaneously emitting alpha particles, beta particles, and gamma rays. Elements with atomic numbers 83 to 92 are all naturally radioactive. The synthetically prepared elements with atomic numbers from 93 to 103 also are all radioactive without exception.

The emission of radiation by radioactive substances is, however, not predictable. When the atomic particles leave the nucleus of the atom of the radioactive substance, they are called nuclear radiations. They thus can be considered as a matter associated with the heart (nucleus) of the atom. Because the atomic particles are leaving the nuclei of the atoms, the nuclear structure of the radioactive atoms is gradually changing. For instance, owing to emitting an alpha particle, the radioactive element Uranium-238 transforms into Thorium-234. Again, emitting an electron (beta ray) twice in succession transforms it into a different isotope, giving off alpha particles. And so forth, until the process finishes with Lead (Pb) of atomic weight 206, a stable atom and does not undergo any further change. The atom becomes quite a different atom due to the change of the atomic number. Radioactivity is the worst problem of atomic energy.

HALF-LIFE

The rate at which a radioactive isotope decays is constant and completely independent of external conditions such as temperature. It means that a constant proportion of the radioactive atoms present will decompose in a given time by giving off an atomic particle entirely independent of how many are present. Also, they are pretty independent of the chemical combination in which the isotope is being handled.

As a result of this behavior, it is possible to express the rate or speed with which the nucleus of an unstable (i.e., radioactive) isotope changes by its so-called 'half-life'. This 'half-life' is the time in which half of the atoms present will have changed. The rate at which nuclei disintegrate varies widely. The 'half-life' of some isotopes is a fraction of a second, while others amount to millions of years. This prolonged activity of radioactive substances is essential. Some of the radioactive fission products distributed over the earth as a fall-out of the atomic and Hydrogen bombs have lengthy half-lives. They may keep on spreading the effects of radioactivity for incredibly lengthy periods. The term 'half-life' means that if we keep a lump of some radioactive element for a period under observation, we find that in a given period (termed as 'half-life'), half of the atoms in the lump will have disintegrated.

NATURAL RADIOACTIVITY

The different radio-isotopes in a decay series are present naturally since they are continuously formed and broken down. The relative amount depends on the rate of their disintegration, and those having a short 'half-life' will only be present in very minute amounts. 'Half-life' of Uranium-238 (chief fissile material in atomic energy and atomic bomb) is 4.5 billion years. Thus, it takes Uranium-238 to convert itself through constant emission of atomic particles through gradual series into Lead four billion years. Because Uranium ore contains always Lead, we thereby surmise that the age of our earth is the same, namely, four billion years.

Moreover, just as the disintegration of Uranium has provided geologists with a unique clock to measure the age of the earth, C^{14} (carbon) has provided anthropologists with a radioactive clock to measure the time after someone's death. It is done so by measuring the concentration of C^{14} in a dead body. The intake of C^{14} stops with death while its disintegration continues. At any time after death, measurement of the concentration of C^{14} in the dead body tells the time elapsed after death.

ARTIFICIAL RADIOACTIVITY

In 1919, Sir Earnest Rutherford discovered that we could disrupt stable nuclei by bombardment with alpha particles. For the first time, nuclear fragmentations were produced under man's control and were no longer entirely confined to the inevitable and unalterable events associated with natural radioactive processes. By bombarding Nitrogen atoms with alpha particles, Sir Rutherford transmuted the Nitrogen atoms into Oxygen-17 and protons that are Hydrogen nuclei. In 1934, Joliot Curie discovered that we could prepare radioisotopes of elements of lower atomic numbers by transformation. Bombarding aluminum with alpha particles resulted in the emission of neutrons, and the process formed a radioisotope of phosphorus. The phosphorus atoms then disintegrated by emitting positrons (positive electrons). This initial discovery paved the way for further investigations, and they formed up to about 1200 radioactive species until 1958. These nuclides decay exactly like those naturally occurring radioactive elements.

THE NEUTRONS

The neutron is the particle now believed to be one of the significant components of the nuclei of atoms. It is ideal for disintegrating nuclei since it carries no charge, and no other particle will repel it. Plutonium-239 and the elements having atomic numbers from 93 to 103 result from neutron bombardment and are all radioactive. Interestingly, the research of these so-called trans-Uranium elements led to the discovery of nuclear fission, the landmark in the history of nuclear science.

ATOMIC OR NUCLEAR RADIATIONS

What are the nuclear radiations? These are the invisible, undetectable, penetrating, and poisonous arrows of damaging subatomic particles and rays thinner than the thinnest needles and emitted by radioactive substances in spontaneous disintegration, and also emitted during the generation of atomic energy in the fission process, and the explosion of the atomic bomb, and after that by the radioactive fission products of the fission explosion.

In-built in the very nature of atomic energy generation's radioactive substances and fission process, these radiations are the deadliest bane and the ugliest plague of atomic energy, both inseparable and uncontrollable on a universal basis. This rebellious generation of inexorable radiations has offended nature, emerging in the form of alpha, beta, and gamma rays, neutrons, and protons, etc. Hence, Mother Nature has outwitted human genius in a retaliative mood and has hitherto defied all human endeavor to discover or devise any means of protection against radiations that might be hundred percent sure or universally applicable.

Inherent in every radioisotope and single fission, most dreadfully hazardous and most inherently rebellious, the main spoilers from the matchlessly excellent potential of atomic energy, these nuclear radiations are the nightmare of the scientist. He stands before these delusive, demoniacal apparitions of a deadly nature: baffled, hesitant, uncertain, and confounded. The scientist heartily wishes all the while for a possibility to control these insurgent and insidious destroyers of humankind. However, he hopes only a little success in achieving any means whatsoever of providing universal protection to all humankind individually (which is the absolute necessity) against them or even discovering some sure cure of the sickness produced by them. However, atomic energy would have proved to be a unique source of energy potential in the absence of these radiations. The relentless interference of these radiations appears as proof without any doubt of the implied spite of the punishing nature of the atomic energy itself.

Of these atomic radiations, usually referred to as ionizing radiations, alpha particles are the nuclei of Helium ($2He^4$), beta particles are electrons, X-rays and gamma rays are electromagnetic waves, while protons and neutrons are nucleons. Alpha particles have a positive charge, whereas beta particles have a negative charge. Hence, magnetic fields could deflect both the alpha and beta particles while gamma rays remain un-deflected. X-rays and gamma rays are precisely the same thing. The only difference, however, between them is regarding their origin. When produced in special high-voltage equipment, they are called X-rays, but we call them gamma rays when given off by radioactive substances. The corpuscular radiations (electrons, protons, etc.), whether given off by radioactive materials or generated in high-voltage equipment, move at extremely high speeds, often close to the speed of light, 186,000 miles per second.

Therefore, we can justly say that the speeds of these particles are incredibly high. Alpha particles move at a speed of about (roughly) 10,000 miles per second. X-rays and gamma rays travel at the speed of light. Gamma rays are highly penetrating neutrons. Being neutral, they can travel long distances within the living body or inanimate matter. Radiations have different depths of penetration. Radiations that do not penetrate deep into the body, e.g., alpha particles or beta particles, can cause considerable harm if the substance emitting them is in close contact with the skin. If ingested, the radioactive substances are sure to cause grievous injury.

FISSION PRODUCTS

When the nucleus of Uranium-235 fissions, it splits into two parts and produces various atoms. Scientists have identified more than 200 isotopes of elements ranging from Zinc with atomic number 30 to Gadolinium with atomic number 64 among the fission products. They are found in an extensively disturbed state of composition and have mass numbers that are too high compared to their atomic numbers to be stable isotopes. They are radioactive and emit beta particles to increase the charge of their nuclei to approach a state of stability. The half-lives of these isotopes range from one second to many million years. Whenever and anywhere fission takes place, it produces radioactive fission products. These fission products from atomic reactors and nuclear bomb explosions constitute a dreadful radiological threat to human health and life. The long half-life of some of these radioactive substances makes the state of affairs still worse.

CLOUD CHAMBER

Sub-atomic particles are too minute to be seen. But there are several ways the tracks along which they have traveled can be made visible. The footprints which reveal their presence are the ionization of the atoms lying within their path. Ionization can result in the fogging of a photographic plate, and this was the effect that led to the original discovery of radioactivity by Henry Becquerel in 1892.

Another way of rendering the sub-atomic particles visible is to direct them against the luminescent screen, which will give off a flash of visible light whenever a sufficiently energetic particle hits it.

What happens when ionizing radiations pass through matter? We obtain most information about it from an ingenious device known as the 'cloud chamber' or 'Wilson chamber', devised by Charles Thomson Rees Wilson at Cambridge. A cloud chamber is just a glass cylinder closed at one end by a glass window and at the other end by a metal piston to form a chamber.

When we pull down the piston, the air becomes supersaturated, and fog tracks form in the presence of radiations. Ions formed by atomic radiations can act as the foci for precipitating the drops from so-called supersaturated vapors. Under suitable conditions, each ion formed will give rise to a droplet.

ROENTGEN

The roentgen (symbol R) is a unit of measurement for exposure to ionizing radiation (X-ray and gamma rays) and is named after the German physicist Wilhelm Roentgen. To adjust for the different impacts of different forms of radiation on biological matter, 'roentgen equivalent in man' or 'rem' was also in use.

The 'rad' is a unit of absorbed radiation dose. The 'rad' was first proposed in 1918 as "that quantity of X rays which will destroy the (malignant mammalian) cells in question when absorbed."

The definition of roentgen adopted by the international commission on radiological units and measurement states Roentgen (R) as:

"The quantity of X or gamma radiation such that the associated corpuscular emission per 0.001293 gram of dry air produces ions (in the air) carrying one electrostatic unit of quantity of electricity of either sign. The amount of energy is equal to 2.58×10^{-4} coulombs/kg air. The Roentgen is a special unit of exposure."

This definition looks very complicated. However, it is enough for the laymen to know that Roentgen is a unit for measuring radiation just as ampere is for measuring current in electricity.

GABRIEL'S EXTINGUISHING THE ATOMIC HELL SERIES

HOW TO MAKE AN ATOMIC BOMB

Things so very formidable in the beginning will gradually become easier to make. Once thought of as an unimaginably formidable proposition even by highly industrialized countries, the atomic bomb may, in time, become a mere plaything. After all, it is a question simply of a small quantity of Uranium-235 or Plutonium-239. Moreover, some skill is involved in enclosing material in a shell.

The news some time ago that a young student in America had built a homemade atomic bomb did not deserve the surprise that excited the world. Sooner or later, the atomic bomb is going to become a household affair. It is so easy to make.

Just take a lump of Uranium-235 in two equal parts, each of which is less in mass than the critical mass, and see that these parts remain apart. That is, they do not touch each other, for if they hit each other, some stray neutron may surprise you by causing your atomic bomb to explode before you essentially wanted it to go off.

This problem of the critical mass is significant. You have to calculate the critical mass of the fissile material you intend to use in your proposed atomic bomb. The critical mass is a chunk of Uranium's mass just large enough to ensure that it will retain more neutrons than lost.

Suppose a mass is so tiny that a neutron placed well within it has a high probability of reaching the surface (boundary of mass). That neutron may escape to the outside without suffering a collision with the nucleus. Hence, instead of participating in the chain process, most fission neutrons would be lost outside. Hence, it would not sustain the chain process. The continuation of chain reaction needs that, on average, for every neutron lost, either by absorption in the system or escape to outside, at least one new neutron should be added by fission.

A system for which the above condition is just satisfied is called 'critical'. For an over-critical (or super-critical) system, which is the actual requirement of the atomic bomb, the number of neutrons added for every neutron lost is more than one, and the chain process builds up at a tremendous rate. While for a sub-critical system, more neutrons will be lost than added. Hence, it cannot sustain the chain reaction.

After you have learned this problem of critical mass and have placed your Uranium-235 in chunks, each consisting of sub-critical mass in a neutron-free chamber, then arrange for a bit of quantity of Radium-Beryllium for the supply of neutrons. This absence of neutrons from the vicinity inside a neutron-free chamber is crucial since the presence of a neutron may cause an explosion.

You could have it from a druggist. However, keep it closed in a pot of Lead lest a neutron escapes before you indeed want your bomb to go off. Keep your Radium-Beryllium mixture beneath the chunks of Uranium.

Your atomic bomb is now ready, and you can reasonably apply for the membership of the club of atomic powers to attain the unique and much-coveted honor so cheaply attained.

Now, whenever you are disposed to see the fun of your atomic toy, just bring the various chunks of Uranium together, and open the lid of the Radium-Beryllium mixture. Neutrons from the Radium-Beryllium mixture jump up into the Uranium mass. In the twinkling of an eye, the world around you will resound with the deafening thunder of the explosion. There is hardly any need to tell you that some automatic device is necessary to open the lid of the Radium-Beryllium mixture to give you sufficient time to consult your safety. Otherwise, you would be the first victim of your terrible toy.

However, suppose you do not care for such a device for your safety. In that case, none could single you out as a typical fool because all those powers that are today making the atomic bombs are doing closely the same, that is, they are not at all minding their safety and have only the destruction of their enemy in view.

Nevertheless, are they in any way safe from the effects of their atomic bomb? No. If they ponder their method over a bit, they will be surprised by their horror to know about one mechanism. The flaw in the contrivance is to follow precisely the same example of leaving the Radium-Beryllium bottle uncovered beneath Uranium chunks or at least nuclear powers have never thought of the automatic device like the time bomb in their process that may provide them with safety.

They would be horrified at their neglect no sooner than they wake up from their stupor at the first detonation of the atomic bomb. However, will these powers try to understand the logic of this example? Alas, the relentless influence of the doom implied by the three evils has rendered them quite insensible to the dire consequences of what they do. In a state of intoxication, they prepare to make a bonfire of their home, health, house, and all without realizing what they did. Along with their foes, they will blow up their friends, near and dear ones, even their own house, country, land, etc.

FUSION

We have previously explained how the fission process generates atomic energy. We also know that atomic energy is appropriately called nuclear energy. We will now explain how the fusion process generates atomic energy.

In the fission process, the nucleus of an atom is divided into parts. In the fusion process, we fuse the nuclei of several atoms to release the atomic that is the nuclear energy. For example, we fuse four Hydrogen ($1H^1$) nuclei to form a Helium ($2He^4$) nucleus with the resultant nuclear energy release. Fission is carried out in atoms with bulkier nuclei, while fusion is undertaken in atoms with light nuclei. We achieve fission with comparative ease, but the question of fusion is indifferent and problematic. All the positively charged protons are the nuclei of Hydrogen. Incredibly high temperatures are required to fuse them; temperatures of the order of millions of degrees, such as are found in the sun and the stars, wherein the fusion process is believed to be going on to generate such tremendous heat.

The fusion process on earth has been made practicable only by the application of the fission process. The atomic fission process develops the temperatures required for the fusion of the positively charged nuclei. Such temperatures have hitherto been possible only by the detonation of the atomic (fission) bombs. Then we apply these temperatures to the fusile material, and the fusion process can feasibly take place.

However, no controlled fusion chain reaction has been possible, and we cannot apply the fusion process to practical utility. The fusion process is radiation-free, but we cannot achieve it without, at the same time, the application of the fission process in which radiations are naturally inherent. There simply exists no container on earth to contain such an intense fire for practical purposes. Any earthly element would no sooner come in contact with such a fire than it would evaporate and disappear. However, the common point between the fission and fusion processes is that both are concerned with the nucleus (atom's heart). Therefore, both generate nuclear energy.

In contrast, chemical energy never touches the atom's nucleus and cannot be called nuclear energy. While in atomic energy, there are two possible processes. Either the nucleus (heart) of the atom is crushed and divided, as is the case in the fission process, or the nuclei (hearts) of several atoms are fused; they are crushed together to release the nuclear energy/atomic fire. We term more adequately atomic energy as nuclear energy, derived from the atom's nucleus. [1]

HOW TO BUILD A FUSION BOMB

Fusion bomb, the Hydrogen bomb, super bomb, supergiant, thermonuclear bomb are all the various appellations of this pride of the superpowers. Fusion bomb, however, is its proper name. The term 'thermonuclear' also is scientifically most appropriate and depicts, in particular, the method of applying the heat for fusion from a separate source. According to the Quranic characterization of 'Al-Hotama' fire, the term 'thermonuclear' reflects an oracular aspect. We shall discuss this critical aspect in its proper place.

To build the fusion bomb, an initial fission detonator such as Plutonium-239 or Uranium-235, a booster detonator containing Tritium, and a main charge of Deuterium, or another relatively stable thermonuclear explosive such as Lithium combined with Hydrogen in the solid compound, are the main accessories. Just place the fission detonator that is the fission bomb within Tritium and Deuterium, and your fusion bomb that is the Hydrogen bomb is ready. Now, detonate the fission bomb in the usual way by releasing neutrons into the fissile material of the fission bomb that is the Uranium or Plutonium chunks.

Detonating the fission device will develop the required temperatures of millions of degrees to impinge on the fusile material to fuse it and cause the explosion of the fusile material. The fusion bomb takes up the radioactive fission products of the fission bomb. Due to the terrific force of the explosion, the fusion bomb throws these radioactive fission products into the highest regions of the atmosphere to be carried by prevailing wind streams around the earth. It thus constitutes the most severe radiological hazard to the entire world, including the country that had exploded the fusion device.

We cannot use fusion energy for any other purpose than destruction. The destruction caused by a fusion bomb is unlimited. The stockpiles of fusion bombs in the world mean the complete extinction of the entire life on earth. Nevertheless, for this obstacle of the incredibly high temperatures required for causing the fusion of atoms, man would have turned all the world's oceans into energy, leaving this world without water, like a barren desert. Such is the instability of the human mind.

THE EFFECTS OF THE ATOMIC BOMB EXPLOSION

The effects of the atomic bomb explosion are as follows.

(1) **HEAT FLASH (THERMAL RADIATIONS)**

The initial heat radiation called 'Heat-Flash' appears with brilliance even more dazzling than that of the sun within a fraction of a second of detonation. In the nominal atomic bomb case, 'Heat-Flash' lasts for two seconds while the ground temperature below the bursting point rises to 3000°C. About one-third of the total energy of the explosion is emitted as thermal radiation.

(2) **BLAST**

The first effect of a blast wave on a structure is that of a gigantic hammer blow. The shock front of the blast wave reaches the rear end of the structure. Now, the structure is surrounded by the wave entirely, and the effect of blast pressure is to squeeze or crush the structure. About two-thirds of the total energy of the explosion goes into the blast.

(3) **RADIOLOGICAL EFFECTS (NUCLEAR RADIATIONS AS NEUTRONS, BETA, AND GAMMA RAYS)**

When the atomic bomb is detonated, gamma rays and neutrons are emitted in the actual fission process. Gamma and beta rays are also emitted by the fission products of the atomic explosion. These radiations carry about 9 percent of the total energy of the explosion. Because of the intense force and heat of the explosion, the fission products are dispersed into tremendously fine particles, and most of them being volatile are reduced to a gaseous state. These radioactive particles continue to fall on earth, and further, because of the wind and weather, they are carried to the farthest ends of the earth. They all being radioactive could be considered as the worst of the problems of atomic energy.

THE EFFECTS OF THE FUSION BOMB

The effects of the fusion bomb are precisely the same as that of the atomic bomb. The difference, however, is in the quantity and intensity and the extent of the areas affected. A Hydrogen or fusion bomb is a thousand times more potent than the atomic bomb. Twenty megaton Hydrogen bombs have also been built and, at present, adorn the stockpiles of superpowers as the symbol of their superiority.

After having estimated the damage to be done by such bomb to life and property, Austrian theoretical physicist Dr. Hans Thirring said:

"God protect the country over which such a bomb would ever be exploded."

There is not a city in the world that may exist after experiencing the explosion of such a bomb, and indeed the fears of Dr. Thirring were not just baseless. The area covered by the blast destruction of a fusion bomb varies with the cube root of the explosion energy. The same law applies to the duration of any particular phase of the blast wave. Thus, the duration of the positive pressure phase of the blast, which is about 1 second for a tiny atom bomb, is about 10 seconds for a 20-megaton bomb. 'Heat-Flash' of a 20-megaton bomb lasts for 20 seconds as against 2 seconds in the case of the little bomb.

The Hydrogen bomb spreads vast quantities of radioactive fission products locally. It also has another aspect of global radiological fall-out. This fall-out undoubtedly constitutes a severe radiological hazard to humankind. Strangely enough, it includes the country which might have exploded such a bomb in any part of the world. The column is a particular characteristic of the atomic bomb. The column of the 20-megaton bomb rises to the height of about 20 miles. There, the prevailing wind streams carry the radioactive fallout to every part of the earth. This fallout gradually settles on the earth to contaminate water sources, trees, crops, and everything with radioactivity. The hydrogen bomb has no radioactivity of its own, but it spreads from its inseparable associate, the fission device.

HIROSHIMA AND NAGASAKI BOMBS

In Hiroshima, the Uranium-235, a 20-kiloton bomb, killed 66,000 persons and injured 69,000, and in Nagasaki, 39,000 were dead and 25,000 wounded by the Plutonium-239, 20-kiloton bomb. In general, most of the casualties were due to the combined effects of burns and mechanical injuries. However, estimates show about 60 percent of deaths (almost 75% of all casualties) were caused by burning through 'Heat-Flash' and fires. About 20% of deaths were due to physical injuries from falling structures and flying debris (resulting from blast damage). And 20% of deaths were due to other causes, including nuclear radiation (gamma rays). Radiation, too, is fire originally. Out of Hiroshima's 75,000 houses, about 55,000 were burnt entirely, and 7000 were utterly destroyed.

These numbers might have seemed colossal to the people in 1945. However, today they may well be regarded as a mere trifle against the numbers that are to be expected in the event of the 20-megaton war when the supergiants, the pride of superpowers, will take up the field to display their powers. Those numbers no one will care to count or record. None perhaps will be left to do the counting, and in case someone was left, whence will anyone redeem either interest or relish enough to do the counting. The counting itself might perhaps be an impossibility in case interest in counting existed. How could anyone salvage the massive wreck of a world lying completely in ruins?

THE HISTORY OF THE ATOMIC BOMB

Although Newton and Boyle believed that matter was atomic, Chemistry did not systematically adopt the atomic theory until John Dalton (1766-1844) took it up for research. Dalton's modernization of the long-neglected atomic theory marked the end of the previous epoch, which had begun with Copernicus three centuries ago.

Dalton's chief contentions are as follows.

(1) Matter consists of atoms that cannot be created or destroyed. The chemical change consists of the combination of previously apart atoms or the separation of those combined. There is no change in the atoms themselves.

(2) The atoms of a given element are all exactly alike, and they differ practically in weight from those of any other element.

It has been necessary to extend and modify his original hypothesis, but they still play a vital part in chemical theory in a modern dress.

Luigi Galvani discovered flowing electricity in the 18th century. Scientists understood that electricity was composed of uniform-sized pieces. They named these pieces electrons. J. J. Thomson, the English physicist, even succeeded in weighing them. In 1886, Eugen Goldstein, a German physicist, discovered proton, a particle positively charged against the negatively charged electron. In 1895 Roentgen, a German physicist accidentally discovered X-rays.

Pray, mark this word 'accidental'. It is imperative. This accidental discovery initiated a period of unprecedented progress in physical science. The French physicist Becquerel sought a possible connection between phosphorescence and X-rays. He chose Uranium nitrate as the substance for investigation by a mere 'chance' and was led unexpectedly in 1896 to discover radioactivity. Pray mark again the play of 'chance' in the discovery of radioactivity.

This discovery, in turn, soon led to the discovery of Radium by Pierre and Madame Curie. In 1905 Einstein enunciated the theory of special relativity, and as a consequence, it established the equivalence between mass and energy. The outstanding work of Rutherford on radiations (named by him as alpha, beta, and gamma rays) emitted by radioactive bodies eventually led to the concept of the atom as made up of a central core, the nucleus (heart) with electrons revolving around it: 'a solar system in miniature'. Bohr incorporated the quantum hypothesis of Plank and Einstein into Rutherford's atom model and formulated his far-reaching quantum theory of the atom. In 1919 Rutherford, for the first time, achieved the disintegration of an element (Nitrogen) by bombarding it with alpha particles. Mr. Blacket soon provided a cloud chamber photograph of the same process. In 1932 Sir John Douglas Cockcroft and Ernest Thomas Sinton Walton working in Rutherford's laboratories, brought about the first artificial nuclear transmutation by bombarding Lithium with protons accelerated to less than a million volts.

Chadwick, in the same laboratory, discovered the neutron in 1932. Other discoveries followed in rapid succession.

The phenomenon of Uranium fission was discovered by the German physical chemists Hahn and Strassman in 1938. The extraordinary significance of the discovery was soon realized and led to a period of intense activity in the study of atomic nuclei. By 1940 more than a hundred papers had appeared on this subject. But, soon after, the whole subject went underground, and no further reference appeared in open scientific literature till the end of the war.

Although the fundamental discoveries leading to the realization of atomic energy came practically all from Western Europe, the U.S.A. (soon followed by the U.S.S.R.), with its colossal industrial and scientific resources, was the first to harness this fundamental knowledge for practical ends.

On August 2, 1939, Albert Einstein wrote his now-famous letter to Mr. Roosevelt, the then President of America. In that letter, Einstein tried to attain Roosevelt's attention to the possibility of utilizing the phenomenon of Uranium fission for the construction of a mighty (weight for weight) bomb of a new type. That bomb had to be a million times more potent than conventional bombs. Some work of Fermi and Szilard had indicated particular progress in this regard.

Einstein wrote: "A single bomb of this type, carried by boat and exploded in a port, might very well destroy the whole port together with some of surrounding territory".

The U.S.A. government decided to explore the possibility.

The first successful realization of a (slow neutron) fission chain reaction in the Graphite-pile built in a converted squash court of the Stagg Field, University of Chicago, was achieved by Enrico Fermi, an Italian physicist, on December 2, 1942.

The design of a workable atom bomb was entrusted to New Loss Alamos Laboratory (New Mexico), working under the leadership of Oppenheimer. They produced three bombs by the middle of 1945. One bomb made of Plutonium was tested on the ground at the Alamogordo sands on July 16, 1945. The other two were dropped on Hiroshima and Nagasaki on August 6 and 9, 1945, respectively. The first Soviet atomic (fission) explosion took place in August 1949.

After that, the U.S.A. first tested a thermonuclear device (Mike) at the Marshall Islands in the Pacific Ocean. The first Soviet thermonuclear test explosion took place in August 1953. Then, on March 1, 1954, the U.S.A. set off a powerful thermonuclear explosion at Bikini Atoll, the energy of the explosion being equivalent to 15 million tons of

TNT. In November 1955, the Russians had a thermonuclear explosion about as powerful as the U.S.A. test of March 1954.

At present, the stockpiles possessed by any of the world's superpowers are individually enough to destroy this world many times in succession according to the competitive vaunts of various superpowers. Their boast is based on reality, but what is not comprehensible is the subsequent series of the world's destruction.

"Who will execute the second series of destruction after carrying out the first round of destruction?"

Not a single soul will be there to stir, and not a leaf to quiver on this earth for millions of years to come. Such is the despotism of the sense of power.

At last, the emulative spirit of Baconian atomism elevated humankind to the cherished position of the godhead. August 6, and August 9, 1945, respectively, were memorable dates in human history when the ultimate 'fruit' of atomism was displayed in the markets of Hiroshima and Nagasaki, respectively.

Inebriated with dizzying thoughts of power and holding in hands destructive trident, humankind on those two days stood over the sky-high precipitous cliffs of Hiroshima and Nagasaki. Soon humanity realized to their real panic that to stay over the edges of those high cliffs was impossible, and to advance a step further meant a fall into the deep bottomless Jehannah of a blazing hell of atomism. At the same time, the economic and military exigencies exerted relentless pressure from behind.

Hence, the only ray of hope appears in the Scriptural prophecy of the Quran, which sounds like a warning. It teaches a method of escaping the atomic hell that may save the distressed humankind in the last.

~~*~*~*~*

PART-2
THE NUCLEAR CORROBORATION OF THE FIRE OF 'AL-HOTAMA'

The description of the fire of 'Al-Hotama' by the Quran is as follows and is identical to the atomic phenomena.

The prophecy of the Quran is as follows.

"Woe unto every backbiter, defamer, who amasseth wealth (of this world) and arrangeth it (against the future). He thinketh that his wealth will render him immortal. Nay, for verily he will be cast into 'Al-Hotama'. And what could teach thee what 'Al-Hotama' is? It is a fire of

Allah enkindled which leapeth up unto the hearts. It is (a fire) closed in on them in outstretched columns."

(Quran: 104 'Al-Homaza')

However, here we are concerned only with that part of the prophecy which explains the fire of 'Hotama' that is:

"What could teach thee what 'Al-Hotama' is? It is a fire of Allah enkindled, which leaps up unto the hearts. It is (a fire) closed in on them in outstretched columns."

(Quran: 'Al-Homaza' 104: 5-9)

We will explain the previous philosophical part of the prophecy later in a separate chapter.

IT IS 'HOTAMA' (A 'CRUSHER')

That 'it leaps up unto the hearts' and 'it is a fire closed in on them in outstretched columns' are the characteristics of the atomic energy and are the distinctive characteristics of atomic energy that distinguish it from other types of energy, namely, the chemical or the electrical. We have to prove this identity between Al-Hotama's and the atomic fire characteristics to prove our project. In another place, we will show the identity existing between the causes of 'Al-Hotama' punishment and the reasons for the appearance of atomic energy.

SECTION-1
'HOTAMA'
(1) 'HOTAMA' AND 'ATOM'

'Hotama' is the qualitative agent formed from the tri-syllabic root-verb 'Hatama' (Ha-Tam). The word 'Hatama' means to 'break something to pieces'. In the language of science, it would mean 'atomizing'. The term 'Hotama', therefore, means a 'crusher'.

Inquiry into the grammatical conjugation reveals that doubling the 'T' of 'Hatama' and rendering it as 'Ha**tt**ama' gives it the meaning of 'shattering something into pieces'.

The next inflection, 'Tahattama', assumes the intransitive form and means 'to go into pieces'.

The inflection 'Inhatama' has the same meanings, while 'Inhitaam' means 'the process of going into pieces'.

The noun is 'Hitma', which means 'broken pieces', 'fragments', 'smithereens' etc.

The phonetic and the functional resemblance between these 'Hatama' inflections and their scientific counterparts deserve note.

The word 'Hatama' and its derivatives are of a pure Arabic origin and were extant in Arabia long before the revelation of the Quran. The word 'Atom' is of Greek origin. It was inherited by modern scientists and adapted from the original Greek 'Atomos'. The phonetic resemblance between this word 'Atom' and the Arabic word 'Hatam' from which the term 'Hotama' is derived is remarkable and is of genuine interest.

Further, the Arabic phrase 'Hitaam-ud-Duniya' means 'the vanities of the world', and 'Hitaam-us-Safina' means the 'wreckage of the ship'.

The words 'Atom' and 'Hatam' are far more similar in pronunciation than they appear in writing. The letter we have written as 'H' in 'Hatama' is not precisely 'H' and merely bears a resemblance to 'H'. We are obliged to write it as 'H' because its exact equivalent is not found in the English alphabet.

Similarly, the letter we have translated as 'T' in the word 'Hatama' is not the equivalent of the English 'T' but somewhat resembles 'TUA' with soft 'T'.

The word 'Hatam' pronounced by an indigenous Arab is far nearer to 'Atom' in sound than it appears in transliteration. These things may appear mere trifles, but they certainly are of much introductory significance to the theme.

NOTE: [For further comprehensive details regarding 'HOTAMA', please refer to Book-1/volume-1/chapter-3.]

'ATOM' IS A MISNOMER

The word 'Atom' means 'not-cuttable', 'indivisible', and 'indestructible'. Early Greek Atomists applied it in their theory of atomism in this very same sense. Nevertheless, when scientists split the atom into various sub-atomic particles in modern times, it lost its right to its previous designation.

Sir James Jeans has, in this context, alluded to it in his book, 'The Mysterious Universe' as follows.

"Just as the 19th century was drawing to a close", says Sir Jeans, "Sir J. J. Thomson and his followers began to break up the atom, which now proved to be no more uncuttable, and so no more entitled to the name of 'atom' than the molecule to which the name had previously been attached."

The scientists, however, were not unmindful of this fundamental change and called a conference to discuss the point and remove the thoughtful discrepancy. However, strangely enough, after an elaborate discussion, they decided, in the end, to leave the word 'Atom' as it were.

In this respect, a reflection by L. W. H. Hull in his "History and Philosophy of Science" is interesting. Says he:

"By derivation, atom means that which cannot be cut up."

The fastidious philologist may reasonably point out that the phrase 'splitting the atom', now so familiar, involves a contradiction in terms. 'Splitting' a thing that 'cannot be split' is like 'uttering' something 'unutterable'. The word 'atom' indeed has become so familiar by now that the inconsistency seldom occurs to anyone. Still, we are obliged to mention it because of a particular bearing it happens to have on our discussion.

Strangely, scientists did not amend the name of 'Atom' after this radical change, but it assumes stranger still when we see that the matter concerns the most hard-headed and exact of all the subjects of knowledge, namely, science. Indeed, nothing short of hypnotizing effect could stop the scientists from affecting the modification in so glaring an inconsistency.

When scientists found it to be in 'rotation', the earth was no longer called 'stationary', nor was it permitted to be termed 'flat' when they knew it was 'round'. When it was known to have been 'cut', why was the atom allowed to continue as 'Atom', meaning 'not-cuttable'?

A message like, "In compliance with your demand sending you a thousand pieces of the 'unbreakable', can further break the 'unbreakable' if you so desire", may sound as fantastic.

Yet, exactly it is what we mean when we say, "In compliance with your demand sending you a thousand particles of 'Atom', can further break the 'Atoms' into particles if you so desire".

Science, due to its particular hard-headed nature, would not brook an inconsistency so glaring as this.

The same we could say about the scientist. Indeed, an omission like this by scientists and the countenance of the word 'Atom' has something very remarkable in it. Also, it is of particular interest to us in this (our) theme. The phonetic resemblance existing between the word 'Atom' and 'Hatam' has excellent meanings. Apart from other things, this resemblance in recognizing this prophecy of the Quran is immense. It essentially plays the legendary role of 'Open Sesame' to the gate of the mystery.

Without laying oneself open to the charge of thaumaturgy, miracle mongering, or any superstition, we could rightly believe that the very same power which had placed the prophecy about the atomic bomb in the Scripture had decreed that the word 'Atom' remained as it were. Moreover, the same power hypnotized scientists despite all their proverbial hard-headedness and the uncompromising rigidity of science dictates. Anyone could not justly label this belief unreasonable or senseless, even if it is a mere conjecture.

Why would Providence show such particular solicitude to retain the word 'Atom' as 'Atom'? The answer to such a question could be that obviously, the phonetic resemblance between words 'Atom' and 'Hatam' did serve as the formula 'Open Sesame' to point to the gate of the mystery of the prophecy. This Providential scheme is considered one of the links to the unbroken chain of miracles establishing this prophecy of the Quran. Such resemblance between the words 'Atom' and 'Hatam' strikes in mind like a flash and leads to revealing the mystery of prophecy. We may take it well as the prophetic counterpart of the 'accidental' discoveries of X-rays and radioactivity attained in nuclear science. These discoveries, too, had served as the formula of 'Open Sesame' to the mysterious gate of atomic energy and the atomic bomb.

Despite the radical change, the scientists left the word 'Atom' without changing its name. This act was in exact contradiction to the basic tenets of science and the recognized practice of the community of scientists. In reality, it may not be as pedantic as it at first appears to those not well conversant with the habit of the scientific mind. Still, instead, it is a veritable indication of a remarkable inconsistency on the scientist's part verifiable by a score of examples in the history of the advancement of science.

We will, however, content ourselves with but one such example, which in itself is highly representative of the class and shows in the best possible manner the truth of our statement. We mean the example that could be quoted from the preface of the book 'Nuclear Theory' by Robert G. Sachs. The example will undoubtedly depict the extreme sense of attentiveness and the degree of care shown by the scientist regarding the correctness in terminology matters.

So writes Mr. Sachs as follows.

"Remarks concerning the selection of the Isotopic spin notation seem to be called for because the subject is the center of some controversy. There are many objections to the term 'Isotopic Spin'. Some are based on the fact that 'Isotopic' is a misleading word; others are based on the fact that the term 'Spin' is misleading. At about the time the author had completed Part-II, a move to replace 'Isotopic' by 'Isobaric' was initiated at the 1952 conference on Nuclear Physics at the University of Pittsburgh. This change was so widely accepted that the new term is used in some recent review articles. However, we found that the change did not meet the most serious objection to the terminology; namely, that very awkward phrasing was sometimes necessary. Such a phrase as SPIN SINGLET, ISOTOPIC SPIN TRIPLET, D-State is both awkward and confusing. The author, therefore, leaped at a suggestion of Fermi that either 'ISOTOPIC', or "ISOBARIC", should be abbreviated to 'I'. Hence the terms 'I-Spin', 'I-Singlet', and so on. Although this solution to the problem has disadvantages (such as the tendency to use 'I' instead of 'T' for the associated quantum number), it seemed reasonable when looked upon as an abbreviation. The reader can read the term 'I' as 'Isotopic' or 'Isobaric' according to his taste."

The above-quoted example best serves our particular purpose. It indicates the sensitivity of scientists to the appropriateness of terms and how essential it is for the scientist to be sure of the appropriateness of the terms. The proper representation and, more essentially, understanding the subject are fundamentally essential to advancing the subject itself.

Another point from the above example is that the inconvenience caused by the improper term serves as a necessary stimulus for correcting and appropriately modifying the term. However, we see that the erroneous term 'Atom' has caused no inconvenience to scientists or the public. That is why the scientist has felt little cause for the concern over the inconsistency of the term 'Atom'.

We can see this fact as yet another influencing factor of the Providential scheme in retaining the term 'Atom', as it were. Any inconvenience experienced by scientists due to the impropriety of the term 'Atom' would have obliged them to affect change and thus deprive the world of such a revealing resemblance between the words 'Atom' and 'Hatam'.

(2) 'HOTAMA': A 'CRUSHER'
(a) A 'CRUSHER'

'Hotama' literally means 'the crusher'. The root verb 'Hatama' from which the term 'Hotama' has been derived means 'to break something to pieces, particles, smithereens' etc. and 'to grind something to powder', as has already been explained in previous pages. Further, we can detect a very suggestive resonance between the scientific term 'atomization' and the translated and anglicized, minor version of the word 'Hatama', namely, 'Hatamization'.

The resemblance shows the phonetic and phenomenal, and functional identity between the two distinctly. It is clear from its name that 'Hotama' is a crusher. The atomic fire and its explosive manifestation, the atomic bomb can fundamentally possess this quality of crushing. We even generate atomic energy by crushing the atoms. The atomic bomb crushes matter into powder. It pulverizes buildings into dust and reduces the dust into a gaseous state. Similarly, atomic radiations crush atoms, molecules, and cells.

(b) 'HOTAMA' THE 'NUCLEAR CRUSHER'

The Quran has said, "Hotama is a fire which leaps up over the hearts." It is well-known that all the reactions of the atomic phenomena from energy generation to its last reactions within the body's cells occur in the nuclei of the atoms and the cells. The nuclear reaction of the atomic phenomena as against the chemical phenomena or any phenomena is its distinctively characteristic feature, distinguishing it from every other type of phenomenon known to man. Anyone acquainted with this distinction will not fail to recognize the marvel of the Quran in this particular characterization of the fire of 'Al-Hotama'.

An apparent resemblance exists between the crushing affected by the atomic phenomena and other ordinary means of crushing such as impact crushers, chemical fire, etc. Yet, there is a marked difference between the crushing done by the atomic phenomena and other means of crushing, either by impact or chemical fire, acids, etc.

It is a well-known fact that atomic action disintegrates the atomic nuclei. It thus crushes the basic sub-atomic structure of the atom, the 'basic building block of the universe', whereas every other means of crushing leaves the atomic nuclei untouched and intact. It shows that the atomic phenomenon is the nuclear crusher (the crusher of hearts) that is the absolute crusher of the fundamental matter. Any substance crushed by ordinary means or consumed by ordinary chemical fire could be brought back to its original form by the synthesis process because the nuclear structure of the atoms thereof is fundamentally intact. Still, it is pretty impossible to re-arrange the nuclear structure of the atoms disintegrated by the atomic energy. It is pretty impossible at present, and there is no apparent probability in the future. It is simply impossible to deny the Quran its miracle, the miracle of describing such mysterious reactions taking place within a matter in an age utterly ignorant of science. This fact alone is enough to open the eyes of an eminent scientist.

The Quran pronounces the fire of 'Al-Hotama' as a crusher. Still, it should further qualify it with the feature of nuclear crushing and that, in a pre-atomic age, it is a revelation that deserves no appellation less than a miracle. It will at the same time be a gross injustice to the modern scientist to deny him the genuine merit of admirable precision and appropriateness in discerning and naming the nucleus. The attribute equally applies to the field of modern science terminology that affords an unmistakable proof of his genius and ability. The correspondence between the word nucleus and the object it represents serves as an example of exactitude and precision. Indeed, the whole terminology of modern science merges at a point of conformity between the term and the object it represents where vision and the fact appear fused.

(c) 'HOTAMA' A 'THERMONUCLEAR CRUSHER'

This term of 'thermonuclear' has enshrined a unique miracle of the Quranic description of 'Al-Hotama' in its bosom. It has furnished yet another marvel of the keen-sightedness of the modern scientist. If the coinage of a term like 'thermonuclear' is a feat on the scientist's part, it is a miracle of the Quran to anticipate this term by fourteen centuries. This term 'thermonuclear' happens to be the most comprehensively representative definition and most characteristically distinct description of the particular process applied in the fusion of the fusile material of the fusion bomb. The scientist applies this term to supplying heat for the fusion of atoms of fusile material (of the fusion bomb) from an outside source.

Thus, the term depicts a peculiar characteristic of the fusion bomb. Scientist has called the 'fusion bomb' the 'thermonuclear bomb' because the fusion therein is caused by the heat of the fission device (atomic bomb) impinging on the surrounding fusile material of the fusion bomb. It is the incredible heat produced by the fission device that causes the fusile material to fuse. Otherwise, the fusile material would not fuse, for the temperatures of such order (millions of ^{0}C) as could only be developed by the fission bombs could feasibly bring about the necessary fusion. Essentially, the fusion or the Hydrogen bomb is no more than a wrapping of Hydrogen material around the fission bomb.

After the reader has understood the thermonuclear process, let us see what this term means philosophically. The word 'thermo' has been combined with the word 'nuclear'. The word 'thermo' is derived from the Greek word, which means 'heat'. 'Nuclear' is the adjective of the nucleus (the central core), the 'heart' of the thing, etc. The term 'thermonuclear' thus means a process that indicates the relation of heat (fire) with the nucleus (the heart).

While explaining the process to a layman, a scientist would say, "It is something concerned with heat which impinges on the nuclei", while the Quran has said, "Hotama is a fire which leaps up over the hearts". Just marvel at this identity. The term 'thermonuclear' that is the scientist's expression and the Quranic expression, 'the fire climbing the heart', could well be interpreted as the same thing. No doubt, it is a marvel of anticipation on the part of the Quran and ingenuity on the scientist's part. It proves that 'Al-Hotama' is a 'thermonuclear crusher'. Imagination just reels at such disclosed wonders.

(d) ATOMIC ENERGY IS GENERATED BY 'CRUSHING' THE BINDING OF ATOM

It is surprising to observe how the Quran should discern and describe such sub-microscopically subtle and mysteriously clandestine nuclear phenomena in an age of no science. It is illuminated indeed in a manner so superhumanly comprehensive that every point would throw the mind of the knowing scientist into convulsions and extract praise from the most fastidious among the critics. The merit of the modern scientist too, to whose keen insight, persevering genius, and un-intermittent toil, goes the credit of discovering such deep mysteries of nature as have appeared to furnish unmistakable proofs of the truth of the sacred word of the prophecy, deserves consideration. The scientist has a keen discernment, remarkable sensitivity, and fantastic knowledge of the subject. Yet how unfortunate, if he should fail to benefit by the superior and supernatural insight, and infallible guidance of the Scripture which has prophesied the appearance of the atomic bomb, and ignore its advice due merely to the overwhelming pressure of the prevailing circumstances.

The atomic energy, in truth, is the binding energy of an atom. For, it is the binding of the atom that breaks to release the atomic energy. Rather more appropriately, it is the nuclear binding of the atom that breaks to release energy. It is a fact well-established and a feature that distinguishes nuclear energy from chemical energy. Because of this fundamental and distinctive nature of the atomic phenomena, we can trace the name of 'Hotama' (the nuclear crusher) to its origin. Every other type of energy is produced either as a result of friction or oxidation, while we produce atomic energy by breaking the nuclear bond of the atoms. This feature is the fundamental characteristic of nuclear energy. Furthermore, it distinguishes atomic energy from every other kind of energy since, in the generation of any other kind of energy, the bond of the atom itself remains untouched.

The atomic energy is only the binding energy of the atom. The nuclear binding of the atom breaks and the binding energy is thereby released. The nuclear binding of the atom is broken both in the fission and fusion processes. Except for Hydrogen, all atoms have more than one proton. The proton is a positively charged nucleon. All protons, therefore, having similar charges repel each other, for like charges always repel. The positively charged protons in an atomic nucleus must be repelling each other with tremendous force because they are closely packed up in the nucleus. Yet, they are all retained there within a minimal space. Therefore, there must be some force needed to keep them pressed together. This force, which we know no more than that it is some kind of force, breaks. When it breaks, energy is released, and hence it is called the binding energy or, more appropriately, the nuclear binding energy. 'Hotama' is the breaker that is the crusher of this binding energy.

(e) NUCLEAR FISSION AND FUSION ARE THE 'CRUSHING' PROCESSES

Fission and fusion are the two processes by which we generate the atomic that is nuclear energy. In both these processes, we crush the nuclei of the atoms to liberate energy.

For example, the neutron attacks the nucleus of a Uranium-235 atom and knocks out two neutrons from it. The atom divides into two daughter nuclei, i.e., Krypton and Barium. Similarly, when we direct a stream of protons against a film of the alkali metal Lithium, alpha particles emerge, traveling at a very high velocity. For each proton that hits a Lithium nucleus, two alpha particles appear. An alpha particle is the Helium nucleus without electrons. Proton is the Hydrogen nucleus. Proton and Lithium atoms together are changed into 2 Helium nuclei. The two Helium nuclei fly apart with great speed. Each collision releases two alpha particles with a combined energy of 27.2 millionths of an Erg for each Lithium atom. Splitting the Uranium-235 nucleus into two pieces severely crushes the Uranium atom. As a result, among the fission products, scientists have identified more than 200 isotopes of elements ranging from Zinc with atomic number 30 to Gadolinium with atomic number 64. They are found in an extensively disturbed state of composition and have mass numbers that are too high compared to their atomic numbers to be stable isotopes.

Similarly, in generating atomic energy through the fusion process, the nuclei of atoms are fused; we crush their nuclei together to liberate energy. For example, we crush four Hydrogen ($1H^1$) nuclei together to form a Helium ($2He^4$) nucleus. Again, remember that this crushing of the nuclei of atoms in generating atomic energy is unique and applies to the generation of no other kind of energy except atomic energy. We have explained the fission and the fusion processes of generating the atomic energy to prove the point that the characteristic of crushing remains as fundamental in every process of generating atomic energy; a fact that testifies the justification of naming this particular fire as 'Hotama', that is the 'crusher'.

(f) ATOMIC RADIATION IS A 'FIRE' AND IT IS A 'CRUSHING' TYPE OF 'FIRE' BY NATURE

Anyone acquainted with the fundamental nature of energy in general and knowing the reactions of the atomic radiations will find no difficulty in realizing the truth of the words of the prophecy that 'Hotama' is a crushing fire. Atomic radiations, alpha, beta, gamma rays, and neutrons, are generally referred to as ionizing radiations. They are inherent in the very nature of atomic energy and atomic bombs and maintain all the most fundamental characteristics of the atomic phenomena. They are one and all characteristically a fire and fundamentally a crushing fire of atomic nature. They crush the basic molecular structure and the nuclear structure of the materials' atoms through which they pass. Beta and gamma rays knock out electrons from the atoms of the molecules, changing them into ions and free radicals, while alpha particles, neutrons, and protons going into a headlong collision with the atoms eject nucleons from their nuclei. The ionizing radiations play atomic havoc within the living body without discriminating between scientists and non-scientists, rich or poor.

The ionizing radiations activate the water content, which is more than 75 percent of the body of a mammal. They crush the biological cells by breaking the chromosomes of the cell nuclei, and they change the whole body into a sackful of curdled blood and minced meat.

Again, it is strange to observe that although the radiation energy (fire) brings about the crushing, there is no sign of apparent burning within the body in the sense of burning, as we generally understand by the word 'burning'. On the other hand, a body burnt by ordinary fire, even if it is reduced to ashes, shows the signs of burning and that its atoms, even if dispersed, have their nuclei intact. While we may find the atoms of the body of a person killed by radiations to have their atomic structure disintegrated without any apparent sign of burning.

(g) **THE INITIAL HEAT RADIATION AND THE BLAST OF THE ATOMIC BOMB ARE BOTH 'CRUSHERS'**

The atomic bomb explosion's initial heat radiation generally referred to as 'Heat-Flash', appears simultaneously with the atomic bomb's detonation. It crushes the hearts of unfortunate people who happen to be near the blast point and sets the area within the effective zone on fire due to the intensity of its heat. The blast of the atomic bomb is even more noticeably crushing, and it hardly needs any explanation except that the effect of the blast wave of the explosion of the atomic bomb on the structure is that of a gigantic hammer blow. The shock front of the blast wave reaches the rear end of the structure.

Now, the structure is surrounded by the wave entirely, and the effect of blast pressure is to squeeze or crush the structure. The atomic explosion crushes the most robust cities to dust. A 20-megaton bomb, for example, would destroy all ordinary buildings within a radius of 80 miles. Buildings within this area would be fractionalized, pulverized, or vaporized. The zone of severe crushing would cover more than 200 square miles, and that of partial crushing extends to 10000 square miles. A single bomb of this kind would virtually mean the wholesale destruction even of the largest city. For instance, a single 20-megaton bomb dropped on New York would cause material damage to the order of 20,000 million dollars and result in about 7.5 million casualties.

The radiological fallout of such a bomb would lay waste areas equal to the most significant states. How befitting would then seem the name of 'Al-Hotama' to represent such a monstrous fire? It is not without reason that Dr. Hans Thirring has said, "God protect the country over which such a bomb would ever be exploded."

Based on rather detailed guess-estimates, H. Hart concluded in 1954 that the total area of vital strategic targets of the U.S.A. was somewhat less than 2000 square miles. It included strategic bombing bases, population, business, industrial centers, coal and oil sources, important transportation centers, etc. Destruction of this vital area would lead to complete national disruption and paralysis. Speaking of the Soviet stockpiles of nuclear weapons, Hart then estimated that it was large enough to inflict severe damage on an area of about 10,000 square miles. Moreover, by 1957 its destruction capacity was likely to be 70,000 square miles, more than thirty times the total area of the U.S.A. vital targets. These estimates did not include the damage done by radiations, which might exceed the damage done by the fire and blast.

Whatever the case, these estimates of Hart might seem mere trifles against the 1977 destruction capacity of the atomic stockpiles of the world's superpowers. Nowadays, the considered damage of existing stockpiles of the world's atomic powers is not discussed in terms of square miles but instead is declared in terms of the number of times this world could be destroyed. Suppose one atomic power, for example, would declare that its stockpiles were enough to destroy this world thirteen times. In that case, some other atomic power might be ready to declare that its atomic stockpiles could simply destroy this world thirty times.

We are not talking mere fancies when we say such things. Nay, but these are indisputable facts endorsed by the topmost atomists of the world. Anyone who will read their reports about the destruction capacities of the atomic bombs and the Hydrogen bombs will see slight exaggeration in our statements. Instead, we find our power of expression unequal to the task that describes the probable havocs exactly. They say the Hydrogen bomb is eternal destruction; we could equally say that it is crushing infinite.

(h) 'HOTAMA' AND ATOMIC HELL ARE 'CRUSHING' GORMANDIZERS

It is interesting to observe that the Arabs nicknamed renowned gormandizer as 'Hotama' before the revelation of the Quran. Atomic hell that is this replica of the 'Hotama' is a gormandizer of exceptional voracity. The largest cities could be but a morsel in the colossal mouth of the atomic bomb, while this entire world could be a dainty feast for one of its stockpiles.

Nor is the atomic energy for peace to be considered far behind in this respect. All this life on earth could eventually be inhaled in secret whiffs by the atomic energy for peace. Yet, although the leading atomists have declared the Hydrogen bomb as the 'destruction unlimited' and a means of complete annihilation of life on earth, the destructive propensities of the atomic energy for peace they have to declare to the world. Their failure in this respect now may leave no more margin, and the circumstances may deem their later warnings untimely.

(i) THE TERMINOLOGY OF NUCLEAR SCIENCE HIGHLY CHARACTERISTIC OF THE QUALITY OF 'CRUSHING'

Throughout, so amazingly appropriate has been the coinage of the terms in the subject of nuclear science. Such exact correspondence exists between the expression and the object. Indeed so precisely descriptive of the crushing quality of atomic phenomena have these terms been that the human mind fills with wonder at the unique ability of the atomist.

No doubt, anyone could seldom expect greater clarity of vision and ability from a human mind. Indeed, the atomist has depicted the crushing characteristics of the atomic phenomena very simply and clearly. Every standard work on the subject of nuclear science is found replete with expressions such as 'bombardment of atoms by sub-atomic particles', 'the particles crashing into the heavy metal targets', 'smashing the atoms', 'hitting the targets', 'breaking energy bonds', etc. These terms and terminologies are all unmistakably reminiscent of the characteristics of crushing.

When the Germans named the continuous spectrum of X-rays 'Bremsstrahlung', the 'braking radiation', the atomists regarded the term as highly descriptive. Indeed, the whole field of nuclear science is dominated by the sense of 'breaking' and 'crushing'. A sense of crushing speeds, crushing impacts, crushing reactions pervades the entire field of nuclear science.

One can observe the same a step further in the subject of Radiobiology: wherein terms like 'the radiation theory of hitting the target', 'breaking of chromosomes', 'electrons being knocked out from atoms', 'headlong collisions of neutrons and protons with nucleons', etc., are usually met with at every step.

Ernest Rutherford conducted his famous experiment of bombarding a gold foil with alpha particles from Radium. As a result, he discovered the nucleus of the atom. During this experiment, he observed that some alpha particles deflected through huge angles; a few even returned to the side of the gold foil from which they came. The astonishment of Rutherford at this was remarkable. Indeed, so great was his astonishment that in his comments, he recorded as is given in the following.

"It was the most incredible event that ever happened to me in my life. It was almost as incredible as if you fired a 15-inch shell at a piece of tissue paper, and it came back and hit you."

Now, mark the reason for the astonishment of this prominent atomist and see that it is no other than the unusual and unexpected, and un-proportional display of the crushing feature of the subatomic particles in the nuclear reaction. Then mark also, how exactly the cause of Rutherford's astonishment corroborates the term 'Al-Hotama' regarding the aspect of crushing.

We may find justification in assuming that when this great genius, Rutherford, sat engrossed in astonishment at the unusual experience, what if someone had recited the Quranic description of the fire of 'Al-Hotama', the crusher? The surprise of Rutherford would have outstripped his astonishment on the unusual display of the alpha particles. The description of 'Al-Hotama' by an ancient Scripture would have seemed to him an even more incredible event of his life.

(j) ATOMIC PHENOMENON IS A BASIC 'CRUSHER'

We have known that the atomic phenomena (fire) crush both: the 'basic building block of the universe' (the atom), as well as the 'basic unit of life' (the cell). We have also known the atomic phenomena in their capacity as nuclear and thermonuclear crushers. Moreover, we may well fear that it might eventually be in the destiny of this tempting gorgon to crush the whole creation of Allah on earth.

SECTION-2
THE CHARACTERIZATION OF THE FIRE OF 'AL-HOTAMA' BY THE QURAN AND THE CORROBORATION THEREOF BY NUCLEAR SCIENCE

No doubt, the first characteristic of the 'Al-Hotama' fire is that it is a crusher. Because we have already dealt with this point at greater length in the previous section, we shall continue to the rest of the 'Al-Hotama' characteristics.

(1) "HOTAMA IS A 'FIRE'." (Quran)

The manifestation of atomic phenomena that is the atomic energy and the atomic bomb is nothing but fire. Atomic energy is fire. The atomic bomb explosion is nothing but fire. Hence, the entire atomic phenomenon is characteristically a fire. The three constituents of the atomic bomb explosion are 'initial heat radiation', 'ionizing radiations', and the 'blast'. The first and the second are both energy and heat and are, therefore, the heat that is fire while the blast is merely a symptom of the explosive force and expansion and is shock wave which essentially being energy is also fire.

There are other colossal and widespread fires started within the effective zones of the atomic bomb explosion. But, such fires are ordinary chemical fires and are started only due to the intense heat spread in the atmosphere by the initial heat radiation of the explosion. Though they may consume entire cities, we cannot yet take such fires as part of the phenomenon of the atomic bomb explosion since they are not atomic in character. It is the fire that takes a tremendous toll on life in the event of the atomic bomb explosion.

In Hiroshima, the Uranium-235, a 20-kiloton bomb, killed 66,000 persons and injured 69,000, and in Nagasaki, 39,000 were dead and 25,000 wounded by the Plutonium-239, 20-kiloton bomb. In general, most of the casualties were due to the combined effects of burns and mechanical injuries. However, estimates show about 60 percent of deaths (almost 75% of all casualties) were caused by burning through 'Heat-Flash' and fires. About 20% of deaths were due to physical injuries from falling structures and flying debris (resulting from blast damage). And 20% of deaths were due to other causes, including nuclear radiation (gamma rays). Radiation, too, is fire originally. Out of Hiroshima's 75,000 houses, about 55,000 were burnt entirely, and 7000 were utterly destroyed.

(2) "HOTAMA IS 'FIRE OF ALLAH'." (Quran)

While everything belongs to Allah, how did Allah mainly link this fire of 'Al-Hotama' to His particular name? How is the fire of 'Al-Hotama' the fire of Allah? The atomic fire is to be taken as the fire of Allah because it has appeared on earth as retribution and punishment for certain evils. It is the retaliation of Nemesis, and it is the manifestation of the wrath of Allah, and it can be employed to no real advantage eventually. The atomic bomb is indisputably destructive, while the doubt about the destructive aspect of atomic energy, even for peaceful purposes, will be cleared one day. The world will be down to its neck in misery due to the pernicious effects of atomic radiation. It will not be able to get out of the fiery swamp. By the time they know that nuclear energy's initial advantages were baiting to entice them into the atomic hell, it will be too late. No amount of repentance will be of any avail, and their cries and wails will remain unheard forever. The indisputable fact is that the disadvantages of atomic energy for peace will un-proportionally outweigh its initial advantages.

Moreover, who can think that threat of atomic war will not remain there as long as there existed atomic energy in any form in this world? The atomic energy for war and peace is but the same thing. Then, the atomic energy features are unusually distinct from all earthly energies that justify linking this kind of fire to the Creator's name. It is a kind of fire that reaches the 'heart' of the basic structure of the 'basic building block of the universe', namely, the atom. The temperatures developed by this fire are solar and stellar and are not at all terrestrial. Celestial temperatures of millions of degrees would reduce everything on earth to a gaseous state and disperse in space. There simply exists no container on earth to contain such fires.

Again, the magnitude of its destruction is without a parallel on earth. Its destruction capacity is yet another marvel. Barely a couple of pounds of Uranium-235 liberate energy equivalent to 20 thousand tons of TNT. A thousand kilograms of Uranium-235 liberates energy equivalent to 20 million tons of TNT. This energy is of the order of large-scale natural phenomena such as hurricanes and earthquakes and resembling the cataclysms, supernaturally raised against some of the froward tribes in the past, e.g., the people of Sodom, Gomorrah, Aad, and Thamud, etc. However, what were those cataclysms against worldwide atomic warfare or the universal epidemic of atomic energy for peace at a later stage in the world. The explosive energy released by a single 15 megaton thermonuclear bomb far exceeds all the explosive energy released during the whole history of humankind. Then imagine a thousand 20 megaton bombs detonated over the earth.

EQUIVALENCE BETWEEN 'WEALTH' AND 'FIRE'

Einstein established the equivalence between Mass and Energy that is between matter and fire. His world-famous equation in this respect is $E=MC^2$. But the way mass can be converted into energy by physical processes; wealth converts into fire caused by the heat of its excessive love at the expense of the love of its giver, the Creator. The Quran has treated the problem of this equivalence of wealth and fire in the clearest of terms.

GABRIEL'S EXTINGUISHING THE ATOMIC HELL SERIES

Read the following.

(a) "They who hoard up gold and silver and spend it not in the way of Allah, unto them give tidings (O Muhammad) of a painful doom. On the day when it will (all) be heated in the fire of hell, and their foreheads and their flanks and their backs will be branded therewith (and it will be said unto them): Here is that which ye hoarded for yourselves. Now taste of what ye used to hoard."

(Quran 9:34-35)

(b) "Lo! Those who devour the wealth of orphans wrongfully, they do but swallow fire into their bellies, and they will be exposed to the burning flame."

(Quran 4:10)

Similarly, the combined effects of the three evils, namely, 'slander', excessive and exclusive engrossment in the pursuit of 'wealth accumulation' as the sole object of life, and a 'belief in immortalizing powers of wealth' convert wealth into a fire. However, wealth is converted not to ordinary chemical fire, rather atomic that is nuclear fire.

The differentiation between the two types of fire must be regarded as vital since it will help understand the difference between the ordinary hellfire and the 'Al-Hotama' fire. The atomic fire appears as a result of a particular process. It proceeds to consume the owner and his wealth both as part of the scientific process and the resultant logical sequence.

Nations initially do spend a considerable portion of their wealth developing atomic energy and building the atomic bomb. The atomic energy and the atomic bomb itself devour the remaining portion of the wealth. Time, the most outstanding judge, will undoubtedly prove that Providence did not mean atomic energy's appearance to be a means of utility and prosperity but rather a means of exacting the retribution. Decidedly it is a manifestation of the wrath of Allah enkindled against a transgressing race engrossed in the particularly relevant set of evils liable to enkindle the atomic fire. Despite the under-estimation of the relevant evils by those involved, it is a fire certainly enkindled due to a scientific and logical process that could scientifically be calculated based on the relevant factors and reduced to equations.

The existing equation of Einstein, $E=MC^2$, could well be further augmented by others such as the following.

(a) **$C = HNC^2$**

Where:

C=**C**hemical fire   H=**H**oarding the wealth

N=**N**ot spending wealth in the way of Allah
C=As usual is the speed of the light

(b) $\underline{A = SWBC^2}$

Where:

A=**A**tomic fire   S=**S**lander   W=**W**ealth-accumulation
B=**B**elief in the immortalizing power of wealth
C=As usual is the speed of light

Humankind can develop a reliable science on these lines through intensive scientific-philosophical research and calculate the quantities in light of the relevant factors. Thus, it could find the equivalent in the fire of a certain quantity of hoarded gold in a chemical and atomic fire in agreement with the existing factors.

(3) "HOTAMA IS A 'FIRE WHICH LEAPS UP OVER THE HEARTS'." (Quran)

(a) AN INTERESTING CHARACTERISTIC OF THIS 'FIRE'

It is indeed an exciting characteristic of fire of 'Hotama' and quaintest-ever quality to be attributed to any fire. Burning a body, a heart, or anything is the quality characteristically attributed to fire, but this quality of rising above the 'hearts' is something quite strange. Some interpreters of the Quran have said in this respect that the fire of 'Al-Hotama' is a fire endued with sagacity as it can peep into the hearts and discern the heart deserving of punishment. No doubt it cannot be the intensity of the fire. Apart from the quality of intensity, this 'leaping up over the hearts' is another exceptional quality.

The novel and distinctive features of atomic energy are nuclear bombs and nuclear radiation. These have been revealed to distinguish atomic energy from every other kind of energy on the atomic basis, the nuclear characteristics and nuclear reactions of the atomic energy, the nuclear bomb, and the nuclear radiations. To wit, the atomic fire is a fire from the initial generation of the atomic energy to the final reactions of the atomic radiations, basically and characteristically of nuclear origin, nuclear characteristic, and nuclear reaction.

Moreover, what is a 'nucleus'? It is but 'heart'. What is 'nuclear'? It is but something related to the 'heart'. Thus, the whole affair of atomic energy from the beginning to the end is the affair of the 'heart'. The Quran has observed this nuclear feature and has described it with astonishing exactitude and has described it in words, "It is a fire which leaps up over the hearts." That is, it leaps up over the 'nuclei', meaning it is nuclear fire.

The subject prophecy of the Quran is a prophetic declaration of so unbelievably mysterious phenomena in an age of no science and without a laboratory or a microscope and any scientific data accumulated by the previous generations. It is the revelation of a category that even the scientists would have been at a loss to understand or believe until they had approached a particular stage in the field of nuclear science. Now, there appears not the slightest reason to doubt that this discovery of the Quran will appear fantastic in the sight of every knowing scientist. What then will you call it if not a miracle?

The atom of Democritus meant no more than the smallest particle of matter which could not further be divided. Democritus and, indeed, even the early modernists, the pioneers of modern science, were entirely ignorant of the sub-atomic particles of the atom and its nucleus. Is it not strange then to see that the description of the atomic phenomena by the Quran should be from the nuclear point of view? A fire rising unto the hearts, described by the Quran, would in the modern atomic description imply, "the impinging of the atomic energy itself or its radiations on the nuclei (hearts) of the atoms, and the nuclei of the cell."

The atoms' 'hearts' (nuclei) are impinged upon by the atomic particles (atomic fires) during atomic energy generation. The 'hearts' (nuclei) of the cells are intruded upon by the atomic radiations during the latter's reactions. The 'Heat-Flash' of the atomic bomb explosion kills its victims by rising unto their 'hearts'. We can see the fire of atomism to rise unto and occupy the 'hearts' of humankind psychologically. From the beginning to the end, the whole theme of atomic energy revolves upon one word, 'nucleus' and its adjective, the 'nuclear', that is of the 'heart'. Yet, the approach of the Quran in this respect is unique enough to startle the most outstanding scientist despite his knowledge of the subject.

(b) **THE NUCLEAR DIFFERENTIATION: A NECESSITY**

The Quran has called this particular fire 'Al-Hotama', which precisely means a 'crusher'. This quality, howsoever correct in this case, is not yet comprehensive enough to show the aimed at complete description and distinction of fire of 'Al-Hotama' because the sheer quality of crushing could be attributed to any kind of a crusher, igneous or otherwise, chemical, or electrical. Any kind of fire can be seen to reduce the consumed object to ashes and could be said to have crushed it.

However, the chemical fire leaves the nuclei of the atoms of the consumed substance intact and undisturbed. In contrast, the atomic or nuclear fire, that is, 'Al-Hotama', does disintegrate the nuclei of the atoms of the substance consumed by it. It was, therefore, further necessary to affect this particular differentiation to distinguish the atomic fire from other ordinary kinds of fire. This mention of the nuclear aspect of the atomic fire has shown complete differentiation between the atomic fire and other kinds of fire.

Indeed, the chemical fire too could have been capable of disintegrating the nuclei of the atoms of the substance consumed by it, provided it could have developed temperatures of the order of millions of degrees. Such temperatures are possibly produced by the atomic fission process, for example, the heat generated by the nuclear fission bomb employed in the fusion of the fusile material of the fusion bomb.

However, neither development of such temperatures by standard chemical processes has been possible, nor is there any possibility of ever achieving success in this respect because every material substance on earth melts and evaporates in the presence of such temperatures. Thus, the distinction of nuclear energy remains there.

Therefore, the real distinction of the fire of 'Al-Hotama' obviously lay in its nuclear characteristics. Hence, the Quran has necessarily characterized it as a 'fire that leaps up over the hearts'; that is, it 'leaps up over the nuclei' of the atoms. The Arab Lexicographers of modern times have translated a 'nucleus' as 'Qalb', accurately a 'heart'.

The English word 'heart' represents the physiological muscle that pumps blood in the body and signifies a source of feelings, emotions, desires, etc. The word 'heart' has a more comprehensive figurative application. For example, when we continuously strike a boulder with a hammer till the boulder breaks, it is said that we have broken the 'heart' of the boulder.

The Quran says:

"Naarullah-Il-Muqadah. Allati Tattalio Alal **Afedha** (أَفْئِدَة)."

The Quran has used the word **'Afedha'** (أَفْئِدَة), which is the synonym of the word 'Qalb' (قلب) in Arabic and 'heart' in English and has broader meanings just as the English word 'heart' has various meanings.

The word 'Afedha' (أَفْئِدَة) is derived from 'Fouad', 'Fuaad', or 'Fawad' (فَؤَاد). 'Fouad' (فَؤَاد) is a masculine Arabic given name, meaning 'heart' - the beating circulating heart, the concept of 'mind and spirit'. Its root word is the Arabic verb 'fa'ada (فَأَد), meaning 'burning' or a 'flame' and 'lahmun fa'eed' - means a 'roasted meat on a fire'. It is used to describe a 'heart that is inflamed with emotion'.

Look at the marvel of the Quran in the choice of words. Instead of using the derivation from the Arabic word 'Qalb' (قلب) for the 'heart', the Quran has used the Arabic word 'Afedha' (أَفْئِدَة). Choice of this word emphasizes the severity of agony of 'heart' like '<u>burning</u>', a '<u>flame</u>', or '<u>roasted meat on a fire</u>'. Note the link between the 'fire leaping up over the heart' and the word used by the Quran for 'hearts' that is 'Afedha' (أَفْئِدَة). The 'fire leaping up over the heart' is '<u>burning</u>' the 'heart' like a '<u>flame</u>', and torture of 'heart' is easily sensed to identify it as a '<u>roasted meat on a fire</u>'.

But look at the difference. The ordinary biological burning fire is visible to human eyes. What type of fire is this one 'Hotama' that "is a fire which leaps up unto the hearts" and burns but no signs either of 'burning' or 'fire itself' are noticeable?

(c) **NUCLEUS' AND THE 'HEART'**

Nucleus means central core, seed, heart, central part, or thing round which others are collected, etc. A particular part in the plant cell, animal cell, and the atom has been given the name of the nucleus by scientists in the light of specific function performed by that particular part and indeed with great appropriateness. This part called 'nucleus' is so delicate, sensitive, and vital to the whole that we could identify it with real plausibility with the 'heart'. Arab Lexicographers indeed translated it as the 'heart'.

The nucleus of the plant cell is the controlling center of all the vital activities of the cell. When we cut a plant cell into two, the nucleus's part continues to live and constructs a wall around itself while the part without the nucleus dies. Similarly, if the nucleus of an animal cell is fatally injured or separated from the cell, the cell dies. The nucleus of the animal cell, when it divides, ensures the exact reproduction of the cell by duplicating the cellular control mechanisms carried by chromosomes. It is highly vulnerable to atomic radiation, and good evidence suggests that the critical initial radiation injury occurs for cells in the active division.

Again, it is the breakdown of the nucleus of an atom that means the extinction of the atom. This fact, if viewed further, would presage the termination of the universe because it is the 'atom' that is the 'basic building block of the universe', and it would destroy the whole structure of the universe if we damaged the nuclear systems of its atoms.

Judging from the particular characteristics of the nucleus and the role nucleus plays relative to the whole, it is easy to establish an evident analogy between it and the heart. It is not our view alone, but the leading scientists who accurately understand the matter have endorsed it. The phrase 'heart of the atom' is commonly used in scientific literature to represent the nucleus. Scientists and the Quran share the use of the word 'heart' between them.

In the following, we reproduce a few excerpts from various scientific and philosophical sources to show how scientists and philosophers of the atomic age identified the nucleus with the heart. On the one hand, this would serve as a testimony for our interpretation, that is, our identification of the nucleus with heart; on the other hand, it would show a real credit to the discerning genius of the scientists and the philosophers. The examples we here cite are not in any way to be considered as mere chance uttering, nay, but rather are one and all well-judged and deliberate pronouncements based on keen discernment of the fact.

Such corroborative testimony of scientists and philosophers to the Quranic concept of the phenomenal 'nucleus-heart' relation, being truly significant, deserves to be highly prized. Because it issues through minds that have peeped deep into mysteries of the subject and have known the true nature of the phenomena concerned.

Further, they are the minds of hard-headed scientists and philosophers never accustomed to resort to a mere symbolic or metaphorical manner of expression in science matters until there existed some exceptional, undeniable, and exact appropriateness justifiable by precise standards set by the science. Even though their writings may contain similes and metaphors, or their style may even be ornate, philosophers are not generally wont to resort to mere impassioned rhetoric. Their similarities and analogies are examples of exactness and, therefore, are credited if they happen to corroborate our point in this respect.

Following are the excerpts in question. Read and see yourself the miraculous anticipation of the Quran and wonder.

(i) OBTAINING THE ENERGY FROM THE 'HEART' OF THE 'ATOM'

"Early in that year (1939), young physicist Teller (eventually destined to make the first Hydrogen bomb in 1952) was required to give a lecture. The subject of the nuclear energy was being widely discussed. Accordingly Teller felt compelled to go on record concerning the probability of obtaining energy from the <u>heart</u> of the 'Atom'. It was later that year that two German physicists Hahn and Strassman split the atomic <u>nucleus</u>."

('The Hydrogen Bomb: The Men, the Menace, the Mechanism'; by James R. and Blair, Clay Jr. Shepley, Page-484)

(ii) THE BREAKUP OF THE VERY 'HEART' OF 'ATOM'

"Examine the luminous dial of a watch in complete darkness, holding the dial only an inch or so from your unaided eye. As your eyes become

dark-adapted, you will see no steady glow but a continual random succession of individual flashes of light, scintillations, like so many tiny fireflies. A magnifying glass will make the flashes appear sharper and clearer. Each flash signals the passage of a single fast particle which originated in the radioactive material. Each fast particle comes from the break-up of the very heart of a single atom - - - the Nucleus - - - of the radioactive material."
(Physics, Physical Science Study Committee, Second Edition, D.C. Heath and Company, Lexington, Massachusetts, July 1965, Page-130)

NOTE: Does it not then prove the identity between 'nucleus' and 'heart'?

(iii) 'HEART-BEATS' OF 'NUCLEUS' (NUCLEAR HEART-BEATS)

"The basic time unit for an atomic nucleus (something like its heartbeat) is of the order of 10^{-22} sec. How many nuclear heart-beats are in the lifetime of a radioactive nucleus which lasts only one billionth of a second?"

(Ibid: Page-21, Short Problems)

Thus, by merely uttering the adjective nuclear, point of the Quran is proved when it calls atomic fire "a fire which leaps up unto the 'hearts'."

(iv) THE 'HEART' OF THE 'ATOM'

"We are dealing, let us tell ourselves again, with mind pictures. Three specially concern us. The first, barely possible to the imagination, is that of the atom waiting to explode at a moment of its own choosing, without any reference to law. The second is that of a city enveloped in darkness, full of men fleeing and burning as they flee. The third is that of a control released, now at the heart of the atom itself, now in mid-air over the doomed city. Faith feels a twinge at the first, hope at the second, charity at the third."

('God and the Atom'; by Ronald Arbuthnott Knox, Page-117)

(v) THE ATOMIC REACTOR TOO HAS 'HEART'

Innumerable and, of course, highly appreciable testimonies to the appropriateness of terms used by the Quran in its prophecy about the atomic bomb have appeared in writings of scientists on this subject. We are desirous of quoting one concerning the term 'heart', whose significance we can judge from the fact that it comes from no less an authority on the subject than Edward Teller, the famous maker of the first-ever Hydrogen bomb himself. Edward Teller has named the region of the atomic reactor in which the process of generation takes place as the 'heart' of the reactor. We reproduce in the following a description from his book, 'Our Nuclear Future', which he conjointly wrote with Dr. L. Latter in 1958.

Their description appearing under a photograph of the reactor, 'The heart of a reactor cutaway section of a nuclear reactor', is given as follows.

"The heart of the reactor is a small region at the center where the fission energy is generated. Most of the weight and volume are needed for cooling apparatus and shielding material to keep in nuclear radiation."

The atomic reactor's region wherein nuclear energy generation takes place is termed by the atomist of the caliber of Edward Teller as 'heart'. He labeled it without in any way or reference to the text, teachings, or knowledge of the Quran. It was merely by dint of the appropriateness suggested by the object.

This fact deserves to be prized as admirably spectral testimony to the authenticity and originality of the expression of the Quran and the incredible genius of the modern scientist for so correctly viewing the fact and so precisely synchronizing it with an appropriate term.

Suppose this eminent atomist, Edward Teller, would ever have a chance to see this writing of ours. In that case, we could surely guess his wonder at the revelation of such a prophecy that would far exceed that satisfaction he might have had when he had received the intelligence regarding the successful detonation of his Hydrogen bomb.

It was not in the destiny of poor Einstein to reap wonders from this Scientifico-Prophetic miracle of the Quran because the hand of death snatched him away before the appearance of this our work. Yet, surely there might be others of requisite caliber fortunate enough to observe this wonder and marvel at this miracle of miracles. Perhaps they might even see the advice and guidance contained in it for this present-day humankind.

(vi) THE URANIUM CORE OF THE REACTOR DESCRIBED AS THE 'HEART' OF THE PROJECT

Margaret O. Hyde, in her book, 'Atoms today and tomorrow', while describing the project of the atomic submarine 'NAUTILUS', writes on page 130:

"The Uranium core of the reactor was the heart of the project."

(vii) PLANTS HAVE 'HEARTS' TOO THAT ARE AFFECTED

In his book 'Jesting Pilate', Aldous Huxley has recorded a fascinating instance regarding demonstrating the 'hearts of plants'. He visited the Botanic Institute of Sir J. C. Bose in Calcutta (India) during his world tour. He witnessed many a miracle of the plant world that resulted from

Sir Bose's creative experimentation and had become perceptible to the human eye.

One of these marvels was the recording of the 'heartbeats' of a plant.

"In one of the laboratories," writes Huxley, "we were shown the instrument which records the beating of a plant's <u>heart</u>. ... The normal vegetable <u>heartbeat</u>, as we saw it recording itself, point by point on the moving plate, is very slow. ... But a grain of caffeine or of camphor affects the plant's <u>heart</u> in exactly the same way as it affects the heart of an animal. The stimulant was added to the plant's water ... the pulse of the plant's <u>heart</u> had become more violent and more rapid. After the pick-me-up, we administered poison. A mortal dose of chloroform was dropped into the water. The graph became the record of a death agony. As the poison paralyzed the <u>heart</u>, the ups and downs of the graph flattened out into a horizontal line halfway between the extremes of undulation. But so long as any life remained in the plant, this medial line did not run level, but was jagged with sharp irregular ups and downs that represented in a visible symbol the spasms of a murdered creature desperately struggling for life. After a little while, there were no more ups and downs. The line of dots was relatively straight. The plant was dead.

The spectacle of a dying animal affects us painfully; we can see its struggles and, sympathetically, feel something of its pain. The unseen agony of a plant leaves us indifferent. To a being with eyes a million times more sensitive than ours, the struggles of a dying plant would be visible and therefore distressing. ... The poisoned flower manifestly writhes before us. The last moments are so distressingly like those of a man that we are shocked by the newly revealed spectacle of them into a hitherto unfelt sympathy."

('Jesting Pilate'; by Aldous Huxley, 1945, Page-153)

A million times more sensitive eye is required to see the death of a flower. How many times is more powerful imagination necessary to see the death of the cities by the shock of the bombs that are a million times more powerful than the conventional bombs?

Sadly, the world is playing quite blind to the spectacle of atomic warfare and the radiation affliction.

(viii) THE 'HEART' OF NATURE

"And now, when two wars lie behind us, and the current of human affairs seems swifter and more ungovernable than ever, we turn despairingly to the scientists who have presented us with the Atom Bomb, and ask, at least, to have their word for it that this cataclysm of history is not a cataclysm in the whole structure of our sublunary existence. 'Tell us at least,' we insist, 'that you have looked through your microscopes into the very heart of nature, and that order still reigns there'."

('God and the Atom'; by Ronald Arbuthnott Knox, Page-47)

THE 'HEART' OF NATURE'S SECRETS

"The days are long past when philosophy was described as the handmaid of theology; the most we can expect nowadays is an occasional little help. And science, equally, has played us false if we had any hopes in that quarter. For nature, more than ever, seems to have been reduced by science to the position of a drudge and an accomplice; she lends herself to our purposes, and such purposes! Yesterday, we pointed to her with reverent fingers, 'See, how her mysteries still baffle us. See, what a lesson we can derive from the majestic leisureliness with which she works out her designs!' Deified yesterday, today she is defied; we are closed to the heart of her secrets, and we know now that she was cheating us; that all her boasted orderliness was but a screen for anarchy. Will they not tell us, the men of the new generation, 'We are atom-children; do not be surprised if we turn out worthy of our breed'?"

('God and the Atom'; by Ronald Arbuthnott Knox, Pages: 80-81)

(d) ATOMIC 'FIRE' LEAPS UP OVER THE 'HEARTS'
(i) THE 'HEART' OF THINGS AND THE INDETERMINATE ELEMENT

"I have tried to analyse my own reactions to the scientific view that there is, after all, an indeterminate element at the heart of things; to the prospect of an age in which the possibilities of evil are increased by an increase in the possibilities of destruction; ..."

('God and the Atom'; by Ronald Arbuthnott Knox, Page-133)

Ronald Arbuthnott Knox was concerned over the indeterminate behavior of the radioactive atom that could explode at any moment at random and would thus affect the established attitude of the trends of philosophy. This indeterminateness, however, is a particular characteristic of this atomic age. At random, it is that the atomic war may start. We are, however, interested in the above-quoted passage of Ronald Arbuthnott Knox for the use of the phrase, 'the heart of things'.

(ii) ATOMIC FISSION AND THE 'LEAPING UP OVER THE HEARTS'

How the atomic fire 'leaps unto the hearts' can be seen in the fission process of generating atomic energy. A neutron leaps up over the nucleus that is the atom's heart and knocks out two neutrons, which attack the nucleus of another atom, and each one ejects two neutrons from the nucleus attacked. Neutron itself is an atomic particle that is atomic radiation energy, or nuclear radiation fire. The four neutrons then further attack the nucleus of another atom, each knocking out two neutrons each and so on, and the process proceeds till the whole lump of Uranium explodes.

Every single fission thus generates energy in the heart of the atom. We have described the 'fission chain reaction' process though the description of single fission serves our purpose. However, the fission chain reaction in the case of the reactor remains under control, and the explosion does not take place while energy is systematically generated. Thus, the tiny little embers of the radioactive fire, that is, the neutrons, keep on 'leaping up over the hearts' of the atoms, and the atomic energy generation continues. Radiations inherent in the very nature of atomic energy are emitted and take the same attitude, for they also 'leap up unto the nuclei' that are 'hearts' of atoms.

Radiations 'leap up unto the nuclei' of the atoms of the inanimate matter. Hence, they thereby disturb the order of the nuclei, causing transmutations of atoms. At the same time, in the living body, they eject nucleons from the nuclei of the atoms and 'leap up unto the nuclei' of the cells and break the chromosomes. Atomic energy is more appropriately called nuclear energy, and atomic radiations likewise are more adequately called nuclear radiations, for both are concerned characteristically and uniquely with the nucleus. Other types of energy have to do nothing with the nucleus, and in all their reactions, the atomic nuclei remain untouched and intact.

(iii) **ATOMIC FUSION AND THE 'LEAPING UP UNTO THE HEARTS'**

In the fusion process, the only other process of atomic energy generation, too, the rule of 'leaping up over the hearts' stands good. The difference is that while the atomic nucleus divides in the fission process, in the fusion process, we fuse the nuclei of several tiny atoms, and the energy liberates.

For instance, we fuse four Hydrogen atoms to form one Helium 'heart'. The case of the Hydrogen bomb, which is the case of fusion, offers a prominent example of the 'leaping up over the hearts'. Intense heat is required to fuse the atoms, and we have to place a fission device within the Hydrogen material. The fission device, when detonated, creates intense heat, which 'leaps up unto the nuclei' of the atoms of Hydrogen material and fuses them.

(iv) **'THERMONUCLEAR': THE TERM, THE PROCESS, AND THE REMINISCENCE**

The term 'thermonuclear' is a marvel of terminology, and the credit goes to the scientist for having coined so wondrous a term. Even more remarkable is the role of the Quran in this respect. The Quran has anticipated this term and has kept it treasured, though unfortunately, without the knowledge of the modern scientist for about fourteen centuries.

The term 'thermonuclear' represents a process in which heat is directed upon the nuclei of atoms to initiate nuclear reactions. The scientists have called the fusion bomb the 'thermonuclear bomb' because the 'thermonuclear' process is applied therein to cause the fusion of the nuclei of the fusile material. The heat produced by the fission bomb is impinged on atoms of the fusion bomb to cause the fusion of the atoms of the fusile material. Thus, we see that the heat supplied from a different source causes the fusion of atoms of the fusion bomb. However, the principle of 'leaping up over the hearts' is there. The atomic fire produced by the fission bomb impinges on the nuclei of the atoms of the fusion bomb.

It will appear something extraordinary to note that the term 'thermonuclear' is the exact translation of the words of the prophecy, namely, that "Al-Hotama is a fire which leaps up over the hearts". The 'thermonuclear' process is the practical demonstration of the words of the prophecy above quoted. 'Thermo' means heat, and 'nuclear' is the adjective of the nucleus. The meaning of this particular structure of the term 'thermonuclear' could be deduced as 'A fire, related to heart' just as we have seen the fire of the fission bomb related to the nuclei of the fusion bomb in a fusion bomb explosion.

If men of medicine might develop a process in which the human heart would receive heat from some external source, they may justly call the process 'thermo-cardiac', for the word 'cardiac' means 'of the heart'. Likewise, suppose we establish a reasonable identity between the 'nucleus' and the 'heart'. In that case, the atomists may find justification in using the term 'thermo-cardiac' as a parallel substitute for 'thermo-nuclear'.

However, remember that no ordinary chemical fire could bring about the fusion of Hydrogen atoms since atomic fission can only develop temperatures of such high order as are required for the fusion of the atoms of the fusile material. Hence, it is necessarily the heat derived from atomic fission that could serve the purpose of fusion of the nuclei of the atoms of the fusile material.

The Quran anticipated the term 'thermonuclear'. This term and the words of the prophecy 'a fire that leaps up over the hearts' are the same things: the translation of each other. This fact is a wonder not to be missed by a knowledgeable scientist. Also, the ingenuity of scientists in contriving a term as 'thermonuclear' could hardly miss the notice of anyone who has an inkling of the subject of nuclear science.

(v) THE 'HEAT-FLASH' OF THE ATOMIC BOMB EXPLOSION 'LEAPS UP OVER THE HEARTS'

The effect of the initial heat radiation of the atomic bomb explosion, generally referred to as 'Heat-Flash', on the human and mammalian body furnishes a remarkably typical example of the peculiar 'leaping up over the hearts' characteristic of the atomic fire. The effect of the 'Heat-Flash' completely overwhelms the heart of the victim, and in certain cases (when the victim happens to be close to ground zero), it kills the heart on the spot, yet leaving it 'un-burnt' and unconsumed in a sense we generally understand from the term burning.

'Heat-Flash' appearing within a fraction of a second of detonation, and with brilliance far more dazzling than the sun, and traveling at a speed of light (186,000 miles per second), strikes like a flash at the bodies of those exposed within effective range of atomic bomb explosion. It burns their skins in various degrees, kills those within a specific range about the grounds, and leaves others to either die within a few hours or escape death with severe or minor burns of the skin.

'Heat-Flash' does not penetrate much beneath the skin, for its duration is too short. In the case of a nominal kiloton bomb, it is only about two seconds, while in the case of a high yield megaton bomb, it extends to about twenty seconds. Despite its severity, therefore, the 'Heat-Flash' effect is confined to the victim's skin. How then does it kill some of its victims on the spot? It kills its victim on the spot by overwhelming the heart with heat, agony, and shock. There can be no doubt that the heat, agony, and shock cause the instantaneous death of 'Heat-Flash' victims. We can here hardly think of any necessity of going into any discussions of the pathological indications. The case is clear-cut. The effect of shock is observable in an irradiated mammal or human being.

(vi) THE 'ATOMIC RADIATIONS' 'LEAP UP OVER THE NUCLEI (HEARTS)'

We have seen that atomic fire 'leaps up over the nuclei' of the atoms in atomic energy generation. Also, the heat of the fission bomb 'leaps up over the nuclei' of the atoms of fusile material of the fusion bomb. We further observe that atomic radiations 'leap up over the nuclei (hearts)' of the atoms that constitute the body's molecules through which these radiations happen to pass. Radiations also 'leap up over the nuclei' of the cells of the body. The reactions of nuclear radiation, whether emitted during the generation of atomic energy or emitted by fission products of atomic energy in a bomb explosion, occur within the electrons and the nuclei of the atoms while passing through a body.

Radiations ionize the atoms that constitute the molecules of the body through which they pass. They ionize the molecules of the mammalian bodies' water content--the water content of the mammalian bodies being above 75 percent--they go in headlong collision with the nuclei of the atoms they come in contact with, and from there eject nucleons. They attack and mount above nuclei of both botanical and biological cells, and break chromosomes of nuclei of cells, thereby killing cells. The chromosomes being the strings of the nucleus of a cell could well be called 'heart-strings' of the cell. So, we can say that the fire of atomic radiations has 'mounted above the cell's heart (nucleus)'. We can see these broken strings (chromosomes) of the 'heart' of the cell under the microscope.

Radiations mount above the 'heart' of both: the 'basic building block of the universe' that is the 'atom', and the 'basic unit of life' that is the 'cell'. To wit, they strike at the very 'heart' of life and the existence of the creation.

The one word around which the theme of nuclear science and atomic radiations revolves is 'nucleus', the exact synonym of 'heart'.

(vii) THE THOUGHT OF ATOMIC ENERGY AND ATOMIC BOMBS SEIZES THE 'HEART' OF ENTIRE HUMANKIND

The most assiduously guarded secret of atomic energy at the beginning of the affair leaked out from the laboratories of the U.S.A. and seized the heart of humanity, inspiring it with dread as well as a passion; the dread of its horrible destruction and passion for its possession. Gradually the idea of atomic energy became a universal craze. So intense is humankind's passion for atomic energy today that it has expelled every trace of serenity, sagacity, and contentment from the human mind. Every window that could afford a glimpse of the frightful hazards and calamities incident on adopting atomic energy is closed. Therefore, the horrific vision of the impending catastrophe that lurks in the wake of the atomic energy potential has been rendered invisible to the human eye. Yet, in the innermost depths of the human mind, the temptation of the atomic energy potential, the hazards incident on the atomic energy for peace, and the terrific possibilities of the atomic war seem to vie with each other for the possession of the human mind.

However, every nation on earth today is longing after atomic reactors and processing plants. At present, the entire world is clamoring for atomic energy despite the hazards, for the impelling force of the necessity is overwhelming. The consideration of necessity has quelled every other consideration within man's mind, and the apprehension of hunger and poverty has blotted out every other apprehension. Despite its apprehension of the ruinous consequences, economic, industrial, and military necessities have forced humankind into adopting atomic energy for peace. The mind of the entire humankind now, it seems, is struggling helplessly in the grip of the inevitable doom of atomic ruin.

(viii) THE SECRET OF THE GLOBAL RADIOLOGICAL HAZARD 'LEAPS UP OVER THE HEART' OF THE ATOMIC POWERS ALONG WITH THE ENTIRE HUMANKIND

Hiroshima and Nagasaki's news had once convulsed the entire world, though something even worse was yet to be heard. The tragic news came in the form of the global radiological hazard of the fall-out of the Hydrogen bomb in the event of the test explosion of the Hydrogen bomb at Bikini Atoll in 1954. Although they adopted every feasible measure to keep the test explosion of the Hydrogen bomb a secret yet, the mysterious Providence of Allah disclosed it. The disclosure caused a shock to the world opinion that out-rivaled the shock even that was of the Hydrogen bomb itself. A secret might for long have remained secret, but the presence of a Japanese fishing boat in the vicinity of the test explosion revealed the horror to the world at large. Thus, another gust of the atomic fire had mounted above their 'hearts'.

However, the shock to the atomic powers was of a particular kind and more grievous manner. That day could have been befittingly named as the day of weeping and mourning for the atomic powers. They realized that their atomic bombs, no matter in what part of the world they detonated, were equally dangerous even to themselves. However, the tragedy was discovered only 'accidentally', like X-rays and radioactivity. Yet, what a tragedy it was? A tragedy over which the tragedy itself would weep.

Providence revealed to humankind that none who lived beneath this blue canopy and over this global earth was safe from the global radiological hazard of the fall-out of the Hydrogen bomb. The scientists soon declared that if these test explosions in the world exceeded a specific limit, so much radioactive substance would have been spread all over the earth that would constitute a serious, rather irreparably ruining hazard to the health of humankind. The heat of these successive shocks served only to increase the intensity and the magnitude of the atomic fire in the 'heart' of humankind.

The story of discovering the hazard of the fall-out of the Hydrogen bomb states that a Japanese fishing boat, 'Daigo Fukuryu Maru' (Lucky Dragon-5), with 23 fishermen on board, was anchored seventy-one miles east-north-east of Bikini Atoll, the test site for the thermonuclear bomb. This location was fourteen miles outside the restricted areas of the U.S.A. Atomic Energy Commission's Pacific Testing grounds.

On the morning of March 1, 1954, at 6:12 AM, the boat crew saw flashes of fire, bright as the sun itself, rising into the sky. Someone yelled to men below, "the sun is rising strangely. Hurry up and see it." They soon realized that it could not be the sun, for the light was coming from the West. Alas, the sun was not rising, but the sun of humanity was setting in forever and never to rise again.

At this moment, they first felt fear and thought of 'PICADON' or 'PIKADON' (the Japanese word for the atomic bomb, meaning a tremendous flash and sound). The glow continued for several minutes-- two to three--then the yellow color seemed to fade away, leaving the dull red color like a hot piece of iron cooling in the air. The sounds of the explosion came about six minutes later. There were two of them, and they went like the sounds of many peals of thunder rolled into one. The crew felt no concussion, but the boat did seem to roll as if it was trying to ward off some blow. Then a pyramid-shaped cloud began to form. None of the fishermen knew how high it went because none could see it stop as it bellowed up and up into the sky. The cloud went through a series of strange bursts and flashes that included nearly every color in the spectrum: red, orange, violet, greenish, and blue. The colors gradually faded, and the sky became clear again. Against the sky, a thin, trailing cloud appeared. The fishermen returned to their nets.

About three hours after the explosion, a cloud of fine white dust or ash-like talc began to fall. The fishermen became warm, and they thought as if they were glowing. The ash had entered the eyes and nostrils of some of them. The frightened crew sailed back to Japan, and after fourteen days, the ill-fated vessel arrived in Yaizu harbor, contaminated with radioactivity. Japanese radiation specialists were called in when the crew revealed that they had become ill near Eniwetok, Marshall Islands.

Before importing Lucky Dragon's cargo of tuna for inspection, much of it was taken ashore in Japan and sold. Japan reacted sensationally after discovering that tuna's men, boat, and cargo were 'Hot' with radioactivity. The resultant campaign to track down and destroy the Lucky Dragon's tuna cargo touched off one of the enormous flash scars in Japan's history.

The news of the tragic incident spread over the earth like a flash. Nations then realized that no one in the world was ever safe from the radiological hazard of the atomic bombs, not even the owners of the largest stockpiles, those staunch, somewhat deluded believers --- in the deterring effects of their giant bombs.

Scientists observed that the fall-out of the high-yield bombs would rise to the height of twenty miles in the stratosphere. There, riding the prevailing currents of air would move around the earth for about ten years, gradually settling out on earth to contaminate the whole surface of the earth with radioactivity and constitute a grievous hazard to the health and life of humankind. Thus, it proved that the atomic bomb was not a defense weapon, but it was a means of complete extermination of life on earth.

In 1955, the atomists declared that when the number of test explosions reached five times the number of test explosions that had by then been conducted, the factor of radioactivity would constitute a severe hazard to the entire humankind. However, inhabitants of the earth had never heeded this timely warning. Since then, test explosions have continued without any restraint or any pangs of conscience. Moreover, because no such effects of radioactivity have been manifested among the present generation, the inhabitants of this earth would not care for any consequences that would appear in some future generations. Therefore, it is difficult for them to sense the future effects of their present global suicide.

(ix) THE 'FIRE' OF UNIVERSAL DISCONTENT MOUNTS ABOVE THE 'HEARTS' OF HUMANKIND

The sensation of heart-burning is nothing new to the human being. It has, since the birth of humankind, accompanied the human heart incessantly. However, the heart-burning in this present age of atomism has assumed such alarming proportions and unrestrained universality that we can fitly liken humankind's heart at present to an oven working on the principle of fission chain reaction and tending with frightening speed towards explosion.

The fission-like necessities of life compel man's heart, and it dreads fusion-like insults incident on poverty in this age of wealth-worship. Hence, the atomic oven of man's heart is nearing the point of final burst into smithereens that may be shot out into outer space even before the man has attained the glory of reaching Mars. Man today is constantly haunted by the fear of poverty and dwindling of wealth, so much that it perpetually sounds in his ears like a death knell.

With atomism as the philosophy of life in this material age of material progress, physical comforts, and hence the accumulation of wealth as the sole object of life, humankind is trudging on the path of material progress toward an illusory utopia of self-sufficiency and deceptive bliss of the earthly Paradise. They are marching in an atmosphere of complete indifference to spiritual, moral, or celestial considerations without any thought of death, Resurrection, Judgment, or the life in Heaven, with hearts, overwhelmed with a multitude of distressing worries, tormenting anxieties, and chafing troubles. Their hearts are seething, sizzling, and raging like an oven convulsed with overbearing loads of agony, grief, anguish, sorrows, and sufferings, and subjected to the tragic possibility either of going to pieces with the suddenness of the atomic explosion or of undergoing a painful and lingering decay to ultimate destruction with the tormenting tediousness of the decay to be brought about by the process of the atomic energy for peace.

The current deluded race is the miserable dupe of the horrible demons of atomism. It is groping its path through the deceptive labyrinths of self-sufficiency with a vision blurred by ill-conceit and a mind possessed by blazing lust, gaping avarice, flaming hoarding, devouring greed, and false pride. This generation is little realizing that a mind engaged in the exclusive pursuit of the world and entirely divested of spiritual solace would essentially be an abode of constant misery and a helpless prey to biting snakes, stinging scorpions, and tormenting wasps without respite. It is a path that leads deeper and deeper into misery without any hope of ever emerging from the pits and dungeons.

Never before in the whole history of humankind was to be seen such intense and universal heart-burning and frustration, worldwide discontent and anxiety, extreme fear of the extinction of the human race and the eradication of the entire life on earth, and the definite threat of so deplorable and disgraceful an end. Humankind has sullied every other consideration on earth for the much-cherished goal of self-sufficiency. They can never achieve their goal if self-sufficiency is taken as the contentment of heart because the hope is false, the method is erroneous, and the object is inaccessible.

The idea of perpetual progress based on the grow-more policy has proved to be a mere delusion. The more it is grown, the more it is consumed with the increased demand for more. The point of satisfaction moves farther in proportion to the advancement in progress in the process of fission chain reaction. The word 'increase' has assumed the opposite meanings, becoming a synonym of 'decrease'. The only commodity which in the world today we witness to increase continually is discontentment and heart-burning.

The dire need for energy or power has impelled the hungry humankind into adopting so dangerously hazardous a bane as atomic energy. Nowhere in the world today, not even in the reputedly prosperous countries, is to be seen any contentment that might have resulted from the centuries-long continual struggle for progress. They may rise to the Moon and Mars, but their hearts grow hungrier every moment, and the contentment quickly leaves their world on this earth. They might bring some minor information from the Moon and Mars, but surely, they will never bring any contentment from there. The only hope is that they will bring more discontentment, more frustrations, and more miseries.

However, let them wait for a little and see. Atomic energy has not yet put its share into the existing frustration of humankind. The real contribution of atomic energy to the heart-burning of man will come with its gradual development in due course. Humankind as yet stands on the horns of a dilemma: whether to adopt atomic energy or not to adopt it? Adopting it forebodes a calamity almost equal to complete ruin; banishing it entails sacrificing an energy potential needed in industrial development and an acute sense of deprivation and grief. Although the developing stage of atomic energy for peace is yet at a distance, conflict in man's mind over the question of its adoption or banishment has caused a peculiar heart-burning, even now. Nuclear energy has its peculiar nuclear way of producing heart-burning.

The heart of the present humankind is indeed sick and miserable. All heartfelt joy seems to have left the human heart. A burst of hearty laughter is only a thing of the past. The inward hope and joy of a faithful heart hopeful of a blissful future abode in the next world and unseen dreamland of a poetic vision could nowhere be seen in the materialistically practical world of today. Even tears, a recognized source of mental relief, have been dried up due to the heat of the modern atmosphere, and lachrymal springs of relief have long since been evaporated. Darwin, I think, confessed that he had lost all the faculty of enjoying poetry.

The beautified vision of a faithful heart rejoicing in Allah's Mercy and yearning for a blissful seat in the next celestial world is a spectacle that human beings today thirst to see and nowhere to be seen. The atmosphere of the present world, on the other hand, is seen reeking with panting breaths, burning eyes, ever hastening movements, panicky gestures, and the constant hustle and bustle of anxious shadows. Every heart is on fire for financial worries, and the image of the goddess of wealth, called the supreme deity of this present age, has possessed every mind. Yet, ills for which wealth is considered a remedy are, on the contrary, worsened by the increase of wealth.

The illusory image of water has moved farther and farther, increasing the thirst of the deluded minds, never once bestowing on them a drop of water to quench their thirst. In its constant search for the material elixir, humankind may fall in perpetual misery due to a nervous breakdown or may suddenly perish under the hail of atomic bombs, bearing the ambition of finding the elixir in its heart or the utopia, or the earthly Paradise. Unfortunately, the path they have adopted leads to neither utopia nor Paradise. Instead, it leads to ultimate ruin. A balanced thought, outlook, and life are the necessity. Thus, in a balanced philosophy, they may find the ultimate reality and may find contentment.

That humankind is suffering from 'heart-sickness' is not my personal view alone. Read the following from Ronald Arbuthnott Knox. He says:

"Be that it may, the Atomic Age will have, no less than ourselves, windows that open on eternity. The true lesson of the five proofs, as of all other proofs devised to establish the fact of God's existence, is that we see his face looking down at us from the end of every avenue of our thought; there is no escaping from it. All our metaphysics play with word-counters and reshuffle our concepts as we will, must necessarily take us back to God. The doubts, hesitations come only when human knowledge is suffering from growing pains, when we have not yet sorted out our ideas and integrated, for the hundredth time, our world picture. Of that inevitability, our own <u>heart-sickness</u> is the best proof. 'Lo, all things fly thee, for thou fliest me'."

('God and the Atom'; by Ronald Arbuthnott Knox, Page-100) This passage of Ronald Arbuthnott Knox is replete with wisdom and hope. Would to Allah his hopes come true and this world return to God. They will be able to do this when they have only sensed their 'heart-sickness' and have also known the actual cause. When the disease has been diagnosed, humanity will seek the remedy, and if applied, health will return. By the way, what may be the remedy? It is a life balanced between the material and the spiritual. It is the whole distilled in the form of an elixir.

Howsoever disconcerting and disturbing the present state of heart-burning in the world might be, it is just nothing compared to that state of heart-burning in the future age of full-fledged atomic energy. That shall be a state which no words can express. The state shall simply be inexpressible. The little gusts of the atomic ill-wind that at present are causing a ripple on the surface of the human mind will in those times turn into raging storms of agonizing radiations that will constantly prey on humankind to fill the cup of human misery to its brim.

So exceedingly wretched and so unbearably miserable will be the state of humankind then immersed in numerous maladies, inexpressible agonies, and unimaginable calamities that the hail of atomic bombs may appear to those life-weary people as a flight of swift redeemers from the unbearable loads of misery and torture. Not the previous facilitations but the current calamities of science will then be the topic of the day. Not the constructive faculty but the destructive capacity of science will be the object of the thought of humankind besieged on all sides by a hundred different varieties of plagues and epidemics, miseries and calamities, sufferings, and sorrows. To them, the scientist will not be a benefactor but an enemy, and science a curse and not a blessing.

The atomic fire has possessed the heart of humanity with such tenacity that it will continue to afflict even future generations. The ill effects of atomic radiation will be insidiously at work even in this present generation. They will be secretly sowing the seeds of misery and igniting the fires that will cause heart-burning to future generations. Thus, as a result of the effects of the atomic radiation on this present generation, future generations will be born as haggard apparitions, imbecile monsters, stinking lepers, and miserable chimeras of infinitely variant forms; kinds and combinations, neither living nor dying and perpetually cursing their fore-fathers and progenitors. It is hard to express their state then.

The wretched, miserable monsters in the extremity of their heart-burning will call upon the scientists and will cry to them:

"You ruthless people, if you had no means of universal protection against the effects of radiation, in the beginning, then why did you recommend the use of the atomic energy for peace before actually discovering the protection and cure? Now, pray, contrive some means of speedy death, and relieve us from the burden of this unbearable existence."

What will then be the answer of the equally miserable scientists? No one at present can tell. However, we may guess that the answer of the scientists will be as follows.

"Your forefathers were mad after wealth and material comforts. So, they compelled the scientists to contrive some means of obtaining wealth and physical comforts. The scientists then had warned them against all the possible hazards of atomic energy. Still, the scientists were forced into submission to recommend using atomic energy for peace. So now, bear the pains with fortitude and courage, for we too are your co-sharers in this ordeal."

There is, however, another possibility equally feasible. In a world of increasing discord, ever-worsening social, political, and economic situation, and ever-increasing heart-burning, the communities in a fit of intense frustration may plunge this world into the atomic war as the surest remedy of all the miseries of the groaning humankind. That case will change the earth into a reeking furnace or heap of ruins within hours. In such circumstances, the human race could consider such a suicidal sacrifice of humankind on the altar of Vulcan [2] good riddance if the whole of humankind were to vanish from the scene.

However, unfortunately, this might not be the case. There might be survivors left stranded on the atomic-war-rent wreckage of the earth to mourn not the death of the parted friends but their (own) survival and envy, in reality, the doom of those having perished in the atomic holocaust. What will be the plight of these unfortunate survivors of the global atomic war? One shudders even to think of that. Wretched, worn, and miserable beyond description, these derelicts will be found struggling through the reeking ruins of the collapsed buildings and the wider-spread heaps of swelling, stinking dead.

They will be shocked almost to the point of death: pathetic, haggard, confounded, and stupefied, hungry, and finding nothing to eat, naked and finding nothing to wear, sick and finding no treatment, shivering with cold and finding nothing to make themselves warm, dying of thirst and having no cold water to drink. But, above all else, they will be calling for death, and death even fleeing from them. Flying and shrieking with horror, the condition of the survivors of the atomic war, the degree of their suffering, and the shattered state of their burning minds are simply impossible for anyone to express in words.

Nevertheless, their sad story does not end with their own lives. If they live, they will be constantly preyed upon by the atomic radiation emitted by the fission products of the atomic bomb explosions. Consequently, they will suffer from radiation sickness. Further, they will be responsible for sowing the seeds of chimeras in succeeding generations due to the mutated genes caused by the action of radiations. The monstrous children will appear in the world as the relics of follies of their inconsiderate ancestors, shadowy incarnations of the sins of their forefathers, the ultimate symbols of the extinction of the human species and the eradication of life on earth. Alas, for their heart burning due to the atomic fire. What Shakespeare, Milton, or Dante is there to portray that in words?

Yet, indeed, all in the present transitory world is nothing compared to that heart-burning from the fire of 'Al-Hotama' that awaits humankind in the next world. If the atomic bomb has emerged in this world as the punishment for certain evils, then they who would be found justly deserving of the heart-burning from the atomic fire would also justify the heart-burning from the fire of 'Al-Hotama' in the next world. Alas! For those who were doomed to the eternal punishment of the next eternal world. Here in this life, death is there to redeem from the torture of life, but who will redeem from the eternal torture?

If excessive greed and the endless pursuit of wealth be the cause of all this heart-burning and discontent in this present age, then know that the human heart was never free from it since the birth of humankind on earth. The love of wealth and the world is inherent in the very nature of man. However, it is not the acquirement of reasonable necessities of life but the entire engrossment in pursuing wealth as the sole object of one's life. It is the only choice of this world against the next world that is objectionable and responsible for dire consequences.

The generations of the pre-modern ages were made to realize the hazards of the exclusive love of wealth. Every religious philosophy has declared the noxiousness of the wealth and has constantly endeavored to place adequate checks on man's inherent love of wealth by constantly reminding him of this world's transitory and perfidious nature and its wealth as against the reliable eternity of the next world. The fear of final judgment and consideration of the eternity of the next world always proved an efficacious check on the evil and excessive indulgence in the world and demonstrated constant guidance.

Men tended to sacrifice this world in the hope of receiving a better reward in the next eternal life. They could bear great hardships and severest vicissitudes with remarkable patience. They made it their point throughout their life to constantly struggle against the love of this world and wealth for the sake of the next world. Their heart-burning, therefore, was not only reduced in intensity but was also mollified peculiarly. It was a mixture of a sense of loss of the current world and gain of the next world. The loss of this world was not given such extreme importance and was forgotten. If the people incurred such a loss for the sake of the next world, it was considered no loss, but rather it was considered an excellent deal and was a source of contentment.

On the other hand, suppose folks incurred the loss of the otherworld to benefit this world. In that case, they took it to heart as an actual loss and much lamented. Thus, the heart-burning of those peoples was influenced by such considerations. The people of this modern age, on the other hand, think to the contrary. They have little or no consideration for the next elusive world. Their only loss is the loss of this present material world. Therefore, their sense of the loss of this world and wealth has assumed an exclusive acuteness. The fuel for their heart-burning is pure, intense, and concentrated. They have put all power of the sense of loss into this channel of loss of the material world. There happens to be no vent hole, no means of emission, and no neutralizing arrangement in their heart to decrease the intensity of their heart-burning. Like a ventless boiler, their heart, therefore, would eventually explode. The loss of the world means death to them.

Indeed, the human race could have never wholly eradicated the love of wealth and the world from their heart in any era. It could, however, have been mellowed down and moderated. The people could have brought it down to its minimum possible in certain exceptional cases. There was the possibility of striking a reasonable balance between love of this world and the next world, greed and sobriety, wealth and poverty, through the ballasting factor of the hatred of this world. In the pre-modern, that is, pre-atomic ages, humankind was able to delimitate the degree of heart-burning. It was possible only due to a balance achieved through mutual neutralization of love of this and otherworld. Also, due to this factor of the limitation of heart-burning, humankind could continue its existence on earth and the development of its mind: stage by stage, degree by degree, despite all the various blights like hunger, poverty, famine, epidemic, war, and anarchy.

It may sound like a paradox that this modern age of knowledge and science has almost lost the true love and appetite for knowledge compared to the past ignorant ages. Today, knowledge is universally sought and constitutes merely a catalog of methods and processes of acquiring wealth and never a piece of knowledge for the sake of finding the ultimate reality. We could best describe it as the catafalque of knowledge. The idea of the acquirement of knowledge purely for knowledge is a matter of the past. Yet, despite its promises to the contrary, modern knowledge has increased the factor of heart-burning beyond all proportions.

All the combined explosive energy appearing during the previous history is no match for the explosive energy liberated by a single 15 megaton bomb. So likewise, all the joint atrocities of priests and princes of past ages could hardly be considered a match for the single atrocity of the invention of the atomic bomb. So also, all the pre-eminent collective dangers in past ages were a trifle against dangers imminent in this modern scientific age. Similarly, there is a little difficulty in observing that the heart-burning of the past ages could be considered a mere triviality compared to the intense and universal heart-burning of this present age.

The attitude of two persons, modern and pre-modern, towards pain and misery can easily be differentiated and traced to the relative philosophies of the two ages. At the appearance of a calamity, ancient people instinctively believed in pangs of conscience that some guilt on their part might be a probable factor for calamity. They thought that because the calamity appeared as the consequence of some fault on their part, it was the manifestation of the divine wrath. The dread of the wrath of Allah possessed the mind to the degree that they forgot the actual calamity. Hence earthquake, solar or lunar eclipse, and the epidemic resulted from the excessive burden of sin on earth and a means of retribution. They attributed calamity to the divine will and the remedy, therefore, was repentance and the avoidance of sins. Irrespective of the partial element of superstition, they did not so severely feel the pangs of the misery brought about by the particular calamity and soon forgot the whole affair. All was the Will of Allah. His Will be done while all credit for this attitude went to the particular philosophy of those times.

The case of the modernist stands on a different panel. He attributes natural and physical laws to the appearance of eclipse, earthquake, or any other natural phenomena. He simply explains them accordingly with a sneer at the superstitious attitude of the ancients. His attitude regarding a calamity of any kind is identical. Instead of attributing the appearance of the calamity to the divine decree as the retribution for sin, he resorts to his (own) power, exercises his right of dominion over Mother Nature, and devises means and methods to combat the calamity for the sake of conquering it. His confidence is in the material agencies' efficacy, so his remedies are of a type, exclusively material. It is seldom that thought of moral guilt would cross his mind at the appearance of calamity. Any connection between sin and calamity is quite incomprehensible to him. It is always the material cause that he looks for and the material remedy that he has to propose. The confidence of modern man in combating and overpowering calamities and surmounting obstacles found some justification initially that men, even like Macaulay, were in their time all praise for the philosophy of Bacon.

However, gradually it was found out to the chagrin of every thoughtful person in the world that the modern attitude towards the calamities was no final remedy, for the calamities even of a worse nature appeared in succession and greater degree after the previous ones were subdued and eradicated. There was simply no end to the line of the calamities, and the modern physical method had produced no panacea efficacious enough to cut their root. Antibiotics were once considered as the final remedy for infections. However, the radiation's appearance and resulting radiation sickness defied all the most effective and sure antibiotics.

The ancients found solace in forgetting the calamity and thus succeeded in mellowing down its effects. On the contrary, instead of forgetting it, the modernist takes it to heart as the most memorable object and thinks it is most worthy of antagonistic concentration. Thus, this object of hostile absorption proves to be a very effective agent in augmenting the intensity of heart-burning.

Self-confidence may not in itself be considered as objectionable, but when man's will collides with the divine will volitionally, the outcome would be terrific. Indeed, the devout acquiescence in the divine judgment and submission to the Will of Allah would be a better course to be adopted. The atomism, however, has no room for such things, and it has produced a race of self-conceited demigods and the proud conquerors of Mother Nature. Still, at the same time, they are embodiments of heart-burning in the igneous picture of misery, looking upward towards high horizons but overlooking the self.

We are not unaware of the evident shortcomings of our differences between the ancient and modern attitudes respecting the calamities. Such differentiation could only be general, and we could not exclude the possibility of exceptions. Ancient history is replete with examples that would refute our differentiation. At the same time, today's world may produce millions that in a bygone age would have figured among the saints as the models of belief in the divine will and disinterestedness in the matters of the world. We cannot simply afford to be unjust to the people of these modern times, and we just consider them as the saints involved in hell. It is a painful age to live in misery. Atomism has set this world on fire in which the inmates are obliged to burn. We are not ignorant of the atrocities perpetrated and most heinous deeds committed in the past ages by notorious characters for the sake of the world and the wealth of the world and power, nor we could in any way be ignorant of all the various and indeed laudable qualities of the people of this present age. But what we mean in our differentiation is a general attitude of age under the influence of a particular philosophy.

In past ages, people considered this world as merely transitory. The actual home was in Heaven and, therefore, persons imparted comparatively less importance to the affairs of this present world, and hence the loss of the next world was considered the actual loss. Under the influence of the philosophy of atomism, the modern world has little thought of the next world. They take it for granted that this world or life is the only one they have: its loss is, therefore, the actual loss. Yet, despite all shortcomings of our differentiation, it is hard to miss the comparative characteristics of two epochs regarding submission to the Will of Allah and the attitude towards the world and the world's wealth.

Yesterday we commonly heard voices like:

"Ill fares the land, to hastening ill a prey,
Where <u>wealth accumulates,</u> and men decay."

('The Deserted Village'; by Oliver Goldsmith)

But today, no such voice is anywhere uttered, and the universal chorus is:

"Well fares the land, to no ills a prey,
Where <u>wealth accumulates</u> by night and day."

No hermits move about in sack-cloth today, and no prince is there to renounce his throne for the sake of achieving Nirvana. Faith is considered an impediment in progress, and the thought of the next world is just something unbelievable. Values, spiritual and moral, are superfluities, and we talk of generalities. There might be many exceptions still existing.

The credit, however, of the entire, particularly atomistic attitude goes to the philosophy of atomism which has flared up like a wildfire and has consumed or at least suppressed every other philosophy. It has substituted the chemical fire with the atomic fire. Also, this philosophy has changed the ordinary heart-burning to an atomic sort of heart-burning and has replaced the ordinary calamities and epidemics with atomic calamities. It has produced the atomic means of the wholesale destruction of the world instead of the previous chemical means. Indeed, the philosophy of atomism has proved to be a perennial source of abounding discontent and eternal destruction. An equally dynamic and all-pervading antidote is necessary to counteract its pernicious effects and quench the universal heart-burning it has produced.

(4) 'ENCOMPASSING FIRE'
"HOTAMA IS A FIRE CLOSED IN ON THEM IN <u>OUTSTRETCHED COLUMNS</u>." (Quran)
(a) MAN'S MIND IS 'ENCOMPASSED' BY THE THOUGHT AND FEAR OF ATOMIC ENERGY

Anyone acquainted with the characteristic features of the atomic energy from its initial generation to the stage of the fall-out of the megaton bomb will hardly find any difficulty in recognizing the encompassing feature of the atomic energy, that is, the replica of the fire of 'Al-Hotama'. Further, indeed anyone utterly devoid of the powers of observation only will fail to see the entire world today fully encompassed by the impending hazards as well as the thought of atomic energy. However, an exceptional faculty of imagination and genuine knowledge of the subject of nuclear science is necessary to imagine the future state of the encompassment of the world by atomic energy in a future age of full-fledged atomic energy to one's actual horror.

The thought of atomic energy today can manifestly be seen encompassing the mind of humankind as a whole. The thought of atomic energy overbearingly prepossesses the minds of nations. The topic of atomic energy has attained universal predominance. It permeates the mind of the world with ever-increasing heat and fast-developing enthusiasm, and uncontrollable fervent. Nations, communities, and kingdoms worldwide are raving mad after atomic reactors and processing plants to process the embers of their atomic misfortunes. Countries are seething with ambitions of atomic designs. Continents are grievously pining for the prosperity expected from the incredible energy potential of nuclear energy.

Moreover, the entire world has lost itself in a reverie of the great utopia of the atomic age. The thought of atomic energy has so bewitched the human mind that human sight completely lost every possibility other than the unlimited prosperity of the nuclear age. Even the scientist, whose diaries overflow with the dreadful ill-omens of the horrific hazards of the atomic radiations, is not behind anyone in this zeal of humanity to adopt atomic energy for peace. Such is the hypnotic hold of this enchantress over the mind of humankind.

Howsoever ignorant the intellectuals or the world leaders might be of the more profound mysteries and the subtle intricacies of nuclear science, the horrors of atomic warfare can be no secret even to the generality of humankind. Even the dire necessity of atomic energy for power and all the too irresistible temptation of the unusually excellent energy potential obtainable from that source has not been able to expel the dread of the horrifying hazards of atomic energy.

Hence, the temptation and apprehension moving like shuttles in opposite directions in the human mind have woven an impregnable network generating at the same time great heat due to friction that adds fuel to the fire and augments the intensity of heart-burning. It is a remarkable feature of the whole affair of atomism, culminating in the hell of atomic energy.

A factor that may prolong the existence of the atomic bombs, perpetuate the threat of atomic devastation, strengthen the hold of atomic energy, and lengthen the siege of the world by nuclear apprehensions is the notion of deterrence associated with the presence of the stockpiles. This notion is identical to that of the immortalizing power of wealth. The atomic powers are obliged to maintain their stockpiles to deter the aggression of their territories by the foe.

Such is the situation of the prevailing rivalry, hostility, and mistrust amongst the world's nations. They are pretty aware that the deterrence afforded by the stockpiles is merely deceptive, it would vanish the moment the atomic war broke out, and it could be regarded as no more than the suspense that precedes a storm. Furthermore, they are not ignorant that the atomic bomb is not a weapon of defense or war but a means of the whole world's wholesale destruction, including their own country.

Yet, despite all such knowledge, the atomic powers cannot destroy their stockpiles, which are the sure means of their destruction. Nay, they even don't find themselves capable of curtailing the amount of their nuclear armament despite their strenuous efforts.

The kind of blight they were to deal with could not be evaded or avoided through treaties and agreements. Instead, the necessity was to remove fundamental causes of the evil which the Quran has depicted and pointed out in an oracular manner in the nick of time. It is pretty challenging to understand that factors so gigantic and glaring should not be understandable to those who claim to rule and regulate the destinies of nations and formulate the world's policies. However, it is not they blamed for the fix. They only are helpless in the grip of the circumstances.

Moreover, indeed the force of the three evils and the influence of the impending doom are irresistible. This influence may render the scientist helpless against the urging wave of the circumstances and coerce him into the recommendation of atomic energy for peace in exact contradiction to the basic tenets of science. It must be an influence of the unusual kind that has hypnotized the entire world of sages, scientists, philosophers, scholars, and the connoisseurs of all kinds into the act of behaving like an ostrich. It could not be taken as lightly. The snare is visible, but the bird cannot help falling into it.

(b) FULL 'ENCOMPASSMENT' IN FUTURE DURING FULL-FLEDGED ATOMIC ENERGY

Although the encompassing features of atomic energy are evident even now, the true spectacle of the encompassment of humanity by atomic energy will be seen in a future perspective of this world when atomic energy will have obtained its total prevalence in the world. The atomic reactors and the processing plants will occupy the entire earth like the besieging forces in a world teeming with all-pervading swarms of atomic radiations, the fiery invisible snakes, adders, serpents, and scorpions of alpha, beta, gamma rays, and neutrons. These flocks of radiation will be shooting in all directions around the globe and encompassing it like a spherical network to enclose all humankind and all the inmates of earth, leaving no exit and no possibility of escape.

People then will endeavor to get out of that net of misery, yet they will not be able to do so and be forced to suffer the unbearable tortures helplessly like within a besieged garrison. Are these all the fancy stories that we are telling? The answer is 'No'. Are the scientists ignorant of these realities? The answer is 'No'. Will the scientists be able to discover universal protection against radiation or a sure cure in time? The answer to this question is that it is neither known nor could it be predicted. Humanity can banish atomic energy at this present stage in the twinkling of an eye. They can destroy all the existing atomic reactors and stockpiles in a matter of minutes. [3]

Why then, despite all the knowledge of the ruin that they will bring about in time, and even though this world can go on without even the atomic energy, are they after it with unrelenting zeal and escalating enthusiasm? There happens to be a factor as subtle as the atom's binding energy that keeps the encompassing feature of the atomic energy and the atomic bomb in force. The delayed effects of atomic radiation also play a prominent part in ignoring the hazards of atomic energy. If the effects of the atomic radiation appeared instantaneously in the present generation itself, then the hazards would have perhaps been regarded differently. [4]

Due mainly to this factor of the delayed effects of radiations, the governments worldwide are engaged like honeybees in either developing the atomic hive or at least pining for their inability to produce the sweet nuclear honey. They do this laudably to safeguard the integrity and solemnity of their countries and acquire means of prosperity for their people. But they never think that they essentially are engaged in an endeavor to throw their dear countries into ruin and their public into poverty, misery, and sickness of the worst type. There could hardly be another example of such a fatal misunderstanding or such a gross outrage on common sense in the whole history of humankind. It is just like setting someone on the throne of fire: handing him a fire wand and placing a crown on his head that is of fire, too.

Today it seems as if humankind has turned blind to any energy source except that of atomic energy. The mind of the entire humankind, it seems, is invited to the idea of atomic energy by some irresistible force; the atomic age appears to them like a garden, though it truly is hell. Atomic energy appears to them like a source of eternal prosperity though it is an endless source of poverty and misery. The atomic stockpiles appear to them as the protectors of the integrity and solemnity of their territories. However, they are the surest means of destroying their lands, cities, and populations. Yet, alas for them, the industrial, economic, and military necessities have chained them to the chair of atomic energy that will prove worse even than the electric chair.

(c) RADIO-GENETIC EFFECTS TO PERSIST LONG AFTER EVEN IF ATOMIC ENERGY IS BANISHED: 'ENCOMPASSMENT'

A remarkable feature of the encompassment of the atomic fire is the tenacity which it exhibits throughout. At some stage of the atomic energy for peace, humankind might decide to banish it in the face of the hazards. But even they banish atomic energy, destroy all reactors, and bury every source of radioactivity in the deep, the effects of the atomic radiation would continue.

For, the genetic effects of radiation are irreversible and irreparable. They persist, are cumulative, and may keep on multiplying through marriages among humankind. That is why the decision to adopt atomic energy warrants utmost caution and extreme far-sightedness. It is simply the question of life and death to the entire humankind, nay even to the whole life on earth.

Therefore, we should never lose sight of or forget the atomic fire's 'encompassing' feature. It is a particular specialty of atomic energy, and we should keep it under consideration. In other things, there might be a chance of retreating the steps or abandoning the project with no after-effects, but it is not so with atomic energy. Your jump into it is the first and the last. There is no coming out, and there is no stepping back. Think, therefore, before you leap.

(d) ATOMIC BOMB EXPLOSION, ENCLOSURE UPON ENCLOSURE: 'ENCOMPASSMENT'

The atomic bomb explosion forms a perfect encompassing enclosure, and we will now describe how. The first enclosure of the atomic bomb explosion is its effective zone in a circular rather semi-spherical form. The radioactive fall-out forms the second enclosure. Its form generally depends on the direction and the intensity of the prevailing winds. In the case of the high yield that is the megaton bomb, it overlaps the effective zone. However, the radiological fall-out of the megaton bomb forms yet another enclosure beside the enclosure of the local fall-out, called the global fall-out, because it envelops the entire globe, thus encompassing the whole earth. We can liken the effective zone of the atomic bomb explosion of any caliber to an inverted cauldron. A column of great height shoots upwards from the base and forms a mushroom-like top upon its head. The atomic bomb explosion's whole phenomenon is like a tree. The effective zone, column, and mushroom represent the roots, the stem, and the top.

Yet, it is the exact antithesis of the tree of life, for it does not give but destroys life. Again, it is the tree of the knowledge of evil only that has no good element in it whatsoever. We will now describe the general pattern of the little kiloton bombs' explosion, such as were dropped on Hiroshima and Nagasaki.

The first announcement of the detonation is a brilliant white flash, many times brighter than the sun. The tremendous energy released in the explosion reduces everything--particularly the contents and the bomb's casing--to a gaseous state. Initially, mass, which has about the same volume as the original size of the bomb, is at a temperature of over a million degrees and pressure over a million atmosphere. At about 0.1 million-second from the instant of detonation, it is an isothermal sphere of diameter about 30 yards and temperature 300,000 ^{0}C, which is 50 times the surface temperatures of the sun.

At this stage, the shock-front of the blast wave coincides with the surface of the sphere but soon, the shock-front breaks away and moves ahead. The fireball surface cools rather rapidly because of energy lost by it on account of radiations into space. In a little more than 0.01 seconds, the surface temperature reaches its minimum value of about 2000 ^{0}C. The interior of the fireball is still sweltering. Like its surrounding, the sphere gets heated and ionized by the advancing shock-front, its transparency falls, and it exerts a 'Blanketing Effect' on the hot sphere. The rate of heat loss from the surface decreases and, as the flow of heat from inside continues, the surface temperature begins to rise. It reaches a maximum of 7000 ^{0}C in about 0.3 seconds, and luminosity is almost extinct at the end of about 10 seconds.

The maximum rate of the ascent of the fireball is about 300 feet per second. The diameter slowly increases and attains its maximum value of about 300 yards in about one second. The break-away of the shock-front is soon followed by a wave of low-pressure causing expansion of the air and consequent condensation of any water vapor contained in it.

"What is seen is a ring of fog, spreading outward at a speed of sound and lit up, like a Chinese lantern, by the red glow of the fireball inside it."

Within a few seconds, the pressure returns to normal, and the condensation cloud suddenly disappears. Then we see the fireball, rushing upwards at a speed of a hundred miles per hour. It is followed by an opaque cloud of turbulent gases mixed with dust drawn from the surroundings by the uprush of the air. The rising cloud reaches the stratosphere in about four minutes and, continuing upwards, rises to its full height of thirty to sixty thousand feet in about seven minutes. By this time, the fireball has disappeared and replaced by a mushroom-shaped cloud of white vapor that eventually reaches two miles in diameter. In a later test at Bikini, the mushroom persisted for many hours and was followed by planes with Geiger-Counters as it slowly drifted downward.

We have likened the effective zone of the atomic bomb explosion to 'an inverted cauldron'. It indeed covers the unfortunate people present within that area like 'an inverted cauldron'. It has a radius of two and a half miles in the case of the 20-kiloton bomb, while its radius in a 20-megaton thermonuclear bomb is 80 miles. Whoever had the ill-luck of being within that area at the instant of detonation has no chance to escape the effects of the explosion until the process of the explosion is complete. The process begins within a fraction of detonation. The 'Heat-Flash' appears within a fraction of a second and lasts for 2 seconds in the case of a tiny kiloton bomb and 20 seconds in a high-yield megaton bomb.

Who could manage the escape in so short a period? The effect of the blast comes to an end in about 10 seconds. The initial effects of nuclear radiation, too, would have been very nearly over by then. In the case of the high yield bomb, these effects would be over in about 100 seconds. It is simply impossible to think of escaping. The fire of the atomic bomb has 'encompassed' them irredeemably.

Moreover, it is not all. We can compare the atomic bomb explosion to an octopus. It has many tentacles. It burns with its 'Heat-Flash' those who are exposed in the open. It buries those who happen to be within the buildings under the very same buildings. It sends after those, its deadly radiations, who happen to have escaped both these ordeals, and kills them. Radiations chase them wherever they would be and pierce through like poisonous nails. There is no outlet. There is no means of escape.

However, the primary and noteworthy fact is the characterization of the 'Al-Hotama' fire by the Quran as 'a fire closed in on them in outstretched columns'. This feature of nuclear fire distinguishes it most clearly from ordinary fire. The Quran has thus described the particular design of nuclear fire, which appears in the atomic bomb form, as distinct from other fires. The fires that occasionally break out in a city or the forests take their shape following the shape of the structure in which they are blazing. However, the fire of the atomic bomb has its particular form and design wherever it appears, and it essentially has an 'outstretched column'. This column is a miracle of prediction, description, and portrayal on the part of the Quran. The mention of a column is the strongest marvel of description and prediction.

How many great scientists engaged in constructing the first atomic bomb could predict and describe this feature of the atomic bomb explosion that of its column, a second before the actual demonstration of the explosion? And how many of the scientists were there who could predict the encompassing global feature of the radiological fall-out of the Hydrogen bomb a day before the actual test explosion of the Hydrogen bomb?

Yet, Scripture has shown all this and much more that is still far beyond the understanding of leading modern scientists. However, miraculously, this has been described fourteen centuries earlier the actual appearance of phenomena, in an age when even dreaming of discoveries of this modern science could not have been supposed as a probability. We are yet traversing through preliminaries of our time in this book, and innumerable myriads of miraculous facts of Scripture remain still to get through in succeeding chapters.

The knowing mind of the scientist, by now, will have realized the glorious vision and unimaginable supremacy of Scripture in this respect. We can reasonably expect that judging from the impartial and frank nature of the scientific mind, ever open to the light of the truth, justice to this warning of the Scripture will be done as is due to it. The appreciation will come with an open mind and generous disposition, for it is the only way left to humankind to break through the disastrous siege of the atomic fire and destroy its forces eternally to eliminate the grievous threat that its presence has implied.

The deceptive snares have to be detected and destroyed. Lest the devil, a confirmed foe of Adam and his posterity may ultimately be witnessed dancing in mocking revelry around the blazing shrine of the atomic hell in which humankind was being broiled as the sacrificial victims on the altar of greed. Hence, the devil may have an occasion to raise his head towards the heavens and say:

"O, Lord, is not that Lordly creature whom you had commanded me to worship, and for whose sake you had turned me out of your Paradise, and did I not say to you then that this moldy creature whom you command me to worship, is not worth that? Now, see what a mess of himself and of your world he has made."

O, hark then fellow humans; will not that be a disgraceful end of the vicegerent of Allah, and one created in the image of Himself?

(e) MEGATON THERMONUCLEAR BOMB'S FALL-OUT IS A FORM OF 'GLOBAL ENCOMPASSMENT'

However, let us revert to our topic, for that as yet is not complete. We still have to describe the global fall-out of the megaton thermonuclear bomb, which brings the encompassing features of the atomic fire to completeness due to its global fall-out. Radioactive fallout is the radioactivity that falls out of the atmosphere after the explosion of a nuclear weapon.

In a surface burst, a substantial part of the fireball comes into contact with the earth producing a gigantic crater, a mile or more in diameter and projecting into the fire-ball about 10-100 million tons of vaporized earth dust and debris. In the first-ever test of the Hydrogen bomb, they blasted a crater more than a mile wide and 175 feet deep in the ocean bed, and consequently, it wiped out the island of Elugelab.[5]

The fireball rapidly moves upward, expanding and cooling as it does. It reaches a diameter of over three miles. Strong upward air currents follow the rapidly rising ball, carrying with them more dust and debris. After a few minutes, the explosion cloud reaches tropopause at the height of 30-40 thousand feet. It meets here a temperature inversion in the atmosphere, which considerably slows down the upward motion. The cloud expands literally into a mushroom about a hundred miles diameter placed on the top of the stem of diameter about the same as the fireball (3 miles). However, the central portion of the cloud (head of the stem) continues to push upwards, reaching 80-90 thousand feet in about 10 minutes. Still, because of the marked increase in the temperature with height in the higher levels of the stratosphere, it does not go much beyond 100,000 feet (20 miles). The fission products condense and collect on the very abundant dust particles present in the explosion cloud. Sooner or later, this massive quantity of contaminated dust and debris returns to the earth.

This rise of the explosion clouds up to and above the tropopause produces significant effects. The height of the tropopause is about 10 miles in tropical latitudes and 5 miles in temperate latitudes. The weather phenomena, e.g., winds and storms, clouds and rain, occur in the troposphere. The region of the atmosphere above the tropopause is called the stratosphere. The stratosphere is a region of calm, free from winds and turbulence. The temperature in the atmosphere (leaving aside the lowermost regions) decreases (in general) with increasing height till the tropopause is reached. Instead of decreasing with increasing height, the temperature shows a rapid increase near the tropopause, called temperature inversion. At some distance above the tropopause, temperature attains a value of about 50^0C and remains constant till 20 miles or so. Then it again begins to rise. The temperature at the tropopause is to retard the motion of the ascending current of air. The result is that unless the convection current is superbly strong, it cannot penetrate the stratosphere. The dust and dirt that go up with convection current are all brought to rest at the tropopause. Sooner or later, these particles of dust again return to the earth.

GLOBAL FALL-OUT

Due to the terrific force and heat released in the case of a high yield atomic bomb (20 megatons), a considerable portion of (the central part) the rapidly ascending explosion cloud can penetrate the tropopause and go to considerable heights into the stratosphere. The relatively large particles will soon return to the tropopause. Still, small particles about a micron or so in diameter will stay in the stratosphere for a long time on an average of about ten years. The proportion of the fission products that go into the stratosphere will return to the earth at a prolonged rate. As the diffusion process and mixing, in this case, will operate for a relatively long time, the fall-out will be more or less at the same rate over the entire surface of the globe. This 'Global Fall-Out' is carried around the earth by the currents of air prevailing in higher regions. Roughly 50 percent of the fission products go into this type of fall-out.

LOCAL FALL-OUT [6]

We still have to consider the proportion of the explosion cloud that remains in the troposphere. The comparatively large particles, 10-500 microns, return to the earth in a few hours to a few days. This phenomenon constitutes the local fall-out. The smaller particles stay in the troposphere for a couple of weeks. During this time, radioactive cloud travels (generally from west to east, possibly due to jet-streams) two or three times around the earth. This occurrence gives rise to fall-out along a fairly wide belt around the earth, roughly running parallel to the latitude of the explosion site.

A very appropriate term has been suggested, viz. the 'Annular (Semi-Global) Fall-Out'. It is more intense near the explosion site than in regions remote from it. The dust particles in the troposphere stay on, on average, for a week or two. In temperate latitudes, rain usually brings them down, which provides the most effective mechanism of wash-out.

The local fall-out covers about 100,000 square miles, and the average dose received by an exposed person for two days is about 670R, which is fatal. Even if we assume the fall-out area is ten times larger, the dose would be one-tenth of the above value that is 67R. This latter figure, too, is a severe dose that would cause severe genetic effects, even more so when we remember that this is an average to which everyone in a vast area of 100,000 square miles would be exposed. It is something terrible to imagine, and only those blinded by the influence of a dreadful doom could ignore it.

A high-yield fission bomb is primarily a radiological weapon, and this constitutes a hazardous feature. The blast of a high yield 20 megaton bomb is a terrible thing. It destroys the largest of cities. Its fires consume the cities in toto, but its radiological hazard is far worse, for it devastates areas equal to large states. Not to speak of its global radiological hazard, its local fall-out is even enough to lay waste area equal to 100,000 square miles, which is not a small area. It is, in reality, only somewhat less than 1/500th part of the total land surface of the earth. The global fall-out of such a bomb constitutes a severe threat to the health and life of the entire population of earth.

Whereas the global fall-out of a high-yield (megaton) bomb encompasses the entire world, the local fall-out of one such bomb encompasses an area of 100,000 square miles. All persons in that area would be exposed to a hefty radiation dose. To escape serious consequences, we must evacuate them in a day following detonation. However, evacuation from a vast area of 100,000 square miles of whatever population survived the blast, 'Heat-Flash' and intense radiation exposure, can hardly be considered a practical thing even for highly industrialized countries.

Further, where would one find a safe area to provide shelter to this massive mass of evacuated people in case of nuclear war? The atomic fire has 'encompassed' them in every way. Besides, it is not essentially one bomb only, but there might be dozens or scores. There might be hundreds. The world, when it will engage in the suicidal holocaust of mutual destruction, the entire atmosphere may be seen quivering under the wings of the dreadfully luminescent flocks of fiery vulture-bombs that now lie in a state of hibernation in the stockpiles of the nations of the world.

(f) **THE OPERATION ALERT: 'ENCOMPASSMENT'**

The encompassing feature of the atomic fire was experienced, not only by the unfortunate inmates of Hiroshima on August 6, 1945, and Nagasaki on August 9, 1945, respectively but was experienced by the people of America too, on June 15, 1955, in the first U.S.A. nationwide civil defense exercise based on a mock attack using nuclear weapons.

"It was assumed that 61 cities were struck by 61 bombs varying in size from a nominal atom bomb to a five-megaton bomb. The warning time (that is, advance information of the attack) allowed was about three hours. Based on the data collected by the bomb damage assessment groups of the Federal Civil Defence administration, it was estimated that at the end of the first day of the attack, more than 8 million people would have been killed, and another 8 million would have died a few weeks later. About the quarter of the deaths would have been caused by the radioactive fallout. It was also estimated that the attack would have damaged more than 11 million dwelling units and about 25 million people rendered homeless. In New York alone, a five-megaton bomb (surface burst) would have killed about 3 million people (38 percent of the population) and injured another 23 percent. Of every 8 New Yorkers, about three were estimated killed and two injured. Civil Defense officials said that the nation was far from being ready to withstand a nuclear attack."

(New York Times: June 18, 1955)

The Civil Defense officials ought actually to have said:

"No nation on earth will ever be able to withstand the nuclear attack."

It is now the year 1977. Could the Civil Defense officials now say that the defensive ability of America has in any way improved since then? No, the defensive ability of America regarding the atomic attack has not improved much since. The fact is that the atomic fire knows no defense. It is invulnerable. Sense would have directed the world to abandon atomic energy after Hiroshima and Nagasaki tragedy. In his testimony to the U.S.A. Senate Sub-Committee investigating comparative airpower, Lt. General James Gavin (Chief of the U.S.A. Army Research & Development) unveiled another crucial fact from the encompassing features of the atomic fire. Referring to a full-scale nuclear assault, he is reported to have said:

"Current planning estimates run on the border of several hundred million deaths that would be either way depending on which way the wind blew. If the wind blew south-east, they would be mostly in the U.S.S.R., although they would extend into the Japanese and perhaps down into the Philippine area. If the wind blew the other way, they would extend well back into Western Europe."

The best surmise of the whole affair seems to be an ill wind that blows no one good.

(g) THE 'GLOBAL ALL-COMPASSING' EDIFICE OF ATOMIC HELL ON EARTH

The construction of the global tower of the atomic hell on earth seems a certainty. Let us form a mental image of that majestic appearance that may surround the earth one day altogether. Just imagine 500, twenty-megaton bombs planted in extreme symmetry all over the earth. We detonate these bombs simultaneously. Every three miles in diameter, you will see five hundred columns instantaneously rising from 500 inverted cauldrons of the effective zone of the explosion, covering a radius of 80 miles each. The columns have risen to a height of 10 miles, and there have developed mushrooms top 100 miles in diameter each. They have shot through the mushroom tops upward into the stratosphere and have reached a height of 20 miles. The heads of 'outstretched columns' spread into a layer and are carried away by prevailing currents around the earth. The layer spreads into a spherical roof over the earth, and it has completely covered the whole of the earth like the eighth heaven. Below at the mushrooms' level, the local fall-out has spread over an area of 100,000 square miles around every column like an inverted cauldron, more significant than the cauldron of the effective zone but more irregular in shape due to the streaming current of air. You are in a new world now. It is different earth and a different sky. However, see the majesty of the tower: the majestic columns, the majestic vaults, and the majestic ceiling. Alas for you. It is the enclosure of the atomic hell, the replica of 'Al-Hotama'.

(5) 'OUTSTRETCHED COLUMNS.'

"Higher still and higher
From the earth thou springest,
Like a cloud of fire;
The blue deep thou wingest,
And singing still dost soar, and soaring ever singest."

(Shelley's 'Ode to a Skylark')

"HOTAMA IS A FIRE CLOSED IN ON THEM IN 'OUTSTRETCHED COLUMNS'." (Quran)

(a) 'Column' is a characteristic feature of the atomic bomb explosion.

(b) SPECTACULAR 'COLUMN' OF THE SHALLOW UNDER-WATER BURST

We have already mentioned such columns in the previous pages in detail. The column of the atomic bomb explosion presents an awful spectacle to the eye of an on-looker. A strange inexpressible feeling of awe overwhelms the mind. Every column of the atomic bomb explosion is spectacular but particularly fascinating to the eye is the column of the shallow underwater burst. Bikini's (1946) test ('Baker') was one of such bursts.

Generally, in the shallow underwater burst, the detonation takes place at a depth of about fifty feet. The first thing seen in the 'Baker' test was a flash of light, much less luminous than that for air burst explosion as the fireball broke through the water surface. A column of water in the form of a hollow cylinder (plume) with a straight stem rushed upwards. In 15 seconds, it was a mile high. It attained its maximum height of about a mile and a half within a minute. Its stem was one-third of a mile in diameter and 'mushroom head' about a mile and a half across. The water contained in the column was of the order of a million tons.

Due to the force of the explosion, the water present in the plume was in a state of clear drops, and the subdivision was carried further as the water column began to fall after it attained its maximum height. There rolled out a white ring of mist (named 'base surge') at a speed of about 50 miles per hour from the base of the column. It was an unexpected phenomenon.

After about three minutes of the explosion, rain began to fall from the bottom of the expanding surge, and soon the outward expansion slowed down and altogether stopped in another two minutes. The base surge probably covered a total area of more than five square miles. It carried a part of the fission products, but a significant fraction of them was likely in the mushroom top.

(c) THIS IS AN AGE OF 'SMOKING COLUMNS'

Before we bring this point of column rising tendencies of nuclear phenomena to an end, we consider it worthwhile to add another point. Apart from the column raising characteristics of the nuclear phenomena as distinct from the chemical phenomena, the particular feature of the column in connection with thermal processes is a particularly characteristic feature of this modern age as distinct from all pre-modern ages.

Praised be the revealing eye of the Quran that in an age in remote antiquity could penetrate through all these centuries to discern a very quaint character that of 'column raising' of this modern age. It is not only the columns of the atomic explosions, the sub-atomic particles, or the packed columns functioning within the reprocessing plants that we observe in connection with the nuclear phenomena. But generally, this age could be named as an age of columns that we see in characteristics preponderance of columns: high and low, from a few feet to several hundred feet stretching toward the sky almost everywhere in the world in the form of smoking chimneys of factories, brick kilns, cement kilns, etc. indeed in conjunction with the igneous process associated with this age. It is worth observing that this age of atomism stands in conspicuous comparison with the pre-modern ages in this particular respect of the columns of the chimneys. Mark also the high columns of the electric power transmission circuits (closed circuits), which remind one of the Quran's words: "The fire closed in on them in outstretched columns." See how the Quran has characterized a far distant age.

SECTION-3
IRVING KAPLAN'S COMPREHENSIVE EXAMPLE

In the following, we give an excerpt from a standard textbook of atomic physics. The reader will find this little excerpt to contain most of the characteristics of 'Al-Hotama'. The characteristics of 'crushing', 'leaping up unto the hearts', and 'encompassing' could easily be discerned in the excerpt in question. It is as follows.

"The concept of a nuclear assertion can be most easily visualized as the cross-sectional area, or target area, presented by a nucleus to an incident particle. If the nuclei are considered as sphere and the incident particles as point projectiles, then the target area of cross section of each nucleus can be calculated."

('Nuclear Physics'; by Irving Kaplan, 2nd Edition, Page-458) We have exhausted the subject of nuclear physics and proved all characteristics of 'Al-Hotama' fire in the fire of atomic energy that is the atomic hell. Now, the subject of Radiobiology opens its heart to us, and we find therein a fascinating study for our theme. The next chapter will augment our argument through the radiobiological confirmation of 'Al-Hotama' characteristics.

~~*~*~*

---

[1] Reader should note that, now, even in 2021, **nuclear fusion** is still an experimental energy source. It differs from nuclear fission, which is what modern nuclear power plants use to generate energy. Whereas fission involves splitting atoms, fusion happens when two atoms collide and form one heavier atom. As a result, commercially viable fusion has been highly sought after, as it would theoretically produce much more power than fission as well as far fewer radioactive byproducts.

[2] **Vulcan** is the Roman god of fire and metalworking: identified with the Greek god Hephaestus.

[3] The people of Italy have consistently voted against the adoption of nuclear energy, whether for war or so-called peaceful purposes. After the most recent tragedy of Fukushima, Germany has closed some of its

nuclear reactors and has announced that by the year 2022, it will shut down all of the nuclear reactors. Chinese people have shown wisdom by waving banners saying, **"We want children, not atoms"**, and their opposition compelled the government to cancel the "Jiangmen Uranium plant" project altogether. A protest and debate have already been in vogue in India in this regard. But who will teach other nations around the globe that are still enthusiastic about nuclear energy, which ultimately devours their children?

[4] The effects of the atomic radiations have already appeared instantaneously in the present generation itself; therefore, the hazards MUST be regarded in a different light by humankind now. The author finished this series in 1982 when there had been no signs of birth abnormalities in the present generation. If there had been some traces visible in this regard, those were neither common nor in the author's knowledge just because of the place where he lived at that time, as there were no social media in vogue or the internet as it is active globally these days. However, throughout this work, the reader comes across the warnings repeated on several occasions regarding abnormal births resulting from genes mutated by nuclear radiation. The author believed that it would appear in some of our 'future generations', but unfortunately, it has already started in the present generation. In this regard, as undeniable proof, at the end of Book-2 of this series, the reader will see dozens of the highly horrifying and disturbing photos of deformed babies born with complex abnormalities as an aftermath of exposure to nuclear radiation. Exerting your 'human' wisdom, decide whether these chequered chimerical loathsome baby-monsters born to poor parents are humans or 'nonhumans'. Moreover, the internet is open for you in this regard.

[5] "**Elugelab** (or Elugelap) was an island, part of the Enewetak atoll in the Marshall Islands. It was destroyed by the world's first test of a hydrogen bomb on November 1, 1952, as part of Operation Ivy. The blast yielded 10.4 megatons of explosive energy, 750 times the explosion that levelled central Hiroshima, leaving only a crater where Elugelab had been." (Wikipedia, the free Encyclopedia)

[6] "Area as large as 100,000 square miles may be dusted with fallout… so large that evacuation may be a bit impractical.

The extent to which the radioactive fallout is spread, is determined, of course, by the winds, the particle size in the cloud, and to a certain degree by the atmospheric and meteorological conditions, such as rainfall. ... When we say that the March 1, 1954 shot in the South Pacific contaminated 7,000 square miles to a dangerous level, it should be borne in mind that these were under the particular weather conditions operating at the time, and that on another occasion, the area might be larger or smaller by a considerable factor. ... At the rate of 100R, about 12 percent of the reproductive cells will be expected to have one or more new gene mutations. ... Exposure of people to dosages like 100R can lead to undesirable genetic effects in later generations. ... Exposure of large numbers of people to dosages like 100R can lead to deaths and mutilations in later generations. ... In the case of a nuclear war, the immediate deaths and the question of survival may somewhat outweigh the genetic effects which will be introduced ... In case of full-scale atomic war, ... there will be additional hazards due to the fallout, additional to the blast and thermal and other better known effects of nuclear weapons, that should be seriously considered. ... There is a possibility that the Strontium-90 in the foodstuffs at such level might increase the occurrence of bone cancer. ... The immediate effects on health would be noticeable. These latter effects, of course, are well-known to those who have studied the unfortunate Japanese people who were subjected to the full effects of the nuclear detonations in Hiroshima and Nagasaki."

(Dr. Willard F. Libby: 'Bulletin of the Atomic Scientists', Sep 1955, Pages: 256-260)

~~*~*~*~*

CHAPTER-3

THE RADIOBIOLOGICAL CORROBORATION OF 'AL-HOTAMA'

In the previous chapter, we have corroborated the characteristic features of 'Al-Hotama' by the nuclear phenomenon of the atomic explosion in the field of nuclear physics. In this chapter, we will see the corroboration by the biological reactions of atomic radiations.

Before we commence the actual task, a brief sketch of the theory of Radiobiology may be deemed necessary to understand the actual subject better. If the reader studies the theoretical part with care, he will find the subsequent treatment of the subject more exciting due to a better understanding.

PART-1
THEORY OF RADIOBIOLOGY
THE CELL STRUCTURE

In Radiobiology, it is reactions of radiations in the cell of the living body and the plant that we generally consider. These reactions of radiation within the cell determine the question of death and sickness. Hence, some basic knowledge of the cell and its response to radiations may be considered essential. In biology, the 'cell' is the basic unit of life, just as an 'atom' is the basic building block of the universe's structure.

The round structure near the center, sharply differentiated from the rest of the cell, is the 'nucleus' of the 'cell'. The remainder of the cell is known as the 'cytoplasm' and contains many granules--most of them not visible under the optical microscope. Both the nucleus and the surrounding cytoplasm are vital to life and the duplication of the cell.

In general, any attempt to separate the nucleus from the cytoplasm kills the cell. Herein is the particular importance of the nucleus. As an extreme over-simplification, we may consider the cell factory's cytoplasm in which food is broken down and converted into energy and small molecules. The primary function of the nucleus is to ensure the exact reproduction of the cell when it divides by duplicating the cellular control mechanisms carried by chromosomes.

'Chromosomes' are thread-like formations in the cell nucleus, and if broken by radiations, the cell's death occurs. The nucleus, as well as its chromosomes, are of particular importance from our point of view.

We may liken the nucleus to the 'heart' of the cell. The nucleus chromosomes are attacked by radiations and broken to cause the cell's death or other damage.

Cells are of various types and have distinct characteristics. The size of the cell is usually of the order of a millimeter that is only 10 microns. Many cells, particularly those in elementary organisms, are spherical or ellipsoid. The cells of highly specialized organs in more advanced forms of life are of many shapes; for example, nerve cells send out thread-like feelers that may extend over several feet. Despite all these diversities, a remarkable unity underlies the basic structure of the cell.

CELL MULTIPLICATION

The increase in the number of cells determines all the growth. In Unicellular organisms, cell multiplication by cell division represents actual reproduction since two new and exactly similar organisms are formed from the original cells. Multicellular organisms also arise from a single cell known as 'Zygote', but this is produced by fertilization of 'Ovum', and reproduction does not occur by dividing the parent's cells. The 'Zygote' divides, and many new cells are produced, which later become the specialized cells that make up specific tissues and organs in the animal and the plant.

CELL DIVISION

Cell division occurs when a 'parent cell' divides into two or more 'daughter cells'. Most cells will divide when placed in a favorable environment. Multiplication by cell division continues until maturity is reached and the organs and tissues have reached their maximum size.

MITOSIS

During the process in cell division known as mitosis, the nucleus duplicates itself; the cytoplasm cleaves into two parts (nuclei), and when it is complete, two cells, each identical with the original one (each of which contains a complete copy of the parental chromosomes), are formed. A superb sequence of changes occurs in the nucleus during mitosis in four distinct phases: prophase, metaphase, anaphase, and telophase.

PROPHASE

In the first stage of cell division, the prophase strands appear in the nucleus, and these gradually condense and contract into distinct threads called chromosomes. Human cells have 46 of these chromosomes while those of beans have 12, and so on. Different species have a different number of these chromosomes. As this division process in the prophase develops, it becomes apparent that these threads are composed of two filaments known as 'chromatids'. Simultaneously with the appearance of chromosomes, the nuclear membrane contracts and finally disappears, leaving the chromosomes packed closely together in the cytoplasm. At this time, a gel-like structure (known as the spindle and stretching out from the center) appears in the cytoplasm.

METAPHASE AND ANAPHASE

In the next metaphase stage, the spindle becomes attached to the chromosomes, which ordinarily arranges at the cell center. During this process, the chromosomes contract and can no longer be composed of two chromatids. It becomes dramatically apparent at anaphase when the chromosomes suddenly divide. The spindle pulls the two sets of chromatids to the opposite end of the cell (i.e., the chromatids from every chromosome move opposite directions, so two identical sets are produced).

TELOPHASE

The division is completed in telophase when the cytoplasm cleaves into two equal masses divided by a new cellular membrane. The nuclear membrane reforms and the chromosomes in the daughter nuclei swell until they can no longer be resolved with the microscope, and the nucleus assumes the appearance of the resting cell.

During mitosis, we may focus our attention on the precision of the chromosome ballet, and we can easily forget the cytoplasm's outwardly more random and haphazard behavior. Yet cytoplasmic has been duplicated, and the granules in the cytoplasm are distributed during telophase between two daughter cells. At prophase, cytoplasmic activity decreases, and cells like those in the tissue culture that are irregular shape become rounded. At telophase, the cytoplasm becomes the center of the action, and bubbles that rapidly swell and shrink, appear on the cell's surface. This irregular movement finishes soon after the division's completion, and the cell behaves normally.

MEIOSIS

Natural cell division ensures duplication of identical cells, and the growth of differentiated organs and unicellular organisms occurs in this way. It is the process of cell division that is of most paramount importance to the health and life of the body, and it is this very process that is most fatally affected by the reactions of the atomic radiation in the cell.

Hence the importance of this study from our point of view is apparent. The reproduction of multi-cellular organisms is brought about by the union of sex cells (the egg and the sperm), which have undergone a unique series of cell divisions to ensure the mixing of chromosomes.

Since the chromosomes carry the elements called 'genes' that determine inherited characteristics, this chromosomes exchange is vital to life. It is the only mechanism whereby the progeny receives characteristics from both parents. Moreover, since radiations affect these genes of the chromosomes to alter the intrinsic form and characteristics of the embryo to produce abnormal births in mammals and human beings, the point assumes unspeakably great significance from the viewpoint of humankind in general.

The sperm and ovum (the gametes) contain only half the usual number of chromosomes, and the original numbers are established during their fusion to give the fertilized egg or zygote. The latter grows by the cell division and differentiation into a new animal. The division that precedes the gametes' formation is called 'meiosis', in which, through a complex mechanism, cells are produced which contain single chromosomes instead of the regular pairs. These single chromosomes pair up to give a cell a double set of identical chromosomes produced in all subsequent cell divisions on fertilization.

We have mentioned the term 'fusion' in connection with the fusion of sperm and ovum, and this term 'fusion' recalls its use in atomic energy generation. We note the difference that happens to exist between the consequences of the two processes. The 'fusion' of sperm and ovum in biology produces life, while the 'fusion' of atoms in the atomic energy process brings death and destroys life. In this coincidence, the function and process of 'fusion' have been changed from life to death.

Hence, it may be entirely appropriate to point out that such a change we may refer to as the denial (by the prophecy) of eternal life to the 'self-conceited slandering wealth-accumulator' who thinks he shall forever live in this world by dint of his wealth. The prophecy warns the wealth-accumulator: "Nay, but you will be thrown into the fire of Al-Hotama", to be consumed thereby to see your belief in your eternity (in this mortal world) negated. This transformation (of the effect) of the term 'fusion' from life to death is another truthful testimonial favoring the truth of prophecy furnished by facts.

ATOMIC RADIATIONS

Atomic radiations usually referred to as ionizing radiations, are high-energy radiations capable of producing ionization in substances through which they pass. These comprise two kinds as follows.
(1) The first kind comprises electromagnetic waves known according to their origin as X-rays or gamma rays.
(2) The second kind comprises other subatomic particles, notably electrons, which move at very high speeds.

Although physically, these two types of radiations are entirely different, their chemical and biological effects are closely similar and often identical: they both knock out electrons from the material's atoms through which they are passing. The loss of an electron confers high chemical reactivity on the atoms involved. It is subsequent reactions of these so-called ionized atoms that initiate the biological effects that we observe. From a biological point of view, X-rays and gamma rays need to be considered merely as a means of releasing high-energy electrons within the object under irradiation, whatever its chemical constitution.

Besides X-rays, gamma rays, and electrons, there are other kinds of radiations, i.e., alpha particles (Helium nuclei without electrons) and neutrons and protons. The alpha particles, neutrons, and protons go into a headlong collision with the nuclei of atoms and eject nucleons from there, thus causing the transmutation of these atoms. In their wandering about, the ejected nucleons of these atoms further produce ionization in the atoms they happen to contact. The nucleus of some atom captures the slow neutron, and the result is the transformation of the atom concerned.

If the neutron is a fast one, it also, like the alpha particle, goes into a headlong collision against the nucleus of an atom, causing the expulsion of a proton, which further brings about ionization of atoms in the usual way. A neutron being neutral and immune from either attraction or repulsion of the charged particles along its passage, can travel comparatively large distances through the material and comparatively does more significant damage.

IONIZATION, FREE RADICALS, AND EXCITATIONS

The energy transferred by the atomic particle to the material through which it passes brings about the ionization of atoms and excitation of molecules. An atom loses one of its electrons and becomes positively charged in ionization since the atomic nucleus remains unaltered. The ejected electron has only a tiny amount of energy. In all biological systems, it is quickly taken up in the outer electron shell of another atom to form a negatively charged molecule.

In chemistry, we have seen that in the compound Sodium Chloride (common salt), two elements, namely, Sodium and Chlorine, have combined to produce a new, different compound. The Sodium atom, which has only one electron in its outer shell, has given this only electron to the Chlorine atom, which has seven electrons in its outer shell. Sodium atom, thus, by losing one electron, has become a positively charged ion. Chlorine, on the other hand, by gaining an electron, has become a negatively charged ion.

Remember that a typical atom has an equal number of protons and electrons. The protons have a positive while the electrons have a negative charge. These opposite charges neutralize each other, and the atom maintains a state of equilibrium.

The removal of an electron from an atom reduces the negative charge; therefore, the atom's positive charge increases. On the other hand, adding an electron to an atom increases the negative charge, decreasing the positive charge. The atom from which an electron is removed is called a positive ion, whereas the atom taking an additional electron is termed the negative ion.

The outer shells of both the ions in the above example of Sodium Chloride have an octet with 8 electrons. The original electron configuration of the Sodium atom is 2, 8, 1, and that of the Chlorine atom is 2, 8, and 7. The configuration after their inter-reaction has changed to 2, 8 for Sodium and 2, 8, 8 for the atom of Chlorine. It is well-known that atoms strive to gain an octet to gain stability. Sodium and Chlorine ions in this example, therefore, are stable ions.

However, Hydrogen and Helium have an exception to this octet rule, and they are pretty stable if they have two electrons. We have said that the Sodium and the Chlorine atoms in the example above quoted are stable ions. We could not say the same about free radicals, which, although they are ions, have a structure in which each atom does not have a stable electron arrangement. The simplest example is the Hydrogen atom 'H', which is tremendously reactive. It tends to become stabilized either by sharing an electron with another atom or losing its sole electron to become a Hydrogen ion.

A free radical important in Radiobiology is the hydroxyl radical. A hydroxyl ion has lost an electron, thereby becoming electrically neutral again but highly reactive. The significant reactivity of activated water is due to these radicals, which attack most organic substances to attain a standard electron configuration. If these radicals do not find something with which to react, they will combine, and in solution, they persist for less than one-thousandth part of a second.

The free radicals form when the ionizing particle (e.g., an electron from a beta ray or electron liberated on irradiation with X-rays or gamma rays) in its passage through water ejects an electron to produce a positive ion. Another water molecule then captures the electron to give a negative ion to complete the formation of an ion pair. Neither of these ions is stable, and they decompose almost immediately.

If the electron is not removed from the atom by atomic particles, the electrons' arrangement is altered within their orbits; the process is known as 'excitation'. The chemical reactivity of these molecules has been increased without the production of a free radical or ion. A molecule cannot remain in an excited state for an appreciable time --- this period is often less than that of a free radical --- and if it has not undergone a reaction in its lifetime, the electrons will return to their most stable arrangement. Then, the molecule will be back in its original state.

RADIATIONS HIT THE CELL

Radiations cause ionizations in the cell or other biological material that is being irradiated. They do this either by a single-hit process if there is one sensitive volume or by a multi-hit process if more than one sensitive volume in the cell or other biological material is irradiated, thus bringing about the observed effect. This theory is called the 'Target Concept'.

Besides this theory, another theory, called the 'Indirect Theory', assumes that radiations first hit and activate the water content in the living body. Then, the activated molecules of water react with dissolved substances or other materials they contact. The activated water molecules inactivate the enzymes of cells. The enzymes are vital to the cell's life, and, therefore, the death of the cell occurs by their inactivation. Activation of water means the splitting up of water molecules into free radicals.

RADIATIONS BREAK THE CELL CHROMOSOMES

The first changes in irradiated cells visible under the microscope occur in the nucleus, and as the cell degenerates and is approaching death, many other changes become apparent. We can classify changes in the cell nucleus as temporary or permanent. Chromosome sickness is one of the most prominent manifestations of the former type. Chromosomes' permanent changes are not repaired, are perpetuated in subsequent divisions, and can lead to delayed degeneration and death, a characteristic feature of radiation injury.

The usual explanation of permanent chromosome changes is that they result from breaks in the irradiated chromosomes. The broken ends are believed to have the ability to rejoin under certain conditions. When they fuse again in the same way as before irradiation, the damage is completely restored, and no permanent injury has occurred.

However, different types of reunion can occur to give new chromosome configurations different from those initially present. These give rise to a large number of different abnormalities that we can see under the microscope. A proportion of the breaks remains open, and these we see as broken chromosomes. On this hypothesis, the exact sequence of events depends on whether the break has occurred before the chromosomes have split to give two chromatids, a process of splitting which probably occurs at the end of the resting stage, or very early in prophase that is at a time when the cell is most sensitive.

We may present the usual process as follows.

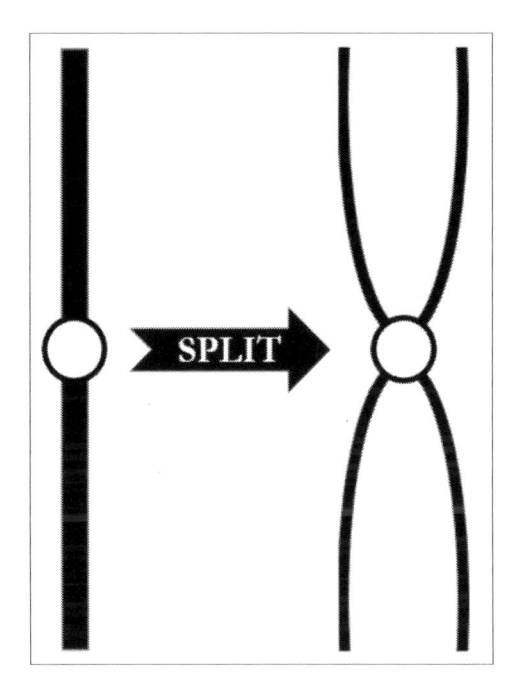

Chromosome chromatid breakage can then be pictured.

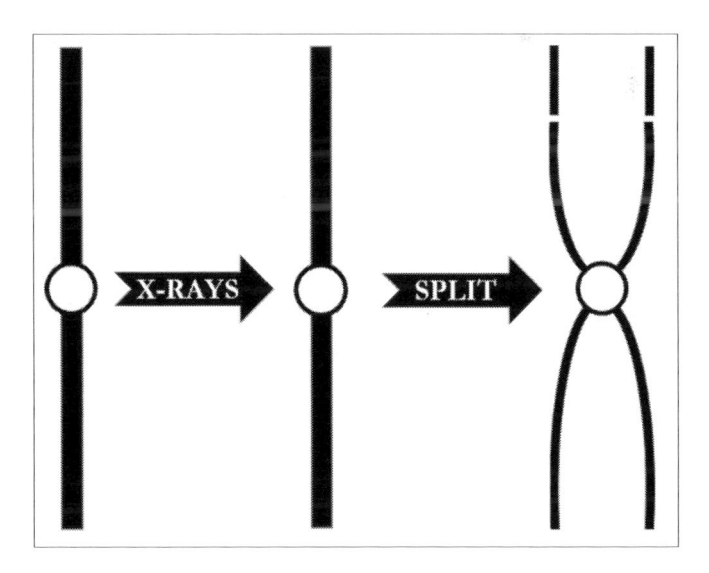

X-rays produce breaks in chromosomes which are followed by splitting to give two broken chromatids. They may rejoin to give the following abnormal structure, which we see at metaphase or anaphase.

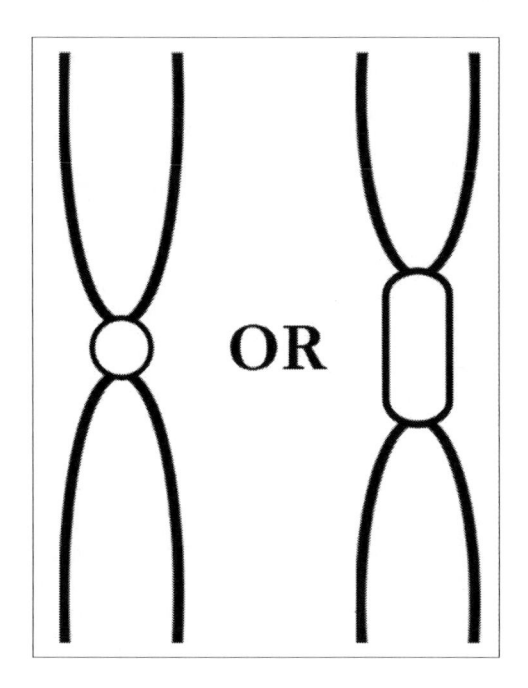

If X-rays act after the split, only one chromatid breaks.

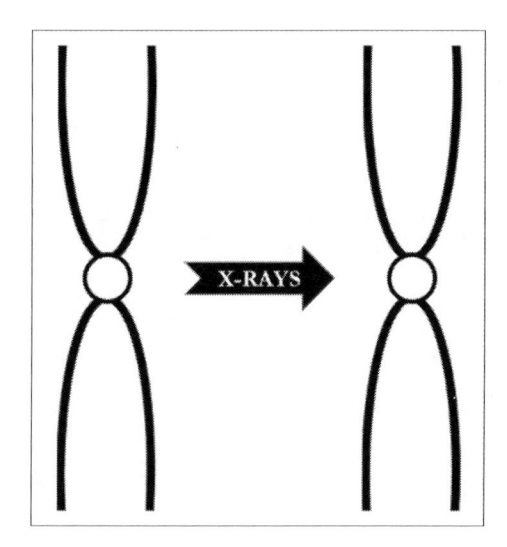

When breaks are formed in chromosomes close together, many types of reunions giving rise to different configurations are possible.

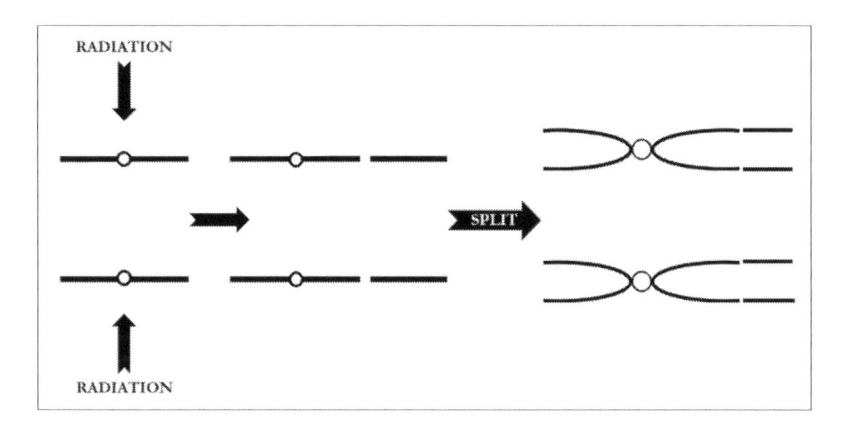

At metaphase, in giving one reunion, the only change is the final metaphase abnormality in irradiated cells. And the earlier stages are inferred. If the reunion occurs before the chromosome splits, structures of the following type are formed.

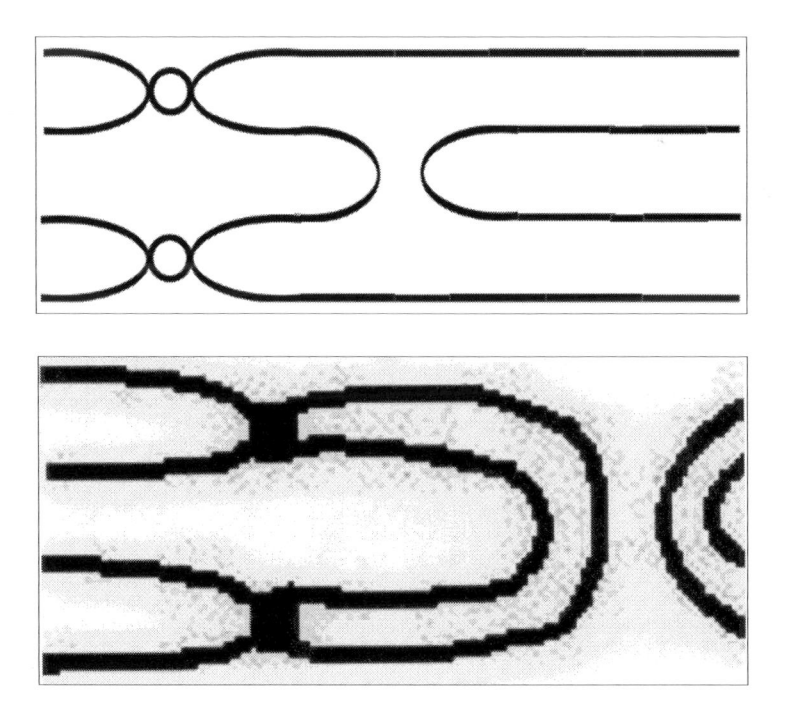

When the cell enters anaphase, the two pairs of each chromosome move apart into opposite sides of the cell. When they join this way, the process is interfered with, forming a bridge between two sets of chromosomes.

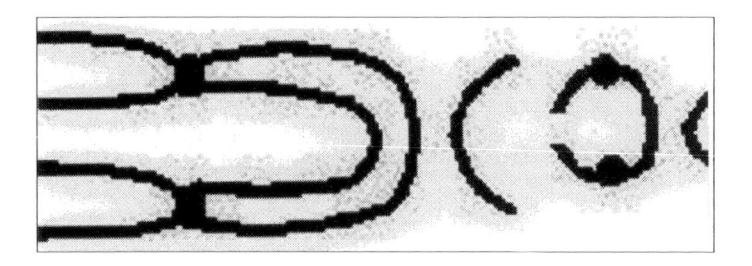

That is, at anaphase, the entire cell looks like this as follows.

Now, this will significantly hinder the completion of the cell division. When it succeeds in dividing, such a cell gives rise to a micro-nucleus formed from the broken-off fragment.

Perhaps we have gone into a little deeper detail. We are endeavoring to show that the radiations break the nucleus cell's chromosomes (the threads). Suppose the dose of irradiation is not sufficient to kill the cell. In that case, the chromosomes try to rejoin, but in this rejoining, distorted forms like stars, bridges, and micronuclei might appear, leading to many abnormalities. The number of chromosome abnormalities increases with increasing doses. It is a significant phenomenon and ought to be read with due care.

DIFFERENT VIEWS REGARDING HOW CHROMOSOME BREAKS OCCUR

Two extreme views regarding chromosome breaks have been adopted. A purely mechanical interpretation would be to consider breaking chromosomes (the threads) as the snapping of a cable by a rifle bullet, and ionizing particle (such as an electron ejected by X-rays or a proton or alpha particle) breaks the thread it hits. The opposite view is to consider that the ionizing radiations interfere with the ability of the cell to make chromosome material. The chromosome break is then a visible manifestation of the interruption in the synthesis.

However, the reader must bear in mind that whatever the controversial aspects of the scientific theories dealt with in this work be, none will ever affect the corroboration of the facts of the prophecy. Instead, all variant views of scientists regarding any phenomena, even seemingly opposing each other, will corroborate the views of the prophecy individually. This expression and verification of the scientific facts is a miracle of the prophecy of the Quran.

THE CAUSES OF CELL DEATH

Radiations kill the cell by rendering the enzymes inactive and decreasing the rigidity of nucleoprotein gels, the material that makes up the chromosomes. Any one of such changes would be sufficient to result in the death of the cell. The immediate death probably is attributed to changes in the physical properties of vital cell structure. Interestingly, a few hundred roentgens kill some cells, and a few thousand roentgens kill most cells. With these doses, cell death only occurs after a time interval, and immediately after irradiation, the cells look and behave quite normally. This delay, one of the characteristic features of radiation injury, can be explained in several chromosome breaks.

RADIATIONS RETARD THE CELLS DIVISION

A dose of more than 100,000 roentgens hits the cells like a sledgehammer. Delivering the dose kills the cells immediately. However, with doses insufficient to kill the cells, e.g., 300R, the most easily detectable change is a 'hold up' in cell division for a limited time and consequently retardation of growth. If the dose of radiation is increased above that necessary to produce only mitotic arrest of the cells which have gone into the division after some delay (cells) are not typical and will degenerate. The radiation has not killed the cells outright but has produced some irreparable permanent effect that the cells cannot overcome. While not preventing one and perhaps two or three divisions, this injury eventually brings about the death of all the cells derived from one that had been initially damaged. The injury which brings about this delayed death is the 'breaking of chromosomes'.

We will treat the rest of the necessary points of the theory of Radiobiology in the second part of this chapter when needed to validate facts.

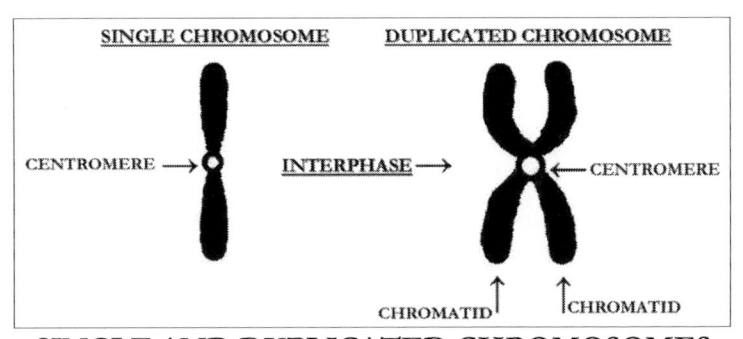

SINGLE AND DUPLICATED CHROMOSOMES

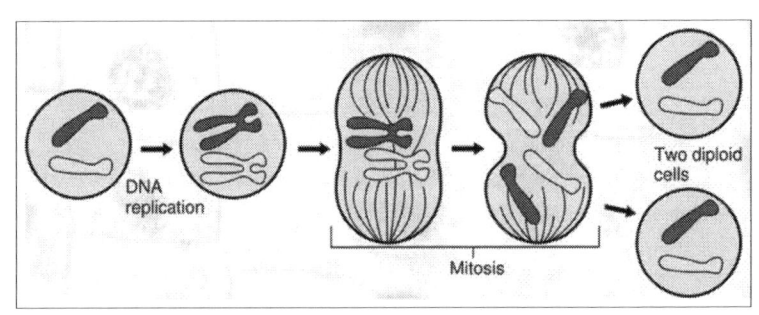

MITOSIS DIVIDES THE CHROMOSOMES IN A CELL NUCLEUS
(http://commons.wikimedia.org/wiki/File:Major_events_in_mitosis.svg)

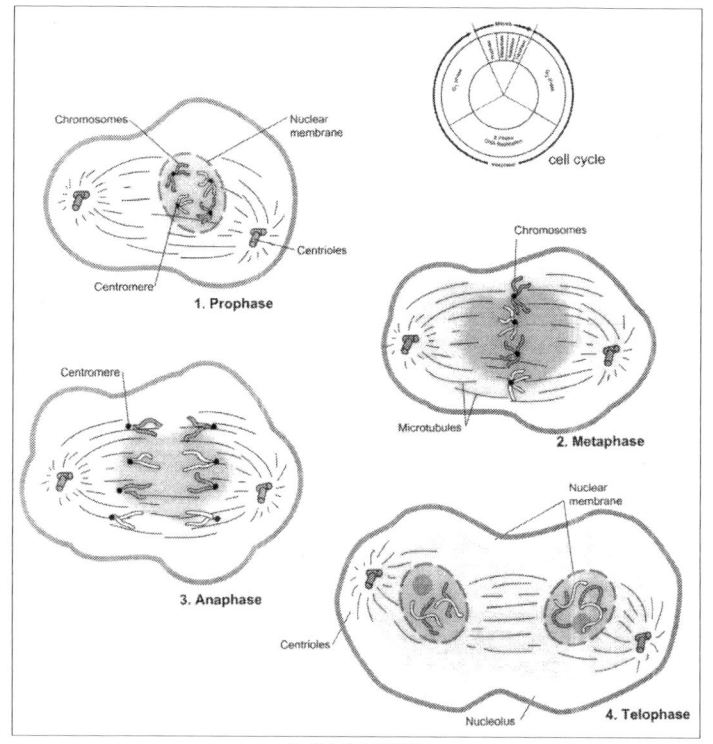

MITOSIS
(Courtesy: "National Human Genome Research Institute.")

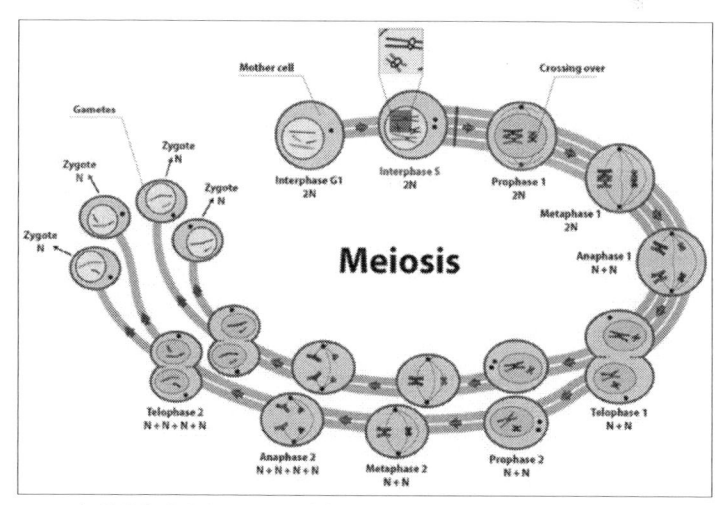

A DIAGRAM OF THE MEIOTIC PHASES
(https://en.wikipedia.org/wiki/File:Meiosis_diagram.jpg)

PART-2
RADIOBIOLOGICAL CORROBORATION OF 'AL-HOTAMA'

We will treat the topic about the knowledge of the subject of Radiobiology as is available at present. Science, as a rule, is a changing subject being the product of the fallible human mind, and scientists might make changes in specific points of present-day science in the future. They might settle controversial issues in the light of reliable proofs for or against any theory.

The confusion at present extant due to the extreme complexity of the subject of Radiobiology is alarming. Yet, the present confusion prevalent in Radiobiology will not affect our proof through the existing knowledge of the subject. Also, no matter what changes appear in due course in the subject, the basic principles that have been discovered and proved with undeniable certainty will forever sufficiently sustain and support the corroborative treatment of the points contained by the prophecy. However, we may assume with certainty that the improved accuracy of the radiologist's knowledge in the future will enhance the authenticity of the corroborative treatment of the points of the prophecy. The prophecy is as follows.

"Woe to every backbiter, defamer, who amasseth wealth (of this world) and storeth it (against the future), he thinketh surely that his wealth will render him immortal. Nay, for verily he shall be cast into 'Al-Hotama'. And what shall teach thee what 'Al-Hotama' is? It is Allah's kindled fire, which rises unto the hearts; it is (a fire) closed in on them, in outstretched columns."

(Quran: 104 'Al-Homaza')

This prophecy will forever be found in the world of science like a distant luminous star ever-present to the sailors and astronauts, no matter to whatever part of the sea or universe they might happen to move. The greater the scientists make advancement in the subject, the nearer will they be to the star, and the brighter will it seem in their sight. Suppose they make no further advancement in the subject. In that case, as is extant of the basic principles, the knowledge is enough to establish the prophecy's truth and corroborate the facts. The atomic war may intervene and destroy the whole prospect of any further research in this subject, instead, in any subject. On the other hand, oppressive circumstances may drown science in the flood of atomic energy for peace at some stage in the future.

Nuclear radiation is inherent in atomic energy. It also has the essential characteristics required to corroborate the facts of the prophecy, just as the atomic energy or atomic bombs. Radiobiology is an exceedingly complicated subject. An endeavor, however, will be made to render the topic as simple and as straightforward as it may be possible, so much so that even the average reader will feel little difficulty in comprehending the facts treated therein. All that hitherto we know about the nature of reactions of radiations within living bodies reveals that such reactions are from the beginning to end a series of 'crushing', 'leaping up over the hearts', and 'closing in on them in outstretched columns', just as the prophecy has described these reactions to be. The discoveries of Radiobiologists seem gratifying when viewed against the features of the fire of 'Al-Hotama' in an authenticating array.

SECTION-1
(1) 'HOTAMA' IS 'FIRE'. (Quran)

(a) **Energy is 'fire'.**

Heat energy and fire are all manifestations of one origin. Even mass and energy have proved to be the same thing initially. The total energy possessed by the molecules of a body represents its heat. The energy causes the motion of the molecules of a body and raises their temperatures. In biology, energy is defined as a sensation of warmth. In space, energy is radiation. Energy produces fire, and fire produces energy. Atomic radiation essentially is energy and can, therefore, be represented as fire.

(b) **The 'fire' of radioactivity burned the skin of the discoverer of the radioactivity itself.**

Becquerel, the discoverer of radioactivity, proved to be the first victim of this fire. He observed that radiations from Radium gave rise to biological effects when he noticed a burn in his skin next to the pocket in which he had carried a vial of Radium. Scientists soon found that the radiations from this element were closely similar to X-rays and could also produce cancer.

(c) **The effect of burning with radiation 'fire' is there, but the victim does not feel burning (heat).**

Radiations burn the body through which they pass, but the victim does not feel burning (heat) in the ordinary sense of the word. Becquerel never had any sensation of burning during the reaction of the radiation of the Radium vial, but all the same, the radiation kept secretly burning the skin of Becquerel, and the burn after a passage of time became visible to prove the fact that atomic radiation was a kind of fire.

(d) **Atomic radiation was called by Edward Teller (the famous inventor of the first Hydrogen bomb) as radioactive 'fire'.**

Describing the behavior of different categories of atomic reactors, he describes atomic radiation as radioactive fire.

The following is his statement.

"At that point a well-behaved dragon (reactor) will perform a harmless action. For instance, it may blow a fuse. But a vicious dragon will spit radioactive fire."

("Our Nuclear Future: Facts, Dangers, and Opportunities"; by Dr. Edward Teller and Dr. Albert. L. Latter, Page-156)

The nickname 'dragon' for 'reactor' is also a very appropriate appellation.

(e) **Radiations are called 'fire' by radiotherapists.**

The classic radiotherapy books use the term 'cross fire' to illustrate a particular method of applying radiation to cancer. The following will serve as an example.

"Deep X-ray therapy is used to assist in the devitalization of scattered cancer cells lying beyond the area of concentrated Radium effect, by means of cross fire in various directions."

('Synopsis of Gynecology'; by Harry Sturgeon Crossen and Robert James Crossen, 1946, Page-144)

The term 'crossfire' not only depicts the igneous quality of the fire of radiations but also, at the same time, represents its destructive capacity as fire. The following from the same book explains the destructive quality of the fire of radiations and their quality of selectivity.

"Radiation treatment is one of our most effective remedies against cancer. It has a selective action on cancer cells insofar that cancer cells may be destroyed without serious injury to adjacent tissue cells. This selective action depends on the fact that cancer cells are younger, less stable, and consequently less resistant to destructive influences than the surrounding nature tissue cells. With proper screening to limit the burning rays, the selective devitalizing action on cancer cells may be extended widely in the pelvis."

(Ibid: Pages: 91-92)

Again, in the same book, the author further identified the differential effect of Radium with heat in general.

"This differential effect is not particular to Radium though Radium gives it most markedly. Heat has this effect to some degree. An incision into a cancer with a cautery kills cancer cells beyond the line of incision; a short distance further than it destroys the mature tissue cells.

That is the reason a cautery incision through a cancerous area is much more likely to heal than a knife incision."

(Ibid: Page-142)

Although a resemblance between the heat of cautery and Radium has been shown, one should not lose sight of the actual difference between ordinary chemical fire and nuclear fire.

(f) **Radiations do but deposit 'energy' in the material through which they pass.**

All kinds of ionizing radiations deposit energy in the material through which they pass and initiate all chemical and biological reactions by this very same act alone. Moreover, we could prove energy to be identical with 'fire'.

(2) 'HOTAMA' IS A 'CRUSHING FIRE'. (Quran)

(a) **Atomic radiation is a 'crushing fire'.**

Atomic radiations are a sort of a crushing fire and show all the characteristics of crushing. The crushing quality of radiations also is peculiarly nuclear. Radiations knock out electrons from the atoms and eject nucleons from the atomic nuclei. Their reactions are identical to crushing in a living body, and so are their reactions in inanimate matter. In a living body, they knock out electrons, eject nucleons from atoms, and thrust nucleons in them; they activate the water content of the living body (the activated water further inactivates the enzymes) and break the cell chromosomes with fatal consequences to the cell.

In inanimate matter, too, they produce transmutations. Thus, they can be seen to crush even the basic structure of 'atom', 'the basic building block of the universe', and 'the basic unit of life' that is the 'cell'. We could appropriately give them the name of 'basic crusher', and further, because they crush the nuclei of the atoms and cells, they could be aptly termed the 'nuclear crusher'.

(b) **The Radiobiologist's terminology indicates the 'crushing' trait of the atomic radiations.**

The appropriateness of high representative terminology of Radiobiologists, like the physicists before them, is remarkable, while the identity between his terminology and that of the prophecy is marvelous. The point of the crushing feature of radiations is understandable by the mere utterance of the terms. It corroborates the points of the prophecy even before any functional or phenomenal scrutiny is attempted.

'Hotama' literally means a crusher. As a term, the Quran has used it to signify a kind of a crushing fire. The 'target concept' is the fundamental mechanism that brings about the radiobiological changes. It is edifying to observe that the Radiobiologist has termed this theory as the 'target concept'. Also, he would frequently apply terms like 'hitting', 'direct action', 'indirect action' etc., just as the physicist would preferably use terms like 'smashing the atoms', etc.

Terms like these suggest military artillery action and most befitting the violence of the actions observed in the described processes. The Radiobiologist rightly treats the 'target concept' above mentioned to describe the impact of radiations under the heading 'hitting the target'. While describing the chromosomes' breaks, he likens the action of the radiations to 'snapping the cable with a bullet'.

The nuclear scientist has universally regarded this crushing concept of atomic energy as a distinctive characteristic of the atomic phenomena. The reader of any standard textbook of nuclear science should frequently expect to encounter statements like the following.

(i) "To transmute a non-radioactive nucleus involves <u>hitting</u> infinitely simply small target nuclei with sub-atomic bullets possessing high kinetic energy."

('General Chemistry'; by John Arrend Timm, Page-606)

(ii) "It seemed possible that if atoms were <u>bombarded</u> with energetic particles, one of the latter might penetrate into a nucleus and cause a disruption."

('Nuclear Physics'; by Irving Kaplan, Page-528)

(iii) "At still higher energies, still more particles are given off, and term '<u>atom smashing</u>' is really appropriate."

(Ibid: Page-277)

(iv) Peter Alexander says that delivering exceedingly massive doses of X-rays; generally, more than 100,000R results in on-the-spot death of all the cells just because of extensive chemical changes produced by a tremendous amount of radiation. He concludes:
"It is comparable to <u>hitting cells with a sledge hammer</u>."

('Atomic Radiation and Life'; by Peter Alexander, Page-53)

The '<u>sledgehammer</u>' action of radiations is of little interest to the Radiobiologist. It is too crude an action of little help to understand the minute reactions of radiations he is interested in to include in his list. Still, strangely enough, this very sledgehammer-like action of radiations is of paramount interest in our theme. We, however, are not chary of the minute aspects of the subject.

(v) "When the target is <u>hit</u>, the cell dies, and there is no halfway house."

(Ibid: Page-202)

Herein then has appeared a miracle of the Scripture; functional and anticipative. Also, credit beyond the power of expression could be due to the scientist for his admirable insight, discernment, and appropriateness. The scientist by the uniqueness of ingenuity of mind, exactitude of vision, keenness of discernment, extreme depth of understanding of the subject, and laudable skill in contriving the terms, and above all else his great sincerity to the profession, well deserves a title like the oracle of the atomism.

Moreover, it may not be wrong to assume that the modern scientist on the dint of the abovementioned qualities is placed in a particular situation. In that situation, he can behold the miracle of the prophecy to his awe and wonder, appreciation and admiration, enlightenment and enjoyment. He can find guaranteed guidelines for his conduct in his field. We do not doubt that his qualities (themselves) will force him to discern the truth of the oracle of the Scripture. Many will be obliged to change their previous view that miracles do not happen.

Those only will deny this miracle of the Quran who can deny the presence of the sun during the day. The conscience-smitten scientist will leap to the occasion with all his heart to save him and this miserable humankind that now stands on the brink of wholesale destruction in which he happens to have the prime share. He shall certainly think that his past acts must be atoned for and will not neglect the prospect of great ills that his discoveries may do to the already miserable humankind.

(c) **The 'target concept' of radiation reactions.**

The target theory is a fundamental theory that illustrates the primary mechanism of Radiobiology changes. The English physicist Growther tentatively put forward this concept in 1924. The unique identity between the 'target concept' and its counterpart, 'the crushing concept' of 'Al-Hotama' of the prophecy, is evident in every respect. The following facts further confirm the resemblance.

SINGLE-HIT AND MULTI-HIT PROCESSES

As with most revolutionary concepts, the idea behind the 'target concept' is simple. It is assumed that in the cell or other biological material being irradiated, there are one or more sensitive volumes within which either one ('single-hit process') or several ('multi-hit process') ionizations have to occur in bringing about the observed effect.

Peter Alexander says that the thick ionization radiations will be less effective for hitting a target that can be inactivated by one ionization since the possibility of missing altogether will be much greater.

The same problem continues in the following where we quote a specimen of the language of the radiologist (Peter Alexander) regarding the 'hitting' characteristics of radiations.

"The same problem confronts the sportsman in deciding between a rifle and a shotgun. Though the total explosive power may be same, the energy loss is different. A target capable of being killed by a small amount of energy is more likely to be brought down by shot, spreading its action over a greater area. In the event of being hit by a bullet, the amount of energy used is greatly in excess of that necessary. In the activation of viruses and enzymes and the other systems to which the Target Theory applies, radiations of low ionization density are more effective than alpha rays or neutrons because only one ionization --- or in our analogy, one bullet of shot --- is necessary. In living system the exact reverse applies. Densely ionizing radiations are much more effective in bringing about all the various types of injury, including both long-term effects like <u>cancer</u> and <u>genetic damage</u>, as well as <u>radiation sickness</u> and <u>acute radiation death</u>." [1]

('Atomic Radiation and Life'; by Peter Alexander, Pages: 206-207)

(d) Indirect theory.

In 1942, Dr. Walter Dale working in Manchester showed that the 'activated water' could inactivate enzymes vital for the cell's life. Later work showed that the free radicals that make up activated water could bring about deep-seated chemical changes in the vital constituents of the cell and must, therefore, be harmful to biological materials. For this reason, the tendency to interpret radiation data on cells in terms of the 'target theory' has become unpopular, and opinion has swung to the other extreme of considering free radicals from water as the primary agent responsible for producing cell damage. This tendency has probably gone too far, and chemical changes from direct action must play an important part.

However, not enough we yet know about fundamental reactions preceding biological injury to estimate how much of the effect can be attributed to reactions of the free radicals formed in water and how much to direct energy absorption by substances of the cell? The experiments in model systems showing direct action being much more efficient than indirect action indicate that changes due to direct action must be essential under the conditions prevailing in the cell.

The indirect theory assumes that the radiations first hit and activate the water content in the living body. Then, the activated molecules of water react with dissolved substances or other material they contact. Changes produced by the activated water molecules are referred to as 'indirect action' of radiation in contrast to the 'direct action', which refers to those changes which occur in the substances which directly absorb the radiation. Much confusion, however, still prevails among the Radiobiologists respecting the two theories, namely, the direct and the indirect.

The activation of water is crucial because most living systems contain a great deal of water, making up as much as 85 percent of the weight of a mammal. Consequently, on irradiation of an animal, most of the energy will initially be deposited on water, and only a tiny proportion will be taken up by the materials which make up the body, such as the skin, bones, muscles, etc. and by the solids dissolved in the fluids such as the proteins in the blood. The energy taken up in the water activates water molecules that then, as already stated, react with dissolved substances or other materials with which they come into contact. The activated water molecules inactivate the enzymes of the cell. Enzymes are vital to the life of a cell. Death, therefore, of the cell occurs if the enzymes are inactivated. Judging from the magnitude of the water content in the living body, it is not difficult to estimate the magnitude of damage to the body's cells by the activated water.

A suggestion made as long ago as 1929 by Risse regarding splitting water into a particular kind of ions called free radicals on irradiation has now been confirmed. These free radicals are highly reactive entities since they do not have the electron configuration required for stable molecules. They have an odd electron: to become stable; they have to lose or gain an electron. The significant reactivity of activated water is due to these radicals, which attack most organic substances to attain a standard electron configuration. If these radicals do not find something with which to react, they will combine, and in solution, they persist for less than one-thousandth part of a second. We can interpret indirect action satisfactorily in terms of the reaction of radicals formed in water and the attack of these radicals on other substances. These reactions are always in completion with the recombination of the radicals to give backwater.

We now know much about the kind of chemical reactions in which these free radicals participate; they may bring about the bridging of two molecules by oxidation of so-called SH groups present in most proteins. Another way in which radicals act is by breaking large molecules into smaller fragments. Some of these reactions can cause the molecule to lose its biological activity, such as enzyme action.

In this indirect theory, too, we see that the basis of all action is the act of 'breaking' and 'crushing'. Radiations by knocking electrons out from the atoms of the water molecules change them into free radicals. The free radicals then bring about bridging molecules, break large molecules into smaller fragments, and cause them to lose their biological activity. Thus, despite controversy among Radiobiologists on the point of direct and indirect action of radiations, the viewpoint of the prophecy remains unaffected till the end since the actions of 'breaking' and 'crushing' are present in both disputed theories.

Let us revert to the point of the terminology of the Radiobiologist and the physicist. Correspondence between radiation's action and the Radiobiologist's expression about radiations' crushing feature might have been clear to the reader. This terminological analogy between the prophecy and the Radiobiologist will continue throughout this chapter.

(e) **Nuclear radiations are possessed of a strangely exceptional characteristic of 'crushing'.**

The dose of radiation sufficient to kill or visibly injure a cell represents such a minute amount of energy that it could affect very few molecules, a change entirely insufficient to directly bring about the pronounced biological effects. Yet, we could examine visibly physical damage in the cells killed by the radiations. Some peculiar and yet unknown crushing faculty must be there to account for this queer factor.

The challenge to the scientist now is to discover the subtle process by which so minute an amount of energy supplied by the ionizing radiations can initiate changes that eventually result in cell injury and death. This peculiar quality of fire of radiation augments the justification of the epithet like 'Hotama' that is the 'crushing fire'.

The discovery of the nature of the process involved in crushing by so minute an amount of energy will lead the scientist into the depths of nature where the boundary of physics may submerge into metaphysics. Such a discovery indeed will be a treat on the part of the scientist. The scientist is justly surprised at highly proportional results of energy of radiations, yet how many points will in his research of Radiobiology appear that will further enhance his surprise at the subtlety of the subject and the wonders of the Creator.

(f) **The strangeness of the 'crushing' faculty of radiations is realized by the scientist but not yet understood.**

The first step involved between exposure to radiation and the first detectable indications of radiation injury is the uptake of energy from sub-atomic particles or radiations. How the mere deposition of energy in a cell can initiate the processes that lead to observed end effects is not yet understood. The energy must bring about some chemical change that modifies some cell constituents. The thing at present is far too subtle for the understanding of the scientist. It is doubtful whether the scientist will ever be able to understand this ultra-subtle fact.

But that the Quran should name the radiations as a 'crushing fire', a fact that carries man's mind into the extreme regions of subtlety ---

means the revealer of the Quran did unmistakably recognize this distinguishing faculty of the fire of 'Al-Hotama'. He named it 'Al-Hotama', the 'crushing fire' and has thus indicated this crushing faculty of the fire of 'Al-Hotama' as its characteristic distinction as distinct from all other types of fire. The quality of crushing is common to all kinds of fires. Still, the distinction of the fire of 'Hotama' is that it crushes the basic nuclear structure of the atom and thus shows a sort of minuteness that does not apply to any other kind of fire.

Moreover, this very minuteness is at play in this present problem, namely, that so tiny an amount of energy deposited by the radiations in the cell should cause such great havoc to the life and structure of the cell thus affected. To understand this problem better, the scientists will have to adopt the same line of thought. The secret remains in the peculiar characteristic feature of the radiations of reaching the innermost depths of the subatomic structure where the atom is most sensitive to the effect and, therefore, the effect of radiations. These parts, where the radiations attack the atom, are extra-sensitive. This extreme sensitivity is responsible for such nonproportional effects of radiations so much so that a minute amount of energy deposited by radiations that could hardly affect a few molecules, visibly injure, or kill the whole cell itself.

(g) **Radiations 'crush' by depositing the energy without raising the temperature of its victim.**
The energy not used for chemical reactions becomes available as heat. But this cannot be responsible for any biological changes in irradiation since the dose of radiation sufficient to kill a man (500R) can raise his temperature by just over one-thousandth part of a degree, which is much less than that the everyday variations. This case may seem crushing without burning. Apparently, yes, but not really, because burning done by radiations is so very minute that has hitherto defied both the senses and the instruments made by man. The body of a man or a mammal killed by radiation is like a burnt corpse. But it is not so since the burning by the fire of 'Al-Hotama' is too minute and excessively subtle to be seen.

(h) **Radiations hit the cells like a 'sledgehammer' and 'crush' them.**
The phrase 'hitting with a sledgehammer' at least appears as a rude expression of someone writing a thrilling film scene, but actually, it is not so. It is the language of the leaders among the Radiobiologists not accustomed to sensational expressions, and they indeed have expressed what they exactly in truth have seen.

They have seen the cells being hit with a sledgehammer by radiations and crushed, and this is what 'Al-Hotama' exactly means: 'Hotama', 'the great crusher'. We can understand how the radiations hit and crush the cells by considering mammalian cells in tissue culture. Delivering doses of more than 100,000 roentgens immediately kills all cells. This instantaneous death is due to widespread chemical changes produced by many radiations. Radiobiologists compare it to 'hitting the cells with a sledgehammer'.

Mark this instance of the analogy that exists between the terminology of Radiobiologist and that of the Quran. The phrase 'widespread chemical changes' is an example of the sophisticated language of the scientist. It seemingly is a very soft expression and causes no one to shudder, but its actual meanings are ruthless enough to terrify someone. It simply means 'wide-spread signs of ruthless crushing'.

(i) **Radiations 'break' the cell chromosomes.**

Visible under the microscope after irradiation, the first changes occur in the cell nucleus, wherein we could visibly see the breaks of the nucleus chromosomes. We can classify changes in the cell nucleus as temporary or permanent. Chromosomes' permanent changes are not repaired and are perpetuated in subsequent divisions and can lead to delayed degeneration and death, a characteristic feature of radiation injury. However, the usual explanation of permanent chromosome changes is that they result from breaks in chromosomes produced by radiations. If the dose is less than the lethal dose, then the broken ends are believed to have the ability to rejoin. Different types of reunion can occur to give new chromosome configurations different from those initially present. These give rise to many different abnormalities that we can see under the microscope. A proportion of the breaks remains open, and these look like broken chromosomes. An ionization particle can break a chromosome if we deposit 700ev of energy in the part of the track which crosses it. This energy is assumed to be equivalent to 20 ionizations; thus, the radiation, true to its fundamental characteristic of 'breaking' and 'crushing', can be seen engaged in its reactions within the cell. Regarding the breakage of chromosomes by radiations, two extreme views which, according to Radiobiologists, can be adopted, are given in the following.

The first, purely mechanical interpretation would consider breakage of chromosomes like the 'snapping of a cable by a rifle bullet'. An ionizing particle (such as an electron ejected by X-rays or a proton or alpha-particle) breaks the thread (of the chromosomes) it hits. It is manifestly in exact accordance with the primary breaking characteristic of radiations.

The second view is to consider that ionizing radiations interfere with the ability of the cell to make chromosome material. It is a process that occurs in the resting stage when the cell is most sensitive to radiation.

The chromosome break is then a visible manifestation of the interruption in synthesis. This latter view, too, in no way interferes with our concept that is the 'breaking' and 'crushing' concept of radiations, for the cell has been rendered incapable of making the chromosome material basically due to the ionization caused by the radiations in the cell.

It is well-known that ionizations are disturbances caused within the atom or the molecules due to the crushing actions of radiations, such as the ejection of electrons and nucleons. As a result, it crushes the basic structure of the atoms and the molecules. In other words, it has crushed the cell to the extent that it has lost the ability to make the chromosome material.

(j) Radiations change the irradiated body into a handful of 'crushed cells', 'crushed blood' and 'crushed bones' etc.

While irradiating, a dose of 200,000 Roentgen wholly crushes the animal internally: cell, sap, bone, blood, and all. Radiation crushes the body's cells to the extent that the whole internal body converts into a handful of minced meat and curdled blood.

The well-known symptoms of radiation sickness are severe hemorrhages (internal blood leaking), leukemia (a blood disorder), anemia (diminished number of red blood cells), diarrhea, vomiting, inflammation, loss of hair, loss of appetite, general disorders, pallor leading to rapid emaciation, asthma, etc.

It is also well-known that radiations destroy the bone marrow, producing cancer of bones and the body. If these are the symptoms of disease, imagine the state of the body that has died of it. What better epithet we could devise for such a dead body than that of:

"A handful of minced meat and curdled blood"?

However, a victim's condition that has succumbed to a dose of 200,000 roentgens would be pretty different. To expose a person to such a dose of radiation is like shooting millions of millions of thin invisible needles of fire through the entire body's cells. Anyone could well imagine the state of such a dead body.

The balance between organs is disturbed by irradiating the whole body, and a vicious circle sets up. A disturbing condition persists for several days, brought about mainly by the fall in blood cells, which the bone marrow has stopped replacing. The action of radiation has entirely crushed the faculty of bone marrow to produce blood cells.

By the time the individual cells have recovered, it is too late for the delicate interplay between the different organs to be re-established, and the complex machine comes to a standstill like crushed wreckage. One must almost say that the diversity and absence of any specific response brought about by radiation's 'crushing' effect is the cause of death.

(k) **The 'crushing' by radiations is widespread, diffused, and ill-defined.**
No complete explanation has hitherto been given for the paradox that although the pathological changes from whole-body irradiation are diffused and ill-defined, yet death occurs with remarkable regularity. From the viewpoint of Radiobiologists, this fact may appear a paradox, yet there is nothing inconsistent in this as far as our perspective is concerned. It is crushing cells, as indicated by the pathological changes brought about by the crushing reactions of radiations within the cells.

However, this paradox, like the paradox of so minute an amount of energy of radiations causing so significant a damage, will call the Radiobiologist to the deeper levels of the atomic structure. Perhaps the Radiobiologist may find the answer, and the riddle solved if possible. The reactions of radiations occur at the atoms' points that are inaccessible to chemical poisons and occur in invisibly minute areas. Such is the complexity of the subject of Radiobiology. As far as our object in this paradox is concerned, it is clear, and we can simply call it by the name of a strange and queer 'crushing' quality of the fire of radiation.

(l) **'Life-crushing' process of radiations is exceptionally minute.**
The symptoms of acute radiation sickness can be summarized, but they tell us little about the cause of death. Suppose a pathologist carries out a postmortem examination on a mammal that has succumbed after a radiation dose of a few hundredth roentgens. In that case, he will find it very difficult to pinpoint death to the failure of a particular organ. He could find the signs of devastation throughout but no severely damaged organ to justify the cause of death. He would find internal hemorrhages of varying severalties, and in some cases, though, they would be considered the cause of death by no means at all. Hemorrhages can kill either by destroying the function of a vital organ or by producing severe anemia. However, the site where hemorrhage occurs varies in different animals. It is confined almost entirely to the intestines in rats and mice, where it would not be lethal. In the pig, hemorrhages always happen near the heart, where they could kill the pigs.

Anemia, observed in all animals after irradiation, though death often occurs before this, is severe. If anemia causes death, then blood transfusions ought to prevent it. Still, in practice, no increase in survival or even a significant increase in time between irradiation and death is found by giving intensive transfusions. The fact is that the reactions of radiations take place at sub-atomic levels, and crushing thereof is so unclearly minute and so minutely wide-spread and universal throughout the body of the irradiated victim that the effects are not observable even in the most robust microscope.

Hence, it is difficult to assess the minute aggregate damage of the whole body that has brought about the death without leaving any signs of damage to any one or more particular organs to whose failure we could pinpoint the cause of death. In contrast, we could see the effect of chemical poisons that happen to do such gross damage to any one of the vital organs that death cause could be pinpointed to the failure of that particular organ.

(m) **Radiations 'crush' life out of the body by putting the organs temporarily out of commission.**

The whole of radiation sickness is a complex interplay between cellular damage and impaired recovery process. It introduces the great diversity and apparent lack of specificity. After whole-body irradiation, mitosis stops, blood production ceases in the bone marrow, and the walls of the intestines are no longer replaced by new cells as they get worn away. Microscopic examination of these organs will show them utterly devoid of new cells a day after whole-body irradiation of several hundred roentgens.

Yet this same effect is produced with doses that do not kill. Indifference can be seen one or two days after irradiation between animals that have received a lethal dose and those given a slightly smaller dose that does not kill. The inhibition of cell division is only temporary. The bone marrow and walls of the intestines begin to fill up with cells again three or four days after irradiation so that at the time of death, these organs do not look severely damaged. Yet, there can be no doubt that the act of putting them temporarily out of commission contributed to the death. Presumably, by the time these radiosensitive organs are producing cells again, the opportunity for repair and recovery of other irradiated cells has been lost.

Radiation has crushed the life within the cells so minutely and undetectably that it (radiation) rendered them (the cells) incapable of availing the opportunity for repair and recovery offered by the revived organs. These organs did not seem severely damaged at the time of death. Yet, their life was insidiously 'crushed' earlier and taken out of them by radiations.

(n) **Radiations 'crush' cell barriers.**

Radiations crush the barriers which exist within the cell. Such barriers require a minimum amount of energy before breaking. Interference with internal structures would bring rapid amplification of a subtle initial effect since the cell contains its particular means for destruction, such as enzymes that break down vital macromolecules. Usually, internal barriers prevent the different components from coming to contact with one another. Once the enzymes are released from their specific location, they act extremely fast, and injuries could become apparent within minutes.

Radiations release the flood-gates, and dammed-up water does the rest. The barriers retaining this structure are tremendously thin, and of the molecular dimensions, the passage of atomic particles through them could create havoc. The diversity of the end-effects of radiations greater than that found after poisoning with most chemical substances would follow naturally if the initial effects were due to the coming together of cellular materials, usually kept apart.

(o) **Radiations destroy the capacity of the body to form antibodies.**
One of the most typical symptoms of radiation sickness is a much greater susceptibility to infection. Small and insignificant wounds turn septic after whole-body irradiation, and many infections set in spontaneously. The reason for this is two-fold; the mucous membranes of the intestines become thin and ulcerated and aided by local hemorrhages, the bacteria from the intestines gain access to other parts of the body. It in itself would probably not be sufficient to make the infections as serious as they are, but the body has at the same time lost its capacity to form antibodies. These substances, probably produced in the blood-forming organs, prepare the animal to combat dangerous organisms immediately.

(p) **Radiations 'crush' as well as cause cancer by 'crushing' the cells.**
Atomic radiations both cure and cause cancer. For this reason, Radiobiologists have named radiation as the 'two-edged sword' and have further called it a 'Tragic Paradox'. To say, however, that radiations cure cancer is erroneous. Radiations, in reality, do not cure cancer, but they only destroy its cells with a probability of recurrence. They, albeit, cause actual cancer by producing a mutation in the normal cell. Mutation, as is well-known, is brought about by a destructive process. By the mutation, radiation confers on the cell the quality of peculiar cancerous malignancy. This quality is further transmissible to every daughter cell of the cell which has been mutated originally.

The Radiobiologists are pretty justified in calling the cancer-causing quality of radiation tragic. Apart from the genetic effects of radiation, the production of cancer by radiation is probably the most unfortunate aspect of radiation exposure. No natural cure for cancer has yet been found, and none is yet in sight. This fact, too, will seem strange to many, for generally, they believe atomic radiation to be a sure cure for cancer. The incidence of cancer due to atomic radiation will increase with the adoption of atomic energy to the extent that atomic radiation treatment will lose much of its significance. Radiation is used in the destruction of cancer because it destroys the less differentiated and, therefore, comparatively less resistant-to-radiation cells of cancer, doing at the same time much hurt to the cells of the neighboring tissues.

(q) **Atomic radiation is 'fire', but it is a kind of a 'crushing fire'.**

A mammal killed by radiation shows no sign of burning in the ordinary sense of the word 'burning'. Not one of its hair is so much as singed. No cell in the body has any indication that the fire has ever touched it. The corpse, however, is inwardly wholly crushed to the cell by the mincing pins of radiations.

However, energy (fire), which ionizing radiations have deposited in the body's cells, has brought about all this crushing. Thus, this strange fire 'crushes' but does not burn in the usual sense of the word 'burning'. The radiations have burned the particles of the body's cells definitely with such minuteness that the effect of burning is not visible, either to man or the microscope.

SECTION-2
"HOTAMA IS A FIRE WHICH LEAPS UP OVER THE HEARTS". (Quran)

At the very outset, it is essential to note that the expression 'heart' which the Quran has used in this context has diverse meanings, both literal and figurative. The expression admits interpretations that may have physical, physiological, or psychological purport. It may mean the muscle that pumps blood in the body, which may also mean the source of desires and thoughts. We will now endeavor to show how the atomic radiations leap up over the hearts, a quaint feature that provides a fascinating study.

(1) **RADIATIONS ATTACK THE 'NUCLEI' THAT ARE THE 'HEARTS' OF ATOMS:** Radiations attack the nuclei of atoms (that constitute the material) through which they pass. They attack the nuclei of the atoms that constitute the biological and botanical cells. Further, mainly, they attack the nuclei of cells. We could see them rise not only above the 'hearts' but further even above the 'hearts' of 'hearts'.

It is a well-known fact that radiations attack the nuclei of the atoms and eject nucleons from there, and they knock out electrons from the atoms, ionizing thereby the atoms. Indeed, all the reactions of radiations take place within the nuclei that are the hearts. The role played by the cell nucleus entitles it with much appropriateness to name as 'heart'. The word nucleus itself is highly suggestive of the word 'heart' philologically. Psychological identity is evident too. The functional justification of the resemblance also is apparent.

The first changes in the irradiated cell visible under the microscope occur in the cell nucleus in chromosome breaks. The cell's nucleus performs the function of ensuring the exact reproduction of the cell when it divides by duplicating the cellular control mechanisms carried by chromosomes. It is highly vulnerable to the effect of atomic radiation. There is good evidence suggesting that the crucial initial radiation injury occurs for cells in the active division. We can visibly see the effects of radiations in the nucleus in the form of chromosomes' breakage.

The chromosomes are thread-like formations in the cell nucleus and could, with remarkable plausibility, be termed heart-strings (nucleus chords). The radiations break these heartstrings of the cell nucleus with fatal consequences to the cell. It either dies instantly or gradually degenerates to death. Even if it survives the ordeal due to the lesser dose of radiation, it forever suffers from heart-sickness after that; yes, even its posterity suffers to the last generation.

(2) **RADIATIONS RISE ON TOP OF THE NUCLEUS CHROMOSOMES JUST AS SOMEONE RISES ON THE TOP OF A HILL:** The Quran, in this context, has used the words 'Tattalio Alal Afedha'. That is, "It rises unto the hearts". 'Tattalio' means to rise above. We derive the word 'Tattalio' from the root verb "Ittalaa". The root verb "Ittalaa" means 'to rise above' like someone climbs up and appears on top of the hill.

Similar is the case of the radiation when it rises on the chromosomes of the cell nucleus. Radiation attacks the cell in its resting stage, but we see nothing of it then. We only observe its presence when it has risen the chromosomes in the metaphase or the anaphase of the cell division. We can thus picture the radiation starting at the bottom of the hill at the resting stage of the cell and then moving uphill to appear on the top (of the hill), that is, the chromosomes where we can view its presence in the chromosome breaks. The cell is most sensitive to the effect of radiation in its resting stage. At this stage, the chromosomes are not visible. But they are very insensitive at metaphase and anaphase when we can see chromosomes very clearly. You must keep in mind that we cannot see what happens to the chromosomes at irradiation time.

Consequently, it is not strictly true that someone has observed a specific chromosome change due to irradiation. The exact statement should be that the effect of the irradiation at the resting stage has given rise to the change seen at metaphase. This point is not as pedantic as it might appear but has an essential bearing on interpreting the results. In light of this explanation, it will be easy to understand how radiation starts climbing up the hill that is the cell's heart. At last, it appears at the top of the peak of chromosomes in metaphase or anaphase of the journey of cell division.

Radiation rises to the extremities of the heart of the cell. It rises above the cell nucleus. Then it rises above the nucleus chromosomes. Lastly, it rises above the chromosome genes that might be considered the utmost extremity of the heart of the cell nucleus.

(3) **THE ACTIONS OF RADIATION ARE LOCALIZED IN SUB-MICROSCOPIC THAT ARE EXTREMELY MINUTE AREAS:** Ionizing radiations are destructive agents who retain action localized in sub-microscopic areas more minor than that obtained by any other method. For example, it is pretty impossible to get a beam of destructive ultraviolet or a jet of toxic chemicals with a cross-section as small as a track of an ionizing particle. It is thus apparent that radiation reaches the point so minute that we could term it as the 'heart' of its existence with plausibility and reason. The incident ray of radiation is a sub-atomistic projectile, extraordinarily sharp, and minutely invisible. It penetrates to the minutest and extra delicate depths of matter. It causes delicately fatal damage to the material. Hence, we could well remark that its action has reached the ultimate 'heart' of existence itself.

(4) **THE 'TARGET CONCEPT' OF RADIATIONS ITSELF IS SUGGESTIVE OF THIS FACT OF RADIATIONS' RISING TO THE 'HEARTS':** The 'target concept' of radiations assumes that either one or more sensitive volumes exist in the cell or other biological material under irradiation. Ionizations must occur within these sensitive volumes in either single-hit or multi-hit processes to bring about the observed effect. These sensitive volumes could be called 'hearts' with much appropriateness since sensitivity is a feature so characteristically associated with 'heart'.

(5) **THE ACTION OF RADIATION REACHES BEYOND THE BRAIN UNTO THE 'HEART' OF LIFE ITSELF:** It is remarkable to note that ionizing radiations hit mammals at their weakest point. They affect the coordination of function at the level where it is beyond the control of the brain. The brain and central nervous system are remarkably radio-resistant, and there is no indication that impairment of these plays any part in radiation sickness. The level where coordination of function is beyond the control of the brain, we could reasonably assume as the level of 'heart'. Clearly, then the radiations could be said to attack the level of the 'heart'.

(6) **THE 'HEART' OF THE MITOTIC CYCLE IN CELL DIVISION:** It is a known fact that if the dose rate exceeds a certain value, the effectiveness of radiation in stopping mitosis falls again. In other words, there is a dose level at which, for a given dose, the mitotic arrest is most outstanding. It suggests a short, specific period in the mitotic cycle when the cell is most susceptible to damage. Therefore, not all cells will be exposed during their critical stage by reducing the time in which radiation is given beyond a specific value. The critical point above-mentioned, at which the damage of radiation is most significant, could with reason be termed as the 'heart' of the mitotic cycle.

(7) **EXCEPTIONAL ATTRACTION OF RADIATION FOR THE 'HEART' IN A BODY; A FACT UNMISTAKABLY DISCERNIBLE:** It is unmistakably observable that radiation shows a selective tendency towards the 'heart' and whatever is related to it in the body.

We will produce a summary of this exciting feature in the following to prove the point.

(a) **The most prominent target of radiation is the bone marrow.**
The function of the bone marrow is to form blood corpuscles. The relation of the bone marrow to the heart through blood is evident.

(b) **A target susceptible to radiation is blood itself.**
The relation of blood to the heart also is apparent.

(c) **All the blood-forming organs are susceptible to radiation.**
All the blood-forming organs are susceptible to the effect of radiation. The relation of blood-forming organs to the heart through blood is evident.

(d) **Unicellular organisms are far less sensitive to radiation than multicellular organisms.**
Unicellular organisms are all, without exception, far less sensitive to the effect of radiation than multi-cellular organisms.

The exact difference between these two kinds is as follows.

The unicellular organisms have circulatory and respiratory systems, far inferior and far less developed than multicellular organisms. The relation of the circulatory and respiratory systems to the heart through blood is no secret. The preference of radiation to the organisms with a more developed circulatory and respiratory system may well be attributed to the particular attraction of radiation for the 'heart'. Probably, this factor that of the degree of development of the heart and lungs might have some influence in determining the relative degree of the sensitivity to radiation.

The Radiobiologists have their viewpoint about this comparative sensitivity of multicellular organisms. They believe that the significant interactions and internal dependence of different organs and cells in multicellular organisms might cause their greater sensitivity to radiation. It might be the basis for why mammals are so much more susceptible to radiation than most unicellular organisms. Radiobiologists might be correct in their opinion. In this respect, we have merely gone a step further to centralize this so-called interdependence of organs and cells of multicellular organisms into the central point of life, the 'heart'.

We have named this visionary something as a heart. The interdependence of organs may bear some particular relation to developing the circulatory and respiratory systems. Since the more elaborate circulatory and respiratory systems may generally accompany the greater interdependence of organs, this elaborateness of the circulatory and respiratory systems can be necessary for greater interdependence and closer interrelation of organs. It may be that the organs have greater dependence and closer inter-relation due to this more significant development of the circulatory and respiratory systems. There might be other factors also, but this particular factor might also play a prominent part.

(e) **The action of radiation is retarded in the absence of Oxygen.**
Radiosensitivity depends on the amount of Oxygen present, and it reaches its limiting value when the amount of Oxygen is the same as its proportion in the air. Enriching the typical atmosphere with Oxygen does not increase the sensitivity to radiation. The removal of Oxygen from the air, however, decreases it. For most systems studied, the radiosensitivity is increased two to three times by changing from an Oxygen-free atmosphere to air. That means that if 100 roentgens in air produce a specific change, 200-300 roentgens will be necessary to achieve the same effect in the absence of Oxygen. The relation between Oxygen (due to its aerating function as regards blood, lungs, and heart) and the heart is a fact of common knowledge. The role of Oxygen in the increase of radiosensitivity goes a step further to establish the 'radiation-heart' relation.

(f) Brain, nerves, and muscles are remarkably less sensitive to the effect of radiation than the heart and whatever in the body are related to it.

(8) **STRESS-REACTION OF RADIATION:** Whenever the body is exposed to a sudden shock --- this may be fright without any physical damage, an accident, an operation, or even exposure to extreme cold --- nerves that control the pituitary gland become stimulated. Secretion of

some hormones, notably those controlling the sex glands, is inhibited while others are increased. Irradiation with fairly heavy doses produces a response of this type, and the changes in specific organs may indirectly bring about changes in different organs. It is well-known that the heart always assumes a central position in the event of a shock and sounds like alarum, its palpitations in panic. The stress reaction of radiation in the irradiated body and the consequent shock to the heart is yet another proof of radiations' particular relation to the 'heart'.

(9) **RADIATION AND THE 'HEART' OF PLANTS:** Modern science has proved that plants have 'cells' and have a 'heart' like animals have. Therefore, whichever we could say of the 'radiation-heart' relations in mammals could almost be said in the case of plants. If plants, too, like people, had the power of expression, they would have related, in heart-touching tones, their painful experiences of radiation effects and stated their agonies that the radiation brings about.

Suppose the plants and beasts had a tongue to express their views. In that case, it is not hard to imagine that what piteous terms would they have used, inducing erring humankind to desist from the determination of adopting atomic energy for peace? What bitterest slogans would they have invented in their protests against the development of stockpiles and the installations of the atomic reactors for peace? And indeed, what gesture they would have displayed in discouraging the misguided human species from perpetuating this ruinous, disastrous, and radiational atrocity on the humans, animals, and the plant world.

SECTION-3

"HOTAMA: A FIRE CLOSED IN ON THEM" Quran)

We will now show another primary feature of atomic radiation. As a part of mother atomic phenomena, atomic radiation is a fire possessed of the 'encompassing' feature.

(1) **WE CANNOT EXPEL RADIOACTIVE MATERIALS FROM BONES:** Once the radioactive material has entered the bones in a body, it is impossible to expel it from there even after the person's death for centuries. Alpha emitters (Radium, Uranium, Plutonium), beta-emitters (Strontium, Tritium), and beta-gamma emitters (Cerium) enter the body through ingestion, inhalation, or injection and deposit in the bone marrow. Scientists nicknamed them 'bone-seekers' because these substances deposit in the bone marrow after entering the body. These substances may produce general weakness, bone changes in the jaw, malignant tumors, and bone cancer (Osteogenic Sarcoma). They may

also induce leukemia. There in the bones, these substances continue to scintillate for ages even after the person has died. The unfortunate women who had died in watch-dial illuminating factories due to the ingestion of radioactive material decades ago, their bones even today, cause the Geiger-Muller counter to glow and click.

(2) **RADIATION KEEPS ITS WATCH OVER THE PERSON FOR DECADES:** By 1909 scientists firmly established that dermatitis, caused by repeated exposures to X-rays, was frequently followed by the developments of warts, which eventually became cancers. Even when they stopped all exposure, the changes continued, and cancer would occur between six and thirty years. It means that radiation had laid siege to the unfortunate persons and lay in wait until after a period, say, of thirty years, it seized the fort and emerged on its ramparts to begin the destruction.

(3) **RADIATION CONTINUES THE SIEGE EVEN AFTER WE FORGET THE IMMEDIATE SIGNS OF RADIATION:** When considering the injuries following doses of radiation that are not lethal, it is necessary to differentiate between long-term and short-term effects. The long-term effects become noticeable only a considerable time after irradiation when all the immediate signs have disappeared and are probably forgotten. These delayed effects may also arise after continuous exposure to radiation at a low intensity so that no immediate symptoms become apparent. Yet radiation is there insidiously concealing its presence. Besides the time factor, there is another characteristic difference in the rate of receiving the radiation. The damage giving rise to immediate effects --- radiation sickness --- is quickly repaired by the body. However, since late changes seem irreparable or incompletely reparable, the injuries become apparent. Hence, these damages are much less dependent on the dose rate. It is why radiation at very low intensity may fail to produce any symptoms typical of radiation sickness while still bringing about long-term injuries. In other words, radiation does not make its presence felt through symptoms of radiation sickness at low dose rates. Yet, it is there 'encompassing' its victim until it has brought about long-term irreparable injuries, thus making its presence felt.

(4) **RADIATION SECRETLY, INSIDIOUSLY, AND INVISIBLY PERSISTS FOR YEARS WITHIN THE BODY:** The symptoms of radiation sickness appear sometime after irradiation. Many months after the irradiation, the incidence of tumors is more significant than in un-irradiated animals, and cancers become prominent as a cause of death. Because of the long latent period between irradiation and the appearance of malignant growths, their effect on the life expectancy of experimental

animals is difficult to determine. Though most pioneer doctors using X-rays died of cancer, most of them lived for twenty to thirty years after severe radiation exposure.

(5) **RADIATION STAGES A HOLD-UP OF CELLS:** When cells are irradiated with doses insufficient to kill them, the most easily detectable change is a hold-up in cell division for a limited time and consequently retardation of growth. Studies of this type have shown that the cell's sensitivity varies depending on the stage it has reached in its mitotic cycle when it is irradiated. Mitosis does not stop immediately after irradiation but goes on for some little time, and then comes a period when there is no division. This delay is because cells that have started division are not particularly sensitive to radiation and the cells most affected are still a little away from division.

(6) **RADIATION KEEPS A GUARD OVER THE CELL FROM ITS RESTING PHASE TO ANAPHASE:** A few hundred roentgens can kill some cells, and a few thousand roentgens may kill most cells. With these doses, cell death only occurs after a time interval, and immediately after irradiation, the cells look and behave seemingly quite normally. This delay, one of the most characteristic features of radiation injury, can be explained in several cases in chromosome breakages.

Mitosis is a most delicate and carefully balanced process, and any disturbance of the chromosome structure can interfere with it. Since chromosomes are self-perpetuating, any chromosome fault will be reproduced in the subsequent division when it has an opportunity to prevent successful mitosis. Chromosome damage, of course, cannot lead to the cell's death until this enters division after irradiation.

If a cell is irradiated at the sensitive stage in the resting phase, it must reach anaphase before a chromosome defect could probably bring about its destruction. It means that radiation struck at the cell in the resting phase but has kept guard over it until the approach of its anaphase, or maybe the observer cannot see the effect of radiation till the appearance of the anaphase of the cell.

The reaction of radiation might have been so extra subtle in the resting phase of the cell that the observer couldn't see it till its effect manifestly appeared in the form of the chromosome fault in anaphase and the subsequent death of the cell due to the chromosome fault. The cell has seemingly looked and behaved quite normally after irradiation to the fatal anaphase. The cell is not sensitive to radiation during its division, and the chromosome breaks occur only in the mitosis following irradiation.

(7) **THE IRRADIATION OF ONE ORGAN 'ENCOMPASSES' THE WHOLE OF THE BODY:** When studying the effect of ionizing radiations on complex organisms, it is often challenging to determine whether the observed effect is due to damage in the cell being irradiated or an effect at a distance is being observed. Such an effect was demonstrated by irradiating certain parts of an animal only and finding that the un-irradiated organs were also affected.

Radiations need no means of transport to permeate the whole of the body. Chemical poisons penetrate through the body and eventually become localized in specific organs. On the other hand, radiation initially acts equally on all cells since it does not have to rely for its dissemination on transport by circulating fluids such as the bloodstream like other chemical poisons. As a result, the damage is pervasive; for example, every part of bone marrow is affected, and no parts are available to undertake the repair.

(8) **RADIATION LAYS A SIEGE TO FROZEN ANIMALS THAT CAN SURVIVE DRASTIC COOLING:** An elegant expedient proves in a very remarkable way the 'encompassing' feature of radiation. After a lethal dose of radiation, frogs will die within three to six weeks if kept at ordinary temperature. However, if we store them in a dormant state at a low temperature just above freezing point, they will survive for many months as if radiation lay watching. However, as soon as the irradiated animals are warmed up, they begin to show radiation symptoms and die in the same time interval as the animals that were not cooled after irradiation. The effect of arresting the course of events following radiation by cooling has been found with many radio-sensitive animals that survive drastic cooling.

(9) **THE EFFECT OF CANCER-PRODUCING SUBSTANCES SUGGESTED BY HADDOW AS DUE TO THEIR PROLONGED AND TENACIOUS 'ENCOMPASSMENT' OF THE TISSUE:** About forty years ago, Professor Alexander Haddow suggested that the cancer-producing action of the cancer-producing substances may result from prolonged interference with average growth. It exactly means a prolonged 'encompassment' of the tissue by the cancer-producing substances. It happens to be an obvious example of the case of encompassment, provided it has been proved.

(10) **THE 'ENCOMPASSMENT' OF HUMANKIND BY GENETIC EFFECTS OF RADIATION EXTENDED TO THE POSTERITY INFINITELY TO THE FINAL EXTINCTION OF SPECIES:** One of the awful consequences of radiation exposure is the effect it may have on future generations. There is every possibility,

instead, certainty, that the world of animals and plants and the human race is ultimately changed into a world of chimeras of innumerable varieties. This conversion may result from the open or insidious exposure of this present generation of humans, beasts, and plants to radiation, even though the parent of the atomic radiation that is the atomic energy at present only is nominal. This hazard constitutes the real headache to every knowing scientist and every man of sense and knowledge worldwide.

Radiation affects the embryonic cell, the embryo, the fetus as well as the genes. Genes, if deformed, are transmitted to posterity. They keep on moving from generation to generation secretly till they manifest their existence in any generation in the form of abnormal birth. This birth itself is inheritable and, therefore, produces abnormal posterity. Hence the number of kinds and varieties of abnormalities keeps multiplying and increasing infinitely due to marriages between persons with different abnormalities.

At last, due to this inheritable and multiplicative factor, the whole humankind, animal world, and plant world are changed into monstrous chequered and multi-featured lot of strange creatures. For example, these abnormal living beings may be creatures with a lion's head, serpent's tail, elephant's eyes, hawk's talons, human beard, etc., in the animal world; and mango trees with foot-longed thorns instead of fruit in the plant world.

Our description of these weird beings may look like a mere fanciful imagination. However, in reality, it is not so. Instead, it is an actual, well-established scientific fact. This point is irrefutable and concrete to the extreme misfortune of future generations. Even their posterity will also be involved who recommend and permit the adoption, use, and development of atomic energy for peace diligently.

The bad luck is that they recommend and push despite knowing all these facts and hazards of such a venture. Any behavior like an ostrich or amount of wishful thinking could in no way avert these hazards to save misguided humankind. This ill-advised human race is moving on its path straight to the flames of blazing atomic hell with two compartments: the explosive compartment of the atomic bombs and the compartment of the slow-burning atomic energy for peace.

The permissive embryonic cell known as the zygote, formed after the entry of the sperm into the ovum, is susceptible to radiation. At first, the embryo grows by cell division without differentiation and becomes firmly implanted in the uterus wall in about eight days in human beings. The differentiation begins, and the individual organs and limbs are formed, and the embryo takes shape. During this period, it is in the greatest danger from radiation. Now, radiation no longer kills the damaged embryo; it is not re-absorbed or aborted but proceeds to a live birth but is abnormal.

These malformations can be very significant to give horrible and distressing monsters which are, however, quite capable of living for a time. The incidence is exceptionally high in the early stage of the active development of the embryo. These malformations can be of almost every kind, ranging from anatomical such as cleft palate, short limbs, a fusion of ribs, etc., to effects on the central nervous system, which reduce intelligence and coordination.

It is well-known that inherited properties are transmitted from parent to offspring by entities called genes. These genes are chromosome parts and determine the type of organ produced. The reshuffling of genes is the most effective mechanism for producing individuals who differ in their genetic makeup. It is responsible for the difference between animals of the same species and between parents and children. In these genes, the radiation causes mutations.

The genetic damage is quite irreversible, and no repair or restitution is possible. It is a point that deserves the utmost attention. You must clearly understand what this point means, for it is a dreadful point. Once the mutation has occurred, it will be passed on to its descendants and recognized in children whose parents, yet, are not born. Gene mutations are independent of dose rate, and it is a hazard that has to be recognized as one of a severe kind and deserves to be surely understood.

A dose of 300R received in less than a day is extremely serious to man, and survival is not sure. Yet, if this same dose is received over thirty years at the rate of 0.2R/week, it is even below the tolerance level for hospital staff who handle radioactive materials and machines.

Nevertheless, the damage is identical from a genetic perspective since the same number of mutations will have been produced even if the dose rate were so low. Strangely, radiation at a high intensity may be genetically less harmful since utterly destroying some of the germ cells prevents mutations from appearing. Just as we say, it is better for them to die instead of living a mutated life of such agony.

At low intensities, the function of the cells as a whole is not impaired, and every mutation in the reproductive organs will give rise to germ cells carrying the mutation. It is worth remembering that every mutation will continue in the subsequent reproduction of cells. These mutations are of a kind that constitutes the greatest danger to the human population since they give us hereditary defectives that in extreme cases go to asylums and hospitals, and in less severe cases, lead the frustrating life of the partially unfit. The worst factor is that these mutations are inheritable and multiply endlessly and infinitely in future generations through marriage.

The Quran has said that 'Hotama' is a fire closed in on them. Indeed, we find to our great distress that atomic radiation encompasses humankind from the embryonic state to the moment of death. Not only this, but furthermore atomic radiation encompasses humankind from the present generation to the future generations. Even it covers humankind to the end. Due to continuous transformation and transmission of the gene mutations that would secretly and gradually multiply in 'kind' and 'numbers' to the consequent abnormalities, simple forms would gradually assume various chimerical features. The disastrous process will continue, and ultimately, every species on earth will lose its original physiological specificity.

Consequently, every species on earth, in the end, would lose the capacity to survive and would perish after a painful but vain struggle in an atmosphere of overwhelming misery, disease, and suffering, cursing the ill-applied and misguided zeal of the enthusiasts who had adopted the atomic energy in the beginning.

A point that deserves note is that gene mutations are secretly transmitted from generation to generation till, in some future generations, they manifest their existence in the form of abnormal birth; such abnormality being inheritable is perpetually multiplied through marriage. Gradually numerous forms of abnormalities appear, which keep on multiplying infinitely.

The following examples will bring the encompassing feature of radiation observable in genetic effects to an end.

(a) Radiations damage a germ cell before fertilization due to genes' mutation. (Encompassment)
(b) Radiations damage an embryo at any stage of its development. (Encompassment)
(c) The recessive mutation is not likely to be detected in the first generation. The presence of the recessive gene will not make itself felt and could only be recognized in subsequent generations. This terrible fact may afford some consolation for the votaries of the atomic energy of present generation. Still, the toll will have to be paid by some future generation, their successors. The horrid fact is that radiation can affect the children of the parents not yet born. [2]

The very nature of a genetic injury will be pretty unknown until it becomes revealed in some future generations in the form of abnormal birth. The nature of a genetic injury keeps itself hidden through several generations. (Encompassment)

(d) The modern theory of inheritance shows how atomic radiation can affect our whole species' makeup for all time. Man's genetic load means a constant and eternal threat due to our hidden recessive genes and is a perpetually tormenting worry of the geneticists with sufficient reason. We must anticipate the dangers of radiation to large sections of the population; once they have shown themselves in the population, it will have done irretrievable damage with disastrous consequences to humankind. (Encompassment)

(e) The damage due to the mutation produced by radiation in germinal tissue is not confined to the immature germ cells then being formed. Still, all subsequent sperms or ova produced by the affected cell will carry the mutation. (Encompassment)

(f) We must repeat it, and every passage of any textbook of Radiobiology ought to be underlined with this remark that 'Radio-Genetic' damage is quite irreversible. Repair or restitution cannot occur. Once a mutation has occurred, it will be passed on to descendants eliminated by natural selection or has appeared in the form of abnormal birth. (Encompassment)

(g) Monsters produced by genetic changes recur exactly in all subsequent generations. It is obvious thus that this monstrosity is inheritable and, therefore, multiplicative through marriage. (Encompassment)

(h) The harmful effects of genetic damage concern the population since all mutations are cumulative and persist. The mutagenic action of radiation is a social problem involving the total number of new mutations in a population to constitute the most significant headache to the world's governments. (Encompassment)

(i) To quote Muller:
"The genetically damaged population will eventually have to pay the cost."
We would like to add to Muller's statement that demurrage of the genetic load will be payable in compound interest. This imminent tragedy recalls to our mind the heart-touching lament of C. H. Waddington, who has said:
"Even if we cannot discover a cure for the ills that we may be inflicting on future generations, we ought at least to take trouble to

find out so that we can decide how far we shall go in running up biological debts which our descendants will have to pay."

This lament of Waddington is in itself the best testimony to the fact that radiation encompasses humankind to future generations till it has exacted its payment in the form of a miserable extinction of the whole of humankind along with the demolition of whole life on earth. Ironically and unfortunately, hitherto, there is no means of estimating the genetic load. Touched by it, and in the light of the wail of Waddington, we view with astonishment and sorrow the attitude of scientists who are in the slightest hesitant to recommend and to permit the use of the atomic energy for peace without having found out any cure for radiation injury. Well-known is the fact that the genetic damage of radiation is quite irreversible and irreparable. However, we find nothing but surprise when we understand that even each type of radiation injury that could heal; after recovery leaves some permanent damage that forever remains. (Encompassment)

(j) The chromosome abnormalities produced by irradiation find expression also as mutations. If the abnormality does not prevent the cell from dividing, each daughter cells produced will carry the abnormality. (Encompassment)

(k) Above all, the most dangerous aspect of the encompassment of humankind by radiation is the secrecy of the genetic load, meaning the threat held over all our heads by our hidden or recessive genes and its undetectable nature. It is impossible to detect the recessive genes in man. None today can tell how much genetic load any individual, male or female, man or beast carries. Nor is it possible for anyone to tell when and in which future generation the recessive gene will manifest its existence in the form of abnormal birth. Nor is there any kind of cure for the recessive genes whatsoever known to anyone.

We cannot exclude the possibility with any proof that the genetic load situation might even be alarming. The only solace in the present situation we find is the present shortage of atomic energy. However, what solace will there be for those people who will reside in a world replete with the sources of atomic energy? This point is worth considering but will anyone consider it? We see a world groping its way through a dark labyrinth that ends in a dark ocean of misery. (Encompassment)

(l) A point that deserves equal consideration and presents the problem of radiation encompassment from a particular angle is that too narrow a margin of safety has been left for humankind. Still, one step and the foot has already been raised forward. If this step is retracted, safety is possible; if placed forward, the fall is complete.

To mean that if now atomic energy is wholly banned, then safety is possible. Otherwise, if it is adopted, humankind is forever doomed. Once the recessive genes have appeared in a certain amount, they will continue their multiplication. Therefore, even if then humanity would banish atomic energy, doom would be inevitable. (Encompassment)

Therefore, to avoid doom, it is essential to avoid the encompassing clutches of the radio octopus from the very outset. Otherwise, radiation's genetic and somatic hazards will soon turn this world into a world of confusion, discord, disease, family disruption, domestic troubles, and untold miseries and sufferings. It will then be like a vast hospital, a gigantic asylum of miserable wretches, and a vast graveyard of a world that once lived.

Then, they shall desire to get out of the trouble and repent of the mistakes made by their progenitors. They will exert frantically to destroy all the atomic setup, but alas, it will then be too late, and it will not then be possible for them to break the encompassment of the punishing fire of the atomic hell. It is neither fancy at all that we talk nor emotional rhetoric that we indulge in now. Nay, it is pure, substantial facts, based on infallible, irrefutable, and undeniable science facts.

Let someone then stand up and say that it is wrong, or it is merely an alarmist view, or there happens to be an exaggeration so much as a scruple. Nevertheless, they only will pay heed to the truth who have the destiny to be saved from the most disgraceful and most painful end by the grace of the Almighty and Merciful Allah.

SECTION-4
"OUTSTRETCHED COLUMNS" (Quran)

Column raising is the distinctive feature of atomic energy. The Quran has said: "Hotama is a fire closed in on them in outstretched columns."

(1) 'OUTSTRETCHED COLUMN' OF ATOMIC BOMB EXPLOSION: The 'outstretched column' is a feature vividly conspicuous in the explosion of the atomic bomb. Folks' ears had failed to hear the ominous rumblings of future transformations in the structure of the atom. Even their eyes could hardly miss the awful spectacle of a column twenty miles high, three miles across and topped with a hundred miles mushroom. This spectacle presented so majestic a picture of the grandeur of man's power over Mother Nature that would cause man's imagination to reel at the view.

(2) RADIOACTIVE ATOMIC PARTICLES RAISE 'COLUMNS' TOO: The words of the Quran are: "Hotama is a fire closed in on them in <u>outstretched columns</u>."

The early authentic interpreters of the Quran inform us that the companions of the Holy Prophet of Islam (peace be upon him) used to discuss the point of a specific description of the fire of 'Hotama' regarding the enclosure in the columns. Some would think these columns were solid, and the doomed were chained to them and then tortured with fire. Some thought that the columns were hollow cylindrical, and the doomed were entered therein and then tortured with fire enkindled within. Some thought these were the columns to encircle the hell of 'Hotama' like the pillars of gates. However, their thought focused on the next world, meaning 'Hotama' was in the next world like hell's thought has always been associated with the next world.

We now see the replica, the transitory, temporal replica of the eternal hell of 'Hotama' of the next world before our very eyes with all its complicated features, and we can see the columns. The column has become a symbol of the atomic bomb explosion and is known to everyone today. The people have well recognized the destroyer of their life and property. Scientists discovered knowledge of columns raised by tiny atomic particles of radioactivity. However, nobody observed the facts from this particular point of view.

The atomic bomb explosions raise the columns, and we could witness the spectacle of columns in the entire field of radioactivity. So also, in the processes of atomic energy generation, anyone could view the raising of columns. Unspeakably small are the atomic particles, and incomparably high are the columns that they raise. It appears as a wonder when judged compared to the physical and visible world's general standards. So small are the atomic particles that the distances traversed by them mean a surprise to anyone. Moreover, so comparatively large is the amount of energy produced by them that comes as no little surprise, e.g., single fission of the Uranium-235 atom liberates enormous energy equal to 200 MeV. It indeed is terrific.

Such is the smallness of the Lilliputian world of atoms that if you could make a row of copper atoms by placing one next to the other, you would need a hundred million to cover an inch. Again, if each atom in grapefruit is measured as one inch in diameter, the grapefruit would be as large as the earth. Taking this latter example as a pattern, we will enter the nuclear world of atomic particles to view the lofty columns raised by the tiny particles. Unfortunately, the atomic parts and even the atoms themselves are not visible to the naked eye and any microscope, howsoever robust it might be. Hence, if we want to see the radiation world, we must have a microscopically strong eye to view the tiny inhabitants of the world of radioactivity.

As we enter the nuclear world of radioactivity, we are stunned to witness the millions of millions of luminescent columns of various heights, from a few yards to sky-high dimensions. They all appear luminous to us, so we have assumed that they appear to us like shooting stars. Thus, to us, the nuclear world of radioactivity appears as a world of shooting stars and rising luminous columns. Here now, before our eyes, is the process of fission chain reaction going on. There Uranium-235 and the fission chain reaction are in progress. It is a very spectacular view. Neutrons, millions of them rising from one nucleus to another and producing a very chequered design.

The neutron is a tiny, very infinite, simply small spec of matter. Its mass has been calculated as equal to 1.0086649156 amu (atomic mass unit). However, it rises from one nucleus of the Uranium-235 atom to the nucleus of the adjacent atom; it has to traverse a distance more than ten thousand times its size. A football may rise ten thousand feet or so high in the air to keep this ratio to its original size. If a football rose to that height truthfully, the entire world would reckon it as a wonder. Also, just calculate how much time it will take to achieve that height. But so fast is the neutron in its motion that it is difficult for the eye to follow it.

So, the spectacle appears marked with lines of light that point to the course of the moving neutrons in millions, and we have to consider that neutrons are stopped in their course by nuclei. Otherwise, they are capable of traversing far greater distances if allowed to move unchecked on their course. Then we see an alpha particle traveling at the speed of (roughly) 10,000 miles per second, rising to the height of four centimeters. Four centimeters might appear a distance very negligible judging from the general physical standards of the visible world. Still, we see the smallness of the size of the alpha particle, a radius of about 10^{-13}cm. Then we compare the distance of four centimeters which it has traveled; the ratio is comparatively large. We may see the particle to have raised millions of millions of times its original diameter. A football rising in the same ratio as its original size would rise far out into outer space.

We then see the electrons of the beta rays rising to heights of several yards. So small is the electron in size, and so great appears the distance of several yards it has traversed comparatively, that if a rocket would rise to a height in the same ratio to its size, then Mars and Neptune would figure as its first and foremost post.

There is as yet the demonstration of the flight of the gamma rays to be seen. It has risen to a height of 200 yards in the air. The size of the gamma rays is not more significant than the alpha particles, while against the 4cm rise of the alpha particle, it has risen to the height of 200 yards. Just imagine then the relative height assumed by the gamma rays.

Still perplexing are the heights the cosmic rays assume from outer space to the earth in showers. These are the distances that appear baffling to man's imagination. While considering these facts, it is justifiable to argue that the column raising is the primary feature of the atomic phenomena itself. The world of radioactivity is a world of columns. It also must be kept in mind that the atomic particles might be regarded as columns while traversing their distances due to their formidable speeds.

(3) **'COLUMNS' INTERPRETED AS ENDLESS AGES:** The earliest, original, and most authentic interpreters of the Holy Quran have interpreted this phrase, 'outstretched columns' figuratively. In this respect, they thus authenticated the permissibility to extend interpretation to figurative aspects and opened an avenue of vaster interpretive application.

'Tafsir al-Jalalayn', one of the leading commentaries of the Quran, asserts that certain interpreters of the Quran have taken the 'outstretched columns' to mean 'chains' (on the necks of the inmates of the hell of 'Hotama'). It further asserts that certain other interpreters of the Quran have meant by the 'outstretched columns' 'fetters' (on the inmates' legs in the hell of 'Hotama'). It also asserts that certain other interpreters of the Quran have maintained that by 'outstretched columns' is meant 'endless age'.

In this age, the appearance of atomic hell has brought to light the truth of all these various interpretations of 'outstretched columns'. All these are to be highly appropriate and exact. How desperately humankind needs nuclear energy, and with what desperateness do the nations seek it? Anyone who knows the impelling necessity of energy, particularly atomic energy worldwide, can hardly fail to observe the 'chains' of necessity and the 'fetters' thereof that have tied this present generation to the peg of the atomic reactor and consequently the column of the atomic bomb.

Also, the nuclear hell is the terrestrial replica of the eternal 'Al-Hotama' of the next eternal world. Therefore, the truth of the interpretations that imply 'chains' and 'fetters' in the case of this nuclear hell could well find justification in the light of the factors that at present have kept humankind fastened to the necessity of nuclear energy.

The question of the 'endless age' also is evident, for the long-term effects of the atomic radiations that we have more than once explained in this work move to the future generations to infinity. Once atomic energy has gained prevalence globally, it is a false delusion to entertain any hope of its effects to be discontinued.

Nay, the world may entertain with suspicion even any thought of discontinuing the atomic energy itself when it has gained its sway in the world. The factors responsible for the emergence of this punishment in nuclear bombs and nuclear radiation will keep on compelling humankind with ever-increasing force and forcing the apprehensions of the hazards of atomic energy out of the human mind.

The world has added the factor of economic necessity to that of military necessity. How helplessly is the world being dragged in chains by the factor of necessity to the atomic hell that can be seen ablaze and raging with thunderous fury? On its way to the atomic hell, humankind has now arrived at a point where a discovery even of a chemical nature may display effects particular to the nuclear reactions and may well be used as auxiliaries to the existing means of nuclear destruction.

(4) **RADIOMIMETIC CARRIES THE 'COLUMN' OF RADIATION HIGHER:** We can cite a striking instance in this respect as the discovery of the so-called 'radiomimetic'. Examples are mustard gas and Nitrogen mustard and their various derivatives. These 'radiomimetic' have effects identical to radiations. They are applied to augment the use of the existing nuclear radiations as extensions of the confining columns of the existing radioactive materials.

The fact that chemicals would produce effects similar to those of nuclear reactions may invite a reasonable suspicion of an acceptance of the influence of the atmosphere sublimated by the causes that have eroded the crust of the nuclear mystery to its ultimate eruptive disclosure. These chemical substances, that is, the radiomimetic, produce biological changes very similar to and often indistinguishable from those produced by atomic radiations. Because they could mimic radiations, they are often referred to as radiomimetic substances used as adjuncts to radiation. We can also call them chemical chains in the necks of the unfortunate inmates of the nuclear hell.

The resemblance between these radiomimetic and radiation is remarkable; both induce cancer, induce true mutations, retard cell division, and find the cells insensitive to the effect of radiation during its division. Both show a delayed effect in bringing about death, and this is the effect that differentiates radiomimetic from common poisons. Both radiation and its mimetic have a selective action on tissue containing rapidly dividing cells. This selectivity is the naturally discernible quality of all the atomic radiations as well as the mimetics. It could be observed in their selection of the raw and rapidly growing cancer cells from well-differentiated cells of healthy neighboring tissue.

This process of first differentiation and then selection reminds one of a particular and much popular interpretation by the interpreters of 'Al-Hotama'. To wit, that fire of 'Al-Hotama' is endowed with a strange understanding in that it can peep into hearts and then mount above those among them that have possessed such qualities as would render them liable to the punishment of the fire of 'Al-Hotama'.

Let us revert to the topic of the resemblance between radiations and the mimetic again. It has been observed that tissues affected first by both are the blood-forming organs such as bone marrow, genital organs, and expandable linings such as those of the stomach and intestines that are continually being replaced. Both cause local graying of hair, and the pigment-producing cells of the hair are susceptible to both. Both produce cancer and malignant tumors in animals.

Essentially all the different biological changes produced by radiation also follow treatment with radiomimetic. Both the radiation and radiomimetic may prove fatal, and science has discovered no antidote for either. Also, one has never to lose sight of this very grievous point mentioned in the previous line.

It constantly has to be borne in mind by every individual member of the whole vast humanity worldwide that no cure, no antidote has been discovered for the effects of radiations, nor any kind of universal protection against the radiations been found. This glaring fact makes it remarkable to think why a considerable proportion of the scientists are not hesitant to recommend and permit atomic energy for peace? How most states' heads worldwide are so anxious to furnish their respective countries with atomic energy?

Mutations produced by radiomimetic are as irreversible and as cumulative as those produced by radiations. The exposure of many people to radiomimetic chemicals would also be harmful to the future of the whole population without noticeably affecting the individual.

The damage done by the radiomimetic will only appear in future generations. However, its extent is even more difficult to evaluate than for radiations. Hence, the problem of radiomimetic is seemingly more dangerous than that of radiation, mainly because it is nobody's particular concern and consequently is ignored.

After knowing the hazards of radiation, anyone wonders at the discovery and application of radiomimetic. It is as if science did not consider the disastrous hazards presented by radiation to miserable humankind enough; the scientist felt the further need to add and augment the ruinous aspects of radiation.

Indeed, the fact may find some justification in the name of research. But the research has revealed frightful truths. What obstacle is left now to impede the complete elimination of the whole affair of atomic energy, radiation, and radiomimetic except the growing needs of fuel and energy? They will, of course, swallow poison if there be any hope of getting some energy out of the poison.

A very amusing (though in no way puerile or superfluous, and one deserving of serious consideration) instance of phonetic resemblance exists between the words 'Mimetic' and the word 'Mumaddadah'. This latter ('Mumaddadah') is the actual word used by the Quran in the prophecy and means 'outstretched columns' or figuratively, (just as some of the worthy commentators of the Quran have interpreted) it means 'extension'.

Noticing this phonetic resemblance of these two words that is the 'Mimetic' and 'Mumaddadah', anyone can understand that the word 'Mimetic' not only represents the mimicking quality of the radiomimetic substance but also is found to mimic the original word of the Quran, i.e., 'Mumaddadah'.

It is then another oracular and anticipative miracle on the part of the Quran. Also, it is a wonder of discernment and aptness of expression on the modern scientist. An experiment could illustrate the phonetic resemblance that exists between these two words.

Let any European pronounce in rapid succession the word 'Mumaddadah'. To your surprise, the word will appear as 'Mimettet', and if the speed of expression is fast enough, soon you will hear the word so pronounced as will make it difficult to discern between 'Mimettet' and 'Mimetic'.

Everybody knows that the words 'Mohammed' and 'Mohammedans' are pronounced and written as 'Mahomet' and 'Mahometan' respectively by Europeans. The alteration is to be sought in the variance of the structure of the vocal organs of various people descending from different origins and living in different climates.

SECTION-5
THE THEORISTS OF RADIOBIOLOGY CONTRIBUTE TO THE CORROBORATION OF THE POINTS OF THE PROPHECY

In the course of the research, theorists and researchers of Radiobiology eventually gathered a multitude of evidence covering the entire range of prophecy of the Quran. They supported the corroboration of the points of the prophecy. They did it, either by advancing a theory or by experimentally proving a point of some kind or the other.

J. A. Crowther, by his target concept of radiation, corroborated the 'crusher' concept of the prophecy. He also presented the possible existence of one or more sensitive volumes in the cell or other biological matter, corroborating the theory of 'radiations leaping up over the hearts' since these sensitive volumes could with much credibility be taken as the representations of heart.

Douglas Lea's conclusion that an ionizing particle breaks a nucleus chromosome by depositing energy on it proved that radiation is fire and is a 'crushing fire'. Further, by dint of rising above the chromosomes of the nucleus (heart), this fire could be termed as 'A fire which leaps up over the hearts' since resemblance between the nucleus of the cell and heart is evident.

The Hungarian scientist George Von Hevesy observed that the enzyme system responsible for synthesizing the critical constituents of chromosomes, deoxyribonucleic acid (DNA), is the most sensitive in the cell to radiation. It further supported the view of radiations' 'rising above the hearts' since the matter is concerned with the chromosomes of the nucleus (heart). Research showed that it extended irradiation effects of one organ in the body to distant organs, and radiation did not depend on any means of transport for its dissemination in the body.

Further, Professor Alexander Haddow suggested that the action of cancer-producing substances might be due to their prolonged interference with average growth. Moreover, the frightening discovery of Hermann Joseph Muller disclosed that radiation could induce mutations and that gene mutations were inheritable. All these references proved beyond any doubt the 'encompassing' feature of radiation.

C. H. Waddington's heart-touching lament regarding the hereditary character of radiation in gene mutations proved the hazardous situation that pointed to the 'encompassing' quality of radiation, though unfortunately, his warning fell on deaf ears.

The discoverers of radiomimetic endowed the subject of Radiobiology with the characteristic of 'outstretched columns'. The observation of Bergonie and Tribondeau that "cells were sensitive to radiation in proportion to their proliferative activity and in inverse proportion to their degree of differentiation" proved the relation of 'wealth accumulation' to the 'punishment' inflicted by the fire of atomic radiations.

Lastly, by discovering various malignant tumors and cancer features like abnormal and infinite growth, exceptional radio-sensitivity, the Radiobiologist has shown cancers and malignant tumors akin to 'slandering wealth accumulators'. Therefore, they deserve exposure to the fire of atomic radiation.

SECTION-6
RADIATIONS TOO NEGATE THE SLANDERING WEALTH ACCUMULATOR'S NOTION OF LIVING FOREVER IN THIS WORLD

The Quran has said:

"The slandering wealth accumulator thinks that his wealth shall render him immortal. Nay, for verily he shall be cast into the fire of 'Al-Hotama' (crushed thereby and destroyed with his wealth)."

We can observe now that it is not only the atomic bomb, but radiation also negates the notion of the 'slandering wealth accumulator' that he will forever live within this world.

Radiations may kill on the spot or leave their victim to die in a few days. In case they are not powerful enough to kill, they shorten the life span of their victim. With 200,000R, the animals die while being irradiated. A dose over 600R brings certain death. Smaller daily doses right shown to 2 or 3R per day certainly shorten the lifespan. In this last case, none of the typical symptoms of radiation sickness such as diarrhea, severe anemia, or loss of appetite and weight are observed. We can best summarize the changes seen as being akin to those generally associated with old age. The notion of eternally living in this world is thus insidiously counteracted by radiation without any suspicion on the part of the unwary victim whose life span radiation has shortened without his knowledge.

Continuous irradiation with doses not exceeding 25R per day may be said to age the animals prematurely. A more helpful way of looking at the results is that continued irradiation of 10R/day lowers the lifespan. A large single dose that does not kill also leaves a permanent mark revealed as premature aging. There is an increase in cancer incidence a long time after irradiation, contributing to decreased life expectancy. The crux of the matter is that so far, no treatment can alter the progress of radiation symptoms, and none as yet is in sight. These are the recognized facts of science and are no mere fantasies, and there is nothing of the alarmist views in it.

Absolutely no sure cure for radiation injury is discovered. Radiations are inherent in atomic energy and are inseparable from it. All the scientific knowledge of such ruinous facts and disastrous aspects is available. Nonetheless, neither hesitation in recommending and adopting atomic energy nor exercising discretion in such a severe matter we observe anywhere.

Atomic energy is being recommended, adopted, and yearned after by every nation on earth as a matter of routine and a sure means of redeeming humankind from poverty, hunger, deprivation, and want of every kind. Of course, every hazardous aspect of the venture is overlooked and forgotten in the belief that adorning the name of atomic energy with the label of 'peace' will make every incident hazard vanish as if by the magical influence of a talisman. If as they say, history repeats itself, and if the superstition of the past ages has ever to recur, anyone could cite no better instance than this belief of the present humankind in the efficacy of a mere label in neutralizing the ill-effects of so dangerous a venom as the atomic energy.

Radiations kill or shorten the lifespan of their present victims. Furthermore, their effects are extended even to future generations. They can produce permanent sterility in their present victims too abruptly and cut their posterity. Also, the formation of recessive genes can cause the extinction of the posterity of the present victims that have not shown any signs of complete sterility themselves. But their posterity rendered abnormal by the pernicious transmitted effects of radiations and deprived of the qualities essential for the successive survival of generations. All this phenomenon negates the notion of the 'slandering wealth-accumulator' that he shall forever live in this world due to the immortality bestowed on him by his goddess of wealth.

The race of the 'slandering wealth-accumulators', that is, the followers of atomism, will perish in a manner that the whole life on earth may become extinct by the effects of atomic radiation. The long-term effects of radiations are transmitted to the progeny of irradiated animals, generation after generation, secretly and insidiously, and are some of the worst features of ionizing radiations. Ovarian tissue is susceptible to radiation, and so are the genetic cells. Doses considerably below those necessary to produce any symptoms of radiation sickness are sufficient to cause damage to germ cells or the embryo. Thus, not only do the children irradiated in the embryonic state have a reduced lifespan but even the children whose parents are not yet born may, due to recessive genes, be born with features similar to those irradiated in an embryonic state. The behavior of atomic radiation in negating the slandering wealth accumulator's notion of forever living in this world will ultimately be found as effective as that of the atomic bombs. The difference only is in duration. Whereas the atomic bombs would cut the Gordian knot of life at once, radiations would work their way to that end slowly, patiently, and gradually. Both the roads, however, do eventually lead to the same Hades. The Quran has said that:

"The slandering wealth accumulator thinks his wealth shall render him immortal."

There is no doubt that this present age of atomism is most fond of prolonging life. The whole age is engaged in a constant endeavor to discover and adopt means that may lengthen life. The most typically spectacular success achieved in this respect is a discovery, hailed by the Radiobiologists as a sure harbinger of the day of prolonging life. It is an undoubted remover of the hitherto insurmountable obstacle that of the immunological incompatibility that stood like a wall in the way of replacing worn-out organs with the new ones.

Foreign cells, if injected into an organism, are rejected, and expelled by it. However, the laws of immunology give way in case an organism is irradiated before the injection of foreign cells into it. Foreign cells can completely take over a specific organ in irradiated organisms. For example, suppose a mouse of strain 'A' is irradiated and then given an injection of cells from a mouse of strain 'B'. In that case, all cells in the bone marrow of 'A' become of the type typical for strain 'B'. Similarly, a mutation is produced in a cell so that one of the cell's chromosomes is distinguishably altered in shape.

Then an ordinary mouse is injected with the bone marrow of the mutant strain. At that point, all the cells of the blood-forming organs of the mouse in whose body the bone-marrow of mutated strain has been injected can be found to contain the sickle-shaped chromosomes. It has also been found that even rat cells could take and multiply in irradiated mice. Thus, the dream of forever living in the world seems to have neared its realization, and strangely enough through the agency of the very same radiation, which is a recognized killer of life.

Thus, the historical discovery that the injected cells flourish in and effectively replace an irradiated worn-out organ has been acclaimed by the Radiobiologists as one to herald the day of the prolongation of life. The worn-out organ will be irradiated, and new cells injected into them. The new cells will then replace the old worn-out organs, and it shall continue the process forever.

However, alas, the doubtful joy of forever living is spoiled by a certain apprehension: the practice introduces chimerical features in the patients thus treated. The mouse which we have quoted in the above example that is the one that has received the injection of the mutated cells turns into a chimera --- the mythological monster with a lion's head, a goat's body, and a serpent's tail.

The chimerical features will gradually multiply into numerous forms and shapes. Thus, the terrible hazard of turning into chimera through generations overshadowed the joy of a long life. Such is a measure of complexity of the subject of radiation, and such meritorious is the knowledge of Radiobiologist. Without a revelation of the danger of chemical metamorphosis, millions in the world would have offered themselves as guinea pigs for a new remarkable experiment. But only to find themselves, or someone in the future generation turned into a chimera of a superb kind, fit perhaps to place in a zoo as an exhibit of the wonder of atomic radiation.

SECTION-7
CANCER IS A TYPICAL 'SLANDERING WEALTH-ACCUMULATOR' OF THE CELL WORLD TO DESERVE ATOMIC FIRE

The formula for humankind's radio-combustibility of slanderous plutolatry, the worship of wealth or material possessions, could be found applicable to cancer in the cell world.

The Quran has given out the fate of human 'slandering wealth-accumulator' as destruction through 'Al-Hotama' fire. The destruction of cancer utilizing atomic radiation in the age of atomism has furnished proof of the universality of this formula. However, let it be remembered from the outset that a person who has cancer and is subjected to the rays of some radioactive substance might not essentially be a 'slandering wealth-accumulator' any more than all others who have escaped the sickness of cancer. Nay, that particular person might even be a model of disinterestedness and utterly pure from the taint of slander.

Our theme from the beginning has had a general aspect, general and universal. It is not concerned with individual and particular cases, and who knows how many innocent people will become the co-victims of the general disorder when the time comes. The emergence of atomic energy and the atomic bombs is the resultant manifestation of a general and universal vogue. Yet, it may or may not spare the innocent, the ones not deserving the atomic punishment. Even some of those deserving may escape the consequences, at least for some time.

However, the actual court is in the next world where no culprit will be able to escape the affliction of the atomic hell that is the real eternal 'Al-Hotama', and Allah will wrongfully cast no innocent person into the flames thereof. The inhabitants of those two ill-starred cities (Hiroshima and Nagasaki) could not be assumed in any way the greater wrongdoers in this respect. They only had the misfortune of being the precedent and example to others, who too, in due course, may follow the same path and meet the same end.

It is only useless to think that this world will keep averting Hiroshima and Nagasaki's destiny by mere treaties of 'No-War'. However, the only actual course to avoid the danger lies in removing the primary causes, as the Quran has revealed in time. Still, unfortunately, the facts have universally been ignored by humanity so that a very narrow margin of escape is left. The innocent people undeservedly forced into the doom with those deserving may have no guilt. Nevertheless, they might fail in seeking the reality of so crucial a subject as atomic energy. In such a grave matter, the reluctance of these innocent people may be accounted for share, at least partly, in affliction with those who became blind to the consequences of so dire a course and inclined entirely toward worldly pursuits.

To assume reticence and fail to raise a voice against the wealth-seeking pursuits of world-hungry humanity and remain a passive spectator in the worldwide designs of the adoption of atomic energy and the construction of atomic bombs in itself is criminal. It may be considered help and encouragement in such nefarious activities as it may destroy faith, wealth, health, life, world, science, and civilization.

Resuming our topic that cancer is the 'slandering wealth-accumulator' of the cell world, we will try, in the following, to prove this point in the light of the most modern research that has proved cancer as such a one beyond any doubt. Modern discoveries have shown cancer as a highly complex disease. The 'slandering wealth-accumulator' wants to live forever, and cancer shows a combination of all of the slanderer's characteristics. The fact is that we cannot define cancer by one characteristic. From a clinical point of view, it is not a single disease but a term that comprises a whole group of conditions, each with its particular characteristic symptoms and differing widely in seriousness.

We will show that cancer is a 'slanderer' engrossed in perpetual and insatiable 'cell accumulation'. It accumulates cells in the fashion that anyone could easily imagine it having a desire to 'live forever'. It has the inward comprehension that cessation of its cell multiplication meant death to it. Therefore, to escape death, it engages itself in constant exertion to live through constant cell multiplication. Radiation being the best possible means of its destruction, it has eventually been exposed to atomic radiation like its human counterpart, the 'slandering wealth-accumulator' in this age of atomism who is also exposed to atomic radiations.

CANCER AS A 'CELL-ACCUMULATOR' IS LIKE ITS TYPICAL HUMAN COUNTERPART AS A 'SLANDERING WEALTH-ACCUMULATOR'

One of the principal features which collectively constitute a malignant growth is a multiplication of cells at a particular point, more than those required by the body. Now, mark these words: 'more than those required by the body'. Cell proliferation occurs typically at several sites. The most common amongst these sites are outer layers such as skin and linings of the stomach and intestines, which must be continually replaced by wear and tear.

Also, in the blood-forming organs, there is continuous division to provide new cells. Cells not generally divided can be stimulated by injury or hormonal excretion to multiply. This growth is not malignant but quite normal, and cell multiplication is not sufficient to define cancer. However, cancer being a malignant growth, the multiplication of its cells is more than those required by the body. The multiplication of cancer cells continues indefinitely, as the constant growth of the wealth of a 'wealth accumulator'. In contrast, the average cell proliferation of healthy cells can be considered as the just requirement of a necessity and stops when no more is needed. Cancer thus could rightly be called a 'cell accumulator'.

Cell multiplication, as has been stated, is not sufficient to define cancer. Its tendency toward excessive cell multiplication more than what is required by the body distinguishes cancer from normal growth. Cell multiplication of cancer goes on indefinitely, but this is not all. The greed of cancer takes it even beyond that. The predatory activities of cancer further expand toward the neighboring tissues. The ability to invade the neighboring tissues by infiltration between cell colonies is an essential property of cancer. It distinguishes it from standard cell multiplication and warts, cysts, and other so-called benign growths.

Another characteristic of cancer that further indicates its ravenous attitude is its forming 'colonies' within the whole body. The most dangerous of all the characteristics of cancer from the medical point of view is the ability of its cells, which have broken off from the primary center, to settle at a new site and form a secondary growth that may be even more harmful than the original tumor. A cancer cell can be transported in the bloodstream, the lymph channels, or across body cavities to distant parts. At the new site, a tumor will grow, which has the characteristics of primary growth. It may be possible to determine the origin of secondary growth; indeed, we may reveal unrecognized primary growth in this way. All these characteristics prove cancer to be a phenomenon of an exceedingly greedy nature.

CANCER CONTINUES CELL MULTIPLICATION AS IF BY THIS MEANS IT WILL 'LIVE FOREVER'

Cancer exerts to live through cell proliferation. The end of cell multiplication is considered by cancer as the end of its very existence, and, therefore, its endeavor constantly is to keep on its cell multiplication. This very same notion pervades the mind of its human counterpart, the 'slandering wealth-accumulator' who also thinks the end of his wealth accumulation would be to him as the end of his life.

CANCER HABITUALLY IS A 'SLANDERER'

The 'wealth accumulator' against whom the threat of the fire of 'Al-Hotama' has been denounced must essentially be a 'slanderer'. Cancer also has to show the essential quality of slander to justify the fire of atomic radiation. It may seem very strange to hear that cancer should 'slander' as if mute organisms have begun to speak like human beings in this age. Cancer, of course, has no tongue like human beings, and it is the particular behavior of cancer that we could interpret as defamatory. Moreover, indeed the behavior of cancer is most typical of a defamatory nature. Cancer, characteristically, is a malignant growth, and further, its malignancy is of a particular type. The key to cancer's malignancy lies in the cell's behavior. The cancer cell's behavior is precisely that of the slanderer's tongue, while the cancer heart is closely like that of a malignant slanderer. This fundamental quality of slanderous malignancy is reflected in the various distinguishing characteristics of cancer, such as the 'indefinite multiplication of cells', 'invading the neighboring tissues', and 'establishing cancer colonies within the whole body'.

In all these various features of cancer, one could minutely discern the shade of slanderous attitude. The epithet of malignant in itself could provide enough justification for attributing the slanderous qualities to cancer. We have known that all the particular characteristics of cancer arise from a mutation peculiar to the cancer cell and the cell's consequent transformation from normal to malignant. The cell has lost the mechanism that brings it under the control of the whole organism.

Due to the loss of this particular mechanism, cancer cells keep multiplying indefinitely even after the body's requirements have been fulfilled. They are not only no more needed but are even harmful. The over-proliferation of cancer cells is indebted to a particular mutation of cancer cells and the consequent loss of the mechanism that keeps the cells under the control of the whole organism, just as the human counterpart of cancer has lost the mechanism that keeps the tongue under the control of modesty. The 'wealth-accumulation' and 'slander' of the human 'slandering wealth-accumulator' are interlinked, so is the case of cancer.

The key to the malignancy of cancer cells relies on indefinite multiplication due to the loss of mechanism that keeps cells under the control of the whole organism. It is the loss of this mechanism that counts. It is not the faculty for unlimited growth that distinguishes cancer cells from normal ones. The capacity to multiply is the property of all cells which have not become too highly differentiated. The growth that occurs when a cut is repaired is much faster than most cancers but stops when the wound has closed. The typical cell is under the control of the organism, while the malignant cell is not. To consider cancer as a deficiency explains why it is relatively easy to make a normal cell malignant, but the reverse process has not been brought about.

The case is precisely analogous to that of the 'wealth accumulation' system of this present modern age in which the accumulation of wealth is continuous, systematic, and eternal. The earning of wealth to the point of necessity is not the aim but rather the mechanism of modesty that keeps the desire of wealth accumulation under control of mind has been lost. Like the continuous and infinite cell multiplication of cancer, the modern man is engaged in continuous, constant, and infinite 'wealth accumulation'.

Moreover, just as the cell multiplication within the reasonable needs of the body is not objectionable, the earning of wealth within the reasonable necessities of life could not be considered objectionable. The objection appears with the loss of mechanism that keeps cells under the control of the whole organism. Similarly, it is objectionable to lose a mechanism that keeps man's mind under the control of modesty.

Just as it is relatively easy to make a normal cell malignant, and the reverse process has not been brought about up to now, it is relatively easier to make a sober mind greedy and a modest tongue malignant. Still, the reverse process has always been found problematic. It is pretty easy for the devil of greed and slander to inspire a person's heart, but exorcising such a devil out of a person's heart would sound like a treat.

Once a person has lost the mechanism that keeps the tongue under conscience control, it would be a marvel to reinstate that mechanism.

So universally prevalent today is the habit of 'slander' that no two persons assemble but to disparage the third, and no three persons come together but to carp at the fourth. Nations are engaged in slandering nations, and Creeds are engrossed in defaming the creeds. Individuals are absorbed in maligning the individuals, and the overall picture is extremely gloomy.

However, let us not lose sight of another fact, namely, that the slanderers could be divided into two categories: natural and induced, just as magnets are of two kinds; permanent and temporary or electromagnet. The permanent magnet is natural, and it is impossible to deprive it of its magnetic quality. However, the electromagnet loses its induced quality no sooner than we switch off the electric current. We have to judge present-day humankind on this principle. We may find a very negligible proportion to be the natural slanderer.

In contrast, the most significant proportion would merely be the subjects of induced slander and induced greed due to the universally and oppressively prevalent current of the present-day circumstances. It is an auspicious omen in that there is a possibility of humankind reverting to senses and escaping the dreadful doom in case the current was switched off, just as at the appearance of electric fire, we at once turn off the main switch. Nevertheless, the analogy between cancer and its human counterpart holds as long as the current and the electromagnetic power persists.

It is with heartfelt regret that this analogy could be summarized as follows.

"Cancer is a **cell-accumulator**, whereas its human counterpart is the **wealth-accumulator**. Cancer debases the cells of its neighboring tissues, whereas its human counterpart, the 'slandering wealth-accumulator', the exact 'Homaza-Lomaza', debases men. Every activity of cancer reflects malignancy, but every act of 'Homaza-Lomaza' is tempered with calumny. The behavior of cancer is voraciously slanderous, and that of 'Homaza-Lomaza' is ravenously cancerous. Both are fated alike to be subjected to atomic fire. Cancer is destroyed by atomic radiation so is its human counterpart. All the treatment methods aim to eradicate cancer cells by killing them or making them incapable of further division. Similarly, its human counterpart may be killed by the atomic bombs or the atomic radiations, or maybe his posterity is rendered incapable of living by the long-term effects of atomic radiations. It is with a heavy heart that we bring this sad analogy to an end. Nor have we concluded it with any relish."

SECTION-8
'URANIUM, TOO, IS THE CHIEF 'SLANDERING NUCLEON-ACCUMULATOR'

If cancer is called the chief slandering 'cell-accumulator' of the cell world, Uranium could be termed the chief 'slandering nucleon-accumulator' among elements. The uranium atom is the bulkiest of all the naturally existing elements, with 92 protons and 146 neutrons in its nucleus. Thus, it is the chief nucleon-accumulator', and because it is radioactive, it is constantly engaged in shooting its atomic radiations like the tongue of a 'slanderer'. Radioactivity is a sort of malignancy, and every radioactive substance is a malignant substance.

Finally, like cancer and the human 'slandering wealth-accumulator', its fate has been exposure to the atomic fire. This very element, Uranium, indeed, had the misfortune of introducing atomic energy and consequently the atomic bomb into this world. This element is the primary source of atomic blight in every form. If the atomic bombs or the atomic radiation consume this world eventually, the credit goes mainly to this very element, the unfortunate Uranium.

SECTION-9
THE NEUTRON BOMB

Recently, benefactors [3] of humanity have developed a new type of bomb called the neutron bomb. The bomb's name originates from the neutral particle in the atom called neutron --- a radioactive component capable of exterminating life without affecting solids, such as buildings, installations, and armory. The neutron bomb is a mini Hydrogen bomb depending technically on the capacity of the Hydrogen bombs to discharge tremendous quantities of high-speed neutrons, which are equivalent to the death rays.

It is possible to procure neutrons on exploding the Hydrogen bomb when two atoms of heavy Hydrogen unite to form an atom of Helium gas. Suppose we could keep the neutrons for a period not exceeding a small fraction of a millionth of a second by neutron reflectors. In that case, the quantity of the neutrons increases, and each one of them bears extreme power and shoots off high power radiation in every direction. The fast neutrons are the horrible so-called death rays. Without assuming that high power, the neutrons seem harmless, but when they acquire it, they can penetrate steel plates and pass through any barriers as though they were dust permeating the barbed wire of a fence. Here lies their deadly effect.

The 'Lance' rockets shoot the Neutron bombs to targets at a range of more than 75 miles. An 18-inches gun may also send them off to a range of 20 miles. Then they explode in the air at an altitude of 130 yards, resulting in death to all human beings within a half-mile radius. Persons within a radius of one mile will be subjected to slow death. As for buildings, machinery, or armaments, these remain safe and intact. Neutron bomb causes death by radiation in the first place. As a result, humans die from a concussion within a few hours by draining off their brains, whereas those more distant die a little later from the bursting of their blood vessels. Now, without seeing the necessity of going into any lengthy details of corroboration, it needs here only to say that the neutron bomb also springs up from the same root as all other nuclear bombs. Its characteristics fully justify its inclusion into the nuclear family in the light of the description of fire of 'Al-Hotama' that prophecy has given.

Some atomists give the impression that they have succeeded in discovering a particular isotope of Uranium that could only be used in the peaceful uses of atomic energy and could not be used to construct atomic weapons. Be it even so. Even if the atomists succeeded in discovering such an isotope, who could stop producing the isotopes of Uranium to be used to manufacture atomic weapons?

Then there is the recent invention of the neutron bomb, which aims at killing the inhabitants but saving the property. Other similar devices may come in due course but do what they can; all nuclear roads lead to nuclear hell. The only remedy lay in removing the primary causes of the trouble, namely, 'the slander', 'the greed for the accumulation of wealth', and 'the notion of forever living in this world'. All these characteristics are the features of the philosophy of modern and ancient atomism. Therefore, the philosophy of atomism has to be struck at and uprooted if this world desires to live.

~~*~*~*~*

---

[1] "H. J. Muller, Nobel prize winner for his famed fruit-fly experiments, said that in the next 1,000 years, there will be as many **'genetic deaths'** in Japan as there were casualties from the bomb blasts themselves. By this he means that unseen internal damage to their genes, or reproductive units, will continue to haunt and plague the Japanese people for the next 30 generations." [(http://blog.modernmechanix.com); with special thanks to Charles Shopsin.]

[2] In this regard, please read the following report that most recently appeared in media on January 7, 2015.

[Residents of a Kazakh village are being relocated because they keep being struck down with a **mystery sleeping illness**, it's been reported.

Villagers in Kalachi, northern Kazakhstan, have been suffering from the unexplained condition for about two years. 'It causes people to fall asleep suddenly, sometimes for several days, and those affected have also complained of memory loss and in some cases hallucinations'. More than 100 cases have been reported in the village, which has been nicknamed **Sleepy Hollow**, and some people have been affected more than once. Now the heads of neighbouring districts are offering to move the villagers to new homes and jobs elsewhere, the Interfax news agency reports. Priority is being given to the families who have children in the village, the deputy head of Esil district, Saule Agymbayeva, tells the agency. More than half of the village's 582 residents plan to relocate, the report says.

The illness has affected both adults and children. 'If you try to wake him, it seems he wants to open his eyes, but can't. He just sleeps and sleeps', Igor Samusenko, whose son was affected by the condition, told 'Russia Today' in December. Doctors haven't been able to work out what's causing the illness, although some have suggested mass psychosis. Other people think the **village's location close to a former uranium mine, which closed more than two decades ago, could be behind it**, although no abnormal readings have been found in samples of the village's water of soil, the TV channel says. **Kalachi is located near an old uranium mine**, but radiation levels are normal in the village.]

NOTE: This report says, "...no abnormal readings have been found in samples of the village's water of soil," and "...radiation levels are normal in the village". Maybe these observations of the report have some truth in them. Still, we may also consider another point of view that the hazardous effects of ionization radiation move on secretly from generation to generation and manifest their existence in some future generations. Maybe the previous generation had been affected by radiation when the production was in progress from the subject **uranium mine**. The symptoms of this disease have now appeared in the next generation. **Researchers should also think about it.**

(www.bbc.com/news/blogs-news-from-elsewhere-30709661)

[3] An ironic remark given by the author.

~~*~*~*

CHAPTER-4

OUR CORROBORATIVE COMMENTS ON THE POINTS OF THE PROPHECY AS EXPLAINED BY THE ORIGINAL INTERPRETERS OF THE QURAN

We may reasonably apprise the reader that it is the only first few authentic and the original among the interpreters of the Quran that have treated the prophecy about 'Al-Hotama'. Later on, they only were quoted by the interpreters of the Quran. The succeeding scholars only summarized all the findings of the pioneer interpreters regarding the prophecy in question till now.

After centuries, we have undertaken to subject the contents of prophecy to a view in the light of nuclear phenomena in an atmosphere of atomistic materialism of this present age. Therefore, our work is of the first kind in this respect; it shall remain in the world as the last original. It could be assumed with a concise reason that the discovery of atomic energy and the development of the atomic bomb have been in a strange mode. We have already mentioned the details in previous chapters and volumes.

Hence, we could expect none of the atomists responsible for the emergence of atomic energy and atomic bomb to see the relation of the prophecy of the Quran about 'Al-Hotama' to atomic energy and the atomic bomb. It was not possible even if the persons in question were thoroughly acquainted with the contents of the Quran until the 'column' of the atomic bomb mainly appeared before the very eyes. But atomists were blind by the hypnotic effects of three evils that prevailed in the world: the Quran's pointed out evils responsible for the emergence of the atomic hell. Therefore, we could not expect them to discover the prophecy even if they had known the Quran. Some mysterious hand dragged them on the path of atomic hell blindfolded.

We will now proceed to examine the interpretations of the original commentators of the Quran regarding 'Al-Hotama'. We have chosen to quote the sources among the most original, authenticated, and authoritative. Remember, as reasonably expected, these commentators treated the topic of 'Al-Hotama' regarding the next eternal world only. They have, therefore, expounded the whole theory based on eternity. Yet, we find their interpretations to corroborate the basic characteristic features of the atomic phenomena with remarkable exactitude. Their characterization of 'Al-Hotama' does establish a perfect identity between 'Al-Hotama' and the terrestrial atomic hell of this present world. And the point of eternity cannot naturally be established in the terrestrial atomic hell of this world in such a manner as is particular to the endless eternity of the next world (deathless). Yet, features are contained even by the transient atomic hell of this transient world that are doubtlessly characteristic of infinitude though within the transient context of this transient world. Although such features should ultimately end with the end of this world, they move infinitely within its span.

Of the Mufassirs [1] (commentators or interpreters) of the Quran, we have quoted from the most widely acknowledged sources listed below.
(1) 'Tafsir Abdullah Ibn-Abbas' (619-687).
(2) 'Tafsir al-Tabari' by 'Abu Jafar Muhammad Ibn-Jarir al-Tabari' (840-923).
(3) 'Tafsir al-Kabir' by 'Imam Fakhr-ud-Din Razi' (1149-1209).
(4) 'Tafsir al-Quran al-Azim (Tafsir Ibn-Kathir)' by 'Ismail Ibn-Kathir' (1301-1373).
(5) 'Tafsir al-Jalalayn' (1460-1505).

May Allah be pleased with all of them. All five are the mainspring of the Quran's commentary and are recognized universally as original, authentic, and authoritative. Their treatment of the topic of 'Al-Hotama' indeed will excite wonder and admiration in the mind of every modern scholar well conversed with the subject of nuclear science. In the light of commentators' interpretations, anyone can find the causes responsible for the emergence of 'Al-Hotama' to prevail in our present age collectively.

We purposely have deferred the causes assigned by the Quran to the emergence of the atomic bomb in this place. Now, we will treat them in the light of the interpretations of the commentators. We may here insert the text of the prophecy for revision.

THE TEXT OF THE PROPHECY OF THE QURAN ABOUT 'AL-HOTAMA' (THE HELL OF THE 'HOTAMA')

(1) ROMAN ARABIC TEXT

"Wail-Ul-Likul-Le-Homazat-Il-Lomazate, Nillazi Jammah Malan-Wa-Addadah. Yahsabo Anna Ma-Lahu Akhladah. Kalla La-Yunbazanna Fil Hotamah. Wa Maa Adraaka Maa Al-Hotama? Naarullah-Il-Muqadah.

Allati Tattalio Alal Afedha. Innaha Alaihim Musadah. Fi Amadim Mumaddadah." (Quran: 104 'Al-Homaza')

(2) ENGLISH TRANSLATION

"Woe unto every backbiter, defamer who heapeth up riches and prepareth the same (for the time to come). He thinketh that his riches will render him immortal (that is, his riches will remain with him forever). By no means shall he surely be cast into Al-Hotama (the crushing fire). And what shall cause thee to understand what Al-Hotama is? (That is how crushingly terrible this fire is? And how incomprehensibly complex is its phenomena?). (It is) the kindled fire of Allah, which leapeth up onto the hearts. Verily it is a fire closed in on them in outstretched columns."

(Quran: 104 'Al-Homaza')

SECTION-1

Quran: "Wail"

It is the original word of the text of the prophecy used by the Quran.

Meaning: 'Woe'

[(1) **Tafsir Al-Jalalayn**

'Wail' is an interjection and exclamation to invoke 'woe'; also, it is a valley in Jehannah (hell).

(2) **Tafsir Al-Tabari**

'Wail' is a vale that overflows with yellow-colored discharge and pus of the inmates of hell.

(3) **Tafsir Abdullah Ibn-Abbas**

'Wail' is the extremity of torment. It also is a vale of blood and pus in Jehannah (hell). It also is a pit of fire.]

ATOMIC HELL DESCRIBED REFERENCED TO THE INTERPRETATION OF 'WAIL'/'WOE'

Now, a valley of blood and pus in hell is a strange phenomenon, for generally, it is the consuming fire associated with hell. Yet there could never be found another description of the atomic hell, more exact. Moreover, although the interpreter had in mind the hell of the next eternal world, the description applies equally and accurately to the atomic hell of this world too. Just imagine for a moment scene of this world during and after the worldwide atomic war and see this earth turned into a valley of blood and pus. About three thousand million people all over the world, including beasts and birds lying dead or dying in heaps, killed or injured by the 'Heat-Flash' of atomic explosions or crushed by the collapsing buildings or hit by the flying debris or burned by the raging city fires; all of them bleeding and issuing pus due to septic wounds; their pus and curdled blood mingling with the bloody vomit and the darkened blood issuing from the noses and the mouths of innumerable victims of radiations. The whole earth drenched with stinking blood and pus and suppuration, till the vivid matter wriggling would move forth slowly and branching itself little by little would cover the earth with a network of loathsomely flowing streamlets. Or at least it would be in such abundance that this earth could figuratively be called the valley of pus and suppuration.

A dreadful scene of millions of the swelling, stinking, and terrifying carcasses of human beings mingled with those of beasts all over the earth would meet your eyes to impress upon your mind the accurate interpretation of 'wail'. The same could be said of a world in an age well-stricken in atomic energy for peace due to radiation. As far as the other interpretation of 'wail', namely, that 'it is a pit of fire' is concerned, there could be no difficulty associating it with the atomic explosion since it essentially is a pit of fire.

And lastly, the meanings of 'wail' that is 'woe' also are pretty apparent in that nothing, but 'woe' is the lot of those unfortunate inmates of the atomic explosion. The thunder of the atomic blast would cry 'woe', and so would the whole world under the hail of atomic bombs utter 'woe'. Even the raging fires, toppling buildings, flying incandescent heaps of debris, choking fumes, and the ringing universal death-knell would cry 'woe'.

SECTION-2

Quran: "Likul-Le-Homazat-Il-Lomazate"
Meaning: "Every backbiter, defamer."
'Likul-Le' means 'to every'; 'Homaza' means the 'backbiter', and 'Lomaza' means 'defamer'.

Interestingly, this expression, namely, 'Homaza-Lomaza', is expressive of contempt and scorn. We could also sense a little touch of the satiric comic therein. Nicknames like, 'Nitwit', 'Mr. Peck-Sniff', 'Mr. Rod-Snap', 'Mr. Worldly-Wise', 'Mr. Hate-Good', and indeed hundreds of such like others, we can cite as examples. A thorough search may perhaps be rewarded with discovering a nickname representing the exact character of the particular 'Homaza-Lomaza' described by the Quran: a backbiting defamer always engaged in pursuing wealth and sowing seeds of discord among friends.

Mr. Doust, a famous artist in his book, 'Looking at the faces', has furnished his readers with one such example:

"I know a man," writes Mr. Doust, "who was very evil. He could take pleasure in separating friends, in breeding hate and jealousy, and he sought but two things, gold and power."

It is a complete and perfect example of identity with the 'Homaza-Lomaza' of the Quran. It shows all the associated characteristics, namely, love of gold and power besides backbiting and slander.

[(1) **Tafsir Al-Kabir**
The meaning of the word 'Homaza' is 'to backbite', and it has assumed the symbolic meanings of 'slander'. The meaning of the word 'Lomaza' is 'to stab', and it has assumed the symbolic meanings of 'defamation', 'incrimination', and 'reviling'. Perpetuity and persistence of a person in these evils is the condition for this appellation, namely, the 'Homaza-Lomaza'.

(2) **Tafsir Abdullah Ibn-Abbas**
'Homaza' is a 'backbiter' who culminates others in their absence, while 'Lomaza' is the one who 'slanders' others to their face.

(3) **Tafsir Al-Jalalayn**
We can include anyone mimicking the others' act, speech, or voice for exciting laughter in the same category as 'slanderers'.

(4) **Tafsir Al-Kabir**
The exposition of (someone's) faults can be of two kinds. Either it shall be prompted by envy and grudge, or it shall be simply a jest (or a joke) in a comic mood. In both cases, religion shall be the object of ridicule or some person's appearance, gait, gesture, etc. It could be further divided into several forms so that the division could proceed infinitely. Further, someone will commit the act of slander, either in the presence or absence of the person thus slandered. In both cases, the act of slander shall be either by word or by the gesture of eye, hand, etc. All such acts are essentially evil and deserve reproof.

(5) **Tafsir Al-Tabari**
'Lomaza' is he 'who eats the flesh of men'. Eating the flesh of men is meant (metaphorically) to backbite, that is, to slander a person in his absence.

(6) **Tafsir Al-Kabir**
In reply to an inquiry regarding the identification of those for whom this denunciation of 'wail' was supposed, Ibn-Abbas said: "They are the slanderers, the sowers of seed of dissension between friends, and are fault-finders, and remember that all such activities originate from the same motive, namely, the exposure of faults of others."

(7) **Tafsir Al-Kabir**
The accepted opinion of competent judges in this matter is that naturally, this denunciation (that of 'wail' that is 'woe') is general and universal and applies to everyone who is habitually guilty of this offense (slander), and no particular person is thereby supposed.

(8) **Tafsir Al-Jalalayn**
The intention of this threat of 'wail' is against every slanderer without any differentiation of caste, creed, faith, or religion. If, however, the accused would die as an unbeliever, hell shall be his abode forever, eternally. If the case is otherwise, then it (the period of his stay in hell) would depend upon the pleasure of Allah.]

The points in the commentaries above quoted are all clear. These are the essential points which we have selected. The basis of various forms of 'slander' and 'backbiting' has been assumed as fault-finding and sowing seeds of discord. No particular person is intended, as it was the opinion of some people in the beginning when the Quran was being revealed. Instead, it is the general and universal formula applicable to anyone in any age irrespective of faith, religion, or creed. There is no distinction made between the believer and the infidel. The universality which 'slandering-wealth-accumulation' has assumed in this age of atomism shows it as a creed in itself. Tragically the two words, namely, 'criticism' and 'propaganda', are the two keywords of this modern age besides the other two keywords, namely, 'fruit' and 'utility'.

H. G. Wells discerned this particular distinctive feature of this age against the pre-modern ages and characterized it as 'evil stuff' in his book 'A Short History of the World'.

"That evil stuff," says he, "the propaganda literature of the present time."

In his book, 'Explaining the atom', Selig Hecht has called it: "The intellectual offensive".

Richard Brinsley Sheridan in 'The School for Scandal' has described a particular group as: "The utterers of forged tales, coiners of scandal, and clippers of reputation."

Mr. Doust, while telling us about the 'gold-and-power-seeking fellow' who could even take pleasure in separating friends, has reminded us of the 'Homaza-Lomaza' described by Ibn-Abbas as the sower of seeds of discord among friends.

Now, leaving the task of observing the habit of slander in individuals to the reader to make his case, we shall proceed to say that the reflections regarding slander quoted above are all precious. However, while the first two characterize the habit of 'propaganda' in this modern age as a distinctive feature and different from the pre-modern ages, the observations of Sheridan and Doust are concerned with individuals.

The fact is that the basis of this age of atomism is characteristically and distinctly on 'criticism' as against the simple faith, rather the 'faith in unseen' of the previous pre-modern ages. Criticism is the keyword of this age of atomism. As we have already said, it is an essential science requirement. Naturally, the whole process of scientific investigation is critical. Blind faith has no room in it.

Criticism could be of two kinds: healthy and tainted. As long as the activity is confined to purely scientific inquiry, the critical judgment remains naturally sound and is essential. But what if the things move into a sphere farther away and beyond the field of science, say in metaphysics, or matters of spiritual nature or blind faith in unseen Allah, Resurrection, Judgment, life in Heaven? In that case, the principle of scientific criticism either darkens into skepticism or takes the form of slander against the unseen things, for it can prove nothing in those spheres by any scientific means.

However, the term 'propaganda' in its modern meanings bespeaks the slanderous attitude according to its modern meanings. Propaganda in this age is the prevailing vogue in its numerous shapes and forms in all the different spheres of human activities. It is a very effective weapon in every struggle — even the weapons of this age exhibit a slanderous attitude. The automatic weapons resemble the tongue of a slanderer, while booby traps and distant missiles imitate the backbiter.

SECTION-3

Quran: "Nillazi Jammah Malan-Wa-Addadah"
Meaning: "He who accumulates wealth and arranges it against the future."

'Nillazi' means 'he who'; 'Jammah' means 'to accumulate'; 'Malan' means 'wealth'; 'Wa' means 'and'; 'Addadah' means 'to arrange and keep it in readiness for future'.

[(1) **Tafsir Al-Tabari**
Accumulates wealth and counts it but never spends in the name of Allah.

(2) **Tafsir Al-Quran Al-Azim (Tafsir Ibn Kathir)**
Accumulates wealth layer upon layer and counts the numbers. He is entirely engrossed, heart and soul, in accumulation during the day, while during the night, he lies like a stinking corpse.

(3) **Tafsir Al-Kabir**
Homaza slanders and slights others due to his pride in his wealth. The particular structure of the word 'Ja**mm**ah' with double 'm', as against

'Ja**m**ah' with single 'm', has special meanings. It means that the wealth is accumulated in every way and from everywhere and that people do not accumulate it within a day, or in two days, or one month or two months. It is grabbed in every way and by every means, and no stone is left unturned in the endeavor. In other words, it is a case of complete engrossment.

Further, the word 'A**dd**adah' with double 'd' as against 'A**d**adah' with single 'd' has due to the double 'd' attained special meanings, to wit; preparedness, storage, hoarding, and keeping as a safeguard against vicissitudes in future times.

Also, those huge numbers are therein involved. The word also alludes to a sort of indiscriminateness in the accumulation of wealth. It is accumulated during the whole of the day, while during the night, it is concealed. Thus, it also means a continuous increase in numbers.]

Pray review these descriptions given by the worthy commentators regarding the modes and methods of wealth accumulation peculiar to 'Homaza', including his wealth features, and examine and judge carefully. The present-day economic and industrial setup of this world wholly-solely is of wealth accumulation.

We could find no better sketch of the economic conditions that prevail in the world to represent the existing picture of this age than the one that has been presented by 'Tafsir al-Kabir'. It is a masterpiece and could be read once more before describing the existing world situation of wealth accumulation.

It is pretty easy to see that wealth, as the great commentator of the Quran has said, is being accumulated in every way and everywhere and that it is accumulated not in one day or two days or one month or two months.

However, it has been continually accumulated for centuries since the beginning of the modern age in a systematic and organized manner based on a particular plan. It intends to continue in five-year plans infinitely with ever-increasing wealth.

People spare not a single method in the world that they could perhaps employ in acquiring wealth. They don't neglect any endeavor in this regard, and no stone is left unturned in the hottest pursuit of wealth by anyone in any corner of the world today. In short, we can conclude that 'systematic wealth accumulation' has become a universal trend.

As the commentators have hinted, it is a case of 'complete engrossment in the pursuit of wealth'. 'Tafsir al-Kabir' indeed, in this respect, has said terrific things so much so that it is hardly possible to admire them fully. The view of the commentators, however, and quite naturally, is confined to individual cases.

Still, their descriptions could be seen applicable to specific individuals and the entire world engrossed in the pursuit of wealth on a collective basis within a universal economic setup. People are absorbed in this course with un-remitting zeal, unrelenting and constant endeavor, incessant toil, gruesome labor, and indeed an unquenchable thirst for wealth as if engaged in achieving the sole object of life.

Man's mind, it may seem, is changed into a reactor in which the desire for wealth is fast increasing like the fission chain reaction with no moderators and may one day explode. Referring to 'Tafsir al-Kabir' statement regarding the immensity of numbers involved in accumulating the wealth of the 'Homaza-Lomaza', we have but to express wonder at the exactness of resemblance.

Anyone acquainted with the features of this modern materialistic age of atomism very well knows that the unimaginable largeness of numbers is a particular feature of this age distinctly observable in every phase. Figures exceed millions, billions, trillions, and so many ciphers have to be dealt with in figures that a new writing system had to be devised.

SECTION-4

Quran: "Yahsabo Anna Ma-Lahu Akhladah"
Meaning: "He thinks his wealth shall render him immortal."
'Yahsabo' means 'thinks'; 'Anna' means 'that'; 'Ma-Lahu' means 'his wealth'; 'Akhladah' means 'shall make him immortal'.

[(1) **Tafsir Al-Jalalayn**

There are two probabilities in this expression of the Quran that the 'Homaza' thinks his wealth shall render him immortal. It either is in the form of the answer to the question:

"Does he think that his wealth shall keep him in the world forever that he is so over-enthusiastic in the accumulation of wealth and is so over-solicitous in its pursuit?"

Or else, it might indeed be his belief that his wealth shall keep him in the world forever. If then, latter be the case, its base is on sheer folly. Due to his folly, he thinks that his wealth could be a means to keep him in the world forever or that he will remain in this world eternally and will never die. It might be by dint of trust in the durability of the structure of his buildings and extraordinary excellence of cultivated lands that he cherishes a belief in the eternity of his name in the world to be perpetuated through his durable structures and memorable lands.]

The worthy commentator says: "Does he think that his wealth shall keep him in the world forever that he is so over-enthusiastic in the accumulation of wealth and is so over-solicitous in its pursuit? Or else, it might indeed be his belief that his wealth shall keep him in the world forever."

It is no hidden secret to anyone who knows about atomism that the atomic theory of Democritus considers this universe as eternal; that is, it will live forever. Therefore, all the vast world of votaries of worldly atomism today implicitly considers this world and this life to continue forever, eternally, and every activity of this modern humankind today breathes the same spirit. Everyone nowadays is engaged in the pursuit of wealth. Nobody ever thinks about death, but the general notion is of forever living in this world. The economic system and economic programs are proof.

Humankind today thinks that this world shall continue to progress eternally, infinitely, gradually, and systematically through five-year plans. They think that it will carry on not for one, two, or more generations, but forever, and as long as this universe sustains. According to the theory of atomism, it sustains forever eternally since the atom itself is immortal.

Man, now, means to conquer the forces of Mother Nature and, by doing so, hopes to become the millionaire, multi-millionaire, and the ruler of the universe with no other purpose but to accumulate wealth through which he hopes to live forever and, therefore, wants to remain forever rich. So powerful is his belief in the immortalizing powers of wealth that he has forgotten every hazard of the atomic war and atomic radiation.

Wealth indeed will provide him with weapons of defense and means of avoiding death. None today need be reminded of the universal pursuit of wealth, and it might be a waste of words to tell the people of it. Yet, we must remind the hypnotized people about things that generally are most conspicuous.

Further, the worthy commentator said that: "It might be by dint of trust in the durability of the structure of his buildings and extraordinary excellence of cultivated lands that he cherishes a belief in the eternity of his name in the world to be perpetuated through his durable structures and memorable lands."

We may not need to point out even a blind in any way to this fact in the present age. Modern civilization has covered the whole earth with sky-high buildings, huge factories, installations, gardens, bridges, stately halls, railways, airports, cultivated lands, harbors, and hundreds of other varieties of structures that may last for centuries. Again, it is not the question of individuals. Instead, the whole world is engaged to perpetuate its name through the durability of structures and excellence of cultivated lands, individually, collectively, and universally. The building process is continuous, and an increase in the structure will go on infinitely till, alas, perhaps atomic bombs will destroy the structures all over the earth along with the name of the owners thereof.

[(2) **Tafsir Al-Kabir**

The hope of 'Homaza' in his wealth has assumed such intensity that a belief has developed in his mind as if ever his wealth came to have dwindled, he would surely die.]

These days, the present-day people have wholly expelled thought of death and the next world from their minds. The slightest apprehension of the decrease of wealth means worse than death to them. Indeed, the whole atmosphere of the world is burning intensely with the heat of material necessities. Fearfully atrocious nowadays are the financial needs of both the rich and the poor. Fiercely economic is the encompassing culture. In such an atmosphere of the world on a global scale, the slightest apprehension of poverty results in a state of the human mind expressed as the worst kind of heart attack, most tormenting and far worse than the pangs of death.

SECTION-5

Quran: "Kalla La-Yunbazanna Fil Hotamah"
Meaning: "Nay, for verily he shall be cast into 'Al-Hotama'."
'Kalla' is a vehement negative which means 'no', 'never', 'it shall not be so'. 'La-Yunbazanna' is an equally forceful affirmative and means, 'shall surely be cast into'. 'Fil' means 'in'. 'Hotamah', of course, is the 'crusher', the nucleus about which the theme of the prophecy revolves. It is a word, terrible and formidable which may be ordained to destroy the whole life on earth.

[(1) **Tafsir Al-Kabir**

By this word that is 'Kalla', Allah means to refute the assumption of the slandering wealth-accumulator that he shall forever live in this world. Perpetuity of name, however, may be achieved through good deeds.]

There is no doubt that the appearance of the atomic bomb is the result of a scientific process and the logical sequence of a particular philosophy. Yet, strangely enough, a mysterious hand too could well be discerned at work in enticing humankind into and leading unto the pit of the atomic hell. That secretive hand did it by playing the role of 'open sesame', as is the case of the preliminary accidental discoveries. It also created appropriate circumstances for advancing the process, such as circulating some rumors, etc. It has ultimately brought humankind to the brink of atomic hell by its peculiar strategy. It now only remains, but the necessity of one more trick and humankind will be shoved down into the blazing atomic hell.

The whole affair of discovering atomic energy and the atomic bomb has been one of doubt, delusion, and mystery throughout. It used to move like a veiled improbability farther and farther, always enticing, and deceptive till it eventually appeared before the world. All the enormous amounts of wealth spent in the enterprise seemed uselessly squandered until they achieved true success in the form of the first atomic bomb or the atomic reactor. All the while, the contest between three prescribed evils and the opposite virtues of humankind could be seen clearly: the former trying energetically for success and the latter endeavoring desperately for the failure thereof. The three evils, however, ultimately triumphed in the contest and the atomic hell appeared. Along with it appeared the justification of the assertion of the prophecy, "Verily he shall be cast into 'Al-Hotama'."

The following abridged summary of hints may illustrate the fact.

TWELVE MECHANICAL FACTORS OF THE APPEARANCE OF THE ATOMIC BOMB

We produce the twelve mechanical factors of the appearance of the atomic bomb as follows.

(a) The chance discovery of X-rays proved to be the root discovery of atomic energy to open the way to subsequent discoveries. Also, we could refer to the accidental discovery of radioactivity as the mother discovery. Scientists could have discovered neither atomic energy nor made the atomic bomb without it. These discoveries accidentally opened the gate of atomic mystery like the legendary formula of 'Open Sesame'. We could attribute these well to the hand of the mysterious power without incurring the charge of superstition.

(b) Scientists could have discovered neither atomic energy nor made the atomic bomb without America's significant 'wealth accumulation'. Therein we could see the necessary relation of 'wealth accumulation' to the atomic bomb.

(c) Even America would never have ventured to spend a cent in an enterprise of so unbelievably dubious a nature as the atomic bomb. Therefore, the cities of Hiroshima and Nagasaki would have been even extant today, flourishing and teeming with life but, for a rumor that Germany was already engaged in the project and in case she succeeded, the consequences for the allies would be catastrophic.

This 'little rumor' proved to be a key that opened up America's treasures, and all the wealth flowed down into the atomic laboratories. It again was the work of the mysterious hand.

(d) Russians could have never dreamed of the atomic bomb had it not been for the hideous appearance of the atomic monster in Hiroshima and Nagasaki.

(e) America would never have contemplated building a bomb as dreadfully monstrous as the hell-bomb (Hydrogen bomb) if the Russians had not detonated their fission device successfully to break the American monopoly in the nuclear field.

(f) The hesitant government of America would have remained hesitant. The reluctant public of America would have remained reluctant to the end and perhaps forever in their move toward the Hydrogen bomb plan till all the raging controversy on this issue had died out. However, a little rumor that a particular scientist had passed some U.S.A. atomic secrets to the U.S.S.R. caused every other consideration to be erased from their minds. The government of America issued urgent orders to go ahead with the Hydrogen bomb plan.

(g) The Russians, too, perhaps, never would have thought of making the Hydrogen bomb were it not for the appearance of the American Hydrogen bomb.

(h) Were it not for the dwindling fuel resources of the world and the extreme industrial and military necessities, humankind would have banished with ease the atomic energy even for peace, the sole root for the growth of atomic bomb and in itself fraught with horrific hazards. Therein we can find a force that keeps humankind fast in the field of atomic energy with future possibilities of the growth of the atomic bombs.

(i) The fundamental discoveries that led to the realization of atomic energy came practically all from Western Europe. However, all discoveries and discoverers wafted across the Atlantic to America by a strange wind raised by the mysterious hand. During World War II, most scientists who later discovered atomic energy and built up the atomic bomb in America were caused to flee before the Nazi oppression. Einstein, Teller (the maker of the Hydrogen bomb), Szilard, Wigner, Newman, and Fermi were the most famous scientists who had reached America as refugees from Western Europe. Fermi, however, had fled from Italy before fascist persecution.

If not wafted to America, all these discoveries would have died in their native lands along with their discoverers for want of suitable soil. Of all the world countries, America could provide soil suitable for such cultivation by her prodigious wealth, enormous resources, vast industrial setup, and outstanding technical facilities, particularly the spirit of the scientific enterprise that abounded amongst her citizens.

No government in the world that lacked these factors could have afforded play host to such a prodigy. No country in the world could ever be induced to adopt such a reckless course of wastefulness to cast all her gold into the river in the hope of catching an imaginary monster that probably could destroy their enemies. Nay, nothing could have easily induced even America to spend her wealth in so dubious an affair, but thanks to the mysterious hand that circulated the 'rumor' of Germany's precedence in the field of atomic research.

(j) The scientists who were engaged in the atomic enterprises remained in doubt about the grievous hazards. Their ignorance never allowed their courage to flag nor their zeal to abate. The hand of destiny dragged them unto the course of a dreadful but well-deserved doom. They only re-joined in the thought of a million times more powerful bomb, a bomb that, if loaded in a boat and exploded in a harbor, could very well destroy even some of the surrounding area along with the whole port. They had hunted for a fox, but a dragon had emerged before them, and they found themselves quite helpless to fly. By the time they realized the fact, it was too late.

(k) A constant dread of the rival powers and the mutual mistrust would not allow humankind to destroy their atomic stockpiles. The prevailing circumstances of the world are coercing even the poorest nations on earth into building up their stockpiles. We can hardly doubt that the presence of the stockpiles and the prevailing distrust of nations will one day bring the latent stockpiles into action to the ultimate wholesale destruction of humankind and all life on earth along with this human race. Atomic powers are indeed endeavoring to the best of their ability to ban the atomic war and curtail the armaments. However, their success in this matter may prove dubious, uncertain, and even impossible. The mysterious hand is still lurking. It is not treaties but rather the removal of the fundamental causes of the trouble that may effectively avert the atomic danger from humankind.

(l) H. Truman, the then President of America, listened to the dramatic news of Russia's first nuclear explosion in silence. At the end of the briefing, he sighed deeply and perceived the whole meaning of the news. The President saw immediately that a monstrous event had overtaken his nation. He might have realized too that a monstrous event had overtaken the entire humankind. However, his sigh availed him naught. The atomic rivalry proceeded with ever-increasing enthusiasm.

The next step for America was to take the direction of the Hydrogen bomb. The General Advisory Committee of the Atomic Energy Commission opposed the plan of the Hydrogen bomb vehemently. They solemnly declared that it was immoral, too expensive, and excessively destructive, might not prove feasible, and no peace-time use for it existed.

Nevertheless, all these arguments availed them naught. The leaders of the 'Anti-Hydrogen Bomb' lobby were the scientists like Einstein, Rabi, Bacher, Conant, Szilard, and others, all of the great status and high prestige, and champion leaders of the U.S.A. science. Yet all their excellent caliber and strenuous efforts in opposition to the Hydrogen bomb availed them naught. Twelve of the nation's leading physicists, including F. Seitz, George Braxton Pegram, F. W. Loomis, Hans Albrecht Bethe, C. C. Lauristen, and others of the American Physical Society, stated on Feb 4, 1950, at the close of the annual meeting in New York. Read the following.

"We believe that no nation has the right to use such a bomb, no matter how righteous its cause. This bomb is no longer a weapon of war but a means of extermination of whole populations. Its use would be a betrayal of all standards of morality and of Christian civilization itself --- to create such an ever-present peril for all the nations of the world is against the interests of Russia and the United States --- In the meantime, we urge that the United States, through its elected government, make a solemn declaration that we shall never use the bomb first."

However, as is apparent, the statement availed these sympathetic scientists naught despite all their worth in the field of science. The sleeping cobra, conjured up by the enchanting tunes of the three gorgonian sirens, had gone unbridled and could not be sobered.

Shortly after this appeal, mighty Einstein made his appeal to the world, saying:

"The idea of achieving security through national armament is, at the present state of military technique, a disastrous illusion...The armament race between the U.S.A. and the U.S.S.R., originally supposed to be a preventive measure, assumes hysterical character. On both sides, the means to mass destruction are perfected with feverish haste ---

behind the respective walls of secrecy. The H-Bomb appears on the public horizon as a probably attainable goal... If successful, radioactive poisoning of the atmosphere, and hence annihilation of any life on earth, has been brought within the range of technical possibilities... In the end there beckons more and more clearly general annihilation."

('Arms can bring no security'; by Albert Einstein) Yet, as is evident, all Einstein's greatness, frightful accuracy of his facts, and sentiments of human sympathy availed him naught. The Hydrogen bomb was made, tested, proved successful, and applauded as a great symbol of strength and atomic monopoly. The world is well aware now that the Hydrogen bomb is not a weapon of war nor an atomic bomb. The larger the stockpiles, the greater the resultant destruction. A single atomic raid will wipe out the countries from the earth.

Yet, that childish and absurd idea of the atomic deterrence of stockpiles still keeps them blind to the dazzling realities. The above-quoted appeal of Einstein that has contained a world of meanings did fall on deaf ears, and the hazards of the atomic radiations have failed to attract the slightest attention of the dizzied humankind.

The ears that had failed to hear the voice of Einstein soon heard a startling echo from the north:

"It is known that abroad the partisans of war have, for a long time, cherished illusions of the United States' monopoly in the production of the atomic bomb. ... The United States of America has long since ceased to have the monopoly in the matter of the production of the atomic bombs. ... The government [Soviet] deems it necessary to report that the United States has no monopoly in the production of the Hydrogen bomb either."

(Georgi M. Malenkov, Premier of U.S.S.R., August 8; Nine months after 'Mike'-The American fission device)

Only, if the people of today had sensed the heat of the exertion of the three evils produced in pushing humankind towards the atomic hell, would they venture to rush out of this world in a mad frenzy like a crowd trapped in a house on fire. How the force of three evils is shoving unwary humankind towards the flames of a burning hell of atomism is a threat to observe but a harrowing one. There is a little joy just because efforts are in progress to ban atomic war, or the nations defer it infinitely. Also, there is no reason for consolation that atomic radiations of the atomic energy for peace have not manifested their effects yet. If these three evils' force continues as usual in its endeavor, the wholesale destruction of this world in the atomic hell is inevitable.

If humankind succeeds in averting the danger of atomic war from the world infinitely, still the radiations of the atomic energy for peace will, due to the preponderance of the atomic energy, prove to be an adequate substitute for the atomic bombs. The ultimate end will be the complete ruin of humankind, the difference being only of duration. Whereas the atomic bomb will give a short shift to humankind, the radiation will subject it to a process of slow decay and lingering death.

The three evils existing in the world in requisite amounts and compounded in correct proportions will undoubtedly cause the emergence of the atomic hell in this world. Their absence, however, will cause the danger of atomic hell to flee just as darkness flees before the sun. The actual stockpiles and every radiation source will disappear from this earth like the mist disappears before the sun's rays. It is no magic formula of the sort of abracadabra, and no witchcraft is involved, but the startling result will appear precisely according to science and logic's hard and fast rules.

Suppose, on the other hand, the three evils did persist in this world as much as they do exist today, or they increased just as they are gradually on the increase. Then, remember that whichever way humankind faced or did move, it will find itself confronted with some new apparition of the atomic demon and some new means of enkindling the atomic hell. The fire of atomic Jehannah (hell) has now encompassed the unfortunate race.

According to the Quran, wealth in a purely worldly pursuit as the main object of life without spending in Allah's name and considering the next world turns into a fire and a means of torture for its owner. When this principle is understood, it is easy to understand that in the presence of slander and wealth worship, the wealth accumulated as the object of life turns instead of ordinary chemical fire into the atomic fire. It proves the truth and certainty of the claim of the prophecy, namely, that "He verily shall be cast into 'Al-Hotama'." No one could deny anyone the needed necessities of life, but if this world alone and the pursuit of wealth in it becomes the sole object of life, then the wealth assumes the character of fire.

In the following, we will quote some of the relevant signs of the Quran that endorse this view. In these signs, the modern ungodly atomistic materialism philosophy is portrayed in the clearest of its colors and condemned in the most explicit terms. Space would not allow us to quote all such signs. But quoted signs are enough to show that the picture is so perfect as if the Omniscient author of the Quran had the modern philosophy of atomism clearly in His view with all its characteristic features, which He has sketched to the minutest detail. He has drawn this depiction with such a skill that the result is a life-like portrait at once recognizable.

Any intelligent reader well acquainted with the philosophy of Bacon will not miss in the following signs and the hints of the Quran, like:

(a) "The <u>fruitlessness</u> of the purely worldly endeavor" of (Quran 11:15-16) with direct reference to the pet phrases of the Baconian philosophy, like '<u>fruit</u>' and '<u>utility</u>'.
(b) "The <u>lords</u> of <u>ease</u> and <u>comfort</u>" of (Quran 73:11-13) with direct reference to the pet utterances of the Baconian philosophy, like "<u>dominion</u> of man over Mother Nature for the attainment of <u>ease</u> and physical <u>comfort</u>".

The reader ought to reflect on these points when we quote these signs in the following pages. These particular signs and every sign of the Quran read with care are replete with incredible miracles.

SEVEN SPECIMENS OF ANALOGY EXIST BETWEEN ENGROSSMENT IN 'WEALTH-ACCUMULATION' AND PUNISHMENT IN 'FIRE', ACCORDING TO THE QURAN

Scriptures, one and all, are blessed works of Allah and breathe the same spirit of divinity. The teachings of Jesus Christ in the Gospel are the exact antithesis and a crushing antidote to worldly materialism.

We could say the same about the teachings of every Prophet of Allah, but only Quran speaks with direct reference to this particular modern philosophy of atomism. It stands up to this modern, science-guided, and machine-ridden age of knowledge in the field of science and philosophy. Likewise, it portrays specific features of particular modern philosophy of atomism with extreme precision to the smallest detail and traces its origin and development.

Quran treats every problem of atomism and offers its specific answer through particular philosophy, and prophecies its end, accepts its challenge in confrontation, and throws its own in the field of science. Hence, Quran champions the cause of faith, religion, and all the Scriptures as the last declared Will of Allah to humankind. It is a standing miracle with the ability to guide the present humankind away from the atomic threat to the path of true peace, prosperity, and joy in this most thoroughly knowledgeable and most complexly problematic of all ages. Only insight, faith, and knowledge are required to discern the facts that we see sparkling through the celestial fabric of ever-scintillating words of the Quran.

GABRIEL'S EXTINGUISHING THE ATOMIC HELL SERIES

You should read the following signs from the Quran with the primary purpose of finding a relationship existing between the 'wealth' of the world as the sole object of life on earth and 'fire'.

(a) "Whoso desireth that (life) which hasteneth away, We hasten for him therein that We will for whom We please. And afterward, We have appointed for him <u>hell</u>; he will endure the heat thereof, condemned, rejected. And whoso desireth the Hereafter and striveth for it with the effort necessary, being a believer; for such, their effort findeth favor (with their Lord). Each do We supply, both these and those, from the bounty of thy Lord. And the bounty of thy Lord can never be walled up."

(Quran 17:18-20)

(b) "Whoso desireth the present life of the world and its pomp, We shall repay them their deeds herein, and therein they will not be wronged. Those are they for whom is naught in the Hereafter save the <u>Fire</u>. (All) that they contrive here (in this life) is vain and shall perish and (all) that they are wont to do is <u>fruitless</u>."

(Quran 11:15-16)

(c) "Those who disbelieve take their comfort in this life and eat even as the cattle eat, and the <u>Fire</u> is their habitation."

(Quran 47:12)

(d) "Leave Me to deal with the deniers, <u>lords</u> of <u>ease</u> and <u>comfort</u> (in this life), and do thou respite them awhile. Lo! With Us are heavy fetters and a <u>raging fire</u>, and food which choketh (the partaker), and a painful doom."

(Quran 73:11-13)

(e) "Let not their wealth nor their children please thee! Allah purposeth only to punish them thereby in the world, and that their souls shall pass away while they are disbelievers."

(Quran 9:85)

(f) "Rivalry in worldly increase distracteth you until ye come to the graves. Nay, but ye will come to know! Nay, but ye will come to know! Nay, would that ye knew (now) with a sure knowledge! For <u>ye will behold hell-fire, Aye, ye will behold it with sure vision</u>. Then, on that day, ye will be asked concerning <u>pleasure</u>."

(Quran 102:1-8)

Mark the word 'pleasure' in the above sign of the Quran and recall to your mind the chief slogan of the Epicureans, namely, 'pleasure'. The Quran is replete with oracular marvels and anticipative miracles. Knowledge and the power of observation are necessary for the discernment thereof. Pray, mark the words, "Ye will behold hell-fire,

Aye, ye will behold it with sure vision." The flare-up of the atomic hell within this world may prove the truth of these words beyond any doubt. Hell-fire in the next world, however, is an indisputable verity.

(g) "They who hoard up gold and silver and spend it not in the way of Allah, unto them give tidings (O Muhammad) of a painful doom. On the day when it will (all) be heated in the <u>fire of hell</u>, and their foreheads and their flanks and their backs will be branded therewith (and it will be said unto them): Here is that which ye hoarded for yourselves. Now taste of what ye used to hoard."

(Quran 9:34-35)

It is now apparent that the only reward for the choice of this world is fire. The hoarded gold and silver will be heated in the fire to brand and torture the hoarder thereof. Further, the Quran has differentiated the fire of nuclear nature from ordinary fire. Specific causes result in the appearance of atomic fire. The particular causes, and distinction of atomic fire from ordinary fire, have been described in the prophecy about 'Al-Hotama'. Thus, anyone can see that the 'conversion of wealth into the fire' is a scientific process and a logical consequence.

THE ATOMIC SAMSON

The Quran has said, "The slandering wealth-accumulator thinks his wealth shall render him immortal." But the Quran further says that he is mistaken; he will undoubtedly be cast into the deadly 'Al-Hotama'.

Now, the whole endeavor of the atomistic world has been basically and practically to gain dominion over the forces of Mother Nature to achieve material progress and fight against death. Spectacular success in this respect has appeared in a substantial and unprecedented increase in the proportion of the world population. The course of natural selection has been attested due to an effective check on the epidemic, famine, and other types of blights. The world's population has unproportionally multiplied to prove the point of prolonging life and constitute a perpetual headache to humankind.

By his frightening estimates of the increase in the world population, Thomas Robert Malthus had called the attention of the thoughtful people to this alarming fact. Darwin discussed at great length the function of natural selection. But how little then did Malthus know of an approaching solution for the alarming problem of the world population on a universal scale? How little could Darwin then anticipate in what terrific manner the repercussive violence of the principle of natural selection will react against the prolonged arrest of its course and the consequent accumulation of the world populations only about eighty-eight years after the publication of his 'Origin of Species'.

Here, we allude to the events of Hiroshima and Nagasaki with a possible repetition of similar events in other parts of the world, perhaps in every part of the world. In Hiroshima and Nagasaki, just with one blow and within a few seconds, the violated and offended Mother Nature produced a veritable proof of the fallacy of the atomistic notion of forever living in this world. And it also denied the belief of enjoying a constant success in perpetual progress and systematic wealth accumulation through five-yearly, ten-yearly, and twenty-yearly plans continuously to eternity.

What a marvel it would be if we awakened ghosts of all pioneers and developers of the modern age of atomism from a deep slumber, taken out of their graves like 'legendary cave-sleepers' [2] and collected in Bikini Atoll; to witness the historic test of the Hydrogen bomb? They could see the demonstration of the Hydrogen bomb dropped on a flourishing city to see with their own eyes the 'fruit' of that philosophy of 'fruit' and 'utility' to which they had devoted their lives. In that philosophy, they had seen the pictures of a universal utopia of peace, plenty, and prosperity on this earth. While, according to their modern advocate, Francis Bacon, pre-modern people had gone astray unto the wrong path of moral philosophy. It would be a treat to imagine the state of their minds at the sight of a city in the fiery grip of the Hydrogen bomb with the inhabitants being roasted alive.

The modern age is a lordly victor of the forces of vengeful Mother Nature, the rebellious believer in this transient world alone, and resembles the modern philistine. Suppose this age has captured the atomic Samson, pulled his eyes out of sockets, and subjected him to abject slavery. Then after serving in obedience to its express commands like a galley slave in reactors and atomic plants, a time will necessarily come when the atomic Samson will someday show an unusual demonstration of his strength in an uncontrolled way in the field of atomic war. He will bring the heavens of this age down on its head and his head himself, killing all the Presidents, Ministers, dignitaries, scientists, philosophers, business magnates, priests, eminent scholars, warmongers, and war chiefs. Like the historical philistine lords, these personalities will have the ill-luck of watching the fantastic feats of the strength of their slave, the 'Atomic Samson'.

However, who was this ancient Samson? He was a famous Israelite in the early history of the people of Israel, reputed for his super-human physical strength. Philistines and antagonist people captured him, plucked his eyes out, and threw him into prison as a captive. On a day of their celebrations, the philistine lords commanded their illustrious captive though blind, to show feats of his strength. They sat under a pavilion, enjoying the fantastic feats of the strength of their helpless captive.

When at last, the tired and exhausted captive stood leaning against the massy pillars that supported the roof of the pavilion to ease his breath, he suddenly cried out, as Milton has described in the following lines.

"As over-tired to let him lean a while
With both his arms on those two massy pillars,
That to the arched roof gave main support.
He unsuspicious led him; which when Samson
Felt in his arms, with head a while inclined,
And eyes fast fixed he stood, as one who prayed,
Or some great matter in his mind revolved.
At last with head erect thus cried aloud:
"Hitherto, Lords, what your commands imposed
I have performed, as reason was, obeying,
Not without wonder or delight beheld;
Now of my own accord, such other trial
I mean to shew you of my strength, yet greater,
As with amaze shall strike all who behold."
This uttered, straining all his nerves he bowed;
As, with the force of winds and waters pent,
When mountains tremble, those two massy pillars
With horrible convulsion to and fro
He tugged, he shook, till down they came and drew
The whole roof after them, with burst of thunder,
Upon the heads of all who sat beneath,
Lords, ladies, captains, counsellors, or priests,
Their choice nobility and flower, not only
Of this but each Philistian city round,
Met from all parts to solemnize this feast.
Samson, with these immixed, inevitably
Pulled down the same destruction on himself;
The vulgar only scaped who stood without."

(Milton's Poetical Works: 'Samson Agonistes': lines 1632-1659) The resemblance between the story of the ancient and the modern philistines as regards Samson is complete with the difference; however, that the theater of the ancient Philistines was but a small one with a few philistine lords in it while the amphitheater of the modern Philistines is going to be this whole earth. In the case of the ancient Samson, the lords only were involved. However, the vulgar had escaped. Neither the lords nor vulgar have a chance to escape the show of modern atomic Samson, except perhaps in a way that some out-of-the-way nations living in remote parts of the earth may escape the blasts of the atomic bombs. However, all will be involved in the radiological hazards, and none living on earth will have a chance to escape.

There is another difference and a very remarkable one indeed. Whereas the philistine lords had pulled the eyes of the giant out, this modern atomic Samson has blinded this conqueror of Mother Nature, the modern lordly humankind. Humanity is riding the atomic python without a bridle; that is, humankind adopted atomic energy without achieving control on the atomic radiations or providing any means of protection from radiations to humankind in general.

[(2) **Tafsir Al-Kabir**

The word 'La-Yunbazanna' (meaning "will certainly be flung into") is expressive of insult as a retaliative measure against the conceit of self-honor due to his wealth entertained by the 'Homaza-Lomaza' (the slandering wealth accumulator).]

The disgraceful compulsion with which the abject necessity of atomic energy is dragging the present world towards the atomic hell of atomic bombs is a process perhaps a little too subtle and discernible only to a subtle vision. The lords, princes, monarchs, scientists, and doctors indeed, along with the commoners, will be flung into the atomic hell of the atomic bombs in the event of atomic war. Furthermore, it will push millions of cancer-ridden victims of atomic radiation into the hands of the shocked staff of the hospitals. This disgraceful spectacle will not be missed even by the most vulgar eye. Now, the vicegerent of Allah on earth, man indeed, then shall be the most despicable creature ever lived on earth.

[(3) **Tafsir Al-Kabir**

We recite the word 'Layunbazanna' (meaning "will be cast into") also as 'La-Yunbazaanne', which is the dual form of 'La-Yunbazanna' and means 'both of them', that is both the owner and his wealth (shall be flung into 'Al-Hotama').]

If flinging his wealth into the fire is meant to torture the 'Homaza-Lomaza', then this particular point of flinging the wealth of 'Homaza-Lomaza' and himself into 'Al-Hotama' shows a plausible bearing on the probability of the appearance of 'Al-Hotama' within this same world: since, in the next world, one's wealth will have little value, and its loss may not bring much pain.

No commentator has hinted in this respect, and it is quite natural because they had only the next world in view. Allah knows precisely the actual reality thereof, but the style of the direct retort of the Quran to the slanderer's claim of living in the world forever may seem to justify the notion of his eradication along with his wealth within this same world and this very life.

Yet, Allah has absolute knowledge. The fact of the appearance of 'Al-Hotama' in the next world, however, stands there glaring into the eyes of man, most certain. Alas, man's mind has moved far away from any consideration of the next unseen world. The warnings of the Scriptures have lost all their value. However, here now is a warning which has come to embrace both worlds. There is a possibility that a hell ablaze not only in their imagination but in a tangible form before their very eyes may affect them, and they may repent and reform.

The celebrated commentator of the Quran, 'Al-Tabari', has named Hassan Al-Basri, who used to recite the word as 'La-Yunbazaanne' in the dual form. Hassan-Al-Basri, as is well-known, is a shining star in the galaxy of the learned in Islam.

[(4) **Tafsir Al-Kabir**

We recite this word also in its plural form that is 'La-Yunbazunna'. It means that Allah will cast even the 'Homaza-Lomaza' supporters into 'Al-Hotama' along with him.]

SECTION-6

Quran: "Al-Hotama"
Meaning: "The meaning of 'Hotama' is a crusher; 'Al' only is a prefix, equivalent to the English 'the'."

[(1) **Tafsir Al-Kabir**
'Al-Hotama': The root verb 'Hatama' from which the word 'Hotama' is derived means 'to break', 'to ground something to pieces'.

(2) **Tafsir Al-Jalalayn**
'Al-Hotama' is named such because it 'breaks', 'crushes', and 'grinds' to pieces.

(3) **Tafsir Al-Tabari**
'Hotama' is the name of a fire. I believe that we call it such because 'it grounds to particles whatever is cast into it'.]

Please mark the phonetic resemblance between the scientific term 'Atomization' and the other one 'Hatomization'. 'Hatomization' is the anglicized form of the Arabic word 'Hatom', Hotama's root verb.

The word we have generally written as 'Hatam' actually is nearer in sound to 'Hatom' than 'Hatam' in its Arabic pronunciation. The rest of the 'Hotama' discussion has passed in the previous chapters and needs not to be repeated here. Mark the identity between our views and those of the venerable commentators.

[(4) **Tafsir Al-Kabir**
'Hotama' is the name of a fire out of various fires.]

Here, the commentator clearly distinguishes between other fires and the particular fire of 'Al-Hotama'. That 'Hotama' is a different and distinct kind of fire is implied by its very name. Generating nuclear energy is quite different from any other kind of energy.

The atomic energy is generated in the atom's nucleus and by crushing the nucleus. In contrast, the chemical energy never touches the atom's nucleus, nor is it generated by crushing the nuclei of the atoms. Nuclei of the atoms of a substance consumed by chemical fire remain intact to the end. The significant difference between the two kinds of fire temperatures, namely, the chemical and the atomic, is conspicuous.

Igniting and extinguishing the atomic fire (that is, the atomic energy) are different. No match or spark is effective in starting the atomic fire. Fission only starts it. No water or any kind of chemical fire extinguisher is of any avail in extinguishing the atomic fire. By stopping fission alone, we can extinguish it. We can stop fission through moderators. However, no one can stop the explosion of the atomic bomb if detonated once. The fires that start in the cities due to the heat radiation of the atomic explosion are not a part of the atomic fire of the atomic bomb explosion.

[(5) **Tafsir Al-Kabir**
'Al-Hotama': Evidently, appropriateness exists in the name of 'Al-Hotama'.

Firstly, the rhyme existing between the words 'Homaza-Lomaza' and 'Hotama' is apparent and is meaningful, as if Allah would say, "be thou Homaza-Lomaza at thy heels in 'Hotama'."

Secondly, a correspondence between the function of 'Homaza-Lomaza' and 'Al-Hotama' exists. The backbiter debases people by giving a black eye (lowering gesture, winking, etc.). In turn, he is lowered (debased) into 'Al-Hotama' to be broken.

Thirdly, 'Homaza-Lomaza' eats the flesh of the people (figuratively, by the act of backbiting); 'Hotama' likewise eats the <u>skin</u> and <u>flesh</u> of men.]

The discussion of the commentator is self-evident. There is a marvelous thing in it: the 'eating up of the skin and flesh of men' by the fire of 'Al-Hotama'.

Atomic radiations do eat up the skin and flesh of their victims. This anticipative description of the fire of 'Al-Hotama' by the commentator could be regarded as a marvel.

[(6) **Tafsir Al-Kabir**
The fire of 'Al-Hotama' crushes bones, eats up flesh, and then attacks the hearts.]

Anyone could expect no better picture of the effects of radiations than that produced by the commentator above.

Radiations 'crush' the bones by producing bone cancers and 'eat up' their victim's flesh during the radiation sickness, leaving the patient as a mere skeleton of bones.

We have already explained the manners in which radiations 'leap up over the hearts' in previous chapters.

[(7) **Tafsir Al-Kabir**
The nickname of Gormandizer is 'Rajul-Hotama', that is 'Man-Hotama'. The gormandizer who eats up the whole of the food stored for a whole people is nicknamed 'Hotama' and is called 'Rajul-Hotama', that is 'Man-Hotama'. It is a general belief that the worse of all the curses is the curse of 'Hotama'.]

Indeed, the atomic hell is the worst of all the gluttons this world has ever seen. In the form of the atomic bomb, it devours up cities, living beings, and wealth, property, plants, shrubs, grass, and all. In a worldwide atomic war, all life on earth will be but a feast to the atomic hell, which will instantly glutton it up. Radiations will eat up all that the atomic bomb will leave, and this earth will be left quite desolate in time.

Nations will spend a part of the world's wealth preparing the atomic bomb, while the atomic bomb itself will devour up the remaining part. The atomic energy for peace, too, though in a more extended period, will take a toll on life. This slow but formidable glutton will swallow whole humankind on earth in time.

Again, this age of atomism in itself is a gormandizer of a rare kind. In less than a century, it has brought to the verge of exhaustion the entire mineral treasures of earth; gold, silver, copper, iron, oil, and indeed everything. So also, it will soon exhaust all the Uranium stores of the world. However, before it has done so, perhaps humankind might have long since been ended by the effects of atomic radiation or the atomic bombs. Nevertheless, for this age, the treasures of earth would have lasted for long ages.

Not a cubit of land is left uncultivated, yet all the food grains are not enough to feed the world's entire population. There is always a cry of hunger and a demand for more. The more is grown; the more is wanted. Woods, as well as wild animals all over the world, have mostly disappeared. They are ransacking oceans for fish, pearls, oil, and mineral wealth, but no signs of appeasement are there. Not even the North and South Poles of the earth are immune from the ravages of this modern age. Nay, nations are searching even the outer worlds of the moon and stars for some valuable commodity. [3]

Pangs of man's hunger in this age, however, are still in the process of aggravation and his range of appetite is infinitely on the increase with no signs whatsoever of any appeasement.

The commentator's remark that 'Rajul-Hotama' is a glutton who eats up the whole of food stored up for a whole people is true to this age of atomistic materialism. In the shortest possible time, this age has devoured up all the materials of earth stored up by Mother Nature for all ages and, in fact, for the whole span of life of the human race on earth to the last age.

This present age is being forced by an un-proportional necessity, having devoured up all the mineral treasures of the earth, to adopt even the most poisonous and most hazardous energy source, which is atomic energy. They will, however, leave recessive genes and genetic loads in abundance to future generations in return for mineral treasures.

[(8) Tafsir Al-Kabir
A ruthless shepherd too is nicknamed as 'Raay-il-Hotama' (the 'Hotama-Shepherd' for his ruthless behavior while driving his herd.)]

Moreover, so also is this age of mechanical driving a race of humans flying about and rushing about like tyrannical and ruthless ghosts: armored mountains-like ships churning the waters of seven seas; millions of engines everywhere in the world seen furiously roaring, cutting, biting, crushing, grinding, kicking, and drilling most ruthlessly. Vehicles crush people and their cattle under the wheels on the road.

Imagine that such a feature of this age is precisely that of a ruthless shepherd. If those pioneers of atomism in this modern age or still better if the early atomists of Greece were revived from their graves to watch a motor car or motorcycle race in a mountainous region and look up into their faces, they would portray the brutality of driving. Then cause them to sit by the cross of a large city and see if they do not lose their sense; those poor inhabitants of the world of bullock carts and laden asses. Then watch the dizziness of their heads due to constant and swift revolving.

SECTION-7
DESCRIPTION OF 'AL-HOTAMA' BY THE HOLY PROPHET (PEACE BE UPON HIM)

(1) "Allah will send over the victims, angels equipped with 'covers of fire', and 'nails of fire', and 'columns of fire'. They will cover the doomed with 'covers of fire', and will transfix them with 'nails of fire', and will 'stretch the columns of fire upward over them'. The entire phenomenon will be made so over airtight that no trace of delight shall enter from outside, nor a trace of agony will escape from inside. Allah will forget them on His throne and will cut them off from His mercy. The inmates of Paradise will begin to enjoy the boons of Allah. The inmates of hell will cease to cry for help, and speech will come to an end. Their speech will then be (as the sound of) inhaling and exhaling".

(Quoted from 'Tafsir al-Jalalayn')

(2) "The angel gets hold of the victim and placing him over the knee, breaks him like a wooden stick, and then casts him into the fire."

(Quoted from 'Tafsir al-Jalalayn')

It could be taken as a superb description and most exact portrayal of the phenomenon of the explosion of the atomic bomb. The atomic bomb explosion spreads like an inverted cauldron and forms a complete cover over the effective zone. The ionizing radiations emitted during the actual explosion and after that by fission products of the atomic explosion could well be likened to extra-fine 'nails of fire' that penetrate and transfix the bodies of those that happen to be within the enclosure. In scientific language, these radiations are called rays, even point projectiles, in which the entanglement of the nails of radiation could be seen.

So, when the atomic bomb bursts, the 'cover of fire' in the form of the effective zone appears to cover the inmates of the area, and radiations appear like delicate nails and transfix the inmates of the enclosure. Then the column of the atomic explosion is stretched upward above them, exactly like that described in 'Al-Hotama' of the next world by the Holy Prophet (peace be upon him). This fact alone could manifest a miracle before the very eyes of skeptics who find it difficult to believe in the possibility of a miracle.

SECTION-8

Quran: "Wa Maa Adraaka Maa Al-Hotama?"
Meaning: "And what could teach thee what 'Al-Hotama' is?"
'Wa' means 'and'; 'Maa' means 'what'; 'Adraaka' means 'cause thee to comprehend'; 'Maa' means 'what'; 'Al-Hotama' is 'Al-Hotama'.

The whole of the sentence means, "What would cause thee to know what 'Al-Hotama' is?" or just as it has been translated, "What could teach thee what 'Al-Hotama' is?"

We have purposely deferred this particular point to here because the point is about the terribleness and the complexity of the theme offered real difficulty in understanding. At this subject stage, we expect the reader to understand better and appreciate the point.

[(1) **Tafsir Al-Jalalayn**
To wit, it is a sort of interrogatory expression that implies negation that you do not have any idea of that horror which 'Al-Hotama' indeed is or the idea of the actual severity of the warning thereof. Nor are you able to understand except through the revelation of Allah.]

The worthy commentator has attributed the questioning mode of expression in "what could teach thee what 'Al-Hotama' is?" which implies unspeakable horror and extreme gravity of the event and also the indescribable complexity of the phenomena of 'Al-Hotama'. Indeed, the horror of the atomic hell of this world, a replica of the eternal 'Al-Hotama' of the next world, is such that there is no possibility of ever expressing it in any language.

The unfortunate survivors of the incident of Hiroshima and Nagasaki who had the ill-luck of experiencing the ordeal themselves always turned pale and dumb at the very mention of the catastrophe they had seen. The journalists found survivors of Hiroshima gathered outside the ruins of the city like a herd of dazed and dumbstruck mutes, staring wildly at the sight of reporters and unable to express as if they had lost the faculty of speech and memory. They gazed at the wilderness of the twitching mouths of the newsmen who endeavored to ask them some questions about the happening.

The pious commentators of the Holy Quran and millions after them would have shuddered in imagination at the horror of the fire of 'Al-Hotama'. However, the actual appearance of the atomic hell on earth has shown that it is not simply possible for anyone to imagine the horrors of 'Al-Hotama' until observed in its manifest appearance and better still personally experienced. The horrors of the atomic hell are such as the horror itself would tremble at their appearance. They are unique in themselves and have no parallel.

Just imagine the scene of the worldwide atomic war. It will be a world caught in a furious storm of blinding flashes and deafening thunderclaps. The whole earth itself will burst into thunder and earthquakes. Cities will be pulled down into heaps of rubble, burying the inmates and crushing them beneath the falling structures. A storm of incandescent debris will be roaring about and beating at the faces and backs of the scurrying crowds. All over the world, heat-flashes of the atomic bomb explosions will spread like hundreds of dazzling suns in the conflagration, hitting millions of people and killing them on the spot. In short, raging fires will consume the whole cities; men, women, children, beasts, and birds roasted alive in fires.

Radiations are invisible, insidious, and deadly, pursuing those who might have escaped all other ordeals and piercing through their bodies like deadly invisible shafts and killing them. None in this atmosphere of the utter hour will listen to the storms of shrieks or render help to millions in trouble. No one will think to extinguish the flaming fires or to mourn the near and dear ones. But everyone will be caught in trouble to remind one of the states of people on the terrible day of Last Judgment.

We can't describe the event correctly. Only the unfortunate victims and witnesses of the catastrophe will understand the actual horror of the atomic hell. The picture of the horrors of the atomic hell which we have drawn is not yet complete. The horrors of the atomic hell will not end with the end of the atomic war. The radiations of the atomic bombs will change the survivals of the atomic war after a few generations into a race of cancer-ridden chimeras, poor, miserable, imbecile, wretched creatures forced to perpetuate their torturous existence on miserable earth on their way to the final extinction of the human race.

A post-atomic war spectacle of the world presents a perspective to the eye of a man so grievous that imagination shuns it, and language trembles to express it. Millions of millions will be rendered homeless, bereaved, mutilated, lying wounded, suffering from radiation sickness amidst epidemics and famines, and all wishing to die, and death would not come. Parents will have lost their children, and husbands, their wives, and vice-versa. All will be crying in a darkened world and wishing to die and envying the doom of those dead, but death would turn her face from them in that hour of need and fly from them away. Shocked at catastrophe and grieved to the core of heart, unfortunate survivors of atomic war would display a picture of misery and desolation to the eyes of an onlooker. It would be the essence of all that misery and desolation that was the lot of sons of Adam during their sojourn on earth.

Dear reader! It indeed is a very distasteful topic and a grievous one. Horrific is the pain and suffering brought by the atomic war and boundless desolation. All the three facets of the atomic bomb explosion, namely, the 'Heat-Flash', the 'blast', and the 'radiations', could be likened to the petrifying faces of the three gorgons. The atomic bomb is the destroyer of flourishing cities, living countries, and populated continents. It is a wholesale dealer in death and misery, the precursor of tormenting agonies and incurable diseases, and an insatiable devourer of life, health, wealth, and peace.

Besides, it is a distortionist of the original pattern of Allah's creation and a monstrous agent mutating flora and fauna into chimeras. In a nutshell, the atomic bomb is a unique, horrifying monster of destruction, devastation, and desolation endowed with all the characteristics of hell. It can destroy this whole earth in a matter of days, hours, even seconds, leaving not a vestige of life. Not even a blade of grass would be growing anywhere. Nor would there be anyone left to gaze at the blade of grass growing anywhere on earth.

The Creator called into being life on earth by millions of processes after the continuation of ages and by coordinating all the forces of the entire universe with abounding love and care. In current circumstances, it could be devastated by fiery catastrophe before the Creator's eyes in the twinkling of an eye. In brief, it will be akin to the garden set on fire in the Gardener's presence and definitely by the folly of those for whom the Creator planted the garden.

The present tendency shows that humankind shall adopt atomic energy for peace unless some miracle happens to the contrary. In that case, no less terrible will be the sight of this earth due to the ravages of the atomic energy for peace on the long-term basis among humankind a few generations removed from now.

Anyone who will know and will have an imagination subtle enough to view the havocs of the atomic war will burst into a fit of blabbing rhetoric in this age of little rhetoric and begin to utter quivering poetry in this age of no poetry. In short, due to the horrors of imagination, the viewer of the havocs of the atomic war will lose sense. As a result of his mental derangement, he will become a desperate victim of a perpetual craze, for the atomic war is nothing short of a terrible hell let loose on the world. Those who think themselves to be very strong-minded today and sit with their necks as stiff as a peg with all the formidable strength of their heart, obstinacy, and conceit will evaporate in the event of the atomic bomb explosion even without their knowledge. The world shuddered at the news of Hiroshima and Nagasaki. Nevertheless, the frightful tales of those two unfortunate cities will seem a mere trifle against the tale of a world subjected to the devastation by the hail of super bombs.

The whole phenomenon of the nuclear explosion is unearthly and unnatural to this humble mold of earthy abode of man; that it is of a nature quite celestial. The intensity of the temperatures developed by the nuclear explosions is not terrestrial but is of a solar and a stellar nature. Also, the energy released by the thermonuclear bombs is of the order of large-scale natural phenomena like hurricanes and earthquakes. The fires starting due to the intense heat produced by the atomic bomb explosion consume whole cities. Cities that had taken centuries, even millenniums to build, would be turned into widespread heaps of ruin in a matter of seconds, along with the ashes of the unfortunate dwellers.

The ionizing radiations of the nuclear explosion could be likened to fiery storms of invisible, insidious, and poisonous nails. They are needles of fire raging in every direction, penetrating the bodies of millions, killing some, and sending others to hospitals to live the rest of their lives as sickly, invalid patients: the pictures of perpetual misery and dying a miserable death. Such indeed will be the misery of the life of the unfortunate survivors of the atomic war. They will sit and envy the doom of those having perished in the event cursing their grievous misfortune for having survived. Their survival will be nothing but suffering and sustaining the horrific catastrophe and living a painful life of misery, disappointment, disease, famine, and a hundred other torments. These pains may include conjugal apathy, domestic discomfort, mistrust, distrust, and hatred besides the distress at abnormal births.

They will wish for death, yet death itself will fly before their misery. The mind recoils from imagining and pen abhors writing the wretched state of the post-atomic-war population of the world. It will be a state of misery that defies exaggeration or overstatement. An entire army of Shakespeares, Miltons, and Dantes combined would simply be dumbstruck and tongue-tied at the inexpressible horrors of the spectacle. All that large repository of phrases contained by their ingenious minds would hardly be sufficient to express even a tithe of that frightening reality which someone would call them upon to express in man's language.

Just imagine the entire world instantly changed into the battlefield of all the furies of a roaring universe. The whole earth has been wholly shrouded in thunder, lightning, fire, smoke, and choking fumes. The whole world changed into a burning, smoking, reeking heap of a ruin, a colossal battlefield with a part of humankind lying burnt and buried under the shattered buildings, and the other lying or wriggling; burnt, wounded, and mutilated.

Yet others, millions of them rushing and screaming in extreme panic through the leaping flames and collapsing buildings and choking fumes, without knowing where to and wherefore. These are not mere fantasies. They, at present, who but gaze in indifference at the possibilities of atomic war and turn themselves deaf to the warnings of the approaching doom may hear one day to their untimely horror a sudden proclamation of a proclaimer with the sound of a trumpet and the beat of drum:

"Awake now, you sound sleepers and face the hail of atomic bombs. Behold super-giants, the pride of your stockpiles in an exquisite array, and ready to destroy this world of heedless and arrogant race that neglected all the friendly counsels and timely warnings. This egotistical generation refrained not from follies pointed out to them as the causes of the emergence of the atomic hell. Trusting in their particular wisdom and in their efforts to make 'No-Atomic-War' pacts, they missed the basic realities and headed toward a burning hell. Their destination has now approached. Here it is, the atomic hell they can see in its true reality. Then, let them taste the fruit of their wrong attitude and erroneous deeds."

Initial heat radiation that is the 'Heat-Flash', the blast, and the fires resulting from the tremendous heat produced by the initial heat-radiation consuming whole cities are all indeed terrible. But far more terrible in a particular way are the radiations emitted by the atomic bomb during its explosion and later on by its radioactive fission products.

Radiations are inherent in the very nature of the atomic (fission) bomb. They are inherent in the very nature of atomic (nuclear) energy. No fission could be caused without at the same time emitting radiation. No atomic energy, therefore, could be generated without at the same time emitting radiations, and no atomic (fission) bomb is exploded without the associated emission of radiations.

Further, because no fusion (Hydrogen) bomb can be detonated without the necessary heat to be produced by some fission device, no radiation-free explosion of Hydrogen that is the thermonuclear bomb is possible. Instead, the fusion bomb is more dangerous in this respect because due to the terrible force of the explosion, the radioactive fission products of the associated fission device scatter over greater distances. The effects of radiation are that they can kill on the spot and produce radiation sickness and cancer.

However, their worst effects are their genetic effects. These genetic effects are irreversible and irreparable. That is, we cannot cure them, and once done, they are forever done. Radiations mutate genes, and these mutated genes are transmitted secretly from generation to generation without anyone's knowledge till they manifest their existence in some future generations in the form of abnormal birth. Also, these abnormalities are further inheritable and multiplicative through marriage.

Miseries inflicted by radiations on their victims are extremely painful, the most benign of these being death. The life of the victims of radiation is far worse than death itself, and death is preferable to living as the victim of heinous effects of radiation. The description of the miseries of the victims of radiation may make Dante mute with horror.

In the event of atomic war, millions may be killed on the spot by radiation, while millions may be left to live a life of pain, misery, and affliction.

However, the worst of all are the long-term effects of radiation. After having passed secretly and insidiously through several successive generations, the recessive genes (that are mutated by the radiations) manifest their existence in some future generations in the form of abnormal birth. A tragedy which the present generation may have the consolation to escape, but certainly their progeny, grandchildren will have to pay the enormous debt bequeathed to them by their unkind ancestors. The human race and the whole of the mammalian world, even the plants, will be turned into chimeras. This world then will be a medley of biological confusion and anatomical anarchy that will render life impossible.

We can compare the spectacle of the world at the event of the atomic war to a furious hell ablaze. The hell at the end of the atomic war or immediately following it, in biological nature, is a hell of wounds and radiation sickness. Millions suffering from bloody hemorrhages, fever, septic wounds, and covered all over with stinking blood, oozing suppuration, and exuding pus, and presenting a horrid spectacle of a horrid hell.

[(2) **Tafsir Al-Kabir**
What could teach thee what 'Al-Hotama' is, means you do not know the reality of this one.]

Quran's Interpreters have interpreted the interrogative mode of sign in terms of the dreadfulness of 'Al-Hotama' and its extreme complexity. We have presented a glimpse of the terribleness of the atomic hell in the previous pages. The factor of its complexity, however, remains to be treated.

Al-Kabir above has rightly said that the meaning of this sign is that you do not know this one. The expression 'this one' has a tone of contempt which reminds one of the expressions 'that thing', an expression used for the atomic reactor by the dissenters in Germany when demonstrating against the installation of an atomic reactor in a particular vicinity. The demonstrators repeatedly shouted:

"We shall not allow <u>that thing</u> to be installed here."

The subject of nuclear science is exceedingly subtle, exceptionally complex, complicated, intricate, and baffling. Most of the reactions taking place therein are invisible and extremely difficult to trace. If, on the one hand, the terrors of the atomic bomb are remarkable in comparison to all other kinds of bombs, the insidious complexity of the nuclear phenomena is regarded as proverbial by the scientists. It has baffled the scientists since the appearance of nuclear science, and it shall keep baffling them to the end.

The subject of nuclear science is inexpressibly complex of all the sciences known to man. The subject moves into the sub-atomic regions of the structure of matter where the human eye and the most powerful microscope turn blind. Any mortal has not hitherto even seen the much-talked-about atom. Even molecules, except a few huge ones of proteins, are as yet invisible. Scientists have derived most of the knowledge of atomic particles and their reactions by indirect means.

Every standard textbook of nuclear science is replete with confessions of ignorance and extraordinary difficulties, and indescribable complexities of the subject. Although we can speak with exactitude and certainty about certain fundamentals of the subject yet there arrives a limit beyond which nothing, but uncertainty and doubt prevail. Thence the subject moves into the regions that are dark, invisible, and ambiguous. In the investigation, we encounter points where even speculation deserts and the human mind is left to blink in a complete void. At that point, the most acute scientific intellects gaze in amazement and are obliged to confess the subject's extreme difficulty and ignorance.

The celebrities among the atomists discovered atomic energy, built atomic bombs, and triumphed over the most significant difficulties in attaining their scientific objects. These luminaries are foremost in their confessions of ignorance regarding the subject and loudest lamenting the unique proclaiming complexities. The truth of the difficulty of the subject of nuclear science is confirmed as a result of continuous research, investigation, and experimentation for centuries, the employment of the ablest of the human intellects, and spectacular achievements in the subject field.

The deeper the research into the subject, the clearer the extent of the complicated nature of the subject. Theories, hypotheses, and suggestions have been advanced in this field only to be partly or wholly rejected. Attempts to construct a theoretical atomic model based on classical physics failed. Eventually, scientists realized that classical physics (Newtonian Mechanics, Electrodynamics of Maxwell, and Thermodynamics) could not explain or describe atomic phenomena.

Bohr's atom theory failed despite the help its relativistic and elliptic orbits provided to explain the fine structure of the Hydrogen and singly ionized Helium spectra. It met serious difficulties in further applying that theory. The interpretation of the nuclear properties of atoms in terms of a theory of nuclear structure presents excessive difficulties.

It has not been possible to analyze the forces which hold neutrons and protons together, nor has it been possible to understand the power which overcomes the mutual repulsion of the positively charged protons to hold them together in the nucleus. Moreover, the structure of the nucleus is not understood.

No picture or theory can unite the nuclei information into a consistent body of knowledge like the quantum-mechanical theory of atomic structure. The complexity of the subject further increases with our entry into the field of Radiobiology. The reactions of the atomic radiations, whether in inanimate matter or a living body, are mostly beyond the power of a microscope to see, and the subject of Radiobiology is one of unusual complexity.

Further, this subject involves many disciplines: physics, chemistry, biology, and the medical sciences are all concerned, and their interdependence adds to the difficulty of the subject. Highly specialized knowledge is required to determine the facts, but their interpretation requires a comprehensive knowledge of all the different sciences involved. No wonder then if the standard books of Radiobiology should contain even a great abundance of the confessions of ignorance and complaints of the difficulty and complexity of the subject.

All the leading authorities agree that our knowledge of the subject is only fragmentary while crucial discoveries lie ahead. Yet, none knows how or when these important discoveries will come. It may be that the world might long since have perished under the effects of radiations before any one of these expected vital discoveries has made its appearance, for such is the difficulty of the subject.

THE 20 EXAMPLES OF THE IGNORANCE OF THE RADIOBIOLOGISTS [4]

Out of the long list of points of ignorance in Radiobiology, the main ones are as follows.

(a) Clues are there indeed numerous, but significant discoveries have yet to be made.

(b) As yet, we know nothing of the nucleus's fine structure in the resting stage.

(c) The division of function between cytoplasm and nucleus is not clear-cut, and there is considerable evidence for some genetic factors in the cytoplasm. At the same time, a considerable amount of synthesis of structural material also occurs in the nucleus.

(d) Neither of the current hypotheses about chromosome breaks is correct, and a theory will have to evolve, incorporating both features.

(e) The nature of the injury, which holds up the normal cell cycle for a time, is not known.

(f) The mechanism by which enzymes can cause a specific chemical reaction to take place is not understood.

(g) The synthesis of proteins from amino acids is a reaction that has wholly defied the ingenuity of chemists.

(h) Scientists have put forward no convincing reason to explain tremendous variations between cells in their response to radiations. Only when this is known will it be possible to base radiotherapy of cancer or methods of protection against radiations on a reliable foundation. It is a measure of difficulty and complexity of the subject that anyone can give, not even a tentative answer to the question.

(i) The critical problem of cancer research is what stimuli cause a cell to stop dividing when an organ reaches a correct size and repair damage after an injury.

(j) The mechanism by which radiation eradicates tumors is exceptionally complex.

(k) How tumor cells are killed or sterilized is not fully understood.

(l) We cannot follow all the stages between the radiation passages through the irradiated organs and the final injury.

(m) It is difficult to predict the course and outcome of radiation treatment.

(n) Death is the most apparent effect of radiation on the cell, but even this drastic change is far from easy to define for the individual cell.

(o) We cannot wholly explain the paradox: although the pathological changes from whole-body irradiation are diffused and ill-defined, death occurs regularly. This mystery is of all the various kinds of poisons is a peculiarly distinctive characteristic of atomic radiations.

(p) The symptoms of acute radiation sickness can be summarized, but they tell us little about the cause of death. Suppose a pathologist carries out a postmortem examination on a mammal who succumbed after a radiation dose of a few hundred roentgens. In that case, he will find it very difficult to pinpoint death to the failure of a particular organ.

(q) We have found no treatment applied sometime after irradiation, which can reduce the number of mutations since no recovery is possible from mutation (a significant point worth noting); we would expect no post-irradiation treatment to restore a mutation. We can consider even little treatment discovered to be of some effect before irradiation for little practical use due to the insidious nature of radiations.

(r) We cannot answer as to whether chemicals can protect against the long-term effects of radiation. Technical difficulties make it extremely hard to measure accurately the mutations produced in mammals.

(s) It is unknown how a dose of radiation sufficient to kill or visibly injure a cell represents such a minute amount of energy that it could only affect very few molecules, a change entirely insufficient to bring about the pronounced biological effects directly. This fact constitutes a challenge to scientists. It is both a disappointment and surprise that we have found no effective substance against radiation effect.

(t) Even the much-talked-about 'permissive dose' [5] is merely hypothetical, and it naturally should be because it needs a sufficient amount of experimental data to confirm the correct dose. The appearance of that data requires the passage of several generations.

Now, this is the picture of our knowledge of the subject of Radiobiology. The Radiobiologists have acquired information about the subject in the face of unspeakable difficulties and unimaginable obstacles. Nevertheless, despite all the notable shortcomings of the Radiobiologists in this field and numerous confessions of ignorance about the reliable fundamental information regarding the subject, all the standard books bespeak the admirable patience and laudable perseverance on their part and their remarkable ingenuity, ability, and skills. We could not attribute their shortcomings to any lack of talent or genius, but the subject's difficulties are great. The nature of difficult points raised by them, which generally constitute the body of their confessions of ignorance, has amply furnished the proof of their talent and understanding of the subject. The scrutiny of these points tells that such points could have been raised only by one who had an accurate understanding of the fundamental nature of the subject and was well aware of its anticipative trends and future necessities.

One confession of a leading Radiobiologist, we shall quote as a specimen. This confession is a masterpiece in itself, comprehensive and indicative of formidable difficulties on the subject and the competence of the Radiobiologist.

THE CONFESSION OF A KNOWING RADIOBIOLOGIST

"The ways in which the complex organisms are affected by radiations are not understood, and the interplay of many factors makes it virtually impossible to relate the final injury to its cellular origin. What is more disappointing is that there is not yet a satisfactory theory which explains how relatively small doses arrest mitosis and kill individual cells sometime after the irradiation is finished. Death follows immediately after extreme irradiation with hundreds of thousands of roentgen, which causes widespread and readily recognized destruction. The real challenge is to discover the subtle process by which a minute amount of energy supplied by ionizing radiations can initiate changes which eventually result in cell death."

('Atomic Radiation and Life'; by Peter Alexander, Page-210)

THE POINTS OF THE CONFESSION REFERRED TO BY THE PROPHECY

Now, this is the most comprehensive confession and quite enough to justify the words of the prophecy, "What could teach thee what 'Al-Hotama' is?" Further, the wonderful thing is that the prophecy has already referred to the points raised by this confession in question.

The following points may be referred to as raised by this confession in question.

(a) **The Radiobiologist:** "The ways in which the complex organisms are affected by radiations are not understood, and the interplay of many factors makes it virtually impossible to relate the final injury to its cellular origin. What is more disappointing is that there is not yet a satisfactory theory which explains how relatively small doses arrest mitosis and kill individual cells sometime after the irradiation is finished."

The Prophecy: "What could teach thee what 'Al-Hotama' is?"

(b) **The Radiobiologist:** "The real challenge is to discover the subtle process by which a minute amount of energy supplied by ionizing radiations can initiate changes which eventually result in cell death."

The Prophecy: "It is a fire which leaps up over the 'hearts'."

It reaches such minute and subtle parts affected by the minutest amount of the energy deposited by the ionizing radiations. We could refer to these parts as 'hearts'.

(c) **The Radiobiologist:** "How radiations arrest mitosis and kill individual cells sometime after the radiation is finished?"

The Prophecy: "It is a fire closed in on them."

That is, this fire keeps the cells 'encompassing' even after irradiation is finished.

(d) **The Radiobiologist:** "Death follows immediately after extreme irradiation with hundreds of thousands of roentgen which causes wide-spread and readily recognized destruction."

The Prophecy: "It is 'Al-Hotama'."

That is, it is a 'crushing fire'.

[(3) **Tafsir Al-Tabari**
"What could cause thee to understand what 'Al-Hotama' is?" Allah, after asking this question (to negate the possibility of one's understanding the phenomena of 'Al-Hotama'), Himself proceeds to define and describe 'Al-Hotama'.]

Indeed, without seeing the description of 'Al-Hotama' in the prophecy, none could ever have been able to know what 'Al-Hotama' is.

[(4) **Tafsir Al-Jalalayn**
"Nor are you able to understand 'Al-Hotama' except through the revealed description given by Allah."]

Nor would the terrestrial atomic hell's corroboration in light of the description of 'Al-Hotama' have been possible without the appearance of the atomic bomb explosion. A question might have emerged in many skeptical minds before reading the complete treatment of prophecy in our work.

Why was the prophecy not understood or proclaimed before the actual appearance of the atomic bomb explosion?

It, however, happens to be a question that justifies an endeavor to furnish an answer to it to alleviate the curiosity of the curious that has origin in doubt again. Indeed, from whatever angle and point of view, the case in question is viewed: the only answer that we could find is that this prophecy could in no way have been discovered before the actual detonation of the atomic bomb and its resulting manifestation in the form of a column. There could be a possibility of guess after the appearance of atomic fire in the light of its nuclear origin. Because the prophecy says: "The fire of 'Al-Hotama' is a fire which leaps up over the hearts", and the generation of the atomic energy being in the 'nucleus' that is the 'heart' might perhaps have led a knowing mind toward the fact, but none ever did it.

If, however, Allah had so willed, He could have easily shown the whole thing to any person any time after the revelation of the Quran, but no such thing ever occurred. Let it be known; the prophecy is a simple description of the most complex of the entire scientific phenomena, the nuclear phenomena. The exposition and proclamation of such a prophecy in any pre-modern age in the light of the nuclear phenomena would not only have been an impossibility but would also have been vain.

At a time when the philosophy of atomistic materialism had gained its ground in the modern age, and its characteristics had visibly appeared in the West: the three evils, namely, slander, wealth-accumulation, and wealth worship, could have been pointed out. These evils are the characteristics of the philosophy of atomism, and one can find them mentioned in the prophecy. Yet, it is hard to believe that anyone would have taken any notice of any such characterizations. Because the people of the West who undoubtedly had forsaken the bitter Anti-Materialistic injunctions of their religion, typically Anti-World Christianity, could hardly have been expected to pay any heed to the injunctions of a seemingly alien religion without the accompanying representation at the same time of the consequential, scientific manifestation of the three evils in the dreadful form of the atomic bomb.

The exposition and proclamation of prophecy before the appearance of the hazards of the nuclear phenomena would have been pretty in vain. It is doubtful that anyone in this world will pay any heed to this prophecy; even after the demons of the hazards of the atomic bombs and the witches of the atomic radiations, everyone could see dancing right before their eyes. How could it be expected that someone would have listened to the warning of prophecy even before any signs of hazards of nuclear phenomena made an appearance in the world?

For sure, it will be considered just a postulate, but suppose scientists and atomists were equally learned in the Quran and had kept it under their perpetual study in a keen spirit of research along with their scientific research. Even then, could they have been expected to recognize and discover prophecy in the light of nuclear development before the actual appearance of atomic explosion with its column at any stage of nuclear development? The sudden answer is 'No'. To a very keen-sighted scientist, however, a dim reflection of reality could have appeared in the nuclear nature of atomic phenomena arising out of the resemblance existing in 'hearts' (as mentioned in prophecy) and 'nucleus' of the atom that appeared as the scene of all the reactions of atomic phenomena. However, whether he would have recognized the reality of atomic phenomena in the light of prophecy seemed a possibility too remote. The recognition could perceptibly come in the presence of the atomic bomb explosion because of its most prominent and distinctive feature, that of the 'outstretched columns'.

However, once someone finds out the clue, the entire course of corroboration moves smoothly to the end. The Western scientists were entirely ignorant of the Quran, not to say of any deep knowledge of that book. There might, however, be some minor exceptions to this rule. Still, we could cite no outstanding scholar of the Quran among the coterie of great scientists, hence the impossibility of their knowing the prophecy to the last.

Again, the atomic phenomena could perhaps afford a clue in this matter. But it appeared at a stage when the blinding influence of the three evils, namely, slander, wealth accumulation, and a belief in the immortalizing powers of wealth with a desire of forever living in this material world, had utterly duped the senses of humankind, including the scientists and the philosophers. Hence, even the presence of an atomic bomb explosion could hardly have convinced the world about the reality of prophecy.

Further, and indeed to the great misfortune of humankind, the course of the development of nuclear science from the beginning to the end, all through the prenatal stages of atomic energy; its birth, and its application to the atomic weapons, had been consistently and everywhere, one strangely haphazard and unpredictable.

Without remaining long under investigation or giving any chance of understanding it after being discovered, the atomic energy went right into constructing the atomic bomb. It (atomic energy) appeared in secrecy, and secretly it went into the atomic bomb and remained in secrecy even sometime after the atomic explosion. It has the strangest history. It was actually in their research on the structure of matter that scientists happened to discover atomic energy. In 1895, Roentgen accidentally discovered X-rays, and there was no thought of atomic energy. In 1896 Becquerel was led unexpectedly to radioactivity, and there was no thought of atomic energy. This discovery, in turn, soon led to the discovery of Radium by Madam Curie, and there was no thought of atomic energy. Rutherford discovered alpha, beta, and gamma rays, and there was no thought of atomic energy.

In 1932 Sir John Douglas Cockcroft (1897-1967) and Ernest Thomas Sinton Walton (1903-1995) brought about the first artificial transmutation of the atom. The first time there appeared the possibility of release of energy in this way. Yet, it was not the release of energy that was the thought in the physicists' minds, but they were essentially concerned with understanding the structure of matter, and they wished to explore the nucleus. Although the transmutation provided one of the earliest proofs of the famous Einstein's mass-energy relationship's validity, the release of atomic energy was then a mere dream.

In 1938 Hahn and Strassman discovered the phenomenon of Uranium fission. Yet, any thought of the generation of atomic energy was a remote consideration. However, the extraordinary significance of the experiment was soon realized and led to a period of intense activity in the study of atomic nuclei. By 1940 more than a hundred papers had appeared on this subject, but after that, the subject was underground, and no open reference appeared in open scientific literature till the end of the war.

In 1942, Fermi successfully realized the first-ever fission chain reaction. Then the possibility of generating atomic energy appeared. But they devoted the whole endeavor to constructing the atomic bomb, bearing on the success of the fission chain reaction. In 1945, three first-ever atomic bombs appeared. They dropped one of them on Hiroshima and the other on Nagasaki and presented the last complete and distinctive feature of the 'sky-high column' to the world. It is hard to believe that in such a history of atomic energy and its abrupt appearance, scientists, even acquainted with Quran, could discern atomic energy as an object of the prophecy contained in the Quran. Further, during all these various stages of the development of the atomic phenomena, the scientists seemed to have been continually and blindly pushed by some mysterious force, the force of three evils that overwhelmingly permeated the entire world.

Such were the circumstances that several atomists lost lives due to nuclear hazards during research. Yet nothing in the world could be deemed enough to open their eyes to the truth in the heat of passion for discoveries of nuclear phenomena. Just imagine that some Quranic interpreter was inspired to expose the secret of prophecy even to the minutest details of the atomic bomb during this period. In that case, it is hard to believe that someone would have lent an attentive ear to this warning. Instead, they would have continued on their course passionately. There is a significant probability that they would have ridiculed the view of such a divine prophecy as fantastic.

Now, we consider the other side of the world that is the Islamic World. Suppose the Islamic world set up an organization in the heart of Europe at the commencement of the Renaissance of the West. It comprised a group of the greatest geniuses that one could find in the entire world of Islam, most learned in the Quran and endowed with the keenest aptitude for science to study the development of science with great care in the light of the Quran. Then this coterie of the scholar scientists labored in a manner from the beginning of modern science. They toiled continually, day in day out, theory after theory, discovery after discovery, development after development, generation after generation, and century after century to the point of the actual explosion of the atomic bomb. It seems hardly possible that any of these great geniuses would have ever anticipated the relationship between the discovery of atomic phenomena and the prophecy before the atomic explosion.

One could attest this surmise by the difficulties professed by the subject, the peculiar haphazard and intricate development of the subject of the atomic phenomena itself. Besides, anyone could construe the text of the prophecy to produce testimony to that effect reading the words, "What could cause thee to understand what 'Al-Hotama' is?". It means nothing can make you understand it until it appears before your eyes in the form of a 'crushing fire' which 'leaps up over the hearts' and 'is closed in on them in outstretched columns'.

That is, it could only be recognized when it has appeared entirely in all its features that the prophecy has described. Now, it remains only to think whether it could be recognized and linked to the prophecy even after it has appeared in its complete form before the eyes. To understand this question, we should know that the most significant barrier to its recognition existed because the idea of hell has always been associated with the otherworld and not this world. Therefore, it has quite naturally been an improbability for man to shift his mind ever toward a postulate as improbable as the appearance of hell within this very world.

It is by Allah's grace alone that He could have shifted man's mind to such an improbable postulate and so unimaginable a presumption. We could compare the strange phenomena to opening a mysterious gate with a blinding flash to expose a world of knowledge, a world metamorphosed into a reality hitherto unexposed and scintillating with dazzling brilliance in an atmosphere of great awe and petrifying charm. The degree of astonishment at such an experience defies expression.

My effort of expressing, expounding, and corroborating the theory of the prophecy has been terrific. It proved to be an experience of being inserted into the jaws of a crusher like a cane-crusher in the endeavor of explaining the crushing fire of 'Al-Hotama' and then gradually being drawn out from the other end in the form of minced meat from toe to head. It was a torturous ordeal for me to translate one entire world into another in an arena where expressions like sweat, tears, and blood lose their meanings.

Apart from the painstaking work of intellectual nature, another experience even of a bitterer nature that attended throughout the gruesome ordeal and never once left was relentless persecution of the terrific force of the world-pervading three evils (the causes of the emergence of the atomic hell). These three furies, on every step and every breath, struggled to the utmost of their might to wreck my prospect, frustrate my plan, and ruin the slightest hope of humankind. This hope was streaked in the warning of prophecy being firstly discovered by a human being for the sake of fellow human beings.

This prophecy produced real cause of alarm for all the antagonistic forces that perhaps the distressed humankind is saved that stood at the brink of destruction, being pushed by the economic pressure from behind and seeing the burning atomic hell in the front. A step further meant a headlong fall into the leaping flames of the nuclear Jehannah ablaze. However, praised be Allah, whose mercy never once forsook me in my abysmal ordeal. It constantly guided me through the darkest of labyrinths and terrific scenes through which I had to grope my terrifying way braving all the horrific apparitions that appeared throughout in their grisly forms to the end of my fateful journey.

SECTION-9

Quran: "Naarullah-Il-Muqadah."
Meaning: "The enkindled fire of Allah."
'Naar' means 'fire'; 'Naarullah' means 'fire of Allah'; 'Muqadah' means 'enkindled'.

[(1) **Tafsir Al-Jalalayn**
Associating the fire of 'Hotama' with the name of Allah enhances the significance of this particular fire. This fire flares up to such an extreme intensity that no one can extinguish it.]

The significance of the fire of 'Hotama' (atomic bomb) and the atomic energy both as regards quality and quantity, multitude and magnitude, features and characteristics is such as may exhaust volumes without itself ever coming to an end. Its association with the name of Allah is indicative both of its substantial significance and its punishing nature. In its latter capacity, we could reasonably label it as the wrath of Allah enkindled against the 'Homaza-Lomaza'.

The commentator has alluded to its intensity. As far as the intensity of the atomic fire in the atomic bomb explosion is concerned, it is just beyond human imagination even to think of it. Temperatures, of the order of millions of degrees that are not at all terrestrial but in reality, are of solar and stellar nature and which reduce everything existing on earth to a gaseous state by mere touch, are developed in fission and fusion explosions.

We can never extinguish the fire of the atomic bomb explosion once we have detonated the bomb until the whole process of the explosion is complete. The process, all of it, namely, initial heat radiation, the blast, and the emission of prompt ionizing radiations, takes but a few seconds. However, the radioactivity of the fission products may stay for millions of years to justify the commentator's statement that we can never extinguish the fire of atomic hell.

Again, there is the point of the continuation of the atomic fire of the atomic energy for peace. This fire will be enkindled and perhaps never extinguished until it has extinguished the human race on earth, or humankind has repented and has forsaken the plan of so hazardous an energy. It will only be possible if humankind has relinquished the habits of slander, wealth accumulation, and wealth worship.

Another instance that we could cite to show the inextinguishable nature, partially though, is atomic fire. In case of a raid of atomic bombs, the extensive fires that start due to the extreme heat of the initial heat radiation of the atomic bomb explosion are to be left to themselves. We cannot make any attempt to extinguish the widespread and colossal fires raging throughout the city. Who will in that event have a mind to undertake a useless and vain task and for what? If they survived the ordeal, you could see the members of the firefighting squads rushing in panic at the heads of other citizens of those unfortunate cities.

Indeed, the fires started by the atomic bomb explosion are pretty different from that fire that occasionally breaks out in a quarter of a city. You can see the firefighting squads rushing towards the fire site with their bells and sirens ringing all the way. But the fires caused by the atomic bomb explosion shall leave neither any vehicles to ride nor a bell to ring. Death-knell alone could peal in plenty, but who could hear that sound in the uproar of raging hell, and who could have the occasion too?

[(2) **Tafsir Al-Kabir**

Linking this fire to the name of Allah is to magnify its significance and distinction, to mean that 'it is a fire that is different from every other kind of fire'. Allah has enkindled it in such a way that somebody will never be capable of extinguishing it, or that it is a fire which the express command of Allah has enkindled.]

The significance of the atomic fire in comparison to any other type of earthly fire is most apparent. It threatens even the existence of life on earth. It has created a problem that means death to humankind. This fire has posed a threat to the present generation, but it threatens the extinction of the generations appearing even in future ages. As far as its distinction is concerned, atomic fire is characteristically distinct from all other types of fire due to its nuclear generation process. It also maintains distinction regarding the intensity of its heat (degree of its temperatures) and the magnitude of destruction wrought. The characteristic distinctions of the atomic fire are that it is generated in the sub-atomic parts of matter and can penetrate to the sub-atomic parts of matter.

Further, its effects in the genetic regions are irreversible and irreparable. So also, the atomic particles of an atom, once disarranged by the reactions of atomic radiations, could not be put back to their original arrangement. The selective faculty of the atomic fire is also remarkable. It kills those exposed in the event of the atomic bomb explosion by its 'Heat-Flash'. Protected by some buildings, it buries those under the same structures by pulling those down over their heads by the blast of the atomic bomb explosion. If some are lucky enough to escape both the ordeals, it sends after them its much subtle atomic radiation that searches them out, pierces their bodies, and kills them. Humankind shall know the real significance of this fire in the event of an atomic war or during the future zenith of atomic energy for peace. Five hundred tons of its fuel (Uranium-235) can obliterate from this earth all life, and not even a blade of grass will be seen anywhere on the face thereof.

The worthy commentator has said that the express command of Allah has enkindled the fire of 'Al-Hotama'. It means that this fire's nature is punishing enkindled as a means of retribution. We could manifestly never use the fire of the atomic explosion for any practical purpose. As far as the atomic energy for peace is concerned, humankind will know just over time that they could use it only for punishment. However, then no amount of repentance might be of any avail. A world is entering hell but only hoping that everything will be all right.

[(3) **Tafsir Al-Kabir**
Ali, may Allah be pleased with him, is quoted to have said, "It is surprising to see that someone persists in his disobedience to Allah on the face of the earth, while fire be burning beneath him."]

It may seem no less surprising to pious Hazrat Ali to see a world under constant threat of worldwide atomic war and be unmindful of it.

SECTION-10

Quran: "Allati Tattalio Alal Afedha"
Meaning: "That rises unto the hearts."
'Allati' means 'that, which'; 'Tattalio' means 'leaps up to', 'rises above' etc.; 'Alal' means 'at'; 'Afedha' means the 'hearts'.

[(1) **Tafsir Al-Jalalayn**
The fire mounts over the hearts and knocks there.]

It indeed is surprising to hear this expression, namely, 'knocks there'. The fire mounts over the hearts and knocks there. We have known now how it knocks at the hearts. Atomic particles mount above the nuclei (hearts) of atoms and knock there, and knock out atomic particles from the nuclei of atoms during the generation for the atomic energy. We have also known the atomic radiations knocking the electrons out from the atoms that constitute the organism's molecules or other material through which radiations pass. We also have known the radiations going in headlong collisions with the nuclei (hearts) of the atoms in the living body and other material and knocking out nucleons from there. Also, we know the radiations to mount above the nuclei of the body's cells and break the chromosomes thereof. We also have seen the 'Heat-Flash' of the atomic bomb explosion mount above the heart of its victim and kill it through heat and shock.

[(2) **Tafsir Al-Jalalayn**
The hearts have been mentioned with particular propriety because the heart is the most sensitive organ in the body endowed with the exceptional faculty of responding to the effect of the slightest agony with remarkable sensitivity.]

We know the extreme sensitivity revealed in the event of cell death brought about by an incomparably negligible amount of radiations (atomic fire). The amount of radiation, in this case, is so unbelievably minute that the enormous effect shown by it in killing the entire cell has emerged as a problem that has confused all the Radiobiologists. In reality, it is not the amount of radiation only but the sensitivity of cells that must count.

[(3) **Tafsir Al-Kabir**
Even though the heart is completely overwhelmed with the fire of Jehannah (hell), the fire does not burn the heart. For, in case the fire of Jehannah (hell) would burn it, man would die. But instead, he will be in a state which the word of Allah in the Quran (elsewhere) has expressed as, "He will neither die nor yet will he live in hell."]

Because there will be no death in the next world, and the fire's consumption of the heart would mean death, the worthy commentator has quite logically inferred that the heart, though overwhelmed with fire, should not be consumed by fire. As has already been observed, anyone could in no way expect complete immunity from death in this transient world. Analogous state, though transiently, could be cited to show that "even though the heart is completely overwhelmed with the fire of Jehannah (hell), the fire does not burn the heart". One could never expect the eternity of anything in a world in which death is the rule.

However, leaving the question of immortality out in this transient world, the heart in all its various functional forms: such as the heart in a mammalian body, or a nucleus in an atom, or the nucleus in the cell, is not burnt, no matter how severely it is overwhelmed by the atomic fire. In the vicinity of the atomic bomb explosion, the 'Heat-Flash' so vehemently crushes the human heart that it may die on the spot. Yet 'there is no sign of burning' whatsoever, as is generally understood by the word, 'burning'. Nor does the cell nucleus show any signs of burning even it has been crushed to death by atomic radiation.

In whole-body irradiation, a mammalian body that has succumbed to a high radiation dose is more of a handful of crushed cells than a sound body. But the post-mortem examination shows not the slightest sign of burning anywhere. However, radiations have killed it by doing nothing more than depositing energy in its cells, and what, after all, is energy, if not heat or fire?

[(4) **Tafsir Al-Jalalayn**
In this respect, another reason for mentioning the 'heart' is that it happens to be the abode of infidelity, evil thoughts, evil intentions, and evil deeds.]

It manifestly is the case of direct retribution. A malignant heart is the source of a malignant tongue that slanders. Again, it is the heart that inspires love and greed for wealth. Further, the heart itself causes one to bow before the goddess of wealth and thus completes the requisite conditions for the appearance of the atomic hell of which it naturally becomes the primary victim.

Following is the observation of Wordsworth (1770-1850).

"To let a creed, built in the 'heart' of things,
Dissolve before a twinkling 'atomy'."

(Wordsworth: Excursion)

Read the above-quoted distich with care. We have already mentioned the verdict of Bertrand Russell in his sentence given as follows.

"Since Adam and Eve ate the apple, man has never refrained from any folly of which he was capable."

Anyone can judge the worth of this sentence in the light of the prophecy of the Quran bout 'Al-Hotama'. It happens to be a criterion of judging thoughts, observations, and remarks of writers and the philosophers of the modern age respecting this particular topic, just as the Quran itself provides a universal criterion for the judgment of whatever is of this modern age.

Suppose the verdict of Bertrand Russell has proved to be a special assessment of the present matter of humankind. In that case, this little distich of Wordsworth shows a particular worth of philosophical insight and observation of the effects of philosophy of atomism in the light of characterization of the fire of 'Al-Hotama' given in the prophecy. This distich of Wordsworth, which at its appearance and long after till this day could have exacted the praise and admiration for its poetic and philosophical merit in general: it is only in the light of the prophecy of the Quran that we could perhaps assess its real great merit.

The phrase, namely, 'the heart of things', appears like the heart of all observations ever made in the modern age respecting the effects of the philosophy of atomism. Wordsworth observes and laments that the creed built in the 'heart' of things would be dissolved before the twinkling 'atomy'. The creed of faith emanated from the heart was to dissolve by the philosophy of atomism, which was the product of the brain and, unlike the creed of the heart, embraced the only present material world. Wordsworth observed that the philosophy of modern material atomism was rising like intoxication to the heart of men, civilizations, and cultures and was eating it up.

The value of Wordsworth's this unique observation has come to be assessed honestly in the light of remark of the prophecy of the Quran, namely, the fire of 'Al-Hotama' is a fire that rises unto the hearts. The term 'twinkling atomy' is also characteristic of atomism's philosophy, which has only an outward show and is vain in reality. Wordsworth lived in an age when a judging eye could well discern the philosophical effects of atomism. Wordsworth found himself in an atmosphere in which scientific research on atoms had begun, and some talented scientists were pursuing the atomic structure of matter.

In 1799, the famous French chemist Joseph Louis Proust had stated the law of definite or constant properties of chemical compounds. The principal credit for finding the modern theory of matter goes to John Dalton. He had given a first indication of the quantitative aspect of his atomic theory in a paper he read at a meeting of the "Manchester Literary and Philosophical Society" in 1803 when Wordsworth was in the thirty-third year of his life. In Wordsworth's time, the matter of atomism had assumed such an explicit form as could have been discerned by any keen observer. Yet, these facts do not distract from the credit of Wordsworth's observation when the matter of the heart he has pointed out is considered.

However, what about the Quran? What sign or omen of atomism or atomic theory was there anywhere in the world when the Quran gave the complete philosophical and scientific characterization of the fire of 'Al-Hotama': the characterization out of which Wordsworth has obliquely hinted upon, but one, namely, that it is a fire which rises unto the hearts?

SECTION-11

Quran: "Innaha Alaihim Musadah"
Meaning: "It is closed in on them."
'Innaha' means 'verily that one'; 'Alaihim' means 'on them'; 'Musadah' means 'closed in'.

[(1) **Tafsir Al-Tabari**
This fire is closed in on the 'backbiting defamer'. 'Musadah' (the original word of the prophecy) means 'Mutbaqah' that is entirely closed without any doors for entrance or exit. Abu Kuraib and Mohammed Ibn-Saeed have quoted Ibn-Abbas, Abid Ibn-Asbaat quoted Attiyya, and Yaqub Ibn-Ibraheem has quoted Hassan: all of them say that by 'Musadah' is meant 'Mutbaqah' that is 'completely covered'. These words, namely, 'Musadah' and 'Mutbaqah', have been taken to mean the same thing.

(2) **Tafsir Al-Kabir**
Allah has said, 'Musadah' (with doors closed) and not 'Mutbaqah' (wholly enclosed without any doors). The particular word 'Musadah' means that the place has doors fitted with it, but the doors are closed, whereas 'Mutbaqah' means an enclosure without any doors. Remember that this specificity of having doors but being closed signifies the magnification, amplification, and universality of the particular torment and the clarity. If Allah had so desired, He could have built the place without any doors. Still, He purposely fitted the place with doors and then closed the doors to awaken in the hearts of the inmates a longing for exit due to the presence of the doors (possible means of escape) and thereby augment their misery.]

Both the commentators quoted above occupy an exceptional place of honor among the most original commentators of the Quran. The difference of opinion existing between them regarding the above-quoted point is also apparent. One has maintained that Al-Hotama's enclosure will be without doors, while the other has considered the enclosure fitted with closed doors. To the people of the pre-atomic age, the point might have appeared as a strange paradox, but the recent appearance of atomic energy and atomic bombs proves both the views and both as correct.

For example, in the case of the atomic bomb explosion, a perfect enclosure encompassing the effective range of the bomb is formed. The explosion truly is like an inverted cauldron that offers no exit to anyone from any side as long as the explosion process is in progress. It forms a complete enclosure without any doors. Yet, there is no circular concrete wall around the enclosure, nor is there any concrete roof above. The enclosure is not walled, yet there is a wall, a boundary drawn by the effective zone of the explosion. The whole thing appears very strange. Then there is the example of the dread of atomic war. Everybody knows the dreadful consequences of such a war, and everyone desires to avert it, but hitherto there appears no sign of successfully averting it. Yet, there are the possibilities of averting it. 'The whole problem seems as if it has doors to escape, yet there are no doors to escape'. [6] Now, it seems as if there were no doors. Again, it seems as if there are doors but closed. As the worthy commentator has said, the purpose is to remind the possibility of exit and thereby augment the agony of internees. The atomic energy for peace provides yet another example. There are other alternative means of energy, yet it seems as if there are no alternative means. The world is doomed to adopt atomic energy despite knowing all the ruinous hazards of a venture of such nature.

[(3) **Tafsir Al-Tabari**
There shall be a man in one of the apartments of hell and crying for a complete millennium:

"Yaa Hannan, Yaa Mannan" (O, Compassionate, O, Bountiful). Gracious Allah will say to the angel Gabriel:

"Go, and take my servant out of the fire."
Gabriel will go, but, finding the fire closed in on him, will return and say to Allah:

"O, Allah! The fire is closed in on him."
Allah will say, "O, Gabriel! Go, open it, and take my servant out."

The man at that time will resemble a mere shadow. Gabriel will place him at the outskirts of the Paradise, till Allah grows his <u>hair</u> and <u>flesh</u> and <u>blood</u> afresh.]

Herein then, a marvel of description is found in the man taken out of the fire of Jehannah (hell). Man's deprivation of <u>hair</u>, <u>flesh</u>, and blood [7] might not have attracted any special notice in the pre-atomic ages. However, after the appearance of the atomic fire, is it not surprising to see such a description of an inmate of hell? Loss of hair, weight loss, anemia, and emaciation are the typical symptoms of radiation sickness. Such a marvelous description will undoubtedly interest the Radiobiologist. As a prodigy of anticipation and attestation, it deserves to have been included in our chapter on radiobiological confirmation.

The world at present is caught up in a strange situation, indeed in a bad situation. If a community would decide to desist from taking part in the race of scientific progress, it would either soon die and disintegrate through modern want or fall prey to some other power advanced in scientific technology and made a slave. On the other hand, if it would strive in scientific progress as is the case today without exception throughout the world, the struggle evidently must lead it straight into the atomic hell and all other nations taking part in the race.

There could not be but two alternatives: the destruction through atomic bombs or radiations of the atomic energy for peace. Thus, this world can today be most vividly seen encompassed by the atomic fire, and none but a doomed race will have no time to pause and look and will have no knowledge thereof to know and find itself helpless to get out of the enclosure of this fire of the atomic hell.

How we could save this mad and helpless world from atomic war or the deadly radiations of atomic energy for peace is a proposition that would stun every pretender of wisdom in the history of the world. None of all the greatest names in the realm of philosophy would hesitate a moment to confess their unspeakable confusion and bewilderment. Some of them might, however, be able to behold the inevitable doom, whipping the present humankind mercilessly unto the blazing hell without allowing them to pause, to see to the right, left, or behind. They are being driven towards the atomic shambles like a herd of miserable victims.

SECTION-12

Quran: "Fi Amadim Mumaddadah"
Meaning: "In outstretched columns."
'Fi' means 'in'; 'Amad', also pronounced as 'Umud', means 'columns'. It is the plural of 'Imaad' or 'Amood'.

(According to 'Tafsir al-Tabari', reciters of Medina and Basra have read this word as 'Amad', while the generality of the reciters of Kufa pronounced it as 'Umud'. In the opinion of Al-Tabari, both the forms are authentic and constitute no difference in meanings); 'Mumaddadah' means 'outstretched'.

In the following quotations from the commentators, the reader will notice the extreme curiosity of the Sahabah [the companions and disciples of the Holy Prophet (peace be upon him)] and the early commentators raised by the strangeness of the phenomenon of columns as a mode of punishment. Interpreters have made observable efforts to explain the punishment by fire amidst the columns.

To explain this mode of punishment, some have thought that the columns will be the gates of hell that are outstretched. Some have thought that the inmates will be tied to these columns with chains and punished with fire. Some have thought that due to the redundancy of such columns in this hell, the intervening parting spaces between columns will look like doors: thus, they shall be tortured in 'outstretched column'.

Others have said that the damned will be entered in the columns and then tortured with fire. Al-Tabari has confessed the uncertainty of all these conjectures and has left the matter to Allah, who knows best.

Yet the conjectures of all these commentators in this matter have been surprisingly ingenious, correctively suggestive, and extremely helpful in understanding the truth of this strangest of the torturing phenomena ever mentioned or appeared. We, the dwellers of the modern age of atomism, were destined to behold this ugly feature.

Also, perhaps we are meant to be unfortunate inmates of the terrestrial replica of 'Al-Hotama' to realize how the angels will enter the inmates of such a hell into these columns. The inhabitants of two cities (Hiroshima and Nagasaki) have already had this experience, and the rest of the cities may any moment, follow suit and realize the reality of the matter.

[(1) **Tafsir Al-Tabari**
Ibn-Zaid has said that columns will be of fire.
(2) **Tafsir Al-Quran Al-Azim (Tafsir Ibn-Kathir)**
Utbat-ul-Aufi has said that columns are to be of iron.
(3) **Tafsir Al-Tabari**
Bashir has quoted Qatadah [a 'Sahabi' that is a companion and disciple of the Holy Prophet (peace be upon him)] as saying, "We used to discuss that these are going to be the columns with which the inmates of the particular hell shall be tortured."
(4) **Tafsir Al-Jalalayn**
It is said the fire will enter the columns with which the inmates thereof shall be covered.

(5) Tafsir Al-Quran Al-Azim (Tafsir Ibn-Kathir)

Ibn-Abbas is quoted to have said, "By the 'outstretched columns' is meant, gates that are outstretched."

(6) Tafsir Al-Kabir

There are two aspects in interpreting this sign (fire closed in on them in 'outstretched columns'). The first is that, just as lanes are closed, the gates are closed with these columns. The word 'Fi' ('in') here is used in the meanings of 'Ba' ('with' or 'by'). It means the fire is closed in on them by the columns stretched above it, and it is not supposed 'by' the columns. Because, due to the redundancy of columns, intervening apertures between them seem as if there were doors in there. The second aspect is that inmates are fastened to columns in the manner just as thieves are fettered.]

NOTE: Obviously, the commentator has taken columns like solid ones and not hollow: hence has construed the meanings of 'Fi' ('in') as 'Ba' ('with' or 'by'). We have in the previous pages mentioned the controversy between two commentators over the point, whether there exist doors that are closed in 'Al-Hotama', or whether this hell is simply closed without any doors. The appearance of the replica of 'Al-Hotama' on earth has proved the views of both the commentators as correct.

Again, a similar situation has appeared in whether the columns are going to be solid or hollow. The columns of the atomic explosion prove both views as correct. These columns consist of fission products and pulverized dust and are thus solid as well as hollow.

Also, we can see that the fission products being radioactive emit energy, and the columns of the atomic explosions could undoubtedly be called 'columns of fire'. The fireball itself is fire.

[(7) Tafsir Al-Jalalayn

It is said that 'outstretched columns' are chains on the necks of internees. It is also said that these are shackles on their feet. Moreover, some say 'outstretched columns' mean endless age.]

The curiosity of the commentators in this matter has been apparent throughout. The companions of the Holy Prophet (peace be upon him) used to discuss this topic, and after that, the recording commentators of the Quran continued it. Columns as a mode of punishment were something unheard of in those days and after that.

The general opinion was that the columns were to be of fire. Some, however, considered that these columns were going to be of iron. Though incompatible with the columns of the atomic explosions, this latter opinion corresponds to the conventional bomb. The outer shell of a giant conventional bomb or a missile is iron and stands like a column.

This interpretation, however, is not of any direct validity, and we have just mentioned it for some remote interest. The particular point of note is that some of the commentators of the Quran have interpreted this phrase, namely, the 'outstretched columns' as figuratively, to mean chains, fetters, endless age, etc.

In the end, we quote a very enlightening and conclusive statement of 'Al-Tabari' in this context.

[(8) **Tafsir Al-Tabari**

There existed a difference of opinion among the commentators regarding the interpretation of this sign (verse of the Quran).

Some have said that the fire has enclosed the inmates of 'Hotama'. This purport is of the reading of Abdullah as has descended to us. At the same time, others have said that the internees will be made to enter the columns, and then 'the columns will be stretched upward, column upon the column'. About their necks shall be chains with which doors shall be fastened. Ibn-Zaid said that the columns would be of fire.

Others have said that these are going to be columns with which they shall be tortured. Bashir has quoted Qatadah as saying, "We used to discuss that these are going to be columns with which they shall be tortured in the fire."

In my opinion, the most plausible among all these interpretations seems to be that they shall be tortured with columns of fire of 'Al-Hotama'. Allah alone knows better the method of torturing them with these columns.

Hitherto no such word has reached us as may be taken as an authority regarding the reality of tormenting them with these columns. Nor have we been granted an 'indicative' that we might know the actual reality of the matter. There is no reliable or authoritative statement, except what I mentioned above and thought it most plausible. Indeed, Allah knows best.]

Alas, we, the generations of the modern age of atomism, were destined to know the reality of how the columns of fire will torture inmates of the hell of 'Hotama'. We have known it in Hiroshima and Nagasaki, and we may in the future know it in every other city in the world.

However, the discerning judgment of Al-Tabari, in this regard, has come nearest the fact of torturing with columns of fire. The column of the atomic bomb explosion has ascertained it. It indeed is edifying to hear the remarks of the interpreters of the Quran about the phenomena of the fire of 'Al-Hotama', which they had made about fourteen hundred years ago and in an age of no knowledge and no science. Their utterances in this respect almost reflect an oracular strain.

SECTION-13
THE PROPHECY TRANSLATED INTO THE TERMS OF THE ATOMIC HELL OF THIS WORLD

By the grace of Almighty Allah, we have brought the exposition of prophecy to an end. We can now translate the prophecy of 'Al-Hotama' expressing its terrestrial replica of the atomic hell of the world as follows.

"Woe to every follower of atomism who backbites and defames the beliefs of true religion against those of atomism. Having Pride in his material progress, he is constantly engaged in pursuing wealth as the sole object of his life and worships it as a deity instead of Allah, and desires to live forever in this world. He considers it his only abode without any thought of Resurrection, Judgment, or the life in the next world. He thinks that his wealth shall infinitely progress and acts as if he had to live forever in this world.

Nay, his scientific research in pursuit of material progress and the doctrinal atmosphere of atomism will eventually lead him to discover atomic fire and the atomic bomb. This atomic fire shall be generated within the 'heart' of the atom, and shall have its subsequent reactions within the 'hearts' of atoms, and will also rise to his 'heart'. It shall 'encompass' him in 'outstretched columns', till it consumed him and thus his notion of taking this world as the eternal world, and that of forever living in this world is practically refuted, negated, and falsified."

~~*~*~*~*

---

[1] An author of Tafsir (Interpretation) is a **'Mufassir'** (Arabic), meaning 'Interpreter'.

[2] **The Seven Sleepers** (Arabic: اصحاب الكهف, romanized: 'ashab al kahf') - a group of young men who, according to Byzantine and Islamic sources, fled the religious persecution of Roman emperor Decius, and slept for a long time in a cave, near Amman, Jordan. Their graves are in the same cave. The Quran has described the story of the 'Companions of the Cave' (18:9-26). It does not state the precise number of sleepers.

Furthermore, the Quran points out that people started to make 'idle guesses' about how many people were in the cave shortly after the incident emerged. To this, the Quran asserts that: "My Sustainer knows best how many they were". People guessed that "they remained in the cave for 300 years and nine added". Regarding the exact period the people stayed in the cave, the Quran, after asserting the guesswork of the people, resolves that "God knows best how long they remained [there]." The Quran says the sleepers included a dog, who sat at the entrance of the cave (verse 18).

[3] Limitless avarice for more and more is inherent in human nature without any boundaries. After conquering it and exhausting recklessly and mercilessly natural resources from the earth's bowels with extraordinary rapidity, they are now thinking about and working on the casting of a noose around the neck of the moon. They are thinking about exploring it in the dubious hope of getting some energy resources, precious metals, and minerals even from there and bringing them down to the earth. Please read the following extract from the magazine of (www.bbc.com), dated March 7, 2013.

What if you could mine the Moon? [by Regan Morris, B.B.C. News, Los Angeles]

— Space exploration has long been about reaching far off destinations but now there's a race to exploit new frontiers by mining their minerals.

— When Neil Armstrong first stepped on the Moon in 1969, it was part of a "flags and footprints" strategy to beat the Soviets, a triumph of imagination and innovation, not an attempt to extract precious metals.

— Mysterious and beautiful, the Moon has been a source of awe and inspiration to mankind for millennia. Now it is the centre of a space race to mine rare minerals to fuel our future - smart phones, space-age solar panels and possibly even a future colony of Earthlings.

— ["...So exploring the Moon commercially is a first step towards making the Moon part of our world, what humanity considers our world," says Bob Richards, C.E.O. of Silicon Valley-based Moon Express.]

— ["The most important thing about the Moon is probably the stuff we haven't even discovered," says Mr. Richards. "But what we do know is that there could be more platinum-group metals on the surface of the Moon than all of the reserves of earth. The race is on."]

— If Moon Express and others are right, it's conceivable that in the future the lunar surface could host a colony of mining robots and astronauts who could use the Moon as a base to explore further into the solar system.

— The potential resources from the Moon are vast. M Darby Dyar, a professor of astronomy at Mount Holyoke College in Massachusetts, says the reservoirs of water ice in the dark, Polar Regions of the Moon probably come from comets that hit the moon over the past four billion years, and that future moon miners could strike it rich with precious metals in ancient lunar rocks.

What might be on the Moon?
— So-called rare-earth minerals, which are used in a range of technologies.
— Water frozen in the dark recesses of polar craters, which according to NASA, can be split into hydrogen for rocket fuel and oxygen for breathing.
— Helium-3 (He-3), which apparently exists in abundance on the Moon. Some believe He-3 could be a future energy source. … … … — Valuable titanium deposits. (www.bbc.com)
[4] These observations (20 examples) had been recorded before 1982 when the author completed this work. Since then, almost more than 39 years have been passed (until 2021). Only scientists or radiobiologists know better whether they have overcome these points of ignorance during this period or there have been any discoveries or improvements made in this regard or not?

But if they have made any progress in this direction, radiobiologists ought to furnish an answer and tell humankind the whole truth about these 20 examples pointed out by the author. Otherwise, the words of the prophecy, "What could teach thee what 'Al-Hotama' is?" are justified.
[5] "There is no safe, low level of radiation." [Margaret Chan, Director-General World Health Organization (WHO): www.iicph.org]
[6] **"The whole problem seems as if it has doors to escape, and yet there are no doors to escape."**
In this context, in addition to the author's words, another interpretation is possible regarding the present-day dilemma of nuclear hell:
(a) **"There are no doors to escape"**. Suppose humanity does not abandon the adoption of nuclear energy, whether for war or so-called peaceful purposes and will continue to show ostrich-like behavior. Then for sure, the nuclear fire will be 'closed in on them in outstretched columns', and indeed there will be 'no doors to escape' from that doom.
(b) **"It has doors to escape"**. If humanity avails this timely warning of the prophecy of the Quran, shows discrete wisdom, and desists from adopting nuclear energy whether for war or so-called peaceful purposes,

another alternative is as well possible, that is, 'It has doors to escape' to avoid nuclear holocaust.

[7] [EFFECTS OF RADIATIONS ON THE HUMAN BODY

(a) **Hair**: The losing of hair quickly and in clumps occurs with radiation exposure at 200 rems or higher.
(b) **Brain**: Since brain cells do not reproduce, they won't be damaged directly unless the exposure is 5,000 rems or greater. Like the heart, radiation kills nerve cells and small blood vessels, and can cause seizures and immediate death.
(c) **Thyroid**: The certain body parts are more specifically affected by exposure to different types of radiation sources. The thyroid gland is susceptible to radioactive iodine. In sufficient amounts, radioactive iodine can destroy all or part of the thyroid. By taking potassium iodide, one can reduce the effects of exposure.
(d) **Blood System**: When a person is exposed to around 100 rems, the blood's lymphocyte cell count will be reduced, leaving the victim more susceptible to infection. This is often referred to as mild radiation sickness. Early symptoms of radiation sickness mimic those of flu and may go unnoticed unless a blood count is done. According to data from Hiroshima and Nagasaki, show that symptoms may persist for up to 10 years and may also have an increased long-term risk for leukemia and lymphoma.
(e) **Heart**: Intense exposure to radioactive material at 1,000 to 5,000 rems would do immediate damage to small blood vessels and probably cause heart failure and death directly.
(f) **Gastrointestinal Tract**: Radiation damage to the intestinal tract lining will cause nausea, bloody vomiting, and diarrhea. This occurs when the victim's exposure is 200 rems or more. The radiation will begin to destroy the cells in the body that divide rapidly. These including blood, G.I. tract, reproductive, and hair cells, and harm their DNA and RNA of surviving cells.
(g) **Reproductive Tract**: Because reproductive tract cells divide rapidly, these areas of the body can be damaged at rem levels as low as 200. Long-term, some radiation sickness victims will become sterile. (Unit of radiation is the rem, or roentgen equivalent in man.)

{(www.atomicarchive.com) with permission, and special thanks to Chris Griffith}]

~~*~*~*

CHAPTER-5

THE QURAN PHENOMENALLY CHARACTERIZES THE ATOMIC HELL AND AVERTS IT

A SUMMARY

A miracle in the field of atomic science and atomism, a miracle undeniable, and the only irrefutable proof of Quran's Divine Origin, and the only guide to escape the atomic doom; indeed Noah's ark in this fiery deluge of atomism, and a redeemer of humankind from this temporal atomic hell as well as its original prototype, the eternal atomic hell ('Hotama') of the next world --- the causes of both these forms of atomic hell being identical --- this 36-word prophecy of the Quran by the Grace of Merciful Allah is my discovery with my three thousand pages explanation of it.

Read the following words of the Quran.

"Woe to every backbiter, defamer, who amasseth wealth (of this world) and arrangeth it (against the future). He thinketh that his wealth will remain with him forever. Nay, for verily he will be cast into 'Al-Hotama'. And what could teach thee what 'Al-Hotama' is? It is the fire of Allah enkindled which leapeth up unto the hearts. It is (a fire) closed in on them in outstretched columns."

(Quran: 104 'Al-Homaza')

Observe now the description of this modern progress of Baconian atomism by the Quran.

(1) Quran says: **"Backbiter and defamer."**

Atomism, both ancient and modern, is a doctrinal slander against divine religion. The spirit of critical rationalism, and the distinguishing philosophical standard of this modern Baconian age against every pre-modern age, being perverted to critical slander, have permeated through every phase of the human affair. This aspect has rendered this period the age of calumny with its intellectualized slander named 'propaganda'. This age itself is the age of slander; everywhere, slander, every way slander.

(2) The Quran says: **"He amasseth wealth (of this world) and arrangeth it against the future."**

Observe this modern, continuous, systematic, organized, ever-increasing, infinite, and universal process of wealth accumulation and increase and arrangement for the future as distinct from the system of every pre-modern age.

(3) The Quran says: **"He thinketh that his wealth will forever remain with him."**

Observe man's faith in the continued eternity of this modern progress.

(4) The Quran says: **"Nay, for verily he will be flung into 'Al-Hotama'."**

Atomic hell as the logical and scientific consequence of this Baconian progress has now appeared. Now, observe the distinguishing phenomenal characteristics of atomic phenomena against every other phenomenon, e.g., chemical, and electrical, in this passage of the Quran.

(5) The Quran says: **"Hotama."**

'Hotama' literally means a crusher, and the same is the atomic phenomenon. It crushes basic atomic structure irreparably. It destroys the atomic nucleus. In no other phenomena, the atomic nucleus is so much as touched. The atomic energy is generated by merely breaking the binding of the atomic nucleus. We generate no other kind of energy in this manner. Atomic radiations follow suit. Radiations cause nuclear transmutations of atoms in the non-living matter, while in living bodies, they break cell nucleus chromosomes that cannot be repaired.

This atomic phenomenon is an absolute, universal crusher. The basic building block of the universe, the atom, and the basic unit of life, the cell nucleus, are absolutely and irreparably crushed. The three manifestations of the atomic bomb 'Heat-Flash', 'Blast', and 'Radiations' are crushers. 'Heat-Flash' crushes the hearts of exposed persons. The 'Blast' crushes structures, while 'Radiations' crush atomic nuclei and cell nuclei. The German physicists' much-appreciated term 'Bremsstrahlung' was highly descriptive when first coined by the Germans for 'the continuous spectrum of rays'. It implied the physicists' realization of the crushing trait of atomic phenomena, for the term meant the 'braking radiation'. To this may be added Rutherford's surprise recorded in his diary after his famous experiment of bombarding the gold foil with alpha particles.

"It was the most incredible event that ever happened to me in my life. It was almost as incredible as if you fired a 15-inch shell at a piece of tissue paper, and it came back and hit you", wrote Rutherford in his diary.

Observe the words like 'bombarding', 'hitting', 'smashing', 'crushing', 'braking' etc., in the standard textbooks of Atomic Physics. Furthermore, mark the phrases like, 'target concept', 'direct action', 'indirect action', 'snapping the cable with a bullet', 'breaking the chromosomes', and sentences like, "Radiations hit the cell like a sledgehammer and crush them" in the standard textbooks of radiobiology. In the end, mark phonetic and functional identity between 'Atomos' of the scientist and 'Hotama' of the Quran, and be surprised at this miracle.

(6) The Quran says: "Hotama is fire."

So also, is the atomic phenomena, exclusively a phenomenon of energy, and energy is fire. The atomic bomb also is a fire. So also, are radiations. The discoverer of radioactivity, Becquerel, was the first to experience a burn on his skin next to the pocket he had carried a vial of Radium. We use the term 'cross-fire' in radiotherapy.

(7) The Quran says: "Hotama is a fire of Allah."

The atomic hell has appeared due to the un-Godly worldly philosophy of Baconian atomism and its Baconian progress as retribution. At the same time, it is a phenomenon beyond any possibility of comparison in intensity and magnitude.

(8) The Quran says: "Hotama is a fire which leaps up unto the hearts."

Atomic phenomena, in reality, are nuclear phenomena, for the atomic nucleus is involved therein. Again, it is a distinguishing feature of the atomic phenomena, for no other phenomena is nuclear phenomena. In no other phenomena, we even touch the nucleus. Quran's description of atomic fire that a fire which "leaps up unto the hearts" or "appears in the hearts" is confirmed merely by uttering the word 'nucleus' since the nucleus and heart are synonymous. Both the orthodox physicists and standard textbooks of atomic physics frequently use the word 'heart' for 'nucleus'.

Two examples only will suffice as follows.

(a) "Each fast particle comes from the breakup of the very heart of a single atom (the 'nucleus') of the radioactive material."
 (Physics, Physical Science Study Committee: second edition, D. C. Heath and Company, Lexington, Massachusetts, July 1965, Page-130)

(b) "How many nuclear heart-beats are in the lifetime of a radioactive nucleus which lasts only billionth of a second?"
(Ibid: Page-21, Short Problems)

Edward Teller, in 1939 spoke of taking energy from the 'heart' of the atom. The atomic radiations follow suit and have their actions in the nuclei of atoms and cells. We may view the most spectacular spectacle of the atomic fire's 'leaping up over the hearts' in the thermonuclear device wherein the fire produced by the inner fission device is directed unto the nuclei that are the hearts of the outer fusile material. The term thermonuclear is the scientific version of the statement of the Quran, namely, a fire that 'leaps up unto the hearts'.

Radiations show a discernible preference for the heart and are all related to the heart in a living body. They affect the coordination of the function at the level where it is beyond the control of the brain. The bone marrow and all the blood-forming organs are more sensitive to the effect of radiations than the brain, nerves, and muscles. The blood relation of bone marrow and blood-forming organs with the heart is known. All the multi-cellular organisms are more sensitive to the effect of radiation than all the unicellular organisms. That the former has a more elaborate circulatory and respiratory system than the latter is well-known. Known also is the blood relation of circulatory and respiratory system with heart. The action of radiation is retarded in the absence of Oxygen, and the blood relation of Oxygen with the heart is well-known.

Lastly, the 'Heat-Flash' of the atomic bomb explosion kills its victim through shock to the heart. Moreover, Wordsworth has an excellent little couplet to show the heart-atom relation. He laments as follows.

"To let a creed built in the 'heart' of things
Dissolve before a twinkling 'atomy'."

(Excursions: Wordsworth)

(9) The Quran says: **"Hotama is a fire closed in on them."** The atomic phenomena show the peculiar and distinctive characteristic of 'encompassing'.

Following are given some of the facts which indicate the distinct 'encompassing features' of atomic phenomena.

(a) The inverted cauldron-like form of the atomic bomb explosion
(b) The continuous series of enclosures of local and global types of radioactive fall-out
(c) The relentless tenacity of the bone-seeking radioactive materials settled in the bones
(d) The appearance of cancers six to thirty-six years after the actual exposure to radiation
(e) The appearance of effects in anaphase despite the attack of radiation on the cell in its resting state
(f) The encompassment of the whole body by the radiation even if only one organ of the body is irradiated

(g) The survival of lethally irradiated frogs for many months instead of dying in a usual time interval of 3 to 6 weeks if kept in a dormant state at a low temperature just above freezing point, and appearance of radiation symptoms as soon as these irradiated frogs are warmed up, and occurrence of their death after that in a usual time interval of 3 to 6 weeks

(h) Alexander Haddow's suggestion that the cancer-producing action of the cancer-producing substances might be the result of prolonged interference with normal growth

(i) The encompassment by radiation of humankind to generations, even to their extinction through long-term radio genetic effects

(j) The encompassment of this earth by radiations in the age of full-fledged atomic energy for peace

(10) The Quran says: **"In outstretched columns."**
Besides the figuratively distinctive feature of the 'outstretched column' associated with the atomic bomb explosion, the atomic phenomena have yet another side of this aspect: the world of radioactivity, which we may regard as a world of columns. The 4 cm rise of the alpha particle would appear as a formidable column if the particle size were seen compared to the height it has assumed; a football rising in the same ratio to its size would disappear in the skies. The cosmic rays present a spectacle of unique columns in showers having heights that may cause man's imagination to reel.

(11) **Description of 'Al-Hotama' by the Holy Prophet of Islam (peace be upon him).**

(a) "Allah will send over the victims, angels equipped with 'covers of fire', and 'nails of fire', and 'columns of fire'. They will cover the doomed with 'covers of fire', and will transfix them with 'nails of fire', and will 'stretch the columns of fire upward over them'. The entire phenomenon will be made so over airtight that no trace of delight shall enter from outside, nor a trace of agony will escape from inside. Allah will forget them on His throne and will cut them off from His mercy. The inmates of Paradise will begin to enjoy the boons of Allah. The inmates of hell will cease to cry for help, and speech will come to an end. Their speech will then be (as the sound of) inhaling and exhaling".

(Quoted from 'Tafsir al-Jalalayn')

(b) "The angel gets hold of the victim and placing him over the knee, breaks him like a wooden stick, and then casts him into the fire."

(Quoted from 'Tafsir al-Jalalayn')

The atomic bomb explosion is a 'cover of fire', and radiations are 'nails of fire'. The outstretched 'columns of fire' miles high are a spectacle of the atomic bomb explosion. No better description of atomic hell we could expect.

(12) The Quran says: **"What could teach thee What 'Al-Hotama' is?"**

According to the early commentators of the Quran, this interrogation mode implies the terribleness of the phenomena. To this may be added the extreme complexity of the subject of atomic science.

The same question today, namely, "What could teach thee what atomic science is" could be addressed to the leading atomists, and their reply would invariably be "Nothing". [1]

So meager is man's knowledge of atomic science, and so complex is atomic science. The most significant point in all this subject is that the causes of this worldly atomic hell and the 'Hotama' of the next eternal world are identical. Those deserving who will escape this transient worldly atomic hell will be cast into the eternal 'Hotama' of the next eternal world.

~~*~*~*

---

[1] World-renowned scientist and Nobel Prize winner Max Planck once made a remarkable comment about the structure of matter that has been widely quoted ever since:

"As a man who has devoted his whole life to the most clearheaded science, to the study of matter, I can tell you as a result of my research about the **atoms** this much: There is **no** matter as such! All matter originates and exists only by virtue of a force which brings the particles of an atom to vibration and holds this most minute solar system of the atom together. . . . We must assume behind this force the existence of a conscious and intelligent **Mind**. This **Mind** is the matrix of all matter."

~~*~*~*

CHAPTER-6

APPLICATION OF THE QURAN'S CHARACTERIZATION OF THE ATOMIC PHENOMENA TO THE ELECTRIC PHENOMENA

We have seen the nuclear characterization of the atomic phenomena by the Quran. Let us now see how far we could apply it to the electric phenomena. The electric phenomena appear as the immediately preceding link to the atomic phenomena in scientific advancement. As initiated by the Quran, the characterization of atomic phenomena could be applied to electric phenomena though not with as much precision and thoroughness as in atomic phenomena, and in points only and vaguely, though exciting and instructive.

Please refer to previous chapters to know the characterization of atomic phenomena by the Quran (Quran: 104 'Al-Homaza').

(1) The Quran says: **"Hotama."**
That is a crusher. The act of crushing is involved in electric phenomena too. Yet, the sense in which the act of crushing we attribute to the atomic phenomena could not be attributed to electric phenomena because electrons are only set in motion in electric phenomena, and the destruction of the atomic nucleus does not occur. The atomic nucleus in electric phenomena remains unaffected, just as in any non-nuclear phenomenon.

(2) The Quran says: **"Hotama is fire."**
The electric phenomenon is fire. It is also a phenomenon of energy, and energy is heat, fire, etc. However, fire is not as conspicuously associated with electric phenomena as atomic phenomena, and we could not imagine the degree and magnitude of atomic fire in electric phenomena.

(3) The Quran says: **"Hotama is a fire of Allah."**
We may regard the electric phenomenon as a phenomenon of facility and utility, and the particular hazards associated with atomic phenomena could not be associated with electric phenomena. If the people so desire, they can use the electric phenomena for constructive purposes only.

Still, the punishing liability of the Baconian culture would force the scientific advancement into the atomic field to ensure the destruction of the atomic and the electric phenomena. The electric phenomenon, just like atomic phenomena, is the product of the Baconian philosophy of modern atomism and is only a link preceding the atomic phenomena and consequent atomic destruction occurring in the manner of retribution.

(4) The Quran says: **"Hotama is a fire which leapeth up unto the hearts."**

The electric phenomena, though not nuclear, yet the target of electric current in the victim's body is the 'heart' in the event of electric shock. The fire of worry and discontent would mount above the hearts of men in the age of materialism in the era of electric phenomena, even if no atomic phenomena had appeared.

(5) The Quran says: **"Hotama is a fire closed in on them."**

Just see the tall poles and columns of hydroelectric lines, and if you know the closed nature of the electric circuit, you will at once see the electric fire closed in on them in 'outstretched columns'. Also, the necessity of electricity at this age 'encompasses' the entire world. It is just closed in on them in 'outstretched columns'.

THE CONCLUDING WORD

Let us conclude that the research reveals and will reveal to infinity that the Quran has in its brief chapter of 'Al-Homaza' covered every phase of this modern, science-guided, and money-oriented culture of atomism. Amazingly, the Quran has covered it entirely from the smoking chimney through the electric pole to the atomic bomb explosion column. It is a fascinating subject and essential for research and study for the philosopher, moralist, economist, theologist, sociologist, and the scientist in this light of the Quran. Many a Russell, Einstein, and James Jeans would have been lost in their life-long preliminary human study against the complete, divine knowledge of the Quran. The times are coming when the sight of a chimney, an electric pole, an electric tower, or the column of the atomic bomb explosion will recall to the mind of man the words of the Quran 'outstretched columns' in association with a feeling of torment. The fire of 'Hotama', according to the Quran, is the fire of Allah enkindled and closed in on them in 'outstretched columns'. The chimneys of factories will become a symbol of torment to honor the views of William Blake.

~~*~*~*

CHAPTER-7

QURAN AND SCIENCE OF METEOROLOGY [1]

QURAN TREATS THE PHENOMENA OF 'RAIN' AND 'HAIL'

The Quran has claimed not once but twice in most explicit terms to contain all knowledge concerning humanity and has challenged the world to bring a chapter like it.

Once, someone asked me if the Quran was not a book of science but religion only. How could the treatment of atomic science, atomic bombs, and atomic radiations be expected in a religious book? [2]

My answer to this question was, and is, that the Quran is a book of religion indeed. Still, it is the book of a perfect and complete religion, and we expect it to answer every question concerned with humanity. The destruction of the habitations of Aad, Thamud, Sodom, and Gomorrah received a mention in it. These habitations were no larger than a negligible part of a modern city. How could the Quran ignore without damaging the claim to universality to mention a destroyer that would not leave even a blade of grass unburnt from one end of the world to the other? We must expect the Quran to answer the question of the atomic obliteration of the world.

Again, someone may ask whether the Quran contains the research of modern science of meteorology. The answer to this question is, "Yes! It does". Quran shows this in one sign (verse) of about forty words.

Read the following English translation from the Quran regarding the phenomena of rain and hail.

"Hast thou not seen how Allah <u>wafteth the clouds</u>, then gathereth them, then maketh them <u>layers</u>, and thou seest the rain come forth from between them; He sendeth down from the heavens, <u>mountains</u> wherein hail is, and smiteth therewith whom He will, and averteth it from whom He will. The flashing of His lightning all but snatcheth away the sight."

[Quran 24 'Surat An-Nūr' (The Light):43]

You have read it now or heard it. And if you happen to be a meteorologist, how much of the science of modern meteorology you have discerned in it so that after we have explained it, you might compare. Whether in translation or original Arabic text of the Quran, most readers consider this reflection just a matter of common observation that Quran has mentioned.

However, remember that mysteries are revealed only in the original Arabic text and never in the translations. The Arabic text of the Quran reveals the essence of the modern science of meteorology about the phenomena of rain and hail. You have read or heard the English translation mentioned above from the [Quran 24 'Surat An-Nūr' (The Light):43].

Now, read or hear its counterpart in the original Arabic text as follows.

أَلَمْ تَرَ أَنَّ ٱللَّهَ يُزْجِى سَحَابًا ثُمَّ يُؤَلِّفُ بَيْنَهُ ثُمَّ يَجْعَلُهُۥ رُكَامًا فَتَرَى ٱلْوَدْقَ يَخْرُجُ مِنْ خِلَٰلِهِۦ وَيُنَزِّلُ مِنَ ٱلسَّمَآءِ مِن جِبَالٍ فِيهَا مِنۢ بَرَدٍ فَيُصِيبُ بِهِۦ مَن يَشَآءُ وَيَصْرِفُهُۥ عَن مَّن يَشَآءُ يَكَادُ سَنَا بَرْقِهِۦ يَذْهَبُ بِٱلْأَبْصَٰرِ (24:43)

At first sight, there appear to be no scientific facts of modern research, but by the grace of Almighty Allah, there are scientific facts to be revealed to those possessed of knowledge and are sincere in their faith in the Quran. The original Arabic text of the Quran has miracles to reveal. We may find the most complex, intricate, and perplexing facts of science and philosophy in words and mysteries discovered. To a knowledgeable reader, the world of the Quran appears like a kaleidoscopic world. The words changing their forms and clues assume new forms and colors, astonishing and perplexing the inferior human intellect.

During my forty years' long research in the Quran, I went to sleep with the satisfaction that I had exhausted the meanings of a particular sign (verse) more than once. But the following day, to my surprise, I saw the same sign blossoming with fresh flowers that had changing colors and delightful fragrances.

Remember that the modern science of meteorology is of recent origin, while Allah revealed the Quran fourteen centuries ago. Suppose; therefore, we find the discoveries of modern meteorology in the Quran. In that case, there remains no doubt about the Divine Origin of the

Quran, and the Quran deserves to assume a unique place among the Divine Scriptures.

We will now interpret the signs (verses) of the Quran, as mentioned earlier, in the light of all the latest discoveries of science in the field of meteorology.

The non-Muslims generally observe that whenever a discovery of science appears, the Muslims prop up the Quran saying, "Lo! Here it is written in the Quran".

These non-Muslim observers put forth a question as follows. "Why can't the Muslims find these facts from the Quran before the science declared discovery?"

The answer to this objection is as follows.
Firstly, the Quran is not the science textbook to teach people how to produce the things created by science. Instead, the Quran observes and regulates the entire life of humanity with every aspect of it. Therefore, the Quran has a specific style of treating the subject of pure science.

Secondly, the Quran would not like the appearance of certain things or their improper use to keep humanity safe from the harmful effects. Therefore, the Quran treats such subjects of science in its peculiar manner. For instance, the Quran has treated atomic science and the entire subject's essence but has not taught to build the atomic bombs.

Thirdly, suppose the Quran had explained the inventions of science as we see them today and had used the terms as we hear them today. In that case, it is not difficult to imagine that the hearers of that time would have stampeded away, thrusting their fingers in their ears, and yelling:

"How impossible and how nonsensical? Away! Away to your rational creed; the creed of your fathers".

The fate of Islam was thus no hidden secret. And it was a miracle of the Quran to say a thing understandable and appealing to its first hearers and conceal within the same language that could answer all that was to come in time in any form; scientific, philosophical, economic, and social.

Yet, understand that the corroboration of the Quran and science is a topic fraught with imminent dangers. Science changes while the Quran is constant. Once said, is forever said. The corroborator, therefore, must have a thorough knowledge of science to discern the recognized facts from mere theories and hypotheses and should, at the same time, have the thorough knowledge of the Quran to its actual mind. Otherwise, there is a great possibility of wrecking the reputation of the Quran and making this word of Allah a butt of ridicule, sealing at the same time the doom of the corroborator himself. I have seen many a corroborator that blundered in this field. Hence, they fell from cliffs to the vales of humiliation. May Allah save us from such doom.

I am a corroborator also. But I weigh a thing a hundred times and pass many a sleepless night before I find the courage to pen or bring on record even a single fact. Yet I pray to Allah, the Most Merciful, to guide me aright in this hazardous field, let me have no personal or other consideration, and forgive any slip or fall. I am obliged to take to this field for no other reason than it has become the inevitable necessity of these days. Otherwise, the early authentic commentators of the Quran have left no point ambiguous.

Now, let us revert to our topic in the name of Allah, the Benign, and the Merciful.

Allah says: "Alam Tara".

It means, "Hast thou not seen?"

People first posed this question to the Holy Prophet (peace be upon him) and his contemporary Arabs. Now, we could pose it to the meteorologist. This feature is marvelous of the all-time pervading and eternal Quran.

Allah says: "Annallaha Yuzji".

It means, "Allah wafteth" that is "Allah drives".

It contradicts those who think that the laws of Mother Nature work independently or that the whole affair of creation is accidental only. Here Allah asserts His complete control of the phenomena.

Allah says: "Sahaban".

'Sahaba' means a 'cloud'. But derivatives formed on its root give meanings: 'to drive along', 'to drag along', 'to withdraw', 'to recall', and 'to retract'.

The modern meteorological science on this point says as follows.

"Previous to a thunder-storm the clouds are in great commotion, great masses [3] being torn asunder, others uniting together; now these clouds being electrified, some more and some less strongly, act inductively on one another, and if a piece happens to be torn away, while more than its fair share of electricity has been induced into it, it may soar away intensely electrified. Several such pieces may unite to form a big cloud charged to the enormous potential necessary to produce a flash of lightning."

('An Elementary Course of Physics'; Chapter-6, 'Atmospheric Electricity', Pages: 707-708, Edited by John Clement Primrose Aldous, Jan1900, Macmillan and Company, Limited.)

Modern meteorological science says:

"… Several such pieces may unite to form a big cloud".

The Quran says:

"Thumma Yuallifu Bainahu", that is, "Then gathereth them together".

We describe the detail in the following paragraph.

Allah says: "Thumma Yuallifu Bainahu".

It means, after that, (Allah) affects harmony between the different parts of the cloud and achieves affinity between them. Generally, we translate it as, "Then gathereth them together".

To know what kind of harmony and affinity is affected and achieved between the various parts of the cloud, let us read the following from the science of meteorology.

"To achieve the coalescence of the minute spherules of water into fallible raindrops, a proper electrical affinity between a particle and a particle within the cloud and further, within the cloud and the earth has to be achieved. In the presence of a strong positive charge in the cloud, the spherules would tend towards separation, excluding any possibility of their coalescence. A charge of a milder sort in the vicinity has been found to be helpful for the desired coalescence for the spherules into raindrops. The necessity of the electric potential and hence the electricity itself having thus been established, a slight acidification of the cloud water is to be understood as a means to impart conductivity to the water, which in a state of its purity is a bad conductor of electricity."

Let the great Masters of Chemistry read these chemical processes explained by the Quran.

Allah says: "Thumma Yajaluhu rukaaman".

That is, "Then maketh them layers" or "Then layeth them in heaps".

Let us read what modern meteorological science says about the 'heaping up' of the cloud. It says as follows.

"When the vapour in the air is condensed, not through contact with cold bodies, but through the cooling of a mass of vapour-laden air, then a cloud is formed. A cloud consists of fine droplets of water; if it be near the ground, it is called a mist or fog. It would, at the outset, seem impossible to classify or account for the myriads forms of the cloud ... But when we come to observe and watch them closely, two main types of cloud-form assert themselves: those which appear in billowy, well-defined shapes, and those which spread over the heavens in a layer, thick or thin, partial, or complete.

The former of these is called Cumulus (a heap), the latter Stratus (a layer); these names are due to Luke Howard (1802), and all cloud observers have used since his time." ('An Elementary Course of Physics'; Chapter-9, 'Hygrometry and the Weather', Pages: 356-357, Edited by

John Clement Primrose Aldous, Jan1900, Macmillan and Company, Limited.)

Meteorological science is of recent origin. It developed within the centuries of this modern age. Luke Howard [4] first used the terms 'Cumulus' and 'Stratus' in 1802.

'Cumulus' [5] and 'Stratus' [6] are both Latin words. 'Cumulus' means 'a heap' or 'a pile', and 'Stratus' means 'a layer'.

The Quran has anticipated the meteorologist for centuries. The word <u>rukaaman</u>, which the Quran has used, means precisely the 'Cumulus'.

So far as the term 'Stratus' is concerned, other than one mentioned above, the Quran has also used it in another sign (verse) about the very same topic. This sign is as follows.

"Allah is He who sendeth the winds so that they raise clouds, and spreadeth them along the sky as pleaseth Him. And <u>forms them in layers</u>, and thou seest the rain downpouring from within them".

(Quran 30:48)

Another translation of the same verse is as follows.

"It is Allah who sends the breezes that raise clouds, then spreads them over the sky as He pleases, <u>folds on the fold</u>, and then you see the drops of rain issue from between them. When He sends it down to those of His creatures as He will, they are filled with joy."

(Quran 30:48)

The actual Arabic word used in the Quran is '<u>Kisafan</u>', which means '<u>to lay in layers</u>', '<u>to stratify</u>', or '<u>to lay layer upon layer</u>', etc. It is precisely the term 'Stratus' used by Luke Howard.

Generally, we translate it as, "Causeth them (clouds) to break into fragments". It is surprising to note that the Quran anticipated Luke Howard by centuries. The words of the Quran thus are not only scientific but also prophetic.

Again, we revert to the verse [Quran 24 'Surat An-Nūr' (The Light):43] under discussion.

Allah says:

"Fataral Wadaqa Yakhruju min <u>khilaalihi</u>".

That is:

"Thou seest the rain which falleth from the midst thereof".

The actual word is 'Min <u>Khilaali</u>hi', that is, "the rain is pouring from the '<u>khilaal</u>' of the cloud".

The meaning of this word is 'pin', 'skewer', or 'spit'. The root of this word is 'khallala', which means 'to acetify'. 'Khalla' means 'vinegar'.

The necessity of the acidification of the cloud water we have already narrated in the previous pages. A charge of the milder sort is essential to achieve the coalescence of the spherules. The charge necessitates electricity. But pure water is a bad conductor of electricity. It is necessary, therefore, to acetify the water to endue water with the quality of conductivity. Thus, the role of the word 'khilaal' in the phenomena becomes apparent, to mean that no 'khilaal' meant no rain and, therefore, no life on earth.

Allah says:

"Wa yunazzilu min assamaae min jibalin fiha min bardin".

That is:

"He (Allah) sendeth down from the heavens mountains wherein hail is"

First, imagine a cloud, like a 'mountain of hail'. How beautiful is the mountain of white pearls, and how exact but novel is the simile? But the point which attracts our attention is hidden in the word 'jibal', which means 'mountains'. The root of this word is 'jabala' which means 'to knead'.

Perhaps the most astonishing discovery of modern meteorological science is that neither mist nor fog could be formed unless there were present in the vapor, laden air particles of dust or sand to act as the nucleus for the spherules of water that constitute the fog. It has been proved since air filtered through cotton wool does not tend to fog formation. The hail pellets likewise are found to have been built around a speck of dust acting as their nucleus, a process distinct from snow formation.

Now, let us see the word 'jibal' that is 'mountains' used by the Quran. As mentioned above, the word 'jibal' has been derived from the root verb 'jabala', which means 'to knead'. Then imagine a cloud of rain or hail wherein every spherule has a speck of dust or sand though invisible to the naked eye. Indeed, the cloud appears like a mountain made of dust particles kneaded with water. Remarkable also is the role of mountains in the formation of rain.

In the end, one may ask that the Quran in this phenomenon has made no mention of the significant role of the air. It is the air that carries the moisture, and it is the air that wafts the clouds. Without the air, no rain would have been possible. The question takes our thought to another sign (verse) of the Quran, which is identical to the sign (verse) we are discussing and has mentioned the role of air. We have mentioned this sign above. Just review it.

"Allah is He who sendeth the <u>winds</u> so that <u>they raise clouds</u>, and spreadeth them along the sky as pleaseth Him. And forms them in layers, and thou seest the rain downpouring from within them".

(Quran 30:48)

The Quran's challenge, "Bring ye a chapter like unto it", stands good for every age, including this age of science. The knowledge of science shown by the Quran is such that no scientist will ever think of being equal to or like the Quern; the great word of Allah, the Allah of the worlds.

~~*~*~*

---

[1] **Meteorology**: The science that deals with the phenomena of the atmosphere, especially weather and weather conditions.

[2] This question refers to an interesting debate between the author and renowned German scholar Ms. Anne Marie Schimmel in 1963 on the Quran's Divine Origin issue. For dialogue details, please read Book-1/volume-1/chapter-6 ["The efficacy of the warning of the Quran about the atomic hell"].

[3] Mark here the exact similarity of the words **great masses** (used by modern meteorological science) with (that used by the Quran) **mountains** when it says, "He sendeth down from the heaven, **mountains** wherein **hail** is."

[4] **Luke Howard** (November 28, 1772 - March 21, 1864) has been called 'the father of meteorology'. His comprehensive weather recordings in the London area from (1801) to (1841) and his writings transformed the science of meteorology. His lasting contribution to science is a 'Nomenclature system for clouds', which he proposed in an 1802 presentation to the Askesian Society.

[5] **Cumulus**: A cloud of a class characterized by dense individual elements in the form of puffs, mounds, or towers, with flat bases and tops that often resemble cauliflower: as such clouds develop vertically, they form cumulonimbus.

[6] **Stratus**: A diffuse, grayish cloud that often produces drizzle formed primarily in altitudes no higher than 2,000 m (6,560 ft.). A stratus cloud close to the ground or water is called fog.

~~*~*~*

VOLUME-3

QURAN VERSUS ANCIENT AND MODERN ATOMISM

TABLE OF CONTENTS

VOLUME-3

PREFACE 589

PART-1
QURAN VERSUS THE ANCIENT ATOMISM OF DEMOCRITUS

Chapter-1
History of atomism 593

Chapter-2
Doctrinal implications of the theory of ancient Greek atomism 612

Chapter-3
The views of the Quran versus
the views of the early Greek atomic theory 614

Chapter-4
The missing link between the
ancient and modern followers of atomism 631

PART-2
QURAN VERSUS BACON'S MODERN ATOMISM

Chapter-5
Who is Bacon? 637

Chapter-6
Baconian and Satanic methods of seduction are identical 641

Chapter-7
Quran versus Bacon's design of atomism 643

Chapter-8
Quran versus Bacon on moral and natural philosophy 663

Chapter-9
Relative views of Bacon and Quran on material utility 674

Chapter-10
Comparative views of Bacon and the
Quran on the purpose of man's creation 705

Chapter-11
Comparative views of Bacon and the
Quran on the contemplation of the works of Allah 708

Chapter-12
Quran on the Baconian right of
man's dominion over Mother Nature 750

Chapter-13
Quran's view of Bacon's philosophy 759

Chapter-14
The views of Bacon, the Bible, and the Quran on 'knowledge' 765

Chapter-15
Bacon's philosophy is antipathetic to religion in general 773

Chapter-16
The natural effects of Baconian philosophy 778

Chapter-17
The causes of the appearance of Baconian culture 783

Chapter-18
The appearance of Baconian culture 788

Chapter-19
The development of atomism 809

Chapter-20
The concluding word 811

BIBLIOGRAPHY 817

PREFACE

The present age is involved in great misunderstandings about this modern Baconian progress and this modern science. Neither the reality of the former is known, nor are the limitations of the latter realized. This age is reputedly the era of knowledge. Yet, it is almost entirely ignorant of the subject on which is staked its existence, namely, the subject of Baconian progress and its appendage, atomic science. Modern progress is not known to any individual in the world today, while the subject of atomic science is known to but a few physicists.

Again, the knowledge of atomic science and Radiobiology available at present is only of the most elementary nature. It may come as a surprise to most, yet the fact is that building the atomic bomb or Hydrogen bomb and designing an atomic reactor is only the first lesson of atomic science. Further, a blind is drawn. The second lesson, the control over radiations, is entirely in the darkness without any hope of a ray of light further in the dark atomic labyrinth. Yet, the scientists have fixed their attention on building up the atomic stockpiles.

It also might come as a surprise to the scholarly world that the name, life history, and works of Francis Bacon (1561-1626), the 'trumpeter of this new age' and the expounder of this philosophy of modern atomism, are almost entirely forgotten to the world. So also, is lost the link existing between Baconian atomism and this modern progress. The thought of this world today is fixed: firstly, on the present situation of progress and, secondly, on the danger of atomic war without knowing anything about either the true origin and exact reality of this modern progress or the connection of the atomic bombs with this modern progress and the origin of both in Bacon's philosophy of modern atomism.

They are blindly engaged in progress. While regarding the atomic hazards, we may see them behaving like an ostrich with their confidence in science for averting the atomic danger. However, science is as helpless as anything else and can afford no remedy for the atomic bomb, other than the atomic bomb itself. No doubt it appears as a mad world with a god other than the actual Creator of the heavens and the earth.

Moreover, the gravest of dangers has plagued this age. The oppressive circumstances are dragging present-day humankind towards the flames of a blazing, braying, and thundering atomic hell to be broiled therein alive. It is, with ever-increasing speed, tending toward the atomic war despite all the wishful thinking, false hopes, and universal behavior like an ostrich. So glaring are their follies thinking that they will avoid the atomic war by specific means and methods. These idiocies excite feelings of pity and remorse. Untold miseries and unheard afflictions that are to be their lot are beside the final consumption by the atomic hell and all-devouring flames that are the devastating atomic blasts and deadly insidious atomic radiations.

We have in this volume tried to explain the reality of the ancient atomic theory against the Quran. Moreover, we have tried to explain the reality of Bacon's philosophy of modern atomism and its manifestation, modern Baconian progress, and its logical and scientific end, the atomic hell against the Quran. We have tried to prescribe the remedy of the relative ills and seek the solution to the relative problems.

We have also tried to show the relation existing between the Quran and the Gospel. In a subsequent Volume, we have written the life history of Bacon referred to his philosophy. In yet another volume, we have tried to glean the traces of the doctrinal implications of ancient Greek theory of atomism in a philosophy based on the discoveries of modern science and its limitations.

The matter and the manner throughout, just as in any other volume ever written by me, is new and original. The reader will always feel a tinge of bitterness in the views. Truth always has been regarded as bitter. Here is a specimen of concentrated truth, concentrated as well as the novel, yet not bitterer than the fumes and burning flames of atomic hell that is the blasting atomic bombs and the stinging heartburning, mistrust, anarchy, and dismay. May Allah guide this humankind aright in this most critical moment in whole human history. Aameen.

YOUSUF GABRIEL

~~*~*~*~*

PART-1

QURAN VERSUS THE ANCIENT ATOMISM OF DEMOCRITUS

CHAPTER-1

HISTORY OF ATOMISM

PHILOSOPHICAL HISTORY OF ATOMISM

This modern age has grown based on atomism. It has derived all fundamental ideas from this very same theory of atomism. Its moral, social, economic, religious, aesthetic, philosophical, and psychological distinctive features as the knowledge, science, civilization, culture, progress, thought, opinions, beliefs, attitudes, and notions are the effects of the atomistic theory and philosophy. It has its unique, universal, systematic, and ever-progressive economic and industrial setup, and lastly, and alas, there is extreme appropriateness of its tragic end in atomic bombs and nuclear radiations. Hence, it is essential to know and comprehend the theory, the philosophy, and the history of atomism to understand this modern age and its distinctive features, as mentioned above.

He can only judge the actual reality of this modern age, who has studied atomism compared to the philosophy of faith. It may appear strange, but it is a fact that a careful study of the Quran from this particular point of view could most easily prove it. The Quran discusses and opposes atomism as if atomism were to appear in the future as a prospective and prominent adversary of faith and hence the Quran itself, and a universal threat to humankind.

The Quran discusses, describes, traces, and confronts atomism to its ultimate end in the atomic hell and sounds a warning accordingly pointing out the causes of the emergence of the atomic bomb, an outcome of the atomism itself. It is not only in its particular prophecy that the Quran has treated the subject of atomism, nay, but the topic spreads throughout the Quran. The prophecy, however, is the essence of the whole subject, just as the atomic bomb is the fruit of the whole theme of atomism. In the light of the treatment of atomism by the Quran, it appears as if the Quran had an entire course of future atomism in view and described the entire affair in a commentary like a keen, omniscient observer.

Anyone who has perceived this view shall find no difficulty in the endorsement thereof. A cursory glance at the writings of the Quran will reveal to any person the truth in the clearest of colors provided indeed that the person possessed the actual knowledge of atomism. After having condemned the worldly doctrines of atomism throughout, the Quran has ultimately shown atomism to culminate in its logical and scientific end in the atomic bomb. Though pointing out the causes of the emergence of the atomic bomb, the Quran has shown a possibility of averting the dreadful doom.

From this particular point of view, a study of the Quran referred to atomism, and consequently to this age of atomism, is essential to the degree that we could hardly overstress. It opens up an avenue of knowledge that is most needed to give the necessary directive to the movement of reform with the object of averting the all-consuming threat of atomic hell.

A study of this kind will also manifest the explicit and implicit capabilities of the Quran and the role of miraculous guidance that this Scripture can play in clearing the misunderstandings of this materialistic age. The Quran can lead it out of all the most impending hazards that are the product of the erroneous philosophy of atomism, onto the path of absolute peace, prosperity, and progress against the delusive peace, prosperity, and progress of atomism that tends toward the deceptive utopia of an illusory bliss.

The plausibility of accepting the word of the Quran by this age lay in the fact that while nothing but the verdict of science would be acceptable to this age of science, the Quran would fulfill this same condition and offer its argument based on science itself. Suppose scientific merit alone could find grace in the eyes of this age. In that case, the Quran will assuredly prove its worth in this field. But let only someone worthy of such an initiative venture on so hazardous a work. If no appeals in the name of divinity and faith could be of any benefit and only the scientific verities were acceptable to the mind of this age, then the Quran would come out with the scientific truths to bring conviction. The Quran has been acclaimed as a standing miracle, and it certainly will work miracles in an age that does not believe in miracles.

The theory of atomism lay buried deep in the strata of history like an old fossil, almost forgotten and far removed from any probability of a revival ever in this world (7th century AD). When the Quran ventured at the prophecy about the atomic bomb, the ultimate fruit of atomism was to appear twelve hundred years later in history. The atomic bomb could never have appeared globally without the revival of atomism (17th century AD).

The revival of atomism itself is one of the strangest events of history. They revived the theory of atomism from a grave that the world

had almost forgotten. Soon, it spread like a flurry with its revival, only likened to a wildfire in the jungle or a petrol dump. Soon, it came to permeate the entire field of science and every sphere of human life.
The prophecy of the Quran is as follows.

"Woe to every backbiter, defamer, who amasseth wealth of (this world) and storeth it (against the future). He thinketh surely that his wealth will render him immortal. Nay, for verily he shall be flung into "Al-Hotama", and what could teach thee what "Al-Hotama" is? It is Allah's kindled fire, which leapeth up over the hearts. It is (a fire) closed in on them in outstretched columns."

(Quran: 104 'Al-Homaza')

We generally attribute the theory of atomism to Democritus (ca. 460 BCE – ca. 370 BCE) of Abdera in Thrace, Greece. He was a younger contemporary of Socrates and nicknamed 'the laughing philosopher' because he found in human life matter only for laughter against Heraclitus (535 BCE – 475 BCE). The later tradition called Heraclitus the 'weeping philosopher' because he always found in human life matter for tears. The theory of atomism is attributed to Democritus though not he, but Leucippus was its actual originator. We know little about Leucippus except that he was a Milesian, most probably born in 'Miletus', and flourished about 440 BC.

"Leucippus or Leukippos (first half of 5th century BC) was the first Greek to develop the theory of atomism — the idea that everything is composed entirely of various imperishable, indivisible elements called atoms — which was elaborated in far greater detail by his pupil and successor, Democritus."

(Wikipedia, the free Encyclopedia)

Democritus received the credit because he was responsible for developing the system and making it known. Both the Leucippus and Democritus were atheists. The association of atheism with their names was responsible for the low esteem of theory in their own time and later. But another fact that undoubtedly has been unobserved is that their theory was of the same dye as their atheism. It was impossible to segregate the 'scientific' part of the theory from the 'atheistic' origin it had sprung. Time has proved this fact.

The pioneers of atomism in the modern age had adopted atomism, thinking that the scientific part of the theory could be separated from the atheistic implications and used in structural interpretation of the universe for the material progress of humankind. It was with this same view in mind that they had ventured to adopt this theory. But unfortunately, their view eventually has proved as a mere delusion. The atheistic implications of the theory have all crept into the field. They have occupied the human mind to the extent that today it is hard to induce a philosopher to study the influence of atomic theory on the faith of humankind.

Even though the theme is far more interesting, absorbing, and indeed more essential than the evolution of Darwin, which treats the origin of humankind. At the same time, it is not the origin but the end in the shadow of the atomic bomb that is more worthy of man's attention.

If ever such research is conducted, humankind would ceremoniously recite the results thereof over the graves of those pioneers of atomism who were mistaken in thinking that they could segregate atheistic elements from the scientific part of the theory.

The process, indeed, was far more complicated than that of separating Uranium-235 from Uranium-238. Atomism was exclusively a theory of the world, and nothing but the world and its wealth today occupy the mind of humankind.

Following are the views of the early atomists.
(1) The atoms are indivisible and indestructible.
(2) They move about in all directions in a fortuitous concourse in an otherwise empty space.
(3) Atoms and space are all that exist.
(4) Differences of shape distinguish different kinds of atoms, but individual atoms are too small to be noticed by the senses.
(5) The arrangement makes the things we touch and see atoms in groups. The change consists of nothing but their arrangement. There is no alteration in the atoms themselves.
(6) The atom's motion persists until checked, presumably in collision with another atom since the theory denies any other cause.

Although both Democritus and Plato lived in the same world, their minds' worlds were quite different from one another. Like Plato, Democritus held the eternal and ultimate reality as the object, not of senses but the understanding. However, he considered the nature of this reality very differently from Plato. It consisted of atoms of inseparable and imperishable bodies of sizes too small to be detected by our senses. They differed in shape (whence Democritus could call them by the same name as Plato gave to his ultimate realities of ideas or forms), moving about in a vacuum or void.

The great contemporary thinkers were apprehensive of the dangers with which atomism was fraught and, therefore, opposed its prevalence. The overbearing influence of Aristotle cast its weight into the scale against the adoption of theory as atomism. Not the influence of

Aristotle alone but also the greatest writing philosopher of ancient times, namely, Plato, was most vehement in his opposition to atomism.

Human civilization made significant scientific progress in mathematics and astronomy during the two hundred years that followed the death of Aristotle in 322 BC. These two centuries were made illustrious by names like Euclid of Alexandria, Greek mathematician, often referred to as the 'Father of Geometry' (300 BC), Eratosthenes of Cyrene (276 BC–195 BC), Archimedes of Syracuse (287 BC–212 BC), and Hipparchus (190 BC–120 BC). Euclid wrote 'Elements' that was the textbook of Geometry for two thousand years. Eratosthenes first used the method to ascertain the size (circumference) of the earth. Archimedes discovered the principle of the lever. Hipparchus has been called the true father of astronomy.

Though these were years of significant progress, yet none of these great thinkers so much as condescended to take the name of atomism, not to speak of any research, investigation, or inquiry.

The opposition of atomism is not limited to the ancient thinkers alone. Francis Bacon was the greatest, the ablest, and the most eloquent advocate of modern atomism. Despite disagreement with Aristotle on many points, he stood in perfect agreement with him in condemning the blindness of atomism to the evidence of design in the world, afforded by the existence of the structures too elaborate ever to be explained satisfactorily by a fortuitous concourse of atoms. Bacon seemed to be keenly sensible of the danger that lay in attempts to start our investigations considering the purpose of nature of which we are about too likely to take a very short-sighted view.

The theory of atomism has brought about the disastrous situation of the world in these present times. In the presence of such a disastrous situation and atomic bombs, we, too, the unfortunate inhabitants of this present age of atomism, are likely to appreciate the apprehensions of the ancient, opposed thinkers and the fears of Bacon, the great modern protagonist of atomism, regarding atomism. At the same time, we mourn the tendency of pioneers who ventured to adopt so dangerous a theory as atomism for material uplift and of their followers who took the short-sighted view of the purpose of nature just as Bacon had feared. The pioneers and their followers fell to the immediate material gains. The result is that the world ultimately has reached a stage where perfect misery and utter destruction billow forth from the horizons towards humankind that stares in terror at the impending catastrophe in utter helplessness.

Amidst the general unpopularity of atomism in ancient Greece, however, a philosophical school adopted atomism as a fundamental part of their system. Its attraction for this school was not its scientific utility so much as its apparent inconsistency with the doctrine of the divine government of the world, which they regarded as the source of worst evil that affected humankind, namely, the fear of death and of what may come after it. This school that adopted atomism as a remedy against the terrors of religion was the Epicurean school of thought. Epicurus (the founder of the Epicurean school), the chief rival of Zeno (the founder of the school of Stoicism), recommended the rational pursuit of pleasure. But people did not follow his ideal, and the excess of the rational pursuit of pleasure became the order of his followers. Epicurus did not preach that one should make the most of his life, eat, drink and be merry, for, tomorrow, we die. He recommended refined pleasures and moderation. Yet, the sensualists found a good chance in his teachings to claim for their lives the sanctions of the Epicurean principle that it is reasonable to aim at 'pleasure' alone which is the chief good.

Thus, the name of an Epicurean very early became a synonym for a 'sensualist' and a reproach. We see that the ancient Epicureans who adopted the atheistic side of atomism and neglected its scientific side failed. We also see that modernists who adopted the scientific side of atomism failed too. Epicureans failed due to the abuse of pleasure, while modernists failed because of the short-sighted view of the purpose of nature and immediate material gain. Atomism, thus in every form, has brought failure and destruction.

Stoic, a school of thought opposed to the theory of Epicureanism, confronted the Epicurean school from its cradle. 'Virtue' against 'pleasure' of Epicureanism was the motto of Stoic, and a strict moral and religious code was to be adhered to as against the loose and lax life of the Epicurean. Although these two schools divided the allegiance of most thoughtful men in the countries that formed the heart of the Roman Empire at the beginning of the Christian era, the Epicureans gradually lost ground, and the Stoics prevailed.

Remember that the philosophers whom the Apostle Paul is related to have encountered on his visit to Athens were representatives of Epicureans and Stoics (The Bible: Acts-17:18-34). When they heard of the Resurrection of the dead from Apostle Paul, some mocked, and others said:

"We will hear thee again of this matter".

Therefore, Paul departed from among them. However, certain men clave unto him and believed. Among them were Dionysius the Areopagite and a woman named Damaris. However, this visit of St. Paul did not augur well for the cult of Epicureanism and atomism both. After the advent of Christianity, an era ushered in those parts that proved fatal to Epicureanism and atomism.

It was not surprising that of all the Greek schools, the Stoic was the one that made itself at home among the Romans who, in less than two centuries after the death of Zeno (the founder of that school), had become the masters of the Greek-speaking world. Love of knowledge and delight in beauty, the indulgence in subtle doubts, and the cultivation of refined pleasures were all alike uncongenial to the Roman temper. It was inclined to charge their representatives among Greek professors of philosophy with a frivolity, dangerous to the sense of discipline and public duty which had been hitherto the ministry of the Roman state.

But such suspicions were less aroused by the Stoics than by any of their rivals. If Stoicism's moral and religious temper thus won it a special welcome at Rome, there was also something in the temper of Roman people that was particularly congenial to the Stoic philosophy. It was called 'The sense of Justice and Law', which marked out the Roman people among their contemporary nations and made the Roman legal system the basis on which the Roman Empire stood for centuries with remarkable stability. The Stoics, rather than either the Epicureans or the Skeptics, exercised, in the long run, the most expansive influence in an era, seeking religious faith. It is to be explained by their attitude of devout acquiescence in the predestined or providential order of the universe.

Epicurus, the founder of Epicureanism, adopted atomism, not for its scientific merit but because its materialism supported his denial of a spiritual life after death. Roman poet Lucretius was an eminent follower of Democritus. He did much by his poem 'De Rerum Natura' to make atomism known. Yet, although the founder seemed to the poet a worthy deliverer of man from the superstitious terrors, the intellectual and scientific activity, except so far as it served to dissipate the superstitious dread, could hardly be more than a refined pastime to a consistent Epicurean. It is not thus surprising to find that the Epicureans contributed little to the advancement of scientific or philosophical inquiry. They adopted as their own the atomic theory of Democritus. However, in their hands, it was neither enabled to meet objections raised against it as a theory of ultimate nature of reality nor made to exhibit its great capacities as an instrument of scientific description and discovery.

Both Stoicism and Christianity were against Epicureanism in their exacting standards of conduct and faith in the divine government of the world. Moreover, whereas the Epicureans saw an eternal play of atoms in the course of nature without any predestined plot, the Stoics and Christians alike looked forward to a configuration in which the current frame of things would perish.

By the 5th Century AD, the period of struggle among numerous competitors ended in the complete victory of Christianity. Every candle except that of Christianity was by then extinguished. The whole of the Roman Empire, along with the emperor, had embraced the faith of Christianity, and it became the state religion.

"The Early Middle Ages span roughly five centuries from 500 to 1000. During this period, most of Europe was Christianized, and the 'Dark Ages' following the fall of Rome took place."

(History of Europe: Wikipedia, the free Encyclopedia) The original contribution of Western thought was essentially complete by about 100 BC, but the decline of philosophy and art began long before this with the eclipse of Athens. The advent of Christianity meant an end to knowledge, Epicureanism, and atomism. The West's so-called 'Dark Ages' are known as the dark ages because intellectual activity for acquiring knowledge was missing.

It is strange to observe that the Quran should make a prophecy about the atomic bomb, the fruit of atomism, in the 7th century AD that is at the zenith of the dark ages of the West at a time when not even a trace of the theory of atomism was extant in the world. At such time, anyone could attribute opinion about the probability of revival of atomism in the world to lunacy. Nay, even an allusion to atomism might have been incomprehensible to most.

In the 4th century BC, Aristotle threw the weight of his authority against the atomic theory in a general atmosphere of the world, which was quite uncongenial to so worldly and atheistic a philosophy as atomism. When Galen, the celebrated physician of the 2nd century AD, added his veto with that of Aristotle, atoms suffered an eclipse that was to last for about fourteen centuries.

The end of atomism was brought about by constant opposition of Stoicism first and then Stoicism and Christianity. This opposition was so forceful that the name of atomism was thrown in oblivion long before the 7th century. Then in the 7th century, Quran ventured its prophecy about 'Al-Hotama' and enumerated as the causes of the appearance of 'Al-Hotama' very same features that were accurately characteristic of the philosophy of atomism.

The eclipse of atoms, however, cleared at last about the 16th century AD. The philosophies of Aristotle and Plato had held the throne for centuries. These had employed the faculties of ablest men in many successive ages, worn many shapes, mingled themselves with many creeds, and survived revolutions. In those revolutions, empires, religions, languages, and races had perished. These philosophies were fated at last to fall before the new philosophy of 'fruit' and 'utility' as a nastily barren and fruitless exercise of the human mind.

The faith of Christianity met the same fate. For more than fifty generations, this faith had occupied the minds and souls of millions of its adherents. It had controlled their lifespans from birth to death, even after that. However, it could not withstand the irresistible urge of its followers for the feast that Mother Nature had spread before them. The doctrinal inconsistencies that had crept into the Christian religion and the excess of the hierarchies' representatives inspired the unquenchable hatred of the faith. The precedent of the sumptuous feasts enjoyed by the ministers of the Church of God further stimulated their desire for wealth and power. At last, atomism's long-lost and forgotten theory had its day to distract the Church with its followers in every community, country, and part of the world.

After its long disappearance, atomists eventually derived the knowledge of atomic theory from a relic of the poem, 'De Rerum Natura', composed by Lucretius in the 1st Century BC. In that poem, the earliest views of atomists were logically marshaled and brilliantly exposed. Considering the information derived from a relevant piece of this poem, Pierre Gassendi (1592-1655), the Provencal philosopher and Roman Catholic priest, introduced the views of the Greek atomists. Gradually atomism was revived, it spread and soon gained the whole field of human activity: manual, mental, social, scientific, economic, domestic, communal, national, and international. After Pierre Gassendi, Francis Bacon rose as a most brilliant and most persuasive advocate of atomism.

Bacon's design was, by means of inquiries, some of which should be experimental like those of the alchemists but purged from all superstitious taint and directed not toward immediate gain but toward thoroughgoing knowledge, vastly to increase in the long run the dominion of man over Mother Nature. To enjoy such a dominion was, he held, the original destiny of our race. But in vain and impious attempt (described in the Biblical story as "eating of the tree of the knowledge of good and evil") to make laws for himself by 'moral philosophy', instead of remaining content with the positive commands of God, the man had turned aside from his proper business of pursuing 'natural philosophy' that is of studying and interpreting the works of God and raising in his own intelligence a true image of the universe; gaining, in other words, such a knowledge of Mother Nature's inner workings as may make it possible to emulate them. The failure of man hitherto to do this and the depressing tradition that the processes of the chemical combination were necessarily beyond the reach of human imitation showed only that, ancient theories of Mother Nature were merely superficial and had not penetrated her true secrets.

However, in the sweat of his brow, man can yet "eat his bread", that is, through resolute and patient persistence in discriminating observation and well-devised experiment, he may wring these secrets from her (Mother Nature) and turn them to his own advantage. For this, however, a new method of approach was necessary. Bacon endeavored to provide this method in his 'Novum Organum', 'The New Instrument' to replace the old organ, namely, the collection of Aristotle's treatises on logic. These treatises on logic were so-called as constituting the proper instrument to be used in reasoning.

Bacon condemned the moral philosophy of the past ages as a vain and impious attempt. The knowledge of good and evil was merely a Biblical story that was misinterpreted and mistaken. The ancient theories of nature, according to him, were merely superficial, for they did not allow the imitation and emulation of the works of God. The real purpose of man's existence on earth was 'natural philosophy' that is the study and interpretation of the works of God, and to raise in his own intelligence a true image of the universe; in other words, affecting the emulation of the works of God through the knowledge of Mother Nature's secret workings.

Bacon interpreted the Biblical injunction, "But in the sweat of his brow man may yet eat his bread", as man's right of obtaining dominion over Mother Nature and wringing the secrets from her and turning them to his advantage through persistent and patient persistence in determining observation and well-devised experimentation. All this happened to be the gist of the philosophy of atomism. There is not the slightest mention of any consideration of celestial or otherworldly directive, control, or guidance regarding man's purpose or material progress. This world alone is the object of all activity and the sole purpose of life. The object of contemplation of works of God is not in any way glorification of the Creator or reflection of the otherworld. Therefore, Bacon's followers soon adopted the idea of eating up the works of God.

Now, undoubtedly, this design of Bacon is the best specimen of 'slander', 'worldly love', 'wealth-accumulation', and a 'faith in the eternity of this world as the sole object of one's life' together with 'the belief in the endless and eternal progress of wealth' through the increasing dominion of man over natural resources. Thus, atomism is the primary source of features as pointed out by the prophecy as causes of the emergence of the atomic bomb. Bacon had openly expressed his apprehensions regarding the danger of man's taking a short-sighted view and falling to the immediate gains. He was concerned about people leaving the vast Baconian design that increased man's dominion over Mother Nature and raised an accurate image of the universe in man's intelligence. Bacon's fears only came too true.

Men soon fell to immediate gain by 'eating' up the works of God instead of 'contemplating' them. Nowadays, atomic reactors and nuclear processing plants are being purchased with intense eagerness and sold too. These installations indeed constitute a source of the worst kind of a plague. Nevertheless, these are merely in progress because the idea of attaining some material gain is associated with the atomic reactors despite all the incident hazards that must follow the deal.

At the commencement of the European Renaissance, pioneers of atomism developed an implicit belief in the possibility of segregation of the 'atheistic' aspect of atomic theory and their explicit belief in the necessity and desirability of such segregation and their determination to adopt the atomic theory purely in its capacity as the instrument of 'scientific' description and discovery. Despite all this endeavor, the toxic and inevitable implications of the philosophy of atomism crept in, till, in due course, faith was gradually expelled from the field by the atheistic views of atomism which prevailed in every human sphere of mental and practical activity.

This assertion may appear strange in the presence of such overwhelming manifestations of religion that even today flourish globally. This point is a topic in itself and would not admit a fuller treatment in a few lines. In various and diverse forms, religion exists in abundance and constitutes a powerful agency in the more significant part of the world. There is no doubt about it. In some parts of the world, it still fully occupies the minds and maintains its sovereignty. Yet, people have reduced the factual sway of faith to almost a private affair. Even where there is a religion as the main object, its followers interpret it in a light favorable to the materialistic tendency of atomism. The necessities of the present times have made it impossible to see the Anti-Materialistic aspect of faith.

When, however, the world neared its destruction by scientific discoveries, nothing but faith could avert the danger and lead humankind out of trouble. Science has oppressed faith, but it is not dead yet, and humankind may invoke it in distress in the face of the atomic ruin. The appearance of the atomic hell may open the eyes of humankind, and there is a possibility that they may revert to faith to save themselves. In case it is suspected that corruption has crept into religion, then not 'renunciation' but 'reform' ought to be the rule. It is hard to deny that wealth today generally figures as a global deity and has a practical hold on the minds. Faith still holds the mind, and it appears as a lamp outdazzled by the light of love or necessity of wealth in an oppressive materialistic atmosphere. If it is in the destiny of this world yet to live, the re-appearance of faith is a certainty. The science left alone in the realm of affairs will never fail to destroy the world.

If civilization had universally adopted atomism at its emergence in the era of its founder, Democritus, humankind would have perished because of evils of immorality and disbelief. These characteristics are inherent in atomism. If, however, scientific inquiry and progress had commenced at the appearance of atomism in the era of Democritus, the atomic bomb would have appeared at its suitable stage on the path of scientific discovery from atom to the atomic bomb.

Whereas in the modern age, the stage of the atomic bomb arrived after about three centuries from the revival of atomism, in ancient times, it probably might have taken a little longer, though its appearance was a certainty. Indeed, the discovery of the atom on the course of atomism would have led to the atomic bomb. If, on the other hand, the ancient world had adopted the atomic energy for peace and had abstained from the atomic war, even then, humankind would have been long extinct on earth, and no modern age would have appeared. Thanks only to the reproached laxity of Epicureans in scientific investigation and the general un-congeniality of the atmosphere to the growth of atomism that the pre-modern world was saved from the wholesale destruction by the atomic bombs and atomic radiations.

The scientific and the philosophical sides of atomism in the modern age progressed in complete mutual harmony. The scientific side beginning with Dalton's atomic hypothesis in 1803, ended after numerous intermediate stages in the appearance of the atomic bomb in 1945. On the other hand, the philosophical influence of atomism has provided the necessary urge to advance the scientific side. It has created the necessary atmosphere to bring about the catastrophic display of the atomic bomb ultimately.

The logical and scientific consequences of atomism must inevitably appear. The ravenous material utility of works of God in the plague of atomism spread worldwide. It touched an extreme extent and compelled every community to adopt materialism for survival and existence in the prevailing atmosphere to the risky point.

Some have made sporadic and meager attempts to interpret the Quran's agreement with materialism after Baconian interpretation of the Bible. These interpreters thought that because the Quran had allowed the material utility of works of Allah for necessities of life, the material progress of this present age also was exactly in conformity to the views of the Quran.

However, time and experience will be the best judge to announce the error of such a view. The reality of the 'materio-spiritual' [1] balance of the teachings of the Quran may appear in its proper form, either under the hail of atomic bombs or in the invisible network of deadly atomic radiations. But then to what avail? The stockpiles of nuclear weapons that exist today are enough to destroy this world many times, and there is little time left to judge the teachings of the Quran on this point and react accordingly. Maybe that the Judgement is near at hand, and we will soon find this world on fire.

There can be no doubt that the pioneers of modern atomism who happened to venture at adopting the long-lost theory did so solely for its capacity as an instrument of scientific description and discovery in the field of material progress. Being aware of its 'atheistic' aspects, they did revive it with caution and believed that the associated factor of atheism could be and had to be separated. It indeed was the view of Pierre Gassendi, who got the credit for introducing the theory of atomism in the modern age. Ralph Cudworth had the same view also. He otherwise represented atomism as the best system on which we could explain all processes. He reiterated his belief that atomism could have no necessary connection with atheism. The same was the belief of most of those pioneers who adopted the theory of atomism. Bacon was the ablest and most discriminating of all the advocates of atomism. He fully realized some dangers of atomism also.

We understand this from his fears and apprehension. He expressed the shortcomings of the theory and the short-sightedness of his fellow humans. Unfortunately, once humanity adopted the theory, it went into their brains like wine and caused them to forget everything except this world and this life. The pioneers had expected faith to exercise as a balancing power against the purely material aspect of atomism. However, their hopes proved false, religion lost its ground, and materialistic atomism prevailed throughout.

Once the forces of atomism were let loose on earth, the humans expelled every thought of faith, Resurrection, Judgement, and life in

Heaven from their minds, and humans turned into a race of 'wisdomized beasts'; [2] selfish and cruel to the possible extremes. All dead of past ignorant ages would rush out from their graves in panic at the sight of a city in the flaming grip of an atomic explosion. At the same time, the home of this present generation has the hearth to roast all this humankind alive in the atomic hell without so much as a wrinkle on its brow yet with the knowledge that its own destruction too was inevitable along with that of others.

SCIENTIFIC HISTORY OF ATOMISM

Newton and Boyle believed that matter was atomic, but the chemistry did not systematically adopt the atomic theory until John Dalton (1766-1844) took it up. Dalton's modernization of the long-neglected atomic theory marked the end of the previous epoch, which had begun with Copernicus three centuries ago.

Dalton's chief contentions are as follows.

(1) Matter consists of atoms that cannot be created or destroyed. The chemical change consists of the combination of previously apart atoms or the separation of those combined. There is no change in the atoms themselves.

(2) The atoms of a given element are all exactly alike, and they differ, practically in weight, from those of any other element.

It has been necessary to extend and modify these original hypotheses. But in modern dress, they still play a vital part in chemical theory.

The theory of atomism fell on its path to the atom bomb unexpectedly with the almost accidental discovery of rays in 1895 by the German physicist Roentgen. These rays, he named X-rays. It initiated a period of unprecedented progress in physical science. In seeking a possible connection between phosphorescence and X-rays, by a mere chance, the French physicist Antoine Henri Becquerel (1852-1908) chose Uranium Nitrate as the substance for investigation. And he was led unexpectedly in 1896 to the discovery of radioactivity. It, in its turn, soon led to the discovery of Radium by Pierre and Madame Curie.

In 1905, Einstein enunciated the theory of special relativity, and consequently, it established the equivalence between mass and energy. The outstanding work of Rutherford on radiations (named by him as alpha, beta, and gamma rays) emitted from radioactive bodies eventually led to the concept of the atom as made up of a central core, the nucleus (heart), with electrons revolving around it; 'a solar system in miniature'. Bohr incorporated the quantum hypothesis of Plank and Einstein into Rutherford's atom model and thus formulated his far-reaching quantum theory of the atom.

GABRIEL'S EXTINGUISHING THE ATOMIC HELL SERIES

In 1919 Rutherford, for the first time, achieved the disintegration of an element (Nitrogen) by bombarding it with alpha particles. Mr. Blacket soon provided a cloud chamber photograph of the same process. Chadwick, working in Rutherford's laboratories, discovered the neutron in 1932. In the same year and laboratory, Sir John Douglas Cockcroft (1897-1967) and Ernest Thomas Sinton Walton (1903-1995) brought about the first artificial nuclear transmutation by bombarding Lithium with protons accelerated to less than a million volts. The novel discoveries followed in rapid succession.

Uranium fission was discovered by the German physical chemists Otto Hahn and Fritz Strassman in 1938. The extraordinary significance of the discovery was soon realized and led to a period of intense activity in the study of atomic nuclei. By 1940 more than a hundred papers had appeared on this subject. Soon after, the whole subject went underground, and no further reference appeared in open scientific literature until World War II.

The fundamental discoveries leading to the realization of atomic energy came practically all from Western Europe. However, it was not Western Europe but the U.S.A. (soon followed by U.S.S.R.), the first to harness this fundamental knowledge to practical ends with its colossal industrial and scientific resources. On August 2, 1939, Albert Einstein wrote his now-famous letter to President Roosevelt. He drew his attention to the possibility, as indicated by some work of Fermi and Szilard, of utilizing the phenomenon of Uranium fission for the construction of mighty (weight for weight) bombs of a new type, a million times more potent than conventional bombs.

"Single bomb of this type carried by boat and exploded in a port, might very well destroy the whole port together with some of the surrounding territory", said Einstein.

The U.S.A. government decided to explore the possibility seriously. Enrico Fermi successfully realized a slow neutron fission chain reaction in the Graphite-pile built in a converted squash court of the University of Chicago's Stagg-field on December 2, 1942. It is a landmark in the history of nuclear science. It led to the construction of a gigantic plant at Hanford on the banks of the Columbia River to produce Plutonium. Following Uranium diffusion, they built a plant to produce Uranium-235 from natural Uranium at Oakridge, and another plant at Oakridge produced Uranium-235 employing the principle of electromagnetic separation. The design of a workable atom bomb was entrusted to the New Los Alamos Laboratory, New Mexico, working under the leadership of Robert Oppenheimer.

They produced three bombs by the middle of 1945. One made of Plutonium was tested on the ground at the Alamogordo sands on July 16, 1945. The other two were dropped on Hiroshima and Nagasaki on August 6 and 9, 1945, respectively. Fermi, who had achieved the first fission chain reaction, successfully failed to protect himself against the deleterious reaction of radiation he had played with and soon succumbed to radiation sickness. [3]

August 6, 1945, is an unforgettable date. On the early morning of this tragic day, the first atomic (U-235) bomb, 'Little Boy', fell on Hiroshima, killing 66,000 persons (on the spot) and injuring another 69,000. It exploded with energy between 13 and 18 kilotons of TNT. [4] The second atomic (Pu-239) bomb 'Fat Man' was dropped on Nagasaki on August 9, 1945. It killed an estimated 39,000 people outright, and a further 25,000 were injured. Thousands more died later from the related blast and burn injuries and hundreds more from radiation sickness from exposure to the bomb's initial radiation. They detonated it at an altitude of about 1,800 feet (550 m). The bomb had a yield of about 21 kilotons of TNT.

The two bombs were average about the same power, but due to Nagasaki's somewhat uneven hilly terrain, casualties were less than Hiroshima. The bombs exploded on average about 2,000 feet above ground to obtain the maximum area of damage as nearly as possible due to the explosion's blast. The death rate was above 90 percent within half a mile of ground zero (the point on the ground immediately below the burst), above 50 percent between half a mile and one and a half miles. Structural damage was complete, including the collapse of earthquake-resistant reinforced concrete buildings within half a mile from ground zero. It destroyed most of the houses within one and a half miles. Houses up to two miles were severely damaged and slightly damaged up to about three miles. Because of the very high temperature produced, the explosions emitted intense heat radiation causing fatal burns (and almost instantaneous deaths due to the intense heat and shock of the 'Heat-Flash') to exposed persons within about three-quarters of a mile of ground zero.

In the Hiroshima and Nagasaki tragedy, most casualties were due to the combined effects of burns and mechanical injuries. However, estimates show about 60 percent of deaths (almost 75% of all casualties) were caused by burning through 'Heat-Flash' and fires. About 20% of deaths were due to physical injuries from falling structures and flying debris (resulting from blast damage). 20% of deaths were due to other causes, including nuclear radiation (gamma rays). Radiation, too, is fire originally. Out of Hiroshima's 75,000 houses, about 55,000 were burnt entirely, and 7000 were utterly destroyed. The damages sounded terrible and the figures imposing, but the later developments in nuclear weapons have dwarfed the Hiroshima and Nagasaki bombs into mere toy bombs. The damages expected from the giant thermonuclear bombs are of a different caliber. They destroy not cities but states.

HELL BOMB

The first Soviet atomic, ordinary fission, like the Hiroshima bomb, took place in August 1949. On September 23, 1949, President Truman announced that the U.S.A. government had incontrovertible proof that the Russians had detonated a fission device. The U.S.A. government immediately decided to go ahead with the thermonuclear bomb (the so-called H or Super bomb). Moreover, on January 31, 1950, Truman directed the atomic energy commission with David Lilienthal as chairman and its general advisory committee with Robert Oppenheimer as chairman, where opinions had sharply divided on the speed and scale of the efforts to go on into the Super bomb. It perhaps put the conscience of the scientists to a severe test.

After seeing the catastrophe in Hiroshima and Nagasaki, even the national defense considerations could, with some difficulty, induce some scientists to produce yet another even more terrific atomic bomb than the Hiroshima patterns. Conscience, after all, smites. And its stings may be painful. Also, another consideration was that producing more powerful atomic bombs was no remedy for the great wrong which nuclear weapons production had already done. The production of a more powerful atomic bomb no doubt meant to bring even greater destruction on their people, too, for a more fantastic bomb would be retaliated by a yet more incredible bomb.

However, the plea of national defense superseded every other consideration. A very brilliant and indeed very enthusiastic atomist named Edward Teller successfully experimented with a thermonuclear device. On November 1, 1952, the U.S.A. first tested the thermonuclear device at Marshal Islands in the Pacific Ocean. Russia followed suit. The first Soviet thermonuclear explosion took place in August 1953. The U.S.A. set off a powerful thermonuclear explosion at Bikini Atoll on March 1, 1954; the energy of the explosion was equivalent to about 15 megatons of TNT. In November 1955, the Russians had a thermonuclear explosion about as powerful as the U.S.A. test of March 1954. Britain, France, China, India, and Israel came in the wake like the legendary.

During the March 1954 explosion at Bikini Atoll in the Pacific Ocean, an unfortunate fact dawned on the atomic powers to their horror, namely, that the atomic bomb was a very treacherous slave. It could also rebound towards its own master who unleashed it on his foe and thus bring about the ruin of both, nay, even of other neutral people all over the globe. It happened that a Japanese fishing boat 'Lucky Dragon' with a crew of 23, was lying 90 miles from the testing site. Its misfortune appeared in the form of powdery fallout of the explosion. It began to settle on it to announce to the world that the thermonuclear bomb constituted a severe radiological hazard that could not be kept secret. The frightened crew of the boat rushed towards Japan and, sailing 2,000 miles in about 13 days, reached the port, all sick with radiations. There, the radio operator died after a few months, but doctors saved the rest eventually.

It was, however, proved beyond any doubt that any nation could maintain no secrecy about the thermonuclear explosion. The news about the potential hazard of radioactive fallout from thermonuclear weapons burst out of deep secrecy. Twenty-three Japanese fishermen announced to the world the first fateful news about the lurking catastrophe that lay in wait for all of us. All the official secrecy proved inept, and the mysterious Providence of Allah decided otherwise. Besides, when the secret came out through unexpected channels, the shock of the world opinion rivaled the blast of the Hydrogen bomb itself. It also proved that no one on the entire earth was safe from the radiation hazards of the thermonuclear bomb explosion, for the air currents in the upper regions of the atmosphere circulated the fallout of the thermonuclear bomb around the earth, the fallout gradually settling all over the globe.

~~*~*~*

---

[1] The term **materio-spiritual** coined by the author means 'material-spiritual'.

[2] The term **wisdomized beasts** coined by the author means 'beasts having the wisdom of human species'.

[3] "**Fermi** died at age 53 of stomach cancer (a result of heavy exposures to radiation) in Chicago, Illinois, and was interred at Oak Woods Cemetery. Two of his graduate students who assisted him in working on or near the nuclear pile also died of cancer. Fermi and his team knew that such work carried considerable risk, but they considered the outcome so vital that they forged ahead with little regard for their safety. Eugene Wigner wrote, 'Ten days before Fermi had died, he told me, 'I hope it won't take long.' He had reconciled himself perfectly to his fate'."

(Wikipedia, the free Encyclopedia)

[4] [(a) "**The Damage:** The atomic bomb dropped on Hiroshima at 8:15 a.m., August 6, 1945. It detonated 580 meters in the air. Though we don't know exactly how many perished in the bombing, it is estimated that 140,000 (plus or minus 10,000) had died by the end of December 1945."

(b) "**Characteristics of A-bomb Damage:** The atomic bomb was quite different from all previous bombs. At the moment of detonation, powerful radiation and a fierce heat ray were emitted. As the rising temperature expanded the surrounding air, it generated a tremendous blast. The complex interaction of these factors amplified the damage. The three energies heat ray, blast, and radiation caused instantaneous mass destruction and indiscriminate mass slaughter."

(c) **Damage from the Heat Ray:** The temperature at the center of the fireball generated by the atomic bomb at the moment of detonation was more than 1 million degrees Celsius. One second later, the fireball had grown to its maximum diameter of 280 meters. The fierce heat ray emitted from that fireball raised surface temperatures at the hypocenter to 3,000 °C to 4000 °C. (The surface temperature of the sun is 5,700 °C; iron melts at 1500 °C.)

(d) **Damage from the A-bomb Blast:** At the instant of detonation, the heat expanded the air suddenly, generating a blast carrying pressure of several hundred thousand atmospheres. At 500 meters from the hypocenter, the atmospheric pressure per square meter was a huge 19 tons (roughly fifteen automobiles), powerful enough to collapse almost every structure. People were killed when the blast threw them or collapsed the buildings they were in.

(e) **Damage from Radiation:** The atomic bomb differed from previous bombs that used chemical explosives. It emitted energy at an entirely different level of magnitude, and it also emitted radiation. In Hiroshima, a vast amount of initial radiation was emitted within a minute after the bomb detonated. It caused terrible injuries to people's bodies. Almost all those who directly absorbed the radiation within one kilometer of the hypocenter died. Residual radiation remained in the city. Because of this, even people who were not directly exposed but who came near the hypocenter for rescue and relief operations or to search for their families absorbed radiation. Many fell ill and some died.

(www.pcf.city.hiroshima.jp]

~~*~*~*

CHAPTER-2

DOCTRINAL IMPLICATIONS OF THE THEORY OF ANCIENT GREEK ATOMISM

Leucippus, the originator, and Democritus, the developer and introducer of the atomic theory, were both atheists. This odious association with the name of these founders of atomism offered a significant setback to the theory. Apart from the atheism of its founders, the theory is, in fact, the mother of atheism. It implies the negation of design, plan, purpose, Resurrection, Judgement, trial, and a divine government. Its atheistic nature was not unknown to the people of those times in which it was advanced. The sect of Epicureans adopted this theory purely for its atheistic aspect. Plato, Aristotle, and all the great contemporary thinkers of Greece opposed and condemned such a theory. Their influence being considerable, their opposition proved to be an effective check on atomism.

Yet, it was reserved for a Scripture, namely, the Holy Quran, to describe modern atomism and give it out as the cause and to infer from it the appearance of atomic hell of the atomic bombs and atomic radiations by describing the characteristics of atomic phenomena. It warned humankind against nuclear danger at a time in the 7th century AD when neither a trace of ancient atomism existed nor any apparent possibility of its revival in the world in any successive age.

We will here discuss the doctrinal implications of the theory of ancient atomism.

THE VIEWS OF EARLY GREEK ATOMISM

(1) "Atoms move about in all directions in a <u>fortuitous</u> concourse in an otherwise empty space."

This notion implies a negation of design, the divine government of the world, the purpose of creation, and the trial of man on earth. These negations further imply the negation of the necessity of Resurrection, Judgement, and life in Heaven.

(2) **"Atoms are <u>indivisible</u> and <u>indestructible</u>."**

This view implies the eternity of this material universe and hence excludes any possibility of Resurrection.

(3) **"The motion of atoms persists until checked presumably in collision with another atom since the theory denies any other cause."**

It again appears to be an attempt to refute the idea of the divine agency since Aristotle's view was that the hand of divine power was necessary to push the things to keep them in motion.

(4) **"Atoms and space are all that exists."**

It is a denial of the existence of any spiritual or divine agency in the creation.

(5) **"The arrangement makes the things, we touch and see, of atoms in groups."**

Scientifically this view indeed bears some truth. However, the philosophical intent behind it appears to negate any spiritual or divine controlling agency. One must consider the arrangement of atoms that move in a fortuitous concourse without any design or control as 'accidental'. It implies a negation of any design or control authority.

(6) **"There are different kinds of atoms distinguished by difference of shape, but individual atoms are too small to be noticed by the senses."**

This view is scientific and is correct, and we may take it as the beginning of the scientific research of the material universe. Indeed, a science to be based exclusively on the purpose of material benefit as the object of man's life on earth is liable to end in a material explosion.

~~*~*~*

CHAPTER-3

THE VIEWS OF THE QURAN VERSUS THE VIEWS OF THE EARLY GREEK ATOMIC THEORY

At times instead of the number of the only part of the Quran quoted, the reader may find the number to refer to a broader text to furnish the occasion of gaining a greater understanding of the point thus referred.

THE VIEWS OF EARLY GREEK ATOMISM

(1) "ATOMS MOVE ABOUT IN ALL DIRECTIONS IN A FORTUITOUS CONCOURSE IN AN OTHERWISE EMPTY SPACE."

The Quran allows no such fortuitous concourse of atoms. Instead, everything moves under strict vigilance and control of the Creator consistent with a perfect design and for an exact purpose.

The Quran says:

(a) "He (Allah) ordereth the course."

(Quran 13:2)

(b) "Our Lord (Allah) is He Who gave unto everything its nature, then guided it aright."

(Quran 20:50)

(c) "And not an atom's weight in the earth or the sky escapeth your Lord, nor what is less than that or greater than that, but it is (written) in a clear Book."

(Quran 10:61)

(d) "... And with Him are the keys of the Invisible. None but He knoweth them. And He knoweth what is in the land and the sea. Not a leaf falleth but He knoweth it, not a grain amid the darkness of the earth, naught of wet or dry but (it is noted) in a clear record."

(Quran 6:59)

(e) "(Luqman to his son) O my dear son! Lo! Though it be but the weight of a grain of mustard seed, and though it be in a rock, or the heavens, or the earth, Allah will bring it forth. Allah is Subtle, Aware."

(Quran 31:16)

(f) "And there is nothing hidden in the heaven or the earth, but it is in a clear Record."

(Quran 27: 75)

(g) "And We have created above you seven paths, and We are never unmindful of creation."

(Quran 23:17)

THE DOCTRINAL IMPLICATIONS OF THE VIEW OF FORTUITOUS CONCOURSE OF ATOMS NEGATED BY THE QURAN

(a) **Fortuitous concourse of atoms negated divine government of the world, design, process, and Resurrection.**

However, the Quran has contradictory views on these points.
It says:

"He (Allah) directeth the ordinance from the heavens unto the earth; then it ascendeth unto Him in a Day, whereof the measure is a thousand years of that ye reckon. Such is the Knower of the invisible and the visible, the Mighty, the Merciful, Who made all things good which He created, and He began the creation of man from clay; Then He made his seed from a draught of despised fluid; Then He fashioned him and breathed into him of His spirit, and appointed for you hearing and sight and hearts. Small thanks give ye! And they say: When we are lost in the earth, how can we then be recreated? Nay, but they are disbelievers in the meeting with their Lord."

(Quran 32:5-10)

(b) **Fortuitous concourse of atoms negates divine command.**
While the Quran says:

(i) "Unto Allah belongeth the Sovereignty of the heavens and the earth. Allah is Able to do all things."

(Quran 3:189)

(ii) "He is the Omnipotent over His slaves, and He is the Wise, the Knower."

(Quran 6:18)

(iii) "Lo! Allah! Unto Him belongeth the Sovereignty of the heavens and the earth. He quickeneth me and He giveth death, and ye have, instead of Allah, no protecting friend, nor helper."

(Quran 9:116)

(iv) "He it is Who created the heavens and the earth in truth. In the day when He saith: Be! It is. His Word is the Truth, and His will be the Sovereignty on the day when the trumpet is blown. Knower of the Invisible and the Visible, He is the Wise, the Aware."

(Quran 6:73)

(v) "Allah is Creator of all things, and He is Guardian over all things. His are the keys of the heavens and the earth, and they who disbelieve the revelations of Allah --- such are they who are the losers."

(Quran 39:62-63)

(vi) "Your Allah is One Allah; there is no God save Him, the Beneficent, the Merciful."

(Quran 2:163)

(vii) "And of His signs is this: The heavens and the earth stand fast by His command, and afterward, when He calleth you, lo! From the earth, ye will emerge. Unto Him belongeth whosoever is in the heavens and the earth. All are obedient unto Him. He it is Who produceth creation then reproduceth it, and it is easier for Him. His is the Sublime Similitude in the heavens and the earth. He is the Mighty, the Wise."

(Quran 30:25-27)

(viii) "Have they not seen in the birds obedient in mid-air (made subservient to the law of Allah)? None holdeth them, save Allah. Lo! Herein, verily, are portents for a people who believe."

(Quran 16:79)

(ix) "He unto Whom belongeth the Sovereignty of the heavens and the earth. He hath chosen no son nor hath He any partner in the Sovereignty. He hath created everything and hath meted out for it a measure."

(Quran 25:2)

(x) "Thy Lord bringeth to pass what He willeth and chooseth. They never have any choice. Glorified be Allah and exalted above all that they associate (with Him)! And thy Lord knoweth what their breasts conceal, and what they publish. And He is Allah; there is no God save Him. His is all praise in the former and the latter (state), and His is the command, and unto Him, ye will be brought back. Say: Have ye thought if Allah made night everlasting for you till the Day of Resurrection, who is a God beside Allah who could bring you light? Will ye not then hear? Say: Have ye thought if Allah made day everlasting for you till the Day of Resurrection, who is a God beside Allah who could bring you night wherein ye rest? Will ye not then see? Of His mercy hath He appointed for you night and day that therein ye may rest, and that ye may seek His bounty, and that haply ye may be thankful."

(Quran 28:68-73)

(xi) "O company of Jinn and men, if ye have power to penetrate (all) regions of the heavens and the earth; then penetrate (them)! Ye will never penetrate them save with (Our) sanction."

(Quran 55:33)

(xii) "Lo! Your Lord is Allah, Who created the heavens and the earth in six Days and then mounted He the Throne. He covereth the night with the day, which is in haste to follow it, and hath made the sun and the moon and the stars subservient by His command. His verily is all creation and commandment. Blessed be Allah, the Lord of the Worlds!"

(Quran 7:54)

(c) **The fortuitous concourse of atoms negates divine control and vigilance.** While the Quran says:

(i) "Lo! Allah hath been a watcher over you."

(Quran 4:1)

(ii) "Lo! Allah graspeth the heavens and the earth, and they deviate not, and if they were to deviate, there is not one that could grasp them after him. Lo! He is ever Clement, Forgiving."

(Quran 35:41)

(iii) "He knoweth all that entereth the earth and all that emergeth therefrom and all that cometh down from the sky and all that ascendeth therein, and He is with you wheresoever ye may be. And Allah is Seer of what ye do."

(Quran 57:4)

(iv) "Lo! Allah is witness over all things." (Quran 22:17)

(v) "And we are never unmindful of creation."

(Quran 23:17)

(vi) "He is the Omnipotent over His slaves. He sendeth guardians over you."

(Quran 6:61)

(d) **Fortuitous concourse of atoms negates divine order of the world, but the Quran negates this negation.**
It says:

(i) "Say (unto them, O Muhammad): Who provideth for you from the sky and the earth, or Who owneth hearing and sight; and Who bringeth forth the living from the dead and bringeth forth the dead from the living; and Who directeth the course? They will say: Allah. Then say: Will ye not then keep your duty (unto Him)? Such then is Allah, your rightful Lord. After the Truth, what is there beyond error? How then have ye turned away?"

(Quran 10:31-32)

(ii) "We have neglected nothing in the Book (of Our decrees)."
(Quran 6:38)
(iii) "It is not for the sun to overtake the moon, nor doth the night over strip the day. They float each in orbit."
(Quran 36:40)
(iv) "My Lord includeth all things in His knowledge; will ye not then remember?"
(Quran 6:80)
(v) "And the sky hath He uplifted, and He hath set the measure that ye exceed not the measure."
(Quran 55:7-8)
(vi) "And everything with Him is measured." (Quran 13:8)
(vii) "He it is Who appointed the sun a splendor and the moon a light and measured for her stages, that ye might know the number of the years and the reckoning."
(Quran 10:5)
(viii) "And for all, there will be ranks from what they do, that He may pay them for their deeds! And they will not be wronged."
(Quran 46:19)

(e) **Fortuitous concourse of atoms negates the plan and design of the Creator.**
While the Quran says:
(i) "Praise be to Allah, Who hath created the heavens and the earth, and hath appointed darkness and light. Yet those who disbelieve ascribe rivals unto their Lord. He it is Who hath created you from clay, and hath decreed a term for you. A term is fixed with Him. Yet still, ye doubt!"
(Quran 6:1-2)
(ii) "He hath created the heavens without supports that ye can see and hath cast into the earth firm hills so that it quakes not with you, and He hath dispersed therein all kinds of beasts. And We send down water from the sky, and We cause (plants) of every goodly kind to grow therein."
(Quran 31:10)
(iii) "And Allah hath created the heavens and the earth with truth, and that every soul may be repaid what it hath earned. And they will not be wronged."
(Quran 45:22)
(iv) "Who hath created life and death that He may try you, which of you is best in conduct; and He is the Mighty, Forgiving."
(Quran 67:2)

(v) "And when thy Lord said unto the angels: Lo! I am about to place a viceroy in the earth."

(Quran 2:30)

(vi) "Allah! There is no God save Him. He gathereth you all unto a Day of Resurrection whereof there is no doubt. Who is truer in statement than Allah?"

(Quran 4:87)

(vii) "And the trumpet is blown, and all who are in the heavens and the earth swoon away, save him whom Allah willeth. Then it is blown a second time, and behold them standing waiting! And the earth shineth with the light of her Lord, and the Book is set up, and the Prophets and the witnesses are brought, and it is judged between them with truth, and they are not wronged. And each soul is paid in full for what it did. And He is best aware of what they do. And those who disbelieve are driven unto hell in troops till, when they reach it and the gates thereof are opened, and the warders thereof say unto them: Came there not unto you messengers of your own, reciting unto you the revelations of your Lord and warning you of the meeting of this your Day? They say Yea, verily. But the word of doom for disbelievers is fulfilled. It is said (unto them): Enter ye the gates of hell to dwell therein. Thus, hapless is the journey's end of the scorners. And those who keep their duty to their Lord are driven unto the Garden in troops till when they reach it, and the gates thereof are opened, and the warders thereof say unto them: Peace be unto you! Ye are good, so enter ye (the Garden of delight), to dwell therein; they say: Praise be to Allah, Who hath fulfilled His promise unto us and hath made us inherit the land, sojourning in the Garden where we will! So bounteous is the wage of workers. And thou (O Muhammad) seest the angels thronging round the Throne, hymning the praises of their Lord. And they are judged aright. And it is said: Praise be to Allah, the Lord of the worlds!"

(Quran 39:68-75)

(f) **Fortuitous Concourse of atoms negates divine process.**
While the Quran says:
(i) "Allah effaceth what He will, and establisheth (what He will), and with Him is the source of ordinance."

(Quran 13:39)

(ii) "Lo! Allah (it is) Who splitteth the grain of corn and the date-stone (for sprouting). He bringeth forth the living from the dead and is the bringer forth of the dead from the living. Such is Allah. How then are ye perverted? He is the Cleaver of the Daybreak, and He hath appointed the night for stillness, and the sun and the moon for reckoning. That is the measuring of the Mighty, the Wise. And He it is Who hath set for you the stars that ye may guide your course by them amid the darkness of the land and the sea. We have detailed Our revelations for people who have knowledge. And He it is Who hath produced you from a single being, and (hath given you) a habitation and a repository. We have detailed Our revelations for people who have understanding. He it is Who sendeth down water from the sky, and therewith We bring forth buds of every kind; We bring forth the green blade from which we bring forth the thick clustered grain; and from the date palm, from the pollen thereof, spring pendant bunches; and (We bring forth) gardens of grapes, and the olive and the pomegranate, alike and unlike. Look upon the fruit thereof, when they bear fruit, and upon its ripening. Lo! Herein verily are portents for a people who believe. Yet they ascribe as partners unto Him the Jinn, although He did create them, and impute falsely, without knowledge, sons, and daughters unto Him. Glorified be He and high exalted above (all) that they ascribe (unto Him)."

(Quran 6:95-100)

(iii) "He it is Who fashioneth you in the wombs as pleaseth Him. There is no Lord save Him, the mighty, the Wise."

(Quran 3:6)

(iv) "Verily We created man from a product of wet earth; Then placed him as a drop (of seed) in a safe lodging; Then fashioned We the drop a clot, then fashioned We the clot a little lump, then fashioned We the little lump bones, then clothed the bones with flesh, and then produced it another creation. So blessed be Allah, the Best of Creators! Then lo! After that, ye surely die. Then lo! On the Day of Resurrection, ye are resurrected (again). And We have created above you seven paths, and We are never unmindful of creation."

(Quran 23:12-17)

(v) "Hast thou not seen how Allah wafteth the clouds, then gathereth them, then maketh them layers, and thou seest the rain come forth from between them; He sendeth down from the heaven mountains wherein is hail, and smiteth therewith whom He will, and averteth it from whom He will. The flashing of His lightning all but snatcheth away the sight."

(Quran 24:43)

(vi) "And thy Lord inspired the bee, saying: Choose thou habitations in the hills and the trees and in that which they thatch; Then eat of all fruits, and follow the ways of thy Lord, made smooth (for thee). There cometh forth from their bellies a drink diverse of hues, wherein is healing for humankind. Lo! Herein is indeed a portent for people who reflect."

(Quran 16:68-69)

(g) **Fortuitous concourse of atoms negates divine purpose, or any purpose of creation, while the Quran has based the creation on a specific purpose.** Read the following.

(i) "And Allah hath created the heavens and the earth with truth, and that every soul may be repaid what it hath earned. And they will not be wronged."

(Quran 45:22)

(ii) "Allah it is Who raised the heavens without visible supports, then mounted the Throne and compelled the sun and the moon to be of service, each runneth unto an appointed term; He ordereth the course; He detaileth the revelations, that haply ye may be certain of the meeting with your Lord."

(Quran 13:2)

(iii) "And We created not the heavens and the earth, and all that is between them, in play. We created them, not save with truth, but most of them know not.

Assuredly the Day of Decision is the term of all of them, a day when a friend can, in naught avail friends, nor can they be helped, save him on whom Allah hath mercy. Lo! He is the Mighty, the Merciful."

(Quran 44:38-42)

(iv) "And We created not the heavens and the earth and all that is between them in vain. That is the opinion of those who disbelieve. And woe unto those who disbelieve, from the fire!"

(Quran 38:27)

(v) "Deemed ye then that we created you for naught and that ye would not be returned unto Us?"

(Quran 23:115)

(vi) "(Allah) Hath created death and life that He may try you, which of you is best in conduct."

(Quran 67:2)

(vii) "He it is Who hath placed you as viceroys of the earth, and hath exalted some of you in rank above others, that He may try you by (the test of) that which He hath given you. Lo! Thy Lord is swift in prosecution, and Lo! He is forgiving, Merciful."

(Quran 6:165)

(viii) "I created the Jinn and humankind only that they might worship Me. I seek no livelihood from them, nor do I ask that they should feed Me."

(Quran 51:56-57)

(ix) "Lo! In the creation of the heavens and the earth and (in) the difference of night and day are tokens (of His Sovereignty) for men of understanding, such as remember Allah, standing, sitting, and reclining, and consider the creation of the heavens and the earth, (and say): Our Lord! Thou createdst not this in vain. Glory be to Thee! Preserve us from the doom of Fire."

(Quran 3:190-191)

(x) "Every soul will taste of death. And ye will be paid on the Day of Resurrection only that which ye have fairly earned. Whoso is removed from the Fire and is made to enter Paradise; he indeed is triumphant. The life of this world is but the comfort of illusion."

(Quran 3:185)

(h) Fortuitous concourse of atoms negates the moral philosophy and moral laws indirectly.

It is a very touchy point. And though the vulgar might find it challenging to comprehend, the subtle advocate of atomism and the founder of atomism in this modern age, namely, Bacon, clearly perceived this delicate point in ancient atomism.

He openly condemned the pursuit of moral philosophy as the repetition of Adam's first transgression of God's commands that forbade him the fruit of the tree of the knowledge of good and evil. He maintained that man had undertaken moral philosophy merely to give himself the law (Bacon's 'Advancement of Learning').

Moreover, ancient Greek atomism had no room for moral philosophy, which is a crucial point. For, the revealed religion is based on the very foundation of moral philosophy. Quran, like every other Scripture, has its basis on moral philosophy. As stated by the Quran, the set of laws that functions in the physical universe emanates from the origin of moral philosophy.

It says:

- "And the sky He hath uplifted; and He hath set the measure. That ye exceed not the measure but observe the measure strictly, nor fall short thereof."

(Quran 55:7-9)

The Quran urges strict adherence to moral laws and man's covenant with Allah.

It says:
- "Lo! Allah enjoineth justice and kindness, and giving to kinsfolk, and forbiddeth lewdness and abomination and wickedness. He exhorteth you in order that ye may take heed. Fulfill the covenant of Allah when ye have covenanted, and break not your oaths after the asseveration of them, and after ye have made Allah surety over you. Lo! Allah knoweth what ye do."

(Quran 16:90-91)

- "Ye are the best community that hath been raised for humankind. Ye enjoin right conduct and forbid indecency, and ye believe in Allah."

(Quran 3:110)

(2) "ATOMS ARE INDIVISIBLE AND INDESTRUCTIBLE."

Now, the modern discoveries of science have repudiated this assertion by dividing and destroying atoms. The Quran explained this fact fourteen hundred years ago. It says:

"Hotama" (Quran 104:4)

'Hotama' is a kind of fire and means crusher, breaker, etc. The Quran's description of this kind of fire shows that it breaks the nuclei of atoms. The notion of the indestructibility of atoms implied the eternity of this physical universe, which further implied a negation of the possibility of Resurrection, Judgement, and life in Heaven. While according to the Quran, this present universe is transient only, and the fact of Resurrection and the other life in Heaven is a certainty.

(a) The universe, according to the Quran, is not eternal but transient.

It says:

"Allah it is Who raised the heavens without visible supports, then mounted the Throne and compelled the sun and the moon to be of service, each runneth unto an appointed term; He ordereth the course; He detaileth the revelations, that haply ye may be certain of the meeting with your Lord."

(Quran 13:2)

(b) Life, according to the Quran, is not eternal.

It says:

(i) "And coin for them the similitude of the life of the world as water which We send down from the sky, and the vegetation of the earth mingleth with it and then becometh dry twigs that the winds scatter. Allah is Able to do all things."

(Quran 18:45)

(ii) "Everyone that is thereon will pass away; there remaineth but the countenance of thy Lord of Might and Glory."

(Quran 55:26-27)

(c) **The notion implied by ancient atomism that the life of this present world is the only life is erroneous, according to the Quran.**
It says:
"And they say: There is naught save our life of the world, and we shall not be raised (again). If thou couldst see when they are set before their Lord! He will say: Is not this real? They will say: Yea, verily, by our Lord! He will say: Taste now the retribution for that ye used to disbelieve."

(Quran 6:29-30)

(d) **The Quran promises the disintegration of this universe.**
It says:
"The Day when We shall roll up the heavens and a recorder rolleth up a written scroll. As We began the first creation, We shall repeat it. (It is) a promise (binding) upon Us. Lo! We are to perform it."

(Quran 21:104)

(e) **Resurrection is asserted by the Quran.**
It says:
"We created not the heavens, and the earth and all that is between them save with truth, and lo! The Hour is surely coming."

(Quran 15:85)

(f) **Resurrection is argued by the Quran.**
It says:
"Thinketh man that he is to be left aimless? Was he not a drop of fluid that gushed forth? Then he became a clot; then (Allah) shaped and fashioned and made of him a pair, the male and female. Is not He (Who doeth so) able to bring the dead to life?"

(Quran 75:36-40)

(g) **Resurrection is exemplified by the Quran.**
It says:
"And Allah it is Who sendeth the winds and they raise a cloud; then We lead it unto a dead land and revive therewith the earth after its death. Such is the Resurrection."

(Quran 35:9)

(h) **The Quran insists upon the necessity of realizing the fact of Resurrection.**
It says:
"Say (O Muhammad): Travel in the land and see how He originated creation, then Allah bringeth forth the later growth. Lo! Allah is Able to

do all things. He punisheth whom He will and showeth mercy unto whom He will, and unto Him, ye will be turned."

(Quran 29:20-21)

According to the Quran, the purpose of discovering the origin of life is to realize the certainty of second life. Darwin is famed for his pursuit of the origin of life. There is no such thought as second life in the course of his research.

(i) **The universe, unlike the early Greek atomists, is regarded desirable by the Quran and is followed inevitably by Resurrection and Judgement and life in Heaven.**

The Quran says:

- "When the sun is overthrown, And when the stars fall, And when the hills are moved, And when the camels big with young are abandoned, And when the wild beasts are herded together, And when the seas rise, And when souls are reunited, And when the girl-child that was buried alive is asked, for what sin she was slain, And when the pages are laid open, And when the sky is torn away, And when the hell is lighted, And when the garden is brought nigh, (Then) every soul will know what it hath made ready."

(Quran 81:1-14)

- "And when the trumpet shall sound one blast, and the earth with the mountains shall be lifted and crushed with one crash, then, on that day will the Event befall. And the heaven will split asunder, for that day it will be frail. And the angels will be on the sides thereof, and eight will uphold the Throne of their Lord that day, above them. On that day, ye will be exposed; not a secret of you will be hidden. Then, as for him who is given his record in his right hand, he will say: Take, read my book! Surely, I knew that I should have to meet my reckoning. Then he will be in a blissful state, in a high Garden whereof the clusters are in easy reach. (And it will be said unto those therein): Eat and drink at ease for that which ye sent on before you in past days. But as for him who is given his record in his left hand, he will say: Oh, would that I had not been given my book. And knew not what my reckoning! Oh, would that it had been death! My wealth hath not availed me; my power hath gone from me. (It will be said): Take him and fetter him, and then expose him to hellfire, and then insert him in a chain whereof the length is seventy cubits. Lo! He used not to believe in Allah the Tremendous and urged not on the feeding of the wretched, nor any food, save filth, which none but sinners eat."

(Quran 69:13-37)

We have described the imageries of hell and Paradise here so that the two paradises, this one of modern Baconian type and one promised by Allah in the next world, may be seen in comparison. Similarly, the two types of hells are this one of this Baconian atomic age and the other one of the next world after death on Resurrection.

(3) "THE MOTION OF ATOMS PERSISTS UNTIL CHECKED PRESUMABLY IN COLLISION WITH ANOTHER ATOM SINCE THE THEORY DENIES ANY OTHER CAUSE."

This idea of early atomism stands in radical opposition to that of Aristotle, whose view was that some pushing hand was necessary to move things. The problem appears more of a pre-disposed imagination than is based on any experimental data. Aristotle believed in God and the divine government of the world. Consequently, he was naturally inclined to the idea of a divine hand's presence in the universe's functioning. However, the early Greek atomists were in the mood of freeing this world from divine implications. The Quran is on the side of Aristotle, and the motion in the universe is essentially attributed to Allah. Modern science, however, has discovered the view of early atomists as a guide to the principle of inertia. However, inertia is perceptible to a particular stage in the realm of physics; after that, the field may presumably be left to the Creator's divine power. Conventionality in such a matter is not objectionable since ultimate reality is out of the pale of science.

The Quran says:

(a) "Hast thou not seen how Allah wafteth the clouds, then gathereth them, then maketh them layers?"

(Quran 24:43)

(b) "O, humankind, Your Lord is He Who driveth for you the ship upon the sea that ye may seek of His bounty. Lo! He was ever Merciful toward you."

(Quran 17:66)

(c) "He (Allah) covereth the night with the day, which is in haste to follow it, and hath made the sun and the moon and the stars subservient by His command. His verily is all creation and commandment. Blessed be Allah, the Lord of the worlds!"

(Quran 7:54)

(d) "Say: Have ye thought if Allah made night everlasting for you till the Day of Resurrection, who is a God beside Allah who could bring you light? Will ye not then hear? Say: Have ye thought if Allah made day everlasting for you till the Day of Resurrection, who is a God beside Allah who could bring you night wherein ye rest? Will ye not then see?"

(Quran 28:71-72)

(e) "And of His portents are the ships, like banners on the sea; if He wills, He calmeth the wind so that they keep still upon its surface Lo! Herein verily are signs for every steadfast grateful (heart)."

(Quran 42:32-33)

(f) "O company of Jinn and men, if ye have power to penetrate (all) regions of the heavens and the earth; then penetrate (them)! Ye will never penetrate them save with (Our) sanction."

(Quran 55:33)

(g) "And of His signs is this: He sendeth herald winds to make you taste His mercy, and that the ships may sail at His command, and that ye may seek His favor, and that haply ye may be thankful."

(Quran 30:46)

Mark that Allah has claimed to do all these things out of man's power, and only Allah can do. See also that there are two ways of saying a thing: either by resorting to the description of a natural process or simply attributing work to the Will and Power of Allah. Moreover, when Allah claims to command the sun, the moon, and other natural phenomena, He speaks as the Originator and the Supervisor of the universe. Quran always speaks from the viewpoint of Allah, the Creator. You may see it when Allah challenges the false gods to create but a piece of straw. It perhaps does not refer to the preparation by some synthetic methods but originally and without taking the material from Allah's world.

(4) "ATOMS AND SPACE ARE ALL THAT EXISTS."

It is a denial of spirituality while, according to the Quran, there are spiritual beings in the world, and it mentions the existence of angels, Jinn, and other unknown creations.

The Quran says:

(a) "Almost might the heavens above be rent asunder while the angels hymn the praise of their Lord and ask forgiveness for those on the earth. Lo! Allah is the Forgiver, the Merciful."

(Quran 42:5)

(b) And (angels) are deputed to take account of man's actions.
The Quran says:
"Lo! There are above you guardians, generous and recording, who know (all) that ye do."

(Quran 82:10-12)

(c) And they (angels) cause men to die.
The Quran says:
"He is the Omnipotent over His slaves. He sendeth guardians over you until, when death cometh unto one of you, Our messengers receive him, and they neglect not."
(Quran 6:61)

(d) And they are rational beings.
The Quran says:
"And when thy Lord said unto the angels: Lo! I am about to place a viceroy in the earth; they said: wilt Thou place therein one who will do harm therein and will shed blood?"
(Quran 2:30)

(e) "And the Jinn did We create aforetime of essential fire."
(Quran 15:27)

(f) "I created the Jinn and humankind only that they might worship Me."
(Quran 51:56)

(g) "And the Jinn did He (Allah) create of smokeless fire."
(Quran 55:15)

(h) "And He createth that which ye knew not." (Quran 16:8)

The atomists may claim the possibility of these spiritual beings' atomic structure. However, this view of early atomism appears too blunt and rigorously rude to explain the spiritual beings atomically.

(5) "THE ARRANGEMENT MAKES THE THINGS, WE TOUCH AND SEE, OF ATOMS IN GROUPS."

Combining the notion of a fortuitous concourse of atoms and their arrangement does not appear as happy congruity or combination. It is undoubtedly a contradiction in terms. The Quran, however, agrees with the idea of the arrangement of atoms, though in a design pre-planned. It says:

"Lo! We have created everything by measure." (Quran 54:49)

The intrinsic arrangement of invisible atoms appears even in visible objects. The Quran says:

"He it is Who sendeth down water from the sky, and therewith We bring forth buds of every kind; We bring forth the green blade from, which we bring forth the thick clustered grain; and from the date palm, from the pollen thereof, spring pendant bunches; and (We bring forth) gardens of grapes, and the olive and the pomegranate, alike and unlike. Look upon the fruit thereof, when they bear fruit, and upon its ripening. Lo! Herein verily are portents for a people who believe."
(Quran 6:99)

(6) "THERE ARE DIFFERENT KINDS OF ATOMS DISTINGUISHED BY DIFFERENCE OF SHAPE, BUT INDIVIDUAL ATOMS ARE TOO SMALL TO BE NOTICED BY THE SENSES."

The Quran says:
"And whatsoever He hath created for you in the earth of diverse hues; Lo! Therein is indeed a portent for people who take heed."
(Quran 16:13)

We may observe this diversity of hues in observable objects.
The Quran says:
"Hast thou not seen that Allah causeth water to fall from the sky, and We produce therewith fruit of divers hues; and among the hills are streaks white and red, of divers hues, and (others) raven-black; And of men and beasts and cattle, in like manner, divers hues? The erudite among His bondsmen fear Allah alone. Lo! Allah is Mighty, Forgiving."
(Quran 35:27-28)

The Spirit, however, is not comprehensible by man.
The Quran says:
"They will ask thee concerning the Spirit. Say: The Spirit is by command of my Lord, and of knowledge, ye have been vouchsafed but little."
(Quran 17:85)

The early atomists gave out the individual atoms as too small to be noticed by the senses. The Quran gives out the Creator as a being incomprehensible by vision.
It says:
(a) "Vision comprehendeth Him not, but He comprehendeth (all) vision, He is the Subtle, the Aware."
(Quran 6:103)
(b) "(Allah is) the knower of the visible, and the invisible."
(Quran 6:73)

ONLY ONE PASSAGE OF THE QURAN TREATS THE ENTIRE THEORY OF EARLY GREEK ATOMISM

The early Greek atomic theory, through its idea of the fortuitous concourse of atoms, excluded the idea of a plan, design, and divine government of the world, purpose, trial, Resurrection, Judgement, second life in Heaven, and indeed the surveillance, vigilance, even interest of the Creator. The idea of persistence of atoms in motion until checked in collision with another atom insidiously implies the absence of any control of divine power. The idea of the non-existence of anything other than atoms and space implies the non-existence of spiritual beings.

The view that the arrangement makes the things (we touch and see) of atoms in groups is yet another hint of the denial of divine influence in the creation.

In short, the entire theory so founded on Anti-Religion and atheistic foundation breathes an air of dark atheism. This theory is purposely set against the established doctrines of revealed faith and formulated with cold-blooded deliberateness. Yet, it presents a unique example of unparalleled success as a deceptive theory in the entire history of philosophy. Its force has been on its scientific basis. Its popularity has its origin in the sweetness of physical comfort. But let us see the wonder of a Scripture that is the Quran, the champion of the Scriptures in this Baconian age; how it has gathered the complete refutation of the entire theory of ancient atomism in but one passage. Read and judge yourself. It says:

"Allah it is Who created the heavens and the earth, and that which is between them, in six Days. Then He mounted the throne. Ye have not, beside Him, a protecting friend or mediator. Will ye not then remember? He directeth the ordinance from the heavens unto the earth; then it ascendeth unto Him in a Day, whereof the measure is a thousand years of that ye reckon. Such is the Knower of the invisible and the visible, the Mighty, the Merciful, Who made all things good which He created, and He began the creation of man from clay; Then He made his seed from a draught of despised fluid; Then He fashioned him and breathed into him of His Spirit, and appointed for you hearing and sight and hearts. Small thanks give ye! And they say: When we are lost in the earth, how can we then be recreated? Nay, but they are disbelievers in the meeting with their Lord. Say: The angel of death, who hath charge concerning you, will gather you, and afterward unto your Lord, ye will be returned. Couldst thou but see when the guilty hang their heads before their Lord, (and say): Our Lord! We have now seen and heard, so send us back; we will do right, now we are sure. And if We had so willed, We could have given every soul its guidance, but the word from Me concerning evildoers took effect: that I will fill hell with the Jinn and humankind together. So, taste (the evil of your deeds). Forasmuch as ye forgot the meeting of this your day, Lo! We forget you. Taste the doom immortality because of what ye used to do."

(Quran 32:4-14)

~~*~*~*~*

CHAPTER-4

THE MISSING LINK BETWEEN THE ANCIENT AND MODERN FOLLOWERS OF ATOMISM

The sect of Epicureans in ancient Greece adopted the theory of atomism as a fundamental part of their system. They adopted it, not indeed for its scientific utility but its apparent inconsistency with the doctrine of the divine government, which they regarded as the source of worst evil that affects humankind, namely, the fear of death and what may come after it. They adopted as their own the atomic theory of Democritus. Still, in their hands, it was neither enabled to meet the objections raised against it as a theory of the ultimate nature of reality nor made it exhibit its great capacities as an instrument of scientific description and discovery. However, the theory of Epicurean pleasure soon had its effects. The name of Epicureans very early became a synonym for sensualists till, at last, this sect was wiped out of existence and, instead, the teachings of Christianity gained ground.

In contrast with the ancient sect of Epicureans, the modern humankind during the Western Renaissance adopted the theory of atomism purely for its 'scientific' aspect with a discreet and determined rejection of its 'atheistic' aspect. They did it with an assurance that it was possible to keep the two aspects apart and adopt the one desired.

However, it is miserable that the 'atheistic' aspect of atomism sustained its existence with the march of modern progress and maintained its ever-increasing effects both openly and insidiously. The ancient sect of Epicureans adopted the 'atheistic' aspect of atomism and, after a short and merry life of debauch, individually and collectively vanished in misery, shame, and affliction.

By adopting the 'scientific' aspect of atomism and obtaining astonishing success in scientific achievements for physical comfort, it may be observed clearly and lamented that this modern age of Baconian atomism is now approaching atomism's logical and scientific consequence: namely, a most grievous, most painful, and most disgraceful end in the flames of atomic hell, the deadly atomic radiations, and devastating atomic bombs.

Atomism has served both the parties ill according to their respective deserts. The features of Epicureanism essentially have been manifested among the followers of the wealth-seeking, comfort-loving philosophy of modern atomism.

A comparison and contrast and resemblance and variance between the human mind of Epicurean and modern age appear to be a subject worthy of observation of a zealous and keen-sighted philosopher. It will help him assess; how far human nature has been 'enlightened' or 'un-enlightened' passing through these centuries under the influence of atomism.

Plato has left us an attempt of a general kind in the form of a very famous and immortal simile, named the 'Simile of the cave'. This simile appears on the title page of 'The Mysterious Universe' by Sir James Jeans with much appropriateness as described follows.

PLATO'S SIMILE

"And now, I said, let me show in a figure how far our nature is enlightened or unenlightened: Behold! Human beings living in an underground den (cave), which has a mouth open toward the light and reaching all along the den; here they have been from their childhood, and have their legs and necks chained so that they cannot move, and can only see before them, being prevented by the chains from turning round their heads. Above and behind them a fire is blazing at a distance, and between the fire and the prisoners there is a raised way; and you will see, if you look, a low wall built along the way, like the screen which marionette-players have in front of them, over which they show the puppets.

I see.

And do you see, I said, men, passing along the wall carrying all sorts of vessels, and statues and figures of animals made of wood and stone and various materials, which appear over the wall? Some of them are talking, others silent.

You have shown me strange images, and they are strange prisoners.

Like ourselves, I replied; and they see only their own shadows, or the shadows of one another, which the fire throws on the opposite wall of the cave?

True, he said; how could they see anything but the shadows if they were never allowed to move their heads?

And of the objects which are being carried in like manner, they would only see the shadows?

Yes, he said.

And if they were able to converse with one another, would they not suppose that they were naming what was actually before them?

Very true.

And suppose further that the prison had an echo which came from the other side, would they not be sure to fancy when one of the passers-by spoke that the voice which they heard came from the passing shadow?

No question, he replied.

To them, I said, the truth would be literally nothing but the shadows of the images."

(Plato's Republic: Book-VII)

QURAN'S SIMILE

It may come as a real surprise to the world that the Quran has a similar simile. It is the first time now in history that I am revealing this astonishing fact which appears as another proof of the Quran's miraculous, all-pervading nature. Following is the text:

"Ya-Sin. By the wise Qur'an, Lo! Thou art of those sent on a straight path, a revelation of the Mighty, the Merciful, that thou mayst warn a folk whose fathers were not warned, so they are heedless. Already hath the word proved true of most of them, for they believe not. Lo! We have put on their necks shackles reaching unto the chins so that they are made stiff-necked. And We have set a bar before them, and a bar behind them, and (thus) have covered them so that they see not. Whether thou warn them or thou warn them not, it is alike for them, for they believe not. Thou warnest only him who followeth the Reminder and feareth the Beneficent in secret. To him bear tidings of forgiveness and a rich reward. Lo! We it is Who bring the dead to life. We record that which they send before (them) and their footprints. And all things We have kept in a clear register."

(Quran 36:1-12)

Unfortunately, the dreaded aspect of ancient atomism, its atheistic feature, has recurred in this age of modern atomism. Time has proved that atomism, a worldly philosophy, is as dangerous and destructive as any atheistic philosophy. Its logical and scientific consequence, the atomic hell, is there as proof.

As far as the two similes quoted above are concerned, it may reasonably apprise the reader of the difference and peculiar in which light they appear. Also, mark the 'chains' of this universal Economico-Industrial setup of this present Baconian age. [1]

~~*~*~*

---

[1] Please read Book-2/volume-6/chapter-7: [The simile of the Quran against Plato's simile of the cave] for a detailed comparison.

~~*~*~*

PART-2

QURAN VERSUS BACON'S MODERN ATOMISM

CHAPTER-5

WHO IS BACON?

What other coveted honor could there be within reach of a mortal than to be selected as an exhibit to the scrutiny of a Scripture: of the two selected by us for this title, Francis Bacon is the one; the other indeed is Sir James Jeans, the author of 'The Mysterious Universe'. [1]

We will now transition from Democritus to Francis Bacon, from ancient Greek atomism to modern Baconian atomism, which is the philosophy of this modern age. Francis Bacon was the author and originator of this modern philosophy of atomism. He was 'The Buccinator Novi Temporis' that is the 'trumpeter of a new age', 'Viscount St Albans', the author of 'Of the Proficience and Advancement of Learning, Divine and Humane', 'New Atlantis', and 'Novum Organum', member English Parliament, Attorney General, and the Lord Chancellor of England. He stands most conspicuous among all the pioneers of Western Renaissance as the chief representative of this modern age and the ablest and most eloquent advocate of modern atomism.

It is exclusively on his design sketched from his famous works 'The Advancement of Learning' and 'The Novum Organum' that all the culture of this modern age and its peculiar pattern of progress are based. Hence, we have selected his works to serve as a basis for inquiry into the emergence of atomic hell.

Modern humankind globally follows the philosophy of Francis Bacon to the letter from the cradle to the grave. It is surprising to note, and it appears to be one of the unique instances in human history that people would not know the name of this prodigy, even those who adhered to his philosophy every moment of their life. Strange though it may sound, it is a fact that a few, a very few even among the learned in this world today could confess to having heard the name of Francis Bacon not to speak of his works.

Equally unique is that Bacon's philosophy should outstrip every religion and every philosophy in popularity and prevalence. Whereas every other religion claims but the allegiance of a part of humanity, Bacon's philosophy has prevailed over the entire earth. And not only does the unanimity of thought and culture need to be observed throughout, but the end of all appears to be identical in the flames of atomic hell, which is the logical and scientific consequence of Bacon's philosophy.

In the 17th century AD in India, Sheikh Ahmad Sir-Hindi, described as Mujaddid Alif Sani, meaning 'the reviver of the second millennium' (1564-1624), contended with the heretic features of emperor Akbar's new religion. These heretic features were the irreverent presentation of the emperor himself and the general corruption among the Muslim community.

At the same time, in England, Francis Bacon formed his new philosophy to remedy all human ills and as an antithetic corrective to the fundamental doctrine of revealed religion. It was in the destiny of his philosophy to outdazzle every other light from one corner of the earth to the other. However, this philosophy was the darkness in itself. Bacon wanted to sit:

"Next the seat of God, … … …

And with their darkness durst affront His light."

['Paradise Lost: Book-I'; by John Milton (Lines number 383 & 391)]
Francis Bacon, the youngest son of Sir Nicholas Bacon, was born at York House (his father's residence) on 22nd January 1561. He had delicate health but intelligent wit, a strong intellect, and an unusual gravity of carriage in the younger days. For Bacon, his father planned a public career as a statesman or diplomatist and, in his sixteenth year, sent him to Paris after spending three years over his books in Cambridge.

Francis Bacon spent some time in France, but his father suddenly died in England, and the tragic event greatly overcast his prospects. He soon returned to England. The death of his father left him a poor man, obliged to work for his living. His father had accumulated a considerable sum of money to purchase an estate for his youngest son. However, his sudden death prevented its accomplishment, and Francis Bacon could get only a fifth part of his father's personal property. He abandoned Diplomacy as a career. Instead of living to study, he was obliged to study how to live.

Soon after his return from France, Bacon entered upon a course of law at Gray's Inn. He was afterward admitted as an Utter Barrister. His struggle from Solicitor General to the highest office of the Lord Keeper is a tale of a success mingled with mortification. It is a specimen of slow and steady triumph. Hardly any man has had a life as stirring as Bacon had from sixteen to sixty. Besides his professional exertion, he sat in parliament, and his life was that of a busy man of the world.

During his worldly business, he snatched some moments for study and his writings. He published the first edition of his 'Essays' when he was thirty-six and 'Advancement of Learning' in 1605 in his forty-fourth year. He published the second edition of his 'Essays' in 1612 in his fifty-first year. Besides, he published his 'Novum Organum' in 1620, six years before his death, for he died on 9th Aril 1626.

In January 1620, Ben Jonson sang of Bacon in his sixtieth year as:

"England's high Chancellor: the destin'd heir,

In his soft cradle, to his father's chair:

Whose even thread the fates spin round and full,

Out of their choicest and their whitest wool."

In January 1621, Bacon reached the zenith of his fortunes. In April, the houses assembled to hold an inquiry. Bacon was tried for bribery and sentenced to a punishment that ended his career in shame. History has remembered him as a man of boundless love for worldly things and ostentation and as a man of flawed principles. Humankind has tried to forget him, but having an unfailing and relentless record of man's deeds, Nemesis [2] would dig Bacon's name out of oblivion. She will do it to intimate this world with his doings in his capacity as the author of the philosophy of atomism. After a span of three hundred years, the result of his philosophy emerged in the form of flames of atomic hell as a logical and scientific consequence of the process of atomism to consume this world.

A renowned and marvelous poet, Alexander Pope, in his 'An Essay on Man', Epistle-IV, made a striking remark on the personality and character of Francis Bacon as follows.

"If parts allure thee, think how Bacon shin'd,
The wisest, brightest, meanest of mankind."

Someone said that:

"Bacon was the wisest because of his worldly wisdom; he was brightest owing to his powerful intellect and the art of writing terse essays, and he was meanest due to his treacherous character."

Macaulay said: "Bacon was a servile advocate, that he might be a corrupt judge."

We may reasonably say:

"Bacon's was a noxious philosophy, that it might produce ruinous results."

We have treated Bacon's life in a subsequent volume-4 referred to his philosophy.

~~*~*~*

---

[1] We will discuss 'The Mysterious Universe' by Sir James Jeans in Book-2/volume-6: [Quran versus the philosophy of the 'Unscientific Scientist Philosopher'].

[2] **Nemesis and Greek Mythology:** Nemesis was the Greek goddess of vengeance, a deity who doled out rewards for noble acts and punished evil ones. The Greeks believed that Nemesis didn't always punish an offender immediately but might wait for generations to avenge a crime. In English, Nemesis originally referred to someone who brought just retribution, but nowadays, people are more likely to see animosity than justice in the actions of a nemesis.

(Courtesy: 'Merriam-Webster')

~~*~*~*

CHAPTER-6

BACONIAN AND SATANIC METHODS OF SEDUCTION ARE IDENTICAL

According to Bible, Satan's temptation is as follows.

"And the serpent said unto the woman, Ye shall not surely die: For God doth know that in the day ye eat thereof, then your eyes shall be opened, and ye shall be as gods, knowing good and evil."

(The Bible: Old Testament: Genesis 3:4-5)

Satan's temptation, according to the Quran, is as follows.

(1) "But the Devil whispered to him, saying: O Adam! Shall I show thee the tree of immortality and power that wasteth not away? Then they twain ate thereof so that their shame became apparent unto them, and they began to hide by heaping on themselves some of the leaves of the Garden. And Adam disobeyed his Lord, so went astray."

(Quran 20:120-121)

(2) "Then Satan whispered to them that he might manifest unto them that which was hidden from them of their shame, and he said: Your Lord forbade you from this tree only lest ye should become angels or become of the immortals. And he swore unto them (saying): Lo! I am a sincere adviser unto you. Thus, did he lead them on with guile? And when they tasted of the tree, their shame was manifest to them, and they began to hide (by heaping) on themselves some of the leaves of the Garden. And their Lord called them, (saying): Did I not forbid you from that tree and tell you: Lo! Satan is an open enemy to you?"

(Quran 7:20-22)

We may record Bacon's temptation in the light of his design as follows.

"Bacon trumpeted to the posterity of Adam, saying 'O Humankind, you were commanded by God to pursue natural philosophy, and He forbade you the pursuit of moral philosophy. But you reversed the edict by denying you the natural philosophy and its fruits and taking to moral philosophy, and you disobeyed the command of your Lord. Pursue, therefore, now the course of natural philosophy, and you will establish your dominion over Mother Nature like that of God Himself. And all the secrets of nature will be revealed to you. You will see everything, and you will hear everything, and this earth will be changed into as good a Paradise as from which your progenitor was expelled, and it will be a Paradise of fruits in which rivers of milk and honey will flow."

(For reference, read 'Bacon's design': 'A history of Philosophy'; by Clement C. J. Webb, Pages: 135-138)

Adam listened to the word of Satan, was expelled from Paradise, and cast into the earth for trial in miseries, sorrows, tears, fears, afflictions, and hope of regaining Paradise and apprehension of eternal hell in the next world.

Adam's posterity listened to the word of Bacon, and this world changed into a hell of misery with manifest expectations that it will soon change into a hell of fire with the probability of eternal punishment in the nuclear hell of the next eternal world. Because the causes of the appearance of Baconian atomic hell in this world and punishment in the eternal atomic hell in the next eternal world (as given by the Quran) are identical, they are alike in a way, the methods of temptation used by Bacon and Satan are matching.

~~*~*~*

CHAPTER-7

QURAN VERSUS BACON'S DESIGN OF ATOMISM

This modern culture, with its science-guided progress, is exclusively the result of Bacon's philosophy. The light of Bacon's philosophy in the form of a blueprint has sketched Bacon's design. Besides, Bacon's philosophy can be clearly and easily understood only from his design. Hence, we must give this design the attention it deserves. A point that appears clearly from this design is that Bacon's philosophy is a complete antithesis of the doctrines of revealed religion. The philosophy of Bacon has turned topsy-turvy the philosophy of religion. Moreover, as a natural philosophy of fruit against all the barren (as per Bacon's thought) moral philosophies, Bacon's philosophy has turned topsy-turvy every philosophy of the past.

We quote Bacon's design from Clement C. J. Webb's 'A history of philosophy' as in the following.

BACON'S DESIGN

"Francis Bacon's design was, by means of inquiries some of which should be experimental like those of alchemists, but purged from all superstitious taint and directed not toward immediate gain, but toward a thoroughgoing knowledge, vastly to increase in the long run the dominion of man over nature. To enjoy such a dominion was, he held, the original destiny of our race. But in a vain and impious attempt (described in the Biblical story as "eating of the tree of knowledge of good and evil") to make laws for himself by "moral philosophy," instead of remaining content with the positive commands of God, man had turned aside from his proper business of pursuing "natural philosophy," that is, of studying and interpreting the works of God and raising in his own intelligence a true image of the universe; gaining, in other words, such a knowledge of nature's inner workings as may make it possible to emulate them. The failure of man hitherto to do this, and the depressing tradition that the processes of chemical combination were necessarily beyond the reach of human imitation, showed only that ancient theories of nature were merely superficial and had not penetrated her true secret. But "in the sweat of his brows" man may yet "eat his bread," that is, through resolute and patient persistence in discriminating observation and well-devised experiment, he may wring these secrets from her and turn them to his own advantage. For this, however, a new method of approach is necessary; and this Bacon endeavored to provide in his Novum Organum, that is "The new Instrument," which was to take the place of the old Organon, namely, the collection of Aristotle's treatises on logic, which were so called as constituting the proper "Instrument" to be used in reasoning, whatever one was reasoning about. ...... Bacon would have the inquirer attend to all facts. He was to "enter the kingdom of nature, like the kingdom of grace, as a little child," to learn, and not to dictate. Nature could only be conquered by obeying her. Nor could she be conquered by isolated efforts. Such discoveries as had been made had frequently been lost again through lack of a provision for recording them. Not until there was a systematic collection and preservation of facts (which could not be without greater expense than private fortunes could support) would it be reasonable to look for a properly based philosophy of nature."

('A history of Philosophy'; by Clement C. J. Webb, Pages: 135-138)
Following are the prominent points of Bacon's Design.
(1) Bacon's design in general.
(2) The place of natural philosophy in Bacon's design.
(3) The place of moral philosophy in Bacon's design.
(4) Man's right of dominion over Mother Nature.
(5) Knowledge.
(6) Contemplation of the works of God according to Bacon's design.
(7) Purpose of man's existence according to Bacon's philosophy.
(8) A comparison between the philosophy of Plato and that of Bacon by Macaulay.
(9) The practical form of Bacon's design and its end.
(10) The process of Baconian design and its end.
(11) Quran's view of Bacon's design.
(12) Bacon's misunderstanding about his philosophy.

We will briefly discuss these points one by one.

(1) BACON'S DESIGN IN GENERAL

Bacon's design stands in radical opposition to revealed religion and every philosophy based on a moral factor, or not based on natural philosophy for material exploitation. It condemns the moral philosophy utterly and entirely as an act of disobedience to God's command and the repetition of Adam's transgression of eating the fruit of the tree of knowledge of good and evil. It gives out the pursuit of natural philosophy as the command of God to man and acquirement of dominion over Mother

Nature as the purpose of man's existence; the object of natural philosophy is knowing the secret working of Mother Nature for turning these secrets to man's material advantage.

It asserts man's right of dominion over Mother Nature as man's preordained destiny. The 'contemplation of the works of God' corresponding to this design is the same as 'exploiting God's works' since it is not concerned with anything other than material exploitation. It is limited to this material and transient world alone without considering spirituality or life after death. The purpose of knowledge, the natural philosophy (science), is to reveal natural secrets for material benefit.

(2) THE PLACE OF NATURAL PHILOSOPHY IN BACON'S DESIGN

The whole structure of Bacon's design is based on natural philosophy. It is the command of God to man. Humankind should pursue it to discover the secrets of Mother Nature to turn them to the advantage of man. Moreover, it is the object of man's existence on earth.

Where does then revealed religion stand in this respect? Natural philosophy, according to religion, is only of secondary status. It must be but the handmaid of moral philosophy. The material utility is allowed by religion as a necessity only and is never the object or the purpose of man's existence. The material world is not to be loved, and people should regard it only as a transitory post on the way back to the next world. Not the natural philosophy, but the moral philosophy is the basis of religion.

Moreover, not this world but the next world is the destination. One must prefer the next world to this transient material world and must sacrifice this world for the next. Christ taught self-abnegation and hatred of this world. Buddha taught the same. Muhammad (peace be upon him) was not behind any, in the condemnation of this world against the next world. If Bacon's view of the pursuit of natural philosophy for material benefit is correct, where do these celebrities stand mentioned above? Which of them is in error? Surely either Bacon or they could be right.

Anybody could not expect the answer to this question from present-day humankind, which is, without exception, entangled in the Baconian net. They certainly will try to seek an argument in favor of Bacon's view and explain the things anyway. The answer to this very crucial question is lamentation in the deafening uproar and silencing thunder and blinding dazzle of the atomic bomb and the deadly, virulent stings of the atomic radiations. Bacon adapted natural philosophy, and nature always speaks the truth. This answer of nature to Bacon's followers is the accurately logical and correctly scientific result of Baconian design.

Also, it is not the revealed religion only that stands opposed to this Baconian view. The philosophers like Socrates, Plato, and Aristotle, and undoubtedly most of the philosophers of the pre-modern ages, would not assent to this view of Bacon regarding the natural philosophy. For, they all stand without any shade of ambiguity, opposed to this entirely materialistic view of Bacon regarding the natural philosophy. The facts have proved them right.

(3) THE PLACE OF MORAL PHILOSOPHY IN BACON'S DESIGN

Bacon says: "In a vain and impious attempt, to make laws for himself by moral philosophy instead of remaining content with the positive commands of God, man had turned aside from his proper business of pursuing 'natural philosophy' (science), that is, of gaining and interpreting the works of God and raising in his own intelligence a true image of the universe; gaining in other words, such a knowledge of nature's inner workings as may make it possible to emulate them. That in the sweat of his brow man may yet eat his bread, that is, through committed and patient persistence in discriminating observation and well-devised experiment, he may wring these secrets from nature and turn them to his own advantage."

Now, this is the position which moral philosophy holds in Bacon's philosophy. According to him:

"In a vain and impious attempt, the man had adopted moral philosophy to give himself the law." The study of Bacon's philosophy reveals that because Adam gave names to the creatures in Paradise, his business and God's command was to pursue natural philosophy when cast on the earth. Because tasting the fruit of the forbidden tree of knowledge of good and evil was the cause of Adam's expulsion from Paradise, it was an act not to be repeated by him; that is, he was not to pursue moral philosophy. For, it was based on the knowledge of good and evil.

Nothing more seems to be necessary to say on it except that revealed religion is manifestly, utterly, and entirely based on moral philosophy and stands in radical opposition to Bacon on this point. Take away moral factors from Christianity, and what remains there? Take away moral factors from Islam, and what remains there? We may say the same about the religion of Buddha and that of Krishna.

Bacon has been so explicit in his view about moral philosophy that if we credit him with the truth, then the Bible, the Quran, and every divine Scripture based on moral philosophy, contained falsity. Hence, every divine Scripture was not the divine word of Allah but was the result of human effort. For, if it were the word of Allah, then indeed it had been based not on moral philosophy, but rather on natural philosophy, and its design would have been the prototype of Bacon's design, which it is not. The philosophy of Socrates, Plato, Aristotle, Zeno, and indeed of most pre-modern philosophers, as far as Bacon's view on moral philosophy is concerned, is opposed to it. Bacon indeed has uttered things entirely novel. How was he tolerated is the question?

The followers of religion might well say:

"Damn him and his darned philosophy; we know not his philosophy; we have not even heard Bacon's name. We follow our religion to the letter."

It is well said and easily but said in ignorance. A blind man holds a snake, plays with it, and knows not by what name people call it. Will the man be thought so safe because he was blind and because he knew not the name? The simile is not complete because the followers of the religion are holding the Baconian adder, and they are not only playing with it, but they are also, and at the same time, being bitten by it with its fiery teeth. They will, in time, perish in acute misery.

Present civilization has adopted this systematic, organized, ever-increasing, infinite, and science-guided process of modern progress, and the net of this modern universal Economico-Industrial setup has entangled it. Whoever adopted this modern progress is only a victim of deception if he entertains the notion that he follows his religion and has to do nothing with Bacon or his philosophy. This modern progress is the practical form of Bacon's design, the blueprint of Bacon's philosophy. This modern progress is a process whose logical and scientific end is the atomic hell. Will the followers of religion guarantee their or their religion's safety against the consequences of this progress? If they can obtain such a guaranty, then only they should take their word with surety. Then only their belief that they only followed their religion would be acceptable.

(4) MAN'S RIGHT OF DOMINION OVER MOTHER NATURE

Bacon has asserted man's right of dominion over Mother Nature as man's destiny. In time, this notion of Bacon emerged as something equivalent to a challenge to Allah's right of dominion. We may see the point to have assumed a philosophical aspect. Religion has allowed the utility of Allah's bounty and has even declared that Allah has rendered to man serviceable whatever is in the heavens and the earth.

However, nowhere is the term 'dominion' employed in how Bacon has used it. Dominion, according to religion, is the right exclusively reserved for Allah. His is the dominion in the heavens and the earth. Humility is for man, and dominion belongs to the Creator; utility is for man, Sovereignty is Allah's alone.

(5) **KNOWLEDGE**

According to Bacon's design, knowledge is the knowledge of the inner workings of Mother Nature only. His design does not mention the subjects of spiritual, religious, or moral knowledge. Knowledge aims to study and interpret God's works and raise an actual image of the material universe in one's intelligence. In other words, to gain such a knowledge of Mother Nature's inner workings may make it possible to emulate them and wring Mother Nature's secrets from her to man's material advantage.

In contrast, according to religion, the purpose of knowledge is to know how to better the next life in Heaven, escape the punishment on the Day of Judgment, and gain the bliss of eternal Paradise in the next eternal life. According to moral and religious philosophy, knowledge is primarily to know oneself and know Allah. The essence of knowledge, according to religion, is the fear of Allah.

(6) **CONTEMPLATION OF THE WORKS OF GOD ACCORDING TO BACON'S DESIGN**

According to Bacon's design, contemplation of the works of God is the synonym of the material exploitation of the works of God. No other purpose whatsoever is mentioned. Nevertheless, according to religion, the general purpose of contemplation of works of God is the glorification of the Creator thereof.

The Quran has given certain particular objects of contemplation of the works of Allah. Most important after Allah's glorification is searching in the workings of Mother Nature of the proofs of the necessity and the certainty of Resurrection.

(7) **PURPOSE OF MAN'S EXISTENCE ACCORDING TO BACON'S PHILOSOPHY**

According to Bacon's philosophy, the purpose of man's existence on earth is to gain dominion over Mother Nature. The object of such dominion is to gain material advantages for humankind in general. While, according to religion, the purpose of man's existence on earth is to undergo the trial of worldly temptation and make an endeavor to gain re-entry into Paradise in the Heaven from which Adam, the progenitor of man, was expelled and cast on this earth. Moreover, the purpose of man's creation is to worship Allah.

(8) A COMPARISON BETWEEN THE PHILOSOPHY OF PLATO AND THAT OF BACON BY MACAULAY

Like all the rest of the modern world, Macaulay has greatly admired Bacon's philosophy. Every point of Bacon's philosophy has been preferable to him as against that of Plato. But the circumstances, at last, have taken so curious a turn and time eventually has so clearly exposed the truth of Bacon's philosophy to man's horror that if Macaulay were revived to read his opinions of Bacon's philosophy today in the presence of the ruinous hazards and unheard miseries that have appeared as the outcome of Baconian philosophy, he would shake his head in amazement at the fallacious judgments of his so keen an insight and so wise a mind, and Plato's philosophy would seem to him a blessing despite faults. However, compared to Plato's, Bacon's views will assume a color, a little more distinct.

Macaulay writes as follows.

"The difference between the philosophy of Bacon and that of his predecessors cannot, we think, be better illustrated than by comparing his views on some important subjects with those of Plato. We select Plato, because we conceive that he did more than any other person towards giving to the minds of speculative men that bent which they retained till they received from Bacon a new impulse in a diametrically opposite direction.

It is curious to observe how differently these great men estimated the value of every kind of knowledge. Take Arithmetic, for example. Plato, after speaking slightly of the convenience of being able to reckon and compute in the ordinary transactions of life, passes to what he considers as a far more important advantage. The study of the properties of numbers, he tells us, habituates the mind to the contemplation of pure truth, and raises us above the material universe. He would have his disciples apply themselves to this study, not that they may be able to buy or sell, not that they may qualify themselves to be shopkeepers or traveling merchants, but that they may learn to withdraw their minds from the ever-shifting spectacle of this visible and tangible world, and to fix them on the immutable essences of things.

Bacon, on the other hand, valued this branch of knowledge only on account of its uses with reference to that visible and tangible world which Plato so much despised. He speaks with scorn of the mystical arithmetic of the later Platonists, and laments the propensity of mankind to employ, on mere matters of curiosity, powers the whole exertion of which is required for purposes of solid advantage. He advises arithmeticians to leave these trifles, and to employ themselves in framing convenient expressions, which may be of use in physical researches. The same reasons which led Plato to recommend the study of arithmetic led him to recommend also the study of mathematics. The vulgar crowd of geometricians, he says, will not understand him. They have practice always in view. They do not know that the real use of the science is to lead men to the knowledge of abstract, essential, eternal truth.

Indeed, if we are to believe Plutarch, Plato carried this feeling so far that he considered geometry as degraded by being applied to any purpose of vulgar utility. Archytas, it seems, had framed machines of extraordinary power on mathematical principles. Plato remonstrated with his friend, and declared that this was to degrade a noble intellectual exercise into a low craft, fit only for carpenters and wheelwrights. The office of geometry, he said, was to discipline the mind, not to minister to the base wants of the body. His interference was successful, and from that time, according to Plutarch, the science of mechanics was considered unworthy of the attention of a philosopher.

Archimedes, in a later age, imitated and surpassed Archytas. But even Archimedes was not free from the prevailing notion that geometry was degraded by being employed to produce anything useful. It was with difficulty that he was induced to stoop from speculation to practice. He was half ashamed of those inventions which were the wonder of hostile nations, and always spoke of them slightingly as mere amusements, as trifles in which a mathematician might be suffered to relax his mind after intense application to the higher parts of his science.

The opinion of Bacon on this subject was diametrically opposed to that of the ancient philosophers. He valued geometry chiefly, if not solely, on account of those uses, which to Plato appeared so base. And it is remarkable that the longer Bacon lived, the stronger this feeling became. When in 1605 he wrote the two books on the Advancement of Learning, he dwelt on the advantages which mankind derived from mixed mathematics; but he at the same time admitted that the beneficial effect produced by mathematical study on the intellect, though a collateral advantage, was "no less worthy than that which was principal and intended." But it is evident that his views underwent a change. When, near twenty years later, he published the De Augmentis, which is the Treatise on the Advancement of Learning, greatly expanded and carefully corrected, he made important alterations in the part which related to mathematics. He condemned with severity the high pretensions of the mathematicians, "delicias et fastum mathematicorum." Assuming the well-being of the human race to be the end of knowledge, he pronounced that mathematical science could claim no higher rank than that of an appendage or auxiliary to other sciences.

Mathematical science, he says, is the handmaid of natural philosophy; she ought to demean herself as such; and he declares that he cannot conceive by what ill chance it has happened that she presumes to claim precedence over her mistress. He predicts -- a prediction which would have made Plato shudder -- that as more and more discoveries are made in physics, there will be more and more branches of mixed mathematics. Of that collateral advantage, the value of which, twenty years before, he rated so highly, he says not one word. This omission cannot have been the effect of mere inadvertence. His own treatise was before him. From that treatise he deliberately expunged whatever was favourable to the study of pure mathematics, and inserted several keen reflections on the ardent votaries of that study. This fact, in our opinion, admits of only one explanation. Bacon's love of those pursuits which directly tend to improve the condition of mankind, and his jealousy of all pursuits merely curious, had grown upon him, and had, it may be, become immoderate. He was afraid of using any expression which might have the effect of inducing any man of talents to employ in speculations, useful only to the mind of the speculator, a single hour which might be employed in extending the empire of man over matter. If Bacon erred here, we must acknowledge that we greatly prefer his error to the opposite error of Plato. We have no patience with a philosophy which, like those Roman matrons who swallowed abortive in order to preserve their shapes, takes pains to be barren for fear of being homely.

Let us pass to astronomy. This was one of the sciences which Plato exhorted his disciples to learn, but for reasons far removed from common habits of thinking. "Shall we set down astronomy," says Socrates, "among the subjects of study?" "I think so," answers his young friend Glaucon: "to know something about the seasons, the months, and the years is of use for military purposes, as well as for agriculture and navigation." "It amuses me," says Socrates, "to see how afraid you are, lest the common herd of people should accuse you of recommending useless studies." He then proceeds, in that pure and magnificent diction which, as Cicero said, Jupiter would use if Jupiter spoke Greek, to explain, that the use of astronomy is not to add to the vulgar comforts of life, but to assist in raising the mind to the contemplation of things which are to be perceived by the pure intellect alone. The knowledge of the actual motions of the heavenly bodies Socrates considers as of little value. The appearances which make the sky beautiful at night are, he tells us, like the figures which a geometrician draws on the sand, mere examples, mere helps to feeble minds. We must get beyond them; we must neglect them; we must attain to an astronomy which is as independent of the actual stars as geometrical truth is independent of the lines of an ill-drawn diagram. This is, we imagine, very nearly if not exactly, the astronomy which Bacon compared to the ox of Prometheus, a sleek, well-shaped hide, stuffed with rubbish, goodly to look at but containing nothing to eat.

He complained that astronomy had, to its great injury, been separated from natural philosophy, of which it was one of the noblest provinces and annexed to the domain of mathematics. The world stood in need, he said, of a very different astronomy, of a living astronomy, of an astronomy which should set forth the nature, the motion, and the influences of the heavenly bodies, as they really are.

Of the greatest and most useful of all human inventions, the invention of alphabetical writing, Plato did not look with much complacency. He seems to have thought that the use of letters had operated on the human mind as the use of the go-cart in learning to walk, or of corks in learning to swim, is said to operate on the human body. It was a support which, in his opinion, soon became indispensable to those who used it, which made vigorous exertion first unnecessary and then impossible. The powers of the intellect would, he conceived, have been more fully developed without this delusive aid. Men would have been compelled to exercise the understanding and the memory and, by deep and assiduous meditation, to make truth thoroughly their own. Now, on the contrary, much knowledge is traced on paper, but little is engraved in the soul. A man is certain that he can find information at a moment's notice when he wants it. He therefore suffers it to fade from his mind. Such a man cannot in strictness be said to know anything. He has the show without the reality of wisdom. These opinions Plato has put into the mouth of an ancient king of Egypt. But it is evident from the context that they were his own; and so they were understood to be by Quinctilian. Indeed they are in perfect accordance with the whole Platonic system.

Bacon's views, as may easily be supposed, were widely different. The powers of the memory, he observes, without the help of writing, can do little towards the advancement of any useful science. He acknowledges that the memory may be disciplined to such a point as to be able to perform very extraordinary feats. But on such feats he sets little value. The habits of his mind, he tells us, are such that he is not disposed to rate highly any accomplishment, however rare, which is of no practical use to mankind. As to these prodigious achievements of the memory, he ranks them with the exhibitions of rope dancers and tumblers. "These two performances," he says, "are much of the same sort. The one is an abuse of the powers of the body; the other is an abuse of the powers of the mind. Both may perhaps excite our wonder; but neither is entitled to our respect."

To Plato, the science of medicine appeared to be of very disputable advantages. He did not indeed object to quick cures for acute disorders or for injuries produced by accidents. But the art which resists the slow sap of a chronic disease, which repairs frames enervated by lust, swollen by gluttony, or inflamed by wine, which encourages sensuality by mitigating the natural punishment of the sensualist, and prolongs existence when the intellect has ceased to retain its entire energy, had no share of his esteem. A life protracted by medical skill he pronounced to be a long death. The exercise of the art of medicine ought, he said, to be tolerated so far as that art may serve to cure the occasional distempers of men whose constitutions are good. As to those who have bad constitutions, let them die, and the sooner, the better. Such men are unfit for war, for magistracy, for the management of their domestic affairs, for severe study and speculation. If they engage in any vigorous mental exercise, they are troubled with giddiness and fullness of the head, all which they lay to the account of philosophy. The best thing that can happen to such wretches is to have done with life at once. He quotes mythical authority in support of this doctrine; and reminds his disciples that the practice of the sons of Aesculapius, as described by Homer, extended only to the cure of external injuries.

Far different was the philosophy of Bacon. Of all the sciences, that which he seems to have regarded with the greatest interest was the science which, in Plato's opinion, would not be tolerated in a well-regulated community. To make men perfect was no part of Bacon's plan. His humble aim was to make imperfect men comfortable. The beneficence of his philosophy resembled the beneficence of the common Father, whose sun rises on the evil and the good, whose rain descends for the just and the unjust. In Plato's opinion, man was made for philosophy; in Bacon's opinion, philosophy was made for man; it was a means to an end; and that end was to increase the pleasures and to mitigate the pains of millions who are not and cannot be philosophers. That a valetudinarian who took great pleasure in being wheeled along his terrace, who relished his boiled chicken, and his weak wine and water, and who enjoyed a hearty laugh over the Queen of Navarre's tales, should be treated as a caput lupinum because he could not read the Timaeus without a headache, was a notion which the humane spirit of the English school of wisdom altogether rejected. Bacon would not have thought it beneath the dignity of a philosopher to contrive an improved garden chair for such a valetudinarian, to devise some way of rendering his medicines more palatable, to invent repasts which he might enjoy, and pillows on which he might sleep soundly; and this though there might not be the smallest hope that the mind of the poor invalid would ever rise to the contemplation of the ideal beautiful and the ideal good. As Plato had cited the religious legends of Greece to justify his contempt for the more recondite parts of the art of healing, Bacon vindicated the dignity of that art by appealing to the example of Christ, and reminded men that the great physician of the soul did not disdain to be also the physician of the body.

When we pass from the science of medicine to that of legislation, we find the same difference between the systems of these two great men. Plato, at the commencement of the Dialogue on Laws, lays it down as a fundamental principle that the end of legislation is to make men virtuous. It is unnecessary to point out the extravagant conclusions to which such a proposition leads. Bacon well knew to how great an extent the happiness of every society must depend on the virtue of its members; and he also knew what legislators can and what they cannot do for the purpose of promoting virtue. The view which he has given of the end of legislation and of the principal means for the attainment of that end has always seemed to us eminently happy, even among the many happy passages of the same kind with which his works abound. -- The end is the well-being of the people. The means are the imparting of moral and religious education; the providing of everything necessary for defence against foreign enemies; the maintaining of internal order; the establishing of a judicial, financial, and commercial system, under which wealth may be rapidly accumulated and securely enjoyed.

Even with respect to the form in which laws ought to be drawn, there is a remarkable difference of opinion between the Greek and the Englishman. Plato thought a preamble essential; Bacon thought it mischievous. Each was consistent with himself. Plato, considering the moral improvement of the people as the end of legislation, justly inferred that a law which commanded and threatened, but which neither convinced the reason, nor touched the heart, must be a most imperfect law. He was not content with deterring from theft a man who still continued to be a thief at heart, with restraining a son who hated his mother from beating his mother. The only obedience on which he set much value was the obedience which an enlightened understanding yields to reason and which a virtuous disposition yields to precepts of virtue. He really seems to have believed that, by prefixing to every law an eloquent and pathetic exhortation, he should, to a great extent, render penal enactments superfluous. Bacon entertained no such romantic hopes; and he well knew the practical inconveniences of the course which Plato recommended.

Each of the great men whom we have compared intended to illustrate his system by a philosophical romance, and each left his romance imperfect. Had Plato lived to finish the Critias, a comparison between that noble fiction and the new Atlantis would probably have furnished us with still more striking instances than any which we have given. It is amusing to think with what horror he would have seen such an institution as Solomon's House rising in his republic: with what vehemence he would have ordered the brew-houses, the perfume-houses, and the dispensatories to be pulled down -- and with what inexorable rigour he would have driven beyond the frontier all the Fellows of the College, Merchants of Light and Depredators, Lamps and Pioneers.

To sum up the whole, we should say that the aim of the Platonic philosophy was to exalt man into a god. The aim of the Baconian philosophy was to provide man with what he requires while he continues to be man. The aim of the Platonic philosophy was to raise us far above vulgar wants. The aim of the Baconian philosophy was to supply our vulgar wants. The former aim was noble; but the latter was attainable. Plato drew a good bow, but, like Acestes in Virgil, he aimed at the stars; and therefore, though there was no want of strength or skill, the shot was thrown away. His arrow was indeed followed by a track of dazzling radiance, but it struck nothing. Bacon fixed his eye on a mark which was placed on the earth and within bow-shot and hit it in the white. The philosophy of Plato began in words and ended in words, noble words indeed, words such as were to be expected from the finest of human intellects exercising boundless dominion over the finest of human languages. The philosophy of Bacon began in observations and ended in arts.

The boast of the ancient philosophers was that their doctrine formed the minds of men to a high degree of wisdom and virtue. This was indeed the only practical good which the most celebrated of those teachers even pretended to effect; and undoubtedly, if they had affected this, they would have deserved far higher praise than if they had discovered the most salutary medicines or constructed the most powerful machines. But the truth is that, in those very matters in which alone they professed to do any good to mankind, in those very matters for the sake of which they neglected all the vulgar interests of mankind, they did nothing, or worse than nothing. They promised what was impracticable; they despised what was practicable; they filled the world with long words and long beards; and they left it as wicked and as ignorant as they found it."

('Critical and Historical Essays': Volume II; by Thomas Babington Macaulay)

Macaulay is reputed to have an angelic pen to write with his works based on truth. You have read the above-quoted treatment of a comparison between the philosophies of Plato and Bacon. No doubt it appears like angelic writing. How lucid? How conniving? One hundred and forty-four years hence when it first appeared, its lights might have dazzled the minds of its readers with even greater brilliance.

However, today in the presence of the mountainous calamities, ruinous hazards, and disastrous catastrophes that have appeared due to Bacon's philosophy, it appears only insipid, ignorant, and spurious. To us, it appears what to the wounded prisoners of a defeated army fighting for a wrong cause might appear on retrospection, the relics of the exhorting speech of their ambitious General.

Macaulay has lamented the incompletion of the philosophical reminisce of Plato and Bacon since the world has missed still more striking instances. We, on our part, have nothing to lament in this respect, for in the philosophy of Plato, we are not much interested, but the 'New Atlantis' of Bacon appears before our eyes with its most minute of features. We glare with trembling hearts at the columns of the atomic bombs rising in a city of destruction bestrewn with shapes of miseries, sorrows, and afflictions and populated with miserable, cancer-ridden chimeras.

(9) THE PRACTICAL FORM OF BACON'S DESIGN AND ITS END

Bacon's design suggested systematic and continuous scientific inquiry, generation after generation. It means an accumulative, ever-increasing process. The results of this inquiry were supposed to apply to the material exploitation of natural sources. It also was consequently to be of nature cumulative and ever-increasing. In this quality that is the quality of ever-increasing lay the core of the entire Baconian affair. Naturally, the process of progress being ever-increasing will gradually increase in magnitude as well as extent. It will gradually occupy phase after phase of human life, and it will steadily occupy a more significant part of man's mind and time. This gradual increase of the occupation of man's mind and time will cause gradual proportional expulsion of every other thought from man's mind, particularly the thought of death, religion, and the otherworld.

Also, with the increase of progress being infinite, every other thought will be elapsed entirely from man's mind. That is what, in reality, is happening, and not extraordinarily keenness of sight is necessary to observe this transition. Science has gradually obtained total control of almost every phase of human life. Machines and factories have covered the entire earth and are on ever-increasing both in, kind and numbers. Man's mind and time are being occupied more and more by progress. The call of prayer from minarets of the mosque or church bells is gradually yielding to the factory hooter and whistle of the workman's train.

Which religion will be willing to allow such progress to sign its (own) warrants of exile and extinction? How then to entertain the thought of a compromise between faith and this progress as it is? It is a miracle that could not be functioned. They, who might think of living without faith, ought to know the impossibility of man's existence without faith in a world with such weapons and such contest to be found in this science-guided age. Faith, moral order, and otherworldliness are the essential requisites for the existence of humanity in such a world.

Moreover, because this process of progress is ever-increasing, its problems are of nature ever-increasing. The transition from Capitalism to Socialism, from the shallow to the unfathomable Baconian hell, is an example of solving its problems. The unequal division of wealth and the class distinction resulting from industrialized Capitalism have necessitated the evolution of a system of apparent equality and no individual property and no religion (Socialism). Besides, because this progress is ever-increasing with its ever-increasing number of machines and factories, therefore, its demands of energy also are of nature forever increasing. Therefore, it has consumed all the available energy resources with fantastic speed, increasing its energy demands. Moreover, because the harmless sources of energy are nearly exhausted, this world has two alternatives now before it: either to close this universal Economico-Industrial setup and face a temporary famine or to restore to the use of atomic energy and face total annihilation.

There is absolutely no possibility of protection against the atomic bombs or the radiation of the atomic energy reactors for peace. Although this world is the victim of false hopes and baseless optimism about the possibility, rather the certainty of a triumph of science over this problem of energy and safety, and protection from the atomic phenomena, facts stand at odds against such hopes. Such hopes as these are entertained by those only who are ignorant of science reality. Moreover, we generally forget the time factor. The clouds of atomic danger are bickering on the horizons of humankind with incredible speed. Moreover, no centuries and no millenniums are there at the disposal for scientific research.

On the other hand, this Baconian progress has failed to appease humankind's hunger, while the atomic phenomena have shattered the Baconian dream of man's dominion over Mother Nature. Ask the atomist, and he will tell you that man at present stands like a helpless and contemptible dwarf against the fiery giant Atumbumb in danger of being consumed by that giant any moment. Mother Nature, at last, has been proved to be too formidable a prey for the presuming posterity of Adam. It appears that it has some thoughts of teaching this humankind a lesson for unreasonable presumptions beyond their capacity. Humankind, however, appears to be in a mode of mortification fused with a fear of helplessness. This ever-increasing quality, regarded as an admirable feature of modern scientific inquiry, has proved ultimately to be its absolute bane.

Macaulay exulted in Baconian philosophy in the following words.

"It is a philosophy which never rests, which has never attained, which is never perfect. Its law is progress. A point which yesterday was invisible is its goal today and will be its starting-post tomorrow."

('Critical and Historical Essays': Volume II; by Thomas Babington Macaulay)

Remember that the adoption of atomic energy is no solution to the problem of energy. It is just as to take to poisoned food in the absence of a healthy one. Yet, the factor of ever-increasing progress will oblige you to adopt atomic energy to your ruin.

(10) THE PROCESS OF BACONIAN DESIGN AND ITS END

The Baconian design suggested a systematic and continuous scientific inquiry and its application to material exploitation of the secrets of Mother Nature. Steam was discovered and employed for locomotion. Then electricity was discovered and employed for various new purposes. Moreover, scientific discovery and material application moved parallel until scientific inquiry reached the atomic phenomena. A closer examination reveals that the scientific inquiry in its course has advanced only in the lines that promised material gain, and never a line has been furthered for merely the sake of gaining knowledge purely for the sake of knowledge. There is also a belief in the eternity of this process of progress. People believe this progress to go on forever through five-year plans. Moreover, indeed this progress is recognized as the sole business of man. The world is utterly, entirely, and wholly engrossed in it.

However, the world is in error regarding the eternity of this progress. Undoubtedly, it has approached its end. The three current elements, namely, 'slander of religion', 'engrossment in wealth accumulation', and 'a belief in the eternity of this progress' will, like the three ingredients of dynamite when mixed up, explode with the difference only that the explosion will not be of chemical but atomic that is nuclear nature.

(11) QURAN'S VIEW OF BACON'S DESIGN

The Quran has taken a grave view of Baconian design and has predicted the appearance of atomic hell from it and the consumption of the Baconian world by the flames of the atomic fire. No doubt it is surprising to see the Baconian atomism categorized and declared as the source of atomic hell, the atomic phenomena characterized, and the atomic bomb portrayed by a book of religion fourteen centuries ago in an age of no sciences, and no expectation ever of the revival of atomism anywhere in the world in any age.

Just read the following.

"Woe to every backbiter, defamer, who amasseth wealth (of this world) and arrangeth it (against the future). He thinketh that his wealth will render him immortal (will forever remain with him), Nay, for verily, he will be cast into "Al-Hotama". And what could teach thee what "Al-Hotama" is? It is a fire of Allah kindled, which leapeth up onto the hearts. It is (a fire) closed in on them in outstretched columns."

(Quran: 104 'Al-Homaza')

No better description of Baconian philosophy, design, and the atomic phenomena is possible than specified by the Quran. We have not seen such a succinct description, neither in any pre-modern age nor in this present age itself when atomic phenomena are before the very eyes of the world and knowledge is touching its highest pinnacles. No doubt Einstein, Rutherford, and Russell are missed to appreciate such a wonder. It has taken me a whole volume to explain the scientific side of the prophecy of the Quran.

Here we will briefly touch on every point referred to in Bacon's philosophy.

(a) The Quran says: "Backbiter, defamer."

Whether ancient or modern Baconian, atomism itself is a glaring example of 'backbiting' and 'defaming' the doctrinal aspects of revealed faith. Besides, the modern Baconian culture itself is steeped in slander to its tongue and pen. The rational criticism, the criterion of judgment in this age, has been cankered into calumny while the spiritual and miraculous side of divine Scriptures according to this modern rationalism is utterly false and mere superstition.

Besides these intellectualized forms of slander, the word 'propaganda' has assumed special meanings of 'slander' in this age. We could witness the habit of universal slander everywhere as a distinctive characteristic feature of this age. From every pen and tongue, in every language and dialect, in every assembly and gathering, in every house and habitation, you will hear slander. Tongues engaged in slander, the whole slander and nothing but the slander, and presenting a peculiar universal spectacle fit for Dante to describe. The spirit of slander characteristically and exclusively possesses this Baconian age.

(b) The Quran says: **"He amasseth wealth (of this world) and arrangeth it (against the future)."**

No better description and definition of this Baconian systematic, organized, ever-increasing, and infinite process of 'wealth-acquirement' and 'wealth accumulation' could be expected. No need appears to spend more words on this factor except that this is a distinctive feature of this present age. It distinguishes this age from every other age of the past. It is the age of systematic and continued 'wealth accumulation' distinctively. Also, there exists a discernible difference between the individual and sporadic instances of 'wealth accumulation' in the pre-modern ages and the systematic, collective, and universal system of 'wealth accumulation' of this Baconian age.

(c) The Quran says: **"He thinketh that his wealth will render him immortal, (that is his wealth will forever remain with him)."**

The general and universal belief of the people of this age in the continued eternity of this present process of 'wealth accumulation' is no hidden secret. So blind is their faith in this respect that even all these most manifest hazards that threaten the very existence of this Baconian humankind have not the most negligible effect on them. We may still hear them cry with Galileo in a chorus, "all the same it continues". However, the Quran has other views about it.

(d) The Quran says: **"Nay, for verily, he will be cast into 'Al-Hotama'."**

The Quran repudiates the belief of 'slandering wealth accumulator' in the 'eternity of wealth' that is the belief of the Baconian age in the eternity of the Baconian process of progress. Nay, says the Quran, he will without fail be cast into 'Al-Hotama'; both he and his wealth to be consumed and ground to powder, for 'Al-Hotama' literally means 'the crusher'.

At last, the truth of this declaration of the Quran appears before the world in the most clear-cut form of atomic crusher. It is ready any moment to crush both the people of this Baconian age and all their accumulated wealth.

However, mark phonetic and functional identity between the scientist's 'Atomos' and the 'Hotama' of the Arabic Quran. The 'phonetic' resemblance between these two words and 'crushing' is a distinguishing characteristic of the atomic that is the nuclear phenomena from every other phenomenon, e.g., chemical, and electrical. We generate atomic energy by crushing the binding of the atomic nucleus. The crushing of the atomic nucleus means complete crushing, defying any attempt at the rearrangement. Atomic phenomena in every way are crushers.

(e) The Quran says: **"What could teach thee what 'Al-Hotama' is?"**
The interrogative mode implied the terribleness and complexity of the phenomena of atomic origin. The terribleness of the atomic phenomena defies expression that no Shakespeare, no Milton was there to describe the atomic horrors and claim perfection. Moreover, it is a lengthy tale of woe. The complexity and intricacy of atomic phenomena are such that if the question, "What could teach thee what the atomic science is?" put to the knowing scientist, his answer invariably will be, "Nothing".

(f) The Quran says: **"It is a fire of Allah enkindled, which leapeth up onto the hearts."**
No doubt, the atomic fire is a fire of retribution. It is the punishment for the evils mentioned above. The atomic fire comes out of the 'nucleus' of the atom. At the same time, radiations have a particular attraction for the 'heart' and all that is related to the 'heart' in a living body compared to nerves, muscles, and the brain.

(g) The Quran says: **"It is a fire closed in on them."**
No doubt, the atomic fire has certain peculiarly characteristic features of 'encompassing' nature. Radiations keep on guarding the victims forever. The genetic effects of radiation encompass their victims to generations secretly. Also, there are so many other factors besides which prove this particular characteristic of atomic fire.

(h) The Quran says: **"In outstretched columns."**
The 'column' of the atomic bomb explosion is a symbolic feature. Besides this, the world of radiations is a world of columns. The four-

centimeter rise of an alpha particle, when regarded in proportion to its tiny size, could be regarded as a column. A football rising to a height in the same proportion to its diameter would disappear in the higher regions of outer space. The cosmic radiation presents a spectacle of columns with heights that may cause the human mind to reel.

(12) BACON'S MISUNDERSTANDING ABOUT HIS OWN PHILOSOPHY

Bacon might have thought that his philosophy would redeem humankind from the double tyranny, that is, of the Christian Church and that of the cruel human wants and needs of life. However, in place of the tyranny of the Church, he imposed on humankind cruelty in the form of the Economico-Industrial system and ever-increasing intensity of appetite that proved to be even severe.

How often would he have imagined a world appearing as the result of his philosophy full of natural saints, cosmic mystics, and terrestrial friars that sat engrossed in the contemplation of the works of God? He would have imagined them discovering secrets of Mother Nature and turning them to the advantage of humankind in an earthy Paradise: in which flowed rivers of milk and honey in an atmosphere free from law or courts, crime, or criminals, since the root of every evil, namely, 'want' had vanished. But, alas! Instead, Bacon's philosophy created a species of human locusts that devoured everything on earth that came in their way and tended toward the blazing flames of Baconian hell, the atomic hell, the logical and scientific consequences of Baconian atomism.

~~*~*~*

CHAPTER-8

QURAN VERSUS BACON ON MORAL AND NATURAL PHILOSOPHY

At the time when Shakespeare's Macbeth was being staged at London's Globe theatre in an atmosphere of sorrow and hate, at the sight of the cold-blooded murder of Duncan (the king of Scotland) by treacherous Macbeth, when tears rolled down the cheeks of many soft-hearted spectators at Macduff's wailing; "O Banquo, O Banquo, Our royal master's murdered", and when the audience was regarding even the actors that acted Macbeth and lady Macbeth with hate and anger: accurately at that time or near about, and in the same city a person was committing a murder; that was without the slightest shadow of a doubt a murder of Mother Nature, far more blasphemous, sinful and of exceedingly far-reaching consequences; indeed the kind of a murder that even if all the murders committed from the beginning to the present-day on this earth were combined, were to be outweighed by that single act of felony.

Such indeed was that murder. Yet, the person did not commit it by a sword; he used the pen only. He murdered Mother Nature in two brief passages, one consisting of seventy-seven, the other of ninety-seven words.

Following are the passages.

(1) "It was not the pure knowledge of nature and universality, a knowledge by the light whereof man did give names unto other creatures in Paradise, as they were brought before him, according unto their proprieties, which gave the occasion to the fall: but it was the proud knowledge of good and evil, with an intent in man to give law unto himself, and to depend no more upon God's commandments, which was the form of the temptation."

(Francis Bacon's 'Advancement of Learning': The first book, Page-7)

(2) "Again, the first acts which man performed in Paradise consisted of the two summary parts of knowledge; the view of creatures, and the imposition of names. As for knowledge which induced the fall, it was, as was touched before, not the natural knowledge of creatures, but the moral knowledge of good and evil; wherein the supposition

was, that God's commandments or prohibitions were not the originals of good and evil but that they had other beginnings, which man aspired to know; to the end to make a total defection from God and to depend wholly upon himself."

(Francis Bacon's 'Advancement of Learning': The first book, Pages: 45-46)

O, Humankind! The revealed religion of Allah that is the religion of Abraham, Moses, Jesus, and Mohammad (peace be upon them all) has been murdered in these two above-quoted brief passages. Also, the religion of Buddha and Krishna, any religion worth the name that ever existed on earth, has been murdered. Humanity has been murdered. Morality has been murdered. In short, the whole truth has been murdered. Pentateuch of Moses, Psalms of David, Gospel of Jesus, and the Quran of Mohammad (peace be upon him); all have been murdered.

Francis Bacon has condemned moral philosophy as a vain, impious innovation of man and forbidden by God, while it is impossible to think of religion without moral philosophy. If Bacon's concept of natural philosophy is correct, then Allah's revealed Scriptures ought to have been the treatises on natural philosophy which they are not. They are rather one and all, the first and the last, basically the treatises on moral philosophy with natural philosophy as a mere handmaid of moral philosophy and regulated by its rules. Bacon thus obviously has condemned all the Scriptures of Allah, which claim to contain the Will of Allah.

The readers of Bacon's works might have overlooked these passages just as pioneers of atomism at the time of Renaissance had hoped to segregate the 'atheistic' part of atomism from its 'scientific' part and had failed. Our opinion is that we should regard every part of the philosophy with suspicion produced by the mind that penned these two passages in question. And we can now see that Baconian progress, despite its apparent dissociation from the doctrinal aspect of Bacon's philosophy, has resulted in misery and destruction. Besides, Bacon has said that man went away from God and depended wholly upon himself by adopting moral philosophy. Our observation is to the contrary rather. Bacon's philosophy has shown this effect. When we see the passages of Bacon minutely, we find the following points.

(1) God commanded 'natural philosophy' to Adam in Paradise.
(2) The fall of Adam occurred not due to natural philosophy but due to his knowledge of 'good' and 'evil'.

(3) Adam pursued the knowledge of 'good' and 'evil' to give himself the law.
(4) God forbade the knowledge of 'good' and 'evil' to Adam.
(5) Commandments and prohibitions of God were not the originals of 'good' and 'evil' but that they had other beginnings that man aspired to know to the end to go entirely away from God and depend wholly upon himself.

It entirely means that Allah's commandments and prohibitions are not based on the principle of good and evil. And that the theory of religion that the commandments and prohibitions of Allah are based on good and evil, "do ye good and ward off evil", is wrong.

Also, because God expelled Adam from Paradise for eating the fruit of the forbidden tree of knowledge of good and evil, pursuing moral philosophy, and gaining the knowledge of good and evil meant repeating the first transgression of Adam and thus defying God's prohibition.

It is hard to believe that Bacon could have said these things. The whole thing appears preposterous. However, if words have any relation to meanings, it is hard to deny the truth of these allegations, howsoever unbelievable they may appear. Bacon's works are still extant, and one may read to confirm the truth or otherwise of these statements, which go much against Bacon in the presence of the dreadful results of Bacon's philosophy.

Bacon has asserted that God's command to man was to pursue natural philosophy (science) and that man, in disobedience to God's commands, took to moral philosophy that was prohibited. It is an exciting postulate for thoughtful persons to imagine. What type of that world would be, where people would excessively pursue the natural philosophy and act tact of moral philosophy to exist therein. It is a strange postulate, and that would be a strange world and strange species that would inhabit such a world: neither human beings at least nor in any way angelic.

When we look a little too minutely into the Baconian doctrine of 'all-natural' and 'no-moral' philosophy: natural philosophy as the command of God to man and moral philosophy forbidden by God, it naturally looks that natural philosophy regards the fall of man on earth as final without any thought of Resurrection, Judgement, or life in the otherworld.

We have no means to ascertain whether to Bacon himself this issue of the affair ever occurred. For, no moral philosophy means not any thought of good and evil. No thought of good and evil means not any possibility of trial. No trial means not any Judgement, and hence neither any Resurrection nor any otherworld. And all this means that there is no truth in religion.

However, an exciting postulate appears when we assume a world of all-natural and not a moral philosophy according to Baconian doctrine. In the absence of the moral factor, the postulate is how and on what criterion Allah would judge men if Resurrection made its appearance? Would the men be judged based on worldly success?

Whatever the case, the law of some kind would make its appearance and make its necessity known. What would then Bacon say to it?

QURAN ON MORAL PHILOSOPHY

Quran, like every true Scripture of Allah, has based its philosophy on morality. The Prophet of Islam (peace be upon him) gave out the purpose of his Prophetic mission as the perfection of moral virtue. Allah, according to the Quran, said to Adam on latter's fall:

"We said: Go down, all of you, from hence; but verily there cometh unto you from Me a guidance; and whoso followeth My guidance, there shall no fear come upon them neither shall they grieve. But they who disbelieve and deny our revelations, such are rightful owners of the Fire. They will abide therein."

(Quran 2:38-39)

This promised guidance we have seen in the form of a Scripture through the messenger of Allah and all of it has been based on moral philosophy, constantly depreciating man's love for this transient world and its wealth against the next world.

QURAN'S DESIGN OF MORAL PHILOSOPHY

According to the Quran, the creation itself is based on moral philosophy and predestined for moral attainment, moral Judgment, and trial. Opposite qualities like darkness against light, cold against hot, good against evil, etc. being the pre-requisites of trial and Judgement, constitute the foundation on which Allah established this creation. Balance being another accessory has been adopted, and everything may be seen created with a certain measure. Natural philosophy is conspicuous, but it is regulated by moral principles and created only subservient to moral philosophy. In the following, we give the moral design of the Quran in twelve passages from the Quran.

(1) "Praise be to Allah, Who hath created the heavens and the earth, and hath appointed darkness and light."

(Quran 6:1)

(2) "Who (Allah) hath created life and death that He may try you, which of you is best in conduct."

(Quran 67:2)

(3) "And He hath set the measure (balance)." (Quran 55:7)

(4) "And We set a just balance for the Day of Resurrection so that no soul is wronged in aught. Though it be of the weight of a grain of mustard seed, We bring it. And We suffice for reckoners."

(Quran 21:47)

(5) "That ye exceed not the measure, but observe the measure strictly, nor fall short thereof."

(Quran 55:8-9)

(6) "We verily sent Our messengers with clear proofs, and revealed with them the Scripture and the balance, that mankind may observe right measure."

(Quran 57:25)

(7) "Now hath come unto you light from Allah and a plain Scripture whereby Allah guideth him who seeketh his good pleasure unto paths of peace. He bringeth them out of darkness unto light by His decree, and guideth them unto a straight path."

(Quran 5:15-16)

(8) "We verily sent Our messengers with clear proofs, and revealed with them the Scripture and the Balance, that humankind may observe right measure; and He revealed iron, wherein is mighty power and (many) uses for humankind, and that Allah may know him who helpeth Him and His messengers, though unseen. Lo! Allah is Strong, Almighty."

(Quran 57:25)

(9) "Lo! Allah enjoineth justice and kindness, and giving to kinsfolk, and forbiddeth lewdness and abomination and wickedness. He exhorteth you in order that ye may take heed. Fulfill the covenant of Allah when ye have covenanted, and break not your oaths after the asseveration of them, and after ye have made Allah surety over you. Lo! Allah knoweth what ye do."

(Quran 16:90-91)

(10) "Recite that which hath been inspired in thee of the Scripture, and establish worship. Lo! worship preserveth from lewdness and iniquity, but verily remembrance of Allah is more important. And Allah knoweth what ye do."

(Quran 29:45)

(11) "Lo! The noblest of you in the sight of Allah is the best in conduct."

(Quran 49:13)

(12) "Successful indeed are the believers who are humble in their prayers, And who shun vain conversation, And who are payers of the poor due; And who guard their modesty save from their wives or the (slaves) that their right hands possess, for then they are not blameworthy, But whoso craveth beyond that, such are transgressors, And who are shepherds of the pledge and their covenant, And who pay heed to their prayers. These are the heirs who will inherit Paradise: There they will abide."

(Quran 23:1-11)

QURAN ON BACONIAN NATURAL PHILOSOPHY

The basis of religion is on moral philosophy, as may be seen from the above-quoted design. That is the Quran's design of moral philosophy. The necessity of natural philosophy, undeniable and indispensable, is recognized by the Quran just as every Scripture and religion, though only a necessity and an agency subservient to moral philosophy.

However, we are here concerned with a particular form of natural philosophy, namely, the Baconian natural philosophy, which is pursued exclusively for worldly ends and purely for attaining the things of this world. No religion allowed such a view, nor did the Quran.

In the following, we quote the views of the Quran regarding Baconian natural philosophy against moral philosophy in twelve passages of the Quran with explanations.

(1) "Say: Shall We inform you who will be the greatest losers by their works? Those whose effort goeth astray in the life of the world, and yet they reckon that they do good work. Those are they who disbelieve in the revelations of their Lord and the meeting with Him. Therefore, their works are vain, and on the Day of Resurrection, We assign no weight to them. That is their reward: hell because they disbelieved and made a jest of Our revelations and Our messengers."

(Quran 18:103-106)

The achievements of science like the accumulation of wealth, worldly facilities, and physical comforts have accrued from Baconian philosophy. These accomplishments are the sole object of people's lives and are contrary to the religious concept due to the complete engrossment in the world and complete forgetfulness of the next world. These are the things to perish within this world. Hence, Allah will not credit these attainments with any weight on the Day of Resurrection and Judgement. Hell, therefore, shall be the reward of the works that carried no weight on that day. Nay, perfect is the example of the Baconian age that hell has appeared in this same world. The world now is ready to be consumed by the flames of atomic hell, the logical and scientific result of the process of the Baconian atomism and the Baconian design.

As far as the question of disbelieving in the revelations of Allah is concerned, the people of this Baconian age are not even willing to believe in the atomic hell which now appears before their very eyes, not to speak of Allah's revelations which only appear in the Scriptures. The question of making a jest of Allah's revelations and His messengers is no hidden secret in this age. People regard the Scriptures as a fardel of ancient, outmoded superstition and religion as opium hindering progress and a source of deterioration. Some great Baconian researchers have declared Jesus Christ as only a mythical fiction. No doubt religion today is a matter of jest. Everyone thinks this philosophy of progress is correct and full of joy, little thinking that these achievements are themselves vanishing and will also become the means of destroying this world.

(2) "See they not that Allah enlargeth the provision for whom He will, and straiteneth (it for whom He will). Lo! Herein indeed are portents for folk who believe. So, give to the relative his due, and the needy, and the wayfarer. That is best for those who seek Allah's countenance. And such are they who are successful. That which ye give in usury in order that it may increase on (other) people's property hath no increase with Allah; but that which ye give in charity, seeking Allah's Countenance, hath increase manifold."

(Quran 30:37-39)

No one in this age of Baconian struggle for material utility is prepared to believe that the distribution of provision is in Allah's hands. Instead, everyone thought of it as the result of one's own ability and endeavor. The charity has vanished because no one today can even think he has a surplus to impart to the needy. Instead, everybody feels needy. Usury is the essential factor of this Baconian culture. However, we are citing these examples from the Quran to show only the general trends of the Quran respecting this Baconian philosophy and the culture based on it.

(3) "They know only some appearance of the life of the world and are heedless of the Hereafter. Have they not pondered upon themselves? Allah created not the heavens and the earth, and that which is between them, save with truth and for a destined end. But truly, many of humankind are disbelievers in the meeting with their Lord."

(Quran 30:7-8)

This Baconian humankind that is these followers of Bacon's exclusively materialistic philosophy, as may be seen, know only the world's outward appearance. The purpose of life they have set before them; namely, the infinite progress only is at variance with the purpose the Quran has set for man.

Moreover, no doubt, there is no real thought of or reasonable belief in the Resurrection and the next life. The entire Baconian world is utterly engrossed in the world, panting, wheezing, chaffing, perspiring, fretting, as the sole purpose of their life so that everyone needs and wants everything and struggles to have it by hook or by crook.

Even though the Baconian mission has succeeded, its success is its failure. Man has succeeded but in what? He has succeeded just in reaching hell. The Baconian enterprise likewise has succeeded but in what? It has succeeded just in reaching the Baconian hell.

(4) "By the declining day, Lo! Man is in a state of loss, save those who believe and do good works, and exhort one another to truth and exhort one another to endurance."

(Quran 103:1-3)

Suppose the truth is Baconian materialism and seeking wealth and spherical comforts, and endurance means the endurance in the worldly struggle. In that case, we may rank people of this age as saints of the highest order, hierarchs, and martyrs. But if by truth is meant which was understood by those who were first recipients of the Quran, and by appeal is meant which they did, then, of course, people of this Baconian age are the losers of the highest order without precedent in human history. The Quran has meant by truth in this instance, the truth of Allah's religion, and the endurance in religion. It has not alluded to worldly matters. Therefore, the truth and endurance to which the first recipients of the Quran encouraged each other was a matter purely of religion.

(5) "The life of the world is but a sport and a pastime. And if ye believe and ward off (evil), He will give you your wages and will not ask of you your worldly wealth."

(Quran 47:36)

The entire theme of Baconian philosophy is limited to the life of the world, which in the sight of the Quran is only a sport and pastime. The Quran has advised belief and warding off evil as preferable and has its peculiar wages. This sign (verse) of the Quran is an exemplary specimen of the Quran's view expressing the natural relative to the moral philosophy.

(6) "Now whatever ye have been given is but a passing comfort for the life of the world, and that which Allah hath is better and more lasting for those who believe and put their trust in their Lord."

(Quran 42:36)

The whole Baconian philosophy revolves around the passing comfort of the life of the world. According to Allah, faith in Allah and good works are a must besides the matter of this world, and that is, to wit, religion. It is another example of the natural against the moral philosophy in the sight of the Quran.

(7) "Wealth and children are an ornament of the life of the world. But the good deeds which endure are better in thy Lord's sight for reward and better in respect of hope." (Quran 18:46)

Baconian philosophy is constrained to wealth and children. It has to do nothing with the type of good deeds as are mentioned in the Quran. It is yet another example of the natural relative to the moral philosophy according to the Quran.

(8) "And it is neither your wealth nor your children that will bring you near unto Us, but he who believeth and doeth good (he draweth near). As for such, theirs will be twofold reward for what they did, and they will dwell securely in lofty halls."

(Quran 34:37)

In this age of Baconian culture, however, nothing but wealth is the source of honor. People regard poverty as the mortifying curse of all the curses that had a name. A paragon of virtue or the one most learned in art is likely to cut a sorry figure without respect, honor, grace, or dignity if he has no wealth. Still, the most wretched thing that ever caused blisters on the breast of the earth with his feet is to consider the wealthiest as most honorable if he is known to have a large sum of money, even without any regard as to how he had gained that wealth. It is in exact accord with the Baconian basis. In the sight of the Quran, however, he who believes and does good deeds is worthy of honor and is nearer to the presence of Allah. It is an example of the natural relative to the moral philosophy according to the Quran's view.

(9) "Beautified for humankind is the love of the joys (that come) from women and offspring, and stored-up heaps of gold and silver, and horses branded (with their mark), and cattle and land. That is the comfort of the life of the world. Allah! With Him is a more excellent abode. Say: Shall I inform you of something better than that? For those who keep from evil, with their Lord, are Gardens underneath which rivers flow, and pure companions, and contentment from Allah. Allah is Seer of His bondmen, those who say: Our Lord! Lo! We believe. So, forgive us our sins and guard us against the punishment of Fire; The steadfast, and the truthful, and the obedient, those who spend (and hoard not), those who pray for pardon in the watches of the night."

(Quran 3:14-17)

More than the eloquence or ability of Bacon, the real cause of the immediate and universal acceptance of his philosophy was this love of the things of the world which is inherent in human nature. The other cause, no doubt, was the disappointment of the West over their religion. In this above-quoted passage, we have yet another example of the Quran's view of the natural against moral philosophy.

(10) "O ye who believe, when the call is heard for the prayer of the day of congregation, haste unto remembrance of Allah and leave your trading. That is better for you if ye did but know. And when the prayer is ended, then you disperse in the land and seek of Allah's bounty, and remember Allah much, that ye may be successful. But when they spy some merchandise or pastime, they break away to it and leave thee standing. Say: That which Allah hath is better than a pastime and merchandise, and Allah is the best of providers."

(Quran 62:9-11)

Here the preference is religious and moral against material and natural. Repeatedly, it tells that there is a difference between worldly things and that which is with Allah. Indeed, worldly things are possessions of the material, but one may gain which is with Allah through religious duty and observation of morality.

(11) "Then verily We shall question those unto whom (Our message) hath been sent, and verily We shall question the messengers. Then verily We shall narrate unto them (the event) with knowledge, for verily We were not absent (when it came to pass). The weighing on that day is the true (weighing). As for those whose scale is heavy, they are successful. And as for those whose scale is light: those are they who lose their souls because they disbelieved Our revelations."

(Quran 7:6-9)

It is about the day of Resurrection. Anyone should weigh neither riches nor the world's material things on the pattern of this material world. Deeds will be weighed. The spirit of deeds will have weight. What weight could be assigned to persons' endeavors to produce wealth in this Baconian progress on that day? To conclude, Allah will assign no weight to this Baconian progress on the Day of Judgments; instead, He will assign the weight to religious and moral deeds and the acts of humility and charity for humanity.

(12) "Then withdraw (O Muhammad) from him who fleeth from Our remembrance and desireth but the life of the world. Such is their sum of knowledge. Lo! Thy Lord is best aware of him who strayeth, and He is best aware of him who goeth right."

(Quran 53:29-30)

The Baconian philosophy has no concern with God's remembrance. The Baconian progress leaves neither mind nor time for the remembrance of God, and no doubt this Baconian philosophy and this Baconian progress and this Baconian culture is a matter of the life of this world alone. Do you think you will superimpose Islam on this Baconian progress and thus affect a balance between the material and spiritual and between this world and the next world? Then you are mistaken. You are the victim of the grossest misunderstanding. This Baconian progress is a witch that yields to no spiritual enchantment. But, since the revelation, the Islamic world has perused the Quran. They are familiar with the punishment in the hell of 'Al-Hotama' for 'wealth accumulation' and a belief in the eternity of riches (Quran: 104 'Al-Homaza'). Yet, the Islamic world has gone headlong into Baconian progress, which is the exact interpretation of the chapter of the Quran alluded to above.

Now that I have pointed out this great prophecy of the Quran and have interpreted it in the clearest of terms, it is still difficult to guess the Quran's followers' attitude regarding this miracle of the Quran.

"So wary held, and wise —

Of whom 'twas said, he scarce received

For Gospel, what the Church believed —"

(Marmion-XXX; by Sir Walter Scott)

It is too spurious a praise for him and too poor accompaniment. Bacon stands too high, towering with his head in the clouds. He did not only not receive for Gospel what the Church believed, but he laid his hand on the very root of the Gospel and caused it to wither in a moment. He drew the entire world towards him by the magical sound of his trumpet while Allah and His Prophets stood looking amazed.

Moreover, he conquered the entire world without striking a blow and without entering into a single controversy. Indeed, he achieved with chalk what Napoleons and Alexanders had failed to achieve with sword and with flame. Yet we are doubtful whether our praise of Bacon could ever reach the true mark or somewhere near it; words of praise just lose their significance. Alas! However, our anger against him subsides to sorrow—we pity his great misfortune and even the afflictions of nature in his life.

~~*~*~*~*

CHAPTER-9

RELATIVE VIEWS OF BACON AND QURAN ON MATERIAL UTILITY

The fundamental difference between the views of Bacon and that of Quran on the point of material utility is that whereas to Bacon, the material utility is the end without any consideration of the next world, to Quran, the material utility is a means only to serve the end which is the next life.

As for the end of Bacon's philosophy though we can see, yet we will cite Macaulay's view as follows.

"The chief peculiarity of Bacon's philosophy seems to us to have been this that it aimed at things altogether different from those which his predecessors had proposed to themselves. This was his own opinion. The more carefully his works are examined, the more clearly, we think, it will appear that this is the real clue to his whole system, and that he used means different from those used by other philosophers, because he wished to arrive at an end altogether different from theirs. What then was the end which Bacon proposed to himself? It was, to use his own emphatic expression, "fruit." It was the multiplying of human enjoyments and the mitigating of human sufferings. It was "the relief of man's estate." This was the object of all his speculations in every department of science, in natural philosophy, in legislation, in politics, in morals. Two words form the key of the Baconian doctrine, Utility and Progress."

('Critical and Historical Essays': Volume-II; by Thomas Babington Macaulay)

Indeed, Bacon's philosophy is opposed to every philosophy and every religion. Bacon has given out 'fruit' as the end of his philosophy. Macaulay points to 'utility' and 'progress', which humankind has achieved through mechanical, economic, social, and political contrivances.

We may further see that humanity has achieved outstanding success in the object of the Baconian philosophy, namely, the material advantage for the world's life. But because the Baconian philosophy has wholly ignored the next world and it was impossible for Baconian philosophy not to ignore the next world, the Quran has a Prophetic pronouncement regarding the Baconian culture. It says their endeavors will become fruitless. Their contrivances will become vain, and Allah will cast them into the fire. Just read:

"Whoso desireth the life of the world and its pomp, We shall repay them their deeds herein, and therein they will not be wronged. Those are they for whom is naught in the Hereafter save the Fire. (All) that they contrive here is vain and (all) that they are wont to do, is fruitless."

(Quran 11:15-16)

See, the Quran has given out the Baconian philosophy of 'fruit' as 'fruitless'. No doubt, suppose even if no atomic hazard had appeared and this humankind suffered a natural death. Even then, all this success of Baconian philosophy would have been regarded as vain and fruitless, being only worldly and also ungodly. Miraculously, the atomic factor has appeared to render these contrivances as vain and make this fruit fruitless. The Quran also has predicted the destruction of this Baconian atomic culture in the flames of atomic hell.

~~*~*~*~*

PART-1
QURAN'S CODE OF MATERIAL UTILITY

As far as the utility of Allah's bounties is concerned, Allah is not averse to His creatures' partaking of his bounties which He has created for their use. Still, the conditions are that they give thanks. Neither they are as engrossed in the material utility as to make it the sole purpose of their life nor forget their duty to Allah or the thought of the next world. Against this transient world, their actual and eternal abode is the next world. The material utility of this transient world is transient. The prince and the slave have both to leave this world. A particular rivalry exists between man's love of this world and his love of Allah. We should say that there has been, there is still, and there shall be forever an almost exclusive temptation for man's disbelief and infidelity, a temptation to the love of this world and its wealth. A Muslim, therefore, while considering the Quran's license of material utility, should always keep these factors in his mind, or else he must be prepared to meet the dire consequences of this neglect.

We will now give in the following the philosophy of the Quran regarding the 'material utility' of this transient world in a manifest array.

(1) **The believers can partake of Allah's bounties, provided they fulfill the conditions of faith.**

According to the Quran, the appearance of good things like food, apparel, gardens, palaces, and other means of luxury, is a representative display of bounties extant in the next eternal world: just as the garden is a representation of Paradise; "gardens beneath which rivers flow". Similarly, the 'fire' is the reminder of 'hellfire'.

If, therefore, the believers partake of Allah's bounties on earth, provided they fulfill the conditions of faith, the gracious and generous Allah is not only not averse to it but is also pleased.
The Quran says:

"Say: <u>Who hath forbidden the adornment</u> of Allah which He hath brought forth for His bondmen and the good things of His providing? Say: Such, on the Day of Resurrection, will be only for those who believed during the life of the world. Thus, do We detail Our revelations for people who have knowledge. Say: My Lord forbiddeth only indecencies, such of them as are apparent and such as are within, and sin and wrongful oppression, and that ye associate with Allah that for which no warrant hath been revealed, and that ye tell concerning Allah that which ye know not."

(Quran 7:32-33)

The style and the language of this above-quoted passage, "<u>Who hath forbidden the adornment?</u>" etc., is apparent inception that it alludes to the practice of seclusion in the monastery and hermitage. Anyone could not make it a sanction for a life of complete engrossment in the material world or this modern material progress. This consent, the sensualists of the Epicurean period had claimed for their short and merry life of debauch, the sanction of Epicurean principle, that pleasure is the chief good at which alone it is reasonable to aim.

The Quran has declared the Holy Prophet of Islam (peace be upon him) as a model and perfect specimen for the followers. It is sufficient to enunciate, to give a short shift to this argument, that even he could not have amply utilized this particular license of the Quran during his Prophetic career. Throughout his Prophetic career, he lived a life of poverty based on self-abnegation. Essentially, there must be some weighty considerations that appeared to check the apparent liberty allowed by the Quran. The Quran must set conditions. There must be considerations worthwhile keeping in mind.

Moreover, the sacred person of the Prophet (peace be upon him) himself and his disciples and men taught and trained by him could be seen to follow the Prophet's example (peace be upon him) in this respect. Why on earth Hazrat Omar (Razi Allah ho taa'la unho), the second Caliph and the absolute emperor of an empire that could be the envy of any monarch, went in a shirt with no less than fourteen patches on it? Why was he seen usually sitting on the steps of the mosque, supping, and inviting the passers-by to a meal that appeared to be repulsive to even the men of the most meager means?

Why would his answer be to those who questioned him for that severe austerity that he feared lest on the Day of Judgment Allah might say:

"Omar! Thou hadst enough of thy share in thy life in the world."?

Why did Hazrat Ali (Razi Allah ho taa'la unho), the fourth Caliph, go about in a dress befitting a dead rather than a living man? Why did he eat a meal so coarse and so hard that a few besides him could chew? Why should Ali challenge all the gold and silver and the apparelling gems of the public treasury during his Caliphate, saying:

"Ye canst adorn the face of anyone but not that of Ali"?

And he did prove his word practically.

It is not at all sufficient to say that they were the paragons of virtue unapproachable and, therefore, could not be followed by ordinary mortals. Indeed, if they are unapproachable, this is not a pretext to plunge headlong into the world as an object and purpose of life vying with each other in the pursuit. Hell is the consequence of such a pursuit. It has now appeared within sight of every pursuer of the world and its wealth.

Does then the Quran allow its followers something which must undoubtedly and inevitably result in the form of the all-consuming atomic hell? Is then the Quran as a book of materialism? A book understood only by Bacon and no one else?

(2) 'Monasticism' and 'Modern Materialism'

In the above-quoted passage of the Quran, we have alluded to the Quran's disapproval of the monastic creeds of the hermitage. According to the Quran, Christians themselves invented monasticism, and Allah did not ordain it for them, and they observed it not with the correct observance.

Mark the difference between the two extremes, namely, 'monasticism' and 'modern materialism'. The world is wholly renounced in the former case, while, in the latter, people wholly adopt this world. Islam allows neither of these forms. The former is difficult to sustain and dangerous; the latter is utterly worldly and one-sided, devoid of spiritualism and otherworldliness. However, the consequences of this Baconian materialism have appeared by far the most heinous than those of monasticism, namely, a blazing atomic hell to consume the Baconian world and miseries of untold and unheard-of denominations.

Now, read the Quran's view of Christianity and Christian monasticism.

The Quran says:

"Then We caused Our messengers to follow in their footsteps; and We caused Jesus, son of Mary, to follow, and gave him the Gospel, and placed compassion and mercy in the hearts of those who followed him. But monasticism they invented. We ordained it not for them. Only seeking Allah's pleasure, and they observed it not with right observance. So, We give those of them who believe their reward, but many of them are evil livers."

(Quran 57:27)

We observe that Western Christendom went from one extreme of monasticism to the other of exclusive materialism and dragged the entire world behind them. Muslims followed them with great willingness, nor did the Hindus or Buddhists stay behind, and for all is a blazing, heaving, roaring hell of atomic fire: the logical and scientific result of Baconian atomism toward which they now hasten speedily vying with each other, waving their banners, raising slogans and beating kettle drums, and carrying one and all an invisible portrait of the originator of this modern age whose name they have seldom heard, and whose works they have never read. Bacon should have taken guidance from Islam instead of imposing on humankind a creed of Anti-Christ that ended in atomic hell.

(3) Everything on the earth is made subservient to man by Merciful Allah.

The Quran says:

"Hast thou not seen how Allah hath made all that is in the earth subservient unto you? And the ship runneth upon the sea by His command, and He holdeth back the heaven from falling on the earth unless by His leave. Lo! Allah is, for humankind, Full of Pity, Merciful."

(Quran 22:65)

(4) All good things are made lawful.

The Quran says:

"They ask thee (O Muhammad) what is made lawful for them. Say: (all) good things are made lawful for you. And those beasts and birds of prey which ye have trained as hounds are trained, ye teach them that which Allah taught you; so, eat of that which they catch for you and mention Allah's name upon it, and observe your duty to Allah. Lo! Allah is swift to take account." (Quran 5:4)

(5) Prodigality is forbidden.

The Quran says:

"O children of Adam! Look to your adornment at every place of worship, and eat and drink, but be not prodigal. Lo! He loveth not the prodigals."

(Quran 7:31)

(6) **Neither (you) forbid yourself good things nor do (you) transgress.**
The Quran says:
"O ye who believe! Forbid not the good things which Allah hath made lawful for you, and transgress not. Lo! Allah loveth, not transgressors. Eat of that which Allah hath bestowed on you as food lawful and good, and keep your duty to Allah in Whom ye are believers."

(Quran 5:87-88)

(7) **Allah's word only is to be taken as the authority on the lawfulness of things or otherwise.**
The Quran says:
"And speak not, concerning that which your own tongues qualify (as clean or unclean), the falsehood: "This is lawful, and this is forbidden," so that ye invent a lie against Allah. Lo! Those who invent a lie against Allah will not succeed. A brief enjoyment (will be theirs); and theirs a painful doom."

(Quran 16:116-117)

(8) **Do not covet other men's property and avoid bribery.**
The Quran says:
"And eat not up your property among yourselves in vanity, nor seek by it to gain the hearing of the judges that ye may knowingly devour a portion of the property of others wrongfully." (Quran 2:188)

(9) **Follow not the footsteps of the devil in material utility.**
The Quran says:
"O, humankind! Eat of that which is lawful and wholesome in the earth, and follow not the footsteps of the devil. Lo! He is an open enemy for you." (Quran 2:168)

(10) **Allah expected gratitude and belief in His unity (oneness) in return for His bounty.**
The Quran says:
"Of His mercy hath He appointed for you night and day that therein ye may rest, and that ye may seek His bounty, and that haply ye may be thankful. And on the Day when He shall call unto them and say: Where are My partners whom ye pretended?" (Quran 28:73-74)

(11) **Let not your wealth and your children distract you from the remembrance of Allah.**
The Quran says:
"O ye who believe! Let not your wealth nor do your children distract you from the remembrance of Allah. Those who do so, they are the losers."

(Quran 63:9)

(12) The best commerce in the sight of the Quran is the belief in Allah and His messenger.

The Quran says:

"O ye who believe! Shall I show you a commerce that will save you from a painful doom? Ye should believe in Allah and His messenger and should strive for the cause of Allah with your wealth and your lives. That is better for you if ye did but know. He will forgive you your sins and bring you into Gardens underneath which rivers flow and pleasant dwellings in Gardens of Eden. That is the supreme triumph."

(Quran 61:10-12)

(13) According to the Quran, the best provision is to ward off evil for fear of Allah.

The Quran says:

"So, make provision for yourselves (hereafter); for the best provision is to ward off evil. Therefore, keep your duty unto Me, O men of understanding."

(Quran 2:197)

(14) Distribution of provisions is in the hands of Allah.

The Quran says:

"Lo! Thy Lord enlargeth the provision for whom He will, and straiteneth (it for whom He will). Lo! He was ever Knower, Seer of His slaves." (Quran 17:30)

(15) Allah provides both for you and your children.

The Quran says:

"Slay not your children, fearing a fall to poverty; We shall provide for them and for you. Lo! The slaying of them is a great sin. And come not near unto adultery. Lo! It is an abomination and an evil way."

(Quran 17:31-32)

(16) Prayers to have precedence over commerce. The Quran says:

"O ye who believe! When the call is heard for the prayer of the day of congregation, haste unto remembrance of Allah and leave your trading. That is better for you if ye did but know. And when the prayer is ended, then disperse in the land and seek of Allah's bounty, and remember Allah much, that ye may be successful." (Quran 62:9-10)

(17) The extra wealth is to be given in charity in consideration of the next world.

The Quran says:

"And they ask thee (O Prophet) what they ought to spend. Say: That which is superfluous. Thus, Allah maketh plain to you (His) revelations that haply ye may reflect upon the world and the Hereafter."

(Quran 2:219-220)

The Bible says:

"Lay not up for yourselves treasures upon earth, where moth and rust doth corrupt, and where thieves break through and steal: But lay up for yourselves treasures in Heaven, where neither moth nor rust doth corrupt, and where thieves do not break through nor steal."

(The Bible: New Testament: Matthew 6:19-20)

See how close to the center is the bare truth. Compare the two above-quoted specimens; one of the Quran and the other that of the Bible. Here indeed is revealed a fundamental truth of the Quran regarding its view of the world and its wealth. Also, see elementary and complete identity between the view of the Quran and the Gospel of Jesus Christ. Wonder then in amazement, for the Quran is no less severe than the Gospel in its opposing view of the wealth of this world and this world itself. If you entertain some doubt, then take up the Quran's copy and read it. Take a copy of the Gospel and read it. Then, look worldwide to find if anyone today is following the policy of the Quran or the Gospel.

(18) **Spend in the name of Allah before the Last Day has arrived.**
The Quran says:

"O ye who believe! Spend of that wherewith We have provided you ere (before) a day come when there will be no trafficking, nor friendship, nor intercession. The disbelievers are the wrongdoers. Allah! There is no God save Him, the Alive, the Eternal."

(Quran 2:254-255)

(19) **Whom to give in charity and how?**
The Quran says:

"Give the kinsman his due, and the needy, and the wayfarer, and squander not (thy wealth) in wantonness. Lo! The squanderers were ever brothers of the devils, and the devil was ever an ingrate to his Lord."

(Quran 17:26-27)

(20) **Avoid extremity in charity.** The Quran says:

"And let thy hand be not chained to thy neck nor open it with a complete opening, lest thou sit down rebuked, denuded."

(Quran 17:29)

(21) **Success is in escaping one's avarice, according to the Quran.**
The Quran says:

"Those who ... prefer (the fugitives) above themselves though poverty become their lot. And whoso is saved from his own avarice such are they who are successful." (Quran 59:9)

Mark the difference between the injunction above noted and the preceding it that urged the avoidance of extremity. The two are concerned with different occasions.

(22) According to the Quran, this world is only a play and idle talk and is transient only. Nor is it the actual mark or the object. The actual mark is the next world.

The Quran says:

"Know that the life of this world is only a play, and idle talk, and pageantry, and boasting among you and rivalry in respect of wealth and children; as the likeness of vegetation after rain, whereof the growth is pleasing to the husbandman, but afterward it drieth up and thou seest it turning yellow then it becometh straw. And in the Hereafter, there is grievous punishment and (also) forgiveness from Allah and His good pleasure, whereas the life of the world is but a matter of illusion. Race one with another for forgiveness from your Lord and a Garden whereof the breadth is as the breadth of the heavens and the earth, which is in store for those who believe in Allah and His messengers. Such is the bounty of Allah, which He bestoweth upon whom He will, and Allah is of infinite bounty."

(Quran 57:20-21)

This above-quoted view of the Quran stands in direct opposition to the view of Bacon regarding this world. To the Quran, the life of this world is only a play and an illusion and is transient. The actual mark is the next world. While to Bacon, this world alone and its wealth is the sole and absolute object without any mention of the next world.

(23) Neither wealth nor ostentation, but piousness and sobriety are the signs of greatness in the sight of Allah.

The Quran says:

"The noblest of you, in the sight of Allah, is the best in conduct. Lo! Allah is Knower, Aware."

(Quran 49:13)

(24) Follow the example of the Holy Prophet (peace be upon him) as a role model.

The best policy for a believer is to seek guidance from the example of the Holy Prophet (peace be upon him) in the matter of utility as in every other matter. That will be infallible guidance.

The Quran says:

"Verily in the messenger of Allah ye have a good example for him who looketh unto Allah and the Last Day, and remembereth Allah much."

(Quran 33:21)

We may know the view and practice of the Prophet (peace be upon him) from the following in the Quran.

"Say (O Prophet): Lo! As for me, my Lord hath guided me unto a straight path, a right religion, the community of Abraham, the upright, who was no idolater. Say: Lo! My worship and my sacrifice and my living and my dying are for Allah, Lord of the Worlds. He hath no partner. This I am commanded, and I am first of those who surrender (unto Him)."

(Quran 6:161-163)

Such an ideology would never allow anyone to stoop to the love of this world or its wealth. The Prophet (peace be upon him) lived a life of self-imposed poverty to the last and lived as one most generous. Either Bacon or his followers could not even imagine so high an ideal. Just Imagine of so high an ideal.

(25) Following is the Prophet's philosophy of life and his view of this world versus Bacon's.

Also, mark the difference between the Prophet's philosophy of life and his view of this world and Bacon's philosophy of life and his view. The two stand at opposite extremes without any possibility whatsoever of any compromise or reconcilement and forever apart. The Quran has perfectly described the pattern of the Baconian view, which we may see against the pattern of the Islamic view. You have read the Prophet's view of life. Quran has described the Baconian view of life too. Read the following.

The Quran says:

"Hast thou seen him who maketh his desire his god, and Allah sendeth him astray purposely, and sealeth up his hearing and his heart, and setteth on his sight a covering? Then who will lead him after Allah (hath condemned him)? Will ye not then heed? And they say: There is naught but our life of the world; we die, and we live, and naught destroyeth us save time; when they have no knowledge whatsoever of (all) that; they do but guess."

(Quran 45:23-24)

If someone asked me this question:

"Hast thou seen him who maketh his desire his god and whose followers are engrossed totally in the pursuit of this world and its progress without ever thinking of the next life?"

My answer would be abrupt:

"I have seen and discerned him. He is Bacon, the originator of the philosophy of modern atomism and the founder of this modern science-guided materialistic culture of progress. His culture is of this present material world entirely, and there is no doubt that his followers have achieved amazing success in that direction. They aim at this world, its wealth, and its physical comforts, which they have fully attained, but only to prove the word of the Quran." Read the following.

"Whoso desireth the life of the world and its pomp, We shall repay them their deeds herein, and therein they will not be wronged. Those are they for whom is naught in the Hereafter save the Fire. (All) that they contrive here is vain and (all) that they are wont to do, is <u>fruitless</u>."

(Quran 11:15-16)

What else is oracular, if not this above-quoted oracle of the Quran? Baconian culture sought this world and its pomp, and they have got it. Their share hereafter of fire has even appeared in this very world in the form of the atomic hell. Atomic fire will consume their mechanical, economic, industrial, and political contrivances. And the Baconian philosophy of '<u>fruit</u>' will become '<u>fruitless</u>' in a world burnt up and rendered desolate by atomic bombs and atomic radiations. It is a matter of time only now. The forces are steadily converging on the point of the final conflict. Humanity has treated the religion of Allah as a joke. It must now be prepared to receive the grievous repartee of nature in the form of 'nuclear Jehannah' (i.e., nuclear hell).

(26) Seek a comparison of this transient world versus the next eternal world.

They, who sought the otherworld, it is they that will find in the next world the things of eternal bliss and felicity, according to the promise of the Quran. Says the Quran:

"Those are they who will be brought nigh in gardens of delight; a multitude of those of old and a few of those of later time on lined couches, reclining therein face-to-face. There wait on them immortal youths with bowls and ewers and a cup from a pure spring wherefrom they get no aching of the head nor any madness and flesh of fowls that they desire. And (there are) fair ones with wide, lovely eyes, like unto hidden pearls, a reward for what they used do. There hear they neither vain speaking nor recrimination (naught) but the saying: Peace (and again) Peace."

(Quran 56:11-26)

Sometimes adversaries took such passages in the Quran (as quoted above) as examples of sensualism and lust in a book that claimed a Divine Origin. But where have those opponents, models of virtue, and seekers of celestial purity disappeared in the waves of the Baconian Ocean of lust that no one can see them anywhere? Indeed, this description of happiness, as has been quoted above, appears to be of celestial hue compared to banquets of modern times. Only if they had waited till the next world, and had abstained from changing this temporary abode, this earth into a Paradise, they would indeed in the next life have found the blissful banquet of celestial odorous in the eternal Paradise of the next world.

The Quran states the banquet of world seekers and disbelievers in the next world as described in the following.

"And those on the left hand: What of those on the left hand? (They will be) in the scorching wind and scalding water and shadow of black smoke, neither cool nor refreshing. Lo! Heretofore they were effete with luxury and used to persist in the awful sin. And they used to say: When we are dead and have come dust and bones, shall we then, forsooth, be raised again, And also our forefathers? Say (unto them, O Muhammad): Lo! Those of old and those of later time will all be brought together to the tryst of an appointed day. Then lo! Ye, the erring, the deniers, ye verily will eat of a tree called Zaqqum and will fill your bellies therewith; and thereon ye will drink of boiling water, drinking even as the camel drinketh. This will be their welcome on the Day of Judgment."

(Quran 56:41-56)

~~*~*~*

PART-2
THIS WORLD AGAINST THE OTHERWORLD, IN THE SIGHT OF THE QURAN

The Gospel of Jesus Christ is generally and reputably regarded as a Scripture strictly Anti-Materialistic and purely spiritual. There can be no doubt that if the followers of the Christian faith did strictly abide by the teachings of the Christian Gospel, they could hardly continue in this program of Baconian progress for a single moment. Anyone who can spare a few minutes can verify our assertion by reading 'Sermon on the Mount' in the Gospel.

In the following sections, we will quote some references from the Quran to compare this world and its wealth to the next world. It may surprise many readers. For, view of the Quran in this respect is not a whit less severe than the Gospel of Jesus Christ.

We will now quote the Quran in the following pages for the people (in 1981) on whose faces one may see the glow of the flames of the fast-approaching atomic hell shimmering and shining with blinding brilliancy. We request people with anxiety, earnestness, and sincerity to read the views of the Quran regarding this world and its wealth. Only then make the honest and sober judgment. Pass your judgment and decide whether Muslims, the avowed adherents of the Quran, could continue in this all-out money-oriented program of Baconian progress for a moment longer than the Christians. Will they continue to follow this progress, particularly when the apostasy of the Christians from the basic principles and doctrines of genuine Christian faith glares in the pitch-black night of the Baconian light of Anti-Christian hues?

However, suppose the mountain-shaking revelations of the Quran fail to shake the stubborn disobedience and relentless stubbornness of its votaries, just as the warnings of the Gospel of Jesus Christ have failed to affect the followers of Christianity. In that case, mere wishful thinking could not stop the infallible course of inevitable laws of Mother Nature, and the inevitable must occur to exempt neither Christian nor the Muslim. Pray read the following.

SECTION-1

(1) "The similitude of the life of the world is only as water which We send down from the sky, then the earth's growth of that which men and cattle eat mingleth with it till, when the earth hath taken on her ornaments and is embellished, and her people deem that they are masters of her, Our commandment cometh by night or by day and we make it as reaped corn as if it had not flourished yesterday. Thus, do We expound the revelations for people who reflect. And Allah summoneth to the abode of peace, and leadeth whom He will to a straight path."

(Quran 10:24-25)

(2) "Know that the life of this world is only a play, and idle talk, and pageantry, and boasting among you and rivalry in respect of wealth and children; as the likeness of vegetation after rain, whereof the growth is pleasing to the husbandman, but afterward it drieth up and thou seest it turning yellow then it becometh straw. And in the Hereafter, there is grievous punishment and (also) forgiveness from Allah and His good pleasure, whereas the life of the world is but a matter of illusion. Race one with another for forgiveness from your Lord and a Garden whereof the breadth is as the breadth of the heavens and the earth, which is in store for those who believe in Allah and His messengers. Such is the bounty of Allah, which He bestoweth upon whom He will, and Allah is of infinite bounty."

(Quran 57:20-21)

(3) "Thereof We created you, and thereunto We return you, and thence We bring you forth a second time." (Quran 20:55)

(4) "And on the day when the Hour (of Reckoning) riseth, the guilty will vow that they did tarry but an hour, thus were they ever deceived. But those to whom knowledge and faith are given will say: The truth is, ye have tarried, by Allah's decree, until the Day of Resurrection. This is the Day of Resurrection, but ye used not to know."

(Quran 30:55-56)

SECTION-2

(1) "Allah enlargeth livelihood for whom He will, and straiteneth (it for whom He will); and they rejoice in the life of the world, whereas the life of the world is but brief comfort as compared with the Hereafter."

(Quran 13:26)

(2) "O, my people! Lo! This life of the world is but a passing comfort, and lo! The Hereafter that is the enduring home."

(Quran 40:39)

(3) "O ye who believe! What aileth you that when it is said unto you: Go forth in the way of Allah, ye are bowed down to the ground with heaviness. Take ye pleasure in the life of the world rather than in the Hereafter? The comfort of the life of the world is but little in the Hereafter."

(Quran 9:38)

(4) "This life of the world is but a pastime and a game. Lo! The home of the Hereafter that is Life if they but knew."

(Quran 29:64)

(5) "And a generation hath succeeded them who inherited the Scriptures. They grasp the goods of this low life (as the price of evil-doing) and say: It will be forgiven us. And if there came to them (again) the offer of the like, they would accept it (and would sin again). Hath not the covenant of the Scripture been taken on their behalf that they should not speak aught concerning Allah save the truth? And they have studied that which is therein. And the abode of the Hereafter is better for those who ward off (evil). Have ye then no sense?"

(Quran 7:169)

SECTION-3

(1) "And when ye have completed your devotions, then remember Allah as ye remember your fathers or with a more lively remembrance. But of humankind is he who saith: "our Lord! Give unto us (Thy bounties) in the world," and he hath no portion in the

Hereafter. And of them (also) is he who saith: "Our Lord! Give unto us in the world that which is good and in the Hereafter that which is good, and guard us against the doom of Fire." For them, there is in store a goodly portion out of that which they have earned. Allah is swift at reckoning."

(Quran 2:200-202)

(2) "Whoso desireth the reward of the world, We bestow on him thereof; and whoso desireth the reward of the Hereafter, We bestow on him thereof. We shall reward the thankful."

(Quran 3:145)

(3) "Whoso desireth that (life) which hasteneth away, We hasten for him therein that We will for whom We please. And afterward, We have appointed for him hell; he will endure the heat thereof, condemned, rejected. And whoso desireth the Hereafter and striveth for it with the effort necessary, being a believer; for such, their effort findeth favor (with their Lord). Each do We supply, both these and those, from the bounty of thy Lord. And the bounty of thy Lord can never be walled up. See how We prefer one above another, and verily the Hereafter will be greater in degrees and greater in preferment. Set not up with Allah any other god (O man) lest thou sit down reproved, forsaken."

(Quran 17:18-22)

SECTION-4

We are quoting passages that reveal the Quran's view about this world which the Muslims recite every day, though seldom with much heed to these passages in question, they skip from these as if they read nothing. Yet these passages about men's love of this world contain threatening and denunciations equal to those for the most terrible sins and most heinous crimes, such as disbelief, infidelity, shirk (polytheism), hypocrisy, murder, felony, theft, etc.

Moreover, what is the nature of this guilt? It is only the desire of this world and its wealth. This guilt nowadays is not regarded as undesirable. Rather it is regarded as a virtue and an unavoidable necessity in a world where every individual is madly pursuing this world and wealth. Wealth today is being worshipped actually; Allah only receives some lip service.

In the name of the dreadful oven of atomic hell, we request the reader to read the views of the Quran regarding this world and its wealth with the care they deserve. The time for inactivity is now long past. Let readers of the Quran now assume a little more realistic attitude and know that the love of this world and its wealth is the worst crime in the sight of the Quran.

Following are given passages from the Quran in this regard.

(1) "Believe ye in part of the Scripture, and disbelieve ye in part thereof? And what is the reward of those who do so save ignominy in the life of the world, and on the Day of Resurrection, they will be consigned to the most grievous doom? For Allah is not unaware of what ye do. Such are those who buy the life of the world at the price of the hereafter. Their punishment will not be lightened, neither will they have support."

(Quran 2:85-86)

(2) "And of humankind is he who would sell himself, seeking the pleasure of Allah; and Allah hath compassion on (His) bondmen. O ye who believe! Come, all of you, into submission (unto Him), and follow not the footsteps of the devil. Lo! He is an open enemy for you. And if ye slide back after the clear proofs have come unto you, then know that Allah is Mighty, Wise."

(Quran 2:207-209)

(3) "Whoso disbelieveth in Allah after his belief save him who is forced thereto and whose heart is still content with Faith but whoso findeth ease in disbelief: On them is wrath from Allah. Theirs will be an awful doom. That is because they have chosen the life of the world rather than the Hereafter and because Allah guideth, not the disbelieving folk. Such are they whose hearts and ears and eyes Allah hath sealed. And such are heedless. Assuredly in the Hereafter, they are the losers."

(Quran 16:106-109)

Mark gradually the correlation between disbelief and the choice of this world. The pity is that the Muslims skip from every sign of the Quran, which appears to be related to the disbelievers or disbelief, thinking it not to apply to them, for they have believed.

However, punishment of atomic hell and all the miseries created by Baconian culture will become transparent with other misunderstandings because Allah will not discriminate between Muslims and non-Muslims or believers and disbelievers. The skeptic and believer will find themselves shoulder to shoulder in the miseries of atomic hell, both in this and the next world. Read the commentaries of the Quran.

"Whoso desireth the life of the world and its pomp, We shall repay them their deeds herein, and therein they will not be wronged. Those are they for whom is naught in the Hereafter save the Fire. (All) that they contrive here is vain and (all) that they are wont to do, is fruitless."

(Quran 11:15-16)

Again, there is no mention of 'faith' or 'no faith' in this above-quoted sign (verse) of the Quran. The question only is of desiring this world. Baconian progress of this age is the money-oriented desires of this world, the entire desires of worldly pursuits, and nothing but materialistic desires. Nor will any discrimination be made between the Muslim and non-Muslim, believer, and non-believer in the logical consequence of this Baconian progress.

(4) "Woe to every backbiter, defamer, who amasseth wealth (of this world) and arrangeth it against the future. He thinketh that his wealth will render him immortal; Nay, for verily he will be cast into 'Al-Hotama'. And what could teach thee what 'Al-Hotama' is? It is a fire of Allah kindled, which leapeth up onto the hearts. It is (a fire) closed in on them in outstretched columns."

(Quran 104:1-9)

Again, in this above-quoted passage, there is no discrimination between the believer and non-believer. Islam is a progressive religion and is not opposed to progress but even enjoins progress on its followers. Why, then, the Quran has such a terrible denunciation against the backbiter and defamer whose only fault is that he is engaged in progress and is persistent therein?

Westerners have always complained that Quran is replete with threats, and threats, and threats. How now has a threat of the Quran appeared in a tangible form in the form of atomic hell? Is it not a miraculous threat that the hell in itself should appear to consume the guilty even within this world? Is not this threat in its tangible form worth paying heed to it?

(5) "As for those who disbelieve, Lo! If all that is in the earth be theirs, and as much again therewith, to ransom them from the doom on the Day of Resurrection, it would not be accepted from them. Theirs will be a painful doom."

(Quran 5:36)

SECTION-5

(1) "Lo! Those who purchase a small gain at the cost of Allah's covenant and their oaths, they have no portion in the Hereafter. Allah will neither speak to them nor look upon them on the Day of Resurrection nor will He make them grow. Theirs will be a painful doom."

(Quran 3:77)

Read this above-quoted passage of the Quran and find that this Baconian worldly gain is small compared to the loss in the next world and mark particularly that people of the present age have almost expelled the thought of Resurrection, otherworld, or the Judgment from their minds. Whether Allah speaks to them or looks upon them on the day of Resurrection or not, they want worldly things, worldly necessities, and worldly comforts. Who in these days remembers the day of Resurrection? Money is the object of remembrance.

(2) "Lo! Allah will cause those who believe and do good works to enter Gardens underneath which rivers flow; while those who disbelieve take their comfort in this life and eat even as the cattle eat, and the Fire is their habitation."

(Quran 47:12)

Mark in the above-quoted passage the correlation between disbelief and the fact of the comfort of this life. People of this age indeed do eat like cattle, and everyone is obliged to eat like cattle. Eating like cattle is the sole object of this present Baconian system. Also, the harsh necessities of life have become more tyrannical due to the much increased and ever-increasing population. Moreover, why has the population so un-proportionally increased in this age? The cause lay in this Baconian culture itself.

(3) "And the dwellers of the Fire cry out unto the dwellers of the Garden; Pour on us some water or some of that wherewith Allah hath provided you. They say: Lo! Allah hath forbidden both to disbelievers (in His guidance), who took their religion for a sport and pastime, and whom the life of the world beguiled. So, this day, We have forgotten them even as they forgot the meeting of this Day and as they used to deny Our tokens. Verily We have brought them a Scripture which We expound with knowledge, guidance and a mercy for a people who believe."

(Quran 7:50-52)

Read the above-quoted passage and see that religion these days is no more than a sport and pastime, and it is the highest place assigned to religion today. The followers of Christianity, Hinduism, and Buddhism have almost forgotten their religions. Islam, no doubt, breathes as yet. However, what could be a lot of a man except disappointment who turns to look at the part played by Islam or the Quran in Muslims' modern affairs?

No doubt, it is not verbally declared a private matter of every individual, but where has it been promulgated or assigned as an influential role, not to speak of a position of super command or sovereignty that essentially is its place among the Muslims. Baconian philosophy, the Baconian culture, and the Baconian progress hold the sway, rather a complete sway. Empty notions and wishful thinking would avail naught against the hard and fast realities that in reality exist.

(4) "Lo! As for those who believe not in the Hereafter, We have made their works fair-seeming unto them so that they are all astray. Those are they for whom is the worst of punishment, and in the Hereafter, they will be the greatest losers."

(Quran 27:4-5)

Read the above-quoted passage of the Quran and mark then the praises of the achievements of science, the ever-advancing progress, the monuments and displays of the modern Baconian culture as the ultimate and the crowning glory of man in which every nation on earth is assiduously engaged to the utmost of their variant ability: Jews, Christians, Muslims, Hindus, Buddhists, the black and the white, and the red and the yellow, in the east and the west, north and south.

Moreover, nowhere was a questioner to ask them what they did? Whither they drifted? What would the result of these excellent achievements be except hell? Even the atomic bombs appear fair in the eyes of the people of this misguided age.

(5) "Those who love the life of the world more than the Hereafter, and debar (men) from the way of Allah and would have it crooked: such are far astray."

(Quran 14:3)

Read the above-quoted passage of the Quran and then look all around and see if those who prefer this world to the next world are not most vigorously engaged in their constant endeavor to stop and destroy religion and never allow its revival.

(6) "Say: Verily, those who invent a lie concerning Allah will not succeed. This world's portion (will be theirs), and then unto Us is their return. Then We make them taste a dreadful doom because they used to disbelieve."

(Quran 10:69-70)

The non-Muslim critics of Islam have always pronounced Islam as a religion of the flesh, devoid of spiritualism. They especially are to be requested to read these passages and judge if their accusation has any truth.

(7) "Lo! Those who expect not the meeting with Us but desire the life of the world and feel secure therein, and those who are neglectful of Our revelations, their home will be the Fire because of what they used to earn."

(Quran 10:7-8)

Read this above-quoted passage of the Quran and see if its truth has not appeared even within this world. Is not this humankind about to have atomic fire as its home due to feeling secure in this life and forgetting the meeting with the Lord?

(8) "Lo! These love fleeting life and put behind them (the remembrance of) a grievous day. We, even We, created them and strengthened thee frame (strengthened their forms). And when We will, We can replace them, bringing others like them in their stead."

(Quran 76:27-28)

SECTION-6

(1) "Every soul will taste of death. And ye will be paid on the Day of Resurrection only that which ye have fairly earned. Whoso is removed from the Fire and is made to enter Paradise; he indeed is triumphant. The life of this world is but the comfort of illusion."

(Quran 3:185)

(2) "Everything will perish, save His countenance. His is the command, and unto Him, ye will be brought back."

(Quran 28:88)

(3) "O humankind! Keep your duty to your Lord and fear a Day when the parent will not be able to avail the child in aught, nor the child to avail the parent. Lo! Allah's promise is the very truth. Let not the life of the world beguile you, nor let the deceiver beguile you, regarding Allah."

(Quran 31:33)

(4) "O humankind! Lo! The promise of Allah is true. So let not the life of the world beguile you, and let not the (avowed) beguiler beguile you about Allah. Lo! The devil is an enemy for you, so treat him as an enemy. He only summoneth his faction to be owners of the Earning Fire."

(Quran 35:5-6)

This above-quoted passage of the Quran reminds us of William Blake's remark about Bacon. He said: "The Prince of Darkness is 'a gentleman and not a man: he is a Lord Chancellor'." 'The Prince of Darkness' is the appellation of the devil. Therefore, let us treat Bacon as an enemy of the human race.

(5) "And on the day when those who disbelieve are exposed to the Fire (it will be said): Ye squandered your good things in the life of the world and sought comfort therein. Now this day, ye are rewarded with the doom of ignominy because ye were disdainful in the land without a right and because ye used to transgress."

(Quran 46:20)

Read the above-quoted passage and see if it could not be proclaimed with propriety to this present-day comfort-seeking humankind when Allah will cast it into the atomic fire. When atomic bombs rain upon them from above, the atomic radiation will sting them from below.

(6) "Take ye pleasure in the life of the world rather than in the Hereafter? The comfort of the life of the world is but little in the Hereafter."

(Quran 9:38)

(7) Abraham's prayer to Allah was: "And abase me not on the day when they are raised, the day when wealth and sons avail not (any man) save him who bringeth unto Allah a whole heart."

(Quran 26:87-89)

(8) "It may be that those who disbelieve ardently wish that they were Muslims. Let them eat and enjoy life, and let (false) hope beguile them. They will come to know!"

(Quran 15:2-3)

We may apply the above-quoted passage to the people of this present age now who eat and enjoy life, and false hopes delude them that there will be no atomic war. They believe that science and scientists will undoubtedly find some remedy for the atomic bombs and atomic radiation.

SECTION-7

(1) "Then withdraw (O Muhammad) from him who fleeth from Our remembrance and desireth but the life of the world. Such is their sum of knowledge. Lo! Thy Lord is best aware of him who strayeth, and He is best aware of him who goeth right."

(Quran 53:29-30)

The above-quoted passage of the Quran is the best advice for Muslims of present times, indeed. Let them withdraw from this worldly Baconian progress which causes them to forget Allah.

(2) "Nay, but ye do love the fleeting now and neglect the Hereafter. That day faces will be resplendent, looking toward their Lord; and that day will other faces be despondent, thou wilt know that some great disaster is about to fall on them."

(Quran 75:20-25)

Even in this world now, they are apprehensive of atomic disasters.

(3) "Verily in the messenger of Allah ye have a good example for him who looketh unto Allah and the Last Day, and remembereth Allah much." (Quran 33:21)

(4) "Then, as for him who rebelled and chose the life of the world, Lo! Hell will be his home. But as for him who feared to stand before his Lord and restrained his soul from lust, Lo! The Garden will be his home."

(Quran 79:37-41)

(5) "Say: Behold what is in the heavens and the earth! But revelations and warnings avail not folk who will not believe."

(Quran 10:101)

~~*~*~*

PART-3
QURAN'S VIEWS ON THE THINGS OF THIS WORLD AGAINST THAT WHICH IS WITH ALLAH

Whatever is with Allah as against the things of this world, Bacon's philosophy is not concerned since it is concerned only with the things of this world. We will, therefore, quote only the Quran, which differentiates between the things of this temporal, transient world and that which is with Allah, everlasting.

(1) "And With Allah is the fairest of rewards."

(Quran 3:195)

(2) "Beautified for humankind is the love of the joys (that come) from women and offspring, and stored-up heaps of gold and silver, and horses branded (with their mark), and cattle and land. That is the comfort of the life of the world. Allah! With Him is a more excellent abode. Say: Shall I inform you of something better than that? For those who keep from evil, with their Lord, are Gardens underneath which rivers flow, and pure companions, and contentment from Allah. Allah is Seer of His bondmen, those who say: Our Lord! Lo! We believe. So, forgive us our sins and guard us against the punishment of Fire; the steadfast, and the truthful, and the obedient, those who spend (and hoard not), those who pray for pardon in the watches of the night."

(Quran 3:14-17)

(3) "No soul knoweth what is kept hid for them of joy, as a reward for what they used to do."

(Quran 32:17)

(4) "And whatsoever ye have been given is a comfort of the life of the world and an ornament thereof, and that which Allah hath is better and more lasting. Have ye then no sense?"

(Quran 28:60)

In this above-quoted passage, the Quran distinguishes between worldly things and those which are with Allah. Then Allah asks whether they had the sense to judge. If we put this same question to the people of this age, their answer invariably would be:

"Our Lord! We have a great sense. Therefore, give us the things of the world's life: wealth, property, bank balance, motor cars, and bungalows. This is the essence of the sense which our teacher, the founder of Baconian culture, has bestowed upon us."

But Allah says:

(5) "That which ye have wasteth away, and that which Allah hath remaineth. And verily, We shall pay those who are steadfast recompense in proportion to the best of what they used to do."

(Quran 16:96)

(6) "Wealth and children are an ornament of the life of the world. But the good deeds which endure are better in thy Lord's sight for reward and better in respect of hope."

(Quran 18:46)

(7) "And be not ye as those who forgot Allah; therefore, He caused them to forget their souls. Such are the evildoers."

(Quran 59:19)

(8) "(Ye have) enjoyment of the life of the world; then unto Us is your return, and We shall proclaim unto you what ye used to do."

(Quran 10:23)

(9) "But ah! Thou soul at peace! Return unto thy Lord, content in His good pleasure! Enter thou among My bondmen! Enter thou My Garden!"

(Quran 89:27-30)

~~*~*~*

PART-4
RIVALRY BETWEEN MAN'S LOVE OF ALLAH AND THAT OF THIS WORLD

The rivalry between man's love of this world and his love of Allah is as old and as persistent a theme as is enmity between Man and Satan. A true believer is basically for Allah, while the Baconian is for this life of the world. No doubt the sense of the people of the age is dulled in this respect, but the disciples of the Holy Prophet of Islam (peace be upon him) and the disciples of Jesus Christ understood this then perfectly. The love of Allah raises a man above the ordinary level of this world. A man possessing the entire world would give it away for the sake of Allah's love.

Thus, it is that generally, the true lovers of Allah could seldom keep worldly wealth along with them, for no sooner would they descry a needy fellow human being than they would part with their wealth purely for the love of Allah. Allah will pay them their love of Him in a manner worthy of Allah.

The Quran says:

"Lo! the righteous shall drink of a cup whereof the mixture is of water of Kafur, a spring wherefrom the slaves of Allah drink, making it gush forth abundantly, because they perform the vow and fear a day whereof the evil is wide-spreading, and feed with food the needy wretch, the orphan, and the prisoner, for love of Him, (saying): We feed you, for the sake of Allah only. We wish for no reward nor thanks from you; Lo! We fear from our Lord a day of frowning and of fate."

(Quran 76:5-10)

However, see how Allah rewards them. The above-quoted statement continues as follows.

"Therefore, Allah hath warded off from them the evil of that day, and hath made them find brightness and joy; and hath awarded them for all that they endured, a Garden and silk attire; reclining therein upon couches, they will find there neither (heat of) a sun nor bitter cold. The shade thereof is close upon them, and the clustered fruits thereof bow down. Goblets of silver are brought round for them and beakers (as) of glass; (bright as) glass but (made) of silver, which they (themselves) have measured to the measure (of their deeds). There are they watered with a cup whereof the mixture is of Zanjabil, the water of a spring therein, named Salsabil. There serve them youths of everlasting youth, whom, when thou seest, thou wouldst take for scattered pearls. When thou seest, thou wilt see there bliss and high estate. Their raiment will be fine green silk and gold embroidery. Bracelets of silver will they wear. Their Lord will slake their thirst with a pure drink. (And it will be said unto them): Lo! This is a reward for you. Your endeavor (upon earth) hath found acceptance."

(Quran 76:11-22)

Now, this is a picture of that Paradise which Allah has prepared in the heavens. Therefore, people of this age will have to choose between the Paradise of Allah and this earthy Baconian Paradise. Know that the latter is about to expose its reality in the form of atomic Jehannah, whose mention even would inspire dread. In comparison, Allah's Paradise would offer pure bliss, unmixed and eternal. The Gospel of Jesus Christ has a statement to this effect. Just read as follows.

"When the Son of man shall come in his glory, and all the holy angels with him, then shall he sit upon the throne of his glory: And before him, shall be gathered all nations: and he shall separate them one from another, as a shepherd divideth his sheep from the goats: And he shall set the sheep on his right hand, but the goats on the left. Then shall the King say unto them on his right hand, Come, ye blessed of my Father, inherit the kingdom prepared for you from the foundation of the world: For I was an hungered, and ye gave me meat: I was thirsty, and ye gave me drink: I was a stranger, and ye took me in: Naked, and ye clothed me: I was sick, and ye visited me: I was in prison, and ye came unto me. Then shall the righteous answer him, saying, Lord, when saw we thee a hungered and fed thee? Or thirsty, and gave thee drink? When saw we thee a stranger, and took thee in? Or naked, and clothed thee? Or when saw we thee sick, or in prison, and came unto thee? And the King shall answer and say unto them, Verily I say unto you, Inasmuch as ye have done it unto one of the least of these my brethren, ye have done it unto me. Then shall he say also unto them on the left hand, Depart from me, ye cursed, into everlasting fire, prepared for the devil and his angels: For I was an hungered, and ye gave me no meat: I was thirsty, and ye gave me no drink: I was a stranger, and ye took me not in: naked, and ye clothed me not: sick, and in prison, and ye visited me not. Then shall they also answer him, saying, Lord, when saw we thee an hungered, or athirst, or a stranger, or naked, or sick, or in prison, and did not minister unto thee? Then shall he answer them, saying, verily I say unto you, Inasmuch as ye did it not to one of the least of these, ye did it not to me. And these shall go away into everlasting punishment: but the righteous into life eternal."

(The Bible: New Testament: Matthew 25:31-46)

Read the following from the Quran to this effect.

(1) "Lo! the righteous shall drink of a cup whereof the mixture is of water of Kafur, a spring wherefrom the slaves of Allah drink, making it gush forth abundantly, because they perform the vow and fear a day whereof the evil is wide-spreading, and feed with food the needy wretch, the orphan, and the prisoner, for love of Him, (saying): We feed you, for the sake of Allah only. We wish for no reward nor thanks from you; Lo! We fear from our Lord a day of frowning and of fate."

(Quran 76:5-10)

(2) "Hast thou observed him who belieth religion? That is he who repelleth the orphan and urgeth not the feeding of the needy. Ah, woe unto worshippers who are heedless of their prayer; who would be seen (at worship) yet refuse small kindnesses!"

(Quran 107:1-7)

About the rivalry of man's love of God and his love of this world, Jesus in his Gospel says:

"And everyone that hath forsaken houses, or brethren, or sisters, or father, or mother, or wife, or children, or lands, for my name's sake, shall receive a hundredfold and shall inherit everlasting life. But many that are first shall be last, and the last shall be first."

(The Bible: New Testament: Matthew 19:29-30)

The Quran on this point says:

"Say: If your fathers, and your sons, and your brethren, and your wives, and your tribe, and the wealth ye have acquired, and merchandise for which ye fear that there will be no sale, and dwellings ye desire are dearer to you than Allah and His messenger and, striving in His way: then wait till Allah bringeth His command to pass. Allah guideth, not wrongdoing folk."

(Quran 9:24)

About the rivalry between the world and God, the Gospel says:

"Ye adulterers and adulteresses, know ye not that the friendship of the world is enmity with God? Whosoever, therefore, will be a friend of the world is the enemy of God. Do ye think that the Scripture saith in vain, the spirit that dwelleth in us lusteth to envy? But he giveth more grace. Wherefore he saith, God resisteth the proud, but giveth grace unto the humble. Submit yourselves, therefore, to God. Resist the devil, and he will flee from you. Draw nigh to God, and he will draw nigh to you. Cleanse your hands, ye sinners, and purify your hearts, ye double minded."

(The Bible: New Testament: James 4:4-8)

The Quran says:

(1) "And of mankind is he who would sell himself, seeking the pleasure of Allah; and Allah hath compassion on (His) bondmen."

(Quran 2:207)

(2) "Lo! Allah hath bought from the believers their lives and their wealth because the Garden will be theirs, they shall fight in the way of Allah and shall slay and be slain. It is a promise which is binding on Him in the Torah and the Gospel and the Quran. Who fulfilleth His covenant better than Allah? Rejoice then in your bargain that ye have made, for that is the supreme triumph."

(Quran 9:111)

BUT:

(3) "Or deemed ye that ye would enter Paradise while yet Allah knoweth not those of you who really strive, nor knoweth those (of you) who are steadfast?"

(Quran 3:142)

(4) "Or think ye that ye will enter Paradise while yet there hath not come unto you the like of (that which came to) those who passed away before you? Affliction and adversity befell them; they were shaken as with earthquake, till the messenger (of Allah), and those who believed along with him said: When cometh Allah's help? Now surely Allah's help is nigh."

(Quran 2:214)

PART-5
INCLINATION TO THIS WORLD IS A CAUSE OF THE DISBELIEF IN THE OTHERWORLD

This world being the adversary of the otherworld is generally the chief cause of a man's disbelief about the otherworld, which is the base of the religion of Allah. Here the Quran stands as always in direct opposition to the view of Bacon, whose sole object is this world and wholly neglects the otherworld. The Quran's gravest imputation is that the love of this world is the cause of man's disbelief about the otherworld.

We will cite the Quran.

(1) "Whoso disbelieveth in Allah after his belief save him who is forced thereto and whose heart is still content with Faith, but whoso findeth ease in disbelief: On them is wrath from Allah. Theirs will be an awful doom. That is because they have chosen the life of the world rather than the Hereafter and because Allah guideth, not the disbelieving folk."

(Quran 16:106-107)

(2) "Lo! Those who expect not the meeting with Us but desire the life of the world and feel secure therein, and those who are neglectful of Our revelations, their home will be the fire because of what they used to earn."

(Quran 10:7-8)

(3) "Then, as for him who rebelled and chose the life of the world, Lo! Hell will be his home. But as for him who feared to stand before his Lord and restrained his soul from lust, Lo! The Garden will be his home."

(Quran 79:37-41)

(4) "Who took their religion for a sport and pastime, and whom the life of the world beguiled; so, this day We have forgotten them even as

they forgot the meeting of this Day and as they used to deny Our tokens."

(Quran 7:51)

(5) "Hast thou observed him who believeth religion? That is he who repelleth the orphan and urgeth not the feeding of the needy. Ah, woe unto worshippers who are heedless of their prayer; who would be seen (at worship) yet refuse small kindnesses!"

(Quran 107:1-7)

The essence of the whole matter is not to entangle your heart in this world and always keep in mind the next world. The utility of the necessities of life is quite a different thing. Eat and give thanks to the Giver. Good food or good clothes are nothing but the love of this world and neglect of the otherworld, and pride in wealth instead of pride in poverty is something else. Love Allah, and He will teach you all the ways.

~~*~*~*

PART-6
WEALTH AGAINST FAITH IN THE SIGHT OF THE QURAN

As far as Bacon's philosophy is concerned, the wealth of this world is its sole object regarded as bliss unmixed. Quran, on the other hand, has a different view. Faith and good deeds are preferable to wealth in the sight of the Quran. We will make the point clear with quotations from the Quran in the following.

(1) **Allah wants to punish disbelievers by their wealth.**

The Quran says:

"So let not their (disbelievers') riches nor their children please thee (O Muhammad). Allah thereby intendeth but to punish them in the life of the world and that their souls shall pass away while they are disbelievers."

(Quran 9:55)

(2) **Disbelievers are mistaken in the fortunateness of their wealth.**

The Quran says:

"Think they that in the wealth and sons wherewith We provide them We hasten unto them with good things? Nay, but they perceive not. Lo! those who go in awe for fear of their Lord, and those who believe in the revelations of their Lord, and those who ascribe not partners unto their Lord, and those who give that which they give with hearts afraid because they are about to return unto their Lord, these race for the good things, and they shall win them in the race. And We task not any soul beyond its scope, and with Us is a Record which speaketh the truth, and they will not be wronged. Nay, but their hearts are in ignorance of this (Quran), and they have other works, besides, which they are doing; till when We grasp their luxurious ones with the punishment, behold! They supplicate. Supplicate not this day! Assuredly ye will not be helped by Us. My revelations were recited unto you, but ye used to turn back on your heels, in scorn thereof. Nightly did ye rave together."

(Quran 23:55-67)

(3) **The wealthy opposed every Prophet of Allah.**
The Quran says:
"And We sent not unto any township a warner, but its pampered ones declared: Lo! We are disbelievers in that which ye bring unto Us. And they say: We are more (than you) in wealth and children. We are not the punished! Say (O Muhammad): Lo! My Lord enlargeth the provision for whom He will and narroweth it (for whom He will). But most of the humankind know not."

(Quran 34:34-36)

(4) **Riches are of no avail to the disbelievers on the Day of Judgment.**
The Quran says:
"(On that Day), neither the riches nor the progeny, of those who disbelieve will aught avail them with Allah. They will be fuel for the fire."

(Quran 3:10)

(5) **They would prefer all as ransom if they had all on the earth on the Day of Judgment.**
The Quran says:
"For those who answered Allah's call is bliss; and for those who answered not His call, if they had all that is in the earth, and therewith the like thereof, they would proffer it as ransom. Such will have a woeful reckoning, and their habitation will be hell, a dire abode."

(Quran 13:18)

(6) **And Allah shall not accept the ransom of disbelievers.**
The Quran says:
"Lo! Those who disbelieve and die in disbelief, the (whole) earth full of gold would not be accepted from such a one if it were offered as a ransom (for his soul). Theirs will be a painful doom, and they will have no helpers." (Quran 3:91)

(7) **Wealth is a cause of rebellion.**
The Quran says:
"And if Allah were to enlarge the provision for His slaves, they would surely rebel in the earth, but He sendeth down by measure as He willeth. Lo! He is Informed, a Seer of His bondmen."

(Quran 42:27)

(8) Wealth and children are a test.
The Quran says:
"And know that your possessions and your children are a test and that with Allah is immense reward."

(Quran 8:28)

(9) There is a terrible punishment for hoarders of wealth.
The Quran says:
"They who hoard up gold and silver and spend it not in the way of Allah, unto them give tidings (O Muhammad) of a painful doom on the day when it will (all) be heated in the fire of hell, and their foreheads and their flanks and their backs will be branded therewith (and it will be said unto them): Here is that which ye hoarded for yourselves. Now taste of what ye used to hoard."

(Quran 9:34-35)

(10) The usurer's condition on Resurrection.
The Quran says:
"Those who swallow usury cannot rise to save as he ariseth whom the devil hath prostrated by (his) touch. That is because they say: Trade is just like usury; whereas Allah permitteth trading and forbiddeth usury. He unto whom an admonition from his Lord cometh, and (he) refraineth (in obedience thereto), he shall keep (the profits of) that which is past, and his affair (henceforth) is with Allah. As for him who returneth (to usury) such are rightful owners of the Fire. They will abide therein."

(Quran 2:275)

(11) The end of Korah (Qaroon), the rich.
The Quran says:
"So, We caused the earth to swallow him and his dwelling place. Then he had no host to help him against Allah, nor was he of those who can save themselves."

(Quran 28:81)

(12) The best provision is piety.
The Quran says:
"And whatsoever good ye do Allah knoweth it. So, make provision for yourselves (hereafter); for the best provision is to ward off evil."

(Quran 2:197)

(13) The punishment of atomic hell for engrossment in wealth accumulation.
The Quran says:
"Woe to every backbiter, defamer, who amasseth wealth (of this world) and arrangeth it (against the future). He thinketh that his wealth will render him immortal; Nay, for verily he will be cast into 'Al-Hotama'."

(Quran 104:1-4)

(14) Not wealth and children but belief and good works that draw anyone near to Allah.

The Quran says:

"And it is not your wealth nor your children that will bring you near unto Us, but he who believeth and doeth good (he draweth near). As for such, theirs will be twofold reward for what they did, and they will dwell securely in lofty halls."

(Quran 34:37)

(15) Wealth means a trial of man on earth.

The Quran says:

"And were it not that humankind would have become one community, We might well have appointed, for those who disbelieve in the Beneficent, roofs of silver for their houses and stairs (of silver) whereby to mount, and for their houses doors (of silver) and couches of silver whereon to recline, and ornaments of gold. Yet all that would have been but a provision of the life of the world. And the Hereafter with your Lord would have been for those who keep from evil."

(Quran 43:33-35)

The above-quoted proposition is exciting and very meaningful. We could hardly exemplify the great temptation of wealth and man's love of it, its significant role in the trial of man on earth, and its position as a rival of Allah in a manner more interesting and more impressive than this example of the Quran.

(16) Treasures of wealth opened to those who forget the reminder of Allah is an excellent example of this modern age.

The Quran says:

"Then, when they forgot that whereof they had been reminded, We opened unto them the gates of all things till, even as they were rejoicing in that which they were given, We seized them unawares, and lo! They were dumbfounded. So, of the people who did wrong, the last remnant was cut off. Praise be to Allah, Lord of the Worlds!"

(Quran 6:44-45)

Now, this is precisely the example of this material age. The speech of the orator in a seminar of modern achievements may be cut short by the atomic wind:

"Ladies and gentlemen, the achievements of this modern science," ... ... **bang.**

~~*~*~*

CHAPTER-10

COMPARATIVE VIEWS OF BACON AND THE QURAN ON THE PURPOSE OF MAN'S CREATION

In Raphael's famous cartoon of the school of Athens, Plato is shown pointing upward to heaven while Aristotle is pointing downward to the earth. The complete validity of the idea of this cartoon, however, has been doubted by critics. Suppose any painter of remarkable ability in this modern age would paint a picture showing Jesus Christ pointing upward to the heavens and Bacon pointing downward to the earth. In that case, any critic could hardly doubt the validity of such a painting.

We have named Jesus only. But Jesus would be assumed to represent all the host of the Prophets of religion and most pre-modern philosophers. Since man's appearance on earth, every religion recommended moral virtue, and the next world was regarded as the object of man's thoughts and as the actual home. In contrast, it assigned this transient world a temporary abode, and the sowing field reaped in the otherworld.

Bacon stands against all the religions and most of the philosophies of the pre-modern age in giving out this same transient world as the sole object and the actual abode in which man was obliged to pursue natural philosophy (science) to obtain dominion over Mother Nature for material advantage. In contrast, moral philosophy was shunned as impious, and man's innovation in disobedience to God's commands.

These are the utterances indeed grievous and charges very serious, but based on truth. All this laid concealed from the eyes of man for more than three centuries because the fruits of Baconian philosophy were exceedingly sweet, and people deemed it entirely proper to ignore the faults of Bacon's philosophy. However, the lie ingress nothing, and the truth appears in its time eventually.

Now that the truth of Bacon's philosophy through the atomic fire, i.e., the logical and scientific result of Baconian progress, has appeared, it appears expedient to voice the reality to the people lest the people say someone never warned them. Indeed, not a voice has been heard against the Baconian philosophy ever since it made its appearance in the seventeenth century. Instead, every voice has commended, extolled, and applauded it as the true redeemer of humankind and the most outstanding philosophy that ever appeared in the world.

The purpose of man's life, according to Baconian philosophy, was to gain dominion over Mother Nature for the material benefit of humankind. The pursuit of natural philosophy (science) was, according to Bacon, the command of God to man. The pursuit of moral philosophy, on the other hand, was undesirable and against the command of God and was the repetition of Adam's transgression of God's command, namely, his eating of the fruit of the forbidden tree of knowledge of good and evil. Baconian philosophy is not at all concerned with the spiritual or the next world. Nor it has to do anything with Allah's worship. However, the Quran has a different view. The purpose of man's life is Allah's worship. Allah in the Quran says:

"I created the Jinn and humankind only that they might worship Me." (Quran 51:56)

The conduct of all creation proves the act of Allah's worship. The Quran says:

(1) "Have they not observed all things that Allah hath created, how their shadows incline to the right and the left, making prostration unto Allah, and they are lowly? And unto Allah maketh prostration whatsoever is in the heavens and whatsoever is in the earth of living creatures, and the angels (also), and they are not proud. They fear their Lord above them and do what they are bidden."

(Quran 16:48-50)

(2) "The seven heavens and the earth and all that is therein, praise Him, and there is not a thing but hymneth his praise; but ye understand not their praise. Lo! He is ever Clement, Forgiving."

(Quran 17:44)

(3) "The thunder hymneth His praise and (so do) the angels for awe of Him. He launcheth the thunderbolts and smiteth with them whom He will while they dispute (in doubt) concerning Allah and He is mighty in wrath." (Quran 13:13)

The purpose is to punish the hypocrites and idolaters and to pardon the believers.

"Lo! We offered the trust unto the heavens and the earth and the hills, but they shrank from bearing it and were afraid of it. And man assumed it. Lo! He hath proved a tyrant and a fool. Allah punisheth hypocritical men and hypocritical women, and idolatrous men and idolatrous women. But Allah pardoneth believing men and believing women, and Allah is Forgiving, Merciful."

(Quran 33:72-73)

Man's object should be removed from fire and entry into Paradise and not the Baconian object of material comfort.

"Every soul will taste of death. And ye will be paid on the Day of Resurrection only that which ye have fairly earned. Whoso is removed from the Fire and is made to enter Paradise; he indeed is triumphant. The life of this world is but the comfort of illusion." (Quran 3:185)

Moreover, the object of man ought to be Paradise, and exertion is the necessity to achieve that object.

"Race one with another for forgiveness from your Lord and a Garden whereof the breadth is as the breadth of the heavens and the earth, which is in store for those who believe in Allah and His messengers."

(Quran 57:21)

Men of understanding contemplate and say Allah could not have created these works without a purpose.

"Lo! In the creation of the heavens and the earth and (in) the difference of night and day are tokens (of His Sovereignty) for men of understanding, such as remember Allah, standing, sitting, and reclining, and consider the creation of the heavens and the earth, (and say): Our Lord! Thou createdst not this in vain. Glory be to Thee! Preserve us from the doom of Fire, Our Lord! Whom Thou causest to enter the Fire: him indeed Thou hast confounded. For evil-doers, there will be no helpers. Our Lord! Lo! We have heard a crier calling unto Faith: "Believe ye in your Lord!" So, we believed. Our Lord! Therefore, forgive us our sins, and remit from us our evil deeds, and make us die the death of the righteous. Our Lord! And give us that which Thou hast promised to us by Thy messengers. Confound us not upon the Day of Resurrection. Lo! Thou breakest not the tryst."

(Quran 3:190-194)

Quran's views on natural versus moral philosophy are clear. The fundamental basis of all religions rests on moral philosophy, whereas natural philosophy is only a handmaid of moral philosophy. The contrast of the view between Bacon and the Quran is obvious.

The difficulty is that people generally always dissociate economics and the necessities of life from religion. It is erroneous in the case of this modern Baconian progress. Instead, it has to be viewed as an article of faith and as a particular creed in itself compared to revealed religion. It has its particular purpose in contrast with the one given by religion.

~~*~*~*

CHAPTER-11

COMPARATIVE VIEWS OF BACON AND THE QURAN ON THE CONTEMPLATION OF THE WORKS OF ALLAH

We are now focusing on a topic that holds a key position in our entire work. It perhaps appears as the key to the future destiny of this humankind. Yet it is of nature indeed exceedingly slippery. It lends itself most simply to the possibility of creating a misunderstanding about it in the minds even of the most learned among men of remarkable shrewdness and wisdom and is highly subtle like a star enclosed in luminous mist. The misunderstanding about it, however, is susceptible to spreading the most catastrophic destruction. No doubt, the entire humankind today is involved in a misunderstanding about it. Instead, humankind has been a victim of this misunderstanding for a long time, that is, since the first appearance of Bacon's philosophy on this earth in the 17th century AD.

The topic in question is that of the contemplation of the works of Allah. The misunderstanding is about its purpose. Bacon gave out its purpose as the material exploitation of the works of God for the material well-being of humankind in general. Everyone on earth has accepted this view of Bacon. The practice of exploitation of the works of God for the material well-being of humankind, in general, has continued since then with the clearest of conscience on the part of the followers of every religion in the world who have discovered complete compatibility to exist (according to their own viewpoint) between the views of Bacon and the views of their religion. Yet, no one cared to look at the effect of this view during these centuries. Till now, it has noticeably appeared though it still is concealed from the eyes of this humankind. It now appears that the spirit of religion has been crushed completely, and the soul of humanity has suffered the same fate. Humankind appears to meet a similar doom at any moment bodily.

We may now regard humankind as a species geared and fattened by a butcher. They will be subjected to the process of nucleo-execution for misunderstanding the purpose of 'contemplation of the works of God'.

They have defied Mother Nature, but the re-appraisal of Mother Nature has appeared in a form too terribly tragic to express in words. Indeed, the Shakespeares, Miltons, and Dantes would lose their wit through horror before the horrible spectacle of the fiery giant Atumbumb, which now is snorting with sinister intentions at this Baconian fed humankind. Dante's inferno (purgatory) might appear only a very childish episode in comparison to the spectacle of this world changed into a dreadful Jehannah (hell) under the hail of atomic bombs and the stings of atomic radiations. From the moral point of humanity, though, this world is even now in no way less than a Jehannah. A hell is ablaze in every heart in discontent and misery, and a tormenting epidemic fever of greed pervades this earth entirely.

The topic of the contemplation of the works of Allah was not new to this world. It was present in the Bible and the Quran. However, Bacon alone may justly deserve the honor of first adopting this notion of the contemplation of God's works for material exploitation. He used the phrases such as 'The Book of God's word' and 'The Book of God's work' and introduced the philosophical idea of material exploitation of the works of God. Earlier, folks invariably and exclusively meant 'contemplation of works of Allah' as a meditation of a religious kind. It was for the adoration and remembrance of the Creator and as a reminder of Allah's truth that is the truth of Allah's religion and as a reminiscence of doomsday and the next world.

The Quran has laid so great a stress on this particular kind of speculation with a particular purpose in such a clear and explicit method that before the modern age, works of poets of the Islamic era are replete with the speculative contemplation of the works of Allah. For instance, read the Persian poetry of Saadi (1184-1283/1291) and Hafez (1315-1390), both of Shiraz. The practice was neither confined to these two great poets nor even to poetry alone. The most significant works of prose have worn contemplation of Allah's works like ornaments. Never once to any Christian or a Muslim appeared the thought of material exploitation associated with the contemplation of God's works until Bacon introduced this idea in his new philosophy of material utility.

The followers of every religion on earth have adopted this new Baconian concept of material exploitation of the works of God. They embraced it in the name of and on the pretext of contemplation of the works of God without any perceptible scruple or effort exporting indeed the early struggle of the Christian Church, which eventually lost the field. Science gained complete sway everywhere and in every way. On the whole, we may reasonably say that humankind has most willingly and gratefully accepted the new idea. The followers of every single religious book appear as victims of misunderstanding about the nature of contemplation of the works of Allah.

Nevertheless, we will treat only the followers of the Quran because of all the Scriptures; the Quran has treated this topic as a whole subject by pointing to the works of Allah and giving most explicitly the objects of the contemplation of the works. The Quran has treated this topic so explicitly that there appeared to be no shadow of any possibility of missing or misunderstanding them. The points have been exhausted and exemplified. Even it has described the mode of contemplation. Further, it has laid considerable stress on the topic of the contemplation of the works of Allah itself. Indeed, the Muslims of the pre-modern age did understand the objects thereof quite well.

The Quran has given numerous objects of contemplation of the works of Allah. But, the only object of material exploitation of the works of Allah does not emerge anyplace like a hint or allusion in the Quran. Undoubtedly, when we view the point in light of the avowed aversion the Quran has manifested to this world and its material wealth, it is not difficult to realize that it could not have been otherwise.

Whence do followers of the Quran discover such relentless zeal and irresistible truth when citing the Quran's signs about contemplation of works of Allah in favor of this Baconian progress? Why do they advance arguments as proof of harmony between the policy of the Quran and the idea of material exploitation of works of God innovated by Bacon? What sincerity, clarity of conscience, and honest zeal, Muslims show to cite signs of the Quran about contemplation of works of Merciful and Bountiful Allah, the Benign and Gracious Creator of the world, as proof of the approval of this progress by the Quran?

Moreover, it is not one Muslim, not two, not two hundred, but the entire Muslim race is the victim of the same misunderstanding excepting no doubt, the Ulema (scholars) of the Muslim nation. With a thankful heart, I contemplate the absence of the effects of the modern knowledge among the Muslim Ulema, whose ignorance of this modern knowledge is a blessing to them and a hope for the future of humankind. Would to Allah there appeared no such thing as modern knowledge and this Baconian progress in the world of Allah so that there had appeared no consequent danger of this humankind being roasted alive in the flames of atomic Jehannah both, in this present life, and the eternal life hereafter. Cursed be the memory of those that were directly or indirectly involved in the appearance and prevalence of Baconian philosophy, the devil's philosophy on this earth, and with what earnestness one ought to wish the instantaneous disappearance of this threat of atomic annihilation to humankind, the disappearance both of the threat and its intrinsic cause.

In the Quran, we find in great profusion the signs that encourage the habit of contemplation of the works of Allah. A close study reveals that the Quran has not inserted these particular signs here and there, just sporadically or haphazardly. Instead, it has treated the subject as a complete entity. It has enunciated in most explicit terms the purpose of contemplation, furnished with the points of contemplation, and has even taught the mode thereof.

It is erroneous to take it for granted that contemplation means only the contemplation of the material works of the universe or the principles on which the material universe is functioning. Nay, but the view of the Quran regarding the contemplation is of a complete, all-pervasive contemplation that embraces the entire field of thought, both concerning the inward mind of man and the outward expanse of the material universe. In modern times, followers of the Quran have utterly lost the sense of the completeness of the subject of contemplation. They have confined the field of contemplation to only Baconian boundaries of material exploitation of Mother Nature's works in the name and on the pretext of blessed activity of contemplation of the Creator's works.

The Muslims of the pre-modern, that is, the pre-Baconian age did contemplate the works of Allah, knowing the purpose of such contemplation instinctively. They were pretty ignorant and innocent of any idea of the association of contemplation with material exploitation or utility. However, nowadays, everyone is dazed with the urge of material exploitation, having eyes fixed on material advantage and overwhelmed with the burden of the material necessities of life. We see no one looking toward the heavens at night. No one has any thought of contemplation during the day. The transition from the pre-modern pattern to this modern one has not been abrupt. Slowly and gradually, though with an accelerating speed, the transformation found its way until today. We can notice no resemblance between the two species: modern and pre-modern contemplation.

When the modern Baconian philosophy appeared in the Islamic world in the form of the Baconian science-guided progress with its rationalistic teachings, the Muslims, indeed without much ado at first and later with a grateful heart, accepted and adopted the beneficial side of the new philosophy. They associated the idea of "<u>material exploitation of the works of God</u>" with the notion of "<u>contemplation of the works of God</u>" ('Ghaur-Fil-Aayaat'). Thus was the conscience unburdened and the mind burdened with ever-increasing worry and discontent, balanced with the joy and satisfaction of modern facilities, physical comforts, and sensual enjoyments. Though the balance is fast being upset for the worst, their zeal shows no signs of abating.

The tragedy of Hiroshima and Nagasaki has not opened their eyes because their faith in the idea of compatibility between 'material exploitation of the works of God' and 'contemplation of the works of God' has not suffered shaking. We may hear war cries of "onward to the progress", "onward to self-sufficiency", and "onward to a position of respect among the advanced nations" everywhere with ever-increasing echo. This misunderstanding of the Muslims may prove dire, not only to the world but also to themselves. This misconception is an inconstancy powerful enough to drag this world and, along with it Muslims, into flames of a blazing atomic Jehannah, in virtue of their misunderstanding, and misinterpreting the sense of the contemplation of the works of Allah and confounding it with the material exploitation of the works of Allah. Earlier, Bacon misinterpreted the Biblical sense of contemplation, and the result is before the world in the form of an all-devouring atomic hell.

The views of the Quran about this world and its wealth have been made known in the previous pages. The Quran shows a manifest aversion to both this world and its wealth. Accordingly, we should judge the topic of contemplation in light of the basic tendency of the Quran regarding the question of material exploitation. The Quran is there. It may be read and referred to for the most authentic of the interpretations. Then, it will reveal the fact most easily that the contemplation of the works of Allah, as is suggested by the Quran, has nothing whatsoever to do with the material exploitation of either of the works of Allah or the material exploitation in general. Also, we could find no word throughout the Quran that we may suspect of urging or encouraging material exploitation or wealth acquisition. Rather everywhere in the Quran, the wealth of this world and this world itself is mentioned as something not to be loved and something not very commendable.

The Holy Prophet of Islam (peace be upon him) likened this world to the dead carrion and its seekers to dogs, and he avowed poverty as his pride and lived up to his word to the last.

No doubt, the subject of the contemplation treated by the Quran has to do nothing with the material utility. The subject of material utility is treated separately by the Quran with a particular name: 'Al-Fadhl' or 'Al-Fazal', which means 'bounty of Allah'. The contemplation has subservient objects to the religious side and nothing to do with the worldly side. The Quran has itself elucidated these objects in a manner quite explicit and without any shadow of ambiguity. These objects generally are: the glorification of the Creator, the recognition of His unshared Sovereignty, His power, His mercy; and His many other attributes like the remembrance of the Creator, His truth, the truth of religion; and remembrance of the doomsday and seeking the proofs of the necessity and certainty of the event of Resurrection; and indeed, seeking the proofs of all the objects that we mentioned above.

We discern not a passing hint or a slight allusion anywhere throughout the Quran that could describe the material utility or exploitation connected with the signs of contemplation. We are at a loss to comprehend how the Quran could cite these signs to confirm the process of modern Baconian progress. The Quran calls the process of contemplation as signs of Allah. No doubt, one has to contemplate the signs of Allah in whatever form they appear. However, we can attribute this misunderstanding only to the atomic misfortune of this humankind. We may regard it as an effect of divine retribution for exclusive engrossment of humankind in the world at the cost of remembrance of the next world and neglect of the religion of Allah.

Howsoever light this inconsistency may be regarded, its retribution has appeared as one of the most grievous natures, namely, the flames of atomic hell and unheard-of miseries and deadly stings of radiations in this world and flames of the atomic hell in the next eternal world. In the future age of full-fledged atomic energy for peace, this earth will be likened to a grave in which snakes and scorpions continued to torment by constantly stinging the bodies of inmates due to erroneous interpretation of the signs of contemplation.

Alas! Allah's sacred word was never supposed to be a herald or the abettor of a system of un-Godly materialism. Nor was it meant to be a champion of worldly philosophy. Nor even was it to take up the role of an attester of a system of knowledge polluted by exclusively materialistic usage or of the contemplation of the works of Allah profaned by exclusive material exploitation.

However, people regard Baconian philosophy, progress, and culture as correct, the naturalist, and noblest. The influence of the love of wealth and luxury has hypnotized the poor, miserable, and unfortunate humankind, and no doubt, the fascinating Baconian culture has blinded this civilization. For, the blind only or the hypnotized could not see the blazing flames of atomic hell that every moment is drifting toward him with perceptible fury. Eight thousand atomic demons stand leashed, waiting hatefully to pounce upon this humankind and consume everything in a matter of moments, friend, and foe alike, and sparing not even their masters. Now, we may see this world visibly moving one step every day to armed atomic conflict. It appears as a mad world suffering from Bacon-mania.

Judging from the state of present humankind, it appears pretty manifestly that the nations which perished through divine vengeance in history were not much different in habits from this present-day humanity. The Creator destroyed them to be a lesson to others. However, when the Creator has destroyed present humankind, who will survive to take the lesson? Moreover, those who survived the atomic war would not be found in a situation to take a lesson. No, but they will only envy those who had died and will mourn their own survival.

Without exception, followers of every religion are vying with one another to show their religion's exact compatibility with Baconian progress and the doctrine of material exploitation of works of God in contemplation's name. We only wonder if they will be ready to blame the havoc on their religion tomorrow when the atomic hell, the logical consequence of this Baconian progress, will have made a medley of their world. On the other hand, will they be putting the whole blame on the behavior of humankind in failing to avoid the war to the mutual recrimination of each other?

Do not recriminate with each other now. The essence and nature of this Baconian process to end in the nuclear explosion is just as every nuclear reactor must end its forty-year span of natural life in explosion and flood the neighboring districts with life-taking radiations. I am not unaware of the prevailing circumstances nor feign ignorance of necessity and helplessness of this humankind. However, the terribleness of the reprisal is too impelling to allow reticence and leave the truth unsaid. Who will judge the difficulty of the situation in which I find myself fallen? Who will have sympathy with me in my afflictions? Indeed, my Allah will. He is the Most Merciful.

As is suggested by the Quran, contemplation is exclusively subservient to religion and is an aid to understanding the fundamental doctrines of religion and, in this case, Islam. The purpose of religion is to teach men to know Allah and Allah-man relations, religious and moral duties of man, religious view of this world and Resurrection and Final Judgment, the next world, and the moral versus the natural philosophy. As suggested by the Quran, contemplation follows religion and probes into phenomena to discover and discern proofs of doctrines taught by the religion besides glorifying the Creator. It is not the business of religion to teach the methods, ways, and processes of acquiring material necessities of life or acquiring the world's wealth. Similarly, it is not the business of the contemplation of the works of Allah to deal with the material exploitation of the works of God, or the means and methods of works of God, or the means and methods of acquiring the necessities of life, or acquiring wealth or accumulating and maintaining it.

According to the Quran, the aim and object of man on earth ought to be to escape the doom of fire and enter Paradise. The object of contemplation ought, in this respect, to be to aid him in obtaining his goal. The acquirement of necessities of life is entirely separate and has to do nothing whatsoever with religious contemplation. People in the pre-modern ages always regarded it as such. No idea of an association between the act of contemplation of works of Allah and material exploitation of works of God had any existence.

However, we now confront the modern Baconian philosophy of atomism, which is purely, exclusively, utterly, and entirely a philosophy of the world and its wealth and material progress. It has nothing but the material exploitation of the works of God in view. It has a peculiar and particularly fixed basic structure that neither would admit any change in itself nor any inclusion in religion's spiritual and moral factor to affect some sort of balance between the material and moral or spiritual.

The Quran, from its beginning to its end, depreciates and condemns this world and enjoins throughout to shun it and its wealth, calling it a play and vanity and comfort of illusion and mere ostentation against the next life, which according to the Quran is the real life. There is neither a word nor a hint in the Quran in favor of this world or its wealth. According to Quran, praiseworthy wealth is spent only in the name of Allah or for the sake of religion.

Supposing this is the case, how is it possible to expect that the Quran would recommend the contemplation of the works of Allah for the material exploitation of the works of Allah. Suppose the Quran abhors this world to such an extent. Then, how could it be expected to suggest a course in which, like Baconian philosophy, no thought could perhaps exist other than that of this material world, its wealth, and its physical comforts? To consider then that we should justly apply the type of contemplation suggested by the Quran to the material exploitation of the works of God in line with the horrific, materialistic, and un-Godly philosophy of Bacon is a libel on the sanctity and the integrity of the Quran. It means to bring the Quran down to the level of a treatise on materialism. Nay, but the contemplation of works of Allah as suggested by the Quran is in every way as spiritual, sacred, and divine as the Quran itself is. There has to be some difference between the contemplation of worldly and materialistic philosophy and divine religion. There ought to be definite discrimination between philosophy exclusively of the material world and religion with its heart in the otherworld.

The Quran has described the act of material utility as 'Al-Fadhl' ('Al-Fazal'). It means 'the bounty of Allah'. The Quran has expressed material utility as seeking the bounty of Allah and fixed its place in the order of precedence after prayers. The Quran has nowhere assumed the duty of teaching any method of seeking bounty and has nowhere explained any process thereof.

It has only enjoined upon its followers to seek the bounty of Allah by fair means and to give charity to those who are needy or who deserve it, to mean that it has treated the moral side of the affair only. On the other hand, the Quran has treated the subject of contemplation completely. It has given out the various purposes of conducting the contemplation and furnished the complete list of the objects to contemplate. We can easily arrange these points in various categories, such as physics, chemistry, botany, astronomy, etc.

As the Quran gives throughout, the object of contemplation is only religious and divine in essence and nature and never once material or worldly. The Quran has pointed to the apparent universe as an object of contemplation. In addition, an introverted contemplation of oneself has been included in the process also. Furthermore, we must also focus on contemplation of the Quran's verses called by the appellation of signs. There are signs in the Quran concerning the 'serviceability' of the universe to man. In these signs, Allah has claimed to have rendered objects in the universe serviceable to man. Hence, we must also include these signs in the subject of contemplation. We will clarify these points with examples from the Quran later.

It was Francis Bacon (1561-1626), a contemporary of Mujaddid Alif Sani, Sheikh Sir-Hindi of India, who first of all did advance the theory of the material exploitation of the works of God on the pretext of the contemplation of the works of Allah by misinterpreting the word of the Bible. The history of philosophy has recorded no such thing before. Before that, people always regarded contemplation as the aesthetic appreciation of the works of Allah. Therein was never any idea of the material exploitation of the works of God. All the time, the thought of the Creator was present there with the idea of contemplation.

However, when the Baconian culture with its science-guided, machine-ridden progress emerged from the West, the people of the entire world sought to satisfy their inner conscience by discovering compatibility between this new progress and the view of their religious book. Indeed, none of them met with much difficulty in finding the cherished quest.

The Muslims found an opportunity to emphasize the factor of compatibility between Islam and achievements of modern science in virtue of great emphasis laid by the Quran on the act of contemplation of works of Allah. They had easily discovered a link between contemplation of works of Allah and material exploitation of His works. Because Islam had the reputation of a religion that had rejected the creed of seclusion in the monastery and hermitage, the Muslims assumed that it allowed progress even if it was of a Baconian kind. However, from first to last till the beginning of the modern age, all authentic interpreters of the Quran have not used a word or passed a hint suggesting the slightest association between the contemplation of works of Allah and their material exploitation.

Nevertheless, Muslims are not the first in history to be involved in a misunderstanding regarding worldly wealth though there is no link between contemplation and material utility whatsoever in the Quran. The Quran says:

"Who (Allah) hath created seven heavens in harmony. Thou (Muhammad) canst see no fault in the Beneficent One's creation; then look again: Canst thou see any rifts? Then look again and yet again, thy sight will return unto thee weakened and made dim."

(Quran 67:3-4)

What if any attempt ever been made to form a possible association between the contemplation and material exploitation of the works of Allah in the Islamic world in pre-modern times? It would have caused a universal uproar among the Islamic Ulema (scholars) as an instance of gross innovation and unacceptable heresy. The negligible social status of the gold-making Alchemists and the little divine reverence they enjoyed among the Muslims in the pre-modern ages affords a sufficient measure of their popularity.

Bacon was extremely lucky in this respect. He found a different and thriving pre-disposed atmosphere. When the Baconian progress emerged from the West, it appeared over the Islamic world like a fateful, hypnotizing victor with flying banners. Muslims were obliged to accept it.

We have alluded to the attitude of interpreters of the Quran in pre-modern ages touching this point that of the material utility in contemplation. We may observe that no Islamic scholar has found an association between contemplation and material exploitation even in this modern age. A little coterie of interpreters of the Quran influenced by

Baconian philosophy, who neither know the Quran nor are familiar with preliminaries of science, are engaged in advocating unanimity of the Quran and modern science and its progress. People, however, would exert in progress even without the inducement of these interpreters in question.

It is not only the Quran that has broached the topic of the contemplation of the works of Allah. The Bible also contains some examples, but the Quran has all or most of the points of Christ's 'Sermon on the Mount' in developed and generalized form. Similarly, the points of contemplation of works of Allah, which appear but in glimpses in the Bible, may be seen in the Quran treated as a complete subject. The Quran pronounced its aims and objects, and the list of the points for contemplation is exhausted. We may also notice that contemplation in the Quran has been treated as thought and encompassed the entire field of thought. Contemplation of material and substantial objects in the universe has been treated with conspicuity and significance and in exact accordance with Quranic views about the world.

The Quranic contemplation has to be judged based on purpose, and it is on the same criterion that one must judge it against the Baconian exploitation of the works of God. It is the purpose itself in this respect that is the decisive factor to judge between sacred and the profane, the spiritual and the material, and it is the purpose itself that makes all the real difference. A controversy that might rage for centuries without deciding about the Quranic and the Baconian contemplation could see termination in a matter of minutes if someone judged the matter upon the criterion of purpose. Why the subject of contemplation should seem such important may be seen in consequence of its erroneous appreciation: A consequence dreadful enough to bring anyone back to senses except him against whom the decree of a horrible doom has gone. We allude to the appearance of atomic hell.

The Prophet of Islam (peace be upon him) was a teacher and a practical model for the Muslims in every respect. Who, more than him, could have contemplated the works of Allah in a manner more proper? There is no sign that he ever hinted at the material exploitation of the works of Allah in connection with their contemplation verbally or ever did anything practically in this respect. Next to him were his disciples as the models. Nor do we find something in any one of them to allude to an association between contemplation and material utility of works of Allah. We can attempt to explain the Holy Prophet's (peace be upon him) and his disciples' attitude in this respect.

But who will explain the consequences of this association between contemplation of works of Allah and material exploitation? The resultant penalties will be unheard afflictions or untold miseries, universal acute discontent and heart-burning, painful and novel diseases, and above all else, the blazing all-consuming atomic hell though not much minded at present. Yet this hell must undoubtedly be recognized when it will broil the people therein once its flames begin to roast and burn them alive. Then, is it not better to foresee the approaching trouble and think about how to avoid it? Nor will be a hell of radiation of the atomic energy for peace in any way the less horrible.

The Quran is the last Scripture, and the last declared Will of Allah. Hence, Allah gave out His works in the universe as miracles in place of the miracles people demanded from pretenders of prophethood to signify the truth of their claim in ancient times. Besides these works of Allah in the universe, He has declared the Quran itself like a standing miracle. It is an object for contemplation presented as a substitute for miracles as the Prophets of pre-Islamic ages worked. Hence, all the enhanced significance of the subject of contemplation and a miracle this Quran indeed is. If it succeeded in guiding this humankind away from the atomic hell, that certainly would be a miracle without a parallel in human history.

Islam is the religion revealed to the Holy Prophet of Islam (peace be upon him) in a form perfected and complete in every way. The peculiar and characteristic innovations of this modern Baconian age in knowledge, science, and other views, are devilish innovations and satanic seductions and Anti-Christic, and not at all in line with Islamic views or teachings and could well be discerned through their gilding enamel by their colors of the Anti-Christic falsehood and deceit.

There is no midway house between this present situation and the early Islamic era. The only alternative now left is either a complete and abrupt mature turn to that same era of early Islam or to move into the grievous punishment of the Baconian falsehood: a punishment which now is no hidden a secret, namely, the flames of a roaring, growling, and bursting atomic hell ready to consume the Jews, the Christians, the Muslims, the Hindus, and the Buddhists and all others that anywhere exist on earth.

If humankind desires to escape dreadful doom and revive religion for safety, the first requisite must be a denial of the materialistic view of contemplation of works of Allah. The Muslims must renew their faith and determination. They have a complete, perfect, intact, and universal religion since the Holy Prophet of Islam (peace be upon him).

Allah has undertaken to guard the Quran, and no doubt He has guarded it to this day.

The Christian Church proscribed acquiring knowledge because eating the fruit of the tree of knowledge of good and evil caused man's expulsion from Paradise. Bacon took up the same point and argued that it was not the pursuit of natural philosophy that had been the cause of man's expulsion from Paradise. However, it was the act of man's eating the fruit of the tree of knowledge of good and evil that had been the cause of expulsion. As the knowledge of good and evil is the basis of the moral philosophy, a man ought to pursue the natural philosophy (science) as God's command and avoid pursuing moral philosophy as proscribed by God to Adam.

This thought of Bacon might appear strange because religion is based exclusively on moral philosophy and not on natural philosophy. Bacon appears to have turned topsy-turvy not only Christian religion but all religions. He went further and gave out the destiny of man and the purpose of his new philosophy as the attainment of man's dominion over Mother Nature for material benefit. He interpreted the purpose of the Bible, the contemplation of God's works, as the material exploitation of the works of God and asserted that man had in a vain and impious attempt resorted to the prohibited philosophy that is moral philosophy merely to give him the law. The name and the philosophy of Bacon, having been long forgotten, vies that we have attributed to him, might appear strange and doubtful. However, his works are still extant, and the reader may well verify his views in his 'Advancement of Learning' and 'Novum Organum'. Still, it is strange that the entire world is adhering entirely to the same views without knowing their origin or reality.

The Quranic concept of contemplation of the works of Allah is purely a concept of a religious kind and has nothing whatsoever to do with material utility. The Quran could never endorse the material view of contemplation. Yet, the religious concept of contemplation has completely been overwhelmed by the material utilization in the world nowadays. Moreover, none today would care. The cry against Baconian progress could be set up only in the presence of havocking consequences of an erroneous view. These devastating outcomes have now appeared in a way too noticeable to be missed: only those will miss it against whom the dreadful decree of providence has gone.

The Quran has obviously laid considerable stress on the act of the contemplation of the works of Allah, but it is only as an aid to faith and cannot initially create faith. In pre-Islamic times, people demanded Prophets to show miracles as proof of the truth of their claim for a divine mission. Now, Allah has pointed to His works as a substitute for such miracles.

Allah presented the Quran to humankind as a 'living miracle' for contemplation besides His works. He brought religion to its ultimate perfection in the shape of Islam as 'the last religion', revealed the Quran as eternal guidance for humankind as 'the last revealed Scripture', and Mohammad, the Prophet of Islam (peace be upon him) as the 'last prophet'. Also, the mind of humankind reached a stage of development where the 'works' of Allah could substitute the 'miracles' shown by the Prophets in pre-Islamic days because there was no prophet to follow Mohammad (peace be upon him) to show such concrete miracles in the future.

When the Baconian material setup with its giant prepared prehensile, flying banners, convincing rationalism, and sweet fruits appeared on the scene of the Islamic world, it was at once accorded a welcome without pointing a finger or without a frown on the brow, as something that accorded with the basic concept of Islam. If there were any differences with the Western conquerors, those were of political or religious nature. The Muslims did neither understand nor even try to understand the actual reality of this modern progress. Now, when its dire and dreadful consequences are there, they are the victims of false optimism with the rest of humankind. Besides that, they are as helpless as the rest are. They are tied in the same chains, and oppressive circumstances drive them to the atomic hell with others.

The people of West took up the contemplation of the works of God for the sake of material exploitation of the works of God. Astonishingly, they did wonders and achieved marvelous success in their initiative due to honesty, sincerity, patience, perseverance, anxiousness, endless labor, and ceaseless toil as the article of faith.

However, they achieved their object by deserting their faith. Their Bible was not the Bible of Moses and Christ; it was the textbook of science. Their guide was neither Jesus Christ nor any of his apostles or saints; it was the scientist. Besides, they achieved their object because they plunged themselves into the battle of material utility with the spirit of a crusade, forgetting everything else; faith, religion, morality, and the next world. Any nation, therefore, that desired to achieve similar success in progress could not succeed as well, unless and until followed the example of the West. Every nation on earth could do that, but there are conditions and requisites. However, the case of Muslims is different. The living religion still lives, but maybe it is at loggerheads with this modern progress and culture.

Indeed, if any of the early commentators of the Quran were to see modern progress as it is, nothing but wonder would be his lot to reap from the attitude of the Muslims in this respect. He would never be able to understand the justification of the material exploitation of the works of Allah through the Quranic concept of the contemplation of the works of Allah. However, the amazement of the present-day Muslims might begin with the bombardment of atomic bombs or the attack of atomic radiation. One may wonder whether they will be ready to attribute the grievous doom to the teachings of the Quran; that is the Quran which, according to them, allowed this modern progress.

However, Nuclear Jehannah (hell) is the inevitable end of this Baconian material setup as just and all-consuming retribution. Also, if the view of modern Muslims regarding utilitarian contemplation is correct, then all the Islamic generations of the pre-modern times had explicitly erred and were regarded as blameable for so gross a neglect and so great an error.

So grossly and universally, the Muslims are involved in the misunderstanding about the Quran's approval of the view of contemplation regarding His 'services' bestowed on humankind as 'bounties' that no sooner one starts the topic than the answer of a Muslim will invariably be, indeed in the sincerest surest of tones, as follows.

"Why, sir, do we not find in the Quran signs that insist to contemplate the works of Allah? Has not the Quran dealt with the topic of the conquest of Mother Nature? Also, is Islam not a progressive and dynamic religion? Moreover, has the Quran not enjoined on the Muslims to keep the war preparation in readiness? Further, is it not essential to have weapons of the same category as the others have?"

Here then, is a situation that deserves note.

There is not a question amongst quoted above that is not perfectly correct. However, it is in the interpretation and the application of these facts that the mistake appears. Quran does not mean material exploitation of the works of Allah by the contemplation thereof. Islam is a progressive religion, not in the sense that it is the religion of materialism. It is dynamic indeed but dynamic only as a religion of Allah and not as a system of materialism. The Quran no doubt has commanded the Muslims to keep the war preparations in readiness as a deterrent. But, whether the atomic bomb, the Hydrogen bomb, or the neutron bomb are weapons of war for defense?

The hydrogen bomb is not a weapon but a means of complete extinction of life on earth to the scientist. To Quran, it is the atomic hell. It is the retributive wrath of Allah. Both the atomic bomb and atomic radiations defy any protection against them. The scientist hitherto has failed absolutely in this respect. The matter is without any doubt beyond the power of the scientist or non-scientist. Neither defense is possible against the divine vengeance and the wrath of Allah, nor can man vanish the atomic threat in the presence of its causes.

We have heard the questions put by the Muslims above. Very genuine questions indeed, but they could be answered with equal genuineness as follows.

Is not the result of this modern progress perceptibly the atomic hell? Could it not be seen even now? Does not this hell encompass the entire humankind? Quite certainly, is it not the wholesale destruction of the entire of humankind? Do not the atomic bomb and the atomic radiation defy every means of defense? Do not the atomic radiations change the creatures to miserable cancer-ridden chimeras before their final extinction?

Neither anyone would be left to call himself the 'victor' after a universal atomic war, nor would anyone be able to live with immunity in a country where they would have fought the atomic war. [1] Radiations make a healthy life impossible therein. Neither the Quran nor any other book, and neither Islam nor any other religion could save this world from the atomic conflagration if this process of modern progress is allowed to continue and complete its stages. The preparation of the means of atomic conflagration is ready while the atomic conflict is quite sure. It is inevitable. Therefore, choose either this progress or safety. That means that humankind shall eradicate this progress, or it will certainly destroy this humankind.

Suppose we assume that the Quran approved this Baconian materialism and that the contemplation suggested by it meant the material exploitation of the works of Allah. Then, if this Baconian materialism ended in the flames of atomic hell, will it not mean that the teachings of the Quran were such as led to the atomic eradication of life?

However, are the teachings of the Quran indeed such? Does not the Quran lead to that path which is the straightest? Is it then the straightest way to reach the inevitable hell of atomic flames? Besides, is Islam not a religion of peace and bliss? Then, is it blissful to enter hell? However, it should be made clear that the atomic hell is the logical, scientific, and inevitable consequence of Baconian materialism and results from this modern progress. The ruins of Hiroshima and Nagasaki churches might serve as a note to those whose eyes are open to seeing and minds to think that the same could and would happen to other churches.

The generality of the Islamic world gratefully ruminates over the thought that scientific discoveries furnished them with proofs of the truth of doctrines of their religion as if the doctrines of Islam were doubtful until proved by science. They do this without ever noticing the scythe science has placed to the roots of their own religion, Islam, Christianity, Hinduism, Buddhism, and all other religions. It is interesting to note that this science could not furnish, as a rule, a proof of any doctrine which happens to be beyond the five senses. Moreover, all the most essential doctrines of religion, e.g., the unseen Allah, Resurrection, and all that is that side of the grave, and spiritual values are beyond the ken of this modern science. She is blind in them. What proofs can she produce to prove religion?

The intelligentsia of the Islamic world, except Ulema (scholars), are happy in the thought that contemplation of the works of Allah as suggested by the Quran results in discoveries of science and implementing the idea of utilization of modern progress and that was creditable to the Quran. So, whenever a fragment of sentimental expression of a natural scientist comes to sight, their hearts are filled with joy. They become lost in reverie, neither ever thinking about the nature of work the scientists did nor giving any attention to results that have appeared from their work in the form of miseries, dissatisfaction; and above all, all-consuming flames of nuclear Jehannah.

We shall quote in the following some examples of such expressions. Judge for yourself, on one hand, the beauty and sublimity of these expressions, and on the other hand, the nature of their field and the results they have produced, and then see if such expressions could be a sufficient bribe for the horrific results of science.

(1) "He who planted ears, shall he not hear? The idea of mind behind and mind within seems like a rational and working hypothesis as any ...."

(2) "The universe is ruled by the mind. Whether it be the mind of a mathematician, of an artist, of a poet or all of them and more; it is the one reality that gives meaning to existence, enriches our daily task, encourages our hope, energizes us with faith and feeling whenever knowledge fails, and illuminates the whole universe with immortal love."

(Sir Oliver Lodge)

(3) "He who can no longer pause to wonder and stand rapt in awe, is as good as dead; his eyes are closed."

(Albert Einstein)

GABRIEL'S EXTINGUISHING THE ATOMIC HELL SERIES

(4) "A final impression we get as we stand and gaze upon the scene before us. We grow to feel part of it. We have a sense of union with it. Something in it communicates with something in us. The communion brings us joy. And the joy brings exaltation."

[Frances (Baker) Mason]

(5) "One plan, many variations; one design, many modifications; one truth, many versions."

[Frances (Baker) Mason]

(6) "Can anyone seriously suggest that this directing and regulating power originated in chance encounter of atoms? Can the stream rise higher than its fountain?"

(Professor William Macberamid)

(7) "The more we know, the more we find there is to know. The farther we go, the greater our joy is. The deeper we penetrate, the higher our exaltation is. So, on and on, we shall go laymen and scientists alike. We shall never stop because the lure is too great."

N. B. No doubt into the atomic hell.

(8) "Our minds are overwhelmed by immensity and majesty of nature."

(David Fraiser)

(9) "We hardly know which to admire the more; the mind that arranged nature, or the mind which interpreted it."

(10) "What a marvelous imagination God Almighty has."

(11) "The universe looks more like a great thought than a great machine."

(Sir James Jeans)

(12) "The trembling universe must have been balanced with unthinkable precision."

(Sir James Jeans)

(13) "O, God! How marvelous are thy works?"

(14) "The very law which molds a tear and bids it trickle from its source. That law preserves the earth and guides the planets in their course."

(Samuel Rogers)

(15) "We are at last to know which to admire the more. The mathematical accuracy of the universe or the beauty of its design."

(Samuel Rogers)

(16) "We must take notice of such qualities of the organism such as varying, growing, multiplying, developing, feeling, and endeavoring; as the study of such facts and interests educates, enriches and helps to keep alive the sense of wonder which we hold to be one of the saving graces of life."

(17) "Open thou mine eyes, that I may behold wondrous things out of thy law."
(The Bible: Old Testament: Psalms 119:18)
(18) "In these things minute what wisdom is displayed, what power, and what unfathomable perfection."
(19) "He who casts himself on nature's fair and full bosoms draws food and drink from a fountain that is never dry."
(20) "In contemplation of created things,
By steps we may ascend to God."
(John Milton)
(21) "How mighty and how majestic are thy works and with what appellant dread they swell the soul."
(22) "It is a wonder that man's brain reels before the infinitely great things of the universe on the one hand and the infinitely small things of nature on the other."
(23) "It is impossible to conceive either the beginning or the continuance of life without an overruling creative power. Overpowering strong proofs of benevolent and intelligent design are to be found around us, teaching that all living things depend on the everlasting Creator and Ruler."
(Lord Colon)
(24) "So work the honey-bees;
Creatures, by a rule in nature, teach
The art of order to a peopled kingdom."
(William Shakespeare)
(25) "The universe is a circle whose center is everywhere, and circumference is nowhere."
(Pickle)
(26) "Mohammad (peace be upon him) was a great king. A mighty conqueror and learned man. From the Quran, we learn that he was a lover of nature and knew something of bees and the value of honey. He speaks of bees building nests for themselves and producing honey of various colors. These things were not obtained without a certain amount of inquiry and observation."
(Kater Lovell)

All these expressions are beautiful and inspiring. We could make interesting comments on them, but here we will cease.

However, the last one of these expressions about Mohammed, the Prophet of Islam (peace be upon him), deserves notice. Kater Lovell has made this observation. There can be no doubt that Kater Lovell's reflections are based on sincerity and must have been meant as a genuine tribute that, in fact, figures as libel. Mohammad (peace be upon him) was neither a king nor a conqueror but was the apostle of Allah, and the Quran owes nothing to his observation or ability. It is the word entirely of Allah revealed to him.

We need not discuss these abovementioned expressions because they are only relics of a by-gone age and past expressions. Today no such sentiments are either thought of or recorded. Now, either the problems of this science-guided age or subjects of textbooks occupy both people's minds and pages of books. Humankind has lost the Wordsworthian touch of contemplation. The practice of material exploitation of works of God has extinguished that light. Man's mind is now entirely occupied by worries of problems created by material exploitation of Allah's works. The constant dread of hazards incident on atomic phenomena has also engaged man's mind. Time is coming when humankind will shun even the idea of contemplation of works of Allah due to the excruciating troubles which this materialistic contemplation will have created for this humankind.

Do we not see that at the beginning of modern Baconian progress, people had in their mind the idea of the contemplation of the works of God in religious spirit even in material exploitation of the works of God? However, gradually the idea of material exploitation prevailed till nothing, but material utility remained without any association with the thought of religion.

The skeptics demanded miracles as proof of the truth of the mission of the Prophets.
The Quran says:
"Their messengers said: Can there be doubt concerning Allah, the Creator of the heavens and the earth? He calleth you that He may forgive you your sins and reprieve you unto an appointed term. They said: Ye are but mortals like us, who would fain turn us away from what our fathers used to worship. Then bring some clear warrant. Their messengers said unto them: We are but mortals like you, but Allah giveth grace unto whom He will of His slaves. It is not ours to bring you a warrant unless by the permission of Allah. In Allah, let believers put their trust!"

(Quran 14:10-11)

If prophets showed a miracle, those who did not want to believe denounced it as mere magic.
The Quran says:
"(Pharaoh) said (to Moses): If thou comest with a token, then produce it, if thou art of those who speak the truth. Then he flung down

his staff and Lo! It was a serpent manifest, and he drew forth his hand (from his bosom): and lo! It was white for the beholders. The chiefs of Pharaoh's people said: Lo! This is some knowing wizard who would expel you from your land. Now, what do ye advise?"

(Quran 7:106-110)

The people of Moses even went further and demanded to see Allah by themselves.

The Quran says:

"And when ye said: O Moses! We will not believe in thee till we see Allah plainly, and even while ye gazed, the lightning seized you. Then We revived you after your extinction, that ye might give thanks."

(Quran 2:55-56)

The denial of the Prophets by the people is the cause of not showing the warnings. Allah, in the Quran, says:

"Naught hindereth Us from sending portents save that the folk of old denied them."

(Quran 17:59)

Even the Prophet of Islam (peace be upon him) was obliged to show a miracle. The moon was rent in twin by the sign of his finger. However, the result was that infidels proclaimed it, as usual, like a magical illusion.

The Quran says:

"The hour drew nigh, and the moon was rent in twain. And if they behold a portent, they turn away and say: Prolonged illusion (the same old magic)."

(Quran 54:1-2)

The Jews, too, demanded a miracle of the Holy Prophet of Islam (peace be upon him), but the answer of the Quran was as follows.

"(The same are) those who say: Lo! Allah hath charged us that we believe not in any messenger until he brings us an offering which fire (from heaven) shall devour. Say (unto them, O Muhammad): Messengers came unto you before me with miracles, and with that (very miracle) which ye describe. Why then did ye slay them? (Answer that) if ye are truthful."

(Quran 3:183)

The people demanded of the Holy Prophet of Islam (peace be upon him) to produce instantly before their eyes the pattern of the Paradise which he promised to the pious people.

The Quran says:

"And they say: We will not put faith in thee till thou cause a spring to gush forth from the earth for us, or thou have a garden of date palms and grapes and cause rivers to gush forth therein abundantly; Or thou cause the heaven to fall upon us piecemeal, as thou hast pretended, or bring Allah and the angels as a warrant; thou have a house of gold, or thou ascend into heaven, and even then we will put no faith in thine ascension till thou bring down for us a book that we can read. Say (O Muhammad): My Lord be glorified! Am I naught save a mortal messenger? And naught prevented humankind from believing when the guidance came unto them save that they said: Hath Allah sent a mortal as (His) messenger?"

(Quran 17:90-94)

People desire an omen from the Prophet of Islam (peace be upon him), but the answer of the Quran is as follows.

(1) "Those who disbelieve say: If only some portent were sent down upon him from his Lord! Thou art a warner only, and for every folk a guide."

(Quran 13:7)

(2) "Say (unto them O Muhammad): I am only a mortal like you. It is inspired in me that your Allah is One Allah, therefore take the straight path unto Him and seek forgiveness of Him. And woe unto the idolaters, who give not the poor a due, and who are disbelievers in the Hereafter."

(Quran 41:6-7)

Quran, revealed to Mohammad (peace be upon him), is declared by Allah as His own standing miracle and a perfect and complete guide to humankind.

Allah, in the Quran, says:

"Say: Verily, though humankind and the Jinn should assemble to produce the like of this Quran, they could not produce the like thereof though they were helpers one of another. And verily We have displayed for humankind in this Quran all kinds of similitudes, but most of the humankind refuse aught save disbelief."

(Quran 17:88-89)

Also, they insist on a miracle such as to: "Cause a spring to gush forth from the earth ... ... messenger."

(Quran 17:90-94) (As mentioned above)

ALTHOUGH:

The Quran comprises 'The sign of the Scripture':

"These are verses of the Scripture. That which is revealed unto thee from thy Lord is the Truth, but most of the humankind believe not."

(Quran 13:1)

YET:

"And when Our clear revelations are recited unto them, who disbelieve say of the Truth when it reacheth them: This is mere magic."

(Quran 46:7)

BUT:

(1) "Proofs have come unto you from your Lord, so whoso seeth, it is for his own good, and whoso is blind, is blind to his own hurt. And I am not a keeper over you."

(Quran 6:104)

(2) "Had it been possible for a Lecture to cause the mountains to move, or the earth to be torn asunder, or the dead to speak, (this Quran would have done so). Nay, but Allah's is the whole command."

(Quran 13:31)

(3) "Will they then not meditate on the Quran, or are there locks on the hearts."

(Quran 47:24)

CONTEMPLATION AS AN AID TO BELIEF

"Lo! In the heavens and the earth are portents for believers. And in your creation, and all the beasts that He scattered in the earth, are portents for a folk whose faith is sure. And the difference of night and day and the provision that Allah sendeth down from the sky and thereby quickeneth the earth after her death, and the ordering of the winds, are portents for a people who have sense. These are the portents of Allah which We recite unto thee (Muhammad) with the truth. Then in what fact, after Allah and His portents, will they believe?"

(Quran 45:3-6)

ALBEIT:

"Say: Behold what is in the heavens and the earth! But revelations and warnings avail not folk who will not believe."

(Quran 10:101)

FOR:

"For indeed it is not the eyes that grow blind, but it is the hearts, which are within the bosoms, that grow blind."

(Quran 22:46)

We find a characteristic instance of the Islamic contemplation of the works of Allah in the example of Hazrat Ibraheem (Abraham). No factor of material utility is involved therein. It is purely a religious matter. The contemplation leads Hazrat Ibraheem to the true Allah after rejecting the false ones.

The Quran says:

"Thus, did We show Abraham the kingdom of the heavens and the earth that he might be of those possessing certainty: When the night grew dark upon him, he beheld a star. He said: This is my Lord. But when it set, he said: I love not things that set, and when he saw the moon uprising, he exclaimed: This is my Lord. But when it set, he said: Unless my Lord guides me, I surely shall become one of the folks who are astray. And when he saw the sun uprising, he cried: This is my Lord! This is greater! And when it set, he exclaimed: O my people! Lo! I am free from all that ye associate (with Him). Lo! I have turned my face toward Him Who created the heavens and the earth, as one by nature upright, and I am not of the idolaters."

(Quran 6:75-79)

Read the above-quoted passage of the Quran carefully. Abraham indeed had the idea of the Creator of the heavens and the earth. He only subjected the object that is the star, moon, and sun to his scrutiny, for these were the very objects worshipped as gods in those days. He set the criterion of 'setting' before him and rejected accepting as Allah anything which did 'set'. It is a specimen of contemplation.

Contemplation does not create faith initially. It only helps to discover the issues, and it helps to make an inference from the facts. This point will clarify when we explain the objects of other contemplations set forth by the Quran.

Abraham left his son in a barren land and not fertile land. He built the house of Allah (in Makkah) and not a laboratory for material utility. Moreover, he seeks the religion of one true Allah as his object and not the world's wealth. The same applies to contemplation. It is subservient to the views of religion and not the material utility.

The duties of the Prophet of Islam (peace be upon him) are enumerated by the Quran as follows.

"Allah verily hath shown grace to the believers by sending unto them a messenger of their own who reciteth unto them His revelations, and causeth them to grow, and teacheth them the Scripture and wisdom; although before (he came to them) they were in flagrant error."

(Quran 3:164)

Also, this is an exact response to the prayer of Abraham as follows.

"Our Lord! And raise in their midst a messenger from among them who shall recite unto them Thy revelations, and shall instruct them in the Scripture and wisdom and shall make them grow. Lo! Thou, only Thou, art the Mighty, Wise."

(Quran 2:129)

The religious and moral side, even in worldly matters, was that only taught by the Prophet of Islam (peace be upon him). He never taught the methods or processes of material utility. Once the Holy Prophet (peace be upon him) observed the people spreading pollen on the palm trees, he forbade them the practice. However, when the fruit product in that season appeared much less, the Prophet (peace be upon him) said:

"You know your worldly matters better".

Hazrat Omer Ibn-ul-Aziz admonished his tax-collectors, saying:

"Allah had sent the Prophet as His Prophet and not as a tax-collector. Desist, therefore, from demanding 'Zimmi' tax from the Muslims, even if the treasury remains empty."

Also, once, the rates had enormously risen in the market. People requested that the Prophet (peace be upon him) issue orders to bring the rates down, but he declined. However, the next day he went to the market and appealed to the merchants. It had an immediate effect, and the rates instantly went down. We must apply the same rules to the contemplation of the works of Allah, which only has the religious ends and objects and not material or worldly ones.

When we view the material contemplation of modern Baconian philosophy against the religious contemplation of the Quranic view, it reminds us about the bird named 'Crane' in English, 'Kraan' in Dutch, and 'Karanich' in German. It is a large wading bird of the family Gruidae characterized by long legs, bill, and neck and an elevated hind toe generally found standing in water near the bank with its head lowered as if in mediation. However, no sooner a frog appears before than it plucks, swallows with a gulp, and again is lost in reverie.

It is an example of modern Baconian utilitarian contemplation of the works of God. We may say that the modern Baconian utilitarian contemplation against the divine contemplation is like the 'crane contemplation' against the 'Quranic contemplation'. Another example is that of a son. From a distant land, he sent to his widowed mother a tiny bird that spoke many languages, and when in a letter, he asked his mother, "How had she liked the bird?"

The reply was, "Very delicious, dear son."

How to do the contemplation of the works of Allah is the question? Indeed, no one we may see in contemplation of works of Allah according to objects of the Quran. In these times, people contemplate following the Baconian pattern of utilitarianism in science laboratories and observatories. The general public, however, is engrossed in financial worries and wants. We must do the Quranic contemplation with Anti-World and Anti-Materialistic views of the Quran and its views about

Allah, Resurrection, Judgement, and the next world in mind. It will be the contemplation on the lines of the Quran though it does not appear possible if this Baconian philosophy and its science-guided progress exits. We will quote the examples from the Quran, which give the various objects of contemplation. We, however, have strained out prayers to the utmost and have viewed the Quran from every angle to find any hint or illusion in any way reminiscent of material utility in connection with the contemplation of the works of Allah, God, or Lord God. But in vain. We have reaped only honor from the sagacity of those millions to whom a conspicuous link between the Quranic contemplation of the works of Allah and the material exploitation of the works of God appears in this modern Baconian progress.

Moreover, alas! A sad misunderstanding is there in every mind that most urgently needs clearance, namely, the general notion that we can accomplish both the glorification of the Creator and the material utility at the same time in the contemplation of the works of Allah. How dearly we wish that it could have been a possibility in this Baconian setup. An equally systematic, organized, ever-increasing, endless, infinite, and eternal kind of science guides the Baconian setup of this systematic, organized, ever-increasing, endless, infinite, and eternal kind of progress.

Gradually, this setup would occupy the more significant part of man's mind and time, expelling simultaneously and respectively the thought of Allah, death, religion, Resurrection, and the next world from the mind and time of man. Eventually, it would end either in an explosion or ruin this life on earth through somatic and genetic effects of the radiations of the atomic energy for peace. Just observe how much thought of Allah, religion, and the next world has been left in man's mind? How much glorification of the Creator is being affected in contemplation of natural objects? Also, remember that this world could only not exist without faith, but also that the inevitable end of this Baconian progress progresses in ruin. The best possible method of distinctly explaining the Quranic view of the contemplation of the works of Allah is to quote examples that show the object thereof, which we will endeavor to do in the following.

(1) The act of contemplation begins with a notion of certainty in the mind of some purpose of this creation. Remembrance of Allah is the object. The works of Allah present objective, substantial view, or the remembrance of the Creator thereof.
The Quran says:
"Lo! In the creation of the heavens and the earth and (in) the difference of night and day are tokens (of His Sovereignty) for men of

understanding, such as remember Allah, standing, sitting, and reclining, and consider the creation of the heavens and the earth, (and say): Our Lord! Thou createdst not this in vain. Glory be to Thee! Preserve us from the doom of Fire. Our Lord! Whom Thou causest to enter the Fire: him indeed Thou hast confounded. For evil-doers, there will be no helpers. Our Lord! Lo! We have heard a crier calling unto Faith: "Believe ye in your Lord!" So, we believed. Our Lord! Therefore, forgive us our sins, and remit from us our evil deeds, and make us die the death of the righteous. Our Lord! And give us that which Thou hast promised to us by Thy messengers. Confound us not upon the Day of Resurrection. Lo! Thou breakest not the tryst."

(Quran 3:190-194)

Read the above-quoted example of the contemplation of the works of Allah and mark that no allusion whatever appears to the material utility of the works of Allah. Mark also the Prophetic fulfillment of the appearance of fire even within this very world. Humankind now stands face-to-face with the confounding hell of atomic fire resulting from their love of the world and wealth and the accumulation of wealth in the name of progress.

Please mark throughout these examples, which we will quote in this context, that:
(a) There is no connection between the objects of Quranic contemplation of the works of Allah and the notion of their material exploitation.
(b) The act of Quranic contemplation of the works of Allah is purely of nature, moral, religious, and divine.
(c) We should accomplish it without the accompaniment of the aids and instruments of this modern science.
(d) The discoveries of science have sided and abetted the contemplation of the works of Allah but little a while. The objects of the two that are the Quran and science, in this respect, have nothing in common and rather stand in radical opposition.

(2) **The purpose is a vision and reminding of Allah's Sovereignty.**
The Quran says:
"Have they not then observed the sky above them, how We have constructed it and beautified it, and how there are no rifts therein? And the earth, have We spread out, and have flung firm hills therein, and have caused of every lovely kind to grow thereon, a vision and a reminder for every penitent slave."

(Quran 50:6-8)

(3) The object is to discern the certainty of man's meeting with the Lord on the Day of Judgement.

The Quran says:

"Allah it is Who raised the heavens without visible supports, then mounted the Throne and compelled the sun and the moon to be of service, each runneth unto an appointed term; He ordereth the course; He detaileth the revelations, that haply ye may be certain of the meeting with your Lord."

(Quran 13:2)

(4) The object is to observe the example of Resurrection.

The Quran says:

"And Allah it is Who sendeth the winds and they raise a cloud; then We lead it unto a dead land and revive therewith the earth after its death. Such is the Resurrection."

(Quran 35:9)

(5) The object is to see through this original creation the fact of the second birth on Resurrection.

The Quran says:

"Say (O Muhammad): 'Travel in the land and see how He originated creation', then Allah bringeth forth the later growth (second birth). Lo! Allah is (Almighty) Able to do all things."

(Quran 29:20)

Read the above-quoted example, which furnishes us with a glaring specimen of comparison in this context between the object of the Quran and Darwin of this modern Baconian era. Darwin exactly did what the Quran has suggested when it says, "Travel in the land and see how He originated creation". Darwin went through the earth in his voyage, and he tried to see how the process had brought the created beings forth. He devoted his life to seeking the origin of species on earth.

However, what was his object? Was it, as the Quran has hinted, like the attainment of the proof of the second birth on Resurrection or something else? It is not without truth that exploring the religious theory of instantaneous birth of creatures was among the objects searching for the origin of species. Whatever might have been the object of the search of Darwin, it was not that which the Quran has given. Furthermore, there appears not any violation of rules or decency if we say that the work of Darwin from beginning to end has been a search, and conclusions reminiscent of something sinister as well as loathsome about it. Whereas science has failed to find the origin of species despite all its knowledge and appendages, as far as the point of the Quran is concerned, it is the easiest thing for any individual to see the possibility of second birth by seeing the example of first birth.

(6) The object is to know the grave and fixed term of the creation and have the consequent certainty of the Resurrection and the Judgement.

The Quran says:

"Have they not pondered upon themselves? Allah created not the heavens and the earth, and that which is between them, save with truth and for a destined end. But truly, many of humankind are disbelievers in the meeting with their Lord."

(Quran 30:8)

(7) The object is to view Allah's government, control, order, power, complete unshared Sovereignty, and the helplessness of those associated with Him as gods.

The Quran says:

"He maketh the night to pass into the day, and He maketh the day to pass into the night. He hath subdued the sun and moon to service. Each runneth unto an appointed term. Such is Allah, your Lord; His is the Sovereignty; and those (gods) unto whom ye pray instead of Him own not so much as the white spot on a date-stone."

(Quran 35:13)

(8) The object is to know the Omnipotence and constant vigilance of the Creator and His compassion and forgiveness.

The Quran says:

"Lo! Allah graspeth the heavens and the earth that they deviate not, and if they were to deviate, there is not one that could grasp them after Him. Lo! He is ever Clement, Forgiving."

(Quran 35:41)

Read the above-quoted example. Newton might attribute the fact of sustaining the solar system members together to the laws of gravity. On the other hand, Einstein might attribute the same fact to relativity. Moreover, there is no doubt that this universe functions according to the Creator's laws ordained for the purpose.

However, there is a subtle distinction in this matter which we like to point out, namely, that Allah appears to insist with particularity upon His claim that every act in the phenomena of the universe must be attributed to Him alone. Every person with a religious bent of mind has adopted this rule.

You will hear him (the person) saying, "Allah has brought the rain", and "Allah has cleared the sky", and so on so forth. However, the scientist stops at the principle of science. There is no doubt that everything ultimately relates to the Will of Allah. The object of a scientist in this respect is short and limited, as well as his view.

(9) **The object is to find a reason to be grateful to Allah for His boons.**

The Quran says:

"A token unto them is the dead earth. We revive it, and We bring forth from it grain so that they eat thereof, and We have placed therein gardens of the date palm and grapes, and We have caused springs of water to gush forth therein. That they may eat of the fruit thereof, <u>and their hand made it not</u>. Will they not, then, give thanks?"

(Quran 36:33-35)

"<u>And their hands made it not</u>", says the Quran in the above-quoted passage. There is something certainly thought-provoking and effective in it.

Also, we may observe that the subject of the passage is the material utility, but it is not the object of contemplation. The object is thanksgiving.

(10) **The object is to realize that the bestowal of wealth is in the hands of Allah.**

The Quran says:

"See they not that Allah enlargeth the provision for whom He will, and straiteneth (it for whom He will). Lo! Herein indeed are portents for folk who believe."

(Quran 30:37)

Read the above-quoted passage to comprehend that apart from all the factors like a struggle, hard work, and ability, there always appears some power which could slight all these factors and distribute wealth in a manner whose reasons a man could hardly understand. It proves the absolute Will and unquestionable Sovereignty of Allah. A Socrates may fret in poverty, but a plodding dunce may play in millions. There might be reasons for that discrimination, but we generally do not know.

(11) **The object is to gain insight and see admonition through the works of Allah to turn to Him.**

The Quran says:

"Have they not then observed the sky above them, how We have constructed it and beautified it, and how there are no rifts therein? And the earth, have We spread out, and have flung firm hills therein, and have caused of every lovely kind to grow thereon, a vision and a reminder for every penitent slave (who loveth to turn to Allah)."

(Quran 50:6-8)

(12) **The object is to observe the dominion of Allah in the heavens and the earth.**

The Quran says:

(a) "Have they not considered the <u>dominion of the heavens and the earth</u>, and what things Allah hath created, and <u>that it may be that their own term draweth nigh? In what fact after this will they believe?</u>"

(Quran 7:185)

(b) "Say: In Whose hand is the dominion over all things and He protecteth, while against Him there is no protection if ye have knowledge?"

(Quran 23:88)

(c) "Glory be to Him in Whose hand is the <u>dominion over all things</u>! Unto Him, ye will be brought back."

(Quran 36:83)

Read these above-quoted passages of the Quran and see that Allah's 'dominion' means a contradiction of Bacon's notion of man's dominion over the universe. Note the Prophetic utterance therein, "that it may be that their own term draweth nigh?". There is no doubt that the disregard of the dominion of Allah in the universe by this present Baconian age due to the notion of their own dominion over Mother Nature has brought the term of this modern humankind near through the atomic ruin.

However, we are concerned with contemplation only but remember that contemplation permeates every subject and object because this thought is concerned with everything that Allah has created.

Let us repeat the question of the Quran in the above-quoted passage:
"In what fact after this will they believe?"

This question may with real aptness be put to this modern humankind saying:

"In what fact, after the manifest appearance of this atomic hell, will you believe?"

Indeed, hitherto, they appear to be quite unmindful of the atomic hazard and hopeful, and nobody is there to tell them of the falsity of their hope.

(13) **The object is to foster fear of Allah, which is the essence of knowledge and piety.**

The Quran says:

"Hast thou not seen that Allah causeth water to fall from the sky, and We produce therewith fruit of divers hues; and among the hills are streaks white and red, of divers hues, and (others) raven black; and of men and beasts and cattle, in like manner, divers hues? The erudite among His bondmen fear Allah alone. Lo! Allah is Mighty, Forgiving."

(Quran 35:27-28)

(14) **The object is to distinguish between the creation and the Creator.**

The Quran says:

"And of His portents are the night and the day and the sun and the moon. Adore neither the sun nor the moon; but adore Allah Who created them, if it is in truth Him whom ye worship."

(Quran 41:37)

Modern humankind has misunderstood the purpose of contemplation because the veil of the world's love blinds their eyes. How comes all this misunderstanding? It is not known. The Muslims read the following saying of the Prophet of Islam (peace be upon him), but the truth is just as the Prophet (peace be upon him) has said, namely:

"The love of the world is the root cause of every mistake."

Therein, we have given most of the objects of contemplation of works of Allah as the Quran has given. Our primary objective here is to show that the Quranic contemplation of the works of Allah is subservient to religion purely and must do nothing with the material utility of the works of Allah. It is in contrast with the Baconian view, which exclusively is concerned with the material utility of the works of God in the name of contemplation. The Quran may be read from beginning to end to find any connection between contemplation and material utility. However, the chance of success is dubious, but realizing the truth needs predisposition of mind. The Quran says:

"Say: Behold what is in the heavens and the earth! But revelations and warnings avail not folk who will not believe."

(Quran 10:101)

FOR:

(a) "Have they not traveled in the land, and have they hearts wherewith to feel and ears wherewith to hear? For indeed it is not the eyes that grow blind, but it is the hearts, which are within the bosoms, that grow blind."

(Quran 22:46)

(b) "Whoso is blind here wilt be blind in the Hereafter, and yet further from the road."

(Quran 17:72)

(c) "He will say: My Lord! Wherefore hast Thou gathered me (hither) blind when I was wont to see? He will say: So (it must be). Our revelations came unto thee, but thou didst forget them. In like manner thou art forgotten this Day."

(Quran 20:125-126)

ALTHOUGH:

(a) "Had it been possible for a Lecture to cause the mountains to move, or the earth to be torn asunder, or the dead to speak, (this Quran would have done so). Nay, but Allah's is the whole command."

(Quran 13:31)

(b) "If We had caused this Quran to descend upon a mountain, thou (O Muhammad) verily hadst seen it humbled, rent asunder by the fear of Allah. Such similitudes coin We for humankind that haply they may reflect."

(Quran 59:21)

In the Quran, there are verses (signs) of the same category as speculative contemplation but are concerned with the subjection of the universe and all in it given to man's service by Allah. Due to the factor of the utility of things appearing in the direct reference to these signs in question, there occurs a considerable probability of man's mind being deluded into subjugation and material utility of the works of God by man; a delusion most likely to appear in the case of this modern much-cherished progress.

These signs generally are called the signs of 'Taskhir-il-Kaayinaat', the 'conquest of the universe', and recited by the Muslims with greater surety, added zest, and enhanced enthusiasm in favor of this Baconian progress. We now seek the actual truth of these signs, which we will endeavor to do.

Following is a specimen of these signs.

"See ye not how Allah hath made 'serviceable' unto you whatsoever is in the skies and whatsoever is in the earth and hath loaded you with His favors both without and within? Yet of humankind is he who disputeth concerning Allah, without knowledge or guidance or a Scripture giving light."

(Quran 31:20)

Read this above-quoted passage of the Quran to find that it is an example of the contemplation, and although the material utility is the object of the topic, yet the act of material utility here, as everywhere else, must follow the basic policy of the Quran about this world and its wealth. If the Quran, as a rule, does not accept modern Baconian progress, it could not in any way be rendered acceptable in this passage of the Quran or any other passage of this kind. In this passage, Allah reminds humankind about His kindness to have rendered all in the universe serviceable to man. He has expressed wonder at those who should dispute Allah's Unity, Sovereignty, and Kindness despite seeing all this.

The phrase 'rendered serviceable' is the translation of the Arabic word 'Sakhara', the word used by the Quran and means: 'subdue', 'to force to do something for nothing', 'to conquer and bring into subjection', 'to overpower by superior force', 'to bring under control', 'render submissive', etc. We need to carefully note that Allah asserts Himself to have left and rendered all these things serviceable to man and, in return, expected allegiance and gratitude of man. There appears no hint at the emulation of Allah on the part of man. However, all the misunderstanding appears as a hasty conclusion made in the heat of inner desire of wealth and urgent necessity. Allah expects 'gratitude'.

The Quran says:

(a) "He who created all the pairs, and appointed for you **ships** and **cattle** whereupon ye ride that ye may mount upon their backs, and may remember your Lord's favor when ye mount thereon and may say: Glorified be He Who hath subdued these unto us, and we were not capable (of subduing them)."

(Quran 43:12-13)

(b) "Allah it is Who hath made the **sea** of 'service' unto you that the ships may run thereon by His command, and that ye may seek of His bounty, and that haply ye may be thankful, and hath made of 'service' unto you whatsoever is in the **heavens** and whatsoever is in the **earth**; it is all from Him. Lo! Herein verily are portents for people who reflect."

(Quran 45:12-13)

Throughout the category of these signs, we will see that Allah asserts His particular declaim to have this life rendered the things serviceable to man and expects gratitude. Read these above-quoted passages to know that firstly Allah has expected gratitude for His kindness. Secondly, He has pointed to His boons as portents for reflection to discover the Sovereignty, unity, mercy, and grace of Allah. Notice that He has not treated the point of material utility as the object. The object instead is the gratitude and Allah's assertion to have done Himself all this for man. Allah expects gratitude.

The Quran says:

"And He, it is, Who hath constrained the **sea** to be of 'service' that ye eat fresh meat from thence, and bring forth from thence ornaments which ye wear. And thou seest the ships plowing it that ye (humankind) may seek of His bounty and that haply ye may give thanks."

(Quran 16:14)

Allah in this above-quoted passage has expected gratitude for these boons and has used the phrase 'seeking the bounty of Allah' for material utility.

In contrast, the functionaries of Baconian progress seek not the bounty of Allah, but they do exact tribute from Mother Nature by force and tact, and they seek dominion over Mother Nature. It, according to the theological views, makes a lot of difference. Portents are therein for people who have sense.

"And He hath constrained the night and the day and the **sun** and the **moon** to be of service unto you, and the **stars** are made 'subservient' by His command. Lo! Herein indeed are portents for people who have sense."

(Quran 16:12)

However, man is 'a wrong-doer' and 'an ingrate'.

"Allah is He Who created the **heavens** and the **earth**, and causeth **water** to descend from the sky, thereby producing fruits as food for you, and maketh the **ships** to be of service unto you, that they may run upon the sea at His command, and hath made of service unto you the **rivers**; and maketh the **sun** and the **moon**, constant in their courses, to be of 'service' unto you, and hath made of service unto you the **night** and the **day**. And He giveth you of all ye ask of Him, and if ye would count the bounty of Allah ye cannot reckon it. Lo! Man is verily a wrongdoer, an ingrate."

(Quran 14:32-34)

Following are given a couple of more examples from the Quran. Allah expects gratitude and glorification for His kindness and boons bestowed upon humankind and mentions His Sovereignty, unity, mercy, and grace.

(1) "And He, it is, Who created the **night** and the **day**, and the **sun** and the **moon**."

(Quran 21:33)

(2) "Hast thou not seen that unto Allah payeth 'adoration' whosoever is in the **heavens** and whosoever is in the **earth**, and the **sun**, and the **moon**, and the **stars**, and the **hills**, and the **trees**, and the **beasts**, and many of humankind, while there are many unto whom the doom is justly due. He whom Allah scorneth, there is none to give him honor. Lo! Allah doeth what He will."

(Quran 22:18)

(3) "Of His mercy hath He appointed for you **night** and **day** that therein ye may rest, and that 'ye may seek His bounty', and that haply 'ye may be thankful'."

(Quran 28:73)

(4) "And if thou were to ask them: Who created the **heavens** and the **earth**, and constrained the **sun** and the **moon** (to their appointed work)? They would say: Allah. How then have they turned away?"
(Quran 29:61)

(5) "And of His signs is this: He sendeth herald **winds** to make you taste His mercy, and that the ships may sail at His command, and that 'ye may seek His favor', and that haply 'ye may be thankful'."
(Quran 30:46)

(6) "Hast thou not seen how Allah causeth the **night** to pass into the **day** and causeth the day to pass into the night, and hath subdued the **sun** and the **moon** (to do their work), each running unto an appointed term; and that Allah is Informed of what ye do?"
(Quran 31:29)

(7) "He hath created the **heavens** and the **earth** with truth. He maketh **night** to succeed **day**, and He maketh day to succeed night, and He constraineth the **sun** and the **moon** to 'give service', each running on for an appointed term. Is not He the Mighty, the Forgiver?"
(Quran 39:5)

(8) "The **sun** and the **moon** are made punctual. The **stars** and the **trees** 'adore'."
(Quran 55:5-6)

Someone may ask if Allah is so averse to material utility, why should He ask man's gratitude for the material utility of His boons? The answer is that Allah is not averse to man partaking of His boons, but it is the kind of the doctrine of material utility and the purpose thereof that counts. We confront this modern Baconian doctrine of material utility which engenders a systematic, organized, ever-increasing, and infinite pattern of progress and is regarded as the purpose of man's life. Also, the basic policy of the Quran, which is averse, has to be kept in mind regarding this world, its wealth, and material utility. In the following, we are quoting some examples of contemplation from the Bible. Note the identity of style and purpose with that of the Quran described in previous paragraphs.

THE GLORY OF GOD IN 'MOTHER NATURE'

(1) "And now, I will remember the works of the Lord, and I will announce what I have seen. The words of the Lord are in his works. The **sun** illuminates and considers all things, and its work shows the fullness of the glory of the Lord. Has not the Lord caused the holy ones to describe all his miracles, which the all-powerful Lord has firmly established in his glory? He has examined the abyss and the

hearts of men. And he has considered their astuteness. For the Lord comprehends all knowledge, and he has gazed upon the signs of the times: announcing the things of the past, as well as the things of the future, and revealing the traces of hidden things. No thought passes by him unnoticed, and no word can conceal itself from him. He has adorned the magnificent works of his wisdom. He is before eternity and even unto eternity. And nothing can be added, and nothing can be taken away. And he has no need of any counselor. O, how desirable are all his works! And all that we consider is but a spark. All these works exist, and they remain in the present age, and they all obey him in every purpose. All things are two-fold, one facing another, and he has not made anything to be lacking. He has confirmed each thing as good. And who would tire of beholding his glory?"

(The Sacred Bible: The Book of Ecclesiasticus: Sirach 42:15-26)

(2) "The firmament on high is his beauty; it is the beauty of heaven in a vision of glory. The **sun**, at its appearance, announces its journey; it is an instrument of wonder, a work of the Most High. At midday, it scorches the earth. And in the presence of its heat, who would be able to endure? It is like the custodian of a furnace in its works of heat. In three ways, the sun acts: scorching the mountains, emitting fiery rays, and shining with its beams that can blind the eyes. Great is the Lord who made it, and at his word, it hurries on its journey."

(Ibid: The Book of Ecclesiasticus: Sirach 43:1-5)

(3) "And the **moon**, in all its phases, serves to mark the seasons and to be a sign of the times. From the moon is the sign of a feast day; it is a light which diminishes at its consummation. A month is named according to its phases, increasing wonderfully at its culmination. It is an instrument of the armies on high, shining gloriously in the firmament of heaven."

(Ibid: The Book of Ecclesiasticus: Sirach 43:6-9)

(4) "The glory of the **stars** is the beauty of heaven; the Lord illuminates the world from on high. At the words of the Holy One, they stand for judgment, and they will never fail in their vigilance."

(Ibid: The Book of Ecclesiasticus: Sirach 43:10-11)

(5) "Consider the **rainbow**, and bless the One who made it; it is very beautiful in its splendor. It encompasses the heavens with the circle of its glory; the hands of the Most High made it appear."

(Ibid: The Book of Ecclesiasticus: Sirach 43:12-13)

(6) "By his order, he hastens the **snow**, and he spurs on the **lightning** to express his judgment. In like manner, his storehouses are opened,

and the **clouds** fly out like birds. By his greatness, he has positioned the clouds, and the hailstones have been broken. At his glance, the **mountains** will be shaken, and by his will, the south **wind** will blow. The voice of his **thunder** will reverberate through the earth, by a **storm** from the north, and by a gathering of the **whirlwind**. And like the birds landing in a flock upon the earth, he sends down the snow; and its descent is like the arrival of a swarm of locusts. The eye is in wonder at the beauty of its whiteness, and the heart is astonished at its falling. He will pour out **frost** like salt upon the earth. And when it freezes, it will become like the tops of thistles. The cold north wind blows, and the water freezes into crystals; it will rest upon every gathering of water, and it will clothe the water like a breastplate. And it will devour the mountains, and burn the wilderness, and extinguish the greenery, like a fire. Relief for all is in the hurried arrival of a cloud. And the lowly **dew** will arrive to meet the heat and overpower it. At his word, the wind grows quiet, and by his thought, he appeases the abyss, for the Lord has planted islands in it. Let those who navigate the **sea** describe its perils. And when we have heard it with our ears, we will wonder. There are illustrious and wondrous works: the various kinds of wild animals, and all manner of cattle, and the great creatures of the sea. Through him, the end of their journey is confirmed, and by his word, all things fit together. We can say much and yet still lack for words. But the consummation of our words is this: He is in all things. What would we be able to do to glorify him? For the Almighty Himself is above all his own works. The Lord is terrible, and exceedingly great, and his power is wonderful. **Glorify the Lord** as much as you are able, yet still he will far exceed this. For his magnificence is beyond wonder. Bless the Lord and exalt him as much as you are able. But he is beyond all praise. When you exalt him, use all your ability, and do not cease in this labor. For you can never comprehend him. Who will see him and explain? And who will magnify him, as he is from the beginning? There are many things hidden from us, which are greater than these things. For we have seen but a few of his works. But the Lord has made all things, and he has given wisdom to those who act with piety."

(Ibid: The Book of Ecclesiasticus: Sirach 43:14-37)

Mark that the praise and the glory of the Creator is the purpose and not the material utility.

"The heavens declare the glory of God; and the firmament sheweth his handywork." (The Bible: Old Testament: Psalms 19:1)

The Bible has never treated contemplation as a complete subject. We will cite an example of the contemplation by Jesus Christ to show that the contemplation reflects the basic tendency of the views.

Jesus Christ famed for the doctrine of poverty says:

"Behold the fowls of the air: for they sow not, neither do they reap, nor gather into barns; yet your heavenly Father feedeth them. Are ye not much better than they? Which of you, by taking thought, can add one cubit unto his stature? And why take ye thought for raiment? Consider the lilies of the field, how they grow; they toil not, neither do they spin: And yet I say unto you, that even Solomon in all his glory was not arrayed like one of these."

(The Bible: New Testament: Matthew 6:26-29)

Then read the following from the Quran to discover the identity of views between the Gospel of Jesus Christ and the Quran.

(1) "And how many an animal there is that beareth not its own provision! Allah provideth for it and you. He is the Hearer, the Knower."

(Quran 29:60)

(2) "And there is not a beast in the earth but the sustenance thereof dependeth on Allah. He knoweth its habitation and its repository. All is in a clear record."

(Quran 11:6)

Now, we will exemplify this Baconian method of contemplation that is the contemplation of the works of God for the material exploitation of the works of God.

The design of Bacon's characteristic contemplation of the works of God is as follows.

"By means of inquirers, some of which should be experimental like those of alchemists, but purged from superstitious taint and directed not toward immediate gain, but toward a thoroughgoing knowledge, vastly to increase in the long run **the dominion of man over nature**.......And through resolute and patient, persistence in discriminating observation and as well devised experiment, **he may wring the secrets from her and turn them to this own advantage**."

('A History of Philosophy'; by Clement C. J. Webb, Page-135)

When the mode of Baconian contemplation is seen compared to the mode of religious contemplation, the following Quranic examples appear to depict the perversion of Baconian contemplation.

(1) The Children of Israel asked Moses to settle in Jericho, or Jerusalem (some commentators suppose it to be Jericho; others Jerusalem). They were allowed and told to enter the city saying, 'Hittaton', which

means "<u>forgive our sins</u>", and moving in humble posture. We may liken it to religious contemplation. However, what they did, in reality, was that instead of saying 'Hittaton', they went saying '<u>Hintaton</u>', which means, "<u>Give us wheat</u>". Instead of entering the gate prostrate, they rudely crept upon their breeches in ridicule of divine command which we may equate to Baconian contemplation for material exploitation. The Quran has recorded this instance as follows.

"And when it was said unto them: Dwell in this township and eat therefrom whence ye will, and say 'Repentance' (Hittaton) and enter the gate prostrate; We shall forgive you your sins; We shall increase (reward) for the right doers. But those of them who did wrong changed the word which had been told them for another saying, and We sent down upon them wrath from heaven for their wrongdoing."

(Quran 7:161-162)

They say that a pestilence broke out among them, which took away 70,000 of them. However, it is difficult to estimate how many will be taken away by the atomic pestilence for this Baconian contemplation.

(2) Another example is as follows.

"In the days of David some Israelites dwelt at Ailah, or Elath, on the Red sea (though some pretend it was Midian, and others, Tiberias), where on the night of the Sabbath the fish used to come in great numbers to the shore, and stay there all the Sabbath, to tempt them; but the night following they returned into the sea again. At length, some of the inhabitants, neglecting GOD's command, caught fish on the Sabbath, and dressed and ate them; and afterward cut canals from the sea for the fish to enter, with sluices which they shut on the Sabbath, to prevent their return to the sea.

The other part of the inhabitants, who strictly observed the Sabbath, used both persuasion and force to stop this impiety, but to no purpose, the offenders growing only more and more obstinate; whereupon David cursed the Sabbath-breakers and GOD transformed them into apes. It is said that one going to see a friend of his that was among them found him in the shape of an ape, moving his eyes about wildly; and asking him whether he was not such a one.

The ape made a sign with his head that it was he: whereupon the friend said to him, did not I advise you to desist? At which the ape wept. These unhappy people remained three days in this condition and were afterward destroyed by a wind which swept them all into the sea."

('The Koran'; Translated by George Sale, Gent. printed by S. and R. Bentley, Dorset Street, Salisbury Square, London, 1821: Chapter-II/Page-13)

The Quran has recorded the tragic event as follows.

"Ask them (O Muhammad) of the township that was by the sea, how they did break the Sabbath, how their big fish came unto them visibly upon their Sabbath day and on a day when they did not keep Sabbath came they not unto them. Thus, did We try them for that they were evil livers. And when a community among them said: Why preach ye to a folk whom Allah is about to destroy and punish with an awful doom, they said: In order to be free from guilt before your Lord, and that haply they may ward off (evil). And when they forgot that whereof they had been reminded, We rescued those who forbade wrong and visited those who did wrong with dreadful punishment because they were evil livers. So, when they took pride in that which they had been forbidden, We said unto them: Be ye apes despised and loathed!"

(Quran 7:163-166)

The Sabbath-breakers who played a trick for material utility were changed to the apes, but the Baconian utilitarian is flung into the atomic hell. Just see the difference and the comparative degree of guilt and wonder, and maybe that:

Darwin might have found some resemblance between the habits of apes and the people of this modern Baconian age. Allah knows better. Radiations, however, do change humankind to chimeras (monkeys). How similar is the end?

(3) An example that bears an exact analogy with the mode of Baconian contemplation is that of Pharaoh. He also wanted to contemplate in an endeavor to see the God of Moses.

The Quran says:

"And Pharaoh said: O chiefs! I know not that ye have a God other than me, so kindle for me (a fire), O Human, to bake the mud; and set up for me a lofty tower so that I may survey the God of Moses, and Lo! I deem him of the liars."

(Quran 28:38)

It appears that Muslims have lost sense of all signs of the Quran and traditions of the Holy Prophet (peace be upon him), which go against this world, its love, and its wealth. Anyone may read the Quran to see that word of Allah has scarcely exhaled a breath throughout without condemning, depreciating, and denouncing the material world, its love, and the love of its wealth against the otherworld. We can say the same of the Holy Prophet of Islam (peace be upon him). Indeed, the hatred of the world had been the fundamental spirit and constant theme both of the Quran and the Holy Prophet (peace be upon him). They perpetually warned the Muslims against the hazards of the love of wealth.

The Prophet (peace be upon him) said:

"O Muslims! I fear not for your poverty, but what I fear is the accumulation of wealth, for I fear that you will be destroyed for your wealth accumulation just as destroyed those in the past for wealth accumulation."

Moreover, he said: "If no one can walk over water without having his feet being wet, no one can be involved in the world and avoid the sin."

He also said: "The love of the world is the root cause of every sin."

The truth of the truthful Prophet (peace be upon him) of Allah has appeared now without any doubt. This world, including the Islamic World, is now on the brink of destruction for no other reason than their love of wealth and wealth accumulation. At the very moment when the Muslims realize the truth of this fact, they will wonder at their previous misunderstanding about the view of the Quran and the Holy Prophet (peace be upon him) regarding this transitory world. When they read the signs concerning the contemplation of the works of Allah, they will see nowhere the factor of material utility therein, and they will wonder at those who cited such signs to prove the compatibility between the view of the Quran and this Baconian materialistic progress. Yet, if once the fire of atomic hell flared up and this world caught in the flames thereof, nothing whatsoever could be of any avail. The gates of repentance will by then have been closed.

~~*~*~*

---

[1] "In a nuclear war there would be **no victors, only victims.**" [Pope Benedict XVI]

~~*~*~*

CHAPTER-12

QURAN ON THE BACONIAN RIGHT OF MAN'S DOMINION OVER MOTHER NATURE

(1) "Have they not considered the **dominion of the heavens and the earth**, and what things Allah hath created, and that it may be that their own term draweth nigh? In what fact after this will they believe?"

(Quran 7:185)

(2) "Say: In Whose hand is the **dominion over all things** and He protecteth, while against Him there is no protection if ye have knowledge?"

(Quran 23:88)

(3) "Glory be to Him in Whose hand is the **dominion over all things**! Unto Him, ye will be brought back."

(Quran 36:83)

Man's dominion over Mother Nature forms the primary article of Bacon's philosophy. Dominion over Mother Nature, according to Bacon, was the original destiny of man. The attainment of man's dominion over Mother Nature as man's destiny and right is the basis of the whole of Bacon's philosophy.

"Francis Bacon's design was, by means of inquiries some of which should be experimental like those of alchemists, but purged from all superstitious taint and directed not toward immediate gain, but toward a thoroughgoing knowledge, vastly to increase in the long run the **dominion of man over nature**. To enjoy such a dominion was, he held, the original destiny of our race. But in a vain and impious attempt (described in the Biblical story as "eating of the tree of knowledge of good and evil") to make laws for himself by "moral philosophy," instead of remaining content with the positive commands of God, man had turned aside from his proper business of pursuing "natural philosophy," that is, of studying and interpreting the works of God and raising in his own intelligence a true image of the universe; gaining, in other words, such a knowledge of nature's inner workings as may make it possible to emulate them."

('A short history of Philosophy'; by Clement C. J. Webb, Page-135)
The moral philosophy is exclusively the basis of the revealed religion that Bacon has condemned as a "vain and impious innovation of man". According to revealed religion, the pursuit of natural philosophy for material utility is not Allah's command as Bacon has given it out. But it is only a means of acquiring the necessities of life. Besides these facts, the notion of man's dominion over Mother Nature is not acceptable to a revealed religion because dominion is only for Allah, and man has only the concession of material utility. Dominion belongs to Allah alone. The purport of dominion in Scriptures and Bacon's philosophy differs.
The Bible says:

"And God said, Let us make man in our image, after our likeness: and let them have **dominion** over the fish of the sea, and over the fowl of the air, and over the cattle, and over all the earth, and over every creeping thing that creepeth upon the earth. So God created man in his own image, in the image of God created he him; male and female created he them. And God blessed them, and God said unto them, be fruitful, and multiply, and replenish the earth, and subdue it: and have dominion over the fish of the sea, and over the fowl of the air, and over every living thing that moveth upon the earth."

(The Bible: Old Testament: Genesis 1:26-28)
The Quran has a relevant passage as follows.

"And the cattle hath He created, whence ye have warm clothing and uses, and whereof ye eat. And wherein is beauty for you, when ye bring them home, and when ye take them out to pasture. And they bear your loads for you unto a land ye could not reach, save with great trouble to yourselves. Lo! Your Lord is Full of Pity, Merciful. And horses and mules and asses (hath He created) that ye may ride them, and for ornament. And He createth that which ye know not. And Allah's is the direction of the way, and some (roads) go not straight. And had He willed, He would have led you all aright."

(Quran 16:5-9)
The Bible has used the term **dominion**. The Quran has treated the point as a **utility**. The Bible is not wrong, for man has been given dominion

over the creatures. However, the dominion of the Bible in this passage and the dominion of Bacon is not one thing. They are different. The Biblical dominion is no more than the right of mere utility. Baconian dominion (of man) appears like the dominion that of God. The difference between the two might appear minute, yet not as minute as could not be discerned by a person of average intelligence.

Biblical dominion is a point of man's gratitude to the Creator; Baconian dominion is a point of man's pride for his own power, ability, and right. There is a difference between Biblical and Baconian dominion. This difference is like the difference between the word 'propaganda' meanings in the pre-modern and modern ages. In the pre-modern age, it meant simply "the propagation of an idea or a religion", etc. In the modern age, its meanings are changed simply to "propagation to intellectualized slander", etc.

The Baconian dominion resembles the notion of Namrud's dominion. The Quran has recorded the debate between Abraham and Namrud as follows.

"Bethink thee of him who had an argument with Abraham about his Lord, because Allah had given him the kingdom; how, when Abraham said: My Lord is He who giveth life and causeth death, he answered: I give life and cause death. Abraham said: Lo! Allah causeth the sun to rise in the East, so do thou cause it to come up from the West. Thus was the disbeliever abashed. And Allah guideth, not wrongdoing folk."

(Quran 2:258)

Bacon has expressed that man detached from God by pursuing the moral philosophy and depended wholly upon himself. Bacon here was in a manifest error. The man did not go away from God and depended wholly upon his life by pursuing moral philosophy.

Instead, he has gone away from God due to his pursuit of natural philosophy (science), as may be seen today. He depends wholly and solely upon himself employing this knowledge of science and his dominion over Mother Nature. By no means may it be regarded as a violation of truth or misstatement if we say that man today aspires to become a god himself. The real God he headlong neglected and discarded due to Baconian philosophy of man's dominion over Mother Nature and material utility.

The Quran reserves the title of dominion exclusively only for one Allah. It is He who claims the right to dominion.

Read the following from the Quran.

(1) "Blessed is He in Whose hand is the Sovereignty, and He is able to do all things."

(Quran 67:1)

(2) "Say: Unto Whom (belongeth) the earth and whosoever is therein if ye know? They will say: Unto Allah. Say: Will ye not then remember? Say: Who is Lord of the seven heavens and Lord of the Tremendous Throne? They will say: Unto Allah (all that belongeth). Say: Will ye not then keep duty (unto Him)? Say: In Whose hand is the **dominion over all things** and He protecteth, while against Him there is no protection if ye have knowledge? They will say: Unto Allah (all that belongeth). Say: How then are ye bewitched? Nay, but We have brought them the Truth, and lo! They are liars."

(Quran 23:84-90)

(3) "And He is Allah; there is no God save Him. His is all praise in the former and the latter (state), and His is the command, and unto Him, ye will be brought back. Say: Have ye thought if Allah made night everlasting for you till the Day of Resurrection, who is a God beside Allah who could bring you light? Will ye not then hear? Say: Have ye thought if Allah made day everlasting for you till the Day of Resurrection, who is a God beside Allah who could bring you night wherein ye rest? Will ye not then see? Of His mercy hath He appointed for you night and day that therein ye may rest, and that ye may seek His bounty, and that haply ye may be thankful."

(Quran 28:70-73)

Who thus could claim a right of dominion except for Allah? Satan made the promise of everlasting dominion to Adam, and similarly, Bacon promised ever-increasing and eternal dominion to the posterity of Adam. The Quran regarding the seduction of Satan says:

"But the Devil whispered to him, saying: O Adam! Shall I show thee the tree of immortality and power that wasteth not away? Then they twain ate thereof so that their shame became apparent unto them, and they began to hide by heaping on themselves some of the leaves of the Garden. And Adam disobeyed his Lord, so went astray."

(Quran 20:120-121)

Bacon, too suggested to the sons of Adam the possibility of an ever-increasing and eternal dominion, and humankind ate the fruit of his philosophy through progress. Consequently, the signs of a shameful end in the flames of the atomic hell have now appeared. This humankind's efforts to avoid the dreadful doom in the atomic hell and Adam's hiding by heaping leaves on him bear a perfect analogy to each other. Adam was cast on earth. Will his posterity be cast into the atomic hell?

Bacon indeed and very falsely has written that man went away from God to depend on himself by his pursuit of moral philosophy wholly. Quite contrary to Bacon's view, we can, with our own eyes, see before us the Baconian humankind, gone completely away from Allah and wholly and solely depending on itself. Instead of Allah, this present humanity has faith in the dependence on science and its own ability. The eclipse of the sun or moon is only caused by either the moon or earth in between. Therefore, there is no cause to fear Allah. If an earthquake occurs, it is merely due to the expulsion of steam from the earth's hot interior and, therefore, no cause to fear Allah or feel distressed about the moral evil. It is science thus to be referred to and preferred everywhere.

However, it is nothing. Just imagine humankind encompassed by the ruinous hazards of the all-consuming hell of nuclear fire and in deadly expectation of a fiery storm of atomic hell to be let loose on it. Yet, it is as confident of the ability of science to avert all these hazards and even bring good out of these evils as a man of Allah in some former pre-modern age could have been confident of Allah's mercy and assistance.

However, the worst feature is their pride in their dominion over Mother Nature. Humankind flushed with the achievements of science has come to regard itself as a god. There is no doubt that humankind today, both in construction and destruction, has assumed powers so unimaginably great that the whole host of Homeric Olympian gods appears as dwarfs trying to hide for awe and shame. The dominion of Mother Nature no longer belongs to Allah; man has usurped that right, but the Quran has a severe warning to the effect. Just read:

"Have they not considered the 'dominion of the heavens and the earth', and what things Allah hath created, and that it may be that their own term draweth nigh? In what fact after this will they believe?"

(Quran 7:185)

Are there not the most manifest signs now of the term of this humankind concerning its end through atomic conflagration because of man's dominion over Mother Nature as against Allah's dominion?

The Quran says:

"We shall show them Our portents on the horizons and within themselves until it will be manifest unto them that it is the Truth. Doth not thy Lord suffice since He is Witness over all things?"

(Quran 41:53)

From the horizons will indeed come leaping the supersonic airplanes carrying the atomic bombs, which will explode to raise their mushroomed columns above the horizons. The people of the atomic age will experience the somatic and genetic afflictions of radiation, cancers, and abnormalities. However, from things just as they appear at present and situation which now exists, it seems likely that no signs and warning will receive the attention of this present-day humankind just as the Quran has said:

(1) "Say: Behold what is in the heavens and the earth! But revelations and warnings avail not folk who will not believe."

(Quran 10:101)

(2) "For indeed it is not the eyes that grow blind, but it is the hearts, which are within the bosoms, that grow blind."

(Quran 22:46)

(3) "Whoso is blind here wilt be blind in the Hereafter, and yet further from the road."

(Quran 17:72)

The acquirement of worldly necessities and physical comforts is exclusively the basis of Bacon's philosophy. Yet, paradoxically enough, no one is satisfied. Everyone in this age of progress, prosperity, and luxury feels poor, hungry, ever-hungry, and uneasy despite all the means of physical comfort. There is no contentment, and the sign of **PAUD** appears written on every face: **P**overty, **A**nxiety, **U**neasiness, and **D**iscontent.

Allah in the Quran reveals the reason for it as follows.

"But he who turneth away from the remembrance of Me, his will be a narrow life, and I shall bring him blind to the assembly on the Day of Resurrection. He will say: My Lord! Wherefore hast Thou gathered me (hither) blind when I was wont to see? He will say: So (it must be). Our revelations came unto thee, but thou didst forget them. In like manner thou art forgotten this Day. Thus, do We reward him who is prodigal and believeth not the revelations of his Lord; and verily the doom of the Hereafter will be sterner and more lasting."

(Quran 20:124-127)

No doubt, the atomic hell ('Hotama') of the next world is more terrible and everlasting than this transient atomic hell of this transient world.

Now, let us try to clear a very grievous misunderstanding of the followers of the Holy Quran regarding a particular species of signs (verses) of the Quran generally known by the appellation of 'Taskhir-il-

Kaayinaat' that is 'the conquest of the universe'. We have mentioned before that the Muslims worldwide quote the signs (verses) of the Quran about the contemplation of the works of Allah, consistently and with one accord as Quran's authority in favor of this modern Baconian progress as it is.

As it is the custom of modern progress, Muslims also quote signs (verses) of the Quran about <u>'Taskhir-il-Kaayinaat'</u> that is the <u>'serviceability of the works of Allah to man'</u>. They do it indeed with greater certainty to the authority of the Quran in favor of material exploitation of works of Allah. The Arabic word <u>'Taskhir'</u> used by the Quran means exploitation or the act of forcing someone to do something for nothing. It is derived from the root verb <u>'Sakhara'</u>, and the Quran has generally used it to signify the act of Allah's having made something serviceable to man as a boon. Allah always says <u>'Sakhara'</u>, that is:

"We have forced the things into man's service".

The first thing that deserves notice in this respect is that in every such instance throughout the Quran, it is Allah Himself who speaks in the first person, always saying 'We': it is 'We' that have made such and such things serviceable to you, and 'We' deserve, therefore, your gratitude. Nowhere is as much a hint or allusion to the act of emulation on the part of man. Nor is any appeal or exhortation to the act of exploitation of things made serviceable by Allah to man. Even for people, more critical is the realization of the true nature of modern progress and its exploitation of the works of Allah.

It is necessary to know whether the Quran approves of this progress as it is or not? And if it approves, does it so even though its inevitable consequence is the destruction of humankind in the flames of atomic hell? Bacon's philosophy certainly is not only opposed to the religion of God but stands as a complete antithesis. As may be seen today, this Baconian progress is the essence of Bacon's un-Godly and materialistic philosophy. It is an exclusively worldly affair, ever-increasing in nature and hence surely to expel in time Islam and Quran from the people's minds, and it has undoubtedly to go up into flames of atomic hell. It is a grave issue. Therefore, that needs the utmost attention of the people. We will, in the following, cite examples to the effect so that the reader may clearly understand the matter.

GABRIEL'S EXTINGUISHING THE ATOMIC HELL SERIES

The Quran says:

(1) "See ye not how Allah hath made **serviceable** unto you whatsoever is in the skies and whatsoever is in the earth and hath loaded you with His favors both without and within? Yet of humankind is he who disputeth concerning Allah, without knowledge or guidance or a Scripture giving light."

(Quran 31:20)

(2) "Allah it is Who hath made the sea of **service** unto you that the ships may run thereon by His command, and that ye may seek of His bounty, and that haply ye may be thankful, and hath made of service unto you whatsoever is in the heavens and whatsoever is in the earth; it is all from Him. Lo! Herein verily are portents for people who reflect."

(Quran 45:12-13)

(3) "And he hath constrained the night and the day and the sun and the moon to be of **service** unto you, and the stars are made subservient by His command. Lo! Herein indeed are portents for people who have sense."

(Quran 16:12)

(4) "And He, it is, Who hath constrained the sea to be of **service** that ye eat fresh meat from thence, and bring forth from thence ornaments which ye wear. And thou seest the ships plowing it that ye (humankind) may seek of His bounty and that haply ye may give thanks."

(Quran 16:14)

(5) "Allah is He Who created the heavens and the earth, and causeth water to descend from the sky, thereby producing fruits as food for you, and maketh the ships to be of service unto you, that they may run upon the sea at His command, and hath made of **service** unto you the rivers; and maketh the sun and the moon, constant in their courses, to be of **service** unto you, and hath made of service unto you the night and the day. And He giveth you of all ye ask of Him, and if ye would count the bounty of Allah ye cannot reckon it. Lo! Man is verily a wrongdoer, an ingrate."

(Quran 14:32-34)

We may see from the style of these signs (verses) of the Quran that Allah asserts that He rendered all things serviceable to man and, in return, expects thanks from man as a token of acknowledgment of the boons. The same is the style of these signs throughout the Quran. They negate any idea or pretension of man's right to or thought of dominion over

Mother Nature. Allah reiterates His sole, exclusive right to such dominion.

The point is more of philosophical nature. It is Allah Himself who has conquered the universe and has made it serviceable to man. It is not for a human being to say without offending the Creator's feelings, "I have conquered the universe", or "I will conquer the universe". The appellation 'Taskhir-il-Kaayinaat' thus in the meanings as is used by the Muslims deserves notice. Allah Himself claims the right to the act of 'Taskhir'; man must be content with material utility. This matter might, at first sight, appear somewhat frivolous. What, after all, is in names and terms? However, it is a matter of gravity, far-reaching in its effect, and worth considering. As follows, Allah gives an example of the requisite attitude that a believer should assume while availing dominion of Allah granted to him over beasts:

"He (Allah) who created all the pairs, and appointed for you ships and cattle whereupon ye ride that ye may mount upon their backs, and may remember your Lord's favor when ye mount thereon and may say: Glorified be He Who hath subdued these unto us, and we were not capable (of subduing them); and lo! Unto our Lord, we are returning."

(Quran 43:12-14)

Opposite, however, is the attitude of the people of this Baconian age. They have long forgotten thought of Allah or His favor. When they invent the machine, it is not Allah, but it is the talent and genius of the Baconian man that is the consideration. How profoundly proud are the nationals of the advanced nations for their national ability? The thought of Allah can hardly enter the mind of an age which has the callousness of heart to make plague bombs, gas bombs, incendiary bombs, atomic bombs, Hydrogen bombs, and neutron bombs, etc. It is all due to the influence of Bacon's un-Godly, selfish, and dominion-seeking philosophy of the world. A most notorious felon of any pre-modern age would shudder at these sophisticated means of destroying the most knowledgeable and civilized age of all human history.

~~*~*~*

CHAPTER-13

QURAN'S VIEW OF BACON'S PHILOSOPHY

In the previous sections, you have viewed a detailed study of the Islamic license of material utility, the Islamic view of this world against the otherworld, the rivalry existing between man's love for Allah and this world, the correlation between the love of this world and infidelity, and the Islamic view of the moral of the disbelievers.

By now, you might have perceived a clear message to realize that Quran is as severe in its policy about the world and its wealth as is the Gospel of Jesus Christ, or any other religion that teaches renunciation of the world, seclusion in the monastery, and being a hermit. Islam has forbidden individual monasticism and renunciation of the world. Yet, its close study reveals that it has aimed at universal monastic order, that is, to change this entire earth into a monastery. Islam has declared all this earth to be the mosque of Allah with the difference only that it has a sort of social monasticism in view in which people live in harmony in a society. They neither entangle hearts with this world nor consider it as their permanent abode. Instead, they constantly look at the next world with such anxiety and longing cherished by a person living in a strange land and yearning for his homeland. It may appear strange, but all pious Muslims in any era have passed their lives on this earth like this.

The heart of Hazrat Omar (Razi Allah ho Taa'la Unho), the second Caliph of Islam, during his tenure of Caliphate, may be seen hardly less detached from this world and its pomp than Diogenes, the tub-dweller of ancient Greek. However, the necessities of life are allowed by Islam without any perceptible severity, as has been the custom in certain other religions, though the authorization is not without conditions and is restricted. The difficulty today is that humankind of these present times has completely lost any sense of guilt or remorse associated with the love of this world.

The Holy Prophet of Islam (peace be upon him) is the first and foremost model for his followers, for his mission embraced the entire human race. The question naturally arises what was his attitude toward the Islamic license and how much did he avail of it? Undoubtedly, his life appears before the world like a clear book. He lived a life of self-imposed poverty and self-abnegation throughout the tenure of his Prophetic office. His motto was, "<u>Poverty is my pride</u>". He publicly gave his opinion of the world and its seekers that this world was dead carrion and its seekers, the dogs.

He preferred to wear coarse apparel. He never once ate a full meal. He and his household frequently suffered starvation. All these sufferings continued even after he was raised to the status of the Head of a State. He distributed a thousand houses among the people, but generally, he went empty-handed. What a home he chose for himself? The head of a man touched the roofs of the cells in which his family members lived. He sat on the floor, and he possessed only one blanket, which during summer, he would spread beneath him while wrapping it about his person during winter. Yet, he was a paragon of piousness, virtue, nobility, and generosity. No needy person ever went empty-handed from him if there existed anything to give in his home. Nay, even he borrowed from the Jews to give it to those in need.

It was the personality of the Prophet (peace be upon him), but he had inspired his disciples with the same views. All of them knew the virtue of poverty and its place in religion. Most of them strove to follow the model. Some have left memorials that whole human history has failed to produce the like of them. Hazrat Abu Bakar Siddique (Razi Allah ho Taa'la unho) was the first Caliph. He lived a life of poverty, such as the envy of the poorest among the people.

Hazrat Omer (Razi Allah ho Taa'la unho), the second Caliph, conquered Iran and Rome and was a sign of terror for the emperors. He used to wear a shirt with fourteen patches and dined on the mosque's steps, inviting the passers-by to his dinner, who generally declined the offer. He used to sleep under a palm tree at hot noon with a whip under his head as a pillow. The drops of sweat trickled down his forehead and were absorbed by the sand below. All this, he suffered intentionally.

Hazrat Othman Ghani (Razi Allah ho Taa'la unho), the third Caliph who was famed for his wealth and generosity, would put out the lamp of his public office and light up his own if the conversation was private.

Hazrat Ali (Razi Allah ho Taa'la unho), the fourth Caliph, was a model of self-imposed poverty and was generous beyond imagination.

Hazrat Omer Ibn-Abdul Aziz also deserves mention. It is enough to mention about him that on his demise, the Roman Emperor wept and wailed aloud, saying: "Today, a saint has departed from the world. If there was a saint, it was Omer. The world was beneath his feet, and he shunned it."

These were the disciples of the Holy Prophet (peace be upon him) or were the disciples of his disciples. Let us see the state of the

Islamic saints after that to this present-day. Poverty has always been their motto and the basis of their cult. It was the decisive, distinctive, and distinguishing feature of their order and the criterion of judgment for their merit. The slightest sign of the world's love or worldly temptation was a signal for their fall in the estimates of the people, and it is still like that.

However, in the case of this Baconian progress, the world has become blind of sight. Even today, the first requisite for saintly life is poverty and disinterestedness. Yet, today's peculiar situation of this Baconian progress system warrants an unusual attitude on this humankind universally. The entire humankind has, individually and collectively, to adopt the saintly attitude of poverty, if escape from the all-devouring flames of the atomic hell, the logical consequence of this Baconian progress, is desired.

This dispute is nothing new. Poverty, humility, and charity have been the features of Allah's religion always. See any religion, and you will find no exception anywhere. Jesus, Mohammed (peace be upon him), Buddha, and every religious teacher has taught this. Controversy, however, appears to be of little avail in the case of this modern Baconian system of progress. Rationalism is the basis of the philosophy of this age, and it is the easiest thing in the world to say:

"This modern progress stops no one from either adopting the religious attitude or from understating religious practices."

Though ages of controversy could hardly succeed in furnishing this humankind with a decisive answer, thanks to the agency of time, the actual decision has appeared without the slightest ambiguity in the form of atomic hell, the logical and scientific result of Baconian progress. The wonderful thing in this respect is that the Quran has contained for all these past fourteen centuries, the subject of Baconian philosophy of modern atomism, a complete characterization thereof, and the resultant atomic hell. The description of the Baconian philosophy of atomism as is given by the Quran is a miracle.

Moreover, to deduce the appearance of atomic hell, that is, atomic bombs and radiations from the Baconian atomism, as the Quran has done, is a miracle. The scientific characterization of the atomic phenomena and its manifestation by the Quran is a miracle. It is a challenge to the scientists as well as the philosophers of this Baconian age. The atomic weapon is not a weapon of defense; it is the wrath of Allah. It is divine vengeance and grievous retribution. It deserves eradication before it has eradicated this life on earth.

Before we quote the answer of the Quran to Baconian philosophy, meaning the prophecy which has been alluded to above, it appears reasonable to question every well-informed person in the world. Could Islam or any other religion, even if it were entirely and perfectly promulgated, save its followers or humanity or even itself from the flames of the atomic hell if this Baconian progress were allowed to continue as it is? The answer is negative. The consumption of this world by the atomic hell is inevitable in the presence of this Baconian progress. The stage by now is set, and the time is long past for such verbal assertions given as follows.

(1) Does not Islam allow the necessities of life and the material utility of the resources of Mother Nature?
(2) Do we not find in the Quran the emphasis laid on the contemplation of the works of Allah? Besides, does the Quran not allude to the conquest of Mother Nature?
(3) Is Islam not a progressive religion?
(4) Is Islam not opposed to monasticism and hermitage?
(5) Is Islam not a dynamic religion?

Such assertions and others of this kind are now long past their age. They are not noteworthy herein, nor can they give the least protection against the blazing reality now advancing toward mistaken humankind like an infallible doom.

Following is the text of prophecy of the Quran about Baconian hell that is the atomic hell, or nuclear hell: most terrible of all the hells. The Quran says:

"Woe unto every backbiter, defamer who amasseth wealth (of this world) and arrangeth it (against the future). He thinketh that his wealth will render him immortal. Nay, for verily, he will be cast into "Al-Hotama." And what could teach thee what "Al-Hotama" is? It is a fire of Allah kindled which leapeth up onto the hearts. It is (a fire) closed in on them in outstretched columns."

(Quran: 104 'Al-Homaza')

What does this mean? The Quran, which allows the material utility, is here seen uttering terrible denunciations against those who, in their own opinion and indeed with a clear conscience, are only utilizing the permissible license of the Quran, keeping within limits, and adhering to the basic policy. It indeed is a postulate that warrants the keenest attention of those who have not as yet acquiesced in the preordained doom: a very terrible, most frightful, and besides that exceedingly shameful doom.

You have read the prophecy of the Quran about the atomic hell. Please re-read it and see the nature of the evils that amazingly implicate such a terrible punishment.

Do you find the most grievous sin 'Disbelief' included therein? No, none of that. It excludes the differentiation between the Muslim and the non-Muslim, believer, and non-believer. It embraces everyone.

Do you see 'Shirk' (Polytheism) as the next grievous sin? No. Not even that.

Is it 'Murder' or 'Felony'? No.
Is it 'Man-slaughter' or 'Fornication'? No, nothing.
What is the crime, then?
It is merely the 'slander'. Only the 'engrossment in wealth accumulation' and just a 'belief in the eternity of riches'.

If you have any regard for Allah's word or realize the true significance of the word of Allah, then look. This Baconian philosophy of modern atomism is a 'slander' of the doctrines of revealed religion; in this age, the habit of slander moves like a spirit from one corner of the earth to another. It is the age of criticism and propaganda. This Baconian progress is no more than a process of systematic, organized, ever-increasing, infinite, and eternal 'wealth-acquirement', 'wealth-increase', and 'wealth-arrangement'. This generation has implicit and explicit 'faith in the ever-increasing eternity of this wealth-acquiring progress'. The case is clear. Above all else, its result is no more a hidden secret. It is there in the form of atomic hell. Now, only its gate has to be thrown open. What remains now only is that you sit alone and think if you are not involved in it.

As you have read in the prophecy of the Quran, the crux of the matter is that the causes of the appearance of this temporal atomic hell of this transient world and the punishment in the eternal atomic hell of the next eternal world, wherein there is no notion of death, are the same. They, who deserved 'Hotama', the atomic hell, even if they escaped this transient atomic hell of this world, could not escape the eternal atomic hell of the next eternal world. The Baconian philosophy is a beautiful snake that appears innocent, harmless, and lovable. In truth, its bite is so deadly, and its breath is so fiery that it would not allow its victim to count there to ask for water or to explain the trouble.

When we see the example of this Baconian philosophy of man's dominion over Mother Nature for material benefit in the Gospel of Jesus, we find the following striking example that the Christian and non-

Christian communities should read with interest and equally for instruction.

"Hear another parable: There was a certain householder, which planted a vineyard, and hedged it round about and digged a winepress in it, and built a tower, and let it out to husbandmen, and went into a far country: And when the time of the fruit drew near, he sent his servants to the husbandmen, that they might receive the fruits of it. And the husbandmen took his servants, and beat one, and killed another, and stoned another. Again, he sent other servants more than the first: and they did unto them likewise. But last of all, he sent unto them his son, saying, they will reverence my son. But when the husbandmen saw the son, they said among themselves; this is the heir; come, let us kill him, and let us seize on his inheritance. And they caught him, and cast him out of the vineyard, and slew him. When the lord, therefore of the vineyard cometh, what will he do unto those husbandmen? They say unto him, He will miserably destroy those wicked men and will let out his vineyard unto other husbandmen, which shall render him the fruits in their seasons."

(The Bible: New Testament: Matthew 21:33-41)
This world is the vineyard of Allah, but he has let it out to humankind. Bacon has sought man's dominion over this vineyard: And poverty, humility, and charity appeared as servants of Allah to take the fruits. But poverty was beaten, humility was killed, and the charity was stoned. Then, the Resurrection idea that appeared as the son of the Master of the vineyard was killed.

Baconian humankind wants to seize on the inheritance, the dominion of Allah. But will it succeed? No. The matter is far beyond human power. It is blasphemous even to think of such a thing. The success of humankind hitherto in scientific achievements has been only an enticement into the final trouble. Steam bent itself to the service of man. Then electricity followed suit and bent its back to the man. Then atomic phenomena appeared before man as an adamant adversary. The folly of man now is to think that he will be able to subdue and trap and tame this fierce, fiery giant Atumbumb. It is a kind of false optimism and blind confidence of the Baconian spirit that will lead this humankind right into the heart of the atomic hell without any hope of redemption, and this will be eternal woe.

~~*~*~*

CHAPTER-14

THE VIEWS OF BACON, THE BIBLE, AND THE QURAN ON 'KNOWLEDGE'

Knowledge, according to Bacon's design, is a systematic accumulation of the results of observational and experimental investigation of the secrets of Mother Nature and turning those results to an advantage for the well-being of humankind in general. Islam has laid great stress on acquiring knowledge so much that it has made it obligatory for every Muslim to acquire knowledge from the cradle to the grave, even if necessary to travel as far as China. The result was an intellectual revolution, the like of which this world had never seen. However, no matter how great it was, the Islamic movement of knowledge could bear no comparison with this modern movement of knowledge so far as the magnitude and prevalence are concerned. If, however, we talk purely of this modern Baconian knowledge, the difference between the Islamic knowledge of Islamic days and this Baconian knowledge is immense. The former was the knowledge subservient only to the doctrines of Islam; the latter is the knowledge purely of the world without any connection with faith or religion.

The question is, did Islam make no distinction between the varieties of knowledge? Was there no discrimination between desirable and undesirable? Magic is also knowledge. Theft, burglary, and swindling all have a particular kind of knowledge to be employed in such activities. Is such a kind of knowledge allowed by Islam? Did Islam exhort to acquire such knowledge? When the Holy Prophet (peace be upon him) uttered these inspiring exhortations to acquire knowledge, was there no distinction made between the various kinds of knowledge? Alternatively, were the followers of Islam to abandon themselves without a reserve in the field of knowledge?

Suppose they made any differentiation, and they undoubtedly made it. In that case, this modern Baconian material knowledge deserves special consideration in the light of basic Islamic differentiations made by the Holy Prophet (peace be upon him). The followers of Islam, however, these days find nothing wrong with this modern Baconian, scientific, material knowledge and deem it in exact accordance with the Islamic view of most desirable knowledge. They have even linked it with the knowledge of the pre-modern Islamic days. Reticence could have been assumed on this misjudgment of the Muslims, for the fruits of this modern knowledge are sweet, and the necessity is acute. However, results of modern knowledge, which have appeared in the form of miseries and atomic hazards, warrant a thorough investigation of the question:

"Does Islam allow this modern Baconian material knowledge, as it is?"

The Holy Prophet (peace be upon him) declared it assiduity incumbent on every Muslim, male and female, to acquire knowledge from the cradle to the grave, even if necessary to travel as far as China in quest of knowledge. However, judging from the present trend of humankind, could the same be said about the Western and other advanced countries of the world where the people go in quest of modern knowledge?

It is essential in this respect to know what this modern knowledge in reality is. Is it merely the knowledge of material utility, or is it something besides that? Remember that modern knowledge is the knowledge of the material utility of the world. It is the knowledge of the particular science; ever-increasing and infinite kind of progress, ever-increasing and gradually occupying the mind and time of man, and expelling the thought of religion and the next world from man's mind proportionally, and exploding eventually as the atomic hell. The question arises:

"Does Islam allow such knowledge or its product, the modern progress?"

The Holy Prophet (peace be upon him) said that the ink inside the inkpot of 'Aalim' (the learned) is as sacred as the blood of a martyr. Is then the ink of the inkpot of the scientists, even that of Robert Oppenheimer and Edward Teller, and all those that have a share in the building of atomic bombs, plague bombs, chemical bombs, and incendiary bombs, is as sacred as the blood of martyr? Maybe the knowledge of procuring the necessities of life was allowed by Islam. But does Islam allow this type of modern knowledge as we have found it to be, and as we have descried it? Or how was the term 'Aalim' (learned) meant for the one learned in the religion of Islam? It appears evident that it was even so. The 'Aalim' meant learned in religion.

The Holy Prophet (peace be upon him) said:

"Sitting with an Aalim (learned) for but a while was better than seventy years' continuous worship."

Could this tenet apply to an atomist, judging from the fact that atomic science was a substantial part of modern science?

The Holy Prophet (peace be upon him) said:

"Angels spread their wings beneath the feet of him who traveled in quest of knowledge."

Do the angels spread their wings beneath the feet of those who travel to the West and other advanced countries in quest of modern knowledge, particularly atomic science, and the science of modern weapons?

The Prophet (peace be upon him) said:

"He, who died on his way to the center of knowledge, died the death of a martyr."

Does anyone who dies on the way to any centers of modern knowledge die the death of a martyr? Just see the difference between the modern school and the Islamic religious school and measure the distance. Knowledge was that of Moses. However, could knowledge of as-Samiri [1] and that of Korah be held equal?

The question is, whether the Quran or the Holy Prophet (peace be upon him) ever alluded to the affair of material gain favorably when speaking of knowledge? The answer is no. Instead of using mud, one companion of the Holy Prophet (peace be upon him) had built a room with materials like bricks, stones, etc., to make it a stable solid structure, signifying to make this transient world a permanent abode. The Holy Prophet (peace be upon him) continued to refuse his salutations until he had demolished that room. Hence, we could hardly expect the Holy Prophet (peace be upon him) to allow the modern knowledge which has covered this earth with the tallest buildings and solid structures.

It is erroneous to assume that the Muslims of the pre-modern ages had neglected the teachings of Islam in neglecting the knowledge of science. Nay, but they knew the views of Islam regarding it. They knew it was undesirable. Now that the attitude of repentance appears in the atomic powers, the Muslims find the zest for scientific advancement. Although the Muslim Scholars (Ulema) have assumed reticence about this modern knowledge, yet we may expect them to understand the correct view of the Quran and the Holy Prophet (peace be upon him) in this respect. The Holy Prophet (peace be upon him) said:

"Whoever gained a kind of knowledge to seek the pleasure of Allah, but he learned the same with the intent of gaining the worldly benefits by it, then on the Day of Judgment, such a man will be denied even the odor of Paradise." (Abu Hurairah vide Abu Daud and Mishkat)

If this is the case of a man who gained a sacred kind of knowledge with the intent of acquiring wealth by it, what will be the condition of him who gained purely worldly knowledge with purely the intent of acquiring wealth? These are the words of the Prophet (peace be upon him) who said:

"The love of the world is the root cause of every evil", and that, "This world is a dead carrion, and its seekers are dogs."

We live in a particular age with its particular kind of culture, the Baconian culture of materialism. It has its particular kind of knowledge, i.e., science for material progress, and has reached a stage nearing the climax, reflecting the total atomic extinction of life on earth. The material world exclusively being the object both for this modern Baconian culture and its modern knowledge, the subject of this modern knowledge like the subject of the contemplation of the works of Allah ought essentially to be judged in the light of the Quran's view about this world. If the Quran rescues from the love of this world, this modern knowledge which is exclusively the knowledge of this material world, we must also see in the same light.

Further, this modern knowledge (science) and its outcome, this modern progress, have peculiar characteristics that distinguish them from the simple love of this world and its wealth, and which indeed aggravate the case grievously. We never should lose sight of the fact and always remember that modern science and progress have particular characteristics. They are systematic, organized, ever-increasing, collective, universal, and infinite as against the individual and sporadic instances of worldly love and wealth-accumulation of the pre-modern that is pre-Baconian ages.

We will now see a view of the Quran regarding the exclusive love of the world, its wealth, and pomp. We may read the following from the Quran about this modern science-guided mechanical, economic, and political devices system and this modern Baconian fruit philosophy. The Quran has uttered something truly Prophetic. It says:

"Whoso desireth the life of the world and its pomp, We shall repay them their deeds herein, and therein they will not be wronged. Those are they for whom is naught in the Hereafter save the Fire. (All) that they contrive here is vain and (all) that they are wont to do, is fruitless." (Quran 11:15-16)

Read the above-quoted passage and see the endeavor of the modern age of fruit and utility has been crowned with remarkable success. However, fire is the end. Still more remarkable is that fire should appear as the retributive result of this modern culture of the world, even within this very world and even before the beginning of the next life. Something is Prophetic in this to prove the truth of the Quran about the fire of the next world. Bacon had called his philosophy the philosophy of 'fruit' compared to the 'barren' philosophy of the pre-modern philosophers, notably Aristotle. Devices of every kind are a conspicuous feature of this Baconian science-guided age, and they will be rendered vain in the last phase of the process. Then what about that knowledge that produced this cursed culture?

According to the Holy Prophet of Islam (peace be upon him), the knowledge is of two kinds: 'religions' and 'bodies', and both are allowed. However, the knowledge of the bodies with the practical application has to be subservient to the knowledge of religions. It has to follow the basic views of Islam regarding this world and the next world. The knowledge of the bodies has to prepare men for the struggle of religion, but this modern scientific knowledge is merely the instrument of material gain. Someone may say that we could use this science and its material gain for the cause of religion. I wish it could have been possible, but it is not possible. It is a delicate point, and we could advance weighty arguments to prove it. But the most potent argument visible to everyone is there. How far has this science and its progress hitherto been used in the service of religion? And how far could it be hoped that someone will ever use it to augment Allah's religion in the future?

Instead, religion has so far been sheared and constricted by this modern Baconian culture to the point that it nears its demise and disappearance. This modern culture has so much dulled only men's sense of religion that whatever of religion has been left is regarded as enough. Anyone, who will see the number of Islamic religious schools against the number of secular schools and their comparative state, will realize religion's situation. Moreover, anyone visiting an Islamic religious school after visiting a secular school will see the difference between secular and religious institutions. To him, the religious school will appear as an institute of knowledge, modesty, piousness, humanity, but the secular school will burst before his view as a nicely kept devil's workshop.

The purpose of this modern knowledge is material gain, while knowledge according to the Quran emanates from the fear of Allah. The Quran says:

"O ye who believe! If ye keep your duty to Allah, He will give you discrimination (between right and wrong) and will rid you of your evil thoughts and deeds, and will forgive you. Allah is of infinite bounty."

(Quran 8:29)

Now, read the above-quoted passage of the Quran, mark the fact of discrimination between right and wrong, and see that the religion of Islam, like other revealed religions, is based on the knowledge of and struggle between right and wrong. But according to Bacon, knowledge of right and wrong and hence the pursuit of moral philosophy has to be avoided as prohibited because it was due to Adam's eating the forbidden fruit of the tree of knowledge of good and evil that God expelled him from Paradise. Post hoc ergo propter hoc, the pursuit of moral philosophy was the repetition of Adam's transgression. Now, this is a queer sort of reasoning, but the sugar of material gain has concealed the bitter pill inside. According to the Quran, this modern knowledge fosters pride and arrogance, but fear of Allah is correlated with knowledge.

It says: "The erudite among His bondsmen fear Allah alone. Lo! Allah is Mighty, Forgiving." (Quran 35:28)
The Bible reckons fear of God as wisdom. It says:

"And make a place for fear of the Most High. For all wisdom is fear of God, and it is wise to fear God, and in all wisdom is the orderly disposition of the law. But the discipline of wickedness is not wisdom. And there is no prudence in the thoughts of sinners. There is a wickedness, and in it, there is abomination. And there is a foolish man who has been diminished in wisdom. Better is a man who has been diminished in wisdom because his mind is failing, but with the fear of God, than he who abounds in intelligence, but with transgression against the law of the Most High."

(The Sacred Bible: The Book of Ecclesiasticus 19:18-21)
Solomon supposed his own model and neglected that of Bacon. He says:

"The fear of the LORD is to hate evil: pride, and arrogancy, and the evil way, and the froward mouth, do I hate."

(The Bible: Old Testament: Proverbs 8:13)
According to the Quran, the criterion of judgment between knowledge and ignorance is Allah's adoration and remembrance of the Hereafter and hope in Allah's mercy. It says:

"Is he who payeth adoration in the watches of the night, prostrate and standing, bewaring of the Hereafter and hoping for the mercy of his Lord (to be accounted equal with a disbeliever)? Say (unto them, O Muhammad): Are those who know equal with those who know not? But only men of understanding will pay heed." (Quran 39:9)

If, however, Bacon's philosophy of the world is considered, the criterion of knowledge will be the ability to turn the secrets of Mother Nature to man's material advantage. Bacon could pose the question as follows: "Are those who know how to wring the secrets of Mother Nature and turn them to their material advantage deemed to be equal to those who know not?" Bacon is all for gold and rubies, so is his wisdom: a means of acquiring gold and rubies.

But Solomon's supposed model is of a different opinion. He says:

"Receive my instruction, and not silver; and knowledge rather than choice gold. For, wisdom is better than rubies, and all the things that may be desired are not to be compared to it."

(The Bible: Old Testament: Proverbs 8:10-11)

Solomon has said that all the things (of this world) that one may desire are not equal to instruction and knowledge. The Quran exemplifies the case of the followers of the Baconian philosophy and sums up their knowledge as follows.

"Hast thou seen him who maketh his desire his god, and Allah sendeth him astray purposely, and sealeth up his hearing and his heart, and setteth on his sight a covering? Then who will lead him after Allah (hath condemned him)? Will ye not then heed? And they say: There is naught but our life of the world; we die, and we live, and naught destroyeth us save time; when they have no knowledge whatsoever of (all) that; they do but guess." (Quran 45:23-24)

Also, the Quran says:

"Then withdraw (O Muhammad) from him who fleeth from Our remembrance and desireth but the life of the world. Such is their sum of knowledge. Lo! Thy Lord is best aware of him who strayeth, and He is best aware of him who goeth right." (Quran 53:29-30)

The Quran in this above-quoted passage says that withdraw from him who desireth but the world's life. However, today in this present world, who should withdraw from whom? The whole world desires but the life of the world. This Baconian culture is one-eyed. It is left-eyed because it is concerned only with matter and this material world and is devoid of spiritual and moral. So also, is this science. It is concerned with matter and the material and is utterly incapable of entering the realm of spirituality, and therefore, is blind entirely to the next world.

The Quran exemplifies this case as follows.

"But of humankind is he who saith: "our Lord! Give unto us in the world," and he hath no portion in the Hereafter." (Quran 2:200)

Not enough time for lengthy discussions is now left. The atomic pyre is quite ready, and it may flare up any moment as the fruit of this modern science. Let the beleaguered humankind now rise to the occasion. Let the nature of the hazards of this deceptive culture be recognized, and people discriminate the absolute reality of this modern knowledge against actual knowledge. Let now humanity carry out the diagnosis, prescription, and treatment without losing a moment. Difficulties are there which we have to encounter. Yet, no difficulty and no affliction are worth considering when we view the flames of atomic hell in comparison. We deem a word with the Ulema (scholars) of Islam will not be out of place. Allah in the Quran has said:

(1) "As for these similitudes, We coin them for mankind, but none will grasp their meaning save the wise." (Quran 29:43)

(2) "The erudite among His bondsmen fear Allah alone." (Quran 35:28)

The Prophet (peace be upon him) declared: "The Ulema of my Ummah (nation) are like the Prophets of the children of Israel."

Judging from these above-quoted expressions, it appears that the Ulema of Islam have a great status and also a great responsibility. Nevertheless, judging from this present situation of the world, it appears that never in the history of Islam had such immense responsibility fallen on the shoulders of the Ulema. They have kept burning the lamp of Islam against every storm in history. We may hope that they will perform their duty against this fiercest storm that ever raged against the religion of Allah and humanity in the form of this most deceptive, seductive, and exceptionally satanic Baconian culture. Will not the sight of the followers of the Prophet of Islam (peace be upon him) discern this Anti-Christic guile of the vilest of the seducers of all times?

~~*~*~*~*

---

[1] **Samiri** or the **as-Samiri** (Arabic: السامري, romanized: as-Samiri) is a phrase used by the Quran to refer to a rebellious follower of **Moses** who created the golden calf and attempted to lead the Hebrews into idolatry. [It is referred to: "the story of the golden calf made and worshipped by the Israelites after their exodus from Egypt while Moses {Musa (a. s.)} was in communion with God on the heights of Mount Sinai, some of the Israelites (under the direction and supervision of a person called 'Samiri') constructed and worshipped a statue of a golden calf. The worshippers of the calf had not turned against religion in and of itself – they were not rejecters of belief in God. They sought the divine but they sought it through the worship of a concrete manifestation - through a visible, tangible object, **'an idol'** – **'one constructed of ornaments that were a symbol of worldly wealth, power, and pleasures'**. They engaged in shirk (idolatry or association). Through this desire of theirs for a worldly, visible, ostentatious representation of the divine, they became deceived. This deception came about through the action of Samiri, a person who was endowed with a degree of knowledge and insight into religion, but who used that insight to falsify rather than clarify matters for the Israelites." (Courtesy: Mr. Irshaad Hussain: www.islamfrominside.com)]

~~*~*~*~*

CHAPTER-15

BACON'S PHILOSOPHY IS ANTIPATHETIC TO RELIGION IN GENERAL

(1) BACON VERSUS BUDDHA

Through inquiries and experimentation, Bacon's object was the attainment of man's dominion over Mother Nature for the material well-being of humankind in general. Through man's conquering the cravings, Buddha's object was the attainment of 'Nirvana', complete emancipation. The two views are manifestly radically opposite to each other. Bacon sought the gratification of worldly desires and gave out the non-gratification of these desires as the source of all ills. On the other hand, Buddha attributed all ills to these worldly desires and saw the remedy in quelling and not gratifying them.

Buddha says: "Unless a man has conquered his cravings, his life is trouble, and his end is sorrow."

Bacon says: "The only way to remove troubles and sorrows is to appease and gratify the worldly desires."

Bacon sought to excite worldly desires and then appease them. Buddha sought to suppress them and escape their ill effects. Buddha looked up toward heaven; Bacon looked downward to the earth. Buddha enumerated three principal forms that he assumed as the craving for life and regarded as evil, which we give as follows.

(1) The desire of the appetite, greed, and all forms of sensuousness.
(2) The desire for personal and egotistic immortality.
(3) The craving for personal success, worldliness, avarice, and the like.

One had to overcome all the three to escape from the distress and chagrin of life. When they were overcome and had vanished altogether, only then one attained the serenity of the soul, the highest good that is the 'Nirvana'. Now, these are the same three principal forms that form the base and the body of Bacon's philosophy, but Bacon does not mean to suppress them; he wants to attain them materially. See how close Buddha and Christ stand and how radically opposite Bacon stands to both of them. It is not Buddha and Christ alone that have taught otherworldliness and self-abrogation. Nay, rather every Prophet of Allah and most eminent philosophers in human history have preached the same views. Bacon alone stands opposed. Though a minor one, the only exception may be seen in Epicurus, the founder of the school of Epicureans in ancient Greece. Howsoever hyperbolic, impractical, and delusional the views of the Buddha and that of Christ may appear to modern Baconian humankind, the fact is that the truth of the Buddhist and Christian views and the Baconian view is now appearing in a form most manifest and undeniable before our eyes. The Baconian view has proved to be the mother of miseries, troubles, and utter ruin.

In contrast, in pre-modern times, the fierce python of man's infinite greed was kept in check to some extent due to the influence of the doctrine of otherworldliness and self-abandonment. Humankind continued its existence in this trial house, at least with hope in the next life, and was comparatively better off. At least the much-dreaded hell had never made its appearance within this very world, nor was this world itself changed into hell. But thanks to Bacon's philosophy of atomism that the atomic hell now glares right into the eyes of humankind, in a world that in itself is nothing short of hell due to Baconian miseries and afflictions. If Buddha has preached the view of 'Nirvana' that is complete emancipation, the Quran too has expressed its view as follows:

"But ah! Thou soul at peace! Return unto thy Lord, content in His good pleasure! Enter thou among My bondmen! Enter thou My Garden!"

(Quran 89:27-30)

According to the Quran, man's objective on earth ought to strive to escape the punishment of fire and gain re-entry into Paradise.
The Quran says:

"Every soul will taste of death. And ye will be paid on the Day of Resurrection only that which ye have fairly earned. Whoso is removed from the Fire and is made to enter Paradise; he indeed is triumphant. The life of this world is but the comfort of illusion." (Quran 3:185)

Fire is the symbol of worldly love. Paradise being the symbol of Allah's love, the escape from fire, and the entry into Paradise meant otherworldliness, the love, and remembrance of Allah.

(2) BACON VERSUS HINDUISM

All said of Buddha is nearly applicable to the original Hindu religion. Hindu religion, as is well-known, is based on otherworldliness and self-abandonment and thus stands in radical opposition to the worldly philosophy of Bacon. However, just as modern Baconian philosophy has deceived the followers of every other religion, the followers of the Hindu religion too have become victims of Baconian delusion. Besides, just as followers of every other religion have endeavored to prove competitively existing conformity between the doctrines of their religion and modern philosophy of worldly progress, Hindus too have not left behind.

We may hear them claim that Germans have gained all the knowledge of science from the Hindu Vedas and that their ancient ancestors used to fly in palanquins, the ancient prototypes of this modern aircraft. However, if and when the Baconian atomic plague breaks out, Hindus too will not be deprived of the share due to them whether Germans had gained their knowledge of science from the Hindu Vedas or not. The Muslims, however, emphasize the topic by dint of supposed Islamic progressiveness and the share of the Muslim physicists of the medieval ages. They, too, will not be denied therein share of the Baconian fire.

(3) **BACON VERSUS SOLOMON**

Bacon has declared Solomon as his model because of the proverbial glory of Solomon. Bacon was mistaken and furnished proof of short-sightedness and shallowness. Jesus, in whom Bacon had professed faith, was more worthy of being taken as a model. Bacon saw only the outer pomp of Solomon and was enamored thereof and neglected the inner heart of Solomon. In contrast, Jesus had seen Solomon's inner heart, having ignored his apparent pomp and glory. After the enjoyment of all the worldly glory, Solomon concluded that it was all vanity and vexation. Bacon ought to have taken a lesson from it. Also, Solomon differed from Bacon on the points of knowledge, wisdom, and dominion. We will quote Solomon's conclusion about the worldly glory, which Bacon too might have read, but the love of its ostentation blinded his heart. Solomon said:

"I made me great works; I builded me houses; I planted me vineyards: I made me gardens and orchards, and I planted trees in them of all kind of fruits: I made me pools of water, to water therewith the wood that bringeth forth trees: I got me servants and maidens, and had servants born in my house; also I had great possessions of great and small cattle above all that were in Jerusalem before me: I gathered me also silver and gold, and the peculiar treasure of kings and of the provinces: I got me men singers and women singers, and the delights of the sons of men, as musical instruments, and that of all sorts. So I was great and increased more than all that were before me in Jerusalem: also, my wisdom remained with me. And whatsoever mine eyes desired I kept not from them, I withheld not my heart from any joy; for my heart rejoiced in all my labour: and this was my portion of all my labour. Then I looked on all the works that my hands had wrought and on the labour that I had laboured to do: and, behold, all was vanity and vexation of spirit, and there was no profit under the sun. And I turned myself to behold wisdom, and madness, and folly: for what can the man do that cometh after the king? Even that which hath been already done. Then I saw that wisdom excelleth folly, as far as light excelleth darkness. The wise man's eyes are in his head; but the fool walketh in darkness: and I myself also perceived that one event happeneth to them all. Then said I in my heart, as it happeneth to the fool, so it happeneth even to me; and why was I then wiser? Then I said in my heart that this also is vanity. For there is no remembrance of the wise more than of the fool forever; seeing that which now is in the days to come shall all be forgotten. And how dieth the wise man? As the fool. Therefore, I hated life; because the work that is wrought under the sun is grievous unto me: for all is vanity and vexation of spirit."

(The Bible: Old Testament: Ecclesiastes 2:4-17)

Bacon has recommended the contemplation of the works of God. Solomon had slain a significant number of the finest horses for no other reason than he, being engrossed in their contemplation, had missed the time of his prayers.

The Quran says:

"When there were shown to him at eventide lightfooted coursers, and he said: Lo! I have preferred the good things (of the world) to the remembrance of my Lord; till they were taken out of sight behind the curtain. (Then he said): Bring them back to me, and fell to slashing (with his sword their) legs and necks."

(Quran 38:31-33)

(4) BACON AND KORAH (QAROON)

If we could find any resemblance, it would be between the philosophy of Bacon and that of Korah. Korah had amassed great riches. It is said that he had acquired all that through his knowledge. He rose in opposition to Moses, but the earth swallowed him with his wealth and household. The Quran has related the event as follows.

"Now Korah was of Moses folk, but he oppressed them, and We gave him so much treasure that the stores thereof would verily have been a burden for a troop of mighty men. When his own folk said unto him: Exult not; lo! Allah loveth not the exultant; but seek the abode of the Hereafter in that which Allah hath given thee and neglect not thy portion of the world, and be thou kind even as Allah hath been kind to thee, and seek not corruption in the earth; lo! Allah loveth not corrupters, he said: I have been given it only on account of knowledge I possess. Knew he not that Allah had already destroyed the generations before him men who were mightier than him in strength and greater in respect of following? The guilty are not questioned of their sins. Then went he forth before his people in his pomp. Those who were desirous of the life of the world said: Ah, would that unto us had been given the like of what hath been given unto Korah! Lo! He is lord of rare good fortune. But those who had been given knowledge said: Woe unto you! The reward of Allah for him who believeth and doeth right is better, and only the steadfast will obtain it. So, We caused the earth to swallow him and his dwelling place. Then he had no host to help him against Allah, nor was he of those who can save themselves. And morning found those who had coveted his place but yesterday crying: Ah, welladay! Allah enlargeth the provision for whom He will of His slaves and straiteneth it (for whom He will). If Allah had not been gracious unto us, He would have caused it to swallow us (also). Ah, welladay! The disbelievers never prosper."

(Quran 28:76-82)

However, we wonder if anyone will survive the outcome of the Baconian philosophy (atomic hell) to see the truth and repent. We will treat the views of Bacon as against the teachings of Jesus Christ in a separate chapter. [1] In this passage of the Quran about Korah, a point has appeared which deserves mention. That is about knowledge.

Says the Quran, they who were given knowledge said:

"The reward of Allah for him who believeth and doeth right is better than wealth."

It shows what the knowledge in the sight of the Quran is. Knowledge to Bacon is only the instrument of gaining wealth, precisely like the knowledge of Korah.

~~*~*~*

---

[1] For details, please read Book-2/volume-5/chapter-6, 'Views of Bacon and Jesus Christ antipathetic'.

~~*~*~*

CHAPTER-16

THE NATURAL EFFECTS OF BACONIAN PHILOSOPHY

Bacon's design was the attainment of man's dominion over Mother Nature through systematic research of science for the material advantage of humankind in general, as the actual business of man on earth, and as the express and exclusive command of God to Adam. Moral philosophy, according to Bacon, having been forbidden as man's persistence in the first transgression of Adam, that of eating the fruit of the forbidden tree of the knowledge of good and evil. It had been a peculiar kind of philosophy and, therefore, has peculiar kind of effects. No doubt, men today do not know the philosophy of Bacon except a few. However, the effects of Baconian philosophy are there through the Baconian progress, which is itself the result of Baconian philosophy. The man who eats poison would experience the effects of poison whether he knew anything about the poison or not.

The effect of the doctrine of man's dominion over Mother Nature as man's birthright is that man has in his pride ventured to become a god himself, and thus defection of man from Allah has occurred. Today, the planting of the banner on the moon is the sign not of the glory of Christ but Bacon. Baconian philosophy has made science the instrument of the contemplation of the works of God, but the object of such contemplation is not the glorification of the Creator. It is purely the manipulation of the works of God for material gain. Material gain is the sole object of science. Science has lost its idea of being science in material attainment. Adoration of the Creator has lost sight of too. Further, under the sway of Baconian philosophy, complete knowledge has been reduced to purely an instrument of physical achievement.

Thus, the knowledge that was a blessing in Islam has become a curse in Baconian culture. We can see the schools of modern knowledge in the East as the devil's workshops against religious education schools. The students of modern knowledge have only one end in view: the certificates or knowledge merely for obtaining employment and making a living or accumulating wealth. The schools of religion produce the students; sober, gentle, Allah-fearing, and respectful.

Science being itself blind of spiritual, supernatural, and miraculous, and the entire philosophy of Bacon being the source of worldly views, the mind of the man of this age has followed suit and has denied or has at least depreciated the idea of spiritual, supernatural, and miraculous. The result is universal discontent and heart-burning for material necessities. As far as moral values are concerned, the attitude of Baconian philosophy regarding the pursuit of moral philosophy itself is not generally known to men. Natural philosophy is the basis of the Baconian philosophy of atomism. The exclusive pursuit of natural philosophy itself is a curse enough to damage the notion of moral philosophy. The disregard of moral values and the neglect of the pursuit of moral philosophy in this age is no longer a hidden secret.

The behavior of this present generation regarding the atomic power behooves not at all to the descendants of Adam and the followers of Abraham, Moses, Jesus, Mohammed (peace be upon them all), Krishna, and Buddha. However, the stomach and never the heart is the object of this Baconian age. This world and not at all the otherworld is the aim of this Baconian culture. Body and not the soul is the subject of this Baconian philosophy. Moral values have fallen to the lowest level and allow me to cry that the moral depravity has reached a point that is enough to sadden the heart of any well-wisher of this humankind. Selfishness and greed have taken the place of everything else. Destruction is the natural consequence.

The state of humanity has now reached a spot where we can vividly observe Baconian philosophy's general effect. Alas, a race of human beings engrossed in the pursuit of material progress: panting, sweating, and ever scared of the goblin of poverty, can be seen as so many clouds of Baconian locusts of various hues, devouring, destroying, wasting whatever came in their way and having devoured up all that existed in the plains, jungles, oceans, deserts, hills, and mountains, now move toward the source of nuclear energy to be sprayed over by the nuclear disinfectant to final extinction despite the disgusting fumes of the flaming nuclear hell.

All ties: fatherly, brotherly, motherly, and sisterly are severed and forgotten in selfishness and greed of wealth and consideration of oneself. The sense of sympathy, pity, mercy, humanity, charity, and every humanitarian feeling has vanished. This earth now appears to be inhabited by a race of 'wisdomized beasts' interspersed with Baconian devils. This earth no doubt never was meant to be an abode of unadulterated bliss or complete joy, no matter whatever the system, civilization, or religion prevailed. This earth is a house for man's trial and is thus the house of sufferings and afflictions, but far grievous is the state of humankind in the Baconian age. People caught up in the universal Economico-Industrial setup and being broiled in the Baconian furnace; still, the victims of misunderstandings, consider this age a great age of great possibilities, not realizing the loss of both worlds.

Their misunderstandings, however, will sooner or later be cleared, for the temperatures of the Baconian furnace are fast increasing and will ultimately become unbearable. The hazards of atomic annihilation through the atomic bombs and radiations trumpet the consequential disapproval of Baconian culture and progress.

If this Baconian system continues for long, this human race, which still shows some humanitarian characteristics, will assume cannibalistic features due to the dwindling resources and intensifying appetite. Falling on each other to appease hunger and tearing into bits, they will devour up flesh, bone, and all. Stronger individuals will devour up the weaker ones. The stronger nations will devour up the frailer ones. All this they will do without a scruple and justifying their acts on this Baconian pretext or that. It will be the unfailing effect and the inevitable result of that philosophy which has given out the pursuit of natural philosophy for material gain as man's actual business. Also, it specified moral philosophy as an impious continuation of the first transgression of Adam that of tasting the fruit of the forbidden tree of the knowledge of good and evil.

All-natural and physical pursuit and no moral restraint was a very unbalanced philosophy of life indeed, and nothing surprising if the results are devastating. Universal anarchy, mistrust, and distrust to mutual devastation were the most natural consequences of a philosophy which had this world alone as its object, having no consideration either of the otherworld or the moral philosophy as the necessary factors of human life. Some people still think that this material progress was the means of attaining merely the necessities of life that their religion allowed and that they could subdue this progress to the dictates of religion. Such folks must open up their eyes a little more to the facts, prevailing circumstances, and impending hazards. They should know that this modern Baconian progress could not be subjected to any religion, howsoever durable and dynamic. Still, it is the religion subjected to this all-pervading and all-devouring type of progress.

Moreover, instead of having some hope of one day subjecting this progress to their religion and working this wonder and showing it to the world, they should consult the safety of their religion itself against the onslaught of the Baconian ever-increasing, continuous, and infinite progress. For, indeed if this progress continues for long, they will eventually find their religion nowhere, and not even the most robust microscope will be able to show any vestige or trace of their religion in their life. For them, it is to pause and ponder over the postulate: whether during the last fifty years it is their religion that has gained on this progress or vice-versa? A few years hence, and people will rush at the call of the factory's hooter while ignoring the call for prayer from the mosque's minaret willingly or helplessly. As proof, let them put this progress to a halt now. They can't do that without complete renunciation of progress which drags them in chains toward the atomic hell.

The Westerners who still talk of God, Christ, or Democracy are not perfect Baconians. We may regard the Muslims, who still believe in their religion with sincerity and are generally eager to revive Islam, as imperfect Baconian. The Hindus and the Buddhists too cannot claim much perfection in Baconian philosophy.

The Communists only, however, can claim with justness the highest attainable perfection in Baconian philosophy. The world has not imported Communism from the heavens; it is only the perfected stage of Baconian philosophy of atomistic materialism that is the philosophy of man's dominion over Mother Nature for material advantage with the idea of moral philosophy as undesirable. In Communist philosophy, we can see the Baconian values to have attained their peak values theoretically and practically.

Bacon sought for man's dominion over Mother Nature as man's right. This view naturally is to bring the man in conflict with God in the matter of dominion. We may see the Communist world have the highest claim of man's dominion over Mother Nature, where the thought of God's dominion is expelled from man's mind altogether. Bacon spoke of the pursuit of natural philosophy (science) for material advantage for humankind in general. We may see the Communist world as a nest of the honey-bees engrossed in preparing honey as one body. Bacon spoke of moral philosophy as a forbidden pursuit. The Communist world has shunned the basic idea of religion as sheer opium, whereas the Westerners had given it out as merely an obstacle in the way of progress.

Bacon had given a philosophy complete in itself. It has a complete system that we may give the name of 'Baconio-Shylockio-Scientifico-Industrial system'. We can see this system in its hitherto perfected picture of Communism which dragged entire life into the Baconian net for dominion over Mother Nature and material advantage. People regard opposition to the dictates of Baconian philosophy in a Baconian society as unpleasant.

Will this cry of mine against the Baconian philosophy and Baconian progress be tolerated? Suppose there is any hope of my word heeded in this world of today. In that case, it is because of the appearance and the presence of the most grievous kind of hazards that were naturally incident on the philosophy of Bacon: the atomic bombs and radiations.

Besides the philosophical and ethical effects of Baconian philosophy, there have appeared some very scientific results too. 'Slander', 'wealth accumulation', and a 'belief in the eternity of this progress of wealth-increase' functioning in modern Baconian progress, the three characteristic features of Baconian philosophy, have acted like the three ingredients of gun powder. But instead, they have produced the peculiar atomic powder.

The three ingredients of Baconian philosophy are **'Slander'**, **'wealth accumulation'**, and the **'belief in the eternity of this process of wealth accumulation'** through Baconian progress. Again, **'Baconian philosophy'**, **'Baconian progress'**, **'cancer'**, and **'Uranium'** could be numbered in one group. All four show similar characteristics and work on the principle of fission chain reaction having the same destiny of destruction through atomic fire.

~~*~*~*

CHAPTER-17

THE CAUSES OF THE APPEARANCE OF BACONIAN CULTURE

The fundamental causes of the appearance, acceptance, and prevalence of Bacon's philosophy and (consequently of) the Baconian culture are two.

Firstly, the peculiar and particular state of the Christian religion, and the state of religion in general, all over the world, was worst at the time of the appearance of Bacon's philosophy in the seventeenth century.

Secondly, a universal wave of the desire for wealth and power and ostentation reached its climax by that time, particularly in the West.

By then divested of higher universal ideals of Islam, Muslims moved in eddy wherein the various sects and archaisms continued naturally harangued over the superfluous matter, revolving all the while in the same eddy engrossed in worldly problems, and engaged in worldly disputes. Politics had superseded the element of religion. They alienated religion and politics, and religion had lost its proper place. Corruption on lower levels was considerable due to the general ignorance of the people about Islam. Sheik Sir-Hindi, a contemporary of Francis Bacon (1561-1626), was seen to affect reform in Islamic religion in general and against the imposture of Emperor Akbar (India) in particular. The fundamental doctrines of Islam could not have been changed or seriously distorted in any age is the miracle of Islam itself and the Quran whose protection Allah Himself has guaranteed.

Far worse, we should say, unutterably and incredibly worse was the state of the religion of Christianity. Christianity in those times turned out to be a massive mass of innovated and framed-up doctrines that went by the name of Christianity. The hierarchical government of the Christian Church functioned in the name of Jesus Christ and wielded limitless power, possessed palaces, treasures, and gardens, ate in utensils of gold and silver, and preached at the same time Christian poverty from the pulpit. It had become a symbol of terror, tyranny, and hypocrisy in the eyes of Western Christendom. It appeared as an anathema, even something worse than that which the followers of the Christian religion wanted to get rid of with most impatient hearts. The hearts of Western Christendom at the same time were burning with the desire of the feast of Mother Nature spread before their eyes, and which they had seen the followers of Islam enjoying in a state of enviable glory. Hinduism and Buddhism were not much different from Christianity, both regarding religion and worldly desires.

As far as the desire for wealth is concerned, it is well-known that it is embedded in the very nature of humankind, and it finds no bounds. No amount of wealth could appease man's desire for wealth. Nevertheless, the few centuries preceding the appearance of Bacon's philosophy show a particular picture of humankind regarding the love of wealth. In their full glory, Muslims presented spectacles of wealth and luxury that were the West's envy. The tale of Arabian Nights had taken all contentment out of the hearts of the Christian West. It rendered the people of the West mad after wealth, power, ostentation, and worldly glory, and they never understood the spirit and the system of Islam. How better it would have been for them to reform their religion and rediscover the pristine beauty and simplicity of Christ's teachings. Some of them indeed tried it. But bones were excavated from their graves by the command of the Church authorities. They burned them for the interest of the Church as heretics for having attempted to re-introduce the original spirit of Christ's religion.

The other alternative was to embrace Islam and partake of the Islamic glory, for indeed, they could have achieved Islamic glory only within the structure of Islamic religion. But they wanted to go on their way to glory independent of religion, and they fell in the ditch, the atomic ditch, and behind they dragged the entire humankind to burn in the atomic pit. These were the world's circumstances then that no sooner Bacon trumpeted his advocating for the fruitful philosophy of materialistic atomism of the world than the predisposed West fell to it with one accord as their redeemer. They did all that was humanly possible to make it a success and succeeded in making it a success. But alas! To what end?

Although the Christian West is directly responsible for adopting Baconian philosophy and its universal prevalence and the consequent appearance of the Baconian hell, we could not entirely absolve other nations from the guilt. Especially the Muslim nation, due to its unique position in the world in those times, stands liable to an especial accusation.

Nay, if Westerners resort to their defense against this charge, it could be shifted onto the Muslims with much plausibility. The duty of teaching and preaching the doctrines of Islam to all humankind and commanding that which is good and forbidding which is evil is a study incumbent on the Muslims. Indeed, all the non-Muslim world never heard of a preacher of Islam, nor a Muslim tried to check them in their march toward the atomic hell on their path of Baconian philosophy. However, Allah has appointed the Muslim nation as a witness against humankind.

Allah, in the Quran, says:

"Thus, We have appointed you a middle nation, that ye may be witnesses against mankind, and that the messenger (prophet) may be a witness against you."

(Quran 2:143)

Moreover, Allah has appointed the Muslim nation as the best community to enjoin good and forbid evil in the world.

The Quran says:

"Ye are the best community that hath been raised for humankind. Ye enjoin right conduct and forbid indecency, and ye believe in Allah."

(Quran 3:110)

Nevertheless, the question is what the Muslims did to stop the Baconian philosophy since it was openly antagonistic to the religion of Allah and posed as a challenge to the community of religion on earth? The answer is nothing whatsoever. They even did not try to understand.

However, the apprehension of the Holy Prophet of Islam (peace be upon him) about the Muslims proved only too true when he said:

(1) "As regards my followers, the thing which I feel most apprehensively is that they will begin to follow their worldly desires and will begin to entertain lengthy and elaborate worldly designs and expectations. And the result of their abiding by the lust of their heart will be that they will be cast away farther from the truth, and their worldly plans will cause them to forget the next world. O, People! This world has left, and it is going. And the next world has left and is coming. And each of these (worlds) has the believers that love it. It is better for you that you do not choose the worship of this world. You are pertinent in the house of deeds, and the time of judgment has not yet come. Tomorrow you should be in the house of reckoning where there will be no possibility of deeds."

(Mishkat: quoted by Jaber)

(2) "O my people, I entertain no apprehensions regarding you that you will fall to idol worship. But what I am apprehensive of about you is that you might be engrossed in the world."

History shows that Muslims have never fallen to idols' worship, but anyone cannot deny their engrossment in the world. The Muslims have a glorious history both secularly and religiously beyond comparison, but there are two standards of judgment. Suppose we see the history of Muslims concerning the general human facilities. In that case, on general human standards, and in comparison to other communities, the case is simply without a parallel. But the standard of Islam is too high and strict: as strict as the rule of nature itself. A minor flaw or the slightest fault has such effects that the blame of the appearance of atomic hell in this world we may put with justice to the shortcomings and failings of the Muslims of medieval ages. The abolition of the Caliphate and reinstatement of the dynastic monarchy by the Muslims is a very dark spot and is a turning point in the history of Muslims. It indicates weakness similar to that of Adam, the progenitor of humankind in Paradise, which influenced the future course of the history of the Muslims and the entire human race.

However, the neglect of the Muslims regarding the Baconian philosophy and the relative events reverberated on them. They were enslaved and subjected to a most disgraceful and painful punishment in abject slavery, servility, and dependence. Besides that, they will share the general doom with humankind in the world's atomic hell and the next world. In this Baconian age, the Jews, once regarded as detestable people, hold the destinies of nations in their hands, and the Muslims are their slavish dependents. The warnings of the Quran have proved only too true, and still, the Muslims are entirely in the dark about the Quran's views of Baconian progress, its reality, and hazards in this world and the next world.

Far worse was the state of Christians at the time of the Renaissance. Because the people's religion was the same as their kings, the condition of the mind of general Christendom of that time may be seen in the condition of their kings and princes then. While the priestly community of the Western Christendom was a symbol of tyranny, hypocrisy, and avarice, the princes of Christendom and the Lords' appointed kings vied with each other in the love of riches and ostentation.

H. G. Wells has left us a description that may serve as a guide. He writes:

"King Louis XIV, 'the Grand Monarque' (1643-1715) … was indeed a pattern king of Europe … He provoked a universal imitation. Every king and Princelets in Europe was building his own Versailles as much beyond his means as his subjects and credits would permit. Everywhere the nobility rebuilt or extended their chateaux to the new pattern. A great industry of beautiful and elaborate fabrics and furnishings developed. The luxurious arts flourished everywhere; sculpture in Alabaster, Faience, gilt woodwork, metalwork, stamped leather, much music, magnificent painting, beautiful printing and bindings, fine crockery, fine vintages. Amidst the mirrors and fine furniture went a strange race of "Gentlemen" in tall powdered wigs, silks and laces, poised upon high red heels, supported by amazing canes; and still more wonderful "ladies", under towers of powdered hair and wearing vast expansions of silk and satin sustained on wire. Through it all, postured the great Louis, the sun of his world, unaware of the meager and sulky and bitter faces that watched him from those lower darknesses to which his sunshine did not penetrate."

('A Short History of the world'; by H. G. Wells, Page-222) How little these princes and Princelets did realize then that they were merely acting as puppets and buffoons of the approaching simulate of Jesus Christ, i.e., 'Messiah-id-Dajjaal', the 'Anti-Christ', and the end of that buffoonery was the atomic hell. King Louis and all his imitations have gone the usual way along with their pomp and show. Even the result of their pomp led the world onto an unusual way into flames of Baconian hell.

With an apology to Voltaire:

"Baconian hell is the worst of all the possible hells."

How hard it is to behold the worst of all possible hells as against Leibnizian best of all possible worlds, which Voltaire in his lifetime had held up to very exquisite ridicule in his romance called 'Candide' (1759). This Baconian culture is the most confounding of all the cultures ever appeared on this earth, yet lends it to the clearest of the analytical explanations. The light of faith, however, is the condition to understand its reality.

~~*~*~*

CHAPTER-18

THE APPEARANCE OF BACONIAN CULTURE

Jewish nation is a phenomenon far beyond the pale of the anthropomorphist and far beyond the ken for the psychologist. It is a phenomenon with its peculiar characteristics and is at least as complex as the nuclear phenomenon. Indeed, we may discover an astonishing resemblance between the two.

Heinrich Heine, the Jewish poet, remarked:

"Judaism is not a religion; it is a misfortune."

Misfortune indeed, it proved to be eventually, still, not only of the Jews but the entire humanity. Nevertheless, neither Judaism itself nor the religion Moses gave, but the Jewish race with its peculiarly Jewish characteristics, unfortunately, appeared as the misfortune of itself and that of the entire humankind, and misfortune at least as significant as discovering nuclear phenomena itself.

When we read the Quran and peruse therein whatever it has said of the children of Israel, peculiar awe, and a sense of apprehension of some great danger may be perceived. Indeed, the Quran has predicted and characterized the nuclear phenomenon that appeared in the 20th century AD. The same Quran has treated the Jews with such attention, apprehension, and profusion as may find Prophetic justification in the light of the hazardous situation in which humankind we may now see having fallen as the result of the Jewish guidance in this modern Baconian enterprise. The resemblance between the Jew and nuclear phenomena may, at first sight, appear obscure and remote. However, the fact is that both are deadly and indispensable in this age. They are ruinous to themselves and this world.

We will now cite the Quran about the Jews. The Quran has given their history and described their character. In the light of narratives of the Quran, we request the reader to see for himself only: if this modern Baconian culture is not the repetition of ancient Jewish history, and if the Jews have not endeavored to achieve all that they had desired in the time of Moses.

Following are the statements of the Quran, which present a picture of the character of Jews.

GABRIEL'S EXTINGUISHING THE ATOMIC HELL SERIES

(1) "Verily Allah heard the saying of those who said, (when asked for contributions to the war): 'Allah, forsooth, is poor, and we are rich!' We shall record their saying with their slaying of the Prophets wrongfully, and We shall say: Taste ye the punishment of burning!"
(Quran 3:181)

They have accomplished this feat in the appearance of the fire of atomic hell. Jews have the primary share in the creation of the atomic bomb.

(2) "The Jews say: Allah's hand is fettered. Their hands are fettered, and they are accursed for saying so. Nay, but both His hands are spread out wide in bounty. He bestoweth as He will. That which hath been revealed unto thee from thy Lord is certain to increase the contumacy and disbelief of many of them, and We have cast among them enmity and hatred till the Day of Resurrection. As often as they light a fire for war, Allah extinguisheth it. Their effort is for corruption in the land, and Allah loveth not corrupters."
(Quran 5:64)

The miserliness of the Jews is proverbial. So is their ability to acquire and accumulate wealth. They have wholly set their heart on the wealth of this world, and they leave no stones unturned in their pursuit.

(3) "The Jews and Christians say: We are sons of Allah and His loved ones. Say, why then doth He chastise you for your sins? Nay, ye are but mortals of His creating. He forgiveth whom He will and chastiseth whom He will. Allah's is the Sovereignty of the heavens and the earth, and all that is between them and unto Him is the journeying."
(Quran 5:18)

Let them now ward off the atomic chastisement or make themselves proof against that punishment of their own creation. There is no protection either against atomic bombs or atomic radiation.

(4) "And they say: None entereth Paradise unless he is a Jew or a Christian. These are their own desires. Say: Bring your proof (of what ye state) if ye are truthful."
(Quran 2:111)

The proof is now there — none of them escapeth the atomic hell, which they have enkindled with their own hands.

(5) "That is because they say: The Fire will not touch us save for a certain number of days. That which they used to invent hath deceived them regarding their religion."
(Quran 3:24)

They invented the atomic fire. But the fire will not respect and spare those, the inventors of the atomic fire, in the next world, for there, the 'Hotama' (atomic hell) is ablaze for those who deserved its fire in this world.

(6) "Hast thou not observed those who were forbidden conspiracy and afterward returned to that which they had been forbidden, and (now) conspire together for crime and wrongdoing and disobedience toward the messenger? And when they come unto thee, they greet thee with a greeting wherewith Allah greeteth thee not, and say within themselves: Why should Allah punish us for what we say? Hell will suffice them; they will feel the heat thereof - a hapless journey's end!"

(Quran 58:8)

The Jews, instead of saying 'Al-Salam-Alaika' (peace be upon you), said 'Al-sam-Alaika' (mischief on thee) to the Prophet (peace be upon him), and thus confounding the utterance. Now, after fourteen centuries, hell is there for them: the atomic hell and they will feel the heat.

(7) "Some of those who are Jews change words from their context and say: "We hear and disobey; hear thou as one who heareth not" and "Listen to us!" distorting with their tongues and slandering religion. If they had said: "We hear and we obey; hear thou, and look at us," it had been better for them and more upright. But Allah hath cursed them for their disbelief, so they believe not, save a few."

(Quran 4:46)

It was one of the devices of the Jews of Medina to annoy the Muslims. By distorting the word of Scripture "Ra'ina" (meaning 'listen to us') by which the Muslims used to call the Prophet's notice, they (Jews) turned it by slightly mispronouncing it into Hebrew word of insult. [1] All this is very characteristic of the Jewish mind.

(8) "The likeness of those who are entrusted with the Law of Moses, yet apply it not, is as the likeness of the ass carrying books. Wretched is the likeness of folk who deny the revelations of Allah. And Allah guideth, not wrongdoing folk."

(Quran 62:5)

Jesus, however, was too aptly severe on them. He addressed them as:

"Ye serpents, ye generation of vipers, how can ye escape the damnation of hell?"

(The Bible: New Testament: Matthew 23:33)

Damnation of hell indeed now is there in view. Now, we will quote from the Quran such signs as show that this modern Baconian culture is only the repetition of the ancient history of the Jews. They have achieved all that they had then desired of Moses. We may see all the tricks they had played in those ancient times reflected in this modern Baconian culture.

(1) "And when it was said unto them: Dwell in this township and eat therefrom whence ye will, and say "<u>Repentance</u>," and enter the gate prostrate; We shall forgive you your sins; We shall increase (reward) for the right-doers. But those of them who did wrong changed the word which had been told them for another saying, and We sent down upon them wrath from heaven for their wrongdoing."

(Quran 7:161-162)

Instead of '<u>Hittaton</u>' (repentance), they uttered '<u>Hintaton</u>', which means "<u>give us wheat</u>", and 70,000 of them were taken away by the pestilence.

(2) "Ask them (O Muhammad) of the township that was by the sea, how they did break the Sabbath, how their big fish came unto them visibly upon their Sabbath day and on a day when they did not keep Sabbath came they not unto them. Thus, did We try them for that they were evil livers. And when a community among them said: Why preach ye to a folk whom Allah is about to destroy and punish with an awful doom, they said: In order to be free from guilt before your Lord, and that haply they may ward off (evil). And when they forgot that whereof they had been reminded, We rescued those who forbade wrong and visited those who did wrong with dreadful punishment because they were evil livers. So, when they took pride in that which they had been forbidden, We said unto them: Be ye apes despised and loathed!"

(Quran 7:163-166)

They dug canals and enclosed the fish in them on the Sabbath day employing sluice gates. And they caught them the following days. But the Creator changed them to apes for the trick.

(3) "And when Moses asked for water for his people, We said: Smite with thy staff the rock. And there gushed out therefrom twelve springs (so that) each tribe knew their drinking-place. Eat and drink of that which Allah hath provided, and do not act corruptly, making mischief in the earth."

(Quran 2:60)

But mischief did they certainly make in the earth.

(4) "And when ye said: O Moses! We are weary of one kind of food; so, call upon thy Lord for us that he brings forth for us of that which

the earth groweth of its herbs and its cucumbers and its corn and its lentils and its onions. He said: Would ye exchange that which is higher for that which is lower? Go down to a settled country; thus, ye shall get that which ye demand. And humiliation and wretchedness were stamped upon them, and they were visited with wrath from Allah. That was because they disbelieved in Allah's revelations and slew the prophets wrongfully. That was for their disobedience and transgression."

(Quran 2:61)

(5) "Listeners for the sake of falsehood! Greedy for illicit gain!"

(Quran 5:42)

Mark this age of 'propaganda' and 'greed' in this regard.

(6) "Those of the children of Israel who went astray were cursed by the tongue of David, and Jesus, son of Mary. That was because they rebelled and used to transgress."

(Quran 5:78)

(7) "And when ye said: O Moses! We will not believe in thee till we see Allah plainly, and even while ye gazed, the lightning seized you. Then We revived you after your extinction, that ye might give thanks."

(Quran 2:55-56)

Mark the scientific investigation of the natural secrets.

(8) "And We decreed for the Children of Israel in the Scripture: Ye verily will work corruption in the earth twice, and ye will become great tyrants. So, when the time for the first of the two came, We roused against you slaves of Ours of great might who ravaged (your) country, and it was a threat performed. Then we gave you once again your turn against them, and We aided you with wealth and children and made you more in soldiery, (saying): If ye do good, ye do good for your own souls, and if ye do evil, it is for them (in like manner). So, when the time for the second (of the judgments) came (We roused against you others of Our slaves) to ravage you, and to enter the Temple even as they entered it the first time, and to lay waste all that they conquered with an utter wasting. It may be that your Lord will have mercy on you, but if ye repeat (the crime), We shall repeat (the punishment), and We have appointed hell a dungeon for the disbelievers."

(Quran 17:4-8)

Undoubtedly, the Jews have repeated the universal crime of aiding and abetting this Baconian culture. And no doubt hell has appeared both for the Jews and others all over the world. It has proved the word of the Quran.

(9) "Then because of their breaking of their covenant, and their disbelieving in the revelations of Allah, and their slaying of the Prophets wrongfully, and their saying: Our hearts are hardened. Nay, but Allah hath set a seal upon them for their disbelief so that they believe not save a few. And because of their disbelief and of their speaking against Mary a tremendous calumny; and because of their saying: We slew the Messiah Jesus, son of Mary, Allah's messenger. They slew him not nor crucified, but it appeared so unto them; and lo! Those who disagree concerning it are in doubt thereof; they have no knowledge thereof save pursuit of a conjecture; they slew him not for certain, but Allah took him up unto Himself. Allah was ever Mighty, Wise. There is not one of the People of the Scripture but will believe in him before his death, and on the Day of Resurrection, he will be a witness against them - because of the wrongdoing of the Jews. We forbade them good things which were (before) made lawful unto them, and because of their much hindering from Allah's way, and of their taking usury when they were forbidden it, and of their devouring people's wealth by false pretenses. We have prepared for those of them who disbelieve a painful doom. But those of them who are firm in knowledge and the believers believe in that which is revealed unto thee, and that which was revealed before thee, especially the diligent in prayer and those who pay the poor, due, the believers in Allah and the Last Day. Upon these, We shall bestow immense reward."

(Quran 4:155-162)

(10) "And thou wilt find them greediest of humankind for life and (greedier) than the idolaters. (Each) one of them would like to be allowed to live a thousand years. And to live (a thousand years) would by no means remove him from the doom. Allah is Seer of what they do."

(Quran 2:96)

See this age of materialism. Is it not the age of the procurements of the worldly necessities of life? Moreover, Jews desired of Moses their necessities of life. See for yourself whether they are not repeating the same Jewish history? No other nation ever asked lentils and onions of their Prophets, and lentils and onions indeed this age has gained.

The Jews, once called by the distinctive appellations of the 'Children of Israel', the 'Chosen seed', and 'People of the God', happened to have a tragic history and an equally awful end. They are unfortunate people indeed, ever miserable, ill-starred, and in general, deemed to a typical antithetical role to humankind in history, like the role of Satan against Adam and the posterity of Adam.

Yet they incite pity instead of wrath: for their life has always been steeped in misery and end woeful. They have eventually made the life of the entire humankind as miserable as their own. They have brought about the end of this humankind as tragic, terrible, and miserable as their own unless Allah takes pity on this humanity and saves it from the horrible atomic doom it now well deserves.

The Jews, however, may justly say:

"We never forced anyone. People followed us due to their own greed."

Maybe Allah will hearken other supplication of Abraham and will produce some means of saving this doomed humankind.

Allah in the Quran repeatedly reminds the Jews of His favors and warns them against the dreadful day, saying:

(1) "O Children of Israel! Remember My favor wherewith I favored you, and fulfill your (part of the) covenant, I shall fulfill My (part of the) covenant and fear Me."

(Quran 2:40)

(2) "O Children of Israel! Remember My favor wherewith I favored you and how I preferred you to (all) creatures. And guard yourselves against a day when no soul will in aught avail another, nor will intercession be accepted from it, nor will compensation be received from it, nor will they be helped. And (remember) when We did deliver you from Pharaoh's folk, who were afflicting you with dreadful torment, slaying your sons and sparing your women: That was a tremendous trial from your Lord. And when We brought you through the sea and rescued you, and drowned the folk of Pharaoh in your sight. And when We did appoint for Moses forty nights (of solitude), and then ye chose the calf, when he had gone from you, and were wrongdoers. Then, even after that, We pardoned you in order that ye might give thanks. And when We gave unto Moses the Scripture and the Criterion (of right and wrong), that ye might be led aright. And when Moses said unto his people: O my people! Ye have wronged yourselves by your choosing of the calf (for worship), so turn in penitence to your Creator and kill (the guilty) yourselves. That will be best for you with your Creator, and He will relent toward you. Lo! He is the Relenting, the Merciful. And when ye said: O Moses! We will not believe in thee till we see Allah plainly, and even while ye gazed, the lightning seized you. Then We revived you

after your extinction, that ye might give thanks. And We caused the white cloud to overshadow you and sent down on you the manna and the quails, (saying): Eat of the good things wherewith We have provided you - they wronged Us not, but they did wrong themselves.

And when We said: Go into this township and eat freely of that which is therein, and enter the gate prostrate, and say: "<u>Repentance</u>." We will forgive you your sins and increase (reward) for the right-doers. But those who did wrong changed the word which had been told them for another saying, and We sent down upon the evil-doers wrath from heaven for their evil-doing. And when Moses asked for water for his people, We said: Smite with thy staff the rock. And there gushed out therefrom twelve springs (so that) each tribe knew their drinking-place. Eat and drink of that which Allah hath provided, and do not act corruptly, making mischief in the earth. And when ye said: O Moses! We are weary of one kind of food; so, call upon thy Lord for us that He brings forth for us of that which the earth groweth of its herbs and its cucumbers and its corn and its lentils and its onions. He said: Would ye exchange that which is higher for that which is lower? Go down to a settled country; thus, ye shall get that which ye demand. And humiliation and wretchedness were stamped upon them, and they were visited with wrath from Allah. That was because they disbelieved in Allah's revelations and slew the prophets wrongfully. That was for their disobedience and transgression. Lo! Those who believe (in that which is revealed unto thee, Muhammad), and those who are Jews, and Christians, and Sabaeans - whoever believeth in Allah and the Last Day and doeth right - surely their reward is with their Lord, and there shall no fear come upon them neither shall they grieve. And (remember, O children of Israel) when We made a covenant with you and caused the mount to tower above you, (saying): Hold fast that which We have given you, and remember that which is therein, that ye may ward off (evil). Then, even after that, ye turned away, and if it had not been for the grace of Allah and His mercy, ye had been among the losers."

(Quran 2:47-64)

(3) "O Children of Israel! Remember My favor wherewith I favored you and how I preferred you to (all) creatures. And guard (yourselves) against a day when no soul will in aught avail another, nor will compensation be accepted from it, nor will intercession be of use to it; nor will they be helped."

(Quran 2:122-123)

(4) "And We verily did allot unto the Children of Israel a fixed abode, and did provide them with good things, and they differed not until the knowledge came unto them. Lo! Thy Lord will judge between them on the Day of Resurrection concerning that wherein they used to differ."

(Quran 10:93)

(5) "And We delivered the Children of Israel from the shameful doom (We delivered them) from Pharaoh. Lo! He was a tyrant of the wanton ones. And We chose them, purposely, above (all) creatures. And We gave them portents wherein was a clear trial. Lo! These, forsooth, are saying: There is naught but our first death, and we shall not be raised again. Bring back our fathers, if ye speak the truth! Are they better, or the folk of Tubb'a and those before them? We destroyed them, for surely, they were guilty. And We created not the heavens and the earth, and all that is between them, in play. We created them, not save with truth, but most of them know not. Assuredly the Day of Decision is the term of all of them, a day when a friend can, in naught avail friend, nor can they be helped, save him on whom Allah hath mercy. Lo! He is the Mighty, the Merciful."

(Quran 44:30-42)

(6) "And verily We gave the Children of Israel the Scripture and the Command and the Prophethood, and provided them with good things and favored them above (all) peoples, and gave them plain commandments. And they differed not until after the knowledge came unto them, through rivalry among themselves. Lo! Thy Lord will judge between them on the Day of Resurrection concerning that wherein they used to differ."

(Quran 45:16-17)

God in their Scripture during the time of Moses says about them:

"Furthermore the LORD spake unto me, saying, I have seen this people, and, behold, it is a stiff-necked people: Let me alone, that I may destroy them, and blot out their name from under heaven: and I will make of thee a nation mightier and greater than they."

(The Bible: Old Testament: Deuteronomy 9:13-14)

The last address of Moses to the Children of Israel on Mount Ebal and Gerizim forebodes the woeful doom of the Jewish people. It is a lengthy address and constitutes the 28th chapter of Deuteronomy.

We will quote the specimen from Henry Hart Milman's 'History of the Jews'.

In a moving historical scene, Milman proceeds as follows.

GABRIEL'S EXTINGUISHING THE ATOMIC HELL SERIES

["Never did human imagination conceive a scene so imposing, so solemn, so likely to impress the whole people with deep and enduring awe, as the final ratification of their polity, commanded by the dying lawgiver. In the territory afterwards assigned to the tribe of Ephraim, a central region, stand two remarkable mountains, separated by a deep and narrow ravine, in which the ancient Sichem, the modern Naplous, stands. Here all Israel was to be assembled six tribes on one height, six on the other. In the open day, and in a theatre, as it were, created by the God of nature for the express purpose, after a sacrifice offered on an altar of stones, the people of Israel testified their free and deliberate acceptance of that constitution which their God had enacted. They accepted it with its inseparable conditions, maledictions the most awful, which they imprecated on their own heads, in case they should apostatise from its statutes—blessings, equally ample and perpetual, if they should adhere to its holy and salutary provisions. The type of either destiny lay before them: Mount Ebal was a barren, stony, arid, and desolate crag; Gerizim a lovely and fertile height, with luxuriant verdure, streams of running water, and cool and shady groves. As God had blasted Ebal, so he would smite the disobedient with barrenness, hunger, and misery; as he crowned Gerizim with beauty and fruitfulness, so he would bless the faithful Israelites with abundance, with peace, with happiness. On Mount Ebal—as the Levites read the heads of the prohibitory statutes, and denounced the curse against the idolater, … the oppressor, the adulterer, the unnatural son, the incestuous, the murderer—the tribes of Reuben, Gad, Asher, Zebulun, Dan, and Naphthali, with one voice, which was echoed back from the opposite height, responded Amen, so be it. On Gerizim stood the tribes of Simeon, Levi, Judah, Issachar, Joseph, and Benjamin, as the blessings of the Law were recited, to give the same unreserved assent.

Having thus appointed all the circumstances of this impressive scene, the law-giver himself enlarged on the blessings of obedience; but with a dark and melancholy foreboding of the final destiny of his people, he laid before them still more at length the consequences of apostasy and wickedness. The sublimity of his denunciations surpasses anything in the oratory or the poetry of the whole world. nature is exhausted in furnishing terrific images; nothing, excepting the real horrors of the Jewish history—the miseries of their sieges, the cruelty, the contempt, the oppressions, the persecutions, which, for ages, this scattered and despised and detested nation have endured—can approach the tremendous maledictions which warned them against the violation of their Law."]

Moses said that if they did not observe the commandments of God and not harkened the voice of God, then Henry Hart Milman continues as follows.

["The LORD shall smite thee with a consumption, and with a fever, and with an inflammation, and with an extreme burning, and with the sword, and with blasting, and with mildew: and they shall pursue thee until thou dost perish. And thy heaven that is over thy head shall be brass, and the earth that is under thee shall be iron. The LORD shall make the rain of thy land powder and dust: from heaven shall it come down upon thee, until thou art destroyed."

(Deuteronomy: 28: 22-24)

"And thou shalt become an astonishment, a proverb, and a by-word; among all nations whither the LORD shall lead thee."

(Deuteronomy: 28: 37)

"A nation of fierce countenance, which shall not regard the person of the old, nor show favor to the young:"

(Deuteronomy: 28: 50)

"And he shall besiege thee in all thy gates, until thy high and fortified walls come down, in which thou didst trust, throughout all thy land; and he shall besiege thee in all thy gates throughout all thy land which the LORD thy God hath given thee. And thou shalt eat the fruit of thy own body, the flesh of thy sons and of thy daughters which the LORD thy God hath given thee, in the siege and in the straitness with which thy enemies shall distress thee:"

(Deuteronomy: 28: 52-53)

"And among these nations shalt thou find no ease, neither shall the sole of thy foot have rest: but the LORD shall give thee there a trembling heart, and failing of eyes, and sorrow of mind: And thy life shall hang in doubt before thee; and thou shalt fear day and night, and shalt have no assurance of thy life: In the morning thou shalt say, O that it were evening, and at evening thou shalt say, O that it were morning! For fear of thy heart with which thou shalt fear, and for the sight of thy eyes which thou shalt see."

(Deuteronomy: 28: 65-67)

"The sequel of our history must furnish an awful comment on these terrific denunciations."]

[{(a) 'The History of the Jews'; by Henry Hart Milman, Pages 88-90} & {(b) Deuteronomy: 28}]

The chapter in question is a frightful series of Denunciations. Allah in the Quran about the trust says:

"Lo! We offered the trust unto the heavens and the earth and the hills, but they shrank from bearing it and were afraid of it. And man assumed it. Lo! He hath proved a tyrant and a fool."

(Quran 33:72)

Now, read the above-quoted denunciations and foreboding against the children of Israel, and this is but a specimen. Therefore, please read the complete 28th chapter of Deuteronomy, judge it, and shudder. Shiver at the frightfulness of the threats and the fact that it is the same state today, not of the Jewish race only, but all humankind in general, from one end of the earth to the other, and the cause no doubt is collective.

In this respect, the Quran has a foreboding, more relevant, appropriate and to the point, touching this present Baconian humankind. It says:

"Woe unto every back-better, defamer, who amasseth the wealth (of this world) and arrangeth it (against the future). He thinketh that this wealth will render him immortal. Nay, for verily he will be cast into 'Al-Hotama' (the crushing hell)."

(Quran: 104 'Al-Homaza')

The dreadful utterances of Moses on Mount Ebal did, over time, prove true henceforth. Misery indeed and affliction was the other name of the Jew. He was chased by this misery and affliction wherever he went in the world. It is a painful thing to dwell on Jewish history. It is a perpetual tale of woe, pillage, hate, persecution, murder, massacre, sacking, betrayal, treachery, atrocity, retaliation, counter retaliation, and obstinacy stretching to a period of centuries. In the early days of Christianity, the Jews themselves, though having eaten the bitter bread of slavery, delighted in the persecution of the rising Christian sect. The early Christians accuse them of having sent messengers throughout the world to slander them in their synagogues and uttering a solemn curse upon the name of Jesus Christ.

However, when the tide turned, and Christianity became an established religion, and the Christians gained power, the Jews had to pay their due along with interest. Despite all the tribulations, scattering, and calamities, the Jews are the people who never forgot their nationality and constantly nursed the hope of regaining their kingdom.

Moreover, the thought of their promised Messiah, who would appear to restore their kingdom and sit on the throne of David, never left them. With their center long-lost and kingdom long-perished, and they scattered all over the earth, it was their Bible, synagogue, and the hope of their promised Messiah that served as the means of keeping them united and in hope for centuries, even millenniums. It is a phenomenon unique in itself in human history.

During these centuries of the ordeal, the promised Messiah has played a very particular role in the history of Jews. Just as the thought of Paradise has never left the posterity of Adam, thought of redemption and restoration of their kingdom and the associated thought of the promised Messiah has never left the Jewish race.

We will quote Henry Hart Milman again on this point, that of Messiah. His work appeared in 1863.

(1) "To Isaiah may be traced the first clear and distinct intimations of the important influence to be exercised by the Jews on the destiny of humankind — the promise of the Messiah, and the remote prospects of future grandeur, which tended so strongly to form their national character, and are still the indissoluble bond which has held together this extraordinary people through centuries of dispersion, persecution, and contempt. Still blind to the fulfillment of all these predictions in the person and spiritual kingdom of Christ, the Jew, in every age and every quarter of the world, dwells on the pages of his great national Prophet, and with undying hope looks forward to the long-delayed coming of the Deliverer, and to his own restoration to the promised land in splendour and prosperity, far surpassing that of his most favoured ancestors."

('The History of the Jews'; by Henry Hart Milman, Page-165)

(2) "Jewish opinion underwent another change no less important: the hope of a Messiah, which had before prevailed but vaguely and indistinctly, had been enlarged and arrayed in the most splendid images by Isaiah, previous to the fall of the city; it had been propagated, and even the time of his appearance dec'ared, by the Prophets of the exiles, Ezekiel and Daniel; it now sunk deep into the popular mind, and contributed, no doubt, to knit the indissoluble tie of brotherhood, by which the Hebrew people was held together, more closely. National pride and patriotism appropriated not merely the lofty privilege of being the ancestors of the great Deliverer but all the advantages and glory which were to attend his coming. In whatever form or character they expected him to appear, king, conqueror, or even God, in this the Jewish race agreed that the Messiah was to be the king, the conqueror, the God of Israel."

(Ibid: Page-186)

N.B: The Jews rejected Christ because he neither wanted to be a king nor a conqueror. He even would not sit on the throne of David. Nor would he reunite the Jews against their Roman masters. They did swarm around him as long as their thought would assume logo as their deliverer from the Roman yoke. However, when they realized that he showed no such signs, they were disappointed in him because their notion of promised Messiah was a king, conqueror, and not a meek dervish.

Henry Hart Milman continues:

(3) "The desperate conviction that they were already committed by the events in Jerusalem—the horrible proofs that in every city every man's hand was armed against them, and every heart steeled against their sufferings : on the other, the bold and lofty tenets of Judas the Galilean, in whose sense their older sacred Scriptures might be made to speak without much violence of interpretation—the universal belief in the immediate coming of the triumphant Messiah, which was so widely diffused as to be mentioned by Suetonius and by Tacitus as a great cause of the war, — all these motives could not but operate in a most powerful manner."

(Ibid: Page-312)

(4) "At this momentous period it was announced that the Messiah had appeared. He had come in power and in glory; his name fulfilled the great prophecy of Balsam. Barcochab, the Son of the Star, was that star which was to 'arise out of Jacob.' Wonders attended upon his person : he breathed flames from his mouth, which, no doubt, would burn up the strength of the proud oppressor, and wither the armies or the tyrannical Hadrian … Barcochab, the Son of a Star, which his disappointed country-men, afterwards, in their bitterness, changed to Bar-cosba, the Son of a Lie. He is said to have been a robber; he had learned a trick of keeping lighted tow, or straw, in his mouth, which was the secret of his breathing flames, to the terror of his enemies, and the unbounded confidence of his partisans."

(Ibid: Page-439)

(5) "We have not thought it expedient to interrupt the course of our history with the account of every adventurer who, from time to time, assumed the name of the Messiah. It is probable that the constant appearance of these successive impostors tended, nevertheless, to keep alive the ardent belief of the nation in this great and consolatory article of their creed. The disappointment in each particular case might break the spirit and confound the faith of the immediate followers of the pretender, but it kept the whole nation incessantly on the watch. The Messiah was ever present to the thoughts and to the visions of the Jews: their prosperity seemed the harbinger of his coming; their darkest calamities gathered around them .only to

display, with the force of stronger contrast, the mercy of their God and the glory of their Redeemer. In vain, the rabbinical interdict repressed the dangerous curiosity which, still baffled, would still penetrate the secrets of futurity. "Cursed is he who calculates the time of the Messiah's coming," was constantly repeated in the synagogue but as constantly disregarded. That chord in the nation feeling was never struck, but it seemed to vibrate through the whole community. A long list of false Messiahs might be produced — in France, in Fez, in Persia, in Moravia, but their career was so short, and their adventures so inseparably moulded up with fiction that we have passed them by."

(Ibid: Page-579)

(6) "In the year 1655, a certain Samuel Brett published a Narrative of a great Meeting of Jewish Rabbins in the plain of Ageda, about thirty miles from Buda, in Hungary, to discuss their long-baffled hopes of the Messiah and to consider the Prophetic passages applied by Christian writers to their Redeemer. The author declared himself an eye-witness of the pomp of this extraordinary general assembly, where 300 Rabbins pitched their tents, and gravely debated, for seven days, this solemn question."

(Ibid: Pages 579-580)

(7) "But a few years after the date of this real or fictitious event, in 1666, the whole Jewish world, co-extensive almost with the globe itself, was raised to the highest degree of excitement by the intelligence of the appearance and rapid progress of a pretender, who had appeared in Smyrna, and assumed the name and the authority of the Messiah. Sabbathai Sevi was the younger son of Mordechai Sevi, who first followed the mean trade of a poulterer at Smyrna, afterwards became broker to some English merchants ... Sabbathai stood before the Grand Seignior; he was ignorant of Turkish, and a Jewish renegade was appointed as interpreter. But the man before whom the awe-struck Agas had trembled, now before the majesty of the Sultan, in his turn, totally lost his presence of mind; when the Sultan demanded whether he was the Messiah, he stood in trembling silence and made no answer. He had some reason for his apprehensions, for the Sultan made him the following truly Turkish proposal: — "That he should shoot three poisoned arrows at the Messiah: if he proved invulnerable, he would himself own his title. If he refused to submit to this ordeal, he had his choice, to be put to death or to embrace Mahometanism." The interpreter urged him to accept the latter alternative — Sabbathai did not hesitate long; he

seized a turban from a page and uttered the irrevocable words, "I am a Mussulman." The Grand Seignior, instead of dismissing him with contempt, ordered him a pelisse of honor, named him Aga Mahomet Effendi, and gave him the title of Capidgi Basha ... At length the Rabbins, dreading the total extinction of Judaism, succeeded in gaining the ear of the Sultan. The Messiah was seized and confined in a castle near Belgrade, where he died of a colic in the year 1676, in the fifty-first year of his age."

(Ibid: Pages 580-584)

(8) "Among the Persian Jesus the excitement was so great that the husbandmen refused to labour in the fields. The governor, a man, it would seem, of unusual mildness, remonstrated with them for thus abandoning their work instead of endeavoring to pay their tribute. "Sir," they answered with one voice, "we shall pay no more tribute - our Deliverer is come." The governor bound them in an obligation, to which they readily acceded, to pay 200 Tomans if the Messiah did not appear within three months."

(Ibid: Page-582)

The meeting of the Jewish Rabbins for discussing the question of Messiah in 1655 was their last meeting. Sabbathai Sevi, who appeared in 1666 as the Messiah, was their last false Messiah. Since then, the thought of promised Messiah has wholly left the mind of the Jewish nation. It seems as if the thirsty had received the water, and their long-wanted Messiah had appeared. The fulfillment of their hope of regaining their kingdom was in sight: their Messiah, called by the Holy Prophet of Islam (peace be upon him) as 'Messiah-id-Dajjaal', had made his appearance. [2]

We have to recall to our mind the year of the appearance of Bacon's 'Novum Organum'. It was 1620, which is 35 years before the last meeting of the Jews and 46 years before the appearance of their last false Messiah. After that, the appearance of Baconian culture established the kingdom of the Jews worldwide. The appearance of the worldly philosophy of Bacon was the cherished goal of the Jews and its achievements the eventual triumph of the Jewish culture. The Jewish race has made this modern age. Jewish was the mind that made it, and the Christian West was only the transformed instrument thereof.

Spinoza, Darwin, Carl Marx, Einstein, Edward Teller, and J. Robert Oppenheimer were Jewish stock. The Jewish atomists were in the van of the discoveries of the atomic phenomena and the makers of atomic bombs and Hydrogen bombs. Nor were the life and writings of Bacon in any way Christian. This modern Baconian culture of science-guided progress, the Economico-Industrial system, banking, wealth accumulation, and wealth worship is purely the Jewish culture, no matter adopted by whom.

However, most surprising is how the entire Christian West reconciled to the Jews after their centuries-long snake-and-mongoose conflict? How did the murderers of Jesus Christ become so endeared to the heart of the followers of Christ? How did all Western nations become real friends of the Jewish nation, all wool and a yard wide, at the beginning of the Renaissance? There can be no reason for this metamorphosis other than that people of the West fell in love with the world and its wealth after being naturally disgusted with religion.

Then the Jews, as the experts of wealth accumulation, were called in to give guidance, and they resolved all the differences on the shared road. Then on the nations of the world, this Baconian culture was thrust by the West. But the convincing rationalism and sweet inebriating taste of the wealth acquiring culture soon captivated all the world's nations, for all were human, and the love of wealth was inherent in their temperament. However, piteous is the outcome, and not much exertion is needed now to cite the proof of the horrid hell of Baconian rationalism.

Power-driven means of mechanical transport that appeared as the result of the science-guided culture offer a fascinating view to the curious as to the modern substitute for the pre-modern donkey. It is an exciting and instructive field of research, beginning with the first-ever power-driven engine to the latest universally equipped airplane. Look around to see the world having the same appearance, aim, ambition, and desires, and engaged in the same practices; everything has the same Baconian cast. Neither the Christ would recognize the present-day Christendom, nor would the present-day Christendom recognize or adopt the Christ just as the Jews of his time did not adopt him. Moreover, see denunciations of Moses against Jews materialized in the case of the world today, entirely to prove identity between the state of the Jews and all the other present nations on earth.

That the Christians and the Jews would forget their centuries-long mutual deep-hearted hatred and become reconciled to each other is nothing short of a wonder in human history. The Christians tolerated and even followed the murderers of Jesus Christ, which we may regard as complete conversion to a new creed. The new creed was the worldly philosophy of Francis Bacon that was purely the creed of the world and its wealth. The desire for worldly wealth had erased every trace of religious hatred against the Jews from the heart of the Christian West. The people, particularly the governments of the West, responded heartily to Jews' wooing for entry into those countries.

There was a rumor that the Jews offered Cromwell of England five hundred thousand pounds to obtain St. Paul's church for their synagogue and the Bodleian Library to begin a business. People also said that certain Asiatic Jews had sent a delegation to inquire whether Cromwell was not the Messiah. Cromwell, however, dared not openly to venture the change, but the necessities of Charles-II and his courtiers quietly accomplished the change, and the Jews insensibly stole into the kingdom.

The case of Bonaparte is made clear-cut. In 1801, this great conqueror was busy distributing to his followers the kingdoms of Europe and consolidating the superiority of France over the whole continent. At that time, the world heard with amazement that almost bordered on ridicule that he had summoned a big herd of Jews to assemble at Paris. He put twelve sham questions to the delegation of the Jews, and the Jews gave equally sham answers. They struck the deal, ratified an agreement, and the Jews moved into the Empire as subjects. Bonaparte had in mind the advantages of the vast extent and rapid correspondence of the Jews throughout the world and the personal ramifications of their trade. This influence of the Jews commanded the supply of the precious metals and much of the internal traffic of Europe and probably made significant inroads on this continental system. At all events in every quarter of Europe, the Jews would be vital auxiliaries of a commissariat, etc. The Jew no doubt was wealth expert, and the wealth it was then wanted by Western Christian.

From this particular point of view, the world's situation deserves more attention than has hitherto been accorded. The human race has entirely neglected some very far-reaching points. Know that the struggle between 'Christ' and 'Anti-Christ' is not of a recent origin. It instead began with the birth of humankind. A Christ with otherworldliness and Resurrection always has his opponent: an Anti-Christ, a lover of the world, and disbeliever in next life. Abraham and Namrud have always been there in the contest. Hussain (Razi Allah ho taa'la unho) and Yazid have always been in opposition.

Since Jews rejected Jesus, spirits of both the Christ and his opponent, the Anti-Christ, have been in the contest for these twenty centuries, and after setbacks, the Anti-Christ's spirit has wholly prevailed in the world. If humankind will not destroy it now, it is about to destroy the world.

The Jew has, in this age of Baconian culture, obtained all that he had expected from promised Messiah to attain for him. Nay, the Jew has obtained even more than that which he had expected from this Messiah. He has not only a kingdom in Palestine, the promised land, but he holds his sway over the entire world mentally and physically. The culture is his; the wealth is his; the honor, power, the policy is his, though all this appears illusive and transitory. However, this Baconian culture is unnatural and, therefore, unstable and subject to decay and destruction. What then is going to be the end of this world? Will it be destroyed? On the other hand, is there any hope of its survival? Humanity has to seek now the answer to this crucial and exceedingly momentous question. Could anyone tell?

That the Jews have obtained their kingdom in Palestine is the first postulate. The Muslims commonly believed that the Jews would never have their kingdom. How is it that they have got the kingdom? No doubt, it appears that the Jews have gained a kingdom of their own. But we have to see what the situation of that kingdom is? Many nations have not recognized it formally. It looks like something of forcible occupation of a piece of land strongly contested so that the kingdom has its roots in the air liable to be blown away any moment. The Palestinian Jews are always in danger of being blown away, and this contest will continue as long as this atmosphere exists, and it will exist as long as the contestant groups exist in the world. Maybe this smoldering conflict dazzles into world-consuming wars. The cessation of hostility and mutual hatred is the condition of peace. It is neither at all in sight nor are there any signs of it.

Therefore, it is not right to assume that the Jews have gained a kingdom of their own. No, the unfortunate Jews have nothing of that sort as yet. The Quran has decreed that they shall exist by the support of some covenant with any people, and the same we could say of their present kingdom, which owes its existence to America and certain other countries of the West.

The words of the Quran are as follows:

"Ignominy shall be their portion wheresoever they are found save (where they grasp) a rope from Allah and a rope from men. They have incurred anger from their Lord, and wretchedness is laid upon them. That is because they used to disbelieve the revelations of Allah and slew the prophets wrongfully. That is because they were rebellious and used to transgress."

(Quran 3:112)

The second postulate is whether the atomic war will destroy this world. No doubt, the atomic fire is involved in the creation of this Baconian-materialistic culture. The present-day humankind justly deserves the punishment, and all the factors of atomic destruction are complete. There appears no apparent hope of escape, yet my conviction is that the atomic hell will not destroy this world; rather, humanity will destroy the atomic hell and its causes.

If you ask me whence, did I find this belief? The Holy Prophet (peace be upon him) has said that a time will come when the Mehdi and Jesus Christ will come, and the entire world will adopt Islam. If the universal atomic war destroys this world and all life on earth, how will the prophecies of the Holy Prophet (peace be upon him) be fulfilled? Whom Mehdi will rule? How will Jesus Christ kill the Anti-Christ?

Apart from this conviction, my view is that neither science nor any power can control the atomic situation by subjecting the atomic phenomena. Nor could we hold the atomic hell at check forever or for long. It is the scientific conclusion. The only way to escape the atomic doom is to eradicate this Baconian, science-guided culture of progress entirely and at any cost.

Humanity may discover the spirit of Abraham to save this humankind from the flames of atomic hell even now. I see this world spread before me like a map. I behold the activity of the spirit of Abraham against the atomic hell. [3] To you, the results might appear only as a surprise, like the stone of Spinoza getting conscious during its flight. [4] Praised be Allah. It is all due to His mercy and His grace on His servant.

~~*~*~*

[1] **Ra'ina** (رَعِنَا): "Ra'ina" is an old Arabic word used to draw attention, meaning 'listen to us' or 'hearken to us'. With a twist in the pronunciation, it can mean 'our sheep herder'. This word is found in the Quran, and the common translation of the verse it is found in is:

[O ye who believe, say not (unto the Prophet): "Ra'ina" (رَعِنَا) "Listen to us" but say "Undhurna" (آنْظُرْنَا) "Look upon us," and be ye, listeners. For disbelievers is a painful doom.]

(Quran 2:104)

"Ra'ina" is equivalent in meaning to 'have regard for us', 'give us your ear', 'hearken', or 'listen to us', but with a slight twist of the accent, the meaning of this word changes and becomes the word for 'livestock tender' (shepherd) - a person who looks after sheep or cows and considered uneducated and unintelligent. The Jews and Pagans used to insult the Holy Prophet (S.A.W.) using it. Therefore, Allah commanded the Muslims to use the clear word 'Undhurna' or 'Unzurna' (آنْظُرْنَا), which means 'grant us some delay' or 'wait for us' when speaking with the Prophet. It is much more respectful and cannot be twisted.

[www.islamic-dictionary.com]

[2] For a detailed study of **'Messiah-id-Dajjaal'** (Anti-Christ), please read Book-2/volume-5/chapter-5: [Anti-Christic features of Baconian culture and 'Messiah-id-Dajjaal'].

[3] In this regard, please refer to Book-2/volume-5/chapter-11: [Abraham-Democritus conflict].

[4] "A stone, while continuing in motion, should be capable of thinking and knowing, that it is endeavoring, as far as it can, to continue to move. Such a stone, being conscious merely of its own endeavor and not at all indifferent, would believe itself to be completely free, and would think that it continued in motion solely because of its own wish."

[Spinoza, Letter to G. H. Schaller, (October 1674)]

~~*~*~*~*

CHAPTER-19

THE DEVELOPMENT OF ATOMISM

The historical development of the theory of atomism has received sufficient treatment in these works. Here we will show only Democritus, Bacon, Spinoza, and Einstein standing in a line of succession in the philosophical history of atomism, engaged in the systematic and gradual preparation of the universal atomic pyre and its final setting on fire. Against them stand Abraham, Moses, Jesus, and Mohammad (peace be upon them all) in a line of succession, engaged in an endeavor to put the fire of this pyre out and save the posterity of Adam.

Democritus, Bacon, Spinoza, and Einstein are famous as prodigies. The writers have written much about them, and in this age, mostly in favor of them. However, hitherto no attempt has been made to link these geniuses collected in a row in the philosophy of atomism. We well recognize Democritus as the patriarch of atomism. We may most justly liken Bacon to Moses, but he has to be discerned and distinguished as the Moses of the Anti-Abrahamic line of atomism from the Moses of Abrahamic line. Spinoza has a great name in the world of philosophy. Still, we have to recognize him as the original prototype of Muhay-ud-Din Arabi and Mansur-Al-Hallaj, the two great and famous expounders of the doctrines of 'Wahdat al-wujud', the unity of existence. The view of Spinoza, however, stands in direct opposition to that of Mansur-Al-Hallaj.

Whereas the view of Mansur-Al-Hallaj was of a spiritual cast, Spinoza's was of material cast in line with the age in which he wrote. The Allah of Mansur-Al-Hallaj was spiritual, and it was the spiritual unity of existence He established in the world. The God of Spinoza was the God appearing in the guise of this material universe. This distinction deserves recognition. This Jewish philosopher, who lived a life of poverty like Jesus and wrote philosophy that smoothed the path of Anti-Jesus's materialism, deserves note. Einstein's works, particularly his theory of relativity, have received scientific treatment though the philosophical side of relativity has been neglected. We may see his universe as an extension of Spinoza's view and the latest portrait of the universe of materialism. His view of the universe would instantaneously vanish with the introduction of God as the observer. He provided the detonator to the Pyre-Bomb of the atomic extermination of all life on earth by his theory of special relativity.

Francis Bacon (1561-1626) and Mujaddid Alif Sani (1564–1624), the reviver of Islam during the second millennium, were contemporaries. We must observe that when Francis Bacon was busy writing the philosophy of atomism in England, Mujaddid Alif Sani, in India, was engaged in a contest with the Akberian view of the Mughal Emperor Akbar of 'the unity of existence'. Instead, he provided the view of 'the unity of observation/vision' ('Wahdat ash-shuhud') against 'the unity of existence' ('Wahdat al-wujud'). [1] Shortly afterward, Spinoza's (1632-1677) view of the unity of material existence appeared. The resultant practical form of modern atomism appeared as the science-guided, systematic, organized, ever-increasing, infinite, and eternal progress as may be universally seen in this world. The ultimate stage of this process logically, scientifically, and inevitably is the appearance and the flare-up of the atomic hell. It is the conclusive view of science, and it has been proved substantially before every man's eyes. Now, let us see what fate the hand of destiny has in store for humankind.

~~*~*~*~*

---

[1] In refuting the extreme monistic position of **'Wahdat al-wujud'** (the concept of divine existential unity of God and the world, and hence man), Mujaddid Alif Sani instead advanced the notion of **'Wahdat ash-shuhud'** (the concept of the unity of observation vision). According to this doctrine, any experience of unity between God and the world He has created is purely subjective and occurs only in the believer's mind; it has no objective counterpart in the real world. The former position, he felt, led to pantheism, which was contrary to the tenets of Sunnite Islam.
(Courtesy: www.britannica.com/Encyclopaedia Britannica)
~~*~*~*~*

CHAPTER-20

THE CONCLUDING WORD

Is it possible to retain the religious and moral values along with this modern science-guided, systematic, organized, ever-increasing, infinite, and eternal progress? Is it possible to reconcile this progress to a religious view and affect a balance? Is it possible to continue eternal control of this science and to use it for constructive purposes only and avoid destruction? Is it possible to escape the doom of atomic annihilation without completely eradicating this science-guided progress? Can Islam or any other religion save their followers from the atomic doom in the presence of this sort of progress? These are the questions that deserve immediate and foremost attention. My answer to all these questions is "No", in contradiction to the universal opinion of the entire humankind. My answer, however, is not based on a whim only but on an argument. If this humankind is unwilling or helpless to pay attention to logic and reason, then time is the best judge to show the decision.

The Quran is a complete and comprehensive philosophy of life and the hereafter. It is perfect and has the backing of a significant party. Therefore, the future of humankind appears based on this book of Allah. However, there are conditions. Under the pressure of modern progress, misunderstandings about the Quran's view of Baconian progress, and general and universal ignorance about the reality of this particular type of progress, the Quran is being interpreted as a book of materialism.

Suppose we Judge from the present situation of the world caused by peculiar Baconian progress, the impending threat of atomic extinction of humankind, and expectation of painful and disgraceful doom. In that case, it appears reasonable that the Quran's views relating to this modern material progress ought to gaze in the light of such otherworldliness and spiritualism as recalls to one's mind the prophecy of the Holy Prophet of Islam (peace be upon him) about Christ's advent among the Muslims for combat with Anti-Christ.

It is in this way only that this atomic conflagration could be dealt with effectively. There is no alternative now except to continue in this progress to its logical and scientific end, that is, the flare-up of atomic hell or going against it and bale out before the plane has caught fire. No doubt, no single nation could do much in these circumstances.

The world, therefore, has to be shown the reality and taught and warned universally. We must mold the world opinion entirely to chalk out some joint program and execute collectively. Perhaps this humankind may yet live and that it may escape the painful and disgraceful doom.

Amidst the all-out confusion and wholesale anarchy in the world, there still appear streaks of hope. This world is awakening with unbelievable rapidity. It realizes the reality of this Baconian culture and its atomic hazards and is rising against it like a storm. The efforts of superpowers, though, to stop atomic conflict will eventually fail in confusion.

I was obliged to discuss people, nations, and individuals during this work and my other works. Let it be made clear that it was not the people, nations, or even individuals who were my subject. Nay, but my works are based on views, principles, and doctrines, in which people, nations, and individuals appear as symbols and emblems only. If, for instance, I was obliged to discuss the Jews, it was not because of their being of Jewish blood, but they served only as symbols and emblems of certain principles and doctrines and deeds. [1] It has to be kept in mind that there are excellent and evil persons in every nation and vice-versa. There are persons in other nations that might even worsen if subjected to scrutiny on the same criterion.

The Quran, on the one hand, if it has incriminated the Jews, it has, on the other hand, discriminated between them.
For instance, the Quran says:
(1) "They are not all alike. Of the People of the Scripture, a staunch community recites Allah's revelations in the night-season, falling prostrate (before Him). They believe in Allah and the Last Day, and enjoin right conduct and forbid indecency, and vie one with another in good works. They are of the righteous. And whatever good they do, they will not be denied the need thereof. Allah is Aware of those who ward off (evil)."

(Quran 3:113-115)

(2) "Among the people of the Scripture, there is he who, if thou trust him with a weight of treasure, will return it to thee. And among them, there is he who, if thou trust him with a piece of gold, will not return it to thee unless thou keep standing over him."

(Quran 3:75)

(3) "Lo! those who believe (in that which is revealed unto thee, Muhammad), and those who are Jews, and Christians, and Sabaeans whoever believeth in Allah and the Last Day and doeth right surely their reward is with their Lord, and there shall no fear come upon them neither shall they grieve."

(Quran 2:62)

Moreover, according to the Quran, everyone is responsible for individual acts and deeds.

It says:

"Those are people who have passed away. Theirs is that which they earned, and yours is that which ye earn. And ye will not be asked of what they used to do."

(Quran 2:134)

This world now faces a great test in the atomic threat, the decline of religion, and the absence of peace and contentment. No one nation or individual but the entire humankind is on the test. Every man's attitude in this universal ordeal individually and collectively is of natural consequence. As a well-wisher and servant, I have produced an argument based on knowledge and truth before this humankind. How, and under what circumstances, by what means, in what manner I have managed it, is exclusively my own concern. Let the product be judged on its merit, for this is the age of knowledge.

The situation of this entire world figures before me, and I descry a deluge like that of Noah; the difference is that whereas Noah's deluge was of water, this present deluge is of fire, the atomic fire.

With my heartfelt prayers for the mercy of Allah for humanity and yearning that He saves humankind from dreadful doom in atomic hell, and for the benefit of the present-day civilization, I intend to end this volume with the following dialogue of Noah with his people as it appears in the Quran.

"I say not unto you: "I have the treasures of Allah" nor "I have knowledge of the unseen," nor say I: "Lo! I am an angel!" Nor say I unto those whom your eyes scorn that Allah will not give them good - Allah knoweth best what is in their hearts, Lo! Then indeed, I should be of the wrongdoers. They said: O Noah! Thou hast disputed with us and multiplied disputation with us; now bring upon us that wherewith thou threatenest us if thou art of the truthful. He said: Only Allah will bring it upon you if He will, and ye can by no means escape. My counsel would not profit you if I were minded to advise you if Allah's Will is to keep you astray. He is your Lord, and unto Him, ye will be brought back. Or say they (again): He hath invented it? Say: If I have invented it, upon me be my crimes, but I am innocent of (all) that ye commit. And it was inspired in Noah, (saying): No one of the folk will believe, save him who hath believed already. Be not distressed because of what they do. Build the ship under Our Eyes and by Our inspiration, and speak not unto Me on behalf of those who do wrong. Lo! They wilt be drowned. And he was building the ship, and every time that, chieftains of his people passed him, they made mock of him. He said: Though ye make mock of us, yet we mock at you even as ye mock; and ye shall know to whom a punishment that will confound him cometh, and upon whom a lasting doom will fall. (Thus it was) till, when Our commandment came to pass, and the oven gushed forth water, We said: Load therein two of every kind, a pair (the male and female), and thy household, save him against whom the word hath gone forth already, and those who believe. And but a few were they who believed with him. And he said: Embark therein! In the name of Allah be its course and its mooring. Lo! My Lord is Forgiving, Merciful."

(Quran 11:31-41)

~~*~*~*

---

[1] **Translated from Urdu**
"It looks that the first largest migration in the known history of the world was that of the Aryans who 5000 years ago, after conquering Eastern Europe and central Asia, entered Iran and India.

The second more extensive migration on a large scale in history is of the children of Israel, which is stated in the Quran also. According to 'Sura (verse) Yousuf', when Hazrat Yaqub (also known as 'Jacob' in the Old Testament) came to know that his beloved son Hazrat Yousuf (also known as 'Joseph' in the Bible) was alive in Egypt, he decided to migrate there. He migrated to Egypt with his tribesmen in 1800-BC, and thus the Israelites inhabited the north bank of river Nile.

The third enormous migration of history is again that of the children of Israel from Jerusalem/Palestine due to the attacks by Bakhat Nasar/Persian 'Bukhtrashah' (Nebuchadnezzar). But in contrast to the past, this time migration was on an individual level rather than a collective one. Passing through Turkey and Khorasan, some of them moved to Russia. Most of them moved to Eastern-Central Europe.

In contrast to their adverse practices, there are some positive characteristics in the Jews as well. After migration to Egypt, they kept remote their Hebrew language from Egyptian and did not let amalgamate both together. They protected the heritage of their civilization and culture up to the limits of racism. Their leaders presented to the nation three ambitions, and the whole nation treaded steadfastly pursuing them.

Firstly, to never let their Hebrew language perish.
Secondly, to return someday to their real homeland (Jerusalem).

Thirdly, to concentrate with full attention on acquiring knowledge and attaining employment through profitable business.

Jewish technocrats trained their generations on this same pattern. As a result of this, Jews though being just 1% of the total population of the world, on average, 60% of them are thinkers, philosophers, and scientists. Either they are the sole owners of the critical and profitable business of the world, or they are the significant shareholders therein. They are only 4% of the whole American population, but the American economy revolves around them. The rise and fall in the international market are bound to their will. They are the most prominent traders of gold and diamonds. They dominate the significant portion of mass communication and important international trade centers. The reason for this is that they have been in transit for the last 4000 years. They have endured twice the tortures of long migrations and have passed through the bitterest of the experiences.

(Mr. Muqtida Mansoor)-(http://www.express.com.pk)

~~*~*~*~*

~

TO BE CONTINUED IN NEXT BOOK-2

~~*~*~*~**~*~*~ ~*~*~*~*~*~*~*~*~*~*~*

In BOOK-2, the reader will explore the topics as follows.

(1) [Anti-Christic features of Baconian culture and Anti-Christ ('Messiah-Id-Dajjaal')]

(2) [The dialogue between the Quran and the 'Unscientific Scientist Philosopher']

(3) [The case of the 'atomic energy for peace' in the Court of Lord Justice Science]

(4) [A Quranic design of the neutralizer of the atomic hell (a 'formula' for the neutralization of nuclear fire having its foundation in the soil of ethics, given by the author at the end of this work)]

~~*~*~*~*

BIBLIOGRAPHY

Scriptures and books in the following list have been consulted and referred to or quoted by the author of 'Gabriel's Extinguishing the Atomic Hell Series' (volume-1 to volume-9).

(1) 'The Glorious Qur'an', Translation by Mohammed Marmaduke Pickthall, published (January 01, 2003) by "Tahrike Tarsile Qur'an, Inc. (www.koranusa.org)"; quoted & reprinted with the permission of "Tahrike Tarsile Qur'an, Inc. 80-08 51st Avenue, Elmhurst, New York 11373-4141, U.S.A." with special thanks to Mr. Aun Ali Khalfan.

(2) **Tafsir (Interpretation/exegesis/commentaries) of the Holy Quran**
   (a) 'Tafsir Abdullah-Ibn-Abbas'.
   (b) 'Tafsir al-Tabari' by 'Abu Jafar Muhammad Ibn-Jarir al-Tabari'.
   (c) 'Tafsir al-Kabir' by 'Imam Fakhr-ud-Din Razi'.
   (d) 'Tafsir al-Quran al-Azim (Tafsir Ibn-Kathir)' by 'Ismail Ibn-Kathir'.
   (e) 'Tafsir al-Jalalayn'.

(3) 'The Koran', translated from Arabic by John Medows Rodwell: by the 'Temple Press Letchworth' for 'J. M. Dent and Sons Ltd.' Aldine House Bedford St. London, 1950 Edition, first published in this edition 1909.

(4) 'The Koran, commonly called The Alcoran of Mohammed', by George Sale, first published in 1734.

(5) The Bible: Old Testament/New Testament [King James Version (KJV) by Public Domain].

(6) The Sacred Bible: The Book of Ecclesiasticus (Catholic Public Domain Version).

(7) 'The Advancement of Learning', by Francis Bacon, Oxford at the Clarendon Press, April 1873, first published in 1605.

(8) 'Sylva Sylvarum: or A Natural Historie: In Ten Centuries', by Francis Bacon, first published in 1627.

(9) 'London past & present: its history, associations, and traditions'; Vol-1, by Henry Benjamin Wheatley, published by 'John Murray, Albemarle Street, London, 1891.

(10) 'Lord Bacon – Critical and Historical Essays', by Thomas Babington Macaulay, 1832/1837.

(11) 'Literary Essays', by Lord Macaulay, Thomas Nelson and Sons Ltd., 1843.

(12) 'The Pilgrim'; by John Fletcher, published in 1621.

(13) 'The Pilgrim's Progress', by John Bunyan, Oxford University Press London, first published in 1678.

(14) 'Theodicy', (Essays on the Goodness of God, the Freedom of Man and the Origin of Evil) by Gottfried Leibniz, 1710.

(15) 'The Mysterious Universe', by Sir James Jeans, at the Cambridge University Press (www.cambridge.org); quoted & reprinted with the permission of "Cambridge University Press, 32 Avenue of the Americas, New York, NY

10013-2473, U.S.A.", vide their Permission Invoice#PO3B 23624, dated January 13, 2014.
(16) 'The Origin of Species', by Charles Darwin, 1859.
(17) 'A Short History of the World', by H. G. Wells.
(18) 'History of the decline and fall of the Roman Empire', by Edward Gibbon, VOL-5, first published in 1776.
(19) 'History of Philosophy of Science', by I. W. H. Hull, Longman Green and Co. Ltd. 7 Clifford Street, London, W. I., 1960.
(20) 'A short history of English Literature', by B. Ifor Evans, Penguin Books, first published in 1940.
(21) 'A history of Philosophy', by Clement. C. J. Webb, Oxford University Press, London, 1915.
(22) 'The History of the Jews', by Henry Hart Milman, J. M. Dent and Sons Ltd. London, 1863.
(23) 'Poetical works of Hafiz Shirazi' (Persian).
(24) 'Zarb-E-Kaleem', [The Rod of the Moses] (Urdu), by Allamah Iqbal.
(25) 'Introduction to Poetical works of John Milton', by William Henry Denham (W. H. D.) Rouse.
(26) The preface to epic "Milton a Poem", by William Blake.
(27) 'Jerusalem', (The Preface to Milton), by William Blake.
(28) Milton's Poetical Works: 'Samson Agonistes'.
(29) 'Paradise Lost', by John Milton.
(30) 'Divine Comedy', by Dante Alighieri.
(31) 'King Henry IV', by William Shakespeare.
(32) 'King Lear', by William Shakespeare.
(33) 'The Excursion', by William Wordsworth.
(34) 'Ozymandias', by Percy Bysshe Shelley.
(35) 'Hellas', by Percy Bysshe Shelley.
(36) 'The Waste Land', by T. S. Eliot.
(37) 'The School for Scandal', by Richard Brinsley Sheridan.
(38) 'Looking at the faces', by Mr. Doust.
(39) 'Jesting Pilate', by Aldous Huxley.
(40) 'An Essay on Man', by Alexander Pope.
(41) 'De Rerum Natura'; (a poem).
(42) 'God and the Atom', by Ronald Arbuthnott Knox, Published 1919 by Sheed and Ward in New York.
(43) 'Explaining the atom', by Selig Hecht.
(44) 'Atoms today and tomorrow', by Margaret O. Hyde.
(45) 'Atomic Radiation and Life', by Peter Alexander, Penguin Books Harmonds-Worth Middlesex, 1957.
(46) 'An Elementary Course of Physics'; Edited by John Clement Primrose Aldous, Jan 1900, Macmillan, and Company, Limited.
(47) 'Physics, Physical Science Study Committee', IInd Edition D.C. Heath and Co. Lexington, Massachusetts, July 1965.

(48) 'Physics of the Atom', by M. Russell and James A. Richards, IInd Edition, Addison-Wesley Publishing Co. Inc. Feb.1967.
(49) 'Nuclear Physics', IInd Edition, by Irving Kaplan, Addison-Wesley Publishing Co. Inc. June 1954.
(50) 'Nuclear Theory', by Robert G. Sachs, Addison-Wesley Publishing Co. Inc. May 1953.
(51) 'Our Nuclear Future', by Edward Teller.
(52) 'Nuclear Explosions and Their Effects', by the Publication Division, Ministry of Information and Broadcasting, Government of India, 1956.
(53) 'The Effects of the Atomic Bombs at Hiroshima and Nagasaki', Report of the British Commission to Japan, His Majesty's Stationary Office London, 1946.
(54) 'The Hydrogen Bomb: The Men, the Menace, the Mechanism', by James R. and Blair, Clay Jr. Shepley, Jarrold Publisher. (London) Ltd. 1955.
(55) 'General Chemistry', by John Arrend Timm.
(56) 'Synopsis of Gynaecology', by Harry Surgeon Crossen and Robert James Crossen, 1946.
(57) 'Philosophical Works of Socrates'.
(58) 'Philosophical Works of Aristotle'.
(59) 'Philosophical Works of Plato'/"Plato's Republic: Book-VII".
(60) 'Galileo's Works'.
(61) 'Scientific Works of Democritus'.
(62) 'Scientific Works of Alexander Haddow'.
(63) 'Scientific Works of Einstein'.
(64) 'Scientific Works of Chadwick'.
(65) 'Scientific Works of Rutherford'.
(66) 'Scientific Works of Fermi'.
(67) 'Scientific Works of Madam Curie'.
(68) 'Scientific Works of Muller'.
(69) 'Scientific Works of Oppenheimer'.
(70) 'Scientific Works of Teller'.
(71) 'Scientific and General Works of Bertrand Russell'.

~~*~*~*

FAMILY TREE OF THE AUTHOR

Abdul Mutlib

- **Abu Taalib**
- **Abdullah**

(1) Hazrat Ali Ibn Abi Talib — Muhammad (peace be upon him)
(2) Abul-Qasim Muhammad Bin Hanfia
(3) Shah Abdul Mannan Ghazi — (4) Shah Battal Ghazi
(5) Syed Malik Asif Ghazi — (6) Shah Umar Ghazi
(7) Shah Muhammad Ghazi — (8) Shah Tayyub Ghazi
(9) Shah Tahir Ghazi — (10) Atta-Ullah Ghazi
(11) Meer Qutub Haider ("Qutub Shah")
(12) Gauhar Shah ("Gor-raa") — (13) Buddhoo — (14) Toor
(15) Muddhoo — (16) Trikh-hoo — (17) Dayyou
(18) Jogee — (19) Deenoo — (20) Rabbee
(21) Gondal — (22) Naddhaa — (23) Jhaam
(24) Khhilchi — (25) Haji — (26) Ipeeloo
(27) Mauroosi — (28) Bhatti — (29) Baaboo
(30) Kamaal Din — (31) Muhammadi — (32) Najab
(33) Daryaa — (34) Malik Azam
(35) Aalim Sher ("Malik Sher") — (36) Malik Allah Yaar
(37) Ghaibah — (38) Fateh Khan
(39) Muhammad Khan
(40) Muhammad Yousuf ("Allamah Muhammad YOUSUF GABRIEL")

LIST OF THE CONTRIBUTORS

PROOF-READING & TYPESETTING

Shaukat Mehmood Awan

COMPILATION, COMPOSITION, EDITING, & END-NOTES

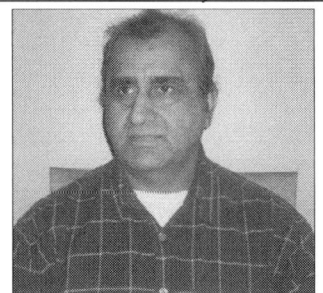

Khalid Mehmood Malik (Co-Author)

GENERAL COORDINATOR

Rizwan Yousuf Awan

Printed in Great Britain
by Amazon